Dictionary
of
Instructional
Programs
and
Careers

J. Michael Farr and LaVerne L. Ludden, Ed.D.

JIST®
Works

Dictionary of Instructional Programs and Careers
© 2000 JIST Works
Published by JIST Works
8902 Otis Avenue
Indianapolis, IN 46216-1033
Phone: 1-800-648-JIST   Fax: 1-800-JIST-FAX   E-Mail: editorial@jist.com

Visit our Web site at http://www.jist.com for more information on JIST, free job search information and book chapters, and ordering information on our many products!

Other JIST books on related topics:
Best Jobs for the 21st Century, 2nd edition
Best Jobs for the 21st Century through Work Experience and On-the-Job Training
Occupational Outlook Handbook (OOH) 2000–2001 Edition

Quantity discounts are available for JIST books. Please call our Sales Department at 1-800-648-5478 for a free catalog and more information.

Library of Congress Cataloging-in-Publication Data
Farr, J. Michael.
  Dictionary of instructional programs and careers / J. Michael Farr and LaVerne L. Ludden.
     p.cm.
  Includes bibliographic references and indexes.
  ISBN 1-56370-609-1
  1. Training—United States—Dictionaries. 2. Professional education—United States—Dictionaries. 3. College majors—United States—Dictionaries. 4. Occupational training—United States—Dictionaries. I. Ludden, LaVerne, 1949- II. Title.
  LB1027.47 .F27 2000

                                                                              00-023826

Printed in the United States of America.
     03 02 01 00   9 8 7 6 5 4 3 2 1

Credits and Acknowledgments

The occupational information used in this book is based on data obtained from both the U.S. Department of Labor and the U.S. Department of Education. These sources provide the most authoritative source of occupational information and instructional programs available. The job descriptions in this book are based on information obtained from the Occupational Information Network (O*NET). The instructional program information in this book is based on the Classification of Instructional Programs (CIP).

     Please consider that the occupational information in this book has its limitations. It should not be used in legal settings as a basis for occupational injuries or other matters. This is because occupational information contained in this book reflects jobs as they have been found to occur in general, but they may not coincide in every respect with the content of jobs as performed in particular establishments or at certain localities. Users of this information demanding specific job requirements should supplement this data with local information detailing jobs within their community.

ISBN 1-56370-609-1

Finally, A Quick Way to Relate Education and Training to Occupations!

We thought it odd that no one had ever put together a book that cross-references two major systems for jobs and instructional programs. So we went ahead and did it, and here it is.

Don't Be Intimidated by the Size of This Book.

We know this book looks complex, but it is really quite easy to use. What it does is cross-reference 885 instructional programs (from short-term through four-year college degrees and beyond) with 1,122 occupations. The U.S. government developed formal systems to collect information on all major instructional programs and jobs—and this book is the first one to cross-reference them. To use it, all you need to do is find one or more instructional programs in Section 1 and then look up the related jobs in Section 2. Or you can look up the jobs that interest you in Section 2 and find the related instructional programs described in Section 1. Simple.

We suggest you begin by browsing the table of contents—it includes one list of all major instructional programs and another listing all major occupations included in this book. Just identify the instructional programs or occupations that interest you and look them up.

Of course, making an important career or educational decision is not as easy, but we hope this book will help you get started.

Where the Information Comes From

It should relieve you to know that we did not make up the substantial information in this book. Most of it comes from our good friends in the Federal government. The information on instructional programs comes from the U.S. Department of Education and uses the Classification of Instructional Programs (CIP) system they developed. The occupational information comes from the O*NET database developed by the U.S. Department of Labor. And the U.S. Census Bureau kindly provided us with the earnings data we used in the occupational descriptions.

But data has its limitations. We used lots of fancy database work to cross-reference the CIP and O*NET data and to construct useful occupational descriptions. We do hope we have created a useful reference to help you in making career, education, and life decisions. Lots of people helped put the information together, but you will now have to figure out what to do with it in making good decisions about your career, education, and life. We wish you well.

Table of Contents

These two tables immediately follow this table of contents and provide listings of the instructional programs and occupations provided in Section 1 and 2. Use them to quickly locate instructional programs or jobs that interest you.

Provides additional information on the sources of data, details on the instructional programs and occupational descriptions and numbering systems, how to best use the book for a variety of purposes, and sources of additional information.

Provides brief descriptions of the 885 instructional programs listed in the U.S. Department of Education's Classification of Instructional Programs. They cover from short-term training programs through four-year college, graduate, and professional degrees. Each program also includes the occupations they lead to. Table A lists these programs within related groupings.

This section provides descriptions for the 1,122 jobs included in the U.S. Department of Labor's O*NET database. These jobs cover all major jobs in our workforce and many of them are cross-referenced in the education and training programs of Section 1. The job descriptions emphasize training or education requirements including earnings, experience, education and training needed, related courses, skills, and other details. Table B lists these occupations within groupings of similar ones.

An alphabetic listing of all 885 instructional programs included in this book, along with the page number where you can find its description.

An alphabetic listing of all 1,122 occupational titles referenced in this book, along with the page number where you can find its description.

Table A: Instructional Groupings Found in Section 1

The listing that follows presents the major groupings of instructional programs found in Section 1. The organizational system it uses was developed by the U.S. Department of Education and is called the "Classification of Instructional Programs" or CIP. Major CIP groupings are presented in **BOLD CAPITAL LETTERS** in Table A, preceded by a two-digit CIP code number used for that group. Subgroups within major CIP program groupings are presented in normal type and have a four-digit CIP code number assigned to them. Specific instructional programs (and their six-digit CIP code numbers) can be found in Section 1 under the appropriate subgroupings.

One way to use Table A is to identify groups of instructional programs that interest you, then review them in more detail in Section 1. The programs are arranged in Section 1 in the same numerical order as in the Table. To find the instructional program you want, look at the top of the page in Section 1 for the instructional program's CIP four-digit subgroup code number—similar to how a Yellow Pages phone book works.

12.04   Cosmetic Services
12.05   Culinary Arts and Related Services
12.99   Personal and Miscellaneous Services, Other

13.   EDUCATION
13.01   Education, General
13.02   Bilingual/Bicultural Education
13.03   Curriculum and Instruction
13.04   Education Administration and Supervision
13.05   Educational/Instructional Media Design
13.06   Educational Evaluation, Research and Statistics
13.07   International and Comparative Education
13.08   Educational Psychology
13.09   Social and Philosophical Foundations of Education
13.10   Special Education
13.11   Student Counseling and Personnel Services
13.12   General Teacher Education
13.13   Teacher Education, Specific Academic and Vocational Programs
13.14   Teaching English as a Second Language/Foreign Language
13.15   Teacher Assistant/Aide
13.99   Education, Other

14.   ENGINEERING
14.01   Engineering, General
14.02   Aerospace, Aeronautical and Astronautical Engineering
14.03   Agricultural Engineering
14.04   Architectural Engineering
14.05   Bioengineering and Biomedical Engineering
14.06   Ceramic Sciences and Engineering
14.07   Chemical Engineering
14.08   Civil Engineering
14.09   Computer Engineering
14.10   Electrical, Electronics, and Communications Engineering
14.11   Engineering Mechanics
14.12   Engineering Physics
14.13   Engineering Science
14.14   Environmental/Environmental Health Engineering
14.15   Geological Engineering
14.16   Geophysical Engineering
14.17   Industrial/Manufacturing Engineering
14.18   Materials Engineering
14.19   Mechanical Engineering
14.20   Metallurgical Engineering
14.21   Mining and Mineral Engineering
14.22   Naval Architecture and Marine Engineering
14.23   Nuclear Engineering
14.24   Ocean Engineering
14.25   Petroleum Engineering
14.27   Systems Engineering
14.28   Textile Sciences and Engineering
14.29   Engineering Design
14.30   Engineering/Industrial Management
14.31   Materials Science
14.32   Polymer/Plastics Engineering
14.99   Engineering, Other

15.   ENGINEERING-RELATED TECHNOLOGIES
15.01   Architectural Engineering Technology
15.02   Civil Engineering/Civil Technology
15.03   Electrical and Electronic Engineering-Related Technology
15.04   Electromechanical Instrumentation and Maintenance Technology
15.05   Environmental Control Technologies
15.06   Industrial Production Technologies
15.07   Quality Control and Safety Technologies
15.08   Mechanical Engineering-Related Technologies
15.09   Mining and Petroleum Technologies
15.10   Construction/Building Technology
15.11   Miscellaneous Engineering-Related Technologies
15.99   Engineering-Related Technologies, Other

16.   FOREIGN LANGUAGES AND LITERATURES
16.01   Foreign Languages and Literatures
16.03   East and Southeast Asian Languages and Literatures
16.05   Germanic Languages and Literatures
16.06   Greek Language and Literature (Modern)
16.07   South Asian Languages and Literatures
16.09   Romance Languages and Literatures
16.11   Middle Eastern Languages and Literatures
16.12   Classical and Ancient Near Eastern Languages and Literatures
16.99   Foreign Languages and Literatures, Other

19.   HOME ECONOMICS, GENERAL
19.01   Home Economics
19.02   Home Economics Business Services
19.03   Family and Community Studies
19.04   Family/Consumer Resource Management
19.05   Foods and Nutrition Studies
19.06   Housing Studies
19.07   Individual and Family Development Studies
19.09   Clothing/Apparel and Textile Studies
19.99   Home Economics, Other

20.   VOCATIONAL HOME ECONOMICS
20.01   Consumer and Homemaking Education
20.02   Child Care and Guidance Workers and Managers
20.03   Clothing, Apparel, and Textile Workers and Managers
20.04   Institutional Food Workers and Administrators
20.05   Home Furnishings and Equipment Installers and Consultants
20.06   Custodial, Housekeeping, and Home Services Workers and Managers
20.99   Vocational Home Economics, Other

21.   TECHNOLOGY EDUCATION/INDUSTRIAL ARTS
21.01   Technology Education/Industrial Arts

22.   LAW AND LEGAL STUDIES
22.01   Law and Legal Studies

23.   ENGLISH LANGUAGE AND LITERATURE/LETTERS
23.01   English Language and Literature, General
23.03   Comparative Literature
23.04   English Composition
23.05   English Creative Writing
23.07   American Literature (United States)
23.08   English Literature (British and Commonwealth)
23.10   Speech and Rhetorical Studies
23.11   English Technical and Business Writing
23.99   English Language and Literature/Letters, Other

45.03 Archaeology	51.03 Community Health Services
45.04 Criminology	51.04 Dentistry (D.D.S., D.M.D.)
45.05 Demography and Population Studies	51.05 Dental Clinical Sciences/Graduate Dentistry (M.S., Ph.D.)
45.06 Economics	
45.07 Geography	51.06 Dental Services
45.08 History	51.07 Health and Medical Administrative Services

45.03 Archaeology
45.04 Criminology
45.05 Demography and Population Studies
45.06 Economics
45.07 Geography
45.08 History
45.09 International Relations and Affairs
45.10 Political Science and Government
45.11 Sociology
45.12 Urban Studies/Affairs
45.99 Social Sciences, Other

46. CONSTRUCTION TRADES
46.01 Masons and Tile Setters
46.02 Carpenters
46.03 Electrical and Power Transmission Installers
46.04 Construction and Building Finishers and Managers
46.05 Plumbers and Pipefitters
46.99 Construction Trades, Other

47. MECHANICS AND REPAIRERS
47.01 Electrical and Electronics Equipment Installers and Repairers
47.02 Heating, Air Conditioning, and Refrigeration Mechanics and Repairers
47.03 Industrial Equipment Maintenance and Repairers
47.04 Miscellaneous Mechanics and Repairers
47.05 Stationary Energy Sources Installers and Operators
47.06 Vehicle and Mobile Equipment Mechanics and Repairers
47.99 Mechanics and Repairers, Other

48. PRECISION PRODUCTION TRADES
48.01 Drafting
48.02 Graphic and Printing Equipment Operators
48.03 Leatherworkers and Upholsterers
48.05 Precision Metal Workers
48.07 Woodworkers
48.99 Precision Production Trades, Other

49. TRANSPORTATION AND MATERIALS MOVING WORKERS
49.01 Air Transportation Workers
49.02 Vehicle and Equipment Operators
49.03 Water Transportation Workers
49.99 Transportation and Materials Moving Workers, Other

50. VISUAL AND PERFORMING ARTS
50.01 Visual and Performing Arts
50.02 Crafts, Folk Art, and Artisanry
50.03 Dance
50.04 Design and Applied Arts
50.05 Drama/Theater Arts and Stagecraft
50.06 Film/Video and Photographic Arts
50.07 Fine Arts and Art Studies
50.09 Music
50.99 Visual and Performing Arts, Other

51. HEALTH PROFESSIONS AND RELATED SCIENCES
51.01 Chiropractic (D.C., D.C.M.)
51.02 Communication Disorders Sciences and Services
51.03 Community Health Services
51.04 Dentistry (D.D.S., D.M.D.)
51.05 Dental Clinical Sciences/Graduate Dentistry (M.S., Ph.D.)
51.06 Dental Services
51.07 Health and Medical Administrative Services
51.08 Health and Medical Assistants
51.09 Health and Medical Diagnostic and Treatment Services
51.10 Health and Medical Laboratory Technologies
51.11 Health and Medical Preparatory Programs
51.12 Medicine (M.D.)
51.13 Medical Basic Sciences
51.14 Medical Clinical Sciences (M.S., Ph.D.)
51.15 Mental Health Services
51.16 Nursing
51.17 Optometry
51.18 Ophthalmic/Optometric Services
51.19 Osteopathic Medicine (D.O.)
51.20 Pharmacy
51.21 Podiatry (D.P.M., D.P., Pod.D.)
51.22 Public Health
51.23 Rehabilitation/Therapeutic Services
51.24 Veterinary Medicine (D.V.M.)
51.25 Veterinary Clinical Sciences (M.S., Ph.D.)
51.26 Miscellaneous Health Aides
51.27 Miscellaneous Health Sciences and Allied Health Services
51.28 Dental Residency Programs
51.29 Medical Residency Programs
51.30 Veterinary Residency Programs
51.99 Health Professions and Related Services, Other

52. BUSINESS MANAGEMENT AND ADMINISTRATIVE SERVICES
52.01 Business
52.02 Business Administration and Management
52.03 Accounting
52.04 Administrative and Secretarial Services
52.05 Business Communications
52.06 Business/Managerial Economics
52.07 Enterprise Management and Operation
52.08 Financial Management and Services
52.09 Hospitality Services Management
52.10 Human Resources Management
52.11 International Business
52.12 Business Information and Data-Processing Services
52.13 Business Quantitative Methods and Management Science
52.14 Marketing Management and Research
52.15 Real Estate
52.16 Taxation
52.99 Business Management and Administrative Services, Other

53. HIGH SCHOOL/SECONDARY DIPLOMAS AND CERTIFICATES
53.01 High School/Secondary Diplomas
53.02 High School/Secondary Certificates

Table B: Occupations in Section 2 Within Groupings of Related Jobs

Table B lists all of the 1,122 occupations that are included in Section 2. It uses an organizational structure developed by the U.S. Department of Labor called the Occupational Information Network (O*NET). Like the system used for instructional programs in Table A, the O*NET jobs are organized within major groups of related jobs, followed by more specific subgroups of related jobs, followed by the job titles within those subgroups.

The O*NET also uses a numerical system to identify the groupings and assigns a unique number to each job title. Like the subgrouping system used for instructional programs, the O*NET system is also easy to use, since it allows you to quickly find the major jobs that are similar to each other. Descriptions for each of the jobs are included in Section 2, arranged in order of its O*NET number. To find the O*NET job descriptions that interest you, look at the top of the page in Section 2 for the O*NET occupation's number you are seeking.

EXECUTIVES, MANAGERS, AND ADMINISTRATORS
General Managers
Treasurers, Controllers, and Chief Financial Officers **(13002a)**
Financial Managers, Branch or Department **(13002b)**
Human Resources Managers **(13005a)**
Training and Development Managers **(13005b)**
Labor Relations Managers **(13005c)**
Employee Assistance Specialists **(13005e)**
Purchasing Managers **(13008)**
Advertising and Promotions Managers **(13011a)**
Sales Managers **(13011b)**
Marketing Managers **(13011c)**
Fundraising Directors **(13011d)**
Property Officers and Contract Administrators **(13014a)**
Administrative Services Managers **(13014b)**
Engineering Managers **(13017a)**
Natural Sciences Managers **(13017b)**
Computer and Information Systems Managers **(13017c)**
Specialty Managers
Postmasters and Mail Superintendents **(15002)**
College and University Administrators **(15005a)**
Educational Program Directors **(15005b)**
Nursing Directors **(15008a)**
Medical and Health Services Managers **(15008b)**
Land Leasing and Development Managers **(15011a)**
Property, Real Estate, and Community Association Managers **(15011b)**
Property Records Managers **(15011c)**
Industrial Production Managers **(15014)**
Landscaping Managers **(15017a)**
Construction Managers **(15017b)**
Mining Superintendents and Supervisors **(15021a)**
Oil and Gas Drilling and Production Superintendents **(15021c)**
Transportation Managers **(15023a)**
Communications Managers **(15023b)**
Utilities Managers **(15023c)**
Storage and Distribution Managers **(15023d)**
Lodging Managers **(15026a)**
Food-Service Managers **(15026b)**

Nursery and Greenhouse Managers **(15031)**
Lawn Service Managers **(15032)**
Executives
Government Service Executives **(19005a)**
Private Sector Executives **(19005b)**
Services Managers
Amusement and Recreation Establishment Managers **(19999a)**
Social and Community Service Managers **(19999b)**
Association Managers and Administrators **(19999c)**
Service Establishment Managers **(19999d)**
Gambling Establishment Managers **(19999e)**
Security Managers **(19999f)**

PROFESSIONAL AND SUPPORT SPECIALISTS—FINANCIAL SPECIALISTS, ENGINEERS, SCIENTISTS, MATHEMATICIANS, SOCIAL SCIENTISTS, SOCIAL SERVICES WORKERS, RELIGIOUS WORKERS, AND LEGAL WORKERS
Financial Specialists
Underwriters **(21102)**
Credit Analysts **(21105)**
Loan Officers and Counselors **(21108)**
Tax Preparers **(21111)**
Accountants **(21114a)**
Auditors **(21114b)**
Data Processing Auditors **(21114c)**
Budget Analysts **(21117)**
Financial Counselors **(21199b)**
Purchasers and Buyers
Wholesale and Retail Buyers, Except Farm Products **(21302)**
Purchasing Agents and Buyers, Farm Products **(21305a)**
Purchasing Agents and Contract Specialists **(21308a)**
Procurement Engineers **(21308b)**
Price Analysts **(21308c)**
Human Resources Workers
Claims Takers, Unemployment Benefits **(21502)**
Special Agents, Insurance **(21505)**
Employment Interviewers, Private or Public Employment Service **(21508)**

Job and Occupational Analysts (21511a)
Employer Relations and Placement Specialists (21511b)
Employee Relations Specialists (21511c)
Employee Training Specialists (21511d)
Personnel Recruiters (21511e)
Labor Relations Specialists (21511f)
Inspectors and Compliance Officers
Cost Estimators (21902)
Management Analysts (21905)
Construction and Building Inspectors (21908a)
Elevator Inspectors (21908b)
Health Officers and Inspectors (21911a)
Environmental Compliance Inspectors (21911b)
Immigration and Customs Inspectors (21911c)
Licensing Examiners and Inspectors (21911d)
Industrial and Occupational Safety and Health Inspectors (21911e)
Equal Opportunity Representatives and Officers (21911f)
Government Property Inspectors and Investigators (21911h)
Financial Examiners (21911j)
Aviation Inspectors (21911k)
Pressure Vessel Inspectors (21911l)
Public Transportation Inspectors (21911m)
Marine Cargo Inspectors (21911n)
Coroners (21911p)
Agricultural Inspectors (21911r)
Radiation-Protection Specialists (21911t)
Tax Examiners, Collectors, and Revenue Agents (21914)
Assessors (21917)
Claims Examiners, Property and Casualty Insurance (21921)
Management Support Workers
Computer Security Specialists (21999a)
Legislative Assistants (21999b)
Executive Secretaries and Administrative Assistants (21999c)
Land Leasing and Permit Agents (21999d)
Meeting and Convention Planners (21999f)
Grant Coordinators (21999g)
Customs Brokers (21999h)
Engineers
Aerospace Engineers (22102)
Ceramic Engineers (22105a)
Metallurgists (22105b)
Welding Engineers (22105c)
Materials Engineers (22105d)
Mining Engineers, Including Mine Safety (22108)
Petroleum Engineers (22111)
Chemical Engineers (22114)
Nuclear Engineers (22117)
Civil Engineers, Including Traffic (22121)
Agricultural Engineers (22123)
Electrical Engineers (22126a)x
Electronics Engineers, Except Computer (22126b)
Computer Engineers (22127)
Industrial Engineers, Except Safety (22128)
Industrial Safety and Health Engineers (22132a)
Fire-Prevention and Protection Engineers (22132b)
Product Safety Engineers (22132c)
Mechanical Engineers (22135)
Marine Engineers (22138)
Production Engineers (22197)

Architects and Surveyors
Architects, Except Landscape and Marine (22302)
Marine Architects (22305)
Landscape Architects (22308)
Cartographers and Photogrammetrists (22311a)
Surveyors (22311b)
Engineering Technologists and Technicians
Civil Engineering Technicians (22502)
Electronics Engineering Technicians (22505a)
Calibration and Instrumentation Technicians (22505b)
Electrical Engineering Technicians (22505c)
Industrial Engineering Technicians and Technologists (22508)
Mechanical Engineering Technicians and Technologists (22511)
Architectural Drafters (22514a)
Electronic Drafters (22514b)
Civil Drafters (22514c)
Mechanical Drafters (22514d)
Estimators and Drafters, Utilities (22517)
Surveying Technicians (22521a)
Mapping Technicians (22521b)
Sound Engineering Technicians (22599a)
Metallurgical Technicians (22599b)
Aerospace Engineering Technicians (22599c)
Agricultural Technicians (22599d)
Chemical Engineering Technicians (22599e)
Laser Technicians (22599f)
Physical Scientists
Physicists (24102a)
Astronomers (24102b)
Chemists, Except Biochemists (24105)
Atmospheric and Space Scientists (24108)
Geologists (24111a)
Geophysicists (24111b)
Geographers (24199a)
Environmental Scientists (24199b)
Materials Scientists (24199c)
Life Scientists
Foresters (24302a)
Soil Conservationists (24302b)
Wood Technologists (24302c)
Range Managers (24302d)
Park Naturalists (24302e)
Animal Scientists (24305a)
Plant Scientists (24305b)
Food Scientists (24305c)
Soil Scientists (24305d)
Biochemists (24308a)
Biologists (24308b)
Biophysicists (24308c)
Botanists (24308d)
Microbiologists (24308e)
Geneticists (24308f)
Physiologists and Cytologists (24308g)
Zoologists (24308h)
Toxicologists (24308j)
Medical Scientists (24311)
Life and Physical Sciences Technologists and Technicians
Biological and Agricultural Technologists (24502a)
Artificial Breeding Technicians (24502b)

Vocational Rehabilitation Coordinators (31517b)
Laboratory Managers (31517c)
Instructional Coordinators (31517d)
Teacher Aides, Paraprofessional (31521)

Diagnosing and Treating Practitioners
Doctors Of Medicine (Md) (32102a)
Doctors Of Osteopathy (Do) (32102b)
Psychiatrists (32102e)
Anesthesiologists (32102f)
Surgeons (32102j)
Pathologists (32102u)
Oral Pathologists (32105a)
Dentists (32105b)
Orthodontists (32105d)
Prosthodontists (32105f)
Oral and Maxillofacial Surgeons (32105g)
Optometrists (32108)
Podiatrists (32111)
Chiropractors (32113)
Veterinary Pathologists (32114a)
Veterinarians (32114b)
Veterinary Inspectors (32114c)

Medical Therapists
Respiratory Therapists (32302)
Occupational Therapists (32305)
Physical Therapists (32308)
Manual Arts Therapists (32311a)
Corrective Therapists (32311b)
Speech-Language Pathologists and Audiologists (32314)
Recreational Therapists (32317)
Exercise Physiologists (32399a)
Orientation and Mobility Therapists (32399b)

Health Care Providers
Registered Nurses (32502)
Licensed Practical Nurses (32505)
Emergency Medical Technicians (32508)
Physician's Assistants (32511)
Opticians, Dispensing and Measuring (32514)
Pharmacists (32517)
Pharmacy Technicians (32518)
Dietitians and Nutritionists (32521)
Dietetic Technicians (32523)

Medical Technologists and Technicians
Medical and Clinical Laboratory Technologists (32902)
Medical and Clinical Laboratory Technicians (32905)
Dental Hygienists (32908)
Medical Records Technicians (32911)
Radiation Therapists (32913)
Nuclear Medicine Technologists (32914)
Radiologic Technologists (32919)
Radiologic Technicians (32921)
Electroneurodiagnostic Technologists (32923)
Cardiology Technologists (32925)
Electrocardiograph Technicians (32926)
Surgical Technologists and Technicians (32928)
Psychiatric Technicians (32931)
Health Service Coordinators (32996a)
Transplant Coordinators (32996b)
Occupational Health and Safety Specialists (32996c)
Orthotists and Prosthetists (32999a)

Pheresis Technicians (32999b)
Optometric and Ophthalmic Technicians (32999c)
Audiometrists (32999d)
Dialysis Technicians (32999e)

Artistic, Creative, and Entertainment Providers
Columnists, Critics, and Commentators (34002a)
Poets and Lyricists (34002b)
Creative Writers (34002c)
Editors (34002d)
Managing Editors (34002e)
Programming and Script Editors and Coordinators (34002f)
Book Editors (34002g)
Readers (34002h)
Caption Writers (34002j)
Copy Writers (34002l)
Dictionary Editors (34002m)
Technical Writers (34005)
Public Relations Specialists and Publicity Writers (34008)
Reporters and Correspondents (34011)
Broadcast News Analysts (34014)
Announcers, Radio and Television (34017)
Announcers, Except Radio and Television (34021)
Professional Photographers (34023a)
Photographers, Scientific (34023b)
Camera Operators, Television and Motion Picture (34026)
Broadcast Technicians (34028b)
Transmitter Engineers (34028c)
Film Editors (34032)
Painters and Illustrators (34035a)
Sketch Artists (34035b)
Graphic Designers (34035c)
Cartoonists and Animators (34035d)
Sculptors (34035e)
Fashion Designers (34038a)
Commercial and Industrial Designers (34038b)
Set Designers (34038c)
Exhibit Designers (34038d)
Art Directors (34038e)
Floral Designers (34038f)
Interior Designers (34041)
Merchandise Displayers and Window Trimmers (34044)
Music Directors (34047a)
Music Arrangers and orchestrators (34047b)
Singers (34047c)
Composers (34047e)
Prompters (34047f)
Musicians, Instrumental (34051)
Dancers (34053a)
Choreographers (34053b)
Actors and Performers (34056a)
Extras/Stand-Ins (34056b)
Amusement Entertainers (34056d)
Equestrian Performers (34056e)
Producers (34056f)
Directors—Stage, Motion Picture, Television, and Radio (34056g)
Program Directors (34056h)
Talent Directors (34056j)
Technical Directors/Managers (34056k)
Coaches and Scouts (34058a)
Athletic Trainers (34058b)

Table B: Occupations in Section 2 Within Groupings of Related Jobs

Office Machine Operators
Billing, Posting, and Calculating Machine Operators **(56002)**
Duplicating Machine Operators **(56005)**
Mail Machine Operators, Preparation and Handling **(56008)**
Computer Operators, Except Peripheral Equipment **(56011)**
Peripheral Edp Equipment Operators **(56014)**
Data-Entry Keyers, Except Composing **(56017)**
Data Keyers, Composing **(56021)**

Communications Equipment Operators
Switchboard Operators **(57102)**
Directory Assistance Operators **(57105)**
Central Office Operators **(57108)**
Telegraph and Teletype Operators **(57111)**

Mail Clerks, Carriers, and Messengers
Mail Clerks, Except Mail Machine Operators and Postal
Service **(57302)**
Postal Mail Carriers **(57305)**
Postal Service Clerks **(57308)**
Couriers and Messengers **(57311a)**

Material Recording, Scheduling, and Distributing Workers
Dispatchers—Police, Fire, and Ambulance **(58002)**
Dispatchers—Except Police, Fire, and Ambulance **(58005)**
Production, Planning, and Expediting Clerks **(58008)**
Transportation Agents **(58011)**
Meter Readers, Utilities **(58014)**
Weighers, Measurers, Checkers, and Samplers—
Recordkeeping **(58017)**
Marking Clerks **(58021)**
Stock Clerks—Stockroom, Warehouse, or Storage Yard **(58023)**
order Fillers, Wholesale and Retail Sales **(58026)**
Shipping, Receiving, and Traffic Clerks **(58028)**
Engineering Clerks **(58099a)**
Transportation Maintenance Clerks **(58099b)**

SERVICE WORKERS

Service Supervisors and Managers
Municipal Fire Fighting and Prevention Supervisors
(61002a)
Forest Fire Fighting and Prevention Supervisors **(61002b)**

Police and Detective Supervisors **(61005)**
Housekeeping Supervisors **(61008)**
Chefs and Head Cooks **(61099a)**
First-Line Supervisors/Managers Of Food Preparation
and Serving Workers **(61099b)**
First-Line Supervisors/Hospitality and Personal Service
Workers **(61099c)**
First-Line Supervisors/Managers Of Housekeeping and
Janitorial Workers **(61099d)**

Private Household Workers
Housekeepers, Private Household **(62031)**
Child Monitors, Private Household **(62041)**
Personal Attendants, Private Household **(62061)**

Protective Service Workers
Fire Inspectors **(63002a)**
Fire Investigators **(63002b)**
Forest Fire Inspectors and Prevention Specialists **(63005)**
Municipal Fire Fighters **(63008a)**
Forest Fire Fighters **(63008b)**
Police Detectives **(63011a)**
Police Identification and Records Officers **(63011b)**
Police Investigators—Patrollers **(63014a)**
Highway Patrol Pilots **(63014b)**
Correction Officers and Jailers **(63017)**
Parking Enforcement Officers **(63021)**
Bailiffs **(63023)**
United States Marshals **(63026)**
Criminal Investigators and Special Agents **(63028a)**
Child Support, Missing Persons, and Unemployment
Insurance Fraud Investigators **(63028b)**
Sheriffs and Deputy Sheriffs **(63032)**
Detectives and Investigators, Except Public **(63035)**
Railroad and Transit Police and Special Agents **(63038)**
Fish and Game Wardens **(63041)**
Crossing Guards **(63044)**
Guards and Watch Guards **(63047)**
Protective Service Workers, Recreational **(63099b)**
Animal Control Workers **(63099c)**
Automatic Teller Machine Servicers **(63099d)**

Introduction

While it is hard to believe, this book presents the very first time that virtually all education and training programs (all 885 of them) have been cross-referenced to all major jobs (1,122 jobs) in one book. At last, you can look up an educational program and find the jobs that are most closely related to it—or look up a job and find the related education or training it requires. In addition, the book includes useful descriptions of all major jobs and educational programs.

While this book contains a lot of information, we've tried hard to make it easy to use. The Table of Contents briefly explains the major sections and how to use them—enough information to begin using the book. This introduction provides additional details about the book, its contents, tips on how best to use it, and other useful information.

A Quick Overview of the Two Major Sections

There are two major sections in this book. The first section presents all major college majors and other instructional programs. All 885 instructional program are organized into groupings that are most easily reviewed in the Table of Contents, Table A. Section 1 briefly describes each of the instructional programs and then lists one or more occupations that are most closely related to it. Section 2 provides descriptions for all major jobs in our economy. Most of these jobs are cross-referenced by the instructional programs in Section 1. The 1,122 job descriptions provided in Section 2 emphasize information related to the education and training requirements for each job. You can review the entire list of occupations by reviewing Table B in the Table of Contents.

A Quick Review of Section 1: Classification of Instructional Programs

The structure used to organize the instructional programs was developed by the good people at the U.S. Department of Education. It's called the "Classification of Instructional Programs" (the CIP) and it is used to classify all instructional programs offered by high schools (including vocational), colleges and universities, junior colleges, business and vocational training programs, apprenticeships, and any other source of training or education that leads to formal certification, diploma, or degree.

As you will see in this book, there are specialized instructional programs that you may not have imagined. It seems that something is available for almost every interest and job objective. If you are considering getting additional training or education, the content of Section 1 will open your mind to the universe of possibilities.

A Sample Instructional Program Entry from Section 1

To best understand what Section 1 does, let's review one of its educational program entries. This entry is followed by notes on each of the entry's component parts.

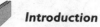
1— ## 01. AGRICULTURAL BUSINESS AND PRODUCTION

2— A summary of groups of instructional programs that prepare individuals to apply scientific knowledge, methods, and techniques to agricultural business and production.

3— ## 01.01 Agricultural Business and Management

A group of instructional programs (see 01.0101).

4— ## 01.0101 Agricultural Business and Management, General

An instructional program that generally prepares individuals to apply modern economic and business principles involved in the organization, operation, and management of farm and agricultural businesses.

5—
15023C	Utilities Managers
15031	Nursery and Greenhouse Managers
27102A	Economists
31210	Social Science Teachers—Postsecondary
31323	Farm and Home Management Advisors
79999K	Agricultural Crop Farm Managers
79999L	Livestock Production Managers
79999M	Fish Hatchery Managers

Notes

1 This is the name of a major group of instructional programs. It is preceded by a two digit number used for programs in this group.

2 A brief description for this group of instructional programs.

3 This is the name of the first subgroup of instructional programs within the major grouping of Agricultural Business and Production group. All subgroups are given a four-digit code number that includes the two-digit number for the major group plus an additional two-digit number for the subgroup.

4 This is the name of the first specific instructional program within the "Agricultural Business and Management" subgroup. Specific instructional programs are given a six-digit code number that begins with the subgroup number followed by a two-digit program number. A brief description follows the program's number and title. There are typically a number of specific instructional programs within each subgroup.

5 These are the occupations for which the "Agricultural Business and Management, General" instructional program prepare you. Each job title is preceded by that job's unique O*NET number (more on this later). You can then look up the descriptions of these jobs in Section Two.

Simple! You can look up an instructional program in one of two ways. You can find it in the Table of Contents or you can also look it up in the alphabetic list included in the appendix. If you are exploring educational or training options, using the Table of Contents Table A will show you groupings of similar programs, a helpful feature. Alphabetic Index of Instructional Programs is a value-added feature that makes it even easier to jump to a specific spot in the book.

As you browse Section 1 (which can be more entertaining that it sounds) you may notice that some instructional programs have many related jobs while others have few or even none. This does not mean that these instructional programs do not prepare you for the labor market, it simply means that there are no specific jobs directly related to that instructional program. One example of this is Liberal Arts, a college major that prepares you to deal with many life situations and jobs rather than a specific occupation. Many business executives, in fact, have graduated from college with a Liberal Arts, education that helps in problem-solving, communications skills, and other areas important for these jobs.

A Quick Review of Section 2: O*NET Job Descriptions

Section 2 provides descriptions of 1,122 jobs, including all major jobs in our economy. The jobs are arranged within groupings of jobs that are similar in nature. Look at Table B in the Table of Contents to see the list of jobs within the groupings. The information we used in these descriptions also comes from our friends in the Federal government, this time from the U.S. Department of Labor. To create these descriptions, we used data from the new database called the "Occupational Information Network"—the O*NET. This is a very large database of information covering all major jobs and quite a few not-so-major ones.

The O*NET database provides an enormous amount of detailed information for each job, including detailed information on over 450 data elements. If you printed all the available information, it would result in a book over seventy feet tall. That is an overwhelming amount of data and certainly more than would hold your reading interest. So we took it upon ourselves to select the information from the O*NET we thought would be most helpful to you. Since the *Dictionary of Instructional Programs and Careers* cross-references instructional programs with occupations, the job descriptions in Section 2 emphasize O*NET data related to that job's training or educational requirements.

A Sample Job Description Entry from Section 2

A picture, it is said, is worth a thousand words. So let's take a look at one of the job descriptions from Section 2.

EXECUTIVES, MANAGERS, AND ADMINISTRATORS

General Managers

1 —— TREASURERS, CONTROLLERS, AND CHIEF FINANCIAL OFFICERS
2 —— (13002A)

3 — Plan, direct, and coordinate the financial activities of an organization at the highest level of management. Include financial reserve officers.

4 — **Average Yearly Earnings:** $54,392. **Experience:** Extensive preparation is needed. Extensive skill, knowledge, and experience are needed for this occupation. It may require more than five years of experience. **Education:** A bachelor's degree is the minimum formal education required for this group of occupations. However, many also require graduate school. For example, they may require a master's degree, and some require a Ph.D., M.D., or J.D. (law degree). **Training:** Employees in this type of occupation may need some on-the-job training, but most of these occupations assume that the person will already have the required skills, knowledge, work-related experience, and/or training. **Examples:** Other occupations like this one often involve coordinating, training, supervising, or managing the activities of others to accomplish goals. Very advanced communication and organizational skills are required. Examples include athletic trainers, lawyers, managing editors, physicists, social psychologists, and surgeons. **Standard Vocational Preparation Range:** 8.0 to 9.0-Four years to more than 10 years. **Major/Instructional Program:** 52.0801 Finance, General; 52.0807 Investments and Securities. **Related Courses:** Administration and Management; Economics and Accounting; Sales and Marketing; Personnel and Human Resources; Mathematics; Psychology; English Language; History and Archeology; Philosophy and Theology; Law, Government, and Jurisprudence; Communications and Media

1 Occupational Title   The U.S. Department of Labor assigns this title as the one that is most often used for this job. But note that the same job can have different titles used by different employers.

2 O*NET Code Number   This five-digit number is assigned to each job by the Department of Labor to help in cross-referencing to other occupational information systems. In some cases, similar jobs have the same five-digit O*NET number plus a letter at the end (for example "Treasurers, Controllers, and Chief Financial Officers (13002A)" and "Financial Managers, Branch or Department (13002B)."

3 Definition   This is a brief statement of the job's basic duties and responsibilities.

4 Average Annual Earnings   This is the average earnings for all people employed in this occupation for 1997 according to the Bureau of Labor Statistics (1997 earnings data was the most recent available from the BLS at the time we went to press). Note that local pay rates will often differ from this national average and that new entrants and those with less experience typically earn much less than the average. **Experience**   This is the amount of work experience typically required to do the job. Note, however, that some people employed in most occupations may have entered with considerably more or less experience. **Education**   This is the level of education typically required for a person to obtain this job though, as with experience, there are often exceptions. **Training**   This is the amount of on-the-job training that would normally be needed to handle this job after it is obtained. **Examples**   This notes key skills required for the job and lists one or more other occupations that require similar skills. **Standard Vocational Preparation**   The SVP is a numeric rating system used in other occupational classification systems. It provides a number rating for the range of education or training time typically required to handle this job. For ease of interpretation, we have translated the SVP ratings into more easily understood time ranges such as "4 years to more than 10 years." **College Major or Instructional Program**   This lists one or more college majors or other instructional program most often used to prepare for this job. A Classification of Instructional Program (CIP) code number follows each entry to allow cross-referencing to Section One and to other systems using the CIP code system. Keep in mind that, for many jobs, Ccreative and persistent individuals have been able to get jobs by gaining the skills needed through means other than formal education or by a combination of related experience and education or training that are not listed. **Related Courses**   The O*NET database provides measures for a variety of knowledge categories that are typically learned through education, training, or extensive on-the-job training. This information will give you a good idea of the types of courses or special knowledge required for the occupation. For each job, we included those knowledge categories that were rated as high or very high (important or very important) for that job.

Beware the Data

It is important to understand that the information provided in the job descriptions represents an "average" or "typical" situation. While the information is obtained from reliable government sources, it does have its limitations. For example, this is part of the warning included in the government's own source for the information we used in this book: "The information reflects jobs as they have been found to occur in general, but they may not coincide in every respect with the content of jobs as performed in particular establishments or at certain localities." Which is to say that you can't apply the "average" to a particular job, because the average job just doesn't exist. In a similar way, the average family may have 1.7 children and four tenths of a cat (or whatever), but I have never personally met a fractional child or cat.

So, unfortunately perhaps, you will have to apply your own common sense to whatever this book's job descriptions tell you. Here are just a few examples: While the job descriptions include the average annual earnings, this means that half of all people earn LESS than the average for a given occupation, and half earn more. New graduates, those with less experience, and those working in smaller organizations typically earn less than average. Local pay rates may also differ substantially from the national average—as may cost of living. So most of us won't get the "average" pay, though the information is interesting, isn't it?

Some people will have substantially different education, training, work experience or other credentials than the typical person holding the job. For example, some Training and

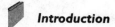

Development Managers do not have a four-year college degree, though most do. There are many ways to enter most occupations, however, employers will typically want the education and experience stated in the job descriptions.

Our point here is that you should use the information in this book to learn more about education and training programs—and their related jobs—but do remember that there are many exceptions. We want you to be encouraged to go after the careers and instructional programs that interest you so, please, don't let any of the information in this book become a barrier to you. Instead, your task is to find creative ways of getting to where you want to go. Barriers can often be overcome with a bit of creativity and hard work.

Tips for Using the Book to Select a Course of Study, Advance on the Job, Write Job Descriptions, and More

It seems odd that, until we did this book, you could not get a cross-reference listing of all college majors and other instructional programs and their related jobs. But we've always thought that such a cross-reference would be useful to a variety of people for a variety of uses, including:

- Job seekers
- People exploring job and career options
- Students, including adults returning to school
- People wanting to advance in their current jobs
- Employers
- Counselors, teachers, and other professionals

Here are some brief tips for using this book in some of the ways we anticipate. If you find other uses, please let us know and we'll mention them in the next edition.

Life Planning, in General

We, the authors, are good examples of people who were not sure about what we wanted to do "when we grew up." We thought about dropping out of school, we changed our majors in college, we changed our jobs and careers several times, and we went back to school when we thought we knew what we wanted to do. And we continue to explore ourselves and our personal and professional options for the future.

We don't think that being unsure about what you want to do with your career or your life is all that unusual. Things change. Even if you were sure at some time in the past, you have probably changed and are likely to have different interests and needs now. We think, then, that the best way to approach this whole career and life-planning thing is to concern yourself with just two questions:

1. What would I really like to be doing in five to ten years?
2. What could I do to help me move in that direction?

Both are practical but very important questions. Whatever your personal situation, we assume that you are reading this book to help you in some practical way. The following are some practical and brief tips on using this book.

Exploring Education and Training Options

A variety of research indicates that your interests are important indicators of what sorts of things you will do well. This book allows you to explore your interests, starting with either jobs that interest you or with education or training options that seem interesting. You may be able to select short-term training that prepares you for a long-term job objective or for additional educational options. Or you may want to consider longer-term education or training, such as a pursuing a college degree, technical certification, or an apprenticeship program.

If you are currently in school, you can use this book to help define possible job objectives related to the college major or other instructional program you are in—or to help define or change your major or area of study to one that makes more sense to you.

We suggest you begin by browsing the list of instructional programs provided in Table A of the Table of Contents. There you will find programs that you may have never known existed—and some will interest you far more than others. We suggest you make a photocopy of that table and checkmark the programs that sound interesting or list them on a separate piece of paper. (Since others may use the book in the same way, our librarian friends ask that you don't mark in the book itself.) Then look over the information we provide on each program in Section 1, including the related jobs. As needed, you can also use Section 2 to learn more about the jobs listed in Section 1. As you learn more, select the one or two college majors or other instructional programs that are MOST interesting to you. Then learn as much as you can about these programs, using the information sources we mention later in this introduction or other sources.

Exploring Career and Job Options

You can use this book to explore career and job options in a similar way described for education and training options. There are two major uses.

The first is for employed folks looking for upward mobility in their current jobs or who want to increase their earnings by upgrading their skills for a related job with the same or a different employer. The second use is for those folks who are trying to figure out, from the universe of possibilities, what sort of job or career they want. Let's take these situations one at a time.

If you are working and want to move up in a similar or related field (so as to increase your earnings, for example), we suggest you begin by finding the job you have now and looking for jobs that are related. The best way to do this is to use the Alphabetic Listing of Occupational Titles. This index lets you locate jobs in Section 2. As you recall from Table B in the Table of Contents, the section organizes all major jobs into clusters of related jobs. This approach allows you to quickly find job titles that are related in some way to what you already do or that you want to do next and obtain additional information on the jobs that interest you from Section 2, including additional training or education those jobs may require.

You may, on the other hand, be among the large group of relatively confused people, career-wise, who are open to the universe of options available but have no good idea of just what to do. If so, don't despair, you are in good company. But you WILL have to limit your options by doing some homework. We suggest you begin with the Table of Contents Table B. Make a copy of this Table and go through each and every grouping of occupations. Put a check mark by those groupings or individual jobs that sound interesting and a line through those

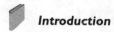

that don't interest you. This won't take all that long to do and, unless you like almost everything (a most unfortunate characteristic shared by one of the authors) this should leave you with a large fraction of all possible occupations crossed off. Then go through the ones you checked and rate each job either "1" (very interested) or "2" (somewhat interested) or "3" (not that interested). The jobs you rated as "1," of course, are those you should focus on, beginning with the information provided on each in Section 2.

Looking for a Job

If you are looking for a job, the descriptions in Section 2 will tell you the requirements for that job and give you key things to emphasize on your resume and in your interviews. Use the Table of Contents Table B to identify possible job targets requiring similar skills and experiences that you may have previously overlooked.

For Counselors, Teachers, and Other Professionals

One obvious use of this book is as a resource for students and adults in helping them plan career and training options. For example, a student can look up a college major and see the jobs it can prepare them for. An adult considering going back to school could use it to identify short term training to help them advance in their career or to develop a long-term educational goal. The job descriptions will help students and adults identify courses or minors that will help them in achieving their career goals.

Instructors and administrators can also use the book to help develop or revise curriculum. The information in Section 1 will identify specific jobs the program should prepare a student for and the job descriptions in Section 2 will identify key skills to address in the program.

Employers and Human Resource Professionals

Professionals and managers in business, government, and nonprofit agencies can use the information in the book to improve their human resource management. Personnel specialists can use it to define the education and experience requirements needed for a job. This can improve the hiring process by helping to identify job candidates with the most relevant education and experience. Human resource staff can also use the material to encourage employees to develop their skills through additional training, education, and on-the-job experience.

As writers and developers of career reference books, we're continually amazed at ideas students, job seekers, teachers, counselors, and others develop for using the book. We're sure that readers will think of many more ways to use the book. If you'd like to share your ideas, please feel free to contact us via the publisher.

The Indexes

The Alphabetic Listing of Instructional Programs index lists all of the instructional programs included in Section 1. The Alphabetic Listing of Occupational Titles lists all of the job titles from Section 2 in alphabetic order. They're not, we admit, exciting indexes but will help you find information in the book quickly.

Source of Information in This Book

The first part of this book is a comprehensive guide to educational programs. The descriptions of instructional programs found in this section are from the Classification of Instructional Programs (CIP), which was developed by the U.S. Department of Education as a system for describing and classifying all education and instructional programs. Each instructional program is assigned a code as a unique identification number. Educators and counselors use CIP numbers for a variety of reasons. The U.S. Department of Labor uses the code when matching instructional programs with occupations. We've chosen to keep the instructional programs organized using these codes for quick and easy reference.

Just what is an instructional program? Well, the Department of Education considers it to be a combination of courses and/or experience designed to prepare a person for a job, additional education, or simply to increase knowledge and understanding. An instructional program must meet several criteria to be included in the system. These are:

1. The program must be offered by an educational institution, business, nonprofit organization, trade association, labor union, or similar provider.

2. A program must be a structured learning activity that leads to a completion point. This means that there is a planned curriculum.

3. Some form of recognition for program completion must be made. This might be a degree, diploma, vocational diploma, certificate of completion, or apprenticeship completion certificate.

The instructional programs can be delivered in a variety of schools, institutions, and other settings including:

- Postsecondary education programs provided by universities, colleges, or career schools that lead to an associate, bachelor's, masters, doctoral degree.

- Secondary education programs provided by high schools or career centers that award either regular or vocational diplomas.

- Adult education programs provided by universities, community colleges, career schools, businesses, or other providers that lead to certificates of completion.

- Apprenticeship programs provided by trade associations or labor unions that result in an apprenticeship completion certificate.

- Residency programs conducted by the dental, medical, and veterinary professions that lead to advanced professional certification.

The second section of this guide uses data from the U.S. Department of Labor. This department provides the most authoritative source of information about jobs available. The job descriptions come from the Occupational Information Network (O*NET). The O*NET database of occupational information was developed by a team of researchers and developers working under the direction of the U.S. Department of Labor. They, in turn, were assisted by thousands of employers who provided details on the nature of work provided in the many thousands of job samplings that were used in the development of this database. There are 1,122 jobs found in the O*NET database.

While the O*NET database was first released in late 1997, it was based on substantial work done on an earlier occupational database that was used to develop the *Dictionary of Occupational Titles* and other information sources. That database was first used in the 1939 edition of the *Dictionary of Occupational Titles* and has been continuously updated since. All of this work over many years has formed the basis for much of the occupational information used by employers, job seekers, career counselors, education and training institutions, researchers, policy makers, and many others.

Sources of Additional Information

This book is designed to help you identify instructional programs or occupations to consider more fully. There are an enormous number of sources of information you can turn to next in your search for information. Check out your library for good reference books and the Internet for sites containing information on occupations, learning, and related topics.

Here are a few of the reference books available from JIST we think will be particularly helpful.

> *The Occupational Outlook Handbook.* Highly recommended. Published by the U.S. Department of Labor and updated every other year. Provides descriptions for about 250 major jobs covering 87% of the workforce. The descriptions are well written and provide information on pay, working conditions, related jobs, projected growth, and more.
>
> *America's Top 300 Jobs.* This is a "bookstore" version of the *Occupational Outlook Handbook* that includes descriptions for all jobs in the OOH plus additional information.
>
> *The Enhanced Occupational Outlook Handbook.* Includes all the descriptions in the *Occupational Outlook Handbook* plus 3,000 descriptions of more specialized jobs and 5,000 additional titles. Easy to use.
>
> *The O*NET Dictionary of Occupational Titles.* The first and only book to provide information on the 1,122 new O*NET jobs from the U.S. Department of Labor. Provides descriptions for each job, including details on related skills, earnings, abilities, education and other requirements for each.
>
> *America's Top Jobs Series.* Each of these books describes about 100 jobs plus a review of job market trends, career planning and job search advice, summary information on hundreds of additional jobs and useful appendices. Titles include: *America's Fastest Growing Jobs; America's Top Jobs for College Graduates; America's Top Jobs for People Without College Degrees; America's Top Medical, Education, and Human Services Jobs; America's Top White Collar Jobs; America's Federal Jobs; and America's Top Military Careers.*
>
> *Best Jobs for the 21st Century.* Lists of jobs for best paying, highest earning at different education levels and other criteria plus hundreds of job descriptions. Additional titles in this series include *Best Jobs for the 21st Century for College Graduates* and, *Best Jobs for the 21st Century Through Work Experience and On-the-Job Training.*
>
> *The Guide for Occupational Exploration, JIST 2000 Edition.* This presents the first major revision of the GOE since the U.S. Department of Labor introduced it in 1979. This new edition introduces a revised Interest Areas and subgroupings to reflect the many changes in our economy. It remains the standard reference for exploring career options based on interests.

Section 1

Instructional Programs and Their Related Jobs

While you may not have thought much about it, there are thousands of formal training and educational programs available nationwide. These programs last from a few weeks to many years and include things like technical training programs, college degrees, apprenticeships, two-year associate's degrees, certificate programs, graduate degrees including the master's and doctor's, and professional degree programs.

One of the functions of government is to collect information that can be used in planning. Since training and education is such an important issue, the government developed an organized way to collect data on the many programs available. This section presents the system developed to collect that information. Called the Classification of Instructional Programs (CIP), it was developed by the U.S. Department of Education to organize all major training or education programs into groups of similar topics.

We use the CIP system in this section and included brief descriptions for each of the CIP group and instructional program. We have also added an important element to each by listing the occupations that relate most closely to each instructional program. Section 2 provides descriptions for each of the occupations listed in Section 1.

Additional information on this section and the Classification of Instructional Programs is provided in the Introduction to this book. Table A, following the Table of Contents, presents the CIP system of groups and subgroups to help you quickly locate the instructional programs that most interest you.

01. AGRICULTURAL BUSINESS AND PRODUCTION

A summary of groups of instructional programs that prepare individuals to apply scientific knowledge, methods, and techniques to agricultural business and production.

01.01 Agricultural Business and Management

A group of instructional programs (see 01.0101).

01.0101 Agricultural Business and Management, General

An instructional program that generally prepares individuals to apply modern economic and business principles involved in the organization, operation, and management of farm and agricultural businesses.

15023C	Utilities Managers
15031	Nursery and Greenhouse Managers
27102A	Economists
31210	Social Science Teachers—Postsecondary
31323	Farm and Home Management Advisors
79999K	Agricultural Crop Farm Managers
79999L	Livestock Production Managers
79999M	Fish Hatchery Managers

01.0102 Agricultural Business/Agribusiness Operations

An instructional program that prepares individuals to apply modern business and economic principles relating to the production and marketing of agricultural products and services.

15031	Nursery and Greenhouse Managers
79999K	Agricultural Crop Farm Managers
79999L	Livestock Production Managers
79999M	Fish Hatchery Managers

01.0103 Agricultural Economics

An instructional program that describes modern business and economic principles relating to the allocation of resources in the production and marketing of agricultural products and services in the domestic and international markets.

| 27102A | Economists |
| 31210 | Social Science Teachers—Postsecondary |

01.0104   Farm and Ranch Management

An instructional program that prepares individuals to manage a farm or ranch. Includes instruction in computer-assisted management analysis, accounting, taxes, production, financing, capital resources, purchasing, government programs, farm inputs, performance records, contracts, estate planning, and marketing.

15031	Nursery and Greenhouse Managers
31323	Farm and Home Management Advisors
79999K	Agricultural Crop Farm Managers
79999L	Livestock Production Managers
79999M	Fish Hatchery Managers

01.0199   Agricultural Business and Management, Other

Any instructional program in agricultural business and management not described above.

01.02   Agricultural Mechanization

A group of instructional programs (see 01.0201).

01.0201   Agricultural Mechanization, General

An instructional program that prepares individuals in a general way to sell, select, and service agriculture or agribusiness technical equipment and facilities, including computers, specialized software, power units, machinery, equipment, structures, and utilities. Includes instruction in agricultural power units, the planning and selection of materials for the construction of agricultural facilities, the mechanical practices associated with irrigation and water conservation, erosion control, and data-processing systems.

19999D	Service Establishment Managers
22121	Civil Engineers, Including Traffic
22599D	Agricultural Technicians
41002	First-Line Supervisors and Manager/Supervisors—Sales and Related Workers
79999B	Irrigation Workers
83002B	Mechanical Inspectors
85123B	Millwrights and Machinery Erectors

85132	Maintenance Repairers, General Utility
85328B	Small Engine Mechanics
85999A	Hand and Portable Power Tool Repairers
87102B	Rough Carpenters
87817	Fence Erectors
89111	Tool Grinders, Filers, Sharpeners, and Other Precision Grinders

01.0204   Agricultural Power Machinery Operator

An instructional program that prepares individuals to install, operate, service, maintain, and repair various agricultural power units, vehicles, machinery, and equipment. Includes instruction in gas, diesel, and electric power units; welding; refrigeration; and hydraulic systems.

41002	First-Line Supervisors and Manager/Supervisors—Sales and Related Workers
79021	Farm Equipment Operators
79036	Sprayers/Applicators
79855	General Farmworkers
79999B	Irrigation Workers
83002B	Mechanical Inspectors
83005A	Production Inspectors, Testers, Graders, Sorters, Samplers, and Weighers
85119A	Machinery Maintenance Mechanics
85311A	Bus and Truck Mechanics and Diesel Engine Specialists
85321	Farm Equipment Mechanics
85328B	Small Engine Mechanics
85999B	Pump Installers and Servicers
87202A	Electricians
87508	Pipelayers
97102A	Truck Drivers, Heavy

01.0299   Agricultural Mechanization, Other

Any instructional program in agricultural mechanization not described above.

15023C	Utilities Managers
72002A	Agricultural Crop Supervisors

01.03   Agricultural Production Workers and Managers

A group of instructional programs (see 01.0301).

01.0301 Agricultural Production Workers and Managers, General

An instructional program that generally prepares individuals to plan and economically use facilities, natural resources, labor, and capital in the production of plant and animal products.

15023A	Transportation Managers
21305A	Purchasing Agents and Buyers, Farm Products
24502B	Artificial Breeding Technicians
24502C	Biological and Agricultural Technicians
31323	Farm and Home Management Advisors
72002A	Agricultural Crop Supervisors
72002B	Livestock Supervisors
72002C	Animal Care Supervisors, except Livestock
72002E	Horticultural Supervisors
72002G	Fishery Supervisors
79015	Animal Breeders
79017A	Animal Caretakers, except Farm
79021	Farm Equipment Operators
79033	Pruners
79036	Sprayers/Applicators
79855	General Farmworkers
79858	Farmworkers, Farm and Ranch Animals
79999A	Weed, Disease, and Insect Control Inspectors
79999B	Irrigation Workers
79999C	Horticultural Specialty Growers
79999D	Farmers
79999E	Commercial Fishery Workers
79999G	Aqua-Culturists
79999J	Gamekeepers
79999K	Agricultural Crop Farm Managers
79999L	Livestock Production Managers
79999M	Fish Hatchery Managers

01.0302 Agricultural Animal Husbandry and Production Management

An instructional program that prepares individuals to select, breed, care for, and market livestock and small farm animals. Includes instruction in the operation of animal production enterprises.

21305A	Purchasing Agents and Buyers, Farm Products
24502B	Artificial Breeding Technicians
24502C	Biological and Agricultural Technicians
31323	Farm and Home Management Advisors

72002A	Agricultural Crop Supervisors
72002B	Livestock Supervisors
72002C	Animal Care Supervisors, except Livestock
79015	Animal Breeders
79017A	Animal Caretakers, except Farm
79855	General Farmworkers
79858	Farmworkers, Farm and Ranch Animals
79999D	Farmers
79999J	Gamekeepers
79999K	Agricultural Crop Farm Managers
79999L	Livestock Production Managers

01.0303   Aquaculture Operations and Production Management

An instructional program that prepares individuals to select, culture, propagate, harvest, and market domesticated fish, shellfish, and marine plants. Includes instruction in the operation of fish farms and related enterprises.

72002G	Fishery Supervisors
79999E	Commercial Fishery Workers
79999G	Aqua-Culturists
79999M	Fish Hatchery Managers

01.0304   Crop Production Operations and Management

An instructional program that prepares individuals to operate enterprises producing cereal grain, fiber, forage, oilseed, tree fruits and nuts, small fruits, vegetables, and other plant products. Includes instruction in soils, plant nutrition, plant diseases, pest management, harvesting, and marketing.

15023A	Transportation Managers
24502C	Biological and Agricultural Technicians
31323	Farm and Home Management Advisors
72002A	Agricultural Crop Supervisors
72002E	Horticultural Supervisors
79021	Farm Equipment Operators
79033	Pruners
79036	Sprayers/Applicators
79855	General Farmworkers
79999A	Weed, Disease, and Insect Control Inspectors
79999B	Irrigation Workers
79999C	Horticultural Specialty Growers
79999D	Farmers
79999K	Agricultural Crop Farm Managers

01.0399 Agricultural Production Workers and Managers, Other

Any instructional program in agricultural production not described above.

01.04 Agricultural and Food Products Processing

A group of instructional programs (see 01.0401).

01.0401 Agricultural and Food Products Processing Operations and Management

An instructional program that prepares individuals to receive, inspect, store, and process agricultural food or products preparatory to marketing. Includes instruction in the characteristics and properties of agricultural products, and processing and storage techniques.

15014	Industrial Production Managers
21911B	Environmental Compliance Inspectors
21911R	Agricultural Inspectors
31314	Teachers and Instructors—Vocational Education and Training
79011	Graders and Sorters, Agricultural Products
81008	First-Line Supervisors and Manager/Supervisors—Production and Operating Workers
83005A	Production Inspectors, Testers, Graders, Sorters, Samplers, and Weighers
89808	Food Batchmakers
92917	Cooking Machine Operators and Tenders, Food and Tobacco
92962	Separating, Filtering, Clarifying, Precipitating, and Still Machine Operators and Tenders
92965	Crushing, Grinding, Mixing, and Blending Machine Operators and Tenders

01.05 Agricultural Supplies and Related Services

A group of instructional programs (see 01.0501).

01.0501 Agricultural Supplies Retailing and Wholesaling

An instructional program that generally prepares individuals to sell supplies for agricultural production, provide agricultural services, and purchase and market agricultural products.

15023A	Transportation Managers
21302	Wholesale and Retail Buyers, except Farm Products
21305A	Purchasing Agents and Buyers, Farm Products
21308A	Purchasing Agents and Contract Specialists
21911B	Environmental Compliance Inspectors

24502B	Artificial Breeding Technicians
31323	Farm and Home Management Advisors
41002	First-Line Supervisors and Manager/Supervisors—Sales and Related Workers
43017	Sales Agents, Selected Business Services
49005A	Sales Representatives, Agricultural
49005B	Sales Representatives, Chemical and Pharmaceutical
49005D	Sales Representatives, Mechanical Equipment and Supplies
49008	Sales Representatives, except Retail and Scientific and Related Products and Services
49011	Salespersons, Retail
49014	Salespersons, Parts
49999A	Merchandise Appraisers and Auctioneers
53505	Investigators, Clerical
67008	Pest Controllers and Assistants
72002A	Agricultural Crop Supervisors
72002B	Livestock Supervisors
79017A	Animal Caretakers, except Farm
79017B	Farriers
79017C	Animal Groomers and Bathers
79021	Farm Equipment Operators
79858	Farmworkers, Farm and Ranch Animals
97102A	Truck Drivers, Heavy
97105	Truck Drivers, Light—Including Delivery and Route Workers
97108	Bus Drivers
97702C	Small Airplane Pilots

01.0505   Animal Trainer

An instructional program that prepares individuals to teach animals to obey commands in order to: perform services, perform in sports and leisure activities, provide security, assist in law enforcement, assist in search and rescue operations, or perform entertainment tricks.

34058L	Umpires, Referees, and Other Sports Officials
63099C	Animal Control Workers
79016	Animal Trainers

01.0507   Equestrian/Equine Studies, Horse Management and Training

An instructional program that prepares individuals to care for horses and horse equipment; to train horses for various work and athletic or entertainment roles; to ride horses; and to manage horse training, breeding, and housing programs and facilities.

34056E	Equestrian Performers
34058G	Horse Riders/Exercisers

34058L	Umpires, Referees, and Other Sports Officials
72002B	Livestock Supervisors
79016	Animal Trainers
79017B	Farriers

01.0599   Agricultural Supplies and Related Services, Other

Any instructional program in agricultural supplies and support services not described above.

01.06   Horticulture Services Operations and Management

A group of instructional programs (see 01.0601).

01.0601   Horticulture Services Operations and Management, General

An instructional program that generally prepares individuals to produce, process, and market plants, shrubs, and trees used principally for ornamental, recreational, and aesthetic purposes and to establish, maintain, and manage horticultural enterprises.

15017A	Landscaping Managers
15031	Nursery and Greenhouse Managers
15032	Lawn Service Managers
24302A	Foresters
49011	Salespersons, Retail
72002D	Landscape Supervisors
72002E	Horticultural Supervisors
79030B	Gardeners and Groundskeepers
79036	Sprayers/Applicators
79041	Laborers, Landscaping and Groundskeeping
79999C	Horticultural Specialty Growers
87899A	Construction Installation Workers

01.0603   Ornamental Horticulture Operations and Management

An instructional program that prepares individuals to produce flowers, foliage, and related plant materials in fields and greenhouses for ornamental purposes, and to arrange, package, and market these materials. Includes instruction in enterprise management.

15032	Lawn Service Managers
49011	Salespersons, Retail
72002D	Landscape Supervisors
72002E	Horticultural Supervisors
79030B	Gardeners and Groundskeepers

| 79041 | Laborers, Landscaping and Groundskeeping |
| 79999C | Horticultural Specialty Growers |

01.0604   Greenhouse Operations and Management

An instructional program that prepares individuals to produce commercial plant species in controlled environments, and to manage commercial and experimental greenhouse operations.

15031	Nursery and Greenhouse Managers
49011	Salespersons, Retail
72002E	Horticultural Supervisors
79030B	Gardeners and Groundskeepers
79041	Laborers, Landscaping and Groundskeeping
79999C	Horticultural Specialty Growers

01.0605   Landscaping Operations and Management

An instructional program that prepares individuals to procure, plant, and maintain grounds and indoor and outdoor ornamental plants. Includes instruction in equipment maintenance and facilities management.

15017A	Landscaping Managers
72002D	Landscape Supervisors
79030B	Gardeners and Groundskeepers
79036	Sprayers/Applicators
87899A	Construction Installation Workers

01.0606   Nursery Operations and Management

An instructional program that prepares individuals to produce turf, shrubs, and trees for the purpose of transplanting or propagation. Includes instruction in enterprise management.

15031	Nursery and Greenhouse Managers
24302A	Foresters
49011	Salespersons, Retail
72002E	Horticultural Supervisors
79036	Sprayers/Applicators
79041	Laborers, Landscaping and Groundskeeping
79999C	Horticultural Specialty Growers

01.0607   Turf Management

An instructional program that prepares individuals to establish, manage, and maintain ornamental or recreational grassed areas, to prepare and maintain athletic playing surfaces, and to produce turf for transplantation.

15032	Lawn Service Managers
72002D	Landscape Supervisors
79030B	Gardeners and Groundskeepers
79036	Sprayers/Applicators
79999C	Horticultural Specialty Growers

01.0699   Horticulture Services Operations and Management

Any instructional program in horticulture management and production not described above.

72002D	Landscape Supervisors
73099A	Tree, Log, and Brush Cutters
79033	Pruners

01.07   International Agriculture

A group of instructional programs (see 01.0701).

01.0701   International Agriculture

An instructional program that describes the application of agricultural principles to problems of global food production and distribution, and to the study of the agricultural systems of other nations.

01.99   Agricultural Business and Production, Other

A group of instructional programs (see 01.9999).

01.9999   Agricultural Business and Production, Other

Any instructional program in agricultural business and production not described above.

02.   AGRICULTURAL SCIENCES

A summary of groups of instructional programs that describe the study of animals and plants as related to agricultural production, the organization of agricultural work, and the processing and distribution of food and fiber products.

02.01   Agriculture/Agricultural Sciences

A group of instructional programs (see 02.0101).

02.0101   Agriculture/Agricultural Sciences, General

An instructional program that generally describes the principles and practices of agricultural research and production, and may prepare individuals to apply such knowledge and skills to the solution of practical agricultural problems. Includes instruction in basic animal, plant, and soil science; animal husbandry and plant cultivation; and soil conservation.

24305A	Animal Scientists
24305B	Plant Scientists
24305C	Food Scientists
31202	Life Sciences Teachers—Postsecondary

02.0102   Agricultural Extension

An instructional program that prepares individuals to provide referral, consulting, assistance, and educational services to farmers and ranchers via local, state, or federal government agencies. Includes instruction in agricultural sciences, agricultural business operations, agricultural law, and administrative regulations, public relations, and communications skills.

15005B	Educational Program Directors
31323	Farm and Home Management Advisors

02.02   Animal Sciences

A group of instructional programs (see 02.0201).

02.0201   Animal Sciences, General

An instructional program that generally describes the scientific principles that underlie the breeding and husbandry of agricultural animals, and the production, processing, and distribution of agricultural animal products.

24305A	Animal Scientists
24305B	Plant Scientists
24502A	Biological and Agricultural Technologists
24502B	Artificial Breeding Technicians
24502C	Biological and Agricultural Technicians

31202	Life Sciences Teachers—Postsecondary
31323	Farm and Home Management Advisors
49005A	Sales Representatives, Agricultural
72002B	Livestock Supervisors
72002C	Animal Care Supervisors, except Livestock

02.0202   Agricultural Animal Breeding and Genetics

An instructional program that describes the application of genetics to the improvement of agricultural animal health, the development of new animal breeds, and the selective improvement of animal populations.

24305A	Animal Scientists
24305B	Plant Scientists
24502B	Artificial Breeding Technicians
31202	Life Sciences Teachers—Postsecondary

02.0203   Agricultural Animal Health

An instructional program that describes the scientific principles that affect the prevention and control of diseases in agricultural animals.

| 24305A | Animal Scientists |
| 31202 | Life Sciences Teachers—Postsecondary |

02.0204   Agricultural Animal Nutrition

An instructional program that describes the biology and chemistry of proteins, fats, carbohydrates, water, vitamins, and feed additives and their relation to animal health and the production of improved animal products.

24305A	Animal Scientists
24502C	Biological and Agricultural Technicians
31202	Life Sciences Teachers—Postsecondary
31323	Farm and Home Management Advisors
49005A	Sales Representatives, Agricultural
72002C	Animal Care Supervisors, except Livestock

02.0205   Agricultural Animal Physiology

An instructional program that describes the application of physiological principles to the study of agricultural animals and production problems. Instruction is provided in lactation, reproduction, digestion, and growth.

| 31202 | Life Sciences Teachers—Postsecondary |

02.0206   Dairy Science

An instructional program that describes the biological theories, principles, and applications that apply to the production and management of dairy animals and the production of milk products.

24305A	Animal Scientists
24502A	Biological and Agricultural Technologists
31202	Life Sciences Teachers—Postsecondary
72002B	Livestock Supervisors

02.0209   Poultry Science

An instructional program that describes the scientific theories, principles, and applications pertaining to the management of poultry populations and the production of poultry products.

24305A	Animal Scientists
31202	Life Sciences Teachers—Postsecondary
49005A	Sales Representatives, Agricultural

02.0299   Animal Sciences, Other

Any instructional program in animal sciences not described above.

02.03   Food Sciences and Technology

A group of instructional programs (see 02.0301).

02.0301   Food Sciences and Technology

An instructional program that describes the biological, chemical, physical, and engineering principles and practices involved in converting agriculture products to forms suitable for direct human consumption or for storage, and the solution of problems relating to product transportation, storage, and marketing.

15014	Industrial Production Managers
21911A	Health Officers and Inspectors
21911B	Environmental Compliance Inspectors
24305C	Food Scientists
24505A	Chemical Technicians and Technologists
24505B	Food Science Technicians and Technologists
31202	Life Sciences Teachers—Postsecondary

| 81008 | First-Line Supervisors and Manager/Supervisors—Production and Operating Workers |
| 83002A | Materials Inspectors |

02.04   Plant Sciences

A group of instructional programs (see 02.0401).

02.0401   Plant Sciences, General

An instructional program that generally describes the scientific theories and principles involved in the production and management of plants for food, feed, fiber, and soil conservation.

15031	Nursery and Greenhouse Managers
19005A	Government Service Executives
21911B	Environmental Compliance Inspectors
21911R	Agricultural Inspectors
24302D	Range Managers
24302E	Park Naturalists
24305B	Plant Scientists
24308D	Botanists
24308G	Physiologists and Cytologists
24502C	Biological and Agricultural Technicians
31202	Life Sciences Teachers—Postsecondary
43017	Sales Agents, Selected Business Services
72002A	Agricultural Crop Supervisors
72002B	Livestock Supervisors
72002E	Horticultural Supervisors
79999K	Agricultural Crop Farm Managers

02.0402   Agronomy and Crop Science

An instructional program that describes the chemical, physical, and biological relationships of crops and the soils nurturing them. Includes instruction in the growth and behavior of agricultural crops, the breeding of improved and new crop varieties, and the scientific management of soils for maximum plant nutrition and health.

24305B	Plant Scientists
24502C	Biological and Agricultural Technicians
31202	Life Sciences Teachers—Postsecondary

02.0403   Horticulture Science

An instructional program that describes the scientific principles involved in the cultivation of garden and ornamental plants, including fruits, vegetables, flowers,

---

landscape, and nursery crops. Includes instruction in specific types of plants, plant breeding, plant physiology, and the management of garden/nursery crops throughout the plant life cycle.

15031	Nursery and Greenhouse Managers
24305B	Plant Scientists
31202	Life Sciences Teachers—Postsecondary
72002A	Agricultural Crop Supervisors
72002E	Horticultural Supervisors
79999K	Agricultural Crop Farm Managers

02.0405   Plant Breeding and Genetics

An instructional program that describes the scientific theories and principles underlying plant breeding, development, and mutation, including hybridization and differential selection for plant improvement. Includes instruction in botanical biometry, statistics, and computer analysis.

24305B	Plant Scientists
31202	Life Sciences Teachers—Postsecondary

02.0406   Agricultural Plant Pathology

An instructional program that describes the scientific principles associated with recognizing diseased plants, identifying causal agents, developing disease response mechanisms and treatments, and preventing or reducing economic loss.

24305B	Plant Scientists
24308D	Botanists
31202	Life Sciences Teachers—Postsecondary

02.0407   Agricultural Plant Physiology

An instructional program that describes the scientific principles involved in the life processes of plants and plant responses to the elements of the physical environment, including nutrition, respiration, growth, photosynthesis, and reproduction.

24308G	Physiologists and Cytologists
31202	Life Sciences Teachers—Postsecondary

02.0408   Plant Protection (Pest Management)

An instructional program that describes the principles and practices of controlling and preventing economic loss caused by plant pests, and related environmental protection measures. Includes instruction in entomology, plant pathology, weed science, crop science, and environmental toxicology.

21911B	Environmental Compliance Inspectors
21911R	Agricultural Inspectors
24305B	Plant Scientists
24308D	Botanists
31202	Life Sciences Teachers—Postsecondary
43017	Sales Agents, Selected Business Services
72002A	Agricultural Crop Supervisors

02.0409   Range Science and Management

An instructional program that describes the scientific principles and practices involved in studying and managing rangelands, arid regions, grasslands, and other areas of low productivity. Includes instruction in livestock grazing systems management, soil science, plant and wildlife ecology, and hydrology.

19005A	Government Service Executives
24302D	Range Managers
24302E	Park Naturalists
31202	Life Sciences Teachers—Postsecondary
72002B	Livestock Supervisors

02.0499   Plant Sciences, Other

Any instructional program in plant sciences not described above.

02.05   Soil Sciences

A group of instructional programs (see 02.0501).

02.0501   Soil Sciences

An instructional program that describes the scientific classification and study of soils and soil properties. Includes instruction in soil chemistry, soil physics, soil biology, soil fertility, morphogenesis, mineralogy and hydrology, and soil conservation and management.

24302B	Soil Conservationists
24305D	Soil Scientists
31202	Life Sciences Teachers—Postsecondary

02.99   Agriculture/Agricultural Sciences, Other

A group of instructional programs (see 02.9999).

02.9999   Agriculture/Agricultural Sciences, Other

Any instructional programs in agriculture/agricultural sciences not described above.

03. CONSERVATION AND RENEWABLE NATURAL RESOURCES

A summary of groups of instructional programs that prepare individuals for activities involving the conservation and/or improvement of natural resources.

03.01 Natural Resources Conservation

A group of instructional programs (see 03.0101).

03.0101 Natural Resources Conservation, General

An instructional program that generally describes activities involving the conservation and/or improvement of natural resources such as air, soil, water, land, fish, and wildlife for economic and recreation purposes.

13017B	Natural Sciences Managers
15023C	Utilities Managers
19005A	Government Service Executives
24199B	Environmental Scientists
24302A	Foresters
24302B	Soil Conservationists
24302D	Range Managers
24599A	Meteorological Technicians
31202	Life Sciences Teachers—Postsecondary
73099D	Cruisers
79002B	Forester Aides

03.0102 Environmental Science/Studies

An instructional program that describes the study of the biological and physical aspects of the environment and environment-related issues, including methods of abating or controlling environmental pollution and collateral damage.

13017B	Natural Sciences Managers
19005A	Government Service Executives
24199B	Environmental Scientists
31202	Life Sciences Teachers—Postsecondary

03.02 Natural Resources Management and Protective Services

A group of instructional programs preparing individuals to engage in activities concerned with monitoring and maintaining the quality of the natural environment.

03.0201 Natural Resources Management and Policy

An instructional program that prepares individuals to plan, develop, and conduct programs to protect and maintain natural habitats and renewable natural resources. Includes instruction in wildlife biology, animal population surveys, economics, conservation techniques, public education, and administration.

31202	Life Sciences Teachers—Postsecondary

03.0203   Natural Resources Law Enforcement and Protective Services

An instructional program that prepares individuals to enforce natural resource and environmental protection regulations and laws; and to perform emergency duties to protect human life, property, and natural resources, including fire prevention and control measures, and emergency and rescue procedures.

19005A	Government Service Executives
61002B	Forest Fire Fighting and Prevention Supervisors
63005	Forest Fire Inspectors and Prevention Specialists
63008B	Forest Fire Fighters
63041	Fish and Game Wardens
79002B	Forester Aides

03.0299   Natural Resources Management and Protective Services, Other

Any instructional program in natural resources management and protective services not described above.

03.03   Fishing and Fisheries Sciences and Management

A group of instructional programs (see 03.0301).

03.0301   Fishing and Fisheries Sciences and Management

An instructional program that describes the scientific study of the husbandry of fish populations for recreational, ecological, and commercial purposes; and the application of such studies to the management of marine life resources and fisheries. Includes instruction in principles of aquatic and marine biology, water resources, fishing production and management operations, fishing regulations, water quality monitoring, and the management of recreational and commercial fishing activities.

31202	Life Sciences Teachers—Postsecondary
63041	Fish and Game Wardens
72002G	Fishery Supervisors
79017D	Aquarists
79999E	Commercial Fishery Workers
79999G	Aqua-Culturists
79999M	Fish Hatchery Managers

03.04 Forest Production and Processing

A group of instructional programs that prepare individuals to assist foresters, scientists, and wood-processing facility managers in the maintenance of forest lands and resources, and the harvesting and processing of forest products.

03.0401 Forest Harvesting and Production Technology/Technician

An instructional program that prepares individuals to assist foresters in managing, protecting, and harvesting timber stands and specialty forest crops. Includes instruction in equipment maintenance and repair, tree planting, selection and identification of trees for special attention, transplantation and harvesting, and forest management and safety procedures.

21305A	Purchasing Agents and Buyers, Farm Products
24302A	Foresters
72002E	Horticultural Supervisors
79002A	Forest and Conservation Workers
79002B	Forester Aides

03.0404 Forest Products Technology/Technician

An instructional program that prepares individuals to assist a manager, engineer, chemist, or forest product scientist in the measurement, analysis of quality, testing, and processing of harvested forest raw materials, and the selection, grading, and marketing of forest products to be used for specific purposes. Includes instruction in identifying, measuring, assessing quality, evaluating commercial value, and strength testing.

24302C	Wood Technologists
24599C	Scientific Helpers
73099D	Cruisers
79008	Log Graders and Scalers
83005A	Production Inspectors, Testers, Graders, Sorters, Samplers, and Weighers

03.0405 Logging/Timber Harvesting

An instructional program that prepares individuals to operate logging equipment and machinery for the direct harvesting of timber crops, including equipment maintenance and the practice of safety procedures.

21911E	Industrial and Occupational Safety and Health Inspectors
73002	Fallers and Buckers
73011	Logging Tractor Operators
73099A	Tree, Log, and Brush Cutters

73099C	Rigging Slingers and Chasers
85935	Riggers
97102B	Tractor-Trailer Truck Drivers
97941	Hoist and Winch Operators

03.0499 Forest Production and Processing, Other

Any instructional program in forestry production and processing not described above.

03.05 Forestry and Related Sciences

A group of instructional programs that prepare individuals to apply scientific, engineering, and management principles to the management and use of natural resources that occur on, and in association with, forest lands.

03.0501 Forestry, General

An instructional program that generally prepares individuals to manage and develop forest areas for economic, recreational, and ecological purposes. Includes instruction in forest-related sciences, mapping, statistics, harvesting and production technology, resource protection, management and economics, ecology and biology, administration, and public relations.

24302A	Foresters
24302B	Soil Conservationists
24302C	Wood Technologists
31202	Life Sciences Teachers—Postsecondary
83005A	Production Inspectors, Testers, Graders, Sorters, Samplers, and Weighers

03.0502 Forestry Sciences

An instructional program that describes the application of scientific principles to the study of environmental factors affecting forests and to the growth and management of forest resources. Includes instruction in forest biology, forest hydrology, forest engineering, silviculture, disease and pest control, and the development of improved tree varieties.

24302A	Foresters
24302B	Soil Conservationists
31202	Life Sciences Teachers—Postsecondary

03.0506 Forest Management

An instructional program that prepares individuals in the management and administration of forests and forest lands. Includes instruction in silviculture, forest protection, forest policy, and forest resources planning and economics.

24302A	Foresters
24302B	Soil Conservationists
31202	Life Sciences Teachers—Postsecondary

03.0509   Wood Science and Pulp/Paper Technology

An instructional program that prepares individuals to apply scientific and engineering principles to analyze the properties and behavior of wood and wood products; to analyze the chemical and physical processes involved in converting wood into paper and other products; and the design and development of related machinery and systems.

| 24302C | Wood Technologists |
| 83005A | Production Inspectors, Testers, Graders, Sorters, Samplers, and Weighers |

03.0599   Forestry and Related Sciences, Other

Any instruction program in forestry and related sciences not described above.

03.06   Wildlife and Wildlands Management

A group of instructional programs (see 03.0601).

03.0601   Wildlife and Wildlands Management

An instructional program that prepares individuals in the principles and practices used in the conservation and management of wildlands and wildlife resources for aesthetic, ecological, and recreational uses.

19005A	Government Service Executives
31202	Life Sciences Teachers—Postsecondary
63041	Fish and Game Wardens
79999J	Gamekeepers

03.99   Conservation and Renewable Natural Resources, Other

A group of instructional programs (see 03.9999).

03.9999   Conservation and Renewable Natural Resources, Other

Any instructional program in conservation and renewable natural resources not described above.

04. Architecture and Related Programs

A summary of groups of instructional programs that describe the principles and methods used to create, adapt, alter, preserve, and control human physical and social surroundings and habitations.

04.02 Architecture

A group of instructional programs (see 04.0201).

04.0201 Architecture

An instructional program that prepares individuals for the independent professional practice of architecture. Includes instruction in architectural design; architectural history and theory; building structures and environmental systems; site planning; construction; professional responsibilities and standards; and the cultural, social, economic, and environmental issues relating to architectural practice.

22302   Architects, except Landscape and Marine

04.03 City/Urban, Community, and Regional Planning

A group of instructional programs (see 04.0301).

04.0301 City/Urban, Community, and Regional Planning

An instructional program that prepares individuals to apply principles of planning and analysis to the development and improvement of urban areas or surrounding regions, including the development of master plans, the design of urban services systems, and the economic and policy issues related to planning and plan implementation.

27105   Urban and Regional Planners

04.04 Architectural Environmental Design

A group of instructional programs (see 04.0401).

04.0401 Architectural Environmental Design

An instructional program that prepares individuals for the independent professional practice of environmental architecture—the processes and techniques of designing total environments and living systems for human populations, both indoor and outdoor.

Includes instruction in relating the structural, aesthetic, and social concerns affecting life and work to the needs of clients and the constraints of the site environment.

22302	Architects, except Landscape and Marine
22308	Landscape Architects

04.05   Interior Architecture

A group of instructional programs (see 04.0501).

04.0501   Interior Architecture

An instructional program that prepares individuals for the independent professional practice of interior architecture—the processes and techniques of designing living, work, and leisure indoor environments as integral components of a building system. Includes instruction in building design and structural systems, heating and cooling systems, safety and health standards, and interior design principles and standards.

22502	Civil Engineering Technicians
34041	Interior Designers

04.06   Landscape Architecture

A group of instructional programs (see 04.0601).

04.0601   Landscape Architecture

An instructional program that prepares individuals for the independent professional practice of landscape architecture. Includes instruction in site planning, site analysis, site engineering, environmental impact, garden and landscape art and design, horticulture, and applicable regulations.

22308	Landscape Architects

04.07   Architectural Urban Design and Planning

A group of instructional programs (see 04.0701).

04.0701   Architectural Urban Design and Planning

An instructional program that prepares individuals for the independent professional practice of urban systems design and planning—the processes and techniques of designing and modifying the physical elements constituting built urban environments. Includes instruction in regional and community site planning, architecture, systems planning, transportation and logistics design, human services planning, legal codes and zoning development, and related economic and policy issues.

27105   Urban and Regional Planners

04.99 Architecture and Related Programs, Other

A group of instructional programs (see 04.9999).

04.9999 Architecture and Related Programs, Other

Any instructional program in architecture and related programs not described above.

05. AREA, ETHNIC, AND CULTURAL STUDIES

A summary of groups of instructional programs that describe the history, society, politics, culture, and economics of a particular geographic region, or a particular subset of the population sharing common characteristics, traits, and customs.

05.01 Area Studies

A group of instructional programs that describe the history, society, politics, culture, and economics of a particular geographic region.

05.0101 African Studies

An instructional program that describes the history, society, politics, culture, and economics of Africa, with emphasis on societies south of the Sahara.

31210   Social Science Teachers—Postsecondary

05.0102 American Studies/Civilization

An instructional program that describes the history, society, politics, culture, and economics of the United States of America and its regions, such as Appalachia, New England, the South, the West, and others.

31210   Social Science Teachers—Postsecondary

05.0103 Asian Studies

An instructional program that describes the general history, society, politics, culture, and economics of the continent of Asia and its borderlands, including related island groups.

31210   Social Science Teachers—Postsecondary

05.0104   East Asian Studies

An instructional program that describes the history, society, politics, culture, and economics of East Asia, including China, Japan, Korea, Mongolia and Eastern Central Asia, Taiwan, and Tibet.

31210   Social Science Teachers—Postsecondary

05.0105   Eastern European Area Studies

An instructional program that describes the history, society, politics, culture, and economics of Eastern Europe, including the Balkans, the Czech Republic, Hungary, Poland, Romania, the European portions of the former U.S.S.R. and its constituent republics, and the region of Germany comprising the former East Germany.

31210   Social Science Teachers—Postsecondary

05.0106   European Studies

An instructional program that describes the general history, society, politics, culture, and economics of the European Continent and its borderlands.

31210   Social Science Teachers—Postsecondary

05.0107   Latin American Studies

An instructional program that describes the history, society, politics, culture, and economics of Mexico, the Caribbean, and Central and South America.

31210   Social Science Teachers—Postsecondary

05.0108   Middle Eastern Studies

An instructional program that describes the history, society, politics, culture, and economics of the Fertile Crescent, Arabic-speaking North Africa, Anatolia, the Caucasus, Iran, the Arabian Peninsula, and the Indo-Soviet borderlands of Central Asia.

31210   Social Science Teachers—Postsecondary

05.0109   Pacific Area Studies

An instructional program that describes the history, society, politics, culture, and economics of Australia, New Zealand, and the Pacific Islands, excluding the Philippines, Taiwan, and Japan.

31210   Social Science Teachers—Postsecondary

05.0110   Russian and Slavic Area Studies

An instructional program that describes the history, society, politics, culture, and economics of the Slavic peoples of Europe, including Russia.

31210   Social Science Teachers—Postsecondary

05.0111   Scandinavian Area Studies

An instructional program that describes the history, society, politics, culture, and economics of Northern Europe and the Baltic, including Denmark, Finland, Iceland, Norway, and Sweden.

31210   Social Science Teachers—Postsecondary

05.0112   South Asian Studies

An instructional program that describes the history, society, politics, culture, and economics of the peoples of the Indian Subcontinent and the Indian Ocean, including Bangladesh, Bhutan, India, Nepal, Pakistan, Sri Lanka, and the Maldive Islands.

31210   Social Science Teachers—Postsecondary

05.0113   Southeast Asian Studies

An instructional program that describes the history, society, politics, culture, and economics of the Southeast Asian Peninsula and the Indonesian and Philippine Archipelagoes, including Burma, Cambodia, Indonesia, Laos, Malaysia, The Philippines, Singapore, Thailand, and Vietnam.

31210   Social Science Teachers—Postsecondary

05.0114   Western European Studies

An instructional program that describes the history, society, politics, culture and economics of the Western European peoples, including the Alpine region, the British Isles, France, the Iberian Peninsula, Italy, the Low Countries, and Germany.

31210   Social Science Teachers—Postsecondary

05.0115   Canadian Studies

An instructional program that describes the history, society, politics, culture, and economics of Canada, including the English, French, and Inuktitut-speaking peoples.

31210   Social Science Teachers—Postsecondary

05.0199   Area Studies, Other

Any instructional program in area studies not described above.

05.02   Ethnic and Cultural Studies

A group of instructional programs that describe the history, society, politics, culture, and economics of subsets of the population sharing common racial characteristics or common traits and customs.

05.0201   Afro-American (Black) Studies

An instructional program that describes the history, society, politics, culture, and economics of the black populations of the Western Hemisphere, with emphasis on the United States and the Caribbean.

31210   Social Science Teachers—Postsecondary

05.0202   American Indian/Native American Studies

An instructional program that describes the history, society, politics, culture, and economics of the original inhabitants of the Western Hemisphere, including American Indians, Aleuts, and Eskimos.

31210   Social Science Teachers—Postsecondary

05.0203   Hispanic-American Studies

An instructional program that describes the history, society, politics, culture and economics of Hispanic Americans in the United States, including Mexican Americans, Puerto Ricans, Cuban Americans, and others.

31210   Social Science Teachers—Postsecondary

05.0204   Islamic Studies

An instructional program that describes the history, traditions, literature, society, politics, culture, and economics of the Islamic peoples.

31210   Social Science Teachers—Postsecondary

05.0205   Jewish/Judaic Studies

An instructional program that describes the history, traditions, literature, society, politics, culture, and economics of the Jewish people.

31210   Social Science Teachers—Postsecondary

05.0206 Asian-American Studies

An instructional program that describes the history, society, politics, culture, and economics of Asian Americans in the United States including immigrants and their descendants from East Asia, South Asia, and Southeast Asia.

31210 Social Science Teachers—Postsecondary

05.0207 Women's Studies

An instructional program that describes the history, society, politics, culture, and economics of women as individuals and social actors. Includes instruction in feminist theory and perspectives, as well as other approaches and methods.

31210 Social Science Teachers—Postsecondary

05.0299 Ethnic and Cultural Studies, Other

Any instructional program in ethnic and cultural studies not described above.

05.99 Area, Ethnic, and Cultural Studies, Other

A group of instructional programs (see 05.9999).

05.9999 Area, Ethnic, and Cultural Studies, Other

Any instructional program in area, ethnic, and cultural studies not described above.

08. MARKETING OPERATIONS/ MARKETING AND DISTRIBUTION

A summary of groups of instructional programs that prepare individuals to plan and execute, at the operational or direct sales level, the promotion and distribution of ideas, goods, and services in order to create exchanges that satisfy individual and organizational objectives.

08.01 Apparel and Accessories Marketing Operations

A group of instructional programs (see 08.0101).

08.0101 Apparel and Accessories Marketing Operations, General

An instructional program that generally prepares individuals to perform marketing tasks specifically applicable to all segments of the apparel and fashion industry.

13011C	Marketing Managers
41002	First-Line Supervisors and Manager/Supervisors—Sales and Related Workers
49008	Sales Representatives, except Retail and Scientific and Related Products and Services
49011	Salespersons, Retail
49032B	Models
49999C	Sales Consultants

08.0102 Fashion Merchandising

An instructional program that prepares individuals to perform wholesaling tasks specifically applicable to promoting product lines to the retail segment of the apparel and fashion industry.

13011C	Marketing Managers
49008	Sales Representatives, except Retail and Scientific and Related Products and Services
49011	Salespersons, Retail
49032B	Models
49999C	Sales Consultants

08.0103 Fashion Modeling

An instructional program that prepares individuals to model (i.e., display) clothing or clothing-related articles for designers, buyers, salespeople, and potential customers.

49032B	Models

08.0199 Apparel and Accessories Marketing Operations, Other

Any instructional program in apparel and accessories marketing operations not described above.

49008	Sales Representatives, except Retail and Scientific and Related Products and Services
49011	Salespersons, Retail

08.02 Business and Personal Services Marketing Operations

A group of instructional programs that prepare individuals to apply marketing concepts in the delivery of services to business or for personal consumption.

08.0204 Business Services Marketing Operations

An instructional program that prepares individuals to perform marketing tasks specifically applicable to business community services.

13011C	Marketing Managers
34008	Public Relations Specialists and Publicity Writers
41002	First-Line Supervisors and Manager/Supervisors—Sales and Related Workers
43014B	Sales Agents, Financial Services
43017	Sales Agents, Selected Business Services
43023B	Sales Agents, Advertising
43099A	Sales Representatives, Service

08.0205   Personal Services Marketing Operations

An instructional program that prepares individuals to perform marketing tasks specifically applicable to personal services.

43099A	Sales Representatives, Service
49999C	Sales Consultants

08.0299   Business and Personal Services Marketing Operations, Other

Any instructional program in business or personal services marketing operations not described above.

39999B	Agents and Business Managers of Artists, Performers, and Athletes
41002	First-Line Supervisors and Manager/Supervisors—Sales and Related Workers
43099A	Sales Representatives, Service
43099B	Fund Raisers and Solicitors
49008	Sales Representatives, except Retail and Scientific and Related Products and Services
49032A	Demonstrators and Promoters
89908D	Exhibit Builders

08.03   Entrepreneurship

A group of instructional programs (see 08.0301).

08.0301   Entrepreneurship

An instructional program that prepares individuals to perform marketing tasks specifically applicable to developing business enterprises.

08.04   Financial Services Marketing Operations

A group of instructional programs (see 08.0401).

08.0401   Financial Services Marketing Operations

An instructional program that prepares individuals to perform marketing tasks specifically applicable to banks, credit unions, and other financial institutions.

21108	Loan Officers and Counselors
43014A	Sales Agents, Securities and Commodities
43014B	Sales Agents, Financial Services
53102	Tellers

08.05   Floristry Marketing Operations

A group of instructional programs (see 08.0503).

08.0503   Floristry Marketing Operations

An instructional program that prepares individuals to perform marketing tasks specifically applicable to the floristry industry.

34038F	Floral Designers
49008	Sales Representatives, except Retail and Scientific and Related Products and Services
49011	Salespersons, Retail

08.06   Food Products Retailing and Wholesaling Operations

A group of instructional programs (see 08.0601).

08.0601   Food Products Retailing and Wholesaling Operations

An instructional program that prepares individuals to perform marketing tasks specifically applicable to food supplies and grocery wholesaling and retailing.

41002	First-Line Supervisors and Manager/Supervisors—Sales and Related Workers
49008	Sales Representatives, except Retail and Scientific and Related Products and Services
49021	Stock Clerks, Sales Floor
49023A	Cashiers, General

08.07   General Retailing and Wholesaling Operations and Skills

A group of instructional programs (see 08.0708).

08.0701   Auctioneering

An instructional program that prepares individuals to sell articles at an auction to the highest bidder.

49999A	Merchandise Appraisers and Auctioneers

08.0704   General Buying Operations

An instructional program that prepares individuals to perform marketing tasks specifically applicable to obtaining goods and services for a business.

21302	Wholesale and Retail Buyers, except Farm Products
21305A	Purchasing Agents and Buyers, Farm Products
21308A	Purchasing Agents and Contract Specialists

08.0705   General Retailing Operations

An instructional program that prepares individuals to perform marketing tasks specifically applicable to retail operations in a wide variety of settings.

13008	Purchasing Managers
13011B	Sales Managers
19005A	Government Service Executives
19005B	Private Sector Executives
19999A	Amusement and Recreation Establishment Managers
21302	Wholesale and Retail Buyers, except Farm Products
41002	First-Line Supervisors and Manager/Supervisors—Sales and Related Workers
43099A	Sales Representatives, Service
49008	Sales Representatives, except Retail and Scientific and Related Products and Services
49011	Salespersons, Retail
49014	Salespersons, Parts
49017	Counter and Rental Clerks
49021	Stock Clerks, Sales Floor
49023A	Cashiers, General
49023B	Cash Accounting Clerks
49026	Telemarketers, Door-to-Door Sales Workers, News and Street Vendors, and Other Related Workers
49032A	Demonstrators and Promoters
49999A	Merchandise Appraisers and Auctioneers
49999C	Sales Consultants
58017	Weighers, Measurers, Checkers, and Samplers—Recordkeeping
97117	Driver/Sales Workers

08.0706   General Selling Skills and Sales Operations

An instructional program that prepares individuals to perform the techniques of direct consumer persuasion, involving planned, personalized communications, as agents for a wide variety of industries and product types.

21305A	Purchasing Agents and Buyers, Farm Products
41002	First-Line Supervisors and Manager/Supervisors—Sales and Related Workers
43008	Sales Agents, Real Estate
43017	Sales Agents, Selected Business Services
43023A	Site Leasing and Promotion Agents
43023B	Sales Agents, Advertising
43099A	Sales Representatives, Service
43099B	Fund Raisers and Solicitors
49005A	Sales Representatives, Agricultural
49005B	Sales Representatives, Chemical and Pharmaceutical
49005C	Sales Representatives, Electrical/Electronic
49005D	Sales Representatives, Mechanical Equipment and Supplies
49005F	Sales Representatives, Medical
49005G	Sales Representatives, Instruments
49008	Sales Representatives, except Retail and Scientific and Related Products and Services
49011	Salespersons, Retail
49014	Salespersons, Parts
49017	Counter and Rental Clerks
49032A	Demonstrators and Promoters
49999A	Merchandise Appraisers and Auctioneers
49999C	Sales Consultants

08.0708   General Marketing Operations

An instructional program that prepares individuals to perform various marketing tasks applicable to a wide variety of industries and commercial settings.

41002	First-Line Supervisors and Manager/Supervisors—Sales and Related Workers
49026	Telemarketers, Door-to-Door Sales Workers, News and Street Vendors, and Other Related Workers
49999A	Merchandise Appraisers and Auctioneers

08.0709   General Distribution Operations

An instructional program that prepares individuals to perform marketing tasks specifically applicable to storing and shipping commodities, either for businesses or retail consumers.

15023A	Transportation Managers
15023D	Storage and Distribution Managers
41002	First-Line Supervisors and Manager/Supervisors—Sales and Related Workers
51002A	First-Line Supervisors, Customer Service
51002B	First-Line Supervisors, Administrative Support
55344	Billing, Cost, and Rate Clerks
58005	Dispatchers—except Police, Fire, and Ambulance
58011	Transportation Agents
58023	Stock Clerks—Stockroom, Warehouse, or Storage Yard
81011	First-Line Supervisors and Manager/Supervisors—Transportation and Material Moving Machine and Vehicle Operators

08.0799   General Retailing and Wholesaling Operations and Skills, Other

Any instructional program in miscellaneous marketing operations skills not described above.

08.08   Home and Office Products Marketing Operations

An instructional program that prepares individuals to perform marketing tasks at all levels relating to the sales of either home or office products.

08.0809   Home Products Marketing Operations

An instructional program that prepares individuals to perform marketing tasks specifically applicable to hardware, building materials and equipment, and household supplies.

41002	First-Line Supervisors and Manager/Supervisors—Sales and Related Workers
49011	Salespersons, Retail
49026	Telemarketers, Door-to-Door Sales Workers, News and Street Vendors, and Other Related Workers
49032A	Demonstrators and Promoters

08.0810   Office Products Marketing Operations

An instructional program that prepares individuals to perform marketing tasks specifically applicable to business equipment and supplies.

41002	First-Line Supervisors and Manager/Supervisors—Sales and Related Workers

| 49005C | Sales Representatives, Electrical/Electronic |
| 49008 | Sales Representatives, except Retail and Scientific and Related Products and Services |

08.0899   Home and Office Products Marketing Operations, Other

Any instructional program in home and office products marketing operations not described above.

08.09   Hospitality and Recreation Marketing Operations

A group of instructional programs (see 08.0901).

08.0901   Hospitality and Recreation Marketing Operations, General

An instructional program that generally prepares individuals to perform marketing tasks applicable to a wide variety of hospitality and leisure industry settings.

13011A	Advertising and Promotions Managers
15026B	Food-Service Managers
19999A	Amusement and Recreation Establishment Managers
39999B	Agents and Business Managers of Artists, Performers, and Athletes
41002	First-Line Supervisors and Manager/Supervisors—Sales and Related Workers
43017	Sales Agents, Selected Business Services
43099A	Sales Representatives, Service
43099B	Fund Raisers and Solicitors
49008	Sales Representatives, except Retail and Scientific and Related Products and Services
49011	Salespersons, Retail
53808	Hotel Desk Clerks
65017	Counter Attendants—Lunchroom, Coffee Shop, or Cafeteria
65041	Combined Food Preparation and Service Workers
68017A	Travel Guides
68017B	Tour Guides and Escorts

08.0902   Hotel/Motel Services Marketing Operations

An instructional program that prepares individuals to perform marketing tasks specifically applicable to hotels and motels.

13011A	Advertising and Promotions Managers
43017	Sales Agents, Selected Business Services
53808	Hotel Desk Clerks

08.0903 Recreation Products/Services Marketing Operations

An instructional program that prepares individuals to perform marketing tasks specifically applicable to the retail sports and recreation equipment and supplies industry.

19999A	Amusement and Recreation Establishment Managers
39999B	Agents and Business Managers of Artists, Performers, and Athletes
41002	First-Line Supervisors and Manager/Supervisors—Sales and Related Workers
43099A	Sales Representatives, Service
43099B	Fund Raisers and Solicitors
49008	Sales Representatives, except Retail and Scientific and Related Products and Services
49011	Salespersons, Retail
68017A	Travel Guides
68017B	Tour Guides and Escorts

08.0906 Food Sales Operations

An instructional program that prepares individuals to perform marketing tasks specifically applicable to the ready-to-eat food and beverage industry.

15026B	Food-Service Managers
65017	Counter Attendants—Lunchroom, Coffee Shop, or Cafeteria
65041	Combined Food Preparation and Service Workers

08.0999 Hospitality and Recreation Marketing Operations, Other

Any instructional program in hospitality and recreation marketing operations not described above.

08.10 Insurance Marketing Operations

A group of instructional programs (see 08.1001).

08.1001 Insurance Marketing Operations

An instructional program that prepares individuals to perform marketing tasks specifically applicable to the insurance industry.

21505	Special Agents, Insurance
41002	First-Line Supervisors and Manager/Supervisors—Sales and Related Workers
43002	Sales Agents and Placers, Insurance

53302	Insurance Adjusters, Examiners, and Investigators
53305	Insurance Appraisers, Auto Damage
53505	Investigators, Clerical

08.11   Tourism and Travel Services Marketing Operations

A group of instructional programs that prepare individuals to perform marketing operations tasks in various travel and tourism settings.

08.1104   Tourism Promotion Operations

An instructional program that prepares individuals to perform marketing tasks specifically applicable to the tourism promotion industry.

43099A	Sales Representatives, Service
51002A	First-Line Supervisors, Customer Service
53802	Travel Clerks
55305	Receptionists and Information Clerks
61099C	First-Line Supervisors/Hospitality and Personal Service Workers
68017B	Tour Guides and Escorts

08.1105   Travel Services Marketing Operations

An instructional program that prepares individuals to perform marketing tasks specifically applicable to the travel industry.

19999D	Service Establishment Managers
43021	Travel Agents
49017	Counter and Rental Clerks
51002A	First-Line Supervisors, Customer Service
53802	Travel Clerks
53805	Reservation and Transportation Ticket Agents
68017A	Travel Guides

08.1199   Tourism and Travel Services Marketing Operations, Other

Any instructional program in tourism and travel services marketing operations not described above.

08.12   Vehicle and Petroleum Products Marketing Operations

A group of instructional programs that prepare individuals to perform marketing tasks applicable to the vehicular sales and retail petroleum industries.

08.1203 Vehicle Parts and Accessories Marketing Operations

An instructional program that prepares individuals to perform marketing tasks specifically applicable to the retail vehicular parts and accessories industry.

41002	First-Line Supervisors and Manager/Supervisors—Sales and Related Workers
49011	Salespersons, Retail
49014	Salespersons, Parts
53123	Adjustment Clerks
58023	Stock Clerks—Stockroom, Warehouse, or Storage Yard
81002	First-Line Supervisors and Manager/Supervisors—Mechanics, Installers, and Repairers

08.1208 Vehicle Marketing Operations

An instructional program that prepares individuals to perform marketing tasks specifically applicable to the retail vehicle sales industry.

13011B	Sales Managers
43099A	Sales Representatives, Service
49011	Salespersons, Retail

08.1209 Petroleum Products Retailing Operations

An instructional program that prepares individuals to perform marketing tasks specifically applicable to the retail petroleum products and service industry.

41002	First-Line Supervisors and Manager/Supervisors—Sales and Related Workers
97805	Service Station Attendants

08.1299 Vehicle and Petroleum Products Marketing Operations, Other

Any instructional program in vehicle and petroleum products marketing operations not described above.

49017	Counter and Rental Clerks

08.13 Health Products and Services Marketing Operations

A group of instructional programs that prepare individuals to market health products and services.

08.1301 Health Products and Services Marketing Operations

An instructional program that prepares individuals to perform marketing tasks specifically applicable to the healthcare supplies and services industry.

41002	First-Line Supervisors and Manager/Supervisors—Sales and Related Workers
49005F	Sales Representatives, Medical
49011	Salespersons, Retail

08.99 Marketing Operations/Marketing and Distribution, Other

A group of instructional programs (see 08.9999).

08.9999 Marketing Operations/Marketing and Distribution, Other

Any instructional program in marketing operations/marketing and distribution not described above.

49008	Sales Representatives, except Retail and Scientific and Related Products and Services
49011	Salespersons, Retail
49021	Stock Clerks, Sales Floor

09. COMMUNICATIONS

A summary of groups of instructional programs that describe the creation, transmission, and evaluation of messages.

09.01 Communications, General

A group of instructional programs (see 09.0101).

09.0101 Communications, General

An instructional program that generally describes the creation, transmission, and evaluation of messages at all levels, for commercial or noncommercial purposes, and that may prepare individuals to apply principles of communications to work in specific media. Includes instruction in modes and behavioral aspects of human communications, and the formal means by which society organizes communications.

| 34021 | Announcers, except Radio and Television |

09.02 Advertising

A group of instructional programs (see 09.0201).

09.0201 Advertising

An instructional program that describes the creation, execution, transmission, and evaluation of commercial messages concerned with the promotion and sale of products and services, and that prepares individuals to function as advertising assistants, technicians, managers, and executives. Includes instruction in advertising theory; marketing strategy; advertising copy/art, layout, and production methods; and media relations.

13011A	Advertising and Promotions Managers
13011B	Sales Managers
34002L	Copy Writers
34038E	Art Directors
43023A	Site Leasing and Promotion Agents
43023B	Sales Agents, Advertising
53908	Advertising Clerks

09.04 Journalism and Mass Communications

A group of instructional programs that describe the study of news production in various media, and the study of the provision of entertainment and information communications to mass audiences.

09.0401   Journalism

An instructional program that describes the methods and techniques for gathering, processing, and delivering news, and that prepares individuals to be professional print journalists. Includes instruction in news writing and editing, reporting, journalism law and policy, professional standards and ethics, and journalism history and research.

31216	English and Foreign Language Teachers—Postsecondary
34002A	Columnists, Critics, and Commentators
34002C	Creative Writers
34002D	Editors
34002E	Managing Editors
34011	Reporters and Correspondents
34014	Broadcast News Analysts

09.0402   Broadcast Journalism

An instructional program that describes the methods and techniques by which radio and television news programs are produced and delivered, and that prepares individuals to be professional broadcast journalists. Includes instruction in principles of broadcast technology, program design and production, broadcast editing, on- and off-camera procedures and techniques, and broadcast media law and policy.

34002A	Columnists, Critics, and Commentators
34002C	Creative Writers
34002D	Editors
34002E	Managing Editors
34002F	Programming and Script Editors and Coordinators

34002H	Readers
34011	Reporters and Correspondents
34014	Broadcast News Analysts
34017	Announcers, Radio and Television

09.0403   Mass Communications

An instructional program that describes the study of the media by which entertainment and information messages are delivered, and the social effects of such messages. Includes instruction in communications theory, communications laws and policies, international communications media, propaganda and political communications, social issues in entertainment and mass communications, and the study of specific media and media organizations.

09.0499   Journalism and Mass Communications, Other

Any instructional program in journalism and mass communications not described above.

09.05   Public Relations and Organizational Communications

A group of instructional programs (see 09.0501).

09.0501   Public Relations and Organizational Communications

A instructional program that describes the methods and techniques for communicating image-oriented corporate and sponsor messages to various audiences, for promoting client interests, and for managing client-media relations, and that prepares individuals to perform public relations and related services.

13011D	Fundraising Directors
34008	Public Relations Specialists and Publicity Writers
39999B	Agents and Business Managers of Artists, Performers, and Athletes

09.07   Radio and Television Broadcasting

A group of instructional programs (see 09.0701).

09.0701   Radio and Television Broadcasting

An instructional program that describes the methods and techniques used to plan, produce, and direct entertainment and informational programs and short subjects in the broadcast media, and that prepares individuals to function as professional announcers, directors, and producers. Includes instruction in scheduling; film and tape editing; on- and off-camera/microphone procedures and techniques; sound mixing; studio direction; personnel and facilities management; and broadcast law, policies, and code regulations.

13011A	Advertising and Promotions Managers
34002C	Creative Writers
34002D	Editors
34002F	Programming and Script Editors and Coordinators
34002H	Readers
34017	Announcers, Radio and Television
34056F	Producers
34056G	Directors—Stage, Motion Picture, Television, and Radio
34056K	Technical Directors/Managers
55302A	Stenotype Operators

09.99　Communications, Other

A group of instructional programs (see 09.9999).

09.9999　Communications, Other

Any instructional program in communications not described above.

10.　COMMUNICATIONS TECHNOLOGIES

A summary of groups of instructional programs (see 10.01).

10.01　Communications Technologies

A group of instructional programs that prepare individuals to support and assist communications professionals and skilled communications workers.

10.0101　Educational/Instructional Media Technology/Technician

An instructional program that prepares individuals to assist instructional media designers and other communications professionals in preparing educational and training films, tapes, recordings, videos, slides, and overheads, and in operating related technical equipment.

31508	Audio-Visual Specialists
39999D	Studio, Stage, and Special Effects Technicians
92905	Motion Picture Projectionists

10.0103　Photographic Technology/Technician

An instructional program that prepares individuals to support photographers and other professionals in preparing still, motion picture, and video products; developing film and related technical processes; and operating specialized equipment.

34026	Camera Operators, Television and Motion Picture
34028B	Broadcast Technicians
83005A	Production Inspectors, Testers, Graders, Sorters, Samplers, and Weighers
89799A	Precision Printing Workers
89914A	Photographic Retouchers and Restorers
89914B	Photographic Reproduction Technicians
89914C	Photographic Hand Developers
89914D	Film Laboratory Technicians
92545	Photoengraving and Lithographing Machine Operators and Tenders
92908	Photographic Processing Machine Operators and Tenders
93947E	Hand Painting, Coating, or Decorating Workers
93997	Intermediate Hand Workers
93998	Elemental Hand Workers

10.0104   Radio and Television Broadcasting Technology/Technician

An instructional program that prepares individuals to support broadcast managers and other professionals in performing tasks related to the production of radio and television programs, films, and recordings. Includes instruction in operating specialized equipment.

22599A	Sound Engineering Technicians
34028B	Broadcast Technicians
34028C	Transmitter Engineers
34032	Film Editors
39999D	Studio, Stage, and Special Effects Technicians

10.0199   Communications Technologies/Technicians, Other

Any instructional program in communications technologies not described above.

II.   COMPUTER AND INFORMATION SCIENCES

A summary of groups of instructional programs that describe the design, development, and operation of electronic data storage and processing systems, including hardware and software.

II.01   Computer and Information Sciences, General

A group of instructional programs (see 11.0101).

II.0101   Computer and Information Sciences, General

An instructional program that generally describes the study of data and information storage and processing systems, including hardware, software, basic design principles, user requirements analysis, and related economic and policy issues.

21999A	Computer Security Specialists
25102	Systems Analysts, Electronic Data Processing
25103A	Database Administrators
31226	Computer Science Teachers—Postsecondary
85123A	Equipment Servicers and Technicians

11.02   Computer Programming

A group of instructional programs (see 11.0201).

11.0201   Computer Programming

An instructional program that prepares individuals to apply methods and procedures used in designing and writing computer programs to developing solutions to specific operational problems and use requirements, including testing and troubleshooting prototype software packages.

21114C	Data Processing Auditors
25102	Systems Analysts, Electronic Data Processing
25103A	Database Administrators
25105	Computer Programmers
25111	Programmers—Numerical, Tool, and Process Control
31226	Computer Science Teachers—Postsecondary

11.03   Data Processing Technology

A group of instructional programs (see 11.0301).

11.0301   Data Processing Technology/Technician

An instructional program that prepares individuals to use and operate computers and associated software packages to perform a variety of tasks, including text processing, number processing, graphics, and database management.

25111	Programmers—Numerical, Tool, and Process Control
25199A	Data Communications Analysts
51002B	First-Line Supervisors, Administrative Support
56011	Computer Operators, except Peripheral Equipment
56014	Peripheral EDP Equipment Operators

11.04   Information Sciences and Systems

A group of instructional programs (see 11.0401).

11.0401   Information Sciences and Systems

An instructional program that describes the scientific study and development of electronic systems for transmitting information via signalling networks, and the study of information transmission from the point of generation to reception and human interpretation. Includes instruction in information systems planning and design, user needs analysis, and provider capacity and requirements analysis.

22127	Computer Engineers
25103A	Database Administrators
25104	Computer Support Specialists
31226	Computer Science Teachers—Postsecondary

11.05   Computer Systems Analysis

A group of instructional programs (see 11.0501).

11.0501   Computer Systems Analysis

An instructional program that prepares individuals to apply computer programming principles to the design and implementation of large-scale computer applications and networking systems. Includes instruction in system design, user prioritization, system and component optimization, and computer security systems.

21999A	Computer Security Specialists
25102	Systems Analysts, Electronic Data Processing
25111	Programmers—Numerical, Tool, and Process Control
31226	Computer Science Teachers—Postsecondary

11.07   Computer Science

A group of instructional programs (see 11.0701).

11.0701   Computer Science

An instructional program that describes the scientific and mathematical study of the algorithms used in designing and building computers, and their application to the development and design of actual computing systems. Includes instruction in computer architecture, assembly and programming languages, numerical and computational analysis, computer systems theory, artificial intelligence and cybernetics, and simulation and modelling.

25104	Computer Support Specialists
31226	Computer Science Teachers—Postsecondary

11.99 Computer and Information Sciences, Other

A group of instructional programs (see 11.9999).

11.9999 Computer and Information Sciences, Other

Any instructional program in computer and information sciences not described above.

12. PERSONAL AND MISCELLANEOUS SERVICES

A summary of instructional programs that prepare individuals to provide a variety of services to individual consumers as well as to organizations such as businesses and industries.

12.02 Gaming and Sports Officiating Services

A group of instructional programs that prepare individuals to conduct and supervise gaming operations, and officiate at sports events.

12.0203 Card Dealer

An instructional program that prepares individuals to operate card games, perform card tricks, and manage table gaming operations at casinos, nightclubs, and other establishments. Includes instruction in the rules and procedures of specific games, and customer relations.

63035	Detectives and Investigators, except Public
68014B	Games-of-Chance Attendants

12.0204 Umpires and Other Sport Officials

An instructional program that prepares individuals to serve as umpires, judges, and other officials for athletic events and specific sports at the school, college, amateur, and professional levels. Includes instruction in the rules and procedures of specific sports, public relations, and related duties.

34058L	Umpires, Referees, and Other Sports Officials

12.0299 Gaming and Sports Officiating Services, Other

Any instructional program in gaming and sports officiating services not described above.

12.03 Funeral Services and Mortuary Science

A group of instructional programs (see 12.0301).

12.0301   Funeral Services and Mortuary Science

An instructional program that prepares individuals to perform and supervise the embalming and cremation of human corpses, to provide funeral and burial services, and to sell funerary equipment to the public. Includes instruction in applicable anatomical, cosmetic, and technical procedures; facilities and equipment management; equipment and services marketing; legal requirements; and professional standards.

21911A	Health Officers and Inspectors
39011	Funeral Directors and Morticians
39014	Embalmers
43099A	Sales Representatives, Service
68005A	Hairdressers, Hairstylists, and Cosmetologists

12.04   Cosmetic Services

A group of instructional programs (see 12.0401).

12.0401   Cosmetic Services, General

An instructional program that generally prepares individuals to render a variety of beauty and grooming services to the general public.

12.0402   Barber/Hairstylist

An instructional program that prepares individuals to cut and care for hair and perform facial shaves, with emphasis on hygiene, sanitation, customer relations, and barbershop management.

68002	Barbers
68005A	Hairdressers, Hairstylists, and Cosmetologists
83005A	Production Inspectors, Testers, Graders, Sorters, Samplers, and Weighers
89999B	Wig Makers

12.0403   Cosmetologist

An instructional program that prepares individuals to care for and beautify hair, care for complexions and perform manicures, and sell cosmetics in commercial or other beauty establishments, or independently. Includes instruction in hygiene, sanitation, customer relations, and salon management. May also include training and supervising assistants.

68005A	Hairdressers, Hairstylists, and Cosmetologists
68005B	Make-Up Artists, Theatrical and Performance
68008	Manicurists

12.0404 Electrolysis Technician

An instructional program that prepares individuals to operate specialized equipment for removing scalp hair, whiskers, body hair, warts, moles, and birthmarks from individuals. Includes instruction in equipment use and maintenance, applications to specific treatments, and customer relations.

68005C   Electrologists

12.0405 Massage

An instructional program that prepares individuals to administer systematic friction, stroking, tapping, slapping and manipulative movements to the human body for therapeutic or relaxation purposes, either independently or under clinical supervision. Includes instruction in any of the various massage disciplines, basic health and first aid principles, customer/patient relations, and applications to specific therapeutic conditions and problems.

69999B   Personal Attendants

12.0406 Make-Up Artist

An instructional program that prepares individuals to apply cosmetics, cosmetic devices, masks, and other materials to the human face and body, to enhance or alter appearance. Includes instruction in specific treatments such as facials, manicures, waxings, pedicures, and others; related techniques and equipment; applications to specific purposes such as acting, television broadcasting, and private cosmetic services; and customer/client relations.

68005B   Make-Up Artists, Theatrical and Performance

12.0499 Cosmetic Services, Other

Any instructional programs in cosmetic services not described above.

12.05 Culinary Arts and Related Services

A group of instructional programs that prepare individuals to provide professional food and beverage services in restaurants, bars, and other commercial establishments.

12.0501 Baker/Pastry Chef

An instructional program that prepares individuals to serve as professional bakers and pastry specialists in restaurants or other commercial baking establishments. Includes

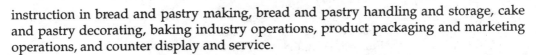
instruction in bread and pastry making, bread and pastry handling and storage, cake and pastry decorating, baking industry operations, product packaging and marketing operations, and counter display and service.

61099A	Chefs and Head Cooks
65021	Bakers, Bread and Pastry
65028	Cooks, Institution or Cafeteria
83005A	Production Inspectors, Testers, Graders, Sorters, Samplers, and Weighers
89805	Bakers, Manufacturing
93997	Intermediate Hand Workers

12.0502   Bartender/Mixologist

An instructional program that prepares individuals to mix and serve alcoholic and non-alcoholic drinks to patrons of bars or other commercial establishments. Includes instruction in standard recipes, cleanliness and safety standards, legal requirements of alcoholic beverage service, and customer relations.

65005	Bartenders

12.0503   Culinary Arts/Chef Training

An instructional program that prepares individuals to provide professional chef and related cooking services in restaurants and other commercial food establishments. Includes instruction in recipe and menu planning, preparing and cooking of foods, supervising and training kitchen assistants, the management of food supplies and kitchen resources, aesthetics of food presentation, and familiarity or mastery of a wide variety of cuisines and culinary techniques.

15026B	Food-Service Managers
61099A	Chefs and Head Cooks
65026	Cooks, Restaurant
93997	Intermediate Hand Workers

12.0504   Food and Beverage/Restaurant Operations Manager

An instructional program that prepares individuals to manage and supervise food and beverage service operations, including catering services, banquet management, and executive chef positions. Includes instruction in food and beverage cost control, food and beverage purchasing and storage, restaurant and food services operation, personnel supervision and management, menu planning and event coordination, and the principles of general hospitality industry management and operations.

15026A	Lodging Managers
15026B	Food-Service Managers

41002	First-Line Supervisors and Manager/Supervisors—Sales and Related Workers
51002A	First-Line Supervisors, Customer Service
55338A	Bookkeepers

12.0505   Kitchen Personnel/Cook and Assistant Training

An instructional program that prepares individuals to serve under the supervision of chefs and other food service professionals as kitchen support staff and commercial food preparation workers. Includes instruction in kitchen organization and operations, sanitation and quality control, basic food preparation and cooking skills, kitchen and kitchen equipment maintenance, and quantity food measurement and monitoring.

65026	Cooks, Restaurant
65028	Cooks, Institution or Cafeteria
65032	Cooks, Specialty Fast Food
65038A	Food Preparation Workers
93947B	Bakery and Confectionery Decorating Workers
93997	Intermediate Hand Workers

12.0506   Meatcutter

An instructional program that prepares individuals to apply technical knowledge and skills to cut, trim, and prepare carcasses and portions of meat for sale in wholesale, retail, or food-service establishments. Includes instruction in the use of meat-cutting tools, identification of and cutting techniques for different cuts of meat, dressing poultry, processing fish, counter display, and refrigeration and sanitation.

65023	Butchers and Meat Cutters
65038A	Food Preparation Workers
89802	Slaughterers and Butchers
93938	Meat, Poultry, and Fish Cutters and Trimmers—Hand

12.0507   Waiter/Waitress and Dining Room Manager

An instructional program that prepares individuals to serve food to customers in formal or informal settings. Includes instruction in formal rules of serving etiquette, table and counter service, dining room operations and procedures, service personnel supervision and management, food and beverage preparation and presentation, communication skills, business math and procedures, and sanitation.

15026B	Food-Service Managers
61099B	First-Line Supervisors/Managers of Food Preparation and Serving Workers
65002	Hosts and Hostesses—Restaurant, Lounge or Coffee Shop
65008A	Waiters/Waitresses

65008B	Wine Stewards/Stewardesses
65011	Food Servers, Outside
65017	Counter Attendants—Lunchroom, Coffee Shop, or Cafeteria

12.0599   Culinary Arts and Related Service, Other

Any instructional program in culinary arts and related services not described above.

12.99   Personal and Miscellaneous Services, Other

A group of instructional programs (see 12.9999).

12.9999   Personal and Miscellaneous Services, Other

Any instructional program in personal and miscellaneous services not described above.

13.   EDUCATION

A summary of groups of instructional programs that describe the theory and practice of learning and teaching, and related research, administrative, and support services.

13.01   Education, General

A group of instructional programs (see 13.0101).

13.0101   Education, General

An instructional program that generally describes the theory and practice of learning and teaching, the basic principles of educational psychology, the art of teaching, the planning and administration of educational activities, and the social foundations of education.

15005A	College and University Administrators
15005B	Educational Program Directors
15014	Industrial Production Managers
19005B	Private Sector Executives
21511E	Personnel Recruiters
27305A	Community Organization Social Workers
31303	Teachers—Preschool
31304	Teachers—Kindergarten
31305	Teachers—Elementary School
31308	Teachers—Secondary School
31311A	Special Education Vocational Training Teachers

31311B	Teachers—Emotionally Impaired, Mentally Impaired, and Learning Disabled
31311C	Teachers—Physically, Visually, and Hearing Impaired
31311D	Special Education Evaluators
31311E	Parent Instructors—Child Development and Rehabilitation
31314	Teachers and Instructors—Vocational Education and Training
31317	Instructors—Nonvocational Education
31321	Instructors and Coaches, Sports and Physical Training
31323	Farm and Home Management Advisors
31511A	Curators
31517D	Instructional Coordinators
31521	Teacher Aides, Paraprofessional
53905	Teacher Aides and Educational Assistants, Clerical
62041	Child Monitors, Private Household

13.02   Bilingual/Bicultural Education

A group of instructional programs (see 13.0201).

13.0201   Bilingual/Bicultural Education

An instructional program that describes the design and provision of teaching and other educational services to bilingual/bicultural children or adults, and/or the design and implementation of educational programs having the goal of producing bilingual/ bicultural individuals. Includes preparation to serve as teachers and administrators in bilingual/bicultural education programs.

31303	Teachers—Preschool
31304	Teachers—Kindergarten
31305	Teachers—Elementary School
31308	Teachers—Secondary School
31311B	Teachers—Emotionally Impaired, Mentally Impaired, and Learning Disabled
31317	Instructors—Nonvocational Education
31514	Vocational and Educational Counselors
31517D	Instructional Coordinators
31521	Teacher Aides, Paraprofessional
53905	Teacher Aides and Educational Assistants, Clerical

13.03   Curriculum and Instruction

A group of instructional programs (see 13.0301).

13.0301　Curriculum and Instruction

An instructional program that describes the study of the curriculum and related instructional processes and tools, and that may prepare individuals to serve as professional curriculum specialists. Includes instruction in curriculum theory, curriculum design and planning, instructional material design and evaluation, curriculum evaluation, and applications to specific subject matter, programs, or educational levels.

15005B	Educational Program Directors
31511A	Curators
31517A	Public Health Educators
31517D	Instructional Coordinators

13.04　Education Administration and Supervision

A group of instructional programs (see 13.0401).

13.0401　Education Administration and Supervision, General

An instructional program that generally describes the study of the principles and techniques of administering a wide variety of schools and other educational organizations and facilities, supervising educational personnel at the school or staff level, and that may prepare individuals as general administrators and supervisors.

15005A	College and University Administrators
15005B	Educational Program Directors
15014	Industrial Production Managers
19005B	Private Sector Executives
21511D	Employee Training Specialists
21511E	Personnel Recruiters
31303	Teachers—Preschool
31304	Teachers—Kindergarten
31305	Teachers—Elementary School
31308	Teachers—Secondary School
31311A	Special Education Vocational Training Teachers
31311B	Teachers—Emotionally Impaired, Mentally Impaired, and Learning Disabled
31311C	Teachers—Physically, Visually, and Hearing Impaired
31311D	Special Education Evaluators
31314	Teachers and Instructors—Vocational Education and Training
31321	Instructors and Coaches, Sports and Physical Training
31514	Vocational and Educational Counselors
31517B	Vocational Rehabilitation Coordinators
31517D	Instructional Coordinators

13.0402   Administration of Special Education

An instructional program that describes the principles and techniques of administering educational facilities and programs provided for children or adults with special learning needs, and that prepares individuals to serve as administrators of such programs. Includes instruction in special education principles, program and facilities planning, personnel management, community and client relations, budgeting and administration, professional standards, and applicable laws and policies.

15005B	Educational Program Directors
31311A	Special Education Vocational Training Teachers
31311B	Teachers—Emotionally Impaired, Mentally Impaired, and Learning Disabled
31311C	Teachers—Physically, Visually, and Hearing Impaired
31311D	Special Education Evaluators
31517B	Vocational Rehabilitation Coordinators
31517D	Instructional Coordinators

13.0403   Adult and Continuing Education Administration

An instructional program that describes the principles and techniques of administering programs and facilities designed to serve the basic education needs of undereducated adults, or the continuing education needs of adults seeking further or specialized instruction, and that prepares individuals to serve as administrators of such programs. Includes instruction in adult education principles, program and facilities planning, personnel management, community and client relations, budgeting and administration, professional standards, and applicable laws and policies.

15005A	College and University Administrators
15005B	Educational Program Directors
15014	Industrial Production Managers
21511D	Employee Training Specialists

13.0404   Educational Supervision

An instructional program that prepares individuals to supervise instructional and support personnel at the school building, facility, or staff level. Includes instruction in the principles of staffing and organization, the supervision of learning activities, personnel relations, administrative duties related to departmental or unit management, and specific applications to various educational settings and curricula.

15005B	Educational Program Directors
31303	Teachers—Preschool
31304	Teachers—Kindergarten
31305	Teachers—Elementary School
31308	Teachers—Secondary School

31311B	Teachers—Emotionally Impaired, Mentally Impaired, and Learning Disabled
31314	Teachers and Instructors—Vocational Education and Training
31321	Instructors and Coaches, Sports and Physical Training
31517D	Instructional Coordinators

13.0405   Elementary, Middle, and Secondary Education Administration

An instructional program that describes the principles and techniques of elementary, middle, or secondary school principalship, and that prepares individuals to serve as principals and other administrative personnel for elementary, middle, or secondary education programs and facilities. Includes instruction in elementary, middle, or secondary-level education, program, and facilities planning, personnel management, community and client relations, budgeting and administration, professional standards, and applicable laws and policies.

15005B	Educational Program Directors
19005B	Private Sector Executives
21511E	Personnel Recruiters
31517D	Instructional Coordinators

13.0406   Higher Education Administration

An instructional program that describes the principles and practice of administration in four-year colleges, universities, and higher education systems, the study of higher education as an object of applied research, and which may prepare individuals to function as administrators in such settings. Includes instruction in higher education economics and finance; policy and planning studies; curriculum; faculty and labor relations; higher education law; college student services; research on higher education; institutional research; marketing and promotion; and issues of evaluation, accountability, and philosophy.

15005A	College and University Administrators
15005B	Educational Program Directors
19005B	Private Sector Executives
31514	Vocational and Educational Counselors

13.0407   Community and Junior College Administration

An instructional program that describes the principles and techniques of administering community and junior colleges and related postsecondary systems, the study of community and junior colleges as objects of applied research, and that may prepare individuals to function as administrators in such settings. Includes instruction in community and junior college finance; policy and planning studies; curriculum; faculty and labor relations; higher education law; student services; research on community and junior colleges; institutional research; marketing and promotion; and issues of evaluation, accountability, and philosophy.

15005A	College and University Administrators
15005B	Educational Program Directors
19005B	Private Sector Executives
31514	Vocational and Educational Counselors

13.0499 Education Administration and Supervision, Other

Any instructional program in education administration and supervision not described above.

13.05 Educational/Instructional Media Design

A group of instructional programs (see 13.0501).

13.0501 Educational/Instructional Media Design

An instructional program that describes the principles and techniques of creating instructional materials and related educational resources in various media or combinations, such as film, video, recording, text, art, software, and three-dimensional objects, and that prepares individuals to function as instructional media designers. Includes instruction in the techniques specific to creating in various media; the behavioral principles applicable to using various media in learning and teaching; the design, testing, and production of instructional materials; and the management of educational/instructional media facilities and programs.

15005B	Educational Program Directors
31502A	Librarians
31508	Audio-Visual Specialists
31511A	Curators
31517D	Instructional Coordinators

13.06 Educational Evaluation, Research and Statistics

A group of instructional programs that describe the application of analytical and evaluation methodologies to educational problems and settings.

13.0601 Educational Evaluation and Research

An instructional program that describes the principles and procedures for generating information about educational programs, personnel, and methods, and the analysis of such information for planning purposes. Includes instruction in evaluation theory, evaluation research design and planning, administering evaluations and related data collection activities, data reporting requirements, data analysis and interpretation, and related economic and policy issues.

15005B	Educational Program Directors
21511E	Personnel Recruiters
31517D	Instructional Coordinators

13.0603 Educational Statistics and Research Methods

An instructional program that describes the application of statistics to the analysis and solution of educational research problems, and the development of technical designs for research studies. Includes instruction in mathematical statistics, research design, computer applications, instrument design, research methodologies, and applications to research problems in specific education subjects.

15005A	College and University Administrators
21511E	Personnel Recruiters
31517D	Instructional Coordinators

13.0604 Educational Assessment, Testing, and Measurement

An instructional program that describes the principles and procedures for designing, developing, implementing, and evaluating tests and other mechanisms used to measure learning, evaluate student progress, and assess the performance of specific teaching tools, strategies, and curricula. Includes instruction in psychometric measurement, instrument design, test implementation techniques, research evaluation, data reporting requirements, and data analysis and interpretation.

15005B	Educational Program Directors
21511E	Personnel Recruiters
27108D	Educational Psychologists
31311D	Special Education Evaluators
31517D	Instructional Coordinators

13.0699 Educational Evaluation, Research, and Statistics, Other

Any instructional program in educational evaluation, research, and statistics not described above.

13.07 International and Comparative Education

A group of instructional programs (see 13.0701).

13.0701 International and Comparative Education

An instructional program that describes the study of educational phenomena, practices, and institutions within different societies and states in comparative perspective, and the study of international educational issues. Includes instruction in comparative research methods, country- or area-specific studies, crossnational studies of learning and teaching styles, international educational policy and development, and analyses of educational migration patterns and experiences.

31517D   Instructional Coordinators

13.08   Educational Psychology

A group of instructional programs (see 13.0802).

13.0802   Educational Psychology

An instructional program that describes the application of psychology to the study of the behavior of individuals in the roles of teacher and learner, the nature and effects of learning environments, and the psychological effects of methods, resources, organization, and non-school experience on the educational process. Includes instruction in learning theory, human growth and development, research methods, and psychological evaluation.

27108D   Educational Psychologists

13.09   Social and Philosophical Foundations of Education

A group of instructional programs (see 13.0901).

13.0901   Social and Philosophical Foundations of Education

An instructional program that describes the systematic study of education as a social and cultural institution, and the educational process as an object of humanistic inquiry. Includes instruction in such subjects as the philosophy of education, history of education, educational literature, educational anthropology, sociology of education, economics and politics of education, educational policy studies, and studies of education in relation to specific populations, issues, social phenomena, and types of work.

13.10   Special Education

A group of instructional programs (see 13.1001).

13.1001   Special Education, General

An instructional program that generally describes the design and provision of teaching and other educational services to children or adults with special learning needs or disabilities, and that may prepare individuals to function as special education teachers. Includes instruction in diagnosing learning disabilities, developing individual education plans, teaching and supervising special education students, special education counseling, and applicable laws and policies.

15005B	Educational Program Directors
27305A	Community Organization Social Workers
31311A	Special Education Vocational Training Teachers
31311B	Teachers—Emotionally Impaired, Mentally Impaired, and Learning Disabled
31311C	Teachers—Physically, Visually, and Hearing Impaired
31311D	Special Education Evaluators
31311E	Parent Instructors—Child Development and Rehabilitation
31517B	Vocational Rehabilitation Coordinators
31517D	Instructional Coordinators
32399B	Orientation and Mobility Therapists

13.1003 Education of the Deaf and Hearing Impaired

An instructional program that describes the study and design of educational services for children or adults with hearing impairments which adversely affect their educational performance, and that may prepare individuals to teach such students. Includes instruction in identifying hearing-impaired students, developing individual education plans, teaching and supervising hearing-impaired students, counseling, and applicable laws and policies.

15005B	Educational Program Directors
31311A	Special Education Vocational Training Teachers
31311B	Teachers—Emotionally Impaired, Mentally Impaired, and Learning Disabled
31311C	Teachers—Physically, Visually, and Hearing Impaired
31311D	Special Education Evaluators
31311E	Parent Instructors—Child Development and Rehabilitation
31517D	Instructional Coordinators

13.1004 Education of the Gifted and Talented

An instructional program that describes the study and design of educational services for children or adults exhibiting exceptional intellectual, psychomotor, or artistic talent or potential, or who exhibit exceptional maturity or social leadership talents, and that may prepare individuals to teach such students. Includes instruction in identifying gifted and talented students, developing individual education plans, teaching and supervising gifted and talented students, counseling, and understanding applicable laws and policies.

31517D	Instructional Coordinators

13.1005 Education of the Emotionally Handicapped

An instructional program that describes the study and design of educational services for children or adults with emotional conditions which adversely affect their educational performance, and that may prepare individuals to teach such students. Includes instruction in identifying emotionally disturbed students, developing individual education plans, teaching and supervising emotionally disturbed students, counseling, and understanding applicable laws and policies.

15005B	Educational Program Directors
27305A	Community Organization Social Workers
31311A	Special Education Vocational Training Teachers
31311B	Teachers—Emotionally Impaired, Mentally Impaired, and Learning Disabled
31311D	Special Education Evaluators
31311E	Parent Instructors—Child Development and Rehabilitation
31517D	Instructional Coordinators

13.1006   Education of the Mentally Handicapped

An instructional program that describes the study and design of educational services for children or adults with mental disabilities which adversely affect their educational performance, and that may prepare individuals to teach such students. Includes instruction in identifying mentally handicapped students, developing individual education plans, teaching and supervising mentally handicapped students, counseling, and applicable laws and policies.

15005B	Educational Program Directors
27305A	Community Organization Social Workers
31311A	Special Education Vocational Training Teachers
31311B	Teachers—Emotionally Impaired, Mentally Impaired, and Learning Disabled
31311D	Special Education Evaluators
31311E	Parent Instructors—Child Development and Rehabilitation
31517D	Instructional Coordinators

13.1007   Education of the Multiple Handicapped

An instructional program that describes the study and design of educational services for children or adults with multiple disabilities which adversely affect their educational performance, and that may prepare individuals to teach such students. Includes instruction in identifying multiple handicapped students, developing individual education plans, teaching and supervising multiple handicapped students, counseling, and understanding applicable laws and policies.

15005B	Educational Program Directors
27305A	Community Organization Social Workers
31311A	Special Education Vocational Training Teachers
31311B	Teachers—Emotionally Impaired, Mentally Impaired, and Learning Disabled

31311D	Special Education Evaluators
31311E	Parent Instructors—Child Development and Rehabilitation
31517D	Instructional Coordinators

13.1008   Education of the Physically Handicapped

An instructional program that describes the study and design of educational services for children or adults with physical disabilities which adversely affect their educational performance, and that may prepare individuals to teach such students. Includes instruction in identifying physically disabled students, developing individual education plans, teaching and supervising physically disabled students, counseling, and understanding applicable laws and policies.

15005B	Educational Program Directors
27305A	Community Organization Social Workers
31311A	Special Education Vocational Training Teachers
31311B	Teachers—Emotionally Impaired, Mentally Impaired, and Learning Disabled
31311C	Teachers—Physically, Visually, and Hearing Impaired
31311D	Special Education Evaluators
31311E	Parent Instructors—Child Development and Rehabilitation
31517D	Instructional Coordinators

13.1009   Education of the Blind and Visually Handicapped

An instructional program that describes the study and design of educational services for children or adults with visual disabilities which adversely affect their educational performance, and that may prepare individuals to teach such students. Includes instruction in identifying visually handicapped students, developing individual education plans, teaching and supervising blind or visually handicapped students, counseling, and understanding applicable laws and policies.

31311A	Special Education Vocational Training Teachers
31311B	Teachers—Emotionally Impaired, Mentally Impaired, and Learning Disabled
31311C	Teachers—Physically, Visually, and Hearing Impaired
31311D	Special Education Evaluators
31311E	Parent Instructors—Child Development and Rehabilitation
31517D	Instructional Coordinators
32399B	Orientation and Mobility Therapists

13.1011   Education of the Specific Learning Disabled

An instructional program that describes the study and design of educational services for children or adults with specific learning disabilities which adversely affect their educational performance, and that may prepare individuals to teach such students. Includes instruction in identifying specific learning disabled students, developing individual education plans, teaching and supervising students with specific learning disabilities students, counseling, and understanding applicable laws and policies.

15005B	Educational Program Directors
27305A	Community Organization Social Workers
31311A	Special Education Vocational Training Teachers
31311B	Teachers—Emotionally Impaired, Mentally Impaired, and Learning Disabled
31311D	Special Education Evaluators
31311E	Parent Instructors—Child Development and Rehabilitation
31517D	Instructional Coordinators

13.1012   Education of the Speech-Impaired

An instructional program that describes the study and design of educational services for children or adults with speech impairments which adversely affect their educational performance, and that may prepare individuals to teach such students. Includes instruction in identifying speech-impaired students, developing individual education plans, teaching and supervising students with speech disabilities, counseling, and understanding applicable laws and policies.

15005B	Educational Program Directors
27305A	Community Organization Social Workers
31311A	Special Education Vocational Training Teachers
31311B	Teachers—Emotionally Impaired, Mentally Impaired, and Learning Disabled
31311D	Special Education Evaluators
31311E	Parent Instructors—Child Development and Rehabilitation
31517D	Instructional Coordinators

13.1013   Education of the Autistic

An instructional program that describes the study and design of educational services for children or adults that are autistic, and that prepares individuals to teach such students. Includes instruction in identifying students with autism, developing individual education plans, teaching and supervising autistic students, counseling, and understanding applicable laws and policies.

31311B	Teachers—Emotionally Impaired, Mentally Impaired, and Learning Disabled

13.1099   Special Education, Other

Any instructional program in special education not described above.

13.11 Student Counseling and Personnel Services

A group of instructional programs (see 13.1101).

13.1101 Counselor Education/Student Counseling and Guidance Services

An instructional program that prepares individuals to apply the theory and principles of guidance and counseling to the provision of support for the personal, social, educational, and vocational development of students, and the organizing of guidance services within elementary, middle and secondary educational institutions. Includes instruction in legal and professional requirements, therapeutic counselor intervention, vocational counseling, and related sociological and psychological foundations.

15005B	Educational Program Directors
27108H	Counseling Psychologists
31514	Vocational and Educational Counselors

13.1102 College/Postsecondary Student Counseling and Personnel Services

An instructional program that describes the organization and provision of counseling, referral, assistance and administrative services to students in postsecondary educational institutions and adult education facilities, and that may prepare individuals to function as professional counselors in such settings. Includes instruction in applicable laws and policies, residential counseling and services, vocational counseling and placement services, remedial skills counseling, and therapeutic counselor intervention.

15005A	College and University Administrators
15005B	Educational Program Directors
27108H	Counseling Psychologists
31514	Vocational and Educational Counselors

13.12 General Teacher Education

A group of instructional programs that prepare individuals to teach at various educational levels.

13.1201 Adult and Continuing Teacher Education

An instructional program that prepares individuals to teach adult students in various settings, including basic and remedial education programs, continuing education programs, and programs designed to develop or upgrade specific employment-related knowledge and skills.

31314	Teachers and Instructors—Vocational Education and Training
31317	Instructors—Nonvocational Education
31321	Instructors and Coaches, Sports and Physical Training

13.1202 Elementary Teacher Education

An instructional program that prepares individuals to teach students in the elementary grades, which may include kindergarten through grade eight, depending on the school system or state regulations. Includes preparation to teach all elementary education subject matter.

31304	Teachers—Kindergarten
31305	Teachers—Elementary School

13.1203 Junior High/Intermediate/Middle School Teacher Education

An instructional program that prepares individuals to teach students in the middle, intermediate, or junior high grades, which may include grades four through nine, depending on the school system or state regulations. May include preparation to teach a comprehensive curriculum or specific subject matter.

31305	Teachers—Elementary School
31308	Teachers—Secondary School

13.1204 Pre-Elementary/Early Childhood/Kindergarten Teacher Education

An instructional program that prepares individuals to teach students ranging in age from infancy through eight years (grade three), depending on the school system or state regulations. Includes preparation to teach all relevant subject matter.

15005B	Educational Program Directors
31303	Teachers—Preschool
31304	Teachers—Kindergarten
31305	Teachers—Elementary School

13.1205 Secondary Teacher Education

An instructional program that prepares individuals to teach students in the secondary grades, which may include grades seven through twelve, depending on the school system or state regulations. May include preparation to teach a comprehensive curriculum or specific subject matter.

31308	Teachers—Secondary School
31314	Teachers and Instructors—Vocational Education and Training

13.1206 Teacher Education, Multiple Levels

An instructional program that prepares individuals to teach students at more than one educational level, such as a combined program in elementary/secondary, early childhood/elementary, elementary/middle school, or junior high/high school teacher education.

31303	Teachers—Preschool
31304	Teachers—Kindergarten
31305	Teachers—Elementary School
31308	Teachers—Secondary School
31314	Teachers and Instructors—Vocational Education and Training
31317	Instructors—Nonvocational Education

13.1299   General Teacher Education, Other

Any instructional program in general teacher education not described above.

13.13   Teacher Education, Specific Academic & Vocational Programs

A group of instructional programs that prepare individuals to teach subject matter in specific academic and vocational programs at various educational levels.

13.1301   Agricultural Teacher Education (Vocational)

An instructional program that prepares individuals to teach vocational agricultural programs at various educational levels.

15005B	Educational Program Directors
31305	Teachers—Elementary School
31308	Teachers—Secondary School
31314	Teachers and Instructors—Vocational Education and Training
31323	Farm and Home Management Advisors

13.1302   Art Teacher Education

An instructional program that prepares individuals to teach art and art appreciation programs at various educational levels.

31303	Teachers—Preschool
31304	Teachers—Kindergarten
31305	Teachers—Elementary School
31308	Teachers—Secondary School
31317	Instructors—Nonvocational Education

13.1303   Business Teacher Education (Vocational)

An instructional program that prepares individuals to teach vocational business programs at various educational levels.

31305	Teachers—Elementary School
31308	Teachers—Secondary School
31314	Teachers and Instructors—Vocational Education and Training

13.1304   Driver and Safety Teacher Education

An instructional program that prepares individuals to teach driver and safety education programs at various educational levels.

21911D	Licensing Examiners and Inspectors
31308	Teachers—Secondary School
31317	Instructors—Nonvocational Education

13.1305   English Teacher Education

An instructional program that prepares individuals to teach English grammar, composition, and literature programs at various educational levels.

31303	Teachers—Preschool
31304	Teachers—Kindergarten
31305	Teachers—Elementary School
31308	Teachers—Secondary School

13.1306   Foreign Languages Teacher Education

An instructional program that prepares individuals to teach foreign-language programs at various educational levels.

31303	Teachers—Preschool
31304	Teachers—Kindergarten
31305	Teachers—Elementary School
31308	Teachers—Secondary School

13.1307   Health Teacher Education

An instructional program that prepares individuals to teach health education programs at various educational levels.

31305	Teachers—Elementary School
31308	Teachers—Secondary School

13.1308   Home Economics Teacher Education (Vocational)

An instructional program that prepares individuals to teach vocational home economics programs at various educational levels.

15005B	Educational Program Directors
31305	Teachers—Elementary School
31308	Teachers—Secondary School
31314	Teachers and Instructors—Vocational Education and Training
31323	Farm and Home Management Advisors

13.1309   Technology Teacher Education/Industrial Arts Teacher Education

An instructional program that prepares individuals to teach technology education/ industrial arts programs at various educational levels.

31305   Teachers—Elementary School
31308   Teachers—Secondary School

13.1310   Marketing Operations Teacher Education/Marketing and Distributive Teacher Education (Vocational)

An instructional program that prepares individuals to teach vocational marketing operations/marketing and distributive education programs at various educational levels.

31308   Teachers—Secondary School
31314   Teachers and Instructors—Vocational Education and Training
31317   Instructors—Nonvocational Education

13.1311   Mathematics Teacher Education

An instructional program that prepares individuals to teach mathematics programs at various educational levels.

31303   Teachers—Preschool
31304   Teachers—Kindergarten
31305   Teachers—Elementary School
31308   Teachers—Secondary School

13.1312   Music Teacher Education

An instructional program that prepares individuals to teach music and music appreciation programs at various educational levels.

31303   Teachers—Preschool
31304   Teachers—Kindergarten
31305   Teachers—Elementary School
31308   Teachers—Secondary School
31317   Instructors—Nonvocational Education

13.1314   Physical Education Teaching and Coaching

An instructional program that prepares individuals to teach physical education programs and/or to coach sports at various educational levels.

31303   Teachers—Preschool
31304   Teachers—Kindergarten
31305   Teachers—Elementary School

31308	Teachers—Secondary School
31321	Instructors and Coaches, Sports and Physical Training
34058A	Coaches and Scouts

13.1315   Reading Teacher Education

An instructional program that prepares individuals to diagnose reading difficulties and to teach reading programs at various educational levels.

31303	Teachers—Preschool
31304	Teachers—Kindergarten
31305	Teachers—Elementary School
31308	Teachers—Secondary School

13.1316   Science Teacher Education, General

An instructional program that prepares individuals to teach general science programs, or a combination of the biological and physical science subject matter areas, at various educational levels.

31303	Teachers—Preschool
31304	Teachers—Kindergarten
31305	Teachers—Elementary School
31308	Teachers—Secondary School

13.1317   Social Science Teacher Education

An instructional program that prepares individuals to teach specific social sciences subjects and programs at various educational levels.

31305	Teachers—Elementary School
31308	Teachers—Secondary School

13.1318   Social Studies Teacher Education

An instructional program that prepares individuals to teach general social studies programs at various educational levels.

31303	Teachers—Preschool
31304	Teachers—Kindergarten
31305	Teachers—Elementary School
31308	Teachers—Secondary School

13.1319   Technical Teacher Education (Vocational)

An instructional program that prepares individuals to teach specific vocational technical education programs at various educational levels.

| 31308 | Teachers—Secondary School |
| 31314 | Teachers and Instructors—Vocational Education and Training |

13.1320   Trade and Industrial Teacher Education (Vocational)

An instructional program that prepares individuals to teach specific vocational trades and industries programs at various educational levels.

| 31308 | Teachers—Secondary School |
| 31314 | Teachers and Instructors—Vocational Education and Training |

13.1321   Computer Teacher Education

An instructional program that prepares individuals to teach computer education programs at various educational levels.

| 31305 | Teachers—Elementary School |
| 31308 | Teachers—Secondary School |

13.1322   Biology Teacher Education

An instructional program that prepares individuals to teach biology programs at various educational levels.

| 31308 | Teachers—Secondary School |

13.1323   Chemistry Teacher Education

An instructional program that prepares individuals to teach chemistry programs at various educational levels.

| 31308 | Teachers—Secondary School |

13.1324   Drama and Dance Teacher Education

An instructional program that prepares individuals to teach drama and/or dance programs at various educational levels.

31303	Teachers—Preschool
31304	Teachers—Kindergarten
31305	Teachers—Elementary School
31308	Teachers—Secondary School
31317	Instructors—Nonvocational Education

13.1325   French Language Teacher Education

An instructional program that prepares individuals to teach French language programs at various educational levels.

31303	Teachers—Preschool
31304	Teachers—Kindergarten
31305	Teachers—Elementary School
31308	Teachers—Secondary School

13.1326   German Language Teacher Education

An instructional program that prepares individuals to teach German language programs at various educational levels.

31303	Teachers—Preschool
31304	Teachers—Kindergarten
31305	Teachers—Elementary School
31308	Teachers—Secondary School

13.1327   Health Occupations Teacher Education (Vocational)

An instructional program that prepares individuals to teach specific vocational health occupations programs at various educational levels.

31308	Teachers—Secondary School
31314	Teachers and Instructors—Vocational Education and Training

---

13.1328   History Teacher Education

An instructional program that prepares individuals to teach history programs at various educational levels.

31305	Teachers—Elementary School
31308	Teachers—Secondary School

13.1329   Physics Teacher Education

An instructional program that prepares individuals to teach physics programs at various educational levels.

31308	Teachers—Secondary School

13.1330   Spanish Language Teacher Education

An instructional program that prepares individuals to teach Spanish language programs at various educational levels.

31303	Teachers—Preschool
31304	Teachers—Kindergarten
31305	Teachers—Elementary School
31308	Teachers—Secondary School

13.1331   Speech Teacher Education

An instructional program that prepares individuals to teach speech and language arts programs at various educational levels.

31303	Teachers—Preschool
31304	Teachers—Kindergarten
31305	Teachers—Elementary School
31308	Teachers—Secondary School

13.1399   Teacher Education, Specific Academic and Vocational Programs, Other

Any instructional program in teacher education, specific academic and vocational programs not described above.

31303	Teachers—Preschool
31304	Teachers—Kindergarten
31305	Teachers—Elementary School
31308	Teachers—Secondary School
31317	Instructors—Nonvocational Education
97702D	Flight Instructors

13.14   Teaching English as a Second Language/Foreign Language

A group of instructional programs (see 13.1401).

13.1401   Teaching English as a Second Language/Foreign Language

An instructional program that describes the principles and practice of teaching English to students who are not proficient in it or who do not speak, read, or write English, and that may prepare individuals to function as teachers and administrators in such programs.

31317	Instructors—Nonvocational Education

13.15   Teacher Assistant/Aide

A group of instructional programs (see 13.1501).

13.1501   Teacher Assistant/Aide

An instructional program that prepares individuals to assist a teacher in regular classroom settings or in providing instruction and supervision to special student populations, such as bilingual/bicultural students, special education students, adult learners, and students learning English. Includes instruction in techniques of general classroom supervision, maintaining order, assisting with lessons, and carrying out related assignments.

31521	Teacher Aides, Paraprofessional
53905	Teacher Aides and Educational Assistants, Clerical

13.99 Education, Other

A group of instructional programs (see 13.9999).

13.9999 Education, Other

Any instructional program in education not described above.

14. ENGINEERING

A summary of groups of instructional programs that prepare individuals to apply mathematical and scientific principles to the solution of practical problems for the benefit of society.

14.01 Engineering, General

A group of instructional programs (see 14.0101).

14.0101 Engineering, General

An instructional program that generally prepares individuals to apply mathematical and scientific principles to solve a wide variety of practical problems in industry, social organization, public works, and commerce.

22123	Agricultural Engineers
22132A	Industrial Safety and Health Engineers
22132B	Fire-Prevention and Protection Engineers
22132C	Product Safety Engineers
22138	Marine Engineers
22197	Production Engineers
22305	Marine Architects
31222	Engineering Teachers—Postsecondary

14.02 Aerospace, Aeronautical and Astronautical Engineering

A group of instructional programs (see 14.0201).

14.0201 Aerospace, Aeronautical, and Astronautical Engineering

An instructional program that prepares individuals to apply mathematical and scientific principles to the design, development, and operational evaluation of aircraft, space vehicles, and their systems; applied research on flight characteristics; and the development of systems and procedures for the launching, guidance, and control of air and space vehicles.

21308B	Procurement Engineers
22102	Aerospace Engineers
31222	Engineering Teachers—Postsecondary
49002	Sales Engineers

14.03 Agricultural Engineering

A group of instructional programs (see 14.0301).

14.0301 Agricultural Engineering

An instructional program that prepares individuals to apply mathematical and scientific principles to the design, development, and operational evaluation of systems, equipment, and facilities used to produce, process, and store agricultural products; to improve the productivity of agricultural methods; and to develop improved agricultural biological systems.

22123	Agricultural Engineers
31222	Engineering Teachers—Postsecondary
49002	Sales Engineers

14.04 Architectural Engineering

A group of instructional programs (see 14.0401).

14.0401 Architectural Engineering

An instructional program that prepares individuals to apply mathematical and scientific principles to the design, development, and operational evaluation of materials, systems, and methods used to construct and equip buildings intended for human habitation or other purposes.

| 22121 | Civil Engineers, Including Traffic |
| 31222 | Engineering Teachers—Postsecondary |

14.05 Bioengineering and Biomedical Engineering

A group of instructional programs (see 14.0501).

14.0501 Bioengineering and Biomedical Engineering

An instructional program that prepares individuals to apply mathematical and scientific principles to the design, development, and operational evaluation of biological and health systems and products such as integrated biological systems, instrumentation, medical information systems, artificial organs and prostheses, and health management and care-delivery systems.

| 22197 | Production Engineers |
| 31222 | Engineering Teachers—Postsecondary |

14.06   Ceramic Sciences and Engineering

A group of instructional programs (see 14.0601).

14.0601   Ceramic Sciences and Engineering

An instructional program that prepares individuals to apply mathematical and scientific principles to the design, development, and operational evaluation of inorganic nonmetallic materials, such as porcelains, cements, industrial ceramics, ceramic superconductors, abrasives, and related materials and systems.

22105A	Ceramic Engineers
31222	Engineering Teachers—Postsecondary
49002	Sales Engineers

14.07   Chemical Engineering

A group of instructional programs (see 14.0701).

14.0701   Chemical Engineering

An instructional program that prepares individuals to apply mathematical and scientific principles to the design, development, and operational evaluation of systems employing chemical processes, such as chemical reactors, kinetic systems, electrochemical systems, energy conservation processes, heat and mass transfer systems, and separation processes; and the applied analysis of chemical problems such as corrosion, particle abrasion, energy loss, pollution, and fluid mechanics.

22114	Chemical Engineers
31222	Engineering Teachers—Postsecondary
49002	Sales Engineers

14.08   Civil Engineering

A group of instructional programs (see 14.0801).

14.0801   Civil Engineering, General

An instructional program that generally prepares individuals to apply mathematical and scientific principles to the design, development, and operational evaluation of structural, load-bearing, material-moving, transportation, water-resource, and material-control systems; and related equipment and environmental safety measures.

13017A	Engineering Managers
21911M	Public Transportation Inspectors
22117	Nuclear Engineers
22121	Civil Engineers, Including Traffic
31222	Engineering Teachers—Postsecondary

14.0802   Geotechnical Engineering

An instructional program that prepares individuals to apply mathematical and scientific principles to the design, development, and operational evaluation of systems for manipulating and controlling surface and subsurface features at or incorporated into structural sites, including earth and rock moving and stabilization, landfills, structural use and environmental stabilization of wastes and by-products, underground construction, and groundwater and hazardous material containment.

22117	Nuclear Engineers
22121	Civil Engineers, Including Traffic
31222	Engineering Teachers—Postsecondary

14.0803   Structural Engineering

An instructional program that prepares individuals to apply mathematical and scientific principles to the design, development, and operational evaluation of materials and systems used in building load-bearing structures for various purposes and in different environments, including buildings, roads, rail lines, bridges, dams, conduits, offshore platforms and work stations, and other structural shells; and the analysis of structural problems such as aging, failure, fabrication, safety, and natural hazards.

22121	Civil Engineers, Including Traffic
31222	Engineering Teachers—Postsecondary

14.0804   Transportation and Highway Engineering

An instructional program that prepares individuals to apply mathematical and scientific principles to the design, development, and operational evaluation of total systems for the physical movement of people, materials, and information, including general network design and planning, facilities planning, site evaluation, transportation management systems, needs projections and analysis, and analysis of costs.

21911M	Public Transportation Inspectors
22121	Civil Engineers, Including Traffic
31222	Engineering Teachers—Postsecondary

14.0805   Water Resources Engineering

An instructional program that prepares individuals to apply mathematical and scientific principles to the design, development, and operational evaluation of systems for collecting, storing, moving, conserving, and controlling surface water and groundwater, including water quality control, water cycle management, management of human and industrial water requirements, water delivery, and flood control.

13017A	Engineering Managers
22121	Civil Engineers, Including Traffic
31222	Engineering Teachers—Postsecondary

14.0899   Civil Engineering, Other

Any instructional program in civil engineering not described above.

14.09   Computer Engineering

A group of instructional programs (see 14.0901).

14.0901   Computer Engineering

An instructional program that prepares individuals to apply mathematical and scientific principles to the design, development, and operational evaluation of computer hardware and software systems and related equipment and facilities; and the analysis of specific problems of computer applications to various tasks.

22126B	Electronics Engineers, except Computer
22127	Computer Engineers
31222	Engineering Teachers—Postsecondary

14.10   Electrical, Electronics, and Communications Engineering

A group of instructional programs (see 14.1001).

14.1001   Electrical, Electronics, and Communications Engineering

An instructional program that prepares individuals to apply mathematical and scientific principles to the design, development, and operational evaluation of electrical, electronic, and related communications systems and their components, including electrical power generation systems; and the analysis of problems such as superconduction, wave propagation, energy storage and retrieval, and reception and amplification.

22126A	Electrical Engineers
22126B	Electronics Engineers, except Computer
31222	Engineering Teachers—Postsecondary
49002	Sales Engineers

14.11   Engineering Mechanics

A group of instructional programs (see 14.1101).

14.1101   Engineering Mechanics

An instructional program that generally describes the application of the mathematical and scientific principles of classical mechanics to the analysis and evaluation of the behavior of structures, forces, and materials in engineering problems. Includes instruction in statics, kinetics, dynamics, kinematics, celestial mechanics, stress and failure, and electromagnetism.

22197	Production Engineers
31222	Engineering Teachers—Postsecondary

14.12   Engineering Physics

A group of instructional programs (see 14.1201).

14.1201   Engineering Physics

An instructional program that generally describes the application of the mathematical and scientific principles of physics to the analysis and evaluation of engineering problems. Includes instruction in high- and low-temperature phenomena, computational physics, superconductivity, applied thermodynamics, molecular and particle physics applications, and space science research.

22197	Production Engineers
31222	Engineering Teachers—Postsecondary

14.13   Engineering Science

A group of instructional programs (see 14.1301).

14.1301   Engineering Science

An instructional program that generally describes the application of various combinations of mathematical and scientific principles to the analysis and evaluation of engineering problems, including applied research in human behavior, statistics, biology, chemistry, the earth and planetary sciences, atmospherics and meteorology, and computer applications.

| 22197 | Production Engineers |
| 31222 | Engineering Teachers—Postsecondary |

14.14 Environmental/Environmental Health Engineering

A group of instructional programs (see 14.1401).

14.1401 Environmental/Environmental Health Engineering

An instructional program that prepares individuals to apply mathematical and scientific principles to the design, development, and operational evaluation of systems for controlling contained living environments and for monitoring and controlling factors in the external natural environment, including pollution control, waste and hazardous material disposal, health and safety protection, conservation, life support, and requirements for the protection of special materials and related work environments.

21911A	Health Officers and Inspectors
22132A	Industrial Safety and Health Engineers
31222	Engineering Teachers—Postsecondary

14.15 Geological Engineering

A group of instructional programs (see 14.1501).

14.1501 Geological Engineering

An instructional program that prepares individuals to apply mathematical and geological principles to the analysis and evaluation of engineering problems, including the geological evaluation of construction sites, the analysis of geological forces acting on structures and systems, the analysis of potential natural resource recovery sites, and applied research on geological phenomena.

| 31222 | Engineering Teachers—Postsecondary |

14.16 Geophysical Engineering

A group of instructional programs (see 14.1601).

14.1601 Geophysical Engineering

An instructional program that prepares individuals to apply mathematical, geophysical, and planetary principles to the analysis and evaluation of engineering problems,

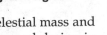
including gravitational and magnetic forces, time and space factors, celestial mass and motion, and their relation to questions of control, movement, function, and design in earthbound and space systems.

31222   Engineering Teachers—Postsecondary

14.17   Industrial/Manufacturing Engineering

A group of instructional programs (see 14.1701).

14.1701   Industrial/Manufacturing Engineering

An instructional program that prepares individuals to apply mathematical and scientific principles to the design, development, and operational evaluation of integrated systems for managing industrial production processes, including the optimization of human work factors, efficiency engineering, logistics and material flow, just-in-time manufacturing, industrial quality control, automation, cost analysis, and production coordination.

22128   Industrial Engineers, except Safety
31222   Engineering Teachers—Postsecondary

14.18   Materials Engineering

A group of instructional programs (see 14.1801).

14.1801   Materials Engineering

An instructional program that prepares individuals to apply mathematical and materials science principles to the design, development, and operational evaluation of materials and related processes used in manufacturing in a wide variety of settings; the synthesis of new industrial materials, including marrying and bonding composites; analysis of materials requirements and specifications; and related problems of system design dependent on materials factors.

31222   Engineering Teachers—Postsecondary

14.19   Mechanical Engineering

A group of instructional programs (see 14.1901).

14.1901   Mechanical Engineering

An instructional program that prepares individuals to apply mathematical and scientific principles to the design, development, and operational evaluation of physical systems used in manufacturing and end-product systems for specific uses, including machine tools, jigs, and other manufacturing equipment; stationary power units and appliances; engines; self-propelled vehicles; housings and containers; hydraulic and electric systems for controlling movement; and the integration of computers and remote control with operating systems.

22135	Mechanical Engineers
31222	Engineering Teachers—Postsecondary
49002	Sales Engineers

14.20 Metallurgical Engineering

A group of instructional programs (see 14.2001).

14.2001 Metallurgical Engineering

An instructional program that prepares individuals to apply mathematical and metallurgical principles to the design, development, and operational evaluation of metal components of structural, load-bearing, power, transmission, and moving systems; and the analysis of engineering problems such as stress, creep, failure, alloy behavior, environmental fluctuations, stability, electromagnetic and thermodynamic characteristics, optimal manufacturing processes, and related design considerations.

22105B	Metallurgists
22105C	Welding Engineers
31222	Engineering Teachers—Postsecondary

14.21 Mining and Mineral Engineering

A group of instructional programs (see 14.2101).

14.2101 Mining and Mineral Engineering

An instructional program that prepares individuals to apply mathematical and scientific principles to the design, development, and operational evaluation of mineral extraction, processing, and refining systems, including open pit and shaft mines, prospecting and site analysis equipment and instruments, environmental and safety systems, mine equipment and facilities, mineral processing and refining methods and systems, and logistics and communications systems.

22108	Mining Engineers, Including Mine Safety
22111	Petroleum Engineers
31222	Engineering Teachers—Postsecondary
49002	Sales Engineers

14.22 Naval Architecture and Marine Engineering

A group of instructional programs (see 14.2201).

14.2201   Naval Architecture and Marine Engineering

An instructional program that prepares individuals to apply mathematical and scientific principles to the design, development, and operational evaluation of self-propelled, stationary, or towed vessels operating on or under the water, including inland, coastal, and ocean environments; and the analysis of related engineering problems such as corrosion, power transfer, pressure, hull efficiency, stress factors, safety and life support, communications and sensing, environmental hazards and factors, and specific use requirements.

22138	Marine Engineers
22305	Marine Architects
31222	Engineering Teachers—Postsecondary
49002	Sales Engineers

14.23   Nuclear Engineering

A group of instructional programs (see 14.2301).

14.2301   Nuclear Engineering

An instructional program that prepares individuals to apply mathematical and scientific principles to the design, development, and operational evaluation of systems for controlling and manipulating nuclear energy, including nuclear power plant design, fission reactor design, fusion reactor design, reactor control and safety systems design, power transfer systems, containment vessels and structures design; and the analysis of related engineering problems such as fission and fusion processes, human and environmental factors, construction, and operational considerations.

22117	Nuclear Engineers
31222	Engineering Teachers—Postsecondary
49002	Sales Engineers

14.24   Ocean Engineering

A group of instructional programs (see 14.2401).

14.2401   Ocean Engineering

An instructional program that prepares individuals to apply mathematical and scientific principles to the design, development, and operational evaluation of systems to monitor, control, manipulate, and operate within coastal or ocean environments, such as underwater platforms, flood control systems, dikes, hydroelectric power systems, tide and current control and warning systems, and communications equipment; the planning and design of total systems for working and functioning in water or underwater environments; and the analysis of related engineering problems such as the action of water properties and behavior on physical systems and people, tidal forces, current movements, and wave motion.

31222	Engineering Teachers—Postsecondary

14.25 Petroleum Engineering

A group of instructional programs (see 14.2501).

14.2501 Petroleum Engineering

An instructional program that prepares individuals to apply mathematical and scientific principles to the design, development, and operational evaluation of systems for locating, extracting, processing, and refining crude petroleum and natural gas, including prospecting instruments and equipment, mining and drilling systems, processing and refining systems and facilities, storage facilities, transportation systems, and related environmental and safety systems.

22108	Mining Engineers, Including Mine Safety
22111	Petroleum Engineers
31222	Engineering Teachers—Postsecondary

14.27 Systems Engineering

A group of instructional programs (see 14.2701).

14.2701 Systems Engineering

An instructional program that prepares individuals to apply mathematical and scientific principles to the design, development, and operational evaluation of total systems solutions to a wide variety of engineering problems, including the integration of human, physical, energy, communications, management, and information requirements as needed, and the application of requisite analytical methods to specific situations.

31222	Engineering Teachers—Postsecondary
49002	Sales Engineers

14.28 Textile Sciences and Engineering

A group of instructional programs (see 14.2801).

14.2801 Textile Sciences and Engineering

An instructional program that prepares individuals to apply mathematical and scientific principles to the design, development, and operational evaluation of systems to test and manufacture fibers and fiber products, both synthetic and natural; to develop new and improved fibers and textiles and their uses; and to the analysis of related engineering problems such as structural factors, molecular synthesis, chemical manufacturing, weaves, strength and stress, useful life, dyes, and applications to composite systems.

15014	Industrial Production Managers
22114	Chemical Engineers
22126A	Electrical Engineers
22128	Industrial Engineers, except Safety
22135	Mechanical Engineers
31222	Engineering Teachers—Postsecondary

14.29 Engineering Design

A group of instructional programs (see 14.2901).

14.2901 Engineering Design

An instructional program that prepares individuals to apply mathematical and scientific principles to engineering problems involving marrying or coordinating multiple dissimilar systems to carry out single functions or achieve common purposes, organizing system components for maximum flexibility and utility, planning engineering projects involving multiple tasks and design solutions, planning design testing and evaluation procedures, resolving specification and requirement conflicts, and choosing among competing theoretical solutions.

31222	Engineering Teachers—Postsecondary

14.30 Engineering/Industrial Management

A group of instructional programs (see 14.3001).

14.3001 Engineering/Industrial Management

An instructional program that describes the application of engineering principles to the planning and operational management of enterprises and organizations, including budgeting, costing, quality control, efficient resource allocation and utilization, product production and distribution, human resource management, systems and plant maintenance, scheduling, storage and security, organization planning, acquisitions, and logistics.

13017A	Engineering Managers
22128	Industrial Engineers, except Safety
31222	Engineering Teachers—Postsecondary

14.31   Materials Science

A group of instructional programs (see 14.3101).

14.3101   Materials Science

An instructional program that generally describes the application of mathematical and scientific principles to the analysis and evaluation of the characteristics and behavior of solids, including internal structure, chemical properties, transport and energy flow properties, thermodynamics of solids, stress and failure factors, chemical transformation states and processes, compound materials, and research on industrial applications of specific materials.

22105D	Materials Engineers
24199C	Materials Scientists
31222	Engineering Teachers—Postsecondary

14.32   Polymer/Plastics Engineering

A group of instructional programs (see 14.3201).

14.3201   Polymer/Plastics Engineering

An instructional program that prepares individuals to apply mathematical and scientific principles to the design, development, and operational evaluation of synthesized macromolecular compounds and their application to specific engineering uses, including the development of industrial materials with tailored properties, the design of lightweight structural components, the use of liquid or solid polymers, and the analysis and control of polymerization processes.

22114	Chemical Engineers
31222	Engineering Teachers—Postsecondary

14.99   Engineering, Other

A group of instructional programs (see 14.9999).

14.9999   Engineering, Other

Any instructional program in engineering not described above.

15. ENGINEERING-RELATED TECHNOLOGIES

A summary of groups of instructional programs that prepare individuals to apply basic engineering principles and technical skills in support of engineering and related projects.

15.01 Architectural Engineering Technology

A group of instructional programs (see 15.0101).

15.0101 Architectural Engineering Technology/Technician

An instructional program that prepares individuals to apply basic engineering principles and technical skills in support of architects, engineers, and planners engaged in designing and developing buildings, urban complexes, and related systems. Includes instruction in design testing procedures, building site analysis, model building and computer graphics, engineering drawing, structural systems testing, analysis of prototype mechanical and interior systems, test equipment operation and maintenance, and report preparation.

21908A	Construction and Building Inspectors
22502	Civil Engineering Technicians
49008	Sales Representatives, except Retail and Scientific and Related Products and Services

15.02 Civil Engineering/Civil Technology

A group of instructional programs (see 15.0201).

15.0201 Civil Engineering/Civil Technology/Technician

An instructional program that prepares individuals to apply basic engineering principles and technical skills in support of civil engineers engaged in designing and executing public works projects such as highways, dams, bridges, tunnels, and other facilities. Includes instruction in site analysis, structural testing procedures, field and laboratory testing procedures, plan and specification preparation, test equipment operation and maintenance, and report preparation.

22502	Civil Engineering Technicians
39005	Traffic Technicians
39999C	City Planning Aides

15.03 Electrical and Electronic Engineering-Related Technology

A group of instructional programs that prepare individuals to apply basic engineering principles and technical skills in support of engineering, research, and industrial applications of electricity, lasers, and computers.

15.0301 Computer Engineering Technology/Technician

An instructional program that prepares individuals to apply basic engineering principles and technical skills in support of computer engineers engaged in designing and developing computer systems and installations. Includes instruction in computer electronics and programming, prototype development and testing, systems installation and testing, solid-state and microminiature circuitry, peripheral equipment, and report preparation.

22505A	Electronics Engineering Technicians
22514B	Electronic Drafters
49005C	Sales Representatives, Electrical/Electronic

15.0303 Electrical, Electronic, and Communications Engineering Technology/Technician

An instructional program that prepares individuals to apply basic engineering principles and technical skills in support of electrical, electronics, and communication engineers. Includes instruction in electrical circuitry and prototype development and testing, systems analysis and testing, systems maintenance, instrument calibration, and report preparation.

21908A	Construction and Building Inspectors
22505A	Electronics Engineering Technicians
22505B	Calibration and Instrumentation Technicians
22505C	Electrical Engineering Technicians
22514B	Electronic Drafters
49005C	Sales Representatives, Electrical/Electronic

15.0304 Laser and Optical Technology/Technician

An instructional program that prepares individuals to apply basic engineering principles and technical skills in support of engineers and other professionals engaged in developing and using lasers and other optical equipment for commercial or research purposes. Includes instruction in laser and optical principles, testing and maintenance procedures, safety precautions, specific applications to various tasks, and report preparation.

22599F	Laser Technicians
89905D	Glass Blowers, Molders, Benders, and Finishers
89917D	Optical Instrument Assemblers

15.0399 Electrical and Electronic Engineering-Related Technologies/Technicians, Other

Any instructional program in electrical and electronic engineering-related technologies not described above.

15.04 Electromechanical Instrumentation and Maintenance Technology

A group of instructional programs that prepare individuals to apply basic engineering and technical skills in support of engineers and other professionals engaged in developing and using industrial systems that rely on electrical power.

15.0401 Biomedical Engineering-Related Technology/Technician

An instructional program that prepares individuals to apply basic engineering principles and technical skills in support of engineers engaged in developing biological or medical systems and products. Includes instruction in instrument calibration, design, and installation testing, system safety and maintenance procedures, procurement and installation procedures, and report preparation.

49005F	Sales Representatives, Medical
66097	Health Equipment Service Workers
83002C	Precision Devices Inspectors and Testers
85908	Electromedical and Biomedical Equipment Repairers

15.0402 Computer Maintenance Technology/Technician

An instructional program that prepares individuals to apply basic engineering principles and technical skills in support of professionals who use computer systems. Includes instruction in basic computer design and architecture, programming, problems of specific computer applications, component and system maintenance and inspection procedures, hardware and software problem diagnosis and repair, and report preparation.

22505A	Electronics Engineering Technicians
49005C	Sales Representatives, Electrical/Electronic
85705	Data Processing Equipment Repairers
85717A	Electronics Mechanics and Technicians

15.0403 Electromechanical Technology/Technician

An instructional program that prepares individuals to apply basic engineering principles and technical skills in support of engineers engaged in developing and testing automated, servomechanical, and other electromechanical systems. Includes instruction in prototype testing, manufacturing and operational testing, systems analysis and maintenance procedures, and report preparation.

22505A	Electronics Engineering Technicians
22505B	Calibration and Instrumentation Technicians
22514D	Mechanical Drafters
83002C	Precision Devices Inspectors and Testers
83002D	Electrical and Electronic Inspectors and Testers
93111B	Electromechanical Technicians

15.0404   Instrumentation Technology/Technician

An instructional program that prepares individuals to apply basic engineering principles and technical skills in support of engineers engaged in developing control and measurement systems and procedures. Includes instruction in instrumentation design and maintenance, calibration, design and production testing and scheduling, automated equipment functions, applications to specific industrial tasks, and report preparation.

22505B	Calibration and Instrumentation Technicians
22514D	Mechanical Drafters
49005C	Sales Representatives, Electrical/Electronic
49005G	Sales Representatives, Instruments

15.0405   Robotics Technology/Technician

An instructional program that prepares individuals to apply basic engineering principles and technical skills in support of engineers and other professionals engaged in developing and using robots. Includes instruction in the principles of robotics, design and operational testing, system maintenance and repair procedures, robot computer systems and control language, specific system types and applications to specific industrial tasks, and report preparation.

22505A	Electronics Engineering Technicians
93111B	Electromechanical Technicians

15.0499   Electromechanical and Instrumentation and Maintenance Technologies/ Technicians, Other

Any instructional program in electromechanical instrumentation and maintenance technologies not described above.

15.05   Environmental Control Technologies

A group of instructional programs that prepare individuals to apply basic engineering principles and technical skills in support of engineers and other professionals engaged in environmental protection and the development of environmental systems.

15.0501   Heating, Air Conditioning, and Refrigeration Technologies/Technicians

An instructional program that prepares individuals to apply basic engineering principles and technical skills in support of engineers and other professionals engaged in developing and using air conditioning, refrigeration, and heating systems. Includes instruction in principles of heating and cooling technology, design and operational testing, inspection and maintenance procedures, installation and operation procedures, and report preparation.

22511	Mechanical Engineering Technicians and Technologists
22514A	Architectural Drafters

15.0503   Energy Management and Systems Technology/Technician

An instructional program that prepares individuals to apply basic engineering principles and technical skills in support of engineers and other professionals engaged in developing energy-efficient systems or monitoring energy use. Includes instruction in principles of energy conservation, instrumentation calibration, monitoring systems and test procedures, energy loss inspection procedures, energy conservation techniques, and report preparation.

22511	Mechanical Engineering Technicians and Technologists

15.0505   Solar Technology/Technician

An instructional program that prepares individuals to apply basic engineering principles and technical skills in support of engineers and other professionals engaged in developing solar-powered energy systems. Includes instruction in solar energy principles, energy storage and transfer technologies, testing and inspection procedures, system maintenance procedures, and report preparation.

22135	Mechanical Engineers

15.0506   Water Quality and Wastewater Treatment Technology/Technician

An instructional program that prepares individuals to apply basic engineering principles and technical skills in support of engineers and other professionals engaged in developing and using water storage, water power, and wastewater treatment systems. Includes instruction in water storage, power and/or treatment systems and equipment; appropriate testing and inspection procedures; appropriate system maintenance procedures; and report preparation.

21911A	Health Officers and Inspectors
21911B	Environmental Compliance Inspectors
22599E	Chemical Engineering Technicians
49005B	Sales Representatives, Chemical and Pharmaceutical
95002A	Water Treatment Plant and System Operators
95002B	Water Treatment Plant Attendants

15.0507 Environmental and Pollution Control Technology/Technician

An instructional program that prepares individuals to apply basic engineering principles and technical skills in support of engineers and other professionals engaged in developing and using indoor and outdoor environmental pollution control systems, and in disposing of hazardous materials. Includes instruction in environmental safety principles, biohazard identification, testing and sampling procedures, laboratory techniques, instrumentation calibration, hazardous waste disposal procedures and systems, safety and protection procedures, equipment maintenance, and report preparation.

21911A	Health Officers and Inspectors
21911B	Environmental Compliance Inspectors

15.0599 Environmental Control Technologies/Technicians, Other

Any instructional program in environmental control technologies not described above.

24505E	Environmental Science Technicians

15.06 Industrial Production Technologies

A group of instructional programs that prepare individuals to apply basic engineering principles and technical skills in support of engineers and other professionals engaged in developing and using industrial processes.

15.0603 Industrial/Manufacturing Technology/Technician

An instructional program that prepares individuals to apply basic engineering principles and technical skills in support of engineers and other professionals engaged in developing and using industrial manufacturing systems and processes. Includes instruction in design and prototype testing, instrument calibration, operational and maintenance procedures, operational diagnosis and repair, applications to specific systems and products, and report preparation.

22128	Industrial Engineers, except Safety
22508	Industrial Engineering Technicians and Technologists
49005D	Sales Representatives, Mechanical Equipment and Supplies
83002A	Materials Inspectors
89398	Standard Precision Woodworkers
89908B	Cutters and Layout Workers
89999A	Color Matchers and Dye Formulators

15.0607 Plastics Technology/Technician

An instructional program that prepares individuals to apply basic engineering principles and technical skills in support of engineers and other professionals engaged in developing and using industrial polymers. Includes instruction in the principles of macromolecular chemistry, polymerization and plastic manufacturing processes and equipment, design and operational testing procedures, equipment maintenance and repair procedures, safety procedures, applications to specific products, and report preparation.

22599E	Chemical Engineering Technicians
49005D	Sales Representatives, Mechanical Equipment and Supplies
83002A	Materials Inspectors
83005A	Production Inspectors, Testers, Graders, Sorters, Samplers, and Weighers
89114B	Pattern Makers, Metal and Plastic
89908C	Model and Mold Makers
89999A	Color Matchers and Dye Formulators
91102	Sawing Machine Tool Setters and Set-Up Operators, Metal and Plastic
91311	Extruding and Drawing Machine Setters and Set-Up Operators, Metal and Plastic
91902	Plastic Molding and Casting Machine Setters and Set-Up Operators
91905	Plastic Molding and Casting Machine Operators and Tenders
93944D	Molders and Casters
93956	Assemblers and Fabricators—except Machine, Electrical, Electronic, and Precision
93997	Intermediate Hand Workers
95008	Chemical Plant and System Operators

15.0611   Metallurgical Technology/Technician

An instructional program that prepares individuals to apply basic engineering principles and technical skills in support of engineers and metallurgists engaged in developing and using industrial metals and manufacturing processes. Includes instruction in principles of metallurgy, related manufacturing systems, laboratory techniques, testing and inspection procedures, instrument calibration, system and equipment maintenance and repair, applications to specific processes, and report preparation.

22599B	Metallurgical Technicians
49005C	Sales Representatives, Electrical/Electronic
49005D	Sales Representatives, Mechanical Equipment and Supplies
83002A	Materials Inspectors

15.0699   Industrial Production Technologies/Technicians, Other

Any instructional program in industrial production technologies not described above.

83002C	Precision Devices Inspectors and Testers
83005A	Production Inspectors, Testers, Graders, Sorters, Samplers, and Weighers
92714	Textile Bleaching and Dyeing Machine Operators and Tenders

15.07   Quality Control and Safety Technologies

A group of instructional programs that prepare individuals to apply basic engineering principles and technical skills in support of engineers and other professionals engaged in monitoring product quality and the health and safety of the workplace.

15.0701   Occupational Safety and Health Technology/Technician

An instructional program that prepares individuals to apply basic engineering principles and technical skills in support of engineers and other professionals engaged in maintaining job-related health and safety standards. Includes instruction in safety engineering principles, inspection and monitoring procedures, testing and sampling procedures, laboratory techniques, applications to specific work environments, and report preparation.

21911A	Health Officers and Inspectors
21911E	Industrial and Occupational Safety and Health Inspectors
24505B	Food Science Technicians and Technologists
32996C	Occupational Health and Safety Specialists
83005B	Construction Checkers

15.0702   Quality Control Technology/Technician

An instructional program that prepares individuals to apply basic engineering principles and technical skills in support of engineers and other professionals engaged in maintaining consistent manufacturing and construction standards. Includes instruction in quality control systems management principles, technical standards applicable to specific engineering and manufacturing projects, testing procedures, inspection procedures, related instrumentation and equipment operation and maintenance, and report preparation.

21911H	Government Property Inspectors and Investigators
22508	Industrial Engineering Technicians and Technologists
22599B	Metallurgical Technicians
24505A	Chemical Technicians and Technologists
24599C	Scientific Helpers
81008	First-Line Supervisors and Manager/Supervisors—Production and Operating Workers
83002D	Electrical and Electronic Inspectors and Testers
83005A	Production Inspectors, Testers, Graders, Sorters, Samplers, and Weighers

15.0799   Quality Control and Safety Technologies/Technicians, Other

Any instructional program in quality control and safety technologies not described above.

15.08   Mechanical Engineering-Related Technologies

A group of instructional programs that prepare individuals to apply basic engineering principles and technical skills in support of engineers and other professionals engaged in developing mechanical systems.

15.0801   Aeronautical and Aerospace Engineering Technology/Technician

An instructional program that prepares individuals to apply basic engineering principles and technical skills in support of engineers and other professionals engaged in developing, manufacturing, and testing aircraft, spacecraft, and their systems. Includes instruction in aircraft/spacecraft systems technology, design and development testing, prototype and operational testing, inspection and maintenance procedures, instrument calibration, test equipment operation and maintenance, and report preparation.

21911K	Aviation Inspectors
22505B	Calibration and Instrumentation Technicians
22599C	Aerospace Engineering Technicians
49005D	Sales Representatives, Mechanical Equipment and Supplies
83002A	Materials Inspectors
83002B	Mechanical Inspectors
83002C	Precision Devices Inspectors and Testers
83005A	Production Inspectors, Testers, Graders, Sorters, Samplers, and Weighers
89908A	Patternmakers and Model Builders
93102D	Aircraft Rigging Assemblers

15.0803   Automotive Engineering Technology/Technician

An instructional program that prepares individuals to apply basic engineering principles and technical skills in support of engineers and other professionals engaged in developing, manufacturing, and testing self-propelled ground vehicles and their systems. Includes instruction in vehicular systems technology, design and development testing, prototype and operational testing, inspection and maintenance procedures, instrument calibration, test equipment operation and maintenance, and report preparation.

22511	Mechanical Engineering Technicians and Technologists
24505A	Chemical Technicians and Technologists
83005A	Production Inspectors, Testers, Graders, Sorters, Samplers, and Weighers

15.0805   Mechanical Engineering/Mechanical Technology/Technician

An instructional program that prepares individuals to apply basic engineering principles and technical skills in support of engineers engaged in the design and development phases of a wide variety of projects involving mechanical systems. Includes instruction in principles of mechanics, applications to specific engineering systems, design testing procedures, prototype and operational testing and inspection procedures, manufacturing system testing procedures, test equipment operation and maintenance, and report preparation.

22135	Mechanical Engineers
22311B	Surveyors
22511	Mechanical Engineering Technicians and Technologists
22514D	Mechanical Drafters
22599C	Aerospace Engineering Technicians

15.0899 Mechanical Engineering-Related Technologies/Technicians, Other

Any instructional program in mechanical engineering-related technologies not described above.

15.09 Mining and Petroleum Technologies

A group of instructional programs that prepare individuals to apply basic principles of engineering and technical skills in support of engineers and other professionals engaged in locating and extracting mineral and petroleum resources.

15.0901 Mining Technology/Technician

An instructional program that prepares individuals to apply basic engineering principles and technical skills in support of engineers and other professionals engaged in the development and operation of mines and related mineral processing facilities. Includes instruction in principles of mineral extraction and related geology, mineral field mapping and site analysis, testing and sampling methods, instrument calibration, assay analysis, test equipment operation and maintenance, mine environment and safety monitoring procedures, mine inspection procedures, and report preparation.

24111A	Geologists

15.0903 Petroleum Technology/Technician

An instructional program that prepares individuals to apply basic engineering principles and technical skills in support of engineers and other professionals engaged in the development and operation of oil and natural gas extraction and processing facilities. Includes instruction in principles of petroleum extraction and related geology, petroleum field mapping and site analysis, testing and sampling methods, instrument calibration, laboratory analysis, test equipment operation and maintenance, environment and safety monitoring procedures for oil/gas fields and facilities, facility inspection procedures, and report preparation.

22599E	Chemical Engineering Technicians
24505A	Chemical Technicians and Technologists
24511B	Geological Data Technicians
24511E	Geological Sample Test Technicians
24599C	Scientific Helpers
49005D	Sales Representatives, Mechanical Equipment and Supplies
83002A	Materials Inspectors
83005A	Production Inspectors, Testers, Graders, Sorters, Samplers, and Weighers

15.0999   Mining and Petroleum Technologies/Technicians, Other

Any instructional program in mining and petroleum engineering-related technologies not described above.

15.10   Construction/Building Technology

A group of instructional programs (see 15.1001).

15.1001   Construction/Building Technology/Technician

An instructional program that prepares individuals to apply basic engineering principles and technical skills in support of engineers, engineering contractors and other professionals engaged in the construction of buildings and related structures. Includes instruction in basic structural engineering principles and construction techniques, building site inspection, site supervision, construction personnel supervision, plan and specification interpretation, supply logistics and procurement, applicable building codes, and report preparation.

21908A	Construction and Building Inspectors
22502	Civil Engineering Technicians
49005D	Sales Representatives, Mechanical Equipment and Supplies

15.11   Miscellaneous Engineering-Related Technologies

A group of instructional programs (see 15.1101).

15.1101   Engineering Technology/Technician, General

An instructional program that generally prepares individuals to apply basic engineering principles and technical skills in support of engineers engaged in a wide variety of projects. Includes instruction in various engineering support functions for research, production, and operations, and applications to specific engineering specialties.

| 31222 | Engineering Teachers—Postsecondary |

15.1102   Surveying

An instructional program that prepares individuals to apply mathematical and scientific principles to the delineation, determination, planning, and positioning of land tracts, land and water boundaries, land contours and features; and the preparation of related maps, charts, and reports. Includes instruction in applied geodesy, computer graphics, photointerpretation, plane and geodetic surveying, mensuration, traversing, survey equipment operation and maintenance, instrument calibration, and basic cartography.

13017A	Engineering Managers
22311A	Cartographers and Photogrammetrists
22311B	Surveyors
22521A	Surveying Technicians
22521B	Mapping Technicians
89908C	Model and Mold Makers

15.1103   Hydraulics Technology/Technician

An instructional program that prepares individuals to apply basic engineering principles and technical skills in support of engineers and other professionals engaged in developing and using fluid power and transportation systems. Includes instruction in fluid mechanics and hydraulics principles, fluid power systems, pipeline and pumping systems, design and operational testing, inspection and maintenance procedures, related instrumentation, and report preparation.

15.99   Engineering-Related Technologies, Other

A group of instructional programs (see 15.9999).

15.9999   Engineering-Related Technologies/Technicians, Other

Any instructional program in engineering-related technologies not described above.

16.   FOREIGN LANGUAGES AND LITERATURES

A summary of groups of instructional programs that describe the study of languages other than English, and the study of related aspects of foreign literatures and cultures.

16.01   Foreign Languages and Literatures

A group of instructional programs (see 16.0101).

16.0101　Foreign Languages and Literatures, General

An instructional program that describes an undifferentiated program in foreign languages and literatures.

27199D	Linguistic Scientists
31216	English and Foreign Language Teachers—Postsecondary
34002J	Caption Writers
39999A	Interpreters and Translators

16.0102　Linguistics

An instructional program that describes the scientific and scholarly study of language and the relationships among languages. Includes instruction in psycholinguistics, anthropological linguistics, historical linguistics, mathematical linguistics, grammatical theory, philosophy of language, philology, sociolinguistics, language and culture studies, and the study of written scripts and their evolution.

27199D	Linguistic Scientists
31216	English and Foreign Language Teachers—Postsecondary

16.0103　Foreign Language Interpretation and Translation

An instructional program that prepares individuals to translate written documents, or to consecutively or simultaneously interpret oral communications. Includes instruction in translating and/or interpreting from a specific foreign language into English, from English into another specific language, or between two foreign languages.

31216	English and Foreign Language Teachers—Postsecondary
34002J	Caption Writers
39999A	Interpreters and Translators

16.03　East and Southeast Asian Languages and Literatures

A group of instructional programs that describe the study of the languages, literatures, and cultures of East and Southeast Asian peoples.

16.0301　Chinese Language and Literature

An instructional program that describes the study of the language, literature, and culture of Chinese-speaking peoples, including dialects such as Cantonese, Taiwanese, and Mandarin.

31216	English and Foreign Language Teachers—Postsecondary

16.0302   Japanese Language and Literature

An instructional program that describes the study of the language, literature, and culture of Japanese-speaking peoples.

31216   English and Foreign Language Teachers—Postsecondary

16.0399   East and Southeast Asian Languages and Literatures, Other

Any instructional program in East and Southeast Asian languages and literatures not described above, such as Korean, Tibetan, Mongolian, Tagalog, Thai, Lao, Vietnamese, Cambodian, Indonesian/Malay, Burmese, or others.

31216   English and Foreign Language Teachers—Postsecondary

16.0402   Russian Language and Literature

An instructional program that describes the study of the language, literature, and culture of Russian-speaking peoples.

31216   English and Foreign Language Teachers—Postsecondary

16.0403   Slavic Languages and Literatures (Other than Russian)

An instructional program that describes the study of one or more of the languages, literatures, and cultures of the non-Russian Slavic peoples, including such languages as Byelorussian, Bulgarian, Czech, Polish, Serbo-Croatian, Old Slavonic, and Ukrainian.

31216   English and Foreign Language Teachers—Postsecondary

16.0406   East European Languages and Literatures

A group of instructional programs that describe the study of the languages, literatures, and cultures of the peoples of Eastern Europe, including Russia, the Baltic Coast, Middle Europe, and the Balkans.

16.0499   East European Languages and Literatures, Other

Any instructional program in East European languages and literatures not described above, such as Finnish, Hungarian, Estonian, Latvian, and Lithuanian.

31216   English and Foreign Language Teachers—Postsecondary

16.05   Germanic Languages and Literatures

A group of instructional programs that describe the study of the languages, literatures, and cultures of peoples speaking Germanic languages other than English.

16.0501   German Language and Literature

An instructional program that describes the study of the language, literature, and culture of German-speaking peoples, including related dialects such as Low German, Swiss-German, and Old or Middle German.

31216   English and Foreign Language Teachers—Postsecondary

16.0502   Scandinavian Languages and Literatures

An instructional program that describes the study of the languages, literatures, and cultures of the Scandinavian peoples, including Danish, Icelandic, Norwegian, Swedish, and Old Norse.

31216   English and Foreign Language Teachers—Postsecondary

16.0599   Germanic Languages and Literatures, Other

Any instructional program in Germanic languages and literatures not described above, such as Yiddish, Dutch, Flemish, Old German, Frisian, Gothic, and Saxon.

31216   English and Foreign Language Teachers—Postsecondary

16.06   Greek Language and Literature (Modern)

A group of instructional programs that describe the study of the language, literature, and culture of Greek-speaking peoples.

16.0601   Greek Language and Literature (Modern)

An instructional program that describes the study of the language, literature, and culture of modern Greece, generally comprising the period from the fall of Byzantium in 1453 to the present.

31216   English and Foreign Language Teachers—Postsecondary

16.07   South Asian Languages and Literatures

A group of instructional programs (see 16.0703).

16.0703   South Asian Languages and Literatures

An instructional program that describes the study of the languages, literatures, and cultures of peoples of South Asia, including such languages as Hindi, Urdu, Bengali, Punjabi, and the Dravidian group, and ancestral languages such as Sanskrit, Pali, and Bactrian.

31216   English and Foreign Language Teachers—Postsecondary

16.09   Romance Languages and Literatures

A group of instructional programs that describe the languages, literatures, and cultures of peoples speaking languages descended from Latin dialects and their modern derivatives.

16.0901   French Language and Literature

An instructional program that describes the study of the language, literature, and culture of French-speaking peoples, including related languages and dialects such as Creole, Provencal and Walloon.

31216   English and Foreign Language Teachers—Postsecondary

16.0902   Italian Language and Literature

An instructional program that describes the study of the language, literature, and culture of Italian-speaking peoples, including dialects and related languages such as Sicilian, Friulian, and Sardinian.

31216   English and Foreign Language Teachers—Postsecondary

16.0904   Portuguese Language and Literature

An instructional program that describes the study of the language, literature, and culture of Portuguese-speaking peoples, including the Luso-Brazilian and African dialects.

31216   English and Foreign Language Teachers—Postsecondary

16.0905   Spanish Language and Literature

An instructional program that describes the study of the language, literature, and culture of Spanish-speaking peoples, including related or derived dialects and languages such as Catalan, Castilian, and various Latin American dialects.

31216   English and Foreign Language Teachers—Postsecondary

16.0999   Romance Languages and Literatures, Other

Any instructional program in Romance languages not described above, such as Romanian and Rhaeto-Romansch.

31216   English and Foreign Language Teachers—Postsecondary

16.11   Middle Eastern Languages and Literatures

A group of instructional programs that describes the languages, literatures, and cultures of peoples of the Middle East, including Turkey, the Arabian Peninsula, Iran, the Fertile Crescent, and Semitic North Africa.

16.1101   Arabic Language and Literature

An instructional program that describes the study of the language, literature, and culture of Arabic-speaking peoples, including Classical, Modern Standard, and related dialects and derivatives.

31216   English and Foreign Language Teachers—Postsecondary

16.1102   Hebrew Language and Literature

An instructional program that describes the study of the language, literature, and culture of Hebrew-speaking peoples, including promodern and modern Hebrew dialects and derivatives.

31216   English and Foreign Language Teachers—Postsecondary

16.1199   Middle Eastern Languages and Literatures, Other

Any instructional program in Middle Eastern languages and literatures not described above, including such languages as Farsi (Iranian), Turkish, Berber, and Armenian.

31216   English and Foreign Language Teachers—Postsecondary

16.12   Classical and Ancient Near Eastern Languages and Literatures

A group of instructional programs that describe the study of the languages, literatures, and cultures of the Greek- and Latin-speaking peoples of the ancient and Medieval West, and of the peoples of the Pre-Islamic Near East.

16.1201   Classics and Classical Languages and Literatures

An instructional program that describes the study of the languages, literatures, and general civilization of the classical Greco-Roman world, including both ancient Greek and Latin, and related studies.

31216   English and Foreign Language Teachers—Postsecondary

16.1202   Greek Language and Literature (Ancient and Medieval)

An instructional program that describes the study of the language, literature, and culture of the ancient and Medieval Greeks, including Archaic Greece, Classical Greece, the Hellenistic World, Byzantium, and related studies.

31216   English and Foreign Language Teachers—Postsecondary

16.1203   Latin Language and Literature (Ancient and Medieval)

An instructional program that describes the study of the language, literature, and culture of the ancient and Medieval Latin-speaking peoples, including Classical Roman Latin, related ancient Italic dialects and languages, Medieval Latin and derivatives, and related studies.

31216   English and Foreign Language Teachers—Postsecondary

16.1299   Classical and Ancient Near Eastern Languages and Literatures, Other

Any instructional program in Classical and ancient Near Eastern languages and literatures not described above, such as Ancient Egyptian/Egyptology, Coptic, Avestan (Old Persian), Akkadian, Aramaic, Ugaritic, Syriac, Phoenician, Hittite and Hurrian, Sumerian, Luwian, Yemeni, Elamite, Cretan, and Urartian.

31216   English and Foreign Language Teachers—Postsecondary

16.99   Foreign Languages and Literatures, Other

A group of instructional programs (see 16.9999).

16.9999   Foreign Languages and Literatures, Other

Any instructional program in foreign languages and literatures not described above, including language groups and individual languages such as the non-Semitic African languages, Native American languages, the Celtic languages, Pacific language groups, the Ural-Altaic languages, Basque, and others.

19.   HOME ECONOMICS, GENERAL

A summary of groups of instructional programs that describe the relationship of the physical, social, emotional, and intellectual environments to the development of individuals, homes, and families, and the effects of these factors on society and the workplace.

19.01   Home Economics

A group of instructional programs (see 19.0101).

19.0101 Home Economics, General

An instructional program that generally describes the study of the relationship between the physical, social, emotional, and intellectual environment and the health and wellness of individuals and families.

19.02 Home Economics Business Services

A group of instructional programs (see 19.0201).

19.0201 Business Home Economics

An instructional program that describes the relationship between the economic environment and the home and family, including instruction in consumption theory and practices, production and distribution of goods and services, and resource uses as these pertain to family resource management and the consumer in the economic system.

19.0202 Home Economics Communications

An instructional program that describes the communication of home economics subject matter and information to a variety of audiences through print and/or non-print media. Includes instruction in the management of home economics-related communications services and materials.

19.03 Family and Community Studies

A group of instructional programs (see 19.0301).

19.0301 Family and Community Studies

An instructional program that describes the study of the cultural, social, and technological influences on families in changing societies, including family programs and support services.

19.04 Family/Consumer Resource Management

A group of instructional programs that describe the concepts, skills, and processes through which decisions about the use and management of resources are made at the individual and family levels, as well as research on general consumer behavior.

19.0401 Family Resource Management Studies

An instructional program that describes the study of the processes used by families and households in balancing needs and wants and in maximizing the use of available resources.

Includes instruction in human behavior, management theory, household planning, financial instruments and planning, and family resource consultative services.

19.0402   Consumer Economics and Science

An instructional program that describes the systematic study of the concepts and skills pertaining to consumer behavior in relation to the social, political, and economic components of market environments; and strategies and methods for responding to identified problems. Includes instruction in consumer activities and behavior that affect the individual, the family, society, and the workplace.

19.0499   Family/Consumer Resource Management, Other

Any instructional program in family/consumer resource management not described above.

19.05   Foods and Nutrition Studies

A group of instructional programs (see 19.0501).

19.0501   Foods and Nutrition Studies, General

An instructional program that generally describes the study of the role of food and nutrition in individual and family health and wellness, and in the study of food production, preparation, and service operations. Includes instruction in food product consumption, nutritional care and education, and the organization and administration of food systems.

15026B	Food-Service Managers
21999F	Meeting and Convention Planners
24305C	Food Scientists
31323	Farm and Home Management Advisors
32521	Dietitians and Nutritionists
32523	Dietetic Technicians
61099B	First-Line Supervisors/Managers of Food Preparation and Serving Workers
69999B	Personal Attendants

19.0502   Foods and Nutrition Science

An instructional program that describes the scientific study of the chemical, physical, and sensory properties of human food, food preservation and safety, nutritional quality, food processing and preparation, food use and diet applications, and food-related logistics management and marketing.

24305C	Food Scientists
32521	Dietitians and Nutritionists
32523	Dietetic Technicians

19.0503   Dietetics/Human Nutritional Services

An instructional program that describes the provision of nutritional services, menu planning, and diet consultation for individuals, families, and institutions. Includes instruction in planning and directing food service activities, diet and nutrition analysis and plan formulation, food preparation management, client education, and related services.

31323	Farm and Home Management Advisors
32521	Dietitians and Nutritionists
32523	Dietetic Technicians
69999B	Personal Attendants

19.0505   Food Systems Administration

An instructional program that describes the principles and practices relating to the administration of institutional food service systems. Includes instruction in service design and organization, resource acquisition and management, personnel resources management and human behavior, and consumer economics.

15026B	Food-Service Managers
21999F	Meeting and Convention Planners
32521	Dietitians and Nutritionists
61099B	First-Line Supervisors/Managers of Food Preparation and Serving Workers

19.0599   Foods and Nutrition Studies, Other

Any instructional program in foods and nutrition studies not described above.

19.06   Housing Studies

A group of instructional programs (see 19.0601).

19.0601   Housing Studies, General

An instructional program that generally describes the study of the behavioral, social, economic, functional, and aesthetic aspects of housing and other environments. Includes instruction in planning, designing, furnishing, and equipping households, and the behavioral, developmental, public policy, and cultural issues related to households.

| 34041 | Interior Designers |

19.0603   Interior Environments

An instructional program that describes the planning and analysis of interior home environments relative to function and quality as related to individual, family, and social development and behavior. Includes instruction in the design of environments and interiors, space utilization, furnishing, and equipment—from the standpoint of enhancing habitability and the quality of life and work.

34041   Interior Designers

19.0699   Housing Studies, Other

Any instructional program in housing studies not described above.

19.07   Individual and Family Development Studies

A group of instructional programs (see 19.0701).

19.0701   Individual and Family Development Studies, General

An instructional program that generally describes the study of the developmental and behavioral characteristics of the individual, within the context of the family, across the life span.

31311E   Parent Instructors—Child Development and Rehabilitation

19.0703   Family and Marriage Counseling

An instructional program that describes the study of the factors affecting marital relationships, parent-child relationships, and the functioning of the family as a whole; the study of separation, divorce and remarriage, death, exceptional children, and health and wellness; and the application of therapeutic intervention strategies in appropriate situations.

19.0704   Family Life and Relations Studies

An instructional program that describes the study of the family unit as it evolves across the lives of its members, with emphasis on identifying and analyzing family structures, family member roles and functions, family interactions, and family conflicts.

19.0705   Gerontological Services

An instructional program that describes the study of the characteristics, attitudes, behavior, and needs of older people in family settings, and the methods of organizing services for them. Includes instruction in providing dependent care; serving the physical, social, economic, and psychological needs and concerns of the elderly; related legislation; and community resources.

19.0706 Child Growth, Care, and Development Studies

An instructional program that describes the study of the intellectual, social, emotional, and physical growth of children from birth through adolescence, and the administration and supervision of services to children and their families. Includes instruction in providing dependent care; related social, behavioral, and biological sciences; and management theory and practice.

31311E   Parent Instructors—Child Development and Rehabilitation

---

19.0799 Individual and Family Development Studies, Other

Any instructional program in individual and family development studies not described above.

19.09 Clothing/Apparel and Textile Studies

A group of instructional programs (see 19.0901).

19.0901 Clothing/Apparel and Textile Studies

An instructional program that describes the study of contemporary and historical ways of meeting psychological, sociological, economic, and physiological needs relative to clothing and textile products, including techniques of design, production, distribution, marketing, and consumption.

15005B   Educational Program Directors
31323   Farm and Home Management Advisors
41002   First-Line Supervisors and Manager/Supervisors—Sales and Related Workers

---

19.99 Home Economics, Other

A group of instructional programs (see 19.9999).

19.9999 Home Economics, Other

Any instructional program in home economics not described above.

---

20. VOCATIONAL HOME ECONOMICS

A summary of groups of instructional programs that describe competencies in home economics which prepare individuals for the occupation of homemaking, for paid employment, and for organizing and managing business undertakings and services.

20.01 Consumer and Homemaking Education

A group of instructional programs that prepares individuals at all education levels for the occupation of homemaking, emphasizing the acquisition of knowledge and the comprehension of attitudes, standards, values, and skills relevant to individual and family life. These programs prepare individuals for the multiple roles of homemaker and wage earner.

20.0101 Comprehensive Consumer and Homemaking Education

An instructional program that generally prepares individuals for the occupation of homemaking, emphasizing the acquisition of knowledge and the development of attitudes, standards, values, and skills relevant to individual and family life and nurturing. Includes instruction in consumer education, food and nutrition, family living and parenthood education, child growth and development, housing and home management (including resource management), and clothing and textiles. Also, prepares individuals for balancing work and family roles and enhancing employability skills.

20.0102 Child Development, Care, and Guidance

An instructional program that prepares individuals to understand children's physical, mental, emotional, and social growth and development. Includes instruction in childcare and guidance and actual experience in supervising children.

20.0103 Clothing and Textiles

An instructional program that prepares individuals to understand the social, psychological, and physiological aspects of clothing and textiles; the nature, acquisition, and use of clothing and textile products; the selection, construction, maintenance, and alteration of clothing and textile products; and the effect of consumer choices on the individual and family as well as the clothing and textile industry.

20.0104 Consumer Education

An instructional program that prepares individuals to understand the values, needs, wants, goals, and resources that enable youth and adults to make rational decisions that contribute to family stability and quality of life. Includes instruction in budgeting and spending plans, use of credit, savings, investments, taxes, consumer buying, and consumer rights and responsibilities.

20.0105   Exploratory Homemaking

An instructional program that provides individuals the opportunity to explore home economics subject matter areas. Includes instruction in the development of positive self-concepts; understanding personal growth and development; and relationships with peers and family members in becoming contributing members in the home, school, and community.

20.0106   Family/Individual Health

An instructional program that prepares individuals to understand the related aspects of health and wellness with special emphasis on nutrition, emotional health, and physical health; the relationship of the health of an individual to the wellness of the family; the prevention of illness; and the basic care of the ill and convalescent in the home, including the elderly, the young child, and the handicapped.

20.0107   Family Living and Parenthood

An instructional program that prepares individuals to understand the nature, function, and significance of human relationships within the family/individual units. Includes instruction in the concepts and principles related to various family living conditions, including abuse prevention; the establishment and maintenance of relationships; the preparation for marriage, parenthood, and family life; and the socialization and developmental needs of individuals.

20.0108   Food and Nutrition

An instructional program that prepares individuals to understand the principles of nutrition; the relationship of nutrition to health and wellness; the selection, preparation, and care of food; meal management to meet individual and family food needs and patterns of living; food economics and ecology; optimal use of the food dollar; understanding and promoting nutritional knowledge; and the application of related math and science skills.

20.0109   Home Management

An instructional program that prepares individuals to understand the establishment and maintenance of a satisfying home and family life, including decision-making regarding human and non-human resources. Includes instruction in the societal and economic influences on individual and family management; values, goals, and standards; family economics; the impact of new technologies on life and work; and the organization of activities in the home as a means of successfully balancing work and family roles.

20.0110   Housing, Home Furnishing, and Equipment

An instructional program that prepares individuals to understand the physical, psychological, and social influences pertaining to the complex housing decisions required for a desirable living environment. Includes instruction in the human and environmental factors influencing the form and use of housing; the varied types of housing; costs; exterior and interior design; home furnishing and equipment; and the selection, use, and care of available resources for achieving improved living space to meet individual and family needs.

20.0199   Consumer and Homemaking Education, Other

Any instructional program in consumer and homemaking education not described above.

20.02   Childcare and Guidance Workers and Managers

A group of instructional programs (see 20.0201).

20.0201   Childcare and Guidance Workers and Managers, General

An instructional program that generally prepares individuals for occupations in childcare and guidance in institutional and residential family settings, often under the supervision of professional personnel. Includes instruction in child growth and development; nutrition; recreation, play, and learning activities planning and supervision; child abuse and neglect prevention; parent-child relationships; and applicable legal and administrative requirements.

15005B	Educational Program Directors
27307	Residential Counselors
27311	Recreation Workers
31303	Teachers—Preschool
62041	Child Monitors, Private Household
68035	Personal and Home Care Aides
68038	Child Care Workers

20.0202   Childcare Provider/Assistant

An instructional program that prepares individuals to be primary providers of home, family, residential or institutionally based childcare services. Includes instruction in planning, organizing, and conducting meaningful play and learning activities; child monitoring and supervision; recordkeeping; and referral procedures.

27307	Residential Counselors
27311	Recreation Workers
62041	Child Monitors, Private Household
68035	Personal and Home Care Aides
68038	Childcare Workers

20.0203   Childcare Services Manager

An instructional program that prepares individuals to develop and manage effective child-care programs and facilities. Includes instruction in the management of financial operations; selecting and developing facilities; selecting staff and staffing patterns; providing for staff development opportunities; developing a total program for children; and working with parents, community organizations, and others concerned with children.

15005B	Educational Program Directors
27307	Residential Counselors
31303	Teachers—Preschool

20.0299   Childcare and Guidance Workers and Managers, Other

Any instructional program in childcare and guidance management and services not described above.

20.03   Clothing, Apparel, and Textile Workers and Managers

A group of instructional programs (see 20.0301).

20.0301   Clothing, Apparel, and Textile Workers and Managers, General

An instructional program that generally prepares individuals for occupations concerned with the entire spectrum of clothing, apparel, and textiles management, production, and services, including but not limited to construction, fabric and fabric care, pattern design, principles in clothing construction and selection, fitting and alterations of ready-to-wear garments, custom tailoring, clothing maintenance, and textiles testing.

13011C	Marketing Managers
19999D	Service Establishment Managers
21302	Wholesale and Retail Buyers, except Farm Products
34038A	Fashion Designers
41002	First-Line Supervisors and Manager/Supervisors—Sales and Related Workers
49008	Sales Representatives, except Retail and Scientific and Related Products and Services
49011	Salespersons, Retail
49017	Counter and Rental Clerks
49032A	Demonstrators and Promoters
49999C	Sales Consultants
51002B	First-Line Supervisors, Administrative Support
58008	Production, Planning, and Expediting Clerks
62061	Personal Attendants, Private Household
68032B	Costumers and Wardrobe Specialists
81008	First-Line Supervisors and Manager/Supervisors—Production and Operating Workers

83005A	Production Inspectors, Testers, Graders, Sorters, Samplers, and Weighers
85956A	Textile Menders
85956C	Hand Weavers
89502A	Fabric and Apparel Patternmakers
89502B	Embroidery Patternmakers and Designers
89502D	Hat Patternmakers
89505A	Shop and Alteration Tailors
89505B	Custom Tailors
89514	Spotters, Dry Cleaning
89517	Pressers, Delicate Fabrics
89521	Precision Dyers
89599B	Fur Garment Workers
89599D	Hat Makers and Repairers
92717	Sewing Machine Operators, Garment
92721	Sewing Machine Operators, Nongarment
92726	Laundry and Dry-cleaning Machine Operators and Tenders, except Pressing
92728	Pressing Machine Operators and Tenders—Textile, Garment, and Related Materials
93923B	Sewers, Hand
93926E	Cutters and Trimmers, Hand
93956	Assemblers and Fabricators—except Machine, Electrical, Electronic, and Precision
93997	Intermediate Hand Workers
93998	Elemental Hand Workers

20.0303   Commercial Garment and Apparel Worker

An instructional program that prepares individuals to construct ready-to-wear garments and apparel. Includes instruction in developing and preparing patterns for standardized sizes, selecting appropriate fabric, cutting fabric with commercial cutting equipment, stitching fabric on commercial power sewing equipment, applying finishes and notions to garments and apparel, and pressing and packing garments or apparel.

51002B	First-Line Supervisors, Administrative Support
58008	Production, Planning, and Expediting Clerks
83005A	Production Inspectors, Testers, Graders, Sorters, Samplers, and Weighers
85956A	Textile Menders
89502A	Fabric and Apparel Patternmakers
89502B	Embroidery Patternmakers and Designers
89502D	Hat Patternmakers
89505A	Shop and Alteration Tailors
89599B	Fur Garment Workers
89599D	Hat Makers and Repairers

92717	Sewing Machine Operators, Garment
92721	Sewing Machine Operators, Nongarment
93926E	Cutters and Trimmers, Hand
93956	Assemblers and Fabricators—except Machine, Electrical, Electronic, and Precision
93997	Intermediate Hand Workers
93998	Elemental Hand Workers

20.0305   Custom Tailor

An instructional program that prepares individuals to design, construct, alter, and repair men's, women's, and children's garments and apparel. Includes instruction in tailoring design; fabric selection; customizing to customer specifications; taking measurements and fitting; preparing patterns; cutting, sewing, altering, refitting, and adjusting; operation of hand and power equipment; and pressing and smoothing seams.

34038A	Fashion Designers
68032B	Costumers and Wardrobe Specialists
81008	First-Line Supervisors and Manager/Supervisors—Production and Operating Workers
83005A	Production Inspectors, Testers, Graders, Sorters, Samplers, and Weighers
89505A	Shop and Alteration Tailors
89505B	Custom Tailors
89599D	Hat Makers and Repairers

20.0306   Fashion and Fabric Consultant

An instructional program that prepares individuals to assist in apparel and fashion selection, style coordination, customer sales and consulting, fabric selection, clothing specifications, and contract buying activities. Includes instruction in supplying regular clothing needs or acting as a consultant for special events such as weddings.

13011C	Marketing Managers
21302	Wholesale and Retail Buyers, except Farm Products
49008	Sales Representatives, except Retail and Scientific and Related Products and Services
49011	Salespersons, Retail
49032A	Demonstrators and Promoters
49999C	Sales Consultants
89505A	Shop and Alteration Tailors

20.0309   Dry Cleaner and Launderer

An instructional program that prepares individuals to perform clothing and apparel cleaning services and to operate and manage laundry and dry-cleaning facilities. Includes instruction in routine clothing repairs, fabric identification, spot removing and special cleaning, dyeing and bleaching, ironing and pressing, equipment operation and maintenance, and business management.

19999D	Service Establishment Managers
49017	Counter and Rental Clerks
81008	First-Line Supervisors and Manager/Supervisors—Production and Operating Workers
83005A	Production Inspectors, Testers, Graders, Sorters, Samplers, and Weighers
89514	Spotters, Dry Cleaning
89517	Pressers, Delicate Fabrics
89521	Precision Dyers
92726	Laundry and Dry-cleaning Machine Operators and Tenders, except Pressing
92728	Pressing Machine Operators and Tenders—Textile, Garment, and Related Materials
93997	Intermediate Hand Workers
93998	Elemental Hand Workers

20.0399   Clothing, Apparel, and Textile Workers and Managers, Other

Any instructional program in clothing, apparel, and textiles management, production, and services not described above.

20.04   Institutional Food Workers and Administrators

A group of instructional programs (see 20.0401).

20.0401   Institutional Food Workers and Administrators

An instructional program that generally prepares individuals in managerial, production, and service skills used in governmental, commercial, or independently owned institutional food establishments and related food industry occupations. Includes instruction in planning, selecting, storing, purchasing, preparing, and serving food and food products; basic nutrition, sanitation, and food safety; the use and care of commercial equipment; serving techniques; and the operation of institutional food establishments.

15026B	Food-Service Managers
21308A	Purchasing Agents and Contract Specialists
21911A	Health Officers and Inspectors
21999F	Meeting and Convention Planners
32521	Dietitians and Nutritionists
32523	Dietetic Technicians
61099A	Chefs and Head Cooks

61099B	First-Line Supervisors/Managers of Food Preparation and Serving Workers
65038A	Food Preparation Workers
69999B	Personal Attendants
89808	Food Batchmakers
92917	Cooking Machine Operators and Tenders, Food and Tobacco

20.0404   Dietician Assistant

An instructional program that prepares individuals to assist registered dieticians in planning, preparing, and serving meals to individuals with specific dietary needs. Includes instruction in equipment use, food preparation, diet regulations, food handling, safety and sanitary standards, and administrative techniques and procedures.

32523	Dietetic Technicians
61099B	First-Line Supervisors/Managers of Food Preparation and Serving Workers
69999B	Personal Attendants

20.0405   Food Catering

An instructional program that prepares individuals to book, plan, and manage the preparation of food and services for special occasions. Includes instruction in arranging for equipment, decorations, entertainment, and transportation of food and equipment to the site of the event.

15026B	Food-Service Managers
21999F	Meeting and Convention Planners
61099B	First-Line Supervisors/Managers of Food Preparation and Serving Workers
65038A	Food Preparation Workers

20.0409   Institutional Food Services Administrator

An instructional program that prepares individuals to manage and supervise institutional food service operations, including school food services and other government-regulated food service operations. Includes instruction in management, purchasing and storage, food preparation, staff supervision, diet and menu planning, and sanitation and safety.

15026B	Food-Service Managers
21308A	Purchasing Agents and Contract Specialists
21911A	Health Officers and Inspectors
32521	Dietitians and Nutritionists
61099B	First-Line Supervisors/Managers of Food Preparation and Serving Workers

20.0499 Institutional Food Workers and Administrators, Other

Any instructional program in institutional food preparation, administration, and related services not described above.

20.05 Home Furnishings and Equipment Installers and Consultants

A group of instructional programs (see 20.0501).

20.0501 Home Furnishings and Equipment Installers and Consultants

An instructional program that generally prepares individuals to assist in the entire spectrum of home furnishings and decorations. Includes instruction in selecting, purchasing, designing, and decorating; home furnishings and equipment; floral design; accessory construction; textiles; and upholstery.

15005B	Educational Program Directors
21302	Wholesale and Retail Buyers, except Farm Products
34038B	Commercial and Industrial Designers
34038D	Exhibit Designers
34038F	Floral Designers
34041	Interior Designers
34044	Merchandise Displayers and Window Trimmers
43099A	Sales Representatives, Service
49011	Salespersons, Retail
49032A	Demonstrators and Promoters
49999B	Home Furnishings Estimators
87899B	Window Treatment Installers
89502A	Fabric and Apparel Patternmakers
89508	Upholsterers
92721	Sewing Machine Operators, Nongarment
93926E	Cutters and Trimmers, Hand
93956	Assemblers and Fabricators—except Machine, Electrical, Electronic, and Precision

20.0502 Window Treatment Maker and Installer

An instructional program that prepares individuals to design, construct, and/or install custom window treatments in residential and commercial facilities. Includes instruction in selecting textiles, fabrics, and finishes; selecting appropriate types of window treatments; and constructing and installing these treatments.

49999B	Home Furnishings Estimators
87899B	Window Treatment Installers
89502A	Fabric and Apparel Patternmakers

92721	Sewing Machine Operators, Nongarment
93926E	Cutters and Trimmers, Hand
93956	Assemblers and Fabricators—except Machine, Electrical, Electronic, and Precision

20.0599   Home Furnishings and Equipment Installers and Consultants, Other

Any instructional program in home furnishings and equipment management, production, and services not described above.

20.06   Custodial, Housekeeping, and Home Services Workers and Managers

A group of instructional programs (see 20.0601).

20.0601   Custodial, Housekeeping, and Home Services Workers and Managers, General

An instructional program that generally prepares individuals for occupations relating to commercial housekeeping and cleaning operations; and for providing housekeeping services to paying clients and to homebound individuals.

27308	Human Services Workers
49999C	Sales Consultants
61008	Housekeeping Supervisors
61099C	First-Line Supervisors/Hospitality and Personal Service Workers
61099D	First-Line Supervisors/Managers of Housekeeping and Janitorial Workers
62031	Housekeepers, Private Household
62041	Child Monitors, Private Household
62061	Personal Attendants, Private Household
66011	Home Health Aides
67005	Janitors and Cleaners, except Maids and Housekeeping Cleaners
68035	Personal and Home Care Aides
87899D	Construction Workers, except Trade

20.0602   Elder Care Provider/Companion

An instructional program that prepares individuals to assist elderly individuals in managing their personal and social needs and their business affairs; to assist the elderly in the maintenance of independent living arrangements; and to promote the well-being of the elderly.

27308	Human Services Workers
62061	Personal Attendants, Private Household
66011	Home Health Aides
68035	Personal and Home Care Aides

20.0604 Custodian/Caretaker

An instructional program that prepares individuals to clean and care for buildings, including their fixtures, furnishings, floor surfaces, and wall coverings. Includes instruction in equipment operation and maintenance, chemical and non-chemical cleaning operations, sanitation, safety, staff supervision, and the management of custodial businesses and services.

61099C	First-Line Supervisors/Hospitality and Personal Service Workers
61099D	First-Line Supervisors/Managers of Housekeeping and Janitorial Workers
62031	Housekeepers, Private Household
62041	Child Monitors, Private Household
62061	Personal Attendants, Private Household
67005	Janitors and Cleaners, except Maids and Housekeeping Cleaners
87899D	Construction Workers, except Trade

20.0605 Executive Housekeeper

An instructional program that prepares individuals to provide comprehensive cleaning and housekeeping services for institutions and to supervise and manage such services. Includes instruction in floor maintenance and care; walls, woodwork, and window cleaning; furnishings and equipment maintenance; laundry and linen services; supply ordering and storage; and recordkeeping.

61008	Housekeeping Supervisors
61099C	First-Line Supervisors/Hospitality and Personal Service Workers
62031	Housekeepers, Private Household

20.0606 Homemaker's Aide

An instructional program that prepares individuals to assist homemakers in the management and operation of the home, including child and convalescent care, cleaning and maintenance, supplies purchasing, and food preparation.

27308	Human Services Workers
49999C	Sales Consultants
62031	Housekeepers, Private Household
62041	Child Monitors, Private Household
62061	Personal Attendants, Private Household

66011	Home Health Aides
68035	Personal and Home Care Aides

20.0699 Custodial, Housekeeping, and Home Services Workers and Managers, Other

Any instructional program in institutional, home management, and supporting programs not described above.

20.99 Vocational Home Economics, Other

A group of instructional programs (see 20.9999).

20.9999 Vocational Home Economics, Other

Any instructional program in vocational home economics not described above.

21. TECHNOLOGY EDUCATION/INDUSTRIAL ARTS

A summary of groups of instructional programs that provide individuals with knowledge and competencies pertaining to aspects of industry and technology, including a variety of learning experiences, and that assist individuals in making informed and meaningful occupational choices as well as preparation for entry into occupational training or education programs.

21.01 Technology Education/Industrial Arts

A group of instructional programs (see 21.0101).

21.0101 Technology Education/Industrial Arts

An instructional program that describes the concepts, processes, and systems that are uniquely technological, such as the evolution, utilization, and significance of technology as related to industry; and its organization, personnel, systems, techniques, resources, and products. Includes instruction in technological literacy, basic applied science, specific technologies and their applications, and related methods of research and experimentation.

22. LAW AND LEGAL STUDIES

A summary of groups of instructional programs that describe the theory, history, and application of the rules of conduct by which societal relations are formally structured and adjudicated.

22.01   Law and Legal Studies

A group of instructional programs that describe the theory, history, and application of the rules of conduct by which societal relations are formally structured and adjudicated.

22.0101   Law (L.L.B., J.D.)

An instructional program that prepares individuals for the independent professional practice of law and for advanced research in jurisprudence. Includes instruction in the theory and practice of the legal system, including the statutory, administrative, and judicial components of civil and criminal law.

28102	Judges and Magistrates
28105	Adjudicators, Hearings Officers, and Judicial Reviewers
28108	Lawyers

22.0102   Pre-Law Studies

An instructional program that prepares individuals for admission to a first-professional program in law.

22.0103   Paralegal/Legal Assistant

An instructional program that prepares individuals to perform research and drafting; and investigatory, recordkeeping, and related administrative functions under the supervision of an attorney. Includes instruction in legal research, drafting legal documents, appraising, pleading, courthouse procedures, and legal specializations.

15011C	Property Records Managers
21999B	Legislative Assistants
28302	Law Clerks
28305	Paralegals and Legal Assistants
28308	Title Searchers
28311	Title Examiners and Abstractors

22.0104   Juridical Science/Legal Specialization (L.L.M., M.C.L., J.S.D., S.J.D.)

An instructional program that prepares attorneys and law school graduates for advanced technical specialization in legal research and practice in law, including such specializations as Tax Law, International Law, Comparative Law, Admiralty, Patents, Contracts, and others.

28108	Lawyers

22.0199   Law and Legal Studies, Other

Any instructional program in law and legal studies not described above.

---

23. ENGLISH LANGUAGE AND LITERATURE/LETTERS

A summary of groups of instructional programs that describe the structure and use of the English language and dialects, speech, writing, and various aspects of the literatures and cultures of the English-speaking peoples.

23.01 English Language and Literature, General

A group of instructional programs (see 23.0101).

23.0101 English Language and Literature, General

An instructional program that generally describes the English language, including its history, structure, and related communications skills; and the literature and culture of English-speaking peoples.

31216   English and Foreign Language Teachers—Postsecondary

23.03 Comparative Literature

A group of instructional programs (see 23.0301).

23.0301 Comparative Literature

An instructional program that describes the study of the literatures of different societies and linguistic groups in comparative perspective, including analyses of cross-cultural influences, national literary styles, the influence of translation, and the shared international literary heritage. Includes instruction in the study of literatures in the original languages as well as in English translation.

31216   English and Foreign Language Teachers—Postsecondary

23.04 English Composition

A group of instructional programs (see 23.0401).

23.0401 English Composition

An instructional program that describes the principles of English vocabulary, grammar, morphology, syntax, and semantics; and techniques of selecting, developing, arranging, combining, and expressing ideas in appropriate written forms.

31216   English and Foreign Language Teachers—Postsecondary

23.05   English Creative Writing

A group of instructional programs (see 23.0501).

23.0501   English Creative Writing

An instructional program that describes the process and techniques of original composition in various literary forms such as the short story, poetry, the novel, and others. Includes instruction in technical and editorial skills, criticism, and the marketing of finished manuscripts.

31216	English and Foreign Language Teachers—Postsecondary
34002A	Columnists, Critics, and Commentators
34002B	Poets and Lyricists
34002C	Creative Writers
34002D	Editors
34002E	Managing Editors
34002F	Programming and Script Editors and Coordinators
34002G	Book Editors
34002M	Dictionary Editors
34005	Technical Writers
34014	Broadcast News Analysts

23.07   American Literature (United States)

A group of instructional programs (see 23.0701).

23.0701   American Literature (United States)

An instructional program that describes the study of the literature and literary development, both formal and folkloric, of the United States from the Colonial Era to the present. Includes instruction in period and genre studies, author studies, literary criticism, and regional and oral traditions.

31216	English and Foreign Language Teachers—Postsecondary

23.08   English Literature (British and Commonwealth)

A group of instructional programs (see 23.0801).

23.0801   English Literature (British and Commonwealth)

An instructional program that describes the study of the literatures and literary developments of the English-speaking peoples of the British Isles and the British Commonwealth, from the origins of English to the present. Includes instruction in period and genre studies, author studies, country and regional specializations, literary criticism, and the study of folkloric traditions.

31216	English and Foreign Language Teachers—Postsecondary

23.10 Speech and Rhetorical Studies

A group of instructional programs (see 23.1001).

23.1001 Speech and Rhetorical Studies

An instructional program that describes the study of human interpersonal communication from the scientific/behavioral and humanistic perspectives. Includes instruction in the theory and physiology of speech, the history of discourse, the structure and analysis of argument and types of public speech, the social role of speech, oral interpretation of literature, interpersonal interactions, and the relation of speech to nonverbal and other forms of message exchanges.

31216	English and Foreign Language Teachers—Postsecondary

23.11 English Technical and Business Writing

A group of instructional programs (see 23.1101).

23.1101 English Technical and Business Writing

An instructional program that describes the theory, methods, and skills needed for writing and editing scientific, technical, and business papers and monographs.

31216	English and Foreign Language Teachers—Postsecondary
34002C	Creative Writers
34002D	Editors
34002E	Managing Editors
34002G	Book Editors
34002M	Dictionary Editors
34005	Technical Writers

23.99 English Language and Literature/Letters, Other

A group of instructional programs (see 23.9999).

23.9999 English Language and Literature/Letters, Other

Any instructional program in English language and literature not described above.

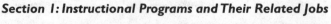

24. LIBERAL ARTS AND SCIENCES, GENERAL STUDIES, AND HUMANITIES

A summary of groups of instructional programs that describe general programs and independent or individualized studies in the liberal arts subjects, the humanities disciplines, and the general curriculum.

24.01 Liberal Arts and Sciences, General Studies, and Humanities

A group of instructional programs (see 24.0101).

24.0101 Liberal Arts and Sciences/Liberal Studies

An instructional program that describes a structured combination of the arts, biological and physical sciences, social sciences, and humanities, emphasizing breadth of study. Includes instruction in independently designed, individualized, or regular programs.

24.0102 General Studies

An instructional program that describes either undifferentiated study for traditional students or continuing education opportunities for adult learners.

24.0103 Humanities/Humanistic Studies

An instructional program that describes combined studies and research in the humanities subjects as distinguished from the social and physical sciences, emphasizing languages, literatures, art, music, philosophy, and religion.

24.0199 Liberal Arts and Sciences, General Studies, and Humanities, Other

Any instructional program in liberal arts and sciences, general studies, and humanities not described above.

25. LIBRARY SCIENCE

A summary of groups of instructional programs that describe the knowledge and skills required to manage and/or maintain libraries and related information and record systems, collections, and facilities for research and general use.

25.01 Library Science/Librarianship

A group of instructional programs (see 25.0101).

25.0101   Library Science/Librarianship

An instructional program that describes the knowledge and skills required to develop, organize, store, retrieve, administer, and facilitate the use of collections of information in such formats as books, documents, manuscripts, machine-readable databases, filmed materials, and recorded materials, and that prepares individuals for professional service as librarians and information consultants.

31502A   Librarians

25.03   Library Assistant

A group of instructional programs (see 25.0301).

25.0301   Library Assistant

An instructional program that prepares individuals to assist professional librarians. Includes instruction in principles, systems, processes, and procedures of library operation; library resources and services; processes of acquisition, cataloging, storage, and display systems; discovery and retrieval of requested materials; and in the management of books, periodicals, and other documents.

31502B   Library Research Workers
31505   Technical Assistants, Library
53902   Library Assistants and Bookmobile Drivers

25.99   Library Science, Other

A group of instructional programs (see 25.9999).

25.9999   Library Science, Other

Any instructional program in library science not described above.

26.   BIOLOGICAL SCIENCES/LIFE SCIENCES

A summary of groups of instructional programs that describe the scientific study of living organisms and their systems.

26.01   Biology, General

A group of instructional programs (see 26.0101).

26.0101   Biology, General

An instructional program that generally describes the scientific study of the structure, function, reproduction, growth, heredity, evolution, behavior, and distribution of living organisms, and their relations to their natural environments.

31202   Life Sciences Teachers—Postsecondary

26.02   Biochemistry and Biophysics

A group of instructional programs (see 26.0202 and 26.0203).

26.0202   Biochemistry

An instructional program that describes the chemical processes of living organisms. Includes instruction in the chemical mechanisms of genetic information storage and transmission; the chemistry of cell components; blood chemistry; the chemistry of biological systems and biological products; and the chemistry of life processes such as respiration, digestion, and reproduction.

24308A   Biochemists
24308C   Biophysicists
24308D   Botanists
24308E   Microbiologists
24308F   Geneticists
24308G   Physiologists and Cytologists
24308J   Toxicologists
24311   Medical Scientists
31202   Life Sciences Teachers—Postsecondary

26.0203   Biophysics

An instructional program that describes the application of physics principles to the study of living cells and organisms, including structures and fine structures, bioelectric phenomena, radiation effects, molecular behavior, photosynthesis, membranes, organic thermodynamics, and quantitative analysis and modelling.

24308A   Biochemists
24308C   Biophysicists
24311   Medical Scientists
31202   Life Sciences Teachers—Postsecondary

26.03   Botany

A group of instructional programs (see 26.0301).

26.0301   Botany, General

An instructional program that generally describes the scientific study of plants, related bacteria, fungi, and algae life forms. Includes instruction in the classification, structure, function, reproduction, growth, heredity, evolution, and pathology of plant life, with particular attention to basic processes such as photosynthesis, plant biochemistry, and plant ecosystems.

24308D	Botanists
24308G	Physiologists and Cytologists
31202	Life Sciences Teachers—Postsecondary

26.0305   Plant Pathology

An instructional program that describes the nature, causes, development, and treatment of plant diseases. Includes instruction in the nature and behavior of disease causal agents, including other life forms and non-biological factors; the study of chemistry and physics of basic pathogens; disease host behaviors; and the development and analysis of disease control and treatment agents.

24308D	Botanists
31202	Life Sciences Teachers—Postsecondary

26.0307   Plant Physiology

An instructional program that describes the scientific study of plant functions and life processes, including such metabolic processes as photosynthesis, respiration, assimilation, and transpiration; and plant systems, including movement, reproduction, digestion, and anatomical system functions.

24308D	Botanists
24308G	Physiologists and Cytologists
31202	Life Sciences Teachers—Postsecondary

26.0399   Botany, Other

Any instructional program in botany not described above.

24308D	Botanists

26.04   Cell and Molecular Biology

A group of instructional programs that describe the cell as a unit of organization in plants and animals, and the molecular structure and processes of living organisms.

26.0401   Cell Biology

An instructional program that describes the scientific study of the cell as a biological system in plants and animals. Includes instruction in cellular structure and function, biosynthesis, enzyme production, cell communication and nutrition, chromosome organization and function, cell life cycles, and cell pathology.

24308E	Microbiologists
24308F	Geneticists
24308G	Physiologists and Cytologists
31202	Life Sciences Teachers—Postsecondary

26.0402   Molecular Biology

An instructional program that describes the scientific study of the molecular structures and processes that underlay the storage and transmission of genetic information, of energy storage and transfer, of hormone generation, and of basic life process such as development, growth, and aging.

24308F	Geneticists
31202	Life Sciences Teachers—Postsecondary

26.0499   Cell and Molecular Biology, Other

Any instructional program in cell and molecular biology not described above.

26.05   Microbiology/Bacteriology

A group of instructional programs (see 26.0501).

26.0501   Microbiology/Bacteriology

An instructional program that describes the scientific study of microorganisms, including bacteria and viruses, as distinguished from the cellular components of larger organisms. Includes instruction in the ecological behavior of microorganisms, their anatomy and physiology, pathogenesis, and microbe evolution and mutation.

24308E	Microbiologists
24311	Medical Scientists
31202	Life Sciences Teachers—Postsecondary

26.06   Miscellaneous Biological Specializations

A group of instructional programs that describe specialized areas of the biological sciences not pertaining exclusively to botany, zoology, microbiology, cell and molecular biology, or related physical sciences.

26.0601   Anatomy

An instructional program that describes the scientific study of the structure and function of living organisms, tissues, organs, and systems. Includes instruction in gross anatomy, histology, ultrastructure, neuroanatomy, microscopy, dissection, electrical and atomic analytical methods, and quantification methods.

24308G	Physiologists and Cytologists
24311	Medical Scientists
31202	Life Sciences Teachers—Postsecondary

26.0603   Ecology

An instructional program that describes the scientific study of ecological systems and the physical interactions among system components. Includes instruction in population biology, large and small ecosystems, environmental factors affecting organisms, evolution and extinction, and symbiotic relationships.

31202	Life Sciences Teachers—Postsecondary

26.0607   Marine/Aquatic Biology

An instructional program that describes the scientific study of marine organisms and their environments. Includes instruction in freshwater and saltwater organisms, physiological and anatomical marine adaptations, ocean and freshwater ecologies, marine microbiology, marine mammalogy, ichthyology, marine botany, and biochemical products of marine life used by humans.

24308B	Biologists
31202	Life Sciences Teachers—Postsecondary

26.0608   Neuroscience

An instructional program that describes the scientific study of the anatomy, physiology, biophysics, biochemistry, molecular biology, and behavior roles of neuron cells and biological nervous systems. Includes instruction in neurological signalling, neuroanatomy and brain research, neuropharmacology, and neuropsychological research.

24308G	Physiologists and Cytologists
31202	Life Sciences Teachers—Postsecondary

26.0609   Nutritional Sciences

An instructional program that describes the scientific study of the biological processes by which organisms ingest, digest, and use the chemical compounds vital to survival, and which cannot be synthesized by the organism itself. Includes instruction in nutritional biochemistry and biophysics, anatomy and physiology of digestive systems, environmental and behavioral aspects of nutrition, and studies of the nutritional problems of specific organisms.

31202   Life Sciences Teachers—Postsecondary

26.0610   Parasitology

An instructional program that describes the scientific study of organisms living on or within biological hosts, their behavioral interactions with host organisms, and defenses against parasitical infestations. Includes instruction in parasitical evolution and community behavior, parasite metabolism, immunization processes, drug development, and drug reactions.

24308D   Botanists
24311   Medical Scientists
31202   Life Sciences Teachers—Postsecondary

26.0611   Radiation Biology/Radiobiology

An instructional program that describes scientific study of the effects of radiation on organisms and biological systems. Includes instruction in particle physics, ionization, biophysics of radiation perturbations, cellular and organismic repair systems, genetic and pathological effects of radiation, and the measurement of radiation dosages.

31202   Life Sciences Teachers—Postsecondary

26.0612   Toxicology

An instructional program that describes the scientific study of the nature, source, effects, identification, and characteristics of poisons, toxic substances, and exogenous chemical agents and their effect on biological organisms. Includes instruction in environmental biology, chemico-physiological mechanisms, genetic toxicology, studies of specific organisms and habitats, and the development of toxic defenses and antidotes.

24308J   Toxicologists
24311   Medical Scientists
31202   Life Sciences Teachers—Postsecondary

26.0613   Genetics, Plant and Animal

An instructional program that describes the scientific study of biological inheritance and variation in organisms, and the mechanisms of gene behavior. Includes instruction in molecular genetics, mutation, gene expression, specification, cloning, the study of inherited diseases and disorders, breeding, genetic biochemistry and biophysics, gene transference, and gene modification.

| 24308F | Geneticists |
| 31202 | Life Sciences Teachers—Postsecondary |

26.0614   Biometrics

An instructional program that describes quantitative measurement methods in the biological and related sciences; the development of biometrics solutions to specific research problems; and related computer applications. Includes instruction in algebraic analysis, matrix algebra, computer methods, and applications to specific biological subdisciplines.

| 31202 | Life Sciences Teachers—Postsecondary |

26.0615   Biostatistics

An instructional program that describes the application of statistical methods and techniques to the study of living organisms and biological systems. Includes instruction in experimental design and data analysis, projection methods, descriptive statistics, and specific applications to biological subdisciplines.

| 25312 | Statisticians |
| 31224 | Mathematical Sciences Teachers—Postsecondary |

26.0616   Biotechnology Research

An instructional program that describes the application of the biological sciences to the development of medical and industrial products and processes, and the methods and equipment used in these procedures. Includes instruction in genetic engineering, cell technology, protein synthesis, applied biology, artificial enzyme production, biomaterial development, and drug therapy mechanisms.

24308A	Biochemists
24308F	Geneticists
24308G	Physiologists and Cytologists
24311	Medical Scientists
31202	Life Sciences Teachers—Postsecondary

26.0617   Evolutionary Biology

An instructional program that describes the scientific study of the generation of organismic traits and of shared traits across taxonomic classifications, and the refinement of related theory and experimental methods. Includes instruction in the process of heredity, genetic mutation and variation, phenotype determination, ecological determinants of species survival and adaptation, population genetics, taxonomic classification, developmental biology, and paleontology.

| 24308F | Geneticists |
| 31202 | Life Sciences Teachers—Postsecondary |

26.0618 Biological Immunology

An instructional program that describes the scientific study of organismic responses to, and defenses against, invasive foreign substances and parasitical life forms. Includes instruction in the anatomy and physiology of immune systems, autoimmune responses, disease response mechanisms and triggers, antigen receptors, membrane transfer, the histocompatibility complex, immunogenetics, immunochemistry, and immune system regulation.

24311	Medical Scientists
31202	Life Sciences Teachers—Postsecondary

26.0619 Virology

An instructional program that describes the scientific study of viruses, a group of parasitical subcellular biologic entities. Includes instruction in viral classification, genetic effects of viral infestations, viral genomes and phenemes, viruses as cancer agents, viral applications in genetic research and engineering, and the development of antiviral drugs and other therapies.

24308E	Microbiologists
31202	Life Sciences Teachers—Postsecondary

26.0699 Miscellaneous Biological Specializations, Other

Any instructional program in miscellaneous biological specializations not described above.

26.07 Zoology

A group of instructional programs that describe the scientific study of animals, including their structure, reproduction, growth, heredity, evolution, behavior, and distribution.

26.0701 Zoology, General

An instructional program that generally describes the scientific study of animals, including their structure, reproduction, growth, heredity, evolution, behavior, and distribution.

24305B	Plant Scientists
24308A	Biochemists
24308B	Biologists
24308G	Physiologists and Cytologists
24308H	Zoologists
24311	Medical Scientists

31202	Life Sciences Teachers—Postsecondary
32102U	Pathologists

26.0702   Entomology

An instructional program that describes the scientific study of insects, including life cycle, morphology, physiology, ecology, taxonomy, population dynamics, genetics, and eco- system relations. Includes instruction in the biological and chemical control of insects and the development of insecticide agents.

24305B	Plant Scientists
31202	Life Sciences Teachers—Postsecondary

26.0704   Pathology, Human and Animal

An instructional program that describes the scientific study of the nature, causes, and devel- opment of human and animal diseases, and the mechanisms of disease infestation and trans- fer. Includes instruction in human and animal pathobiology, disease morphology, disease biochemistry, physiology of disease and cell injury, and immunopathology.

31202	Life Sciences Teachers—Postsecondary
32102U	Pathologists

26.0705   Pharmacology, Human and Animal

An instructional program that describes the scientific study of the therapeutic and toxic effects of drugs on living tissues and entire organisms. Includes instruction in pharma- codynamic behavior, drug metabolism, chemical pharmacology, the physiological ef- fects of chemical substances on human beings and animals, therapeutic applications, chemical profile analysis, and rational drug design.

24308A	Biochemists
24311	Medical Scientists
31202	Life Sciences Teachers—Postsecondary

26.0706   Physiology, Human and Animal

An instructional program that describes the scientific study of organismic and systemic function and behavior in humans and animals, including processes such as respiration, circulation, digestion, excretion, and reproduction.

24308G	Physiologists and Cytologists
31202	Life Sciences Teachers—Postsecondary

26.0799   Zoology, Other

Any instructional program in zoology not described above.

26.99   Biological Sciences/Life Sciences, Other

A group of instructional programs (see 26.9999).

26.9999   Biological Sciences/Life Sciences, Other

Any instructional program in biological sciences not described above.

27.   MATHEMATICS

A summary of groups of instructional programs that describe the systematic study of logical symbolic language and its applications.

27.01   Mathematics

A group of instructional programs (see 27.0101).

27.0101   Mathematics

An instructional program that describes the rigorous analysis of quantities, magnitudes, forms, and their relationships, using symbolic logic and language. Includes instruction in algebra, calculus, functional analysis, geometry, number theory, logic, topology, and other mathematical specializations.

25312	Statisticians
25319A	Mathematicians
31224	Mathematical Sciences Teachers—Postsecondary

27.03   Applied Mathematics

A group of instructional programs (see 27.0301).

27.0301   Applied Mathematics, General

An instructional program that describes the application of mathematical principles to the solution of functional area problems, using the knowledge base of the subject or field for which the analytical procedures are being developed. Includes instruction in computer-assisted mathematical analysis and the development of tailored algorithms for solving specific research problems.

25302	Operations and Systems Researchers and Analysts, except Computer
25312	Statisticians

25319A	Mathematicians
25319B	Weight Analysts
25323	Mathematical Technicians
31224	Mathematical Sciences Teachers—Postsecondary

27.0302 Operations Research

An instructional program that describes the development and application of complex mathematical or simulation models to solve problems involving operational systems, where the system concerned is subject to human intervention. Includes instruction in advanced multivariate analysis, application of judgement and statistical tests, optimization theory and techniques, resource allocation theory, mathematical modelling, control theory, statistical analysis, and applications to specific research problems.

| 25302 | Operations and Systems Researchers and Analysts, except Computer |
| 31224 | Mathematical Sciences Teachers—Postsecondary |

27.0399 Applied Mathematics, Other

Any instructional programs in applied mathematics not described above.

27.05 Mathematical Statistics

A group of instructional programs (see 27.0501).

27.0501 Mathematical Statistics

An instructional program that describes the mathematical theory and proofs forming the basis of probability and inference, and their applications to the collection, analysis, and description of data. Includes instruction in statistical theory, experimental analysis, sampling techniques, survey research, projections, and related evaluations of numerical data.

| 25312 | Statisticians |
| 31224 | Mathematical Sciences Teachers—Postsecondary |

27.99 Mathematics, Other

A group of instructional programs (see 27.9999).

27.9999 Mathematics, Other

Any instructional program in mathematics not described above.

28. RESERVE OFFICERS' TRAINING CORPS (R.O.T.C.)

A summary of groups of instructional programs preparing individuals for entry into the armed forces of the United States as cadets or commissioned officers.

28.01   Air Force R.O.T.C

A group of instructional programs (see 28.0101).

28.0101   Air Force R.O.T.C./Air Science

An instructional program that prepares individuals for commissioning as reserve or active-duty officers in the United States Air Force, or for entry into an approved senior A.F.R.O.T.C. commissioning program.

28.03   Army R.O.T.C

A group of instructional programs (see 28.0301).

28.0301   Army R.O.T.C./Military Science

An instructional program that prepares individuals for commissioning as reserve or active-duty officers in the United States Army, or for entry into an approved senior A.R.O.T.C. commissioning program.

28.04   Navy/Marine Corps R.O.T.C

A group of instructional programs (see 28.0401).

28.0401   Navy/Marine Corps R.O.T.C./Naval Science

An instructional program that prepares individuals for commissioning as reserve or active-duty officers in the United States Navy or Marine Corps, or for entry into an approved senior N.R.O.T.C. commissioning program.

29. MILITARY TECHNOLOGIES

A summary of groups of instructional programs that prepare individuals in specialized and advanced subject matter for the armed services and related national security organizations.

29.01   Military Technologies

A group of instructional programs (see 29.0101).

29.0101   Military Technologies

An instructional program that prepares individuals to undertake advanced and specialized leadership and technical responsibilities for the armed services and related national security organizations. Includes instruction in such areas as weapons systems and technology, communications, intelligence, management, logistics, and strategy.

30.   MULTI/INTERDISCIPLINARY STUDIES

A summary of groups of instructional programs, the components of which derive from two or more separate instructional programs.

30.01   Biological and Physical Sciences

A group of instructional programs (see 30.0101).

30.0101   Biological and Physical Sciences

An instructional program that describes either a general synthesis of one or more of the biological and physical sciences, or a specialization that draws from the biological and physical sciences.

| 31202 | Life Sciences Teachers—Postsecondary |
| 31206 | Physics Teachers—Postsecondary |

30.05   Peace and Conflict Studies

A group of instructional programs (see 30.0501).

30.0501   Peace and Conflict Studies

An instructional program that describes the study of the origins, resolution, and prevention of international and inter-group conflicts. Includes instruction in peace research methods and related social scientific and psychological knowledge bases.

| 31210 | Social Science Teachers—Postsecondary |

30.06   Systems Science and Theory

A group of instructional programs (see 30.0601).

30.0601　Systems Science and Theory

An instructional program that describes a multidisciplinary approach to the analysis and solution of complex problems, requiring a combined approach using data and models from the natural, social, technological, behavioral, and life sciences and other specialized fields.

30.08　Mathematics and Computer Science

A group of instructional programs (see 30.0801).

30.0801　Mathematics and Computer Science

An instructional program that describes a general synthesis of mathematics and computer science or a specialization that draws from mathematics and computer science.

31224	Mathematical Sciences Teachers—Postsecondary
31226	Computer Science Teachers—Postsecondary

30.10　Biopsychology

A group of instructional programs (see 30.1001).

30.1001　Biopsychology

An instructional program that describes the study of the biological linkages to psychological phenomena, especially the linkages between biochemical and biophysical activity and the functioning of the central nervous system.

31202	Life Sciences Teachers—Postsecondary

30.11　Gerontology

A group of instructional programs (see 30.1101).

30.1101　Gerontology

An instructional program that describes the study of the human aging process and aged human populations, using the knowledge and methodologies of the social sciences, psychology, and the biological and health sciences.

31202	Life Sciences Teachers—Postsecondary
31210	Social Science Teachers—Postsecondary
31212	Health Specialties Teachers—Postsecondary

30.12   Historic Preservation, Conservation, and Architectural History

A group of instructional programs (see 30.1201).

30.1201   Historic Preservation, Conservation, and Architectural History

An instructional program that describes the architectural design principles and building techniques used in historic structures and environments, and the process of saving and restoring old buildings and districts for contemporary use and enjoyment. Includes instruction in architectural history; building conservation techniques; real estate, land-use, and tax laws and codes; economics and public policy; and public relations.

30.13   Medieval and Renaissance Studies

A group of instructional programs (see 30.1301).

30.1301   Medieval and Renaissance Studies

An instructional program that describes the study of the Medieval and Renaissance periods in European and circum-Mediterranean history from the perspective of various disciplines in the humanities and social sciences, including history and archeology, as well as studies of period art and music.

31210   Social Science Teachers—Postsecondary

30.14   Museology/Museum Studies

A group of instructional programs (see 30.1401).

30.1401   Museology/Museum Studies

An instructional program that describes the attitudes, knowledge, and skills required to develop, prepare, organize, administer, conserve, store, and retrieve artifacts, exhibits, and entire collections in museums and galleries, and that prepares individuals to assume curatorial, technical, and managerial positions in museums. Includes instruction in institutional management, acquisition, exhibit design, conservation, packing techniques, and public relations.

31511A   Curators
31511B   Archivists
31511C   Museum Research Workers
31511D   Museum Technicians and Conservators

30.15   Science, Technology, and Society

A group of instructional programs (see 30.1501).

30.1501   Science, Technology, and Society

An instructional program that describes the contemporary social and public policy ramifications of science and technology, the interrelationship of science and engineering with the public policy process, and the social and ethical dimensions of scientific and technological enterprises.

31210   Social Science Teachers—Postsecondary

30.99   Multi/Interdisciplinary Studies, Other

A group of instructional programs (see 30.9999).

30.9999   Multi/Interdisciplinary Studies, Other

Any instructional program in multi/interdisciplinary studies not described above.

31.   PARKS, RECREATION, LEISURE, AND FITNESS STUDIES

A summary of groups of instructional programs that describe the principles and practices of managing parks and other recreational and fitness facilities; providing recreational, leisure, and fitness services; and the study of human fitness.

31.01   Parks, Recreation, and Leisure Studies

A group of instructional programs (see 31.0101).

31.0101   Parks, Recreation, and Leisure Studies

An instructional program that describes the study of the principles underlying recreational and leisure activities, and the practices involved in providing indoor and outdoor recreational facilities and services for the general public.

27311   Recreation Workers
68017B   Tour Guides and Escorts

31.03   Parks, Recreation, and Leisure Facilities Management

A group instructional programs (see 31.0301).

31.0301   Parks, Recreation, and Leisure Facilities Management

An instructional program that prepares individuals to develop and manage park facilities and other indoor and outdoor recreation and leisure facilities. Includes instruction in supervising support personnel, health and safety standards, public relations, and basic business and marketing principles.

19005A	Government Service Executives
19999A	Amusement and Recreation Establishment Managers
27311	Recreation Workers
34056G	Directors—Stage, Motion Picture, Television, and Radio
68017A	Travel Guides

31.05   Health and Physical Education/Fitness

A group of instructional programs that describe the study of human physiology and behavior as applied to sports, and the leadership and management of physical fitness and sports services.

31.0501   Health and Physical Education, General

An instructional program that generally describes the study and practice of activities and principles that promote physical fitness, achieve and maintain athletic prowess, and accomplish related research and service goals. Includes instruction in human movement studies, motivation studies, rules and practice of specific sports, exercise and fitness principles and techniques, basic athletic injury prevention and treatment, and organizing and leading fitness and sports programs.

31210	Social Science Teachers—Postsecondary
31212	Health Specialties Teachers—Postsecondary
31321	Instructors and Coaches, Sports and Physical Training
32308	Physical Therapists
32311B	Corrective Therapists
32317	Recreational Therapists
32399A	Exercise Physiologists
34058B	Athletic Trainers

31.0502   Adapted Physical Education/Therapeutic Recreation

An instructional program that describes the provision of physical education and fitness instruction and therapy to children and adults with special learning needs, disabilities, or diagnosed medical conditions, and that prepares individuals to provide and supervise appropriate activities for such persons. Includes instruction in the planning and administration of adapted and therapeutic fitness programs; the supervision of special fitness and rehabilitative students and clients; student and patient counseling and referral; record-keeping; and applicable legal and administrative regulations.

31212	Health Specialties Teachers—Postsecondary
32311B	Corrective Therapists
32317	Recreational Therapists
32399A	Exercise Physiologists

31.0503   Athletic Training and Sports Medicine

An instructional program that prepares individuals to prevent and treat athletic injuries, to perform related rehabilitative therapy, and to manage the provision of health and treatment services to athletes. Includes instruction in basic sports medicine, dietetics, movement and motivation sciences, administering preventive and treatment remedies, equipment maintenance, clinic management, and patient education and counseling.

31212	Health Specialties Teachers—Postsecondary
32399A	Exercise Physiologists
34058B	Athletic Trainers

31.0504   Sport and Fitness Administration/Management

An instructional program that prepares individuals to apply business, coaching, and physical education principles to the organization, administration, and management of athletic programs and teams, fitness/rehabilitation facilities and health clubs, sport recreation services, and related services. Includes instruction in program planning and development; business and financial management principles; sales, marketing, and recruitment; event promotion, scheduling, and management; facilities management; public relations; legal aspects of sports; and applicable health and safety standards.

31.0505   Exercise Sciences/Physiology and Movement Studies

An instructional program that describes the scientific study of the anatomy, physiology, biochemistry, and biophysics of human movement, and applications to exercise and therapeutic rehabilitation. Includes instruction in biomechanics, motor behavior, motor development and coordination, motor neurophysiology, performance research, rehabilitative therapies, the development of diagnostic and rehabilitative methods and equipment, and related analytical methods and procedures.

31212	Health Specialties Teachers—Postsecondary
32308	Physical Therapists
32311B	Corrective Therapists
32399A	Exercise Physiologists

31.0506   Socio-Psychological Sports Studies

An instructional program that describes the scientific study of human motivation as applied to athletic performance, and the related social and cultural factors affecting the organization and behavior of sports and participants. Includes instruction in sports psychology, sociology of sports, studies of sports and coaching theory, motivational research, and the psychological aspects of motor behavior.

31210   Social Science Teachers—Postsecondary

31.0599 Health and Physical Education/Fitness, Other

Any instructional program in health and physical education/fitness not described above.

31.99 Parks, Recreation, Leisure, and Fitness Studies, Other

A group of instructional programs (see 31.9999).

31.9999 Parks, Recreation, Leisure, and Fitness Studies, Other

Any instructional program in parks, recreation, leisure, and fitness studies not described above.

32. BASIC SKILLS

A summary of groups of instructional programs that describe fundamental knowledge and skills that individuals need in order to function productively in society.

32.01 Basic Skills

A group of instructional programs (see 32.0101).

32.0101 Basic Skills, General

An instructional program that generally describes fundamental knowledge and skills that individuals need in order to function productively in society.

32.0104 Computational Skills

An instructional program that describes the development of computing and other mathematical reasoning abilities.

32.0105 Job-Seeking/Changing Skills

An instructional program that describes the development of skills related to job searches and self-marketing. Includes instruction in assessing one's own capabilities and skills, filling out an application, and handling an interview.

32.0107   Career Exploration/Awareness Skills

An instructional program that describes the linkage between individual capabilities and needs and the job market. Includes instruction in the variety and scope of available employment, how to access job information, and techniques of self-analysis.

32.0108   Reading, Literacy, and Communication Skills

An instructional program that describes the development of reading, writing, and speaking abilities that are needed to perform day-to-day tasks. Includes instruction in the use of basic communication skills to develop and transmit ideas and thoughts.

32.0199   Basic Skills, Other

Any instructional program in basic skills not described above.

33.   CITIZENSHIP ACTIVITIES

A summary of groups of instructional programs that prepare individuals for citizenship and describe how citizens may engage in civic activities.

33.01   Citizenship Activities

A group of instructional programs (see 33.0101).

33.0101   Citizenship Activities, General

An instructional program that generally prepares individuals for citizenship and describes how citizens may engage in civic activities.

33.0102   American Citizenship Education

An instructional program that prepares individuals to take the oath of United States citizenship and to exercise the attendant rights and responsibilities of citizenship.

33.0103   Community Awareness

An instructional program that describes local government and history, current issues, and how individuals can keep abreast of important issues that may affect them.

33.0104   Community Involvement

An instructional program that describes how individuals may become actively involved in the social, economic, and political issues and events affecting them; and the roles and methods that are available to influence community life and public policy.

33.0199   Citizenship Activities, Other

Any instructional program in citizenship activities not described above.

34.   HEALTH-RELATED KNOWLEDGE AND SKILLS

A summary of groups of instructional programs that describe the promotion of personal and family health.

34.01   Health-Related Knowledge and Skills

A group of instructional programs that describe the promotion of personal and family health.

34.0102   Birthing and Parenting Knowledge and Skills

An instructional program that describes all facets of the mother's and father's roles in family planning, prenatal preparation and care, the birthing experience, post-natal care, and the raising of children.

34.0103   Personal Health Improvement and Maintenance

An instructional program that describes the principles, techniques, and methods by which individuals can maintain or improve their overall physical and emotional well-being, as well as work on specific areas of personal health.

34.0104   Addiction Prevention and Treatment

An instructional program that describes how individuals can avoid addictive substances and behaviors; the methods by which individuals can be treated for various addictions and related behavior problems; and the knowledge and coping skills needed by relatives and associates of addicted individuals.

34.0199   Health-Related Knowledge and Skills, Other

Any instructional program in health-related knowledge and skills not described above.

35.   INTERPERSONAL AND SOCIAL SKILLS

A summary of groups of instructional programs that describe how to effectively interact with others in private, social, and business settings.

35.01   Interpersonal and Social Skills

A group of instructional programs (see 35.0101).

35.0101   Interpersonal and Social Skills, General

An instructional program that generally describes how to effectively interact with others in private, social, and business settings.

35.0102   Interpersonal Relationships Skills

An instructional program that describes how to increase one's ability to establish and maintain mutually satisfactory ties with other human beings.

35.0103   Business and Social Skills

An instructional program that describes how to increase one's ability to function effectively in social and business settings where interpersonal communication is required.

35.0199   Interpersonal and Social Skills, Other

Any instructional program in interpersonal and social skills not described above.

36.   LEISURE AND RECREATIONAL ACTIVITIES

A summary of groups of instructional programs that describe the development of an appreciation for and competency in recreational and leisure-related activities.

36.01   Leisure and Recreational Activities

A group of instructional programs (see 36.0101).

36.0101   Leisure and Recreational Activities, General

An instructional program that generally describes the development of an appreciation for and competency in recreational and leisure-related activities.

36.0102   Handicrafts and Model-Making

An instructional program that describes the fashioning of objects of decoration, utility, or representation from various materials, including related matters of research, tool use, and appreciation.

36.0103 Board, Card, and Role-Playing Games

An instructional program that describes the rules and techniques of participation and skill-building in competitive activities of skill or chance, such as board games, card games, or role-playing activities.

36.0105 Home Maintenance and Improvement

An instructional program that describes the knowledge and skills associated with maintaining living space and related equipment and furnishings, as well as do-it-yourself repairs and improvement projects of varying complexity.

36.0106 Nature Appreciation

An instructional program that describes how to increase one's understanding and knowledge of the natural environment in which we live, as well as techniques of wildlife observation and management.

36.0107 Pet Ownership and Care

An instructional program that describes how to increase one's ability to care for domesticated animals kept for pleasure or work.

36.0108 Sports and Exercise

An instructional program that describes the rules and techniques of participation and skill-building in competitive physical activities, as well as non-competitive physical fitness programs.

36.0109 Travel and Exploration

An instructional program that describes particular geographic areas or phenomena and provides opportunities for organized trips or tours, including related knowledge and skills.

36.0110 Art

An instructional program that describes the techniques and methods of creative self-expression in visual or plastic media, such as painting or sculpture.

36.0111   Collecting

An instructional program that describes the knowledge and techniques necessary for acquiring and maintaining personal collections of objects, such as autographs, stamps, models, specimens, vehicles, and antiques.

36.0112   Cooking and Other Domestic Skills

An instructional program that describes the knowledge and skills related to food buying and preparation, home decoration, sewing, and other domestic activities, either as hobbies or as routine tasks.

36.0113   Computer Games and Programming Skills

An instructional program that describes the knowledge and skills associated with creating, acquiring, maintaining, and using computer hardware and software, as well as the playing of computer-based games.

36.0114   Dancing

An instructional program that describes the knowledge and skills related to recreational dance, such as square dancing, ballroom dancing, classical dance, or modern dance.

36.0115   Music

An instructional program that describes the knowledge and skills associated with personal music appreciation, the playing of a musical instrument, singing, or recreational composition.

36.0116   Reading

An instructional program that describes the activity of reading for pleasure, either alone or as part of a group experience.

36.0117   Theater

An instructional program that describes the knowledge and skills associated with participation in amateur theatrical productions, drama appreciation, and writing amateur plays.

36.0118   Writing

An instructional program that describes the knowledge and skills related to creative writing and poetry composition for pleasure or profit, including methods of publication.

36.0199   Leisure and Recreational Activities, Other

Any instructional program in leisure and recreational activities not described above.

37. PERSONAL AWARENESS AND SELF-IMPROVEMENT

A summary of groups of instructional programs that describe how to develop improved self-awareness, avoid stressful behavior, and improve decision-making skills.

37.01   Personal Awareness and Self-Improvement

A group of instructional programs that describe how to develop improved self-awareness, avoid stressful behavior, and improve decision-making skills.

37.0101   Self-Awareness and Personal Assessment

An instructional program that describes how to be aware of one's feelings, to use methods of assessing one's personal attributes, and to be aware of how others perceive one's self.

37.0102   Stress Management and Coping Skills

An instructional program that describes the knowledge and skills useful in avoiding stressful situations and managing them when they occur, including dealing with complex and long-term stressful relationships.

37.0103   Personal Decision-Making Skills

An instructional program that describes how to develop individuals' abilities to assess decisions affecting their lives and to make life choices consistent with needs and beliefs.

37.0104   Self-Esteem and Values Clarification

An instructional program that describes the development of personal philosophies and ideas of self-worth, and how to apply such knowledge and skills in everyday circumstances.

37.0199   Personal Awareness and Self-Improvement, Other

Any instructional program in personal awareness and self-improvement not described above.

38. PHILOSOPHY AND RELIGION

A summary of groups of instructional programs that describe the study of modes, methods, and types of logical inquiry; and the study of organized systems of belief and related practices.

38.01 Philosophy

A group of instructional programs (see 38.0101).

38.0101 Philosophy

An instructional program that describes the study of ideas and their logical structure, including arguments and investigations about abstract and real phenomena. Includes instruction in logic, ethics, aesthetics, epistemology, metaphysics, symbolism, history of philosophy, and applications to the theoretical foundations and methods of other disciplines.

38.02 Religion/Religious Studies

A group of instructional programs (see 38.0201).

38.0201 Religion/Religious Studies

An instructional program that describes the study of the nature of religious belief and specific religious and quasi-religious systems. Includes instruction in phenomenology; the sociology, psychology, philosophy, anthropology, literature, and art of religion; mythology; scriptural and textual studies; religious history and politics; and specific studies of particular faith communities and their behavior.

38.99 Philosophy and Religion, Other

A group of instructional programs (see 38.9999).

38.9999 Philosophy and Religion, Other

Any instructional program in philosophy and religion not described above.

39. THEOLOGICAL STUDIES AND RELIGIOUS VOCATIONS

A summary of groups of instructional programs that describe the study of religious beliefs, doctrines, and practices from the intramural standpoint of a particular faith; and that prepare individuals for the professional practice of religious vocations.

39.01   Biblical and Other Theological Languages and Literatures

A group of instructional programs (see 39.0101).

39.0101   Biblical and Other Theological Languages and Literatures

An instructional program that describes the study of liturgical, scriptural, and historical languages and literatures used by Christianity, Judaism, and other major faiths as vehicles for communicating doctrine, forms of worship, rules, and traditions. Includes instruction in translation techniques, textual analysis and criticism, the study and preservation of ancient manuscripts, and studies of specific languages such as Hebrew, Koine Greek, Biblical Aramaic, and others.

39.02   Bible/Biblical Studies

A group of instructional programs (see 39.0201).

39.0201   Bible/Biblical Studies

An instructional program that describes the study of the Bible and its component books from the standpoint of the Christian or Jewish faiths, with an emphasis on understanding and interpreting the theological, doctrinal, and ethical messages contained within it. May include preparation for applying these studies in various church-related vocations.

27502	Clergy
27505	Directors, Religious Activities and Education

39.03   Missions/Missionary Studies and Misology

A group of instructional programs (see 39.0301).

39.0301   Missions/Missionary Studies and Misology

An instructional program that describes the theory and practice of Christian or other religious outreach, social service, and proselytization, and that prepares individuals for mission vocations.

27502	Clergy
27505	Directors, Religious Activities and Education

39.04   Religious Education

A group of instructional programs (see 39.0401).

39.0401   Religious Education

An instructional program that describes the theory and practice of providing educational services to members of faith communities, within the context of a particular religion, and that prepares individuals to serve as religious educators. Includes instruction in planning and teaching lessons; organizing and supervising instructional activities; designing and developing instructional materials; and administering religious education programs and facilities.

27505   Directors, Religious Activities and Education

39.05   Religious/Sacred Music

A group of instructional programs (see 39.0501).

39.0501   Religious/Sacred Music

An instructional program that describes the history, theory, composition, and performance of music for religious or sacred purposes, and that prepares individuals for religious musical vocations such as choir directors, Cantors, organists, and chanters.

34047A   Music Directors
34051   Musicians, Instrumental

39.06   Theological and Ministerial Studies

A group of instructional programs that prepare individuals for the professional study and practice of theology and ministry.

39.0601   Theology/Theological Studies

An instructional program that describes the study of the beliefs and doctrine of a particular religious faith from the intramural point of view of that faith. Includes instruction in systematic theology, historical theology, moral theology, doctrinal studies, dogmatics, apologetics, and applications to specific questions of ecclesiastical polity and religious life.

39.0602   Divinity/Ministry (B.D., M.Div.)

An instructional program that prepares individuals for ordination as ministers or priests in any of the Christian religious traditions. Includes instruction in the theology and polity of a particular church, liturgy, principles of pastoral ministry, homiletics, basic church/parish organization and management, and related studies.

27502   Clergy

39.0603   Rabbinical and Talmudic Studies (M.H.L./Rav.)

An instructional program that prepares individuals for ordination as Rabbis in the Orthodox, Conservative, and Reformed Jewish traditions; and that describes the specialized devotional study of Jewish law and sacred writings.

39.0604   Pre-Theology/Pre-Ministerial Studies

An instructional program that prepares individuals to enter a seminary or other program leading to religious ordination, or a related religious vocation.

39.0699   Theological and Ministerial Studies, Other

Any instructional program in theological and ministerial studies not described above.

39.07   Pastoral Counseling and Specialized Ministries

A group of instructional programs (see 39.0701).

39.0701   Pastoral Counseling and Specialized Ministries

An instructional program that prepares ordained ministers, priests, and rabbis and other religious vocations in the principles and methods of pastoral practice in such areas as clinical pastoral counseling, marriage and family therapy, youth ministry, outreach and evangelism, ministry to special populations, advanced leadership and management skills, and other studies.

27502	Clergy
27505	Directors, Religious Activities and Education

39.99   Theological Studies and Religious Vocations, Other

A group of instructional programs (see 39.9999).

39.9999   Theological Studies and Religious Vocations, Other

Any instructional program in theological studies and religious vocations not described above.

40. PHYSICAL SCIENCES

A summary of groups of instructional programs that describe the scientific study of inanimate objects, processes of matter and energy, and associated phenomena.

40.01   Physical Sciences, General

A group of instructional programs (see 40.0101).

40.0101   Physical Sciences, General

An instructional program that generally describes the major topics, concepts, processes, and interrelationships of physical phenomena as studied in any combination of physical science disciplines.

31204	Chemistry Teachers—Postsecondary
31206	Physics Teachers—Postsecondary

40.02   Astronomy

A group of instructional programs (see 40.0201).

40.0201   Astronomy

An instructional program that describes the scientific study of matter and energy in the universe, using observational techniques such as spectroscopy, photometry, interferometry, radio astronomy, and optical astronomy. Includes instruction in celestial mechanics, cosmology, and stellar physics; and applications to research on lunar, planetary, solar, stellar, and galactic phenomena.

24102A	Physicists
24102B	Astronomers

40.03   Astrophysics

A group of instructional programs (see 40.0301).

40.0301   Astrophysics

An instructional program that describes the scientific and mathematical study of the behavior of astronomical phenomena and related physico-chemical interactions, and the experimental laboratory simulation of these phenomena. Includes instruction in cosmology, plasma kinetics, stellar physics, convolution and nonequilibrium radiation transfer theory, non-Euclidian geometries, mathematical modeling, galactic structure theory, and relativistic astronomy.

| 24102A | Physicists |
| 24102B | Astronomers |

40.04   Atmospheric Sciences and Meteorology

A group of instructional programs (see 40.0401).

40.0401   Atmospheric Sciences and Meteorology

An instructional program that describes the scientific study of the composition and behavior of the atmospheric envelopes surrounding the earth and other planets, the effect of earth's atmosphere on terrestrial weather, and related problems of environment and climate. Includes instruction in atmospheric chemistry and physics, atmospheric dynamics, climatology and climate change, weather simulation, weather forecasting, climate modeling and mathematical theory, and studies of specific phenomena such as clouds, weather systems, storms, and precipitation patterns.

| 24108 | Atmospheric and Space Scientists |

40.05   Chemistry

A group of instructional programs (see 40.0501).

40.0501   Chemistry, General

A group of instructional programs that generally describe the scientific study of the composition and behavior of matter, including its micro- and macro-structure, the processes of chemical change, and the theoretical description and laboratory simulation of these phenomena.

24102A	Physicists
24105	Chemists, except Biochemists
24308J	Toxicologists
31204	Chemistry Teachers—Postsecondary

40.0502   Analytical Chemistry

An instructional program that describes the scientific study of techniques for analyzing and describing matter, including its precise composition and the interrelationships of constituent elements and compounds. Includes instruction in spectroscopy, chromatography, atomic absorption, photometry, chemical modeling, mathematical analysis, laboratory analysis procedures and equipment maintenance, and applications to specific research, industrial, and health problems.

| 24105 | Chemists, except Biochemists |
| 31204 | Chemistry Teachers—Postsecondary |

40.0503　Inorganic Chemistry

An instructional program that describes the scientific study of the elements and their compounds, other than the hydrocarbons and their derivatives. Includes instruction in the characterization and synthesis of non-carbon molecules, including their structure and their bonding, conductivity, and reactive properties; research techniques such as spectroscopy, X-ray diffraction, and photoelectron analysis; and the study of specific compounds, such as transition metals, and compounds composed of inorganic and organic molecules.

24105	Chemists, except Biochemists
31204	Chemistry Teachers—Postsecondary

40.0504　Organic Chemistry

An instructional program that describes the scientific study of the properties and behavior of hydrocarbon compounds and their derivatives. Includes instruction in molecular conversion and synthesis, the molecular structure of living cells and systems, the mutual reactivity of organic and inorganic compounds in combination, the spectroscopic analysis of hydrocarbon compounds, and applications to specific problems in research, industry, and health.

24105	Chemists, except Biochemists
31204	Chemistry Teachers—Postsecondary

40.0505　Medicinal/Pharmaceutical Chemistry

An instructional program that describes the scientific study of the structural and reactive properties of natural and synthetic compounds intended for applications to human or animal medicine, pharmaceutical industrial uses, or treatment of plant disease. Includes instruction in molecular synthesis, drug design, properties of natural organic compounds, cosmetic chemistry, chemical manufacturing systems, drug behavior and host metabolism, and specific applications to health and industrial problems.

24105	Chemists, except Biochemists
24308J	Toxicologists
31204	Chemistry Teachers—Postsecondary

40.0506　Physical and Theoretical Chemistry

An instructional program that describes the scientific study of the theoretical properties of matter, and the relation of physical forces and phenomena to the chemical structure and behavior of molecules and other compounds. Includes instruction in reaction theory, calculation of potential molecular properties and behavior, computer simulation of structures and actions, transition theory, statistical mechanics, phase studies, quantum chemistry, and the study of surface properties.

24102A	Physicists
24105	Chemists, except Biochemists
31204	Chemistry Teachers—Postsecondary

40.0507   Polymer Chemistry

An instructional program that describes the scientific study of synthesized macromolecules and their interactions with other substances. Includes instruction in molecular bonding theory, polymerization, properties and behavior of unstable compounds, the development of tailored polymers, transition phenomena, and applications to specific industrial problems and technologies.

| 31204 | Chemistry Teachers—Postsecondary |

40.0599   Chemistry, Other

Any instructional program in chemistry not described above.

40.06   Geological and Related Sciences

A group of instructional programs that describe the natural history and physical properties of the earth.

40.0601   Geology

An instructional program that describes the scientific study of the earth; the forces acting upon it; and the behavior of the solids, liquids, and gases comprising it. Includes instruction in historical geology, geomorphology, sedimentology, the chemistry of rocks and soils, stratigraphy, mineralogy, petrology, geostatistics, volcanology, glaciology, geophysical principles, and applications to research and industrial problems.

| 24111A | Geologists |
| 24111B | Geophysicists |

40.0602   Geochemistry

An instructional program that describes the scientific study of the chemical properties and behavior of the silicates and other substances forming and formed by geomorphological processes of the earth and other planets. Includes instruction in chemical thermodynamics, equilibria in silicate systems, atomic bonding, isotopic fractionation, geochemical modeling, specimen analysis, and studies of specific organic and inorganic substances.

| 24111A | Geologists |

40.0603   Geophysics and Seismology

An instructional program that describes the scientific study of the physics of solids and its application to the study of the earth and other planets. Includes instruction in gravimetrics, seismology, earthquake forecasting, magnetrometry, electrical properties of solid bodies, plate tectonics, thermodynamics, remote sensing, and laboratory simulations of geological processes.

24111A	Geologists
24111B	Geophysicists

40.0604   Paleontology

An instructional program that describes the scientific study of extinct life forms and associated fossil remains, and the reconstruction and analysis of ancient life forms, ecosystems, and geologic processes. Includes instruction in sedimentation and fossilization processes, fossil chemistry, evolutionary biology and paleobiology, field research methods, and laboratory research and conservation methods; as well as studies of specific subjects such as paleoecology, paleoclimatology, trace fossils, micropaleontology, invertebrate paleontology, vertebrate paleontology, paleobotany, and paleoceanography.

24111A   Geologists

40.0699   Geological and Related Sciences, Other

Any instructional program in geological and related sciences not described above.

40.07   Miscellaneous Physical Sciences

A group of instructional programs that describe specialized areas of the physical sciences not in the other physical sciences groupings.

40.0701   Metallurgy

An instructional program that describes the scientific study of the chemical and physical properties of metals and related compounds in their solid, liquid, and gaseous states, together with applications to industrial problems. Includes instruction in X-ray diffraction, metallurgical microscopy, solid-state chemistry, thermodynamics of solids and solutions, crystallography, surface physics, molecular bonding, electrodynamics of metals, elasticity and mechanical properties, and processing behavior.

22105B   Metallurgists

40.0702   Oceanography

An instructional program that describes the scientific study of the oceans and associated phenomena, including the land/water and water/atmosphere boundaries. Includes instruction in physical oceanography, marine chemistry, marine geology, and biological oceanography; and applications to specific research problems such as coastal erosion, seawater corrosion and reactive behavior, seafloor volcanism, underwater acoustics and optics, oceanic environments and conservation, and global climate change.

24111A	Geologists
24111B	Geophysicists

40.0703   Earth and Planetary Sciences

An instructional program that describes the scientific study of the earth and other planets as comprehensive physical systems incorporating solid, liquid, gas, and radiation constituents, as well as exhibiting interactions with other systems. Includes instruction in planetary evolution, gravitational physics, atmospheric evolution, volcanism and crustal movement studies, organic systems and ecologies, orbital mechanics, radiation physics, and the study of planetary and satellite systems.

24102A	Physicists
24102B	Astronomers

40.08   Physics

A group of instructional programs (see 40.0801).

40.0801   Physics, General

An instructional program that generally describes the scientific study of matter and energy, and the formulation and testing of the laws governing the behavior of the matter-energy continuum. Includes instruction in classical and modern physics, electricity and magnetism, thermodynamics, mechanics, wave properties, nuclear processes, relativity and quantum theory, quantitative methods, and laboratory methods.

24102A	Physicists
24105	Chemists, except Biochemists
25319A	Mathematicians
31206	Physics Teachers—Postsecondary

40.0802   Chemical and Atomic/Molecular Physics

An instructional program that describes the scientific study of the behavior of matter-energy phenomena at the level of atoms and molecules. Includes instruction in chemical physics, atomic forces and structure, fission reactions, molecular orbital theory, magnetic resonance, molecular bonding, phase equilibria, quantum theory of solids, and applications to the study of specific elements and higher compounds.

24102A	Physicists
24105	Chemists, except Biochemists
31206	Physics Teachers—Postsecondary

40.0804 Elementary Particle Physics

An instructional program that describes the scientific study of the basic constituents of subatomic matter and energy, and the forces governing fundamental processes. Includes instruction in quantum theory, field theory, single-particle systems, perturbation and scattering theory, matter-radiation interaction, symmetry, quarks, capture, Schroedinger mechanics, methods for detecting particle emission and absorption, and research equipment operation and maintenance.

24102A	Physicists
31206	Physics Teachers—Postsecondary

40.0805 Plasma and High-Temperature Physics

An instructional program that describes the scientific study of the properties and behavior of matter at high temperatures, such that molecular and atomic structures are in a disassociated ionic or electronic state. Includes instruction in magnetohydrodynamics, free electron phenomena, fusion theory, electromagnetic fields and dynamics, plasma and non-linear wave theory, instability theory, plasma shock phenomena, quantitative modeling, and research equipment operation and maintenance.

24102A	Physicists
31206	Physics Teachers—Postsecondary

40.0806 Nuclear Physics

An instructional program that describes the scientific study of the properties and behavior of atomic nuclei instruction in nuclear reaction theory, quantum mechanics, energy conservation, nuclear fission and fusion, strong and weak atomic forces, nuclear modeling, nuclear decay, nucleon scattering, pairing, photon and electron reactions, statistical methods, and research equipment operation and maintenance.

24102A	Physicists
31206	Physics Teachers—Postsecondary

40.0807 Optics

An instructional program that describes the scientific study of light energy, including its structure, properties, and behavior under different conditions. Includes instruction in wave theory, wave mechanics, electromagnetic theory, physical optics, geometric optics, quantum theory of light, photon detecting, laser theory, wall and beam properties, coherence and chaotic light, non-linear optics, harmonic generation, optical systems theory, and applications to engineering problems.

24102A	Physicists
31206	Physics Teachers—Postsecondary

40.0808 Solid-State and Low-Temperature Physics

An instructional program that describes the scientific study of solids and related states of matter at low energy levels, including liquids and dense gases. Includes instruction in statistical mechanics, quantum theory of solids, many-body theory, low temperature phenomena, electron theory of metals, band theory, crystalline structures, magnetism and superconductivity, equilibria and dynamics of liquids, film and surface phenomena, quantitative modeling, and research equipment operation and maintenance.

| 24102A | Physicists |
| 31206 | Physics Teachers—Postsecondary |

40.0809 Acoustics

An instructional program that describes the scientific study of sound, and the properties and behavior of acoustic wave phenomena under different conditions. Includes instruction in wave theory, the acoustic wave equation, energy transformation, vibration phenomena, sound reflection and transmission, scattering and surface wave phenomena, singularity expansion theory, ducting, and applications to specific research problems such as underwater acoustics, crystallography, and health diagnostics.

| 24102A | Physicists |
| 31206 | Physics Teachers—Postsecondary |

40.0810 Theoretical and Mathematical Physics

An instructional program that describes the scientific and mathematical formulation and evaluation of the physical laws governing, and models describing, matter-energy phenomena, and the analysis of related experimental designs and results. Includes instruction in classical and quantum theory, relativity theory, field theory, mathematics of infinite series, vector and coordinate analysis, wave and particle theory, advanced applied calculus and geometry, analyses of continuum, cosmology, and statistical theory and analysis.

24102A	Physicists
25319A	Mathematicians
31206	Physics Teachers—Postsecondary

40.0899 Physics, Other

Any instructional program in physics not described above.

40.99 Physical Sciences, Other

A group of instructional programs (see 40.9999).

40.9999   Physical Sciences, Other

Any instructional program in physical sciences not described above.

41.   SCIENCE TECHNOLOGIES

A summary of groups of instructional programs that prepare individuals to apply scientific principles and technical skills in support of scientific research and development.

41.01   Biological Technologies

A group of instructional programs (see 41.0101).

41.0101   Biological Technology/Technician

An instructional program that prepares individuals to apply scientific principles and technical skills in support of biologists in research and industrial settings. Includes instruction in field research and laboratory methods.

24502A	Biological and Agricultural Technologists
24502C	Biological and Agricultural Technicians
24502D	Biology Specimen Technicians
24599C	Scientific Helpers

41.02   Nuclear and Industrial Radiologic Technologies

A group of instructional programs that prepare individuals to apply scientific principles and technical skills in support of design, testing, and operational procedures related to the industrial use of radioisotopes and nuclear energy.

41.0204   Industrial Radiologic Technology/Technician

An instructional program that prepares individuals to apply scientific principles and technical skills to the operation of industrial and research testing equipment using radioisotopes. Includes instruction in X-ray analysis of materials, nondestructive testing and inspection of materials, and continuous measurement of paper or metal thicknesses.

24508A	Nuclear Equipment Operation Technicians
24599C	Scientific Helpers
85717A	Electronics Mechanics and Technicians

41.0205   Nuclear/Nuclear Power Technology/Technician

An instructional program that prepares individuals to apply scientific principles and technical skills in support of research scientists and operating engineers engaged in the running of nuclear reactors, and in nuclear materials processing and disposal. Includes instruction in basic nuclear physics and nuclear engineering, monitoring and safety procedures, radioactive materials handling and disposal, equipment maintenance and operation, and recordkeeping.

24508B	Nuclear Monitoring Technicians
24599C	Scientific Helpers
58005	Dispatchers—except Police, Fire, and Ambulance
83005A	Production Inspectors, Testers, Graders, Sorters, Samplers, and Weighers
95026	Power Reactor Operators
97989B	Irradiated-Fuel Handlers

41.0299 Nuclear and Industrial Radiologic Technologies/Technicians, Other

Any instructional program in nuclear and industrial radiologic technologies not described above.

24508A	Nuclear Equipment Operation Technicians
24508B	Nuclear Monitoring Technicians

41.03 Physical Science Technologies

A group of instructional programs that prepare individuals to apply scientific principles and technical skills in support of physical science research and development projects.

41.0301 Chemical Technology/Technician

An instructional program that prepares individuals to apply scientific principles and technical skills in support of chemical research and industrial operations. Includes instruction in laboratory research methods, industrial processing methods and equipment, and instrumentation and test equipment operation and maintenance.

24505A	Chemical Technicians and Technologists
24505B	Food Science Technicians and Technologists
24505C	Assayers
24505D	Textile Science Technicians and Technologists
24505E	Environmental Science Technicians
24511E	Geological Sample Test Technicians
24599C	Scientific Helpers
49005B	Sales Representatives, Chemical and Pharmaceutical
83005A	Production Inspectors, Testers, Graders, Sorters, Samplers, and Weighers
92935	Chemical Equipment Controllers and Operators
93997	Intermediate Hand Workers
95005A	Gas Processing Plant Operators
95008	Chemical Plant and System Operators
97953	Pump Operators

41.0399 Physical Science Technologies/Technicians, Other

Any instructional program in physical science technologies not described above.

24511E	Geological Sample Test Technicians
24599A	Meteorological Technicians
24599C	Scientific Helpers

41.99 Science Technologies, Other

A group of instructional programs (see 41.9999).

41.9999 Science Technologies/Technicians, Other

Any instructional program in science technologies not described above.

42. PSYCHOLOGY

A summary of groups of instructional programs that describe the scientific study of the behavior of individuals, independently or collectively, and the physical and environmental bases of mental, emotional, and neurological activity.

42.01 Psychology, General

A group of instructional programs (see 42.0101).

42.0101 Psychology, General

An instructional program that generally describes the scientific study of individual and collective behavior, the physical and environmental bases of behavior, and the analysis and treatment of behavior problems and disorders. Includes instruction in the principles of the various subfields of psychology, research methods, and psychological assessment and testing methods.

27108A	Developmental Psychologists
27108C	Experimental Psychologists
27108D	Educational Psychologists
27108E	Social Psychologists
27108G	Clinical Psychologists
27108H	Counseling Psychologists
27108J	Industrial-Organizational Psychologists
31210	Social Science Teachers—Postsecondary

42.02 Clinical Psychology

A group of instructional programs (see 42.0201).

42.0201   Clinical Psychology

An instructional program that prepares individuals for the independent professional practice of clinical psychology, involving the analysis, diagnosis, and clinical treatment of psychological disorders and behavioral pathologies. Includes instruction in clinical assessment and diagnosis, personality appraisal, psychopathology, clinical psychopharmacology, behavior modification, therapeutic intervention skills, patient interviewing, personalized and group therapy, child and adolescent therapy, cognitive and behavioral therapy, supervised clinical practice, ethical standards, and applicable regulations.

27108D	Educational Psychologists
27108G	Clinical Psychologists
27108H	Counseling Psychologists
27302	Social Workers, Medical and Psychiatric
27305B	Social Workers
31210	Social Science Teachers—Postsecondary

42.03   Cognitive Psychology and Psycholinguistics

A group of instructional programs (see 42.0301).

42.0301   Cognitive Psychology and Psycholinguistics

An instructional program that describes the scientific study of the mechanisms and processes of learning and thinking, and associated information on encoding, decoding, processing and transmitting systems. Includes instruction in theories of cognition and intelligence; studies of cognitive processes such as memory, sensation, perception, pattern recognition, problem solving, and conceptual thinking; cybernetics; psycholinguistics; and the study of biological and social communications mechanisms and processes.

27108A	Developmental Psychologists
27108C	Experimental Psychologists
27108D	Educational Psychologists
31210	Social Science Teachers—Postsecondary

42.04   Community Psychology

A group of instructional programs (see 42.0401).

42.0401   Community Psychology

An instructional program that prepares individuals to apply psychological principles to the analysis of social problems, and the implementation of intervention strategies for addressing these problems. Includes instruction in social ecology, primary and secondary prevention of social pathologies, social intervention strategies and tactics, large group counseling, social services systems behavior, creating settings, cultural stress, and the dynamics of social change.

| 27108E | Social Psychologists |
| 31210 | Social Science Teachers—Postsecondary |

42.06   Counseling Psychology

A group of instructional programs (see 42.0601).

42.0601   Counseling Psychology

An instructional program that prepares individuals for the independent professional practice of psychological counseling, involving the rendering of therapeutic services to individuals and groups experiencing psychological problems and exhibiting distress symptoms. Includes instruction in counseling theory, therapeutic intervention strategies, patient/counselor relationships, testing and assessment methods and procedures, group therapy, marital and family therapy, child and adolescent therapy, supervised counseling practice, ethical standards, and applicable regulations.

19005A	Government Service Executives
27108D	Educational Psychologists
27108G	Clinical Psychologists
27108H	Counseling Psychologists
27302	Social Workers, Medical and Psychiatric
31210	Social Science Teachers—Postsecondary

42.07   Developmental and Child Psychology

A group of instructional programs (see 42.0701).

42.0701   Developmental and Child Psychology

An instructional program that describes the scientific study of the psychological growth and development of individuals from infancy through adulthood. Includes instruction in cognitive and perceptual development, emotional development, personality development, the effects of biological maturation on behavior, theories of cognitive growth and related research methods, testing and assessment methods for different age levels, research on child and adolescent behavior therapy, and the psychology of aging.

| 27108A | Developmental Psychologists |
| 31210 | Social Science Teachers—Postsecondary |

42.08   Experimental Psychology

A group of instructional programs (see 42.0801).

42.0801   Experimental Psychology

An instructional program that describes the scientific study of behavior under experimental conditions, and the analysis of controlled behavioral responses. Includes instruction in learning theory, research design and experimental methods, psychological measurement, statistical design and methods, analysis of cognitive and behavioral variables, and the conduct of specialized and large-scale studies.

27108C	Experimental Psychologists
31210	Social Science Teachers—Postsecondary

42.09   Industrial and Organizational Psychology

A group of instructional programs (see 42.0901).

42.0901   Industrial and Organizational Psychology

An instructional program that describes the scientific study of individual and group behavior in institutional settings, applications to related problems of organization and industry, and that may prepare individuals to apply such principles in industrial and organizational settings. Includes instruction in group behavior theory, organizational theory, reward/punishment structures, human-machine and human-computer interactions, motivation dynamics, human stress studies, environmental and organizational influences on behavior, alienation and satisfaction, and job testing and assessment.

27108D	Educational Psychologists
27108E	Social Psychologists
27108J	Industrial-Organizational Psychologists
31210	Social Science Teachers—Postsecondary

42.11   Physiological Psychology/Psychobiology

A group of instructional programs (see 42.1101).

42.1101   Physiological Psychology/Psychobiology

An instructional program that describes the scientific study of the biological bases of psychological functioning and their application to experimental and therapeutic research problems. Includes instruction in functional neuroanatomy, neural system development, biochemical neural regulatory mechanisms, neurological biophysics, memory storage and retrieval, physiology of cognition and perception, physiological bases of psychopathology and behavioral disorders, psychopharmacology, comparative psychobiology, and specialized experimental design and research methods.

| 27108C | Experimental Psychologists |
| 31210 | Social Science Teachers—Postsecondary |

42.16   Social Psychology

A group of instructional programs (see 42.1601).

42.1601   Social Psychology

An instructional program that describes the scientific study of individual behavior in group contexts, group behavior, and associated phenomena. Includes instruction in social learning theory, group theory and dynamics, sex roles, social cognition and inference, attribution theory, attitude formation, criminal behavior and other social pathologies, altruistic behavior, social development, and social ecology.

27108D	Educational Psychologists
27108E	Social Psychologists
27108J	Industrial-Organizational Psychologists
31210	Social Science Teachers—Postsecondary

42.17   School Psychology

A group of instructional programs (see 42.1701).

42.1701   School Psychology

An instructional program that prepares individuals to apply clinical and counseling psychology principles to the diagnosis and treatment of student behavioral problems. Includes instruction in child and/or adolescent development; learning theory; testing, observation, and other procedures for assessing educational, personality, intelligence, and motor skill development; therapeutic intervention strategies for students and families; identification and classification of disabilities and disorders affecting learning; school psychological services planning; supervised counseling practice; ethical standards; and applicable regulations.

27108D	Educational Psychologists
31210	Social Science Teachers—Postsecondary
31514	Vocational and Educational Counselors

42.99   Psychology, Other

A group of instructional programs (see 42.9999).

42.9999   Psychology, Other

Any instructional program in psychology not described above.

43. PROTECTIVE SERVICES

A summary of groups of instructional programs that describe the principles and procedures for providing police, fire, and other safety services, and for managing penal institutions.

43.01 Criminal Justice and Corrections

A group of instructional programs that describe the principles and procedures for conducting and supervising law enforcement, corrections, and security services.

43.0102 Corrections/Correctional Administration

An instructional program that prepares individuals to apply the theories, principles, and techniques of correctional science to the development, administration, and implementation of procedures for the incarceration, supervision, and rehabilitation of legal offenders.

15014	Industrial Production Managers
19005A	Government Service Executives
31210	Social Science Teachers—Postsecondary
61005	Police and Detective Supervisors
63017	Correction Officers and Jailers

43.0103 Criminal Justice/Law Enforcement Administration

An instructional program that prepares individuals to apply the theories and practices of criminal justice to structuring, managing, directing, and controlling criminal justice agencies, including police departments, sheriff's departments, law enforcement divisions and units, and private protective services.

19005A	Government Service Executives
31210	Social Science Teachers—Postsecondary
51002A	First-Line Supervisors, Customer Service
51002B	First-Line Supervisors, Administrative Support
61005	Police and Detective Supervisors

43.0104 Criminal Justice Studies

An instructional program that describes the study of the criminal justice system, its organizational components and processes, and its legal and public policy contexts. Includes instruction in criminal law and policy, police and correctional systems organization, the administration of justice and the judiciary, and public attitudes regarding criminal justice issues.

27199B	Sociologists
31210	Social Science Teachers—Postsecondary

43.0106   Forensic Technology/Technician

An instructional program that prepares individuals to conduct crime scene and laboratory analyses and evaluations of evidentiary materials, including human remains, under the supervision of a pathologist, forensic administrator, or other law enforcement personnel. Includes instruction in principles of pathology, laboratory technology and procedures, dusting and fingerprinting, reconstructive analysis, and related skills.

24599B	Criminalists and Ballistics Experts
34035B	Sketch Artists
39999G	Polygraph Examiners

43.0107   Law Enforcement/Police Science

An instructional program that prepares individuals to perform the duties of police and public security officers, including patrol and investigative activities, traffic control, crowd control and public relations, witness interviewing, evidence collection and management, basic crime prevention methods, weapon and equipment operation and maintenance, report preparation, and other routine law enforcement responsibilities.

19005A	Government Service Executives
21911C	Immigration and Customs Inspectors
21911D	Licensing Examiners and Inspectors
21911H	Government Property Inspectors and Investigators
31314	Teachers and Instructors—Vocational Education and Training
63011A	Police Detectives
63011B	Police Identification and Records Officers
63014A	Police Investigators—Patrollers
63017	Correction Officers and Jailers
63023	Bailiffs
63026	United States Marshals
63028A	Criminal Investigators and Special Agents
63028B	Child Support, Missing Persons, and Unemployment Insurance Fraud Investigators
63032	Sheriffs and Deputy Sheriffs
63099C	Animal Control Workers

43.0109   Security and Loss Prevention Services

An instructional program that prepares individuals to perform routine inspection, patrol, and crime-prevention services for private clients. Includes instruction in the provision of personal protection as well as property security.

19999F	Security Managers
21911C	Immigration and Customs Inspectors
63002B	Fire Investigators
63035	Detectives and Investigators, except Public

63038	Railroad and Transit Police and Special Agents
63044	Crossing Guards
63047	Guards and Watch Guards

43.0199   Corrections and Criminal Justice, Other

Any instructional program in corrections and criminal justice not described above.

63017	Correction Officers and Jailers
63099B	Protective Service Workers, Recreational
63099C	Animal Control Workers

43.02   Fire Protection

A group of instructional programs that prepare individuals to perform firefighting and related services.

43.0201   Fire Protection and Safety Technology/Technician

An instructional program that prepares individuals to apply a knowledge of fire prevention and control skills to problems of reducing fire risk, loss limitation, supervising substance removal, conducting fire investigations, and advising on matters of safety procedures and fire prevention policy.

15023A	Transportation Managers
21908A	Construction and Building Inspectors
21911E	Industrial and Occupational Safety and Health Inspectors
61002A	Municipal Firefighting and Prevention Supervisors
63002A	Fire Inspectors
63002B	Fire Investigators

43.0202   Fire Services Administration

An instructional program that prepares individuals to structure, manage, direct, and control fire departments, fire prevention services, fire inspection and investigation offices, and ancillary rescue services.

19005A	Government Service Executives
61002A	Municipal Firefighting and Prevention Supervisors
61002B	Forest Firefighting and Prevention Supervisors
63002B	Fire Investigators
63005	Forest Fire Inspectors and Prevention Specialists

43.0203   Fire Science/Firefighting

An instructional program that prepares individuals to perform the duties of firefighters. Includes instruction in firefighting equipment operation and maintenance, principles of fire science and combustible substances, methods of controlling different types of fires, hazardous material handling and control, fire rescue procedures, public relations, and applicable laws and regulations.

31317	Instructors—Nonvocational Education
61002B	Forest Firefighting and Prevention Supervisors
63002B	Fire Investigators
63005	Forest Fire Inspectors and Prevention Specialists
63008A	Municipal Firefighters
63008B	Forest Firefighters

43.0299   Fire Protection, Other

Any instructional program in fire protection not described above.

43.99   Protective Services, Other

A group of instructional programs (see 43.9999).

43.9999   Protective Services, Other

Any instructional program in protective services not described above.

63099C	Animal Control Workers

44.   PUBLIC ADMINISTRATION AND SERVICES

A summary of groups of instructional programs that prepare individuals to analyze, manage, and deliver public programs and services.

44.02   Community Organization, Resources, and Services

A group of instructional programs (see 44.0201).

44.0201   Community Organization, Resources, and Services

An instructional program that describes the theories, principles, and practice of providing services to communities, organizing communities and neighborhoods for social action, serving as community liaisons to public agencies, and using community resources to furnish information, instruction, and assistance to all members of a community. May prepare individuals to apply such knowledge and skills in community service positions.

19005A	Government Service Executives
19999B	Social and Community Service Managers

21911F	Equal Opportunity Representatives and Officers
27305A	Community Organization Social Workers
53502	Welfare Eligibility Workers and Interviewers

44.04   Public Administration

A group of instructional programs (see 44.0401).

44.0401   Public Administration

An instructional program that prepares individuals to serve as managers in the executive arm of local, state, and federal government; and that describes the systematic study of executive organization and management. Includes instruction in the roles, development, and principles of public administration; the management of public policy; executive-legislative relations; public budgetary processes and financial management; administrative law; public personnel management; professional ethics; and research methods.

13005B	Training and Development Managers
13014A	Property Officers and Contract Administrators
15002	Postmasters and Mail Superintendents
15023C	Utilities Managers
19005A	Government Service Executives
19999B	Social and Community Service Managers
21117	Budget Analysts
21502	Claims Takers, Unemployment Benefits
21511D	Employee Training Specialists
21911D	Licensing Examiners and Inspectors
21911F	Equal Opportunity Representatives and Officers
21999G	Grant Coordinators

44.05   Public Policy Analysis

A group of instructional programs (see 44.0501).

44.0501   Public Policy Analysis

An instructional program that describes the systematic analysis of public policy issues and decision processes. Includes instruction in the role of economic and political factors in public decision-making and policy formulation; microeconomic analysis of policy issues; resource allocation and decision modeling; cost/benefit analysis; statistical methods; and applications to specific public policy topics.

21999B	Legislative Assistants
27105	Urban and Regional Planners

44.07   Social Work

A group of instructional programs (see 44.0701).

44.0701   Social Work

An instructional program that prepares individuals for the professional practice of social welfare administration and counseling, and that describes the study of organized means of providing basic support services for vulnerable individuals and groups. Includes instruction in social welfare policy; case work planning; social counseling and intervention strategies; administrative procedures and regulations; and specific applications in areas such as child welfare and family services, probation, employment services, and disability counseling.

19999B	Social and Community Service Managers
27302	Social Workers, Medical and Psychiatric
27305A	Community Organization Social Workers
27305B	Social Workers
27305C	Probation and Correctional Treatment Specialists
28105	Adjudicators, Hearings Officers, and Judicial Reviewers
32399B	Orientation and Mobility Therapists
53502	Welfare Eligibility Workers and Interviewers
63028B	Child Support, Missing Persons, and Unemployment Insurance Fraud Investigators

44.99   Public Administration and Services, Other

A group of instructional programs (see 44.9999).

44.9999   Public Administration and Services, Other

Any instructional program in public administration and services not described above.

45.   SOCIAL SCIENCES AND HISTORY

A summary of groups of instructional programs that describe the systematic study of social systems, social institutions, and social behavior, as well as the study of the human past.

45.01   Social Sciences, General

A group of instructional programs (see 45.0101).

45.0101   Social Sciences, General

An instructional program that generally describes the study of human social behavior and social institutions using any of the methodologies common to the social sciences and/or history, or an undifferentiated program of study in the social sciences.

31210   Social Science Teachers—Postsecondary

45.02   Anthropology

A group of instructional programs (see 45.0201).

45.0201   Anthropology

An instructional program that describes the systematic study of human beings, their antecedents and related primates, and their cultural behavior and institutions, in comparative perspective. Includes instruction in biological/physical anthropology, primatology, human paleontology and prehistoric archaeology, hominid evolution, anthropological linguistics, ethnography, ethnology, ethnohistory, socio-cultural anthropology, psychological anthropology, research methods, and applications to areas such as medicine, forensic pathology, museum studies, and international affairs.

24111A   Geologists
27199B   Sociologists
27199C   Anthropologists
27199D   Linguistic Scientists
27199H   Archaeologists
31210   Social Science Teachers—Postsecondary

45.03   Archaeology

A group of instructional programs (see 45.0301).

45.0301   Archaeology

An instructional program that describes the systematic study of extinct societies, and the past of living societies, via the excavation, analysis, and interpretation of their artifactual, human, and associated remains. Includes instruction in archaeological theory, field methods, dating methods, conservation and museum studies, cultural and physical evolution, and the study of specific selected past cultures.

27199C   Anthropologists
27199D   Linguistic Scientists
27199H   Archaeologists
31210   Social Science Teachers—Postsecondary

45.04   Criminology

A group of instructional programs (see 45.0401).

45.0401   Criminology

An instructional program that describes the systematic study of crime as a sociopathological phenomenon, the behavior of criminals, and the social institutions that have evolved to respond to crime. Includes instruction in the theory of crime, psychological and social bases of criminal behavior, social value systems and the theory of punishment, criminal law and criminal justice systems, penology, rehabilitation and recidivism, studies of specific types of crime, social attitudes and policy, and applications to specific issues in law enforcement administration and policy.

24599B	Criminalists and Ballistics Experts
27199B	Sociologists
31210	Social Science Teachers—Postsecondary

45.05   Demography and Population Studies

A group of instructional programs (see 45.0501).

45.0501   Demography and Population Studies

An instructional program that describes the systematic study of population models and population phenomena, and related problems of social structure and behavior. Includes instruction in population growth, spatial distribution, mortality and fertility factors, migration, dynamic population modeling, population estimation and projection, mathematical and statistical analysis of population data, population policy studies, and applications to problems in economics and government planning.

25312	Statisticians
27199B	Sociologists
27199C	Anthropologists
31210	Social Science Teachers—Postsecondary

45.06   Economics

A group of instructional programs (see 45.0601).

45.0601   Economics, General

An instructional program that generally describes the systematic study of the production, conservation, and allocation of resources in conditions of scarcity, together with the organizational frameworks related to these processes. Includes instruction in economic theory, micro- and macroeconomics, comparative economic systems, money

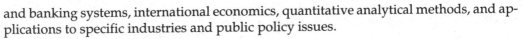

and banking systems, international economics, quantitative analytical methods, and applications to specific industries and public policy issues.

19005A	Government Service Executives
25312	Statisticians
27102A	Economists
27102B	Market Research Analysts
31210	Social Science Teachers—Postsecondary

45.0602   Applied and Resource Economics

An instructional program that describes the application of economic principles and analytical techniques to the study of particular industries or activities, or to the exploitation of particular resources. Includes instruction in economic theory, microeconomic analysis and modeling of specific industries, commodities, the economic consequences of resource allocation decisions, regulatory and consumer factors, and the technical aspects of specific subjects as they relate to economic analysis.

27102A	Economists
27102B	Market Research Analysts
31210	Social Science Teachers—Postsecondary

45.0603   Econometrics and Quantitative Economics

An instructional program that describes the systematic mathematical and statistical analysis of economic phenomena and problems. Includes instruction in economic statistics, optimization theory, cost/benefit analysis, price theory, economic modeling, and economic forecasting and evaluation.

25312	Statisticians
27102A	Economists
27102B	Market Research Analysts
31210	Social Science Teachers—Postsecondary

45.0604   Development Economics and International Development

An instructional program that describes the systematic study of the economic development process and its application to the problems of specific countries and regions. Includes instruction in economic development theory; industrialization; land reform; infrastructural development; investment policy; the role of governments and business in development; international development organizations; and the study of social, health, and environmental influences on economic development.

19005A	Government Service Executives
27102A	Economists
31210	Social Science Teachers—Postsecondary

45.0605   International Economics

An instructional program that describes the systematic study and analysis of international commercial behavior and trade policy. Includes instruction in international trade theory, tariffs and quotas, commercial policy, trade factor flows, international finance and investment, currency regulation and trade exchange rates and markets, international trade negotiation, and international payments and accounting policy.

19005A	Government Service Executives
27102A	Economists
31210	Social Science Teachers—Postsecondary

45.0699   Economics, Other

Any instructional program in economics not described above.

27102A	Economists

45.07   Geography

A group of instructional programs (see 45.0701).

45.0701   Geography

An instructional program that describes the systematic study of the spatial distribution and interrelationships of people, natural resources, and plant and animal life. Includes instruction in historical and political geography, cultural geography, economic and physical geography, regional science, cartographic methods, remote sensing, spatial analysis, and applications to areas such as land-use planning, development studies, and analyses of specific countries, regions, and resources.

22311B	Surveyors
24111A	Geologists
24199A	Geographers

45.0702   Cartography

An instructional program that describes the systematic study of mapmaking and the application of mathematical, computer, and other techniques to the science of mapping geographic information. Includes instruction in cartographic theory and map projections; computer-assisted cartography; map design and layout; photogrammetry; air photo interpretation; remote sensing; cartographic editing; and applications to specific industrial, commercial, research, and governmental mapping problems.

22311A	Cartographers and Photogrammetrists
22311B	Surveyors
22521B	Mapping Technicians

45.08   History

A group of instructional programs (see 45.0801).

45.0801   History, General

An instructional program that generally describes the study and interpretation of the past, including the gathering, recording, synthesizing, and criticizing of evidence and theories about past events. Includes instruction in historiography; historical research methods; studies of specific periods, issues, and cultures; and applications to areas such as historic preservation, public policy, and records administration.

27199E	Historians
27199G	Genealogists
31210	Social Science Teachers—Postsecondary
31511A	Curators
31511B	Archivists
31511C	Museum Research Workers
31511D	Museum Technicians and Conservators

45.0802   American (United States) History

An instructional program that describes the study of the development of American society, culture, and institutions from the Pre-Columbian period to the present. Includes instruction in American historiography, American history sources and materials, historical research methods, and applications to the study of specific themes, issues, periods, and institutions.

27199E	Historians
31210	Social Science Teachers—Postsecondary

45.0803   European History

An instructional program that describes the study of the development of European society, culture, and institutions from the origins to the present. Includes instruction in European historiography, European history sources and materials, historical research methods, and applications to the study of specific themes, issues, periods, and institutions.

27199E	Historians
31210	Social Science Teachers—Postsecondary

45.0804   History and Philosophy of Science

An instructional program that describes the study of the historical evolution of scientific theories and science applications and technologies, as well as the philosophy of science and its historical socioeconomic context. Includes instruction in the concepts and methods of philosophical inquiry, historiography of science, and research methods in the history of the scientific and engineering disciplines, including mathematics.

27199E	Historians
31210	Social Science Teachers—Postsecondary

45.0805   Public/Applied History and Archival Administration

An instructional program that describes the application of history and administrative skills to the recording of public events and the management of related historical resources. Includes instruction in historical research methods, archives and records management, the planning and administration of public records services and history projects, and applications to specific problems in public organizations, government agencies, foundations, and records facilities.

27199E	Historians
27199G	Genealogists
31210	Social Science Teachers—Postsecondary
31511A	Curators
31511B	Archivists
31511C	Museum Research Workers
31511D	Museum Technicians and Conservators

45.0899   History, Other

Any instructional program in history not described above.

45.09   International Relations and Affairs

A group of instructional programs (see 45.0901).

45.0901   International Relations and Affairs

An instructional program that describes the systematic study of international politics and institutions, and the conduct of diplomacy and foreign policy. Includes instruction in international relations theory, foreign policy analysis, national security and strategic studies, international law and organization, the comparative study of specific countries and regions, and the theory and practice of diplomacy.

19005A	Government Service Executives
27199A	Political Scientists
27199C	Anthropologists
27199D	Linguistic Scientists
27199E	Historians
27199F	Intelligence Specialists
31210	Social Science Teachers—Postsecondary

45.10   Political Science and Government

A group of instructional programs (see 45.1001).

45.1001   Political Science and Government, General

An instructional program that describes the systematic study of political institutions and behavior. Includes instruction in political philosophy, political theory, comparative government and politics, political parties and interest groups, public opinion, political research methods, studies of the government and politics of specific countries, and studies of specific political institutions and processes.

27199A	Political Scientists
27199B	Sociologists
27199E	Historians
27199F	Intelligence Specialists
31210	Social Science Teachers—Postsecondary

45.1002   American Government and Politics (United States)

An instructional program that describes the systematic study of United States political institutions and behavior. Includes instruction in American political theory, political parties and interest groups, state and local governments, Constitutional law, federalism and national institutions, executive and legislative politics, judicial politics, popular attitudes and media influences, political research methods, and applications to the study of specific issues and institutions.

27199A	Political Scientists
31210	Social Science Teachers—Postsecondary

45.1003   Political Science and Government, Other

Any instructional program in political science and government not described above.

45.11   Sociology

A group of instructional programs (see 45.1101).

45.1101   Sociology

An instructional program that describes the systematic study of human social institutions and social relationships. Includes instruction in social theory, sociological research methods, social organization and structure, social stratification and hierarchies, dynamics of social change, family structures, social deviance and control, and applications to the study of specific social groups, social institutions, and social problems.

27199B	Sociologists
27199C	Anthropologists
27199F	Intelligence Specialists
31210	Social Science Teachers—Postsecondary

45.12   Urban Studies/Affairs

A group of instructional programs (see 45.1201).

45.1201   Urban Studies/Affairs

An instructional program that describes the application of social science principles to the study of urban institutions and the forces influencing urban social and political life. Includes instruction in urban theory, the development and evolution of urban areas, urban sociology, principles of urban and social planning, and the politics and economics of urban government and services.

| 27199B | Sociologists |
| 31210 | Social Science Teachers—Postsecondary |

45.99   Social Sciences, Other

A group instructional programs (see 45.9999).

45.9999   Social Sciences, Other

Any instructional program in social sciences not described above.

46.   CONSTRUCTION TRADES

A summary of groups of instructional programs that prepare individuals to apply technical knowledge and skills in the building, inspecting, and maintaining of structures and related properties.

46.01   Masons and Tile Setters

A group of instructional programs (see 46.0101).

46.0101   Mason and Tile Setter

An instructional program that prepares individuals to apply technical knowledge and skills in the laying and/or setting of brick, concrete block, hard tile, marble, and related materials, using trowels, levels, hammers, chisels, and other hand tools.

83005A	Production Inspectors, Testers, Graders, Sorters, Samplers, and Weighers
87302	Brick Masons
87305B	Stone Masons
87308	Hard Tile Setters
87605	Floor Layers—except Carpet, Wood, and Hard Tiles
89905A	Molders and Casters
89905C	Stone Cutters and Carvers
89908B	Cutters and Layout Workers
93926B	Rock Splitters
93953	Grinding and Polishing Workers, Hand
93997	Intermediate Hand Workers

46.02   Carpenters

A group of instructional programs (see 46.0201).

46.0201   Carpenter

An instructional program that prepares individuals to apply technical knowledge and skills to lay out, fabricate, erect, install, and repair wooden structures and fixtures, using hand and power tools. Includes instruction in areas such as common systems of framing, construction materials, estimating, blueprint reading, and finish carpentry techniques.

39999D	Studio, Stage, and Special Effects Technicians
83002A	Materials Inspectors
87102A	Construction Carpenters
87102B	Rough Carpenters
87102C	Tank Builders and Coopers
87102D	Carpenter Assemblers and Repairers
87102E	Boat and Ship Builders
87102F	Ship Carpenters and Joiners
87105	Ceiling Tile Installers and Acoustical Carpenters
87121	Brattice Builders
87899A	Construction Installation Workers
87899L	House Movers
89908D	Exhibit Builders
93956	Assemblers and Fabricators—except Machine, Electrical, Electronic, and Precision

46.03   Electrical and Power Transmission Installers

A group of instructional programs (see 46.0301).

46.0301   Electrical and Power Transmission Installer, General

An instructional program that prepares individuals to apply technical knowledge and skills to install, operate, maintain, and repair residential, commercial, and industrial electrical systems, and the power lines that transmit electricity from its source of generation to its place of consumption.

21908A	Construction and Building Inspectors
39999D	Studio, Stage, and Special Effects Technicians
83002D	Electrical and Electronic Inspectors and Testers
83005A	Production Inspectors, Testers, Graders, Sorters, Samplers, and Weighers
83005B	Construction Checkers
85511	Signal or Track Switch Maintainers
85599A	Communication Equipment Mechanics, Installers, and Repairers
85702	Telephone and Cable Television Line Installers and Repairers
85714A	Electric Motor and Switch Assemblers and Repairers
85714B	Battery Repairers
85714C	Transformer Repairers
85721	Powerhouse, Substation, and Relay Electricians
85723	Electrical Power Line Installers and Repairers
85728A	Aircraft Electricians
85728B	Ground Transportation Electricians
87202A	Electricians
87202C	Electrical Utility Troubleshooters
93997	Intermediate Hand Workers
98102	Helpers—Mechanics and Repairers

46.0302   Electrician

An instructional program that prepares individuals to apply technical knowledge and skills to install, operate, maintain, and repair electric apparatus and systems such as residential, commercial, and industrial electric-power wiring; and D.C. and A.C. motors, controls, and electrical distribution panels. Includes instruction in the use of test equipment.

21908A	Construction and Building Inspectors
39999D	Studio, Stage, and Special Effects Technicians
83002D	Electrical and Electronic Inspectors and Testers
85511	Signal or Track Switch Maintainers
85599A	Communication Equipment Mechanics, Installers, and Repairers
85714A	Electric Motor and Switch Assemblers and Repairers
85714B	Battery Repairers
85714C	Transformer Repairers
85721	Powerhouse, Substation, and Relay Electricians
85728A	Aircraft Electricians
85728B	Ground Transportation Electricians

87202A	Electricians
87202C	Electrical Utility Troubleshooters
98102	Helpers—Mechanics and Repairers

46.0303   Lineworker

An instructional program that prepares individuals to apply technical knowledge and skills to install, operate, maintain, and repair local, long-distance, and rural electric power cables and communication lines; erect and construct pole and tower lines; and install underground lines and cables.

83002D	Electrical and Electronic Inspectors and Testers
83005A	Production Inspectors, Testers, Graders, Sorters, Samplers, and Weighers
83005B	Construction Checkers
85511	Signal or Track Switch Maintainers
85599A	Communication Equipment Mechanics, Installers, and Repairers
85702	Telephone and Cable Television Line Installers and Repairers
85723	Electrical Power Line Installers and Repairers
87202C	Electrical Utility Troubleshooters
93997	Intermediate Hand Workers

46.0399   Electrical and Power Transmission Installers, Other

Any instructional program in electrical and power transmission installation not described above.

46.04   Construction and Building Finishers and Managers

A group of instructional programs that prepare individuals to apply technical knowledge and skills to the finishing, inspection, and maintenance of structures and related properties.

46.0401   Building/Property Maintenance and Manager

An instructional program that prepares individuals to apply technical knowledge and skills in order to keep a building functioning, and to service a variety of types of structures including commercial and industrial buildings and mobile homes. Includes instruction in the basic maintenance and repair skills required to service building air conditioning, heating, plumbing, electrical, major appliances, and other mechanical systems.

67005	Janitors and Cleaners, except Maids and Housekeeping Cleaners
85132	Maintenance Repairers, General Utility
85938	Installers and Repairers—Manufactured Buildings, Mobile Homes, and Travel Trailers

93956	Assemblers and Fabricators—except Machine, Electrical, Electronic, and Precision

46.0403   Construction/Building Inspector

An instructional program that prepares individuals to apply technical knowledge and skills to inspect and oversee construction of buildings, dams, highways, and other structures, to ensure that procedures and materials comply with plans, specifications, codes, and regulations.

21908A	Construction and Building Inspectors
21908B	Elevator Inspectors
83002A	Materials Inspectors
83005A	Production Inspectors, Testers, Graders, Sorters, Samplers, and Weighers
83005B	Construction Checkers

46.0408   Painter and Wall Coverer

An instructional program that prepares individuals to apply technical knowledge and skills to finish exterior and interior surfaces by applying protective or decorative coating materials such as paint, lacquer, and wallpaper. Includes instruction in surface preparation; selecting, preparing, and applying paints and other coatings; hanging wallpaper; and equipment operation and maintenance.

83005A	Production Inspectors, Testers, Graders, Sorters, Samplers, and Weighers
87402A	Painters, Construction and Maintenance
87402B	Paperhangers
87505	Pipelaying Fitters
87508	Pipelayers
87608	Floor-Sanding Machine Operators
87899D	Construction Workers, except Trade
92947	Painters, Transportation Equipment
93947E	Hand Painting, Coating, or Decorating Workers

46.0499   Construction and Building Finishers and Managers, Other

Any instructional program in construction and building finishing and management not described above.

83005A	Production Inspectors, Testers, Graders, Sorters, Samplers, and Weighers
87311	Concrete and Terrazzo Finishers
87314	Reinforcing Metal Workers
89908C	Model and Mold Makers
93944D	Molders and Casters

46.05   Plumbers and Pipefitters

A group of instructional programs (see 46.0501).

46.0501   Plumber and Pipefitter

An instructional program that prepares individuals to apply technical knowledge and skills to lay out, assemble, install, and maintain piping fixtures and piping systems for steam, hot water, heating, cooling, drainage, lubricating, sprinkling, and industrial processing systems. Includes instruction in material selection and use of tools to cut, bend, join, and weld pipes.

21908A	Construction and Building Inspectors
83002A	Materials Inspectors
83005A	Production Inspectors, Testers, Graders, Sorters, Samplers, and Weighers
85928D	Utilities Representatives
87502A	Pipe Fitters
87502B	Plumbers
87511	Septic Tank Servicers and Sewer Pipe Cleaners
87899A	Construction Installation Workers
93997	Intermediate Hand Workers

46.99   Construction Trades, Other

A group of instructional programs (see 46.9999).

46.9999   Construction Trades, Other

Any instructional program in construction trades not described above.

83005A	Production Inspectors, Testers, Graders, Sorters, Samplers, and Weighers
87108	Drywall Installers
87111	Tapers
87114	Lathers
87317	Plasterers and Stucco Masons
87505	Pipelaying Fitters
87508	Pipelayers
87602	Carpet Installers
87605	Floor Layers—except Carpet, Wood, and Hard Tiles
87608	Floor-Sanding Machine Operators
87802	Insulation Workers
87808	Roofers
87811	Glaziers
87814	Structural Metal Workers

87899A	Construction Installation Workers
87899C	Swimming Pool Installers and Servicers
87899D	Construction Workers, except Trade
87899F	Conduit Mechanics
89132	Sheet-Metal Workers
89905A	Molders and Casters
93926D	Glass Cutters and Finishers
93956	Assemblers and Fabricators—except Machine, Electrical, Electronic, and Precision

47. MECHANICS AND REPAIRERS

A summary of groups of instructional programs that prepare individuals to apply technical knowledge and skills in the adjustment, maintenance, part replacement, and repair of tools, equipment, and machines.

47.01   Electrical and Electronics Equipment Installers and Repairers

A group of instructional programs (see 47.0101).

47.0101   Electrical and Electronics Equipment Installer and Repairer, General

An instructional program that generally prepares individuals to apply technical knowledge and skills to operate, maintain, and repair electrical and electronic equipment. Includes instruction in electrical circuitry, simple gearing, linkages and lubrication of machines and appliances, and the use of testing equipment.

22505A	Electronics Engineering Technicians
25104	Computer Support Specialists
39008	Radio Operators
81008	First-Line Supervisors and Manager/Supervisors—Production and Operating Workers
83002A	Materials Inspectors
83002D	Electrical and Electronic Inspectors and Testers
83005A	Production Inspectors, Testers, Graders, Sorters, Samplers, and Weighers
85123A	Equipment Servicers and Technicians
85128A	Machinery Maintenance Servicers
85502	Central Office and PBX Installers and Repairers
85505	Frame Wirers, Central Office
85508	Telegraph and Teletype Installers and Maintainers
85514	Radio Mechanics
85599A	Communication Equipment Mechanics, Installers, and Repairers

85599B	Telecommunications Facility Examiners
85599C	Sound Technicians
85708	Electronic Home Entertainment Equipment Repairers
85711A	Electric Home Appliance and Power Tool Repairers
85711B	Home Appliance Installers
85714A	Electric Motor and Switch Assemblers and Repairers
85714B	Battery Repairers
85714D	Armature and Salvage Repairers
85717A	Electronics Mechanics and Technicians
85717B	Test Card and Circuit Board Repairers
85726	Station Installers and Repairers, Telephone
85914	Camera and Photographic Equipment Repairers
85926	Office Machine and Cash Register Servicers
85944	Gas Appliance Repairers
87899A	Construction Installation Workers
92902A	Electronic Semiconductor Processors
92902B	Electronic Semiconductor Wafer Etchers and Engravers
92902C	Electronic Semiconductor Test and Development Technicians
92902D	Electronic Semiconductor Crystal-Growing Technicians and Equipment Operators
92902E	Electronic Semiconductor Sawyers, Abraders, and Polishers
93111A	Electromechanical Equipment Assemblers—Precision
93114	Electrical and Electronic Equipment Assemblers—Precision
93905A	Battery Assemblers
93905B	Electronic Components Assemblers
93905C	Electric Motor Assemblers
93905D	Electrical Components Assemblers
93908	Coil Winders, Tapers, and Finishers
93944D	Molders and Casters
93951B	Etchers, Hand
93956	Assemblers and Fabricators—except Machine, Electrical, Electronic, and Precision
93997	Intermediate Hand Workers

47.0102 Business Machine Repairer

An instructional program that prepares individuals to apply technical knowledge and skills to maintain and repair a wide variety of office machines such as electric typewriters, word processing and dictation machines, calculators, data-processing equipment, duplicating machines, and mailing machines. Includes instruction in diagnostic techniques, the use of testing equipment, and the principles of mechanics, electricity, and electronics as they relate to the repair of business machines.

81008	First-Line Supervisors and Manager/Supervisors—Production and Operating Workers
83002A	Materials Inspectors

83005A	Production Inspectors, Testers, Graders, Sorters, Samplers, and Weighers
85717A	Electronics Mechanics and Technicians
85926	Office Machine and Cash Register Servicers
93111A	Electromechanical Equipment Assemblers—Precision
93114	Electrical and Electronic Equipment Assemblers—Precision

47.0103   Communications Systems Installer and Repairer

An instructional program that prepares individuals to apply technical knowledge and skills to assemble, install, operate, maintain, and repair one- and two-way communications equipment and systems, including television cable systems and mobile or stationary communication devices. Includes instruction in diagnostic techniques, the use of testing equipment, and the principles of mechanics, electricity, and electronics as they relate to the repair of communications systems.

39008	Radio Operators
83002D	Electrical and Electronic Inspectors and Testers
85502	Central Office and PBX Installers and Repairers
85505	Frame Wirers, Central Office
85508	Telegraph and Teletype Installers and Maintainers
85514	Radio Mechanics
85599A	Communication Equipment Mechanics, Installers, and Repairers
85599B	Telecommunications Facility Examiners
85599C	Sound Technicians
85708	Electronic Home Entertainment Equipment Repairers
85717A	Electronics Mechanics and Technicians
85726	Station Installers and Repairers, Telephone
87899A	Construction Installation Workers
93114	Electrical and Electronic Equipment Assemblers—Precision
93905B	Electronic Components Assemblers
93905D	Electrical Components Assemblers

47.0104   Computer Installer and Repairer

An instructional program that prepares individuals to apply technical knowledge and skills to assemble, install, operate, maintain, and repair computers and related instruments. Includes instruction in power supplies, number systems, memory structure, buffers and registers, microprocessor design, peripheral equipment, programming, and networking.

25104	Computer Support Specialists
85599A	Communication Equipment Mechanics, Installers, and Repairers
85717A	Electronics Mechanics and Technicians
85914	Camera and Photographic Equipment Repairers
85926	Office Machine and Cash Register Servicers

47.0105   Industrial Electronics Installer and Repairer

An instructional program that prepares individuals to apply technical knowledge and skills to assemble, install, operate, maintain, and repair electrical/electronic equipment used in industry and manufacturing. Includes instruction in installing, maintaining, and testing various types of equipment.

22505A	Electronics Engineering Technicians
83002D	Electrical and Electronic Inspectors and Testers
83005A	Production Inspectors, Testers, Graders, Sorters, Samplers, and Weighers
85123A	Equipment Servicers and Technicians
85128A	Machinery Maintenance Servicers
85714A	Electric Motor and Switch Assemblers and Repairers
85717A	Electronics Mechanics and Technicians
85717B	Test Card and Circuit Board Repairers
85914	Camera and Photographic Equipment Repairers
92902A	Electronic Semiconductor Processors
92902B	Electronic Semiconductor Wafer Etchers and Engravers
92902C	Electronic Semiconductor Test and Development Technicians
92902D	Electronic Semiconductor Crystal-Growing Technicians and Equipment Operators
92902E	Electronic Semiconductor Sawyers, Abraders, and Polishers
93114	Electrical and Electronic Equipment Assemblers—Precision
93908	Coil Winders, Tapers, and Finishers
93944D	Molders and Casters
93951B	Etchers, Hand
93956	Assemblers and Fabricators—except Machine, Electrical, Electronic, and Precision
93997	Intermediate Hand Workers

47.0106   Major Appliance Installer and Repairer

An instructional program that prepares individuals to apply technical knowledge and skills to repair, install, and service major gas, electric, and microwave consumer appliances such as stoves, refrigerators, dryers, water heaters, washers, dishwashers, and commercial units such as ice makers and coffee makers.

85711A	Electric Home Appliance and Power Tool Repairers
85711B	Home Appliance Installers
85944	Gas Appliance Repairers
93956	Assemblers and Fabricators—except Machine, Electrical, Electronic, and Precision

47.0199   Electrical and Electronics Equipment Installers and Repairers, Other

Any instructional program in electrical and electronics equipment installation and repair not described above.

83002D	Electrical and Electronic Inspectors and Testers
83005A	Production Inspectors, Testers, Graders, Sorters, Samplers, and Weighers
85113	Machinery Maintenance Mechanics, Sewing Machines
85328B	Small Engine Mechanics
85711A	Electric Home Appliance and Power Tool Repairers
85714A	Electric Motor and Switch Assemblers and Repairers
85714C	Transformer Repairers
85714D	Armature and Salvage Repairers
85947	Coin and Vending Machine Servicers and Repairers
93111A	Electromechanical Equipment Assemblers—Precision
93114	Electrical and Electronic Equipment Assemblers—Precision
93908	Coil Winders, Tapers, and Finishers

47.02 Heating, Air Conditioning, and Refrigeration Mechanics and Repairers

A group of instructional programs (see 47.0201).

47.0201 Heating, Air Conditioning, and Refrigeration Mechanic and Repairer

An instructional program that prepares individuals to apply technical knowledge and skills to repair, install, service, and maintain the operating condition of heating, air conditioning, and refrigeration systems. Includes instruction in diagnostic techniques, the use of testing equipment, and the principles of mechanics, electricity, and electronics as they relate to the repair of heating, air-conditioning, and refrigeration systems.

21908A	Construction and Building Inspectors
83002A	Materials Inspectors
83005A	Production Inspectors, Testers, Graders, Sorters, Samplers, and Weighers
85119A	Machinery Maintenance Mechanics
85302B	Automotive Specialty Technicians
85711A	Electric Home Appliance and Power Tool Repairers
85902A	Heating and Air-Conditioning Mechanics
85902B	Refrigeration Mechanics
87505	Pipelaying Fitters
87508	Pipelayers
87608	Floor-Sanding Machine Operators
87899D	Construction Workers, except Trade
95032	Stationary Engineers
98102	Helpers—Mechanics and Repairers

47.03 Industrial Equipment Maintenance and Repairers

A group of instructional programs (see 47.0302 and 47.0303).

47.0302   Heavy Equipment Maintenance and Repairer

An instructional program that prepares individuals to apply technical knowledge and skills in the field maintenance and repair of heavy equipment, and in the general maintenance and overhaul of such equipment. Includes instruction in inspection, maintenance, and repair of tracks, wheels, brakes, operating controls, pneumatic and hydraulic systems, electrical circuitry, engines, and in techniques of welding and brazing.

83005A	Production Inspectors, Testers, Graders, Sorters, Samplers, and Weighers
83008A	Railroad Inspectors
85311A	Bus and Truck Mechanics and Diesel Engine Specialists
85314	Mobile Heavy Equipment Mechanics, except Engines
85317	Railcar Repairers
87714C	Railroad Brake Repairers
97317A	Train Crew Members
97805	Service Station Attendants
98102	Helpers—Mechanics and Repairers

47.0303   Industrial Machinery Maintenance and Repairer

An instructional program that prepares individuals to apply technical knowledge and skills to repair and maintain industrial machinery and equipment such as cranes, pumps, engines and motors, pneumatic tools, conveyor systems, production machinery, marine deck machinery, and steam propulsion, refinery, and pipeline-distribution systems.

21911L	Pressure Vessel Inspectors
49005D	Sales Representatives, Mechanical Equipment and Supplies
83002A	Materials Inspectors
83005A	Production Inspectors, Testers, Graders, Sorters, Samplers, and Weighers
85112	Machinery Maintenance Mechanics, Textile Machines
85118	Machinery Maintenance Mechanics, Water or Power Generation Plants
85119A	Machinery Maintenance Mechanics
85119B	Machinery Maintenance Repairers
85123A	Equipment Servicers and Technicians
85123B	Millwrights and Machinery Erectors
85128A	Machinery Maintenance Servicers
85128B	Oilers
85928A	Valve and Regulator Repairers
85928C	Mechanical Door Repairers
85932	Elevator Installers and Repairers
85999B	Pump Installers and Servicers
87899H	Pipeline Maintenance Workers
89135	Boilermakers
92702	Textile Machine Setters and Set-Up Operators

92914	Paper Goods Machine Setters and Set-Up Operators
92941A	Fiber Product Machine Cutters
92941B	Stone Sawyers
92951	Coating, Painting, and Spraying Machine Setters and Set-Up Operators
92968	Extruding, Forming, Pressing, and Compacting Machine Setters and Set-Up Operators
92971	Extruding, Forming, Pressing, and Compacting Machine Operators and Tenders
93114	Electrical and Electronic Equipment Assemblers—Precision
98102	Helpers—Mechanics and Repairers

47.0399   Industrial Equipment Maintenance and Repairers, Other

Any instructional program in industrial equipment maintenance and repair not described above.

85119A	Machinery Maintenance Mechanics
85119B	Machinery Maintenance Repairers
85128B	Oilers
85928A	Valve and Regulator Repairers
87921	Roustabouts
87949B	Service Unit Operators—Oil, Gas, and Mining
87989A	Miners and Petroleum and Gas Extractive Workers
97908	Oil Pumpers, except Well Head
97911	Well Head Pumpers
97941	Hoist and Winch Operators
97953	Pump Operators
98999B	Production Helpers

47.04   Miscellaneous Mechanics and Repairers

A group of instructional programs that prepare individuals to apply technical knowledge and skills to repair and maintain a wide variety of items other than those described elsewhere in the Mechanics and Repairers series.

47.0401   Instrument Calibration and Repairer

An instructional program that prepares individuals to apply technical knowledge and skills to repair and maintain testing equipment, calibration equipment, instrumentation, meters, measuring devices, and control devices.

22505B	Calibration and Instrumentation Technicians
83002C	Precision Devices Inspectors and Testers
83002D	Electrical and Electronic Inspectors and Testers

83005A	Production Inspectors, Testers, Graders, Sorters, Samplers, and Weighers
83005B	Construction Checkers
85317	Railcar Repairers
85905	Precision Instrument Repairers
85911	Electric Meter Installers and Repairers
85928A	Valve and Regulator Repairers
85928B	Meter Mechanics
85999A	Hand and Portable Power Tool Repairers
89114A	Model Makers, Metal and Plastic
93114	Electrical and Electronic Equipment Assemblers—Precision
93956	Assemblers and Fabricators—except Machine, Electrical, Electronic, and Precision

47.0402   Gunsmith

An instructional program that prepares individuals to apply technical knowledge and skills to make, repair, maintain, and modify firearms according to blueprints or customer specifications, using specialized hand tools and machines.

83002A	Materials Inspectors
83005A	Production Inspectors, Testers, Graders, Sorters, Samplers, and Weighers
85998	Product Repairers
85999D	Gunsmiths
89111	Tool Grinders, Filers, Sharpeners, and Other Precision Grinders
89397B	Custom Precision Woodworkers
92311	Woodworking Machine Setters and Set-Up Operators, except Sawing
92314	Woodworking Machine Operators and Tenders, except Sawing
93917A	Solderers
93953	Grinding and Polishing Workers, Hand
93956	Assemblers and Fabricators—except Machine, Electrical, Electronic, and Precision
93997	Intermediate Hand Workers

47.0403   Locksmith and Safe Repairer

An instructional program that prepares individuals to apply technical knowledge and skills to make, repair, maintain, modify, and open locks; to make keys; to enter and change lock and safe combinations; and to install and repair safes.

85923	Locksmiths and Safe Repairers
93956	Assemblers and Fabricators—except Machine, Electrical, Electronic, and Precision

47.0404   Musical Instrument Repairer

An instructional program that prepares individuals to apply technical knowledge and skills to make, repair, maintain, and tune acoustic and electric musical instruments. Includes instruction in methods and equipment for making musical instruments, electronic instrument amplification systems, techniques of cleaning, and methods of tuning musical instruments.

83005A	Production Inspectors, Testers, Graders, Sorters, Samplers, and Weighers
85708	Electronic Home Entertainment Equipment Repairers
85921A	Keyboard Instrument Repairers and Tuners
85921B	Stringed Instrument Repairers and Tuners
85921C	Reed or Wind Instrument Repairers and Tuners
85921D	Percussion Instrument Repairers and Tuners
89397A	Custom Precision Woodworkers, Musical Instruments
89398	Standard Precision Woodworkers
91321	Machine Forming Operators and Tenders, Metal and Plastic
93114	Electrical and Electronic Equipment Assemblers—Precision
93197A	Musical Instrument Makers, Metal
93926E	Cutters and Trimmers, Hand
93953	Grinding and Polishing Workers, Hand
93956	Assemblers and Fabricators—except Machine, Electrical, Electronic, and Precision

47.0408   Watch, Clock, and Jewelry Repairer

An instructional program that prepares individuals to apply technical knowledge and skills to make, repair, and maintain timepieces, time-measuring devices, and jewelry items. Includes instruction in mechanical timekeeping systems, digital timekeeping systems, timesetting, casting, engraving, polishing, stonesetting, soldering, fine microscopic work, equipment and tool maintenance, redesign and restyling techniques, and customer relations.

31314	Teachers and Instructors—Vocational Education and Training
49017	Counter and Rental Clerks
58008	Production, Planning, and Expediting Clerks
83002A	Materials Inspectors
83002C	Precision Devices Inspectors and Testers
83005A	Production Inspectors, Testers, Graders, Sorters, Samplers, and Weighers
85917	Watchmakers
89114A	Model Makers, Metal and Plastic
89123A	Jewelers
89126C	Model and Mold Makers, Jewelry
89126E	Bench Workers, Jewelry

89128	Precision Etchers and Engravers, Hand or Machine
89926A	Gem and Diamond Workers
91105	Lathe and Turning Machine Tool Setters and Set-Up Operators, Metal and Plastic
91111	Milling and Planing Machine Setters and Set-Up Operators, Metal and Plastic
91114A	Grinding, Honing, Lapping, and Deburring Machine Set-Up Operators
91117	Machine Tool Cutting Operators and Tenders, Metal and Plastic
91321	Machine Forming Operators and Tenders, Metal and Plastic
91505	Combination Machine Tool Setters and Set-Up Operators, Metal and Plastic
91932	Heat Treating, Annealing, and Tempering Machine Operators and Tenders, Metal and Plastic
93117	Watch, Clock, and Chronometer Assemblers, Adjusters, and Calibrators—Precision
93947E	Hand Painting, Coating, or Decorating Workers
93953	Grinding and Polishing Workers, Hand
93956	Assemblers and Fabricators—except Machine, Electrical, Electronic, and Precision
93997	Intermediate Hand Workers

47.0499   Miscellaneous Mechanics and Repairers, Other

Any instructional program in miscellaneous mechanics and repairers not described above.

83002C	Precision Devices Inspectors and Testers
83005A	Production Inspectors, Testers, Graders, Sorters, Samplers, and Weighers
85914	Camera and Photographic Equipment Repairers
85998	Product Repairers
92905	Motion Picture Projectionists
93956	Assemblers and Fabricators—except Machine, Electrical, Electronic, and Precision

47.05   Stationary Energy Sources Installers and Operators

A group of instructional programs that prepare individuals to install, operate, and maintain large power sources for such purposes as generating electricity, pumping, and heating.

47.0501   Stationary Energy Sources Installer and Operator

An instructional program that prepares individuals to apply technical knowledge and skills to install, repair, operate, and maintain large power sources for such purposes as generating electricity, pumping, and heating.

21911L	Pressure Vessel Inspectors
58005	Dispatchers—except Police, Fire, and Ambulance
83002D	Electrical and Electronic Inspectors and Testers
83005A	Production Inspectors, Testers, Graders, Sorters, Samplers, and Weighers
83005B	Construction Checkers
85118	Machinery Maintenance Mechanics, Water or Power Generation Plants
85119A	Machinery Maintenance Mechanics
85714A	Electric Motor and Switch Assemblers and Repairers
85714C	Transformer Repairers
85721	Powerhouse, Substation, and Relay Electricians
85928A	Valve and Regulator Repairers
85928D	Utilities Representatives
87899D	Construction Workers, except Trade
92926	Boiler Operators and Tenders, Low-Pressure
95005A	Gas Processing Plant Operators
95005B	Gas Distribution Plant Operators
95011	Petroleum Pump System Operators
95014	Petroleum Refinery and Control Panel Operators
95017	Gaugers
95021	Power Generating Plant Operators, except Auxiliary Equipment Operators
95023	Auxiliary Equipment Operators, Power
95028	Power Distributors and Dispatchers
95032	Stationary Engineers
97914	Main-Line Station Engineers
97917	Gas Pumping Station Operators
97921	Gas Compressor Operators
97953	Pump Operators

47.06 Vehicle and Mobile Equipment Mechanics and Repairers

A group of instructional programs that prepare individuals to apply technical knowledge and skills to maintain and repair aircraft, land vehicles, ships, construction equipment, and portable power equipment.

47.0603 Auto/Automotive Body Repairer

An instructional program that prepares individuals to apply technical knowledge and skills to repair, reconstruct, and finish automobile bodies, fenders, and external features. Includes instruction in all phases of bodywork preparation and finishing.

83002B	Mechanical Inspectors
83005A	Production Inspectors, Testers, Graders, Sorters, Samplers, and Weighers

85305A	Automotive Glass Installers and Repairers
85305B	Automotive Body Repairers
85305C	Truck and Trailer Body Repairers
85305D	Automotive Body Repair Estimators
85998	Product Repairers
92947	Painters, Transportation Equipment
93947E	Hand Painting, Coating, or Decorating Workers
93953	Grinding and Polishing Workers, Hand
93956	Assemblers and Fabricators—except Machine, Electrical, Electronic, and Precision

47.0604   Auto/Automotive Mechanic/Technician

An instructional program that prepares individuals to apply technical knowledge and skills to repair, service, and maintain all types of automobiles, trucks, vans and buses. Includes instruction in the diagnosis of malfunctions in and repair of engines; fuel, electrical, cooling, and brake systems; and drive train and suspension systems.

83002A	Materials Inspectors
83002B	Mechanical Inspectors
83005A	Production Inspectors, Testers, Graders, Sorters, Samplers, and Weighers
83008C	Automobile and Truck Inspectors
85302A	Automotive Master Mechanics
85302B	Automotive Specialty Technicians
85311A	Bus and Truck Mechanics and Diesel Engine Specialists
85714A	Electric Motor and Switch Assemblers and Repairers
85728B	Ground Transportation Electricians

47.0605   Diesel Engine Mechanic and Repairer

An instructional program that prepares individuals to apply technical knowledge and skills to repair, service, and maintain diesel engines in vehicles such as automobiles, buses, ships, trucks, railroad locomotives, and construction equipment; as well as stationary diesel engines in electrical generators and related equipment.

83002A	Materials Inspectors
83002B	Mechanical Inspectors
83008C	Automobile and Truck Inspectors
85311A	Bus and Truck Mechanics and Diesel Engine Specialists
85311B	Diesel Engine Erectors

47.0606   Small Engine Mechanic and Repairer

An instructional program that prepares individuals to apply technical knowledge and skills to repair, service, and maintain small internal-combustion engines used on portable power equipment such as lawnmowers, chain saws, rotary tillers, and snow-mobiles.

83005A	Production Inspectors, Testers, Graders, Sorters, Samplers, and Weighers
85328B	Small Engine Mechanics

47.0607   Aircraft Mechanic/Technician Airframe

An instructional program that prepares individuals to apply technical knowledge and skills to repair, service, and maintain all aircraft components other than engines, propellers, avionics, and instruments. Includes instruction in the layout and fabrication of sheet metal, fabric, wood, and other materials into structural members, parts, and fittings, and replacement of damaged or worn parts such as control cables and hydraulic units.

83002A	Materials Inspectors
83002B	Mechanical Inspectors
83002D	Electrical and Electronic Inspectors and Testers
85323A	Aircraft Mechanics
85323B	Aircraft Body and Bonded Structure Repairers
85326	Aircraft Engine Specialists
85728A	Aircraft Electricians
85998	Product Repairers
89599C	Canvas, Nets, and Related Materials Workers
93102B	Aircraft Structure Assemblers, Precision
93102C	Aircraft Systems Assemblers, Precision
93102D	Aircraft Rigging Assemblers
93956	Assemblers and Fabricators—except Machine, Electrical, Electronic, and Precision

47.0608   Aircraft Mechanic/Technician Power Plant

An instructional program that prepares individuals to apply technical knowledge and skills to repair, service, and maintain all types of aircraft power plants and related systems. Instruction includes engine inspection and maintenance, lubrication and cooling, electrical and ignition systems, carburetion, fuels and fuel systems, and propeller and fan assemblies.

31314	Teachers and Instructors—Vocational Education and Training
83002B	Mechanical Inspectors
83005A	Production Inspectors, Testers, Graders, Sorters, Samplers, and Weighers
85323A	Aircraft Mechanics
85326	Aircraft Engine Specialists
85728A	Aircraft Electricians
93102C	Aircraft Systems Assemblers, Precision

| 93111A | Electromechanical Equipment Assemblers—Precision |
| 93111B | Electromechanical Technicians |

47.0609   Aviation Systems and Avionics Maintenance Technologist/Technician

An instructional program that prepares individuals to apply technical knowledge and skills to repair, service, and maintain all types of aircraft operating, control, and electronic systems. Includes instruction in flight instrumentation, aircraft communications and homing systems, radar and other sensory systems, navigation aids, and specialized systems for various types of civilian and military aircraft.

21911K	Aviation Inspectors
83002C	Precision Devices Inspectors and Testers
83002D	Electrical and Electronic Inspectors and Testers
85717A	Electronics Mechanics and Technicians
93944D	Molders and Casters

47.0610   Bicycle Mechanic and Repairer

An instructional program that prepares individuals to apply technical knowledge and skills to repair, service, and maintain bicycles and other human-powered vehicles. Includes instruction in lubrication, adjustments of moving parts, and wheel building.

| 85951 | Bicycle Repairers |
| 93956 | Assemblers and Fabricators—except Machine, Electrical, Electronic, and Precision |

47.0611   Motorcycle Mechanic and Repairer

An instructional program that prepares individuals to apply technical knowledge and skills to repair, service, and maintain motorcycles and other similar powered vehicles. Includes instruction in lubrication and cooling systems, electrical and ignition systems, carburetion, fuel systems, and adjustments of moving parts.

83002B	Mechanical Inspectors
83005A	Production Inspectors, Testers, Graders, Sorters, Samplers, and Weighers
85308	Motorcycle Repairers
93956	Assemblers and Fabricators—except Machine, Electrical, Electronic, and Precision

47.0699   Vehicle and Mobile Equipment Mechanics and Repairers, Other

Any instructional program in vehicle and mobile equipment mechanics and repairers not described above.

47.99   Mechanics and Repairers, Other

A group of instructional programs (see 47.9999).

47.9999   Mechanics and Repairers, Other

Any instructional program in mechanics and repairs not described above.

85132	Maintenance Repairers, General Utility

48.   PRECISION PRODUCTION TRADES

A summary of groups of instructional programs that prepare individuals to apply technical knowledge and skills to create products using techniques of precision craftsmanship or technical illustration.

48.01   Drafting

A group of instructional programs (see 48.0101).

48.0101   Drafting, General

An instructional program that generally prepares individuals to apply technical knowledge and skills to plan and prepare scale pictorial interpretations of engineering and design concepts. Includes instruction in the use of precision drawing instruments, computer-assisted design programs, sketching and illustration, and specification interpretation.

22311A	Cartographers and Photogrammetrists
22511	Mechanical Engineering Technicians and Technologists
22514A	Architectural Drafters
22514B	Electronic Drafters
22514C	Civil Drafters
22514D	Mechanical Drafters
22517	Estimators and Drafters, Utilities
22521B	Mapping Technicians

48.0102   Architectural Drafting

An instructional program that prepares individuals to apply technical knowledge and skills to plan and prepare scale pictorial interpretations of plans and design concepts for buildings or other structures. Includes instruction in creating layouts and designs, architectural blueprints and renderings, and in the use of computer-assisted design programs.

22514A	Architectural Drafters

48.0103　Civil/Structural Drafting

An instructional program that prepares individuals to apply technical knowledge and skills to plan and prepare scale pictorial interpretations of plans and design concepts for construction projects, including topographical profiles, related maps, and specifications sheets for use by civil engineers and other land-use-planning specialists. Includes instruction in performing all stages of design illustration and interpretation from initial concept to prototype, and the use of computer-assisted design programs.

22311A	Cartographers and Photogrammetrists
22514A	Architectural Drafters
22514C	Civil Drafters
22517	Estimators and Drafters, Utilities
22521B	Mapping Technicians

48.0104　Electrical/Electronics Drafting

An instructional program that prepares individuals to apply technical knowledge and skills to plan and prepare scale pictorial interpretations of plans and design concepts for wiring diagrams and schematics used by electrical/electronics engineers, electrical contractors, and repairers to plan, install, and modify electrical equipment and systems. Includes instruction in performing all stages of design illustration and interpretation from initial concept to prototype, and the use of computer-assisted design programs.

22514B	Electronic Drafters
22514D	Mechanical Drafters
22517	Estimators and Drafters, Utilities

48.0105　Mechanical Drafting

An instructional program that prepares individuals to apply technical knowledge and skills to plan and prepare scale pictorial interpretations of plans and design concepts for mechanical devices and machinery, including vehicles and other major systems. Includes instruction in performing all stages of design illustration and interpretation from initial concept to prototype, and the use of computer-assisted design programs.

22511	Mechanical Engineering Technicians and Technologists
22514D	Mechanical Drafters

48.0199　Drafting, Other

Any instructional program in drafting not described above.

48.02　Graphic and Printing Equipment Operators

A group of instructional programs (see 48.0201).

48.0201   Graphic and Printing Equipment Operator, General

An instructional program that generally prepares individuals to apply technical knowledge and skills to plan, prepare, and execute commercial and industrial visual image and print products using mechanical, electronic, and digital graphic and printing equipment.

56021	Data Keyers, Composing
58008	Production, Planning, and Expediting Clerks
83005A	Production Inspectors, Testers, Graders, Sorters, Samplers, and Weighers
89128	Precision Etchers and Engravers, Hand or Machine
89702	Hand Compositors and Typesetters
89705	Job Printers
89707	Electronic Pagination System Operators
89712	Photoengravers
89713	Camera Operators
89715	Scanner Operators
89717	Strippers
89718	Platemakers
89719A	Dot Etchers
89719B	Electronic Masking System Operators
89799A	Precision Printing Workers
89799B	Electrotypers and Stereotypers
89911E	Tracers and Letterers
91911	Metal Molding, Coremaking, and Casting Machine Operators and Tenders
92512	Offset Lithographic Press Setters and Set-Up Operators
92515	Letterpress Setters and Set-Up Operators
92522A	Design Printing Machine Setters and Set-Up Operators
92522B	Marking and Identification Printing Machine Setters and Set-Up Operators
92524	Screen Printing Machine Setters and Set-Up Operators
92529A	Embossing Machine Set-Up Operators
92529B	Casting Machine Set-Up Operators
92529C	Plate Finishers
92529D	Engraver Set-Up Operators
92541	Typesetting and Composing Machine Operators and Tenders
92543	Printing Press Machine Operators and Tenders
92545	Photoengraving and Lithographing Machine Operators and Tenders
92908	Photographic Processing Machine Operators and Tenders
93951B	Etchers, Hand
93997	Intermediate Hand Workers

48.0205   Mechanical Typesetter and Composer

An instructional program that prepares individuals to apply technical knowledge and skills to lay out, compose, and make up typesetting and typecast, by hand and by machine.

56021	Data Keyers, Composing
58008	Production, Planning, and Expediting Clerks
89128	Precision Etchers and Engravers, Hand or Machine
89702	Hand Compositors and Typesetters
89705	Job Printers
89707	Electronic Pagination System Operators
89799A	Precision Printing Workers
89799B	Electrotypers and Stereotypers
92529A	Embossing Machine Set-Up Operators
92529B	Casting Machine Set-Up Operators
92541	Typesetting and Composing Machine Operators and Tenders

48.0206   Lithographer and Platemaker

An instructional program that prepares individuals to apply technical knowledge and skills to make prints from chemically prepared stone or metal plane surfaces. Includes instruction in platemaking, stripping, lithographic photography, and related processes.

83005A	Production Inspectors, Testers, Graders, Sorters, Samplers, and Weighers
89707	Electronic Pagination System Operators
89712	Photoengravers
89713	Camera Operators
89715	Scanner Operators
89717	Strippers
89718	Platemakers
89719A	Dot Etchers
89719B	Electronic Masking System Operators
89799A	Precision Printing Workers
91911	Metal Molding, Coremaking, and Casting Machine Operators and Tenders
92529C	Plate Finishers
92529D	Engraver Set-Up Operators
92545	Photoengraving and Lithographing Machine Operators and Tenders
92908	Photographic Processing Machine Operators and Tenders
93951B	Etchers, Hand

48.0208   Printing Press Operator

An instructional program that prepares individuals to apply technical knowledge and skills to make ready, operate, and maintain printing presses.

83005A	Production Inspectors, Testers, Graders, Sorters, Samplers, and Weighers
89799A	Precision Printing Workers
92512	Offset Lithographic Press Setters and Set-Up Operators
92515	Letterpress Setters and Set-Up Operators
92522A	Design Printing Machine Setters and Set-Up Operators
92522B	Marking and Identification Printing Machine Setters and Set-Up Operators
92524	Screen Printing Machine Setters and Set-Up Operators
92529A	Embossing Machine Set-Up Operators
92543	Printing Press Machine Operators and Tenders
93997	Intermediate Hand Workers

48.0211   Computer Typography and Composition Equipment Operator

An instructional program that prepares individuals to apply technical knowledge and skills to design and execute page formats, layouts, and text composition, and to make typographical selections using computer graphics and other computer-assisted design programs.

56021	Data Keyers, Composing
89707	Electronic Pagination System Operators
89799A	Precision Printing Workers
89911E	Tracers and Letterers
92541	Typesetting and Composing Machine Operators and Tenders

48.0212   Desktop Publishing Equipment Operator

An instructional program that prepares individuals to apply technical knowledge and skills to plan and execute entire publication tasks using desktop publishing equipment and software, including designing, printing, and binding.

89799A	Precision Printing Workers

48.0299   Graphic and Printing Equipment Operators, Other

Any instructional program in graphic and printing equipment operation not described above.

83005A	Production Inspectors, Testers, Graders, Sorters, Samplers, and Weighers
89712	Photoengravers
89721	Bookbinders

92524	Screen Printing Machine Setters and Set-Up Operators
92525	Bindery Machine Setters and Set-Up Operators
92543	Printing Press Machine Operators and Tenders
92545	Photoengraving and Lithographing Machine Operators and Tenders
92546	Bindery Machine Operators and Tenders
92956	Cementing and Gluing Machine Operators and Tenders
93923B	Sewers, Hand
93951C	Printers, Hand
93956	Assemblers and Fabricators—except Machine, Electrical, Electronic, and Precision

48.03   Leatherworkers and Upholsterers

A group of instructional programs that prepare individuals to apply technical knowledge and skills to fabricate and repair all types of upholstery and leather goods.

48.0303   Upholsterers

An instructional program that prepares individuals to apply technical knowledge and skills to install springs, filling, padding, covering, and finishing on items such as furniture, automobile seats, caskets, mattresses, and bedsprings.

49999B	Home Furnishings Estimators
83005A	Production Inspectors, Testers, Graders, Sorters, Samplers, and Weighers
89508	Upholsterers
92721	Sewing Machine Operators, Nongarment
93956	Assemblers and Fabricators—except Machine, Electrical, Electronic, and Precision
93997	Intermediate Hand Workers
93998	Elemental Hand Workers

48.0304   Shoe, Boot, and Leather Repairer

An instructional program that prepares individuals to apply technical knowledge and skills to repair all types of footwear, including replacement and mending of worn parts; repairing orthopedic footwear; refinishing and dyeing leather; and repairing other leather goods such as handbags, belts, and luggage.

83005A	Production Inspectors, Testers, Graders, Sorters, Samplers, and Weighers
89502A	Fabric and Apparel Patternmakers
89511	Shoe and Leather Workers and Repairers—Precision
92723	Shoe Sewing Machine Operators and Tenders
93926E	Cutters and Trimmers, Hand

| 93956 | Assemblers and Fabricators—except Machine, Electrical, Electronic, and Precision |
| 93997 | Intermediate Hand Workers |

48.0399   Leatherworkers and Upholsterers, Other

Any instructional program in leatherworking and upholstering not described above.

83005A	Production Inspectors, Testers, Graders, Sorters, Samplers, and Weighers
89511	Shoe and Leather Workers and Repairers—Precision
89599E	Fur Dressers
93926E	Cutters and Trimmers, Hand
93956	Assemblers and Fabricators—except Machine, Electrical, Electronic, and Precision
93997	Intermediate Hand Workers

48.05   Precision Metal Workers

A group of instructional programs (see 48.0501).

48.0501   Machinist/Machine Technologist

An instructional program that prepares individuals to apply technical knowledge and skills to plan, manufacture, assemble, test, and repair parts, mechanisms, machines, and structures in which materials are cast, formed, shaped, molded, heat treated, cut, twisted, pressed, fused, stamped, or worked.

25111	Programmers—Numerical, Tool, and Process Control
49005D	Sales Representatives, Mechanical Equipment and Supplies
81008	First-Line Supervisors and Manager/Supervisors—Production and Operating Workers
83002A	Materials Inspectors
83005A	Production Inspectors, Testers, Graders, Sorters, Samplers, and Weighers
83005B	Construction Checkers
85119B	Machinery Maintenance Repairers
85302B	Automotive Specialty Technicians
85998	Product Repairers
85999C	Blacksmiths
87899K	Ornamental Iron Workers
89102	Tool and Die Makers
89108	Machinists
89114A	Model Makers, Metal and Plastic
89114B	Pattern Makers, Metal and Plastic

89117	Precision Layout Workers, Metal
89126C	Model and Mold Makers, Jewelry
89126K	Pewter Casters and Finishers
89905B	Molders and Casters, Nonferrous Metals
89908A	Patternmakers and Model Builders
89908B	Cutters and Layout Workers
91102	Sawing Machine Tool Setters and Set-Up Operators, Metal and Plastic
91105	Lathe and Turning Machine Tool Setters and Set-Up Operators, Metal and Plastic
91108	Drilling and Boring Machine Tool Setters and Set-Up Operators, Metal and Plastic
91111	Milling and Planing Machine Setters and Set-Up Operators, Metal and Plastic
91114A	Grinding, Honing, Lapping, and Deburring Machine Set-Up Operators
91114B	Buffing and Polishing Set-Up Operators
91302	Punching Machine Setters and Set-Up Operators, Metal and Plastic
91305	Press and Press Brake Machine Setters and Set-Up Operators, Metal and Plastic
91308	Shear and Slitter Machine Setters and Set-Up Operators, Metal and Plastic
91311	Extruding and Drawing Machine Setters and Set-Up Operators, Metal and Plastic
91314	Rolling Machine Setters and Set-Up Operators, Metal and Plastic
91317	Forging Machine Setters and Set-Up Operators, Metal and Plastic
91505	Combination Machine Tool Setters and Set-Up Operators, Metal and Plastic
91714	Metal Fabricators, Structural Metal Products
91928	Heating Equipment Setters and Set-Up Operators, Metal and Plastic
92941A	Fiber Product Machine Cutters
92951	Coating, Painting, and Spraying Machine Setters and Set-Up Operators
93944D	Molders and Casters
93956	Assemblers and Fabricators—except Machine, Electrical, Electronic, and Precision
93997	Intermediate Hand Workers
93998	Elemental Hand Workers

48.0503   Machine Shop Assistant

An instructional program that prepares individuals to apply technical knowledge and skills to fabricate and modify metal parts in support of other manufacturing, repair, or design activities, or as an independent business.

83002A	Materials Inspectors
83002C	Precision Devices Inspectors and Testers
83005A	Production Inspectors, Testers, Graders, Sorters, Samplers, and Weighers
87714B	Rail-Track Maintenance Workers
89105	Precision Instrument Makers
89108	Machinists
89111	Tool Grinders, Filers, Sharpeners, and Other Precision Grinders
89114A	Model Makers, Metal and Plastic
89117	Precision Layout Workers, Metal
89908A	Patternmakers and Model Builders
91117	Machine Tool Cutting Operators and Tenders, Metal and Plastic
91321	Machine Forming Operators and Tenders, Metal and Plastic
91502	Numerical Control Machine Tool Operators and Tenders, Metal and Plastic
91508	Combination Machine Tool Operators and Tenders, Metal and Plastic
91932	Heat Treating, Annealing, and Tempering Machine Operators and Tenders, Metal and Plastic
91935	Furnace Operators and Tenders
92971	Extruding, Forming, Pressing, and Compacting Machine Operators and Tenders
93108	Fitters, Structural Metal—Precision
93926E	Cutters and Trimmers, Hand
93947E	Hand Painting, Coating, or Decorating Workers
93953	Grinding and Polishing Workers, Hand
93956	Assemblers and Fabricators—except Machine, Electrical, Electronic, and Precision
93997	Intermediate Hand Workers
93998	Elemental Hand Workers

48.0506   Sheet Metal Worker

An instructional program that prepares individuals to apply technical knowledge and skills to form, shape, bend, and fold extruded metals, including the creation of new products, using hand tools and machines such as cornice brakes, forming rolls, and squaring shears.

83005A	Production Inspectors, Testers, Graders, Sorters, Samplers, and Weighers
89132	Sheet-Metal Workers
91302	Punching Machine Setters and Set-Up Operators, Metal and Plastic
91305	Press and Press Brake Machine Setters and Set-Up Operators, Metal and Plastic
91308	Shear and Slitter Machine Setters and Set-Up Operators, Metal and Plastic

| 91314 | Rolling Machine Setters and Set-Up Operators, Metal and Plastic |
| 91321 | Machine Forming Operators and Tenders, Metal and Plastic |

48.0507   Tool and Die Maker/Technologist

An instructional program that prepares individuals to apply technical knowledge and skills to operate machine tools used in the forming of metal components, as well as the fabrication of special tools, dies, jigs, and fixtures used in cutting, working, and finishing metal components.

83002A	Materials Inspectors
83005A	Production Inspectors, Testers, Graders, Sorters, Samplers, and Weighers
85119A	Machinery Maintenance Mechanics
89102	Tool and Die Makers
89111	Tool Grinders, Filers, Sharpeners, and Other Precision Grinders
89114B	Pattern Makers, Metal and Plastic
89908A	Patternmakers and Model Builders
91114A	Grinding, Honing, Lapping, and Deburring Machine Set-Up Operators
91317	Forging Machine Setters and Set-Up Operators, Metal and Plastic
91505	Combination Machine Tool Setters and Set-Up Operators, Metal and Plastic
93953	Grinding and Polishing Workers, Hand

48.0508   Welder/Welding Technologist

An instructional program that prepares individuals to apply technical knowledge and skills to unite or separate metal parts by heating, using a variety of techniques and equipment, such as brazing, arc, gas, and laser operations.

49005D	Sales Representatives, Mechanical Equipment and Supplies
83002A	Materials Inspectors
83005A	Production Inspectors, Testers, Graders, Sorters, Samplers, and Weighers
83005B	Construction Checkers
91702	Welding Machine Setters and Set-Up Operators
91705	Welding Machine Operators and Tenders
91708	Soldering and Brazing Machine Setters and Set-Up Operators
91711	Soldering and Brazing Machine Operators and Tenders
93914A	Welders, Production
93914B	Welders and Cutters
93914C	Welder-Fitters
93917A	Solderers
93917B	Brazers
93953	Grinding and Polishing Workers, Hand

48.0599   Precision Metal Workers, Other

Any instructional program in precision metal work not described above.

83002A	Materials Inspectors
83005A	Production Inspectors, Testers, Graders, Sorters, Samplers, and Weighers
85999A	Hand and Portable Power Tool Repairers
85999C	Blacksmiths
89902	Precision Foundry Mold and Core Makers
89905B	Molders and Casters, Nonferrous Metals
91314	Rolling Machine Setters and Set-Up Operators, Metal and Plastic
91321	Machine Forming Operators and Tenders, Metal and Plastic
91908	Metal Molding, Coremaking, and Casting Machine Setters and Set-Up Operators
91911	Metal Molding, Coremaking, and Casting Machine Operators and Tenders
91917	Electrolytic Plating and Coating Machine Setters and Set-Up Operators, Metal and Plastic
91921	Electrolytic Plating and Coating Machine Operators and Tenders, Metal and Plastic
91923	Nonelectrolytic Plating and Coating Machine Setters and Set-Up Operators, Metal and Plastic
91926	Nonelectrolytic Plating and Coating Machine Operators and Tenders, Metal and Plastic
91932	Heat Treating, Annealing, and Tempering Machine Operators and Tenders, Metal and Plastic
91935	Furnace Operators and Tenders
91938	Heaters, Metal and Plastic
92935	Chemical Equipment Controllers and Operators
92941A	Fiber Product Machine Cutters
92951	Coating, Painting, and Spraying Machine Setters and Set-Up Operators
93941	Metal Pourers and Casters, Basic Shapes
93953	Grinding and Polishing Workers, Hand
93997	Intermediate Hand Workers

48.07   Woodworkers

A group of instructional programs that prepare individuals to apply technical knowledge and skills to lay out, shape, assemble, finish, and repair articles made of wood.

48.0701   Woodworker, General

An instructional program that prepares individuals to apply technical knowledge and skills to lay out and shape stock; assemble wooden articles or subassemblies; mark, bind, saw, carve, and sand wooden products; repair wooden articles; and use a variety of hand and power tools.

21911A	Health Officers and Inspectors
83005A	Production Inspectors, Testers, Graders, Sorters, Samplers, and Weighers
89302A	Pattern Makers, Wood
89302C	Jig Builders
89305	Woodworking Layout Workers
89308	Wood Machinists
89311	Cabinetmakers and Bench Carpenters
89314	Furniture Finishers
89397B	Custom Precision Woodworkers
89398	Standard Precision Woodworkers
92302	Sawing Machine Setters and Set-Up Operators
92305	Head Sawyers
92308	Sawing Machine Operators and Tenders
92311	Woodworking Machine Setters and Set-Up Operators, except Sawing
92314	Woodworking Machine Operators and Tenders, except Sawing
93953	Grinding and Polishing Workers, Hand
93956	Assemblers and Fabricators—except Machine, Electrical, Electronic, and Precision

48.0702   Furniture Designer and Maker

An instructional program that prepares individuals to apply technical knowledge and skills to prepare and execute furniture design projects; assemble and finish furniture articles or subassemblies; repair furniture; and use a variety of hand and power tools.

21911A	Health Officers and Inspectors
83005A	Production Inspectors, Testers, Graders, Sorters, Samplers, and Weighers
89302A	Pattern Makers, Wood
89314	Furniture Finishers
89397B	Custom Precision Woodworkers
93953	Grinding and Polishing Workers, Hand
93956	Assemblers and Fabricators—except Machine, Electrical, Electronic, and Precision

48.0703   Cabinet Maker and Millworker

An instructional program that prepares individuals to apply technical knowledge and skills to set up, operate, and repair industrial woodworking machinery, and to use such machinery to design and fabricate wooden components and complete articles.

89302A	Pattern Makers, Wood
89302C	Jig Builders

89305	Woodworking Layout Workers
89308	Wood Machinists
89311	Cabinetmakers and Bench Carpenters
89398	Standard Precision Woodworkers
92302	Sawing Machine Setters and Set-Up Operators
92305	Head Sawyers
92308	Sawing Machine Operators and Tenders
92311	Woodworking Machine Setters and Set-Up Operators, except Sawing
92314	Woodworking Machine Operators and Tenders, except Sawing
93956	Assemblers and Fabricators—except Machine, Electrical, Electronic, and Precision

48.0799   Woodworkers, Other

Any instructional program in woodworking not described above.

93953	Grinding and Polishing Workers, Hand

48.99   Precision Production Trades, Other

A group of instructional programs (see 48.9999).

48.9999   Precision Production Trades, Other

Any instructional programs in precision production not described above.

83002A	Materials Inspectors
83005A	Production Inspectors, Testers, Graders, Sorters, Samplers, and Weighers
89908A	Patternmakers and Model Builders
89908C	Model and Mold Makers
92941A	Fiber Product Machine Cutters
92951	Coating, Painting, and Spraying Machine Setters and Set-Up Operators
92968	Extruding, Forming, Pressing, and Compacting Machine Setters and Set-Up Operators
93944A	Mold Makers, Hand
93944D	Molders and Casters
93997	Intermediate Hand Workers

49. TRANSPORTATION AND MATERIALS MOVING WORKERS

A summary of groups of instructional programs that prepare individuals to apply technical knowledge and skills to perform tasks and services that facilitate the movement of people or materials.

49.01   Air Transportation Workers

A group of instructional programs that prepare individuals to apply technical knowledge and skills to provide in-flight, ground, and administrative services to the aviation industry.

49.0101   Aviation and Airway Science

An instructional program that generally describes the study of aviation and the aviation industry, including in-flight and ground support operations. Includes instruction in the technical, business, and general aspects of air transportation systems.

49.0102   Aircraft Pilot and Navigator (Professional)

An instructional program that prepares individuals to apply technical knowledge and skills to the flying and/or navigation of commercial passenger and cargo, agricultural, public service, corporate, and rescue aircraft. Includes instruction in principles of aircraft design and performance, aircraft flight systems and controls, flight crew operations and procedures, radio communications and navigation procedures and systems, airways safety and traffic regulations, and governmental rules and regulations pertaining to piloting aircraft. Programs may qualify individuals to sit for the FAA commercial aircrew examinations.

21911D	Licensing Examiners and Inspectors
21911K	Aviation Inspectors
63014B	Highway Patrol Pilots
97702B	Airplane Pilots, Commercial
97702C	Small Airplane Pilots
97702D	Flight Instructors
97702E	Flight Navigators
97702H	Flight Engineers
97702J	Helicopter Pilots

49.0104   Aviation Management

An instructional program that prepares individuals to apply technical knowledge and skills to the management of aviation industry operations and services. Includes instruction in airport operations, ground support and flightline operations, passenger and cargo operations, flight safety and security operations, aviation industry regulations, and related business aspects of managing aviation enterprises.

| 15023A | Transportation Managers |

49.0105   Air Traffic Controller

An instructional program that prepares individuals to apply technical knowledge and skills to air traffic management and control, usually with additional training at the FAA

Flight Control Center in a cooperative education program. Includes instruction in flight control, the use of radar and electronic scanning devices, plotting of flights, radio communication, interpretation of weather conditions affecting flights, flight instrumentation used by pilots, and maintenance of flight-control center or control-tower log books.

39002	Airplane Dispatchers and Air Traffic Controllers

49.0106   Flight Attendant

An instructional program that prepares individuals to apply technical knowledge and skills to the performance of a variety of personal services conducive to the safety and comfort of airline passengers during flight, including verifying tickets, explaining the use of safety equipment, providing passenger services, and responding to in-flight emergencies.

53805	Reservation and Transportation Ticket Agents
61099C	First-Line Supervisors/Hospitality and Personal Service Workers
68026	Flight Attendants

49.0107   Aircraft Pilot (Private)

An instructional program that prepares individuals to fly aircraft for personal use, and qualifies individuals to sit for the FAA pilot's license examination. Includes instruction in principles of aircraft design and performance, aircraft flight systems and controls, flight crew operations and procedures, radio communications and navigation procedures and systems, airways safety and traffic regulations, and governmental rules and regulations pertaining to piloting aircraft.

49.0199   Air Transportation Workers, Other

Any instructional program in aviation and air transportation services not described above.

97899A	Airport Utility Workers

49.02   Vehicle and Equipment Operators

A group of instructional programs that prepare individuals to apply technical knowledge and skills to operate commercial and construction vehicles and mobile equipment.

49.0202   Construction Equipment Operator

An instructional program that prepares individuals to apply technical knowledge and skills to operate and maintain a variety of heavy equipment, such as crawler tractors, motor graders and scrapers, and shovels, including draglines, hoes, and cranes. Includes instruction in digging, ditching, sloping, stripping, grading, backfilling, clearing, and excavating.

49005D	Sales Representatives, Mechanical Equipment and Supplies
85935	Riggers
87705	Pile Driving Operators
87708	Paving, Surfacing, and Tamping Equipment Operators
87714A	Rail-Track Laying and Maintenance Equipment Operators
87714B	Rail-Track Maintenance Workers
87899E	Concrete and Utility Cutters and Drillers
87899G	Hydraulic Jack Setters and Operators
87899H	Pipeline Maintenance Workers
87902A	Construction Drillers
87902B	Well and Core Drill Operators
87905	Blasters and Explosives Workers
87943	Mine Cutting and Channeling Machine Operators
87949A	Mining Machine Operators and Tenders
97399A	On-Track Mobile Equipment Operators
97399B	Railroad Control Tower Switching and Car Retarding Operators
97923A	Excavating and Loading Machine Operators
97926	Dragline Operators
97928	Dredge Operators
97938	Grader, Bulldozer, and Scraper Operators
97941	Hoist and Winch Operators
97944	Crane and Tower Operators
97956	Operating Engineers

49.0205   Truck, Bus, and Other Commercial Vehicle Operator

An instructional program that prepares individuals to apply technical knowledge and skills to drive trucks and buses, delivery vehicles, for-hire vehicles, and other commercial vehicles. Includes instruction in operating gas, diesel, or electrically powered vehicles; loading and unloading cargo or passengers; reporting delays or accidents on the road; verifying load against shipping papers; arranging transportation for personnel; and keeping records of receipts and fares.

31314	Teachers and Instructors—Vocational Education and Training
97102A	Truck Drivers, Heavy
97102B	Tractor-Trailer Truck Drivers
97105	Truck Drivers, Light—Including Delivery and Route Workers
97108	Bus Drivers
97111	Bus Drivers, School
97114	Taxi Drivers and Chauffeurs

49.0299 Vehicle and Equipment Operators, Other

Any instructional program in vehicle and equipment operation not described above.

87902A	Construction Drillers
87905	Blasters and Explosives Workers
87908	Rock Splitters, Quarry
87911	Rotary Drill Operators, Oil and Gas Extraction
87914	Derrick Operators, Oil and Gas Extraction
87917	Service Unit Operators
87923	Roof Bolters
87941	Continuous Mining Machine Operators
87943	Mine Cutting and Channeling Machine Operators
87949A	Mining Machine Operators and Tenders
87989A	Miners and Petroleum and Gas Extractive Workers
97308	Rail Yard Engineers, Dinkey Operators, and Hostlers
97314	Subway and Streetcar Operators
97399A	On-Track Mobile Equipment Operators
97902	Longshore Equipment Operators
97923A	Excavating and Loading Machine Operators
97926	Dragline Operators
97932	Loading Machine Operators, Underground Mining
97935	Shuttle Car Operators
97941	Hoist and Winch Operators
97944	Crane and Tower Operators
97951	Conveyor Operators and Tenders
97953	Pump Operators
97956	Operating Engineers

49.03 Water Transportation Workers

A group of instructional programs that prepare individuals to apply technical knowledge and skills to perform tasks on or in the water, including diving, fishing, and ship operation and repair services.

49.0303 Fishing Technology/Commercial Fishing

An instructional program that prepares individuals to apply technical knowledge and skills to function as commercial fishermen, fishing operations supervisors, or in related fishing industry operations. Includes instruction in fishing vessel operation; fishing equipment operation and maintenance; equipment repair; catch identification, sorting, and storage; safety procedures; recordkeeping; and applicable legal regulations.

79999E	Commercial Fishery Workers
97502A	Ship and Boat Captains
97505	Mates—Ship, Boat, and Barge

49.0304   Diver (Professional)

An instructional program that prepares individuals to apply technical knowledge and skills to function as professional deep-water or scuba divers, diving instructors, or diving support personnel. Includes instruction in the use of diving equipment and related specialized gear; diving safety procedures; operation and maintenance of underwater life-support systems; underwater communication systems; decompression systems; underwater salvage; exploration, rescue, and photography; and installation of underwater mechanical systems and their maintenance, repair or demolition.

24599A	Meteorological Technicians
34056D	Amusement Entertainers

49.0306   Marine Maintenance and Ship Repairer

An instructional program that prepares individuals to apply technical knowledge and skills to repair outboard and inboard engines; test, maintain, and repair steering devices and electrical systems; repair metal, wood, and fiberglass hulls and vessel components; fabricate and maintain sails; and repair and balance propellers and drive shafts.

83002A	Materials Inspectors
83005A	Production Inspectors, Testers, Graders, Sorters, Samplers, and Weighers
85116A	Marine Machinists, Maintenance
85116B	Marine Engine Mechanics
85116C	Marine Services Technicians
85328A	Motorboat Mechanics
85935	Riggers
85956A	Textile Menders
87102E	Boat and Ship Builders
87102F	Ship Carpenters and Joiners
87202A	Electricians
87402A	Painters, Construction and Maintenance
89121	Shipfitters
89502A	Fabric and Apparel Patternmakers
89599C	Canvas, Nets, and Related Materials Workers
93926E	Cutters and Trimmers, Hand
93956	Assemblers and Fabricators—except Machine, Electrical, Electronic, and Precision
97517	Ordinary Seamen and Marine Oilers

49.0309   Marine Science/Merchant Marine Officer

An instructional program that prepares individuals to serve as captains, executive officers, engineers, and ranking mates on commercially licensed inland, coastal, and ocean-going vessels. Includes instruction in maritime traditions and law; maritime policy; economics and management of commercial marine operations; basic naval architecture and engineering; shipboard power systems engineering; crew supervision; and administrative procedures.

81011	First-Line Supervisors and Manager/Supervisors—Transportation and Material Moving Machine and Vehicle Operators
85116A	Marine Machinists, Maintenance
97502A	Ship and Boat Captains
97505	Mates—Ship, Boat, and Barge
97508	Pilots, Ship
97521	Ship Engineers

49.0399   Water Transportation Workers, Other

Any instructional program in water transportation not described above.

58005	Dispatchers—except Police, Fire, and Ambulance
97502A	Ship and Boat Captains
97505	Mates—Ship, Boat, and Barge
97511	Motorboat Operators
97514	Able Seamen
97517	Ordinary Seamen and Marine Oilers
97928	Dredge Operators

49.99   Transportation and Materials Moving Workers, Other

A group of instructional programs (see 49.9999).

49.9999   Transportation and Materials Moving Workers, Other

Any instructional program in transportation and materials moving not described above.

50.   VISUAL AND PERFORMING ARTS

A summary of groups of instructional programs that describe the creation and interpretation of works and performances that use auditory, kinesthetic, and visual phenomena to express ideas and emotions in various forms, subject to aesthetic criteria.

50.01   Visual and Performing Arts

A group of instructional programs (see 50.0101).

50.0101   Visual and Performing Arts

An instructional program that generally describes an undifferentiated program in the visual and performing arts, and that may prepare individuals in any of the visual artistic media or performing disciplines.

50.02   Crafts, Folk Art, and Artisanry

A group of instructional programs (see 50.0201).

50.0201   Crafts, Folk Art, and Artisanry

An instructional program that describes the aesthetics, techniques, and creative processes for designing and fashioning objects in one or more of the handcraft or folk art traditions, and that prepares individuals to create in any of these media.

19999A	Amusement and Recreation Establishment Managers
31218	Art, Drama, and Music Teachers—Postsecondary
31511D	Museum Technicians and Conservators
31511E	Craft Demonstrators
34035D	Cartoonists and Animators
89123A	Jewelers
89123B	Silversmiths
89314	Furniture Finishers
89397B	Custom Precision Woodworkers
89511	Shoe and Leather Workers and Repairers—Precision
89905C	Stone Cutters and Carvers
89905D	Glass Blowers, Molders, Benders, and Finishers
89911C	Engravers/Carvers
93926D	Glass Cutters and Finishers
93944D	Molders and Casters
93956	Assemblers and Fabricators—except Machine, Electrical, Electronic, and Precision
93997	Intermediate Hand Workers

50.03   Dance

A group of instructional programs (see 50.0301).

50.0301   Dance

An instructional program that prepares individuals to express ideas, feelings, and/or inner visions through the performance of one or more of the dance disciplines, including but not limited to ballet, modern, jazz, ethnic, and folk dance, and that describes the study and analysis of dance as a cultural phenomenon. Includes instruction in choreography, labanotation, dance history and criticism, and dance production.

31218	Art, Drama, and Music Teachers—Postsecondary
34053A	Dancers
34053B	Choreographers

50.04 Design and Applied Arts

A group of instructional programs (see 50.0401).

50.0401 Design and Visual Communications

An instructional program in the applied visual arts that describes the general principles and techniques for effectively communicating ideas and information, and packaging products, to business and consumer audiences, and that may prepare individuals in any of the applied art media.

34044	Merchandise Displayers and Window Trimmers

50.0402 Graphic Design, Commercial Art, and Illustration

An instructional program in the applied visual arts that prepares individuals to use artistic techniques to effectively communicate ideas and information to business and consumer audiences via illustrations and other forms of printed media. Includes instruction in concept design, layout, pasteup, and techniques such as engraving, etching, silk screen, lithography, offset, drawing and cartooning, painting, collage, and computer graphics.

34035A	Painters and Illustrators
34035B	Sketch Artists
34035C	Graphic Designers
34035D	Cartoonists and Animators
34038A	Fashion Designers
34038B	Commercial and Industrial Designers
34038D	Exhibit Designers
34038E	Art Directors
89706	Paste-Up Workers
89799A	Precision Printing Workers
89908B	Cutters and Layout Workers
89911A	Precision Painters
89911B	Silk Screen Process Decorators
89911C	Engravers/Carvers
89911E	Tracers and Letterers
89911G	Gilders

89914A	Photographic Retouchers and Restorers
93947E	Hand Painting, Coating, or Decorating Workers
93951A	Pantograph Engravers
93951D	Engravers, Hand

50.0404   Industrial Design

An instructional program in the applied visual arts that prepares individuals to use artistic techniques to effectively communicate ideas and information to business and consumer audiences via the creation of effective forms, shapes, and packaging for manufactured products. Includes instruction in designing in a wide variety of media, prototype construction, design development and refinement, principles of cost-saving, and product structure and performance criteria relevant to aesthetic design parameters.

| 34038B | Commercial and Industrial Designers |
| 89908B | Cutters and Layout Workers |

50.0406   Commercial Photography

An instructional program in the applied visual arts that prepares individuals to use artistic techniques to effectively communicate ideas and information to business and consumer audiences, and recording events and people, via film, still and video photography. Includes instruction in specialized camera and equipment operation and maintenance, applications to commercial and industrial needs, and photography business operations.

34023A	Professional Photographers
34023B	Photographers, Scientific
34026	Camera Operators, Television and Motion Picture
89713	Camera Operators
93998	Elemental Hand Workers

50.0407   Fashion Design and Illustration

An instructional program in the applied visual arts that prepares individuals to apply artistic principles and techniques to the professional design of commercial fashions, apparel, and accessories; the illustration of fashion concepts; and the management of fashion development projects. Includes instruction in apparel design; accessory design; the design of men's, women's, and children's wear; flat pattern design; computer-assisted design; concept planning; designing in specific materials; labor and cost analysis; history of fashion; fabric art and printing; and the principles of management and operations in the fashion industry.

34038A	Fashion Designers
34038B	Commercial and Industrial Designers
89502A	Fabric and Apparel Patternmakers

50.0408   Interior Design

An instructional program in the applied visual arts that prepares individuals to apply artistic principles and techniques to the professional planning, designing, equipping, and furnishing of residential and commercial interior spaces. Includes instruction in drafting and graphic techniques; principles of interior lighting, acoustics, systems integration, and color coordination; furniture and furnishings; textiles and their finishing; the history of interior design and period styles; basic structural design; building codes and inspection regulations; and applications to office, hotel, factory, restaurant and housing design.

34038C	Set Designers
34038D	Exhibit Designers
34041	Interior Designers

50.0499   Design and Applied Arts, Other

Any instructional program in design and applied arts not described above.

50.05   Drama/Theater Arts and Stagecraft

A group of instructional programs that describe the study of drama and the theater, and the professional production and performance of dramatic works.

50.0501   Drama/Theater Arts, General

An instructional program that generally describes the study of dramatic works and their performance. Includes instruction in major works of dramatic literature, dramatic styles and types, and the principles of organizing and producing full productions.

27199E	Historians
31218	Art, Drama, and Music Teachers—Postsecondary
31317	Instructors—Nonvocational Education
34002A	Columnists, Critics, and Commentators
34002C	Creative Writers
34002F	Programming and Script Editors and Coordinators
34035A	Painters and Illustrators
34038C	Set Designers
34038D	Exhibit Designers
34056A	Actors and Performers
34056B	Extras/Stand-Ins
34056F	Producers
34056G	Directors—Stage, Motion Picture, Television, and Radio
34056H	Program Directors
34056J	Talent Directors

| 39999D | Studio, Stage, and Special Effects Technicians |
| 89908A | Patternmakers and Model Builders |

50.0502 Technical Theater/Theater Design and Stagecraft

An instructional program that prepares individuals to apply artistic, technical, and dramatic principles and techniques to the communication of dramatic information, ideas, moods, and feelings through technical theater methods. Includes instruction in set design, lighting design, sound effects, theater acoustics, scene painting, property management, costume design, and technical direction and production.

31218	Art, Drama, and Music Teachers—Postsecondary
34035A	Painters and Illustrators
34038C	Set Designers
34038D	Exhibit Designers
34056F	Producers
34056G	Directors—Stage, Motion Picture, Television, and Radio
39999D	Studio, Stage, and Special Effects Technicians
89908A	Patternmakers and Model Builders

50.0503 Acting and Directing

An instructional program that prepares individuals to communicate dramatic information, ideas, moods, and feelings through the achievement of naturalistic and believable behavior in imaginary circumstances; and to supervise dramatic performance. Includes instruction in voice and acting speech, stage dialects, movement, improvisation, acting styles, theater history, rehearsal management, scene work, directing concepts, script interpretation, and actor coaching.

31218	Art, Drama, and Music Teachers—Postsecondary
31317	Instructors—Nonvocational Education
34056A	Actors and Performers
34056B	Extras/Stand-Ins
34056F	Producers
34056G	Directors—Stage, Motion Picture, Television, and Radio
34056H	Program Directors
34056J	Talent Directors

50.0504 Playwriting and Screenwriting

An instructional program that describes the principles and techniques for communicating dramatic information, ideas, moods, and feelings through the composition of creative written works for the theater and/or film. Includes instruction in creative writing craft, scene writing, script development, stage and/or camera instructions, line and moment analysis, script reading, script editing, and the creation of full productions.

31218	Art, Drama, and Music Teachers—Postsecondary
34002C	Creative Writers
34002F	Programming and Script Editors and Coordinators

50.0505 Drama/Theater Literature, History, and Criticism

An instructional program that describes the study of the history, literature, theory, and analysis of written plays, theatrical productions, and theater methods and organization. Includes instruction in historical method; critical theory; literary analysis; the study of themes and archetypes in dramatic literature; the history of acting, directing, and technical theater; and the study of specific historical and cultural styles and traditions.

27199E	Historians
31218	Art, Drama, and Music Teachers—Postsecondary
34002A	Columnists, Critics, and Commentators

50.0599 Dramatic/Theater Arts and Stagecraft, Other

Any instructional program in dramatic/theater arts and stagecraft not described above.

| 34038C | Set Designers |

50.06 Film/Video and Photographic Arts

A group of instructional programs (see 50.0601).

50.0601 Film/Cinema Studies

An instructional program in the visual arts that describes the study of the history, development, theory, and criticism of the film/video arts, as well as the basic principles of filmmaking and film production.

| 31218 | Art, Drama, and Music Teachers—Postsecondary |
| 34002A | Columnists, Critics, and Commentators |

50.0602 Film—Video Making/Cinematography and Production

An instructional program that prepares individuals to communicate dramatic information, ideas, moods, and feelings through the making and producing of films and videos. Includes instruction in theory of film, film technology and equipment operation, film production, film directing, film editing, cinematographic art, film audio, techniques for making specific types of films and/or videos, and the planning and management of film/video operations.

| 13011A | Advertising and Promotions Managers |
| 31218 | Art, Drama, and Music Teachers—Postsecondary |

34026	Camera Operators, Television and Motion Picture
34032	Film Editors
34056F	Producers
34056G	Directors—Stage, Motion Picture, Television, and Radio
34056H	Program Directors
34056K	Technical Directors/Managers
39999D	Studio, Stage, and Special Effects Technicians

50.0605   Photography

An instructional program that describes the principles and techniques of communicating information, ideas, moods, and feelings through the creation of images on photographic film or plates, and that may prepare individuals to be professional photographic artists. Includes instruction in camera and equipment operation and maintenance, film and plate developing, light and composition, films and printing media, color and special effects, photographic art, photographic history, and applications to the photography of various subjects.

31218	Art, Drama, and Music Teachers—Postsecondary
34023A	Professional Photographers
34023B	Photographers, Scientific
34026	Camera Operators, Television and Motion Picture

50.0699   Film/Video and Photographic Arts, Other

Any instructional program in film/video and photographic arts not described above.

50.07   Fine Arts and Art Studies

A group of instructional programs that prepare individuals as professional studio artists and arts managers, and that describe the study of art.

50.0701   Art, General

An instructional program that generally describes art, including its development and practice. Includes instruction in art appreciation, a basic knowledge of art history, fundamental principles of design and color, and an introduction to various media and studio techniques.

13011D	Fundraising Directors
19005A	Government Service Executives
27199E	Historians
31218	Art, Drama, and Music Teachers—Postsecondary
31511A	Curators

31511B	Archivists
31511C	Museum Research Workers
31511D	Museum Technicians and Conservators
34035A	Painters and Illustrators
34035B	Sketch Artists
34035C	Graphic Designers
34035E	Sculptors
43099B	Fundraisers and Solicitors
49032A	Demonstrators and Promoters
49999A	Merchandise Appraisers and Auctioneers
89123A	Jewelers
89126C	Model and Mold Makers, Jewelry
89126E	Bench Workers, Jewelry
89126K	Pewter Casters and Finishers
89905F	Throwers
89911A	Precision Painters
89911D	Etchers
89926A	Gem and Diamond Workers
93947E	Hand Painting, Coating, or Decorating Workers
93956	Assemblers and Fabricators—except Machine, Electrical, Electronic, and Precision
93997	Intermediate Hand Workers
93998	Elemental Hand Workers

50.0702   Fine/Studio Arts

An instructional program that prepares individuals to function as creative artists in the visual and plastic media. Includes instruction in the traditional fine arts media (drawing, painting, sculpture, printmaking) and/or modern media (ceramics, textiles, intermedia, photography); theory of art; color theory; composition and perspective; anatomy; the techniques and procedures for maintaining equipment and managing a studio; and art portfolio marketing.

31218	Art, Drama, and Music Teachers—Postsecondary
34035A	Painters and Illustrators
34035E	Sculptors

50.0703   Art History, Criticism, and Conservation

An instructional program that describes the study of the historical development of art as a social and intellectual phenomenon, the analysis of works of art, and art conservation. Includes instruction in the theory of art, art history research methods, connoisseurship, the preservation and conservation of works of art, and the study of specific periods, cultures, styles, and themes.

31218	Art, Drama, and Music Teachers—Postsecondary
31511A	Curators
31511B	Archivists
31511C	Museum Research Workers
31511D	Museum Technicians and Conservators

50.0704   Arts Management

An instructional program that prepares individuals to organize and manage art organizations, operations, and facilities. Includes instruction in business and financial management; marketing and fundraising; personnel management and labor relations; event promotion and management; public relations and arts advocacy; arts law; and applications to specific arts activities such as galleries, museums, studios, foundations, and community organizations.

13011D	Fundraising Directors
19005A	Government Service Executives
27199E	Historians
31218	Art, Drama, and Music Teachers—Postsecondary
43099B	Fundraisers and Solicitors
49999A	Merchandise Appraisers and Auctioneers

50.0705   Drawing

An instructional program that prepares individuals creatively and technically to express emotions, ideas, or inner visions through representation by lines made on a surface. Includes instruction in eye-hand coordination; line, value, shape, and perspective; figure and still-life drawing; the use of media such as pen and ink, pencil, charcoal, pastel, and brush; and personal style development.

31218	Art, Drama, and Music Teachers—Postsecondary
34035A	Painters and Illustrators
34035B	Sketch Artists

50.0706   Intermedia

An instructional program that prepares individuals creatively and technically to express emotions, ideas, or inner visions in either two or three dimensions, through simultaneous use of a variety of materials and media.

| 31218 | Art, Drama, and Music Teachers—Postsecondary |

50.0708   Painting

An instructional program that prepares individuals creatively and technically to express emotions, ideas, or inner visions by the application of paints and related chemical color substances to canvases or other materials. Includes instruction in color and color mixing, surface preparation, composition, oil and acrylic media, watercolor media, painting techniques, and personal style development.

31218	Art, Drama, and Music Teachers—Postsecondary
34035A	Painters and Illustrators
34035B	Sketch Artists
49032A	Demonstrators and Promoters

50.0709   Sculpture

An instructional program that prepares individuals creatively and technically to express emotions, ideas, or inner visions by creating three-dimensional artworks. Includes instruction in the analysis of form in space; round and relief concepts; sculptural composition; modern and experimental methods; different media such as clay, plaster, wood, stone, and metal; techniques such as carving, molding, welding, casting, and modeling; and personal style development.

| 31218 | Art, Drama, and Music Teachers—Postsecondary |
| 34035E | Sculptors |

50.0710   Printmaking

An instructional program that prepares individuals creatively and technically to express emotions, ideas, or inner visions by rendering art concepts onto surfaces and transferring images, via ink or dyes, onto paper or fabric. Includes instruction in monochrome and color printing; tonality; chemistry; equipment setup and maintenance; techniques such as serigraphy, lithography, intaglio, woodcut, block, stencil, relief, etching, and composite; and personal style development.

31218	Art, Drama, and Music Teachers—Postsecondary
34035A	Painters and Illustrators
34035C	Graphic Designers

50.0711   Ceramic Arts and Ceramics

An instructional program that prepares individuals creatively and technically to express emotions, ideas, or inner visions by producing artworks out of clay and similar materials. Includes instruction in handbuilt and wheelthrown techniques, molding, slips and glazes, trimming and decorating, firing and kiln operation, oxidation, mixed media, ceramic murals, and personal style development.

| 31218 | Art, Drama, and Music Teachers—Postsecondary |
| 31511D | Museum Technicians and Conservators |

89126E	Bench Workers, Jewelry
89905F	Throwers
89911A	Precision Painters
89911D	Etchers
93947E	Hand Painting, Coating, or Decorating Workers
93956	Assemblers and Fabricators—except Machine, Electrical, Electronic, and Precision
93997	Intermediate Hand Workers
93998	Elemental Hand Workers

50.0712 Fiber, Textile, and Weaving Arts

An instructional program that prepares individuals creatively and technically to express emotions, ideas, or inner visions by constructing artworks from woven or nonwoven fabrics and fibrous materials. Includes instruction in weaving techniques and loom operation; nonwoven techniques such as knitting, coiling, netting, and crocheting; quilting; dyeing and pigmentation; printing and other finishing techniques; pattern design; tapestry; and personal style development.

31218	Art, Drama, and Music Teachers—Postsecondary
49032A	Demonstrators and Promoters
93997	Intermediate Hand Workers
93998	Elemental Hand Workers

50.0713 Metal and Jewelry Arts

An instructional program that prepares individuals creatively and technically to express emotions, ideas, or inner visions by fashioning artworks from gems, other stones, and precious metals. Includes instruction in gemology; metalsmithing and finishing; stone cutting and polishing; metal and nonmetal casting and molding; electroforming; metal coloring; enameling; photo etching; lapidary technique and art; design concepts; and personal style development.

31218	Art, Drama, and Music Teachers—Postsecondary
89123A	Jewelers
89126C	Model and Mold Makers, Jewelry
89126E	Bench Workers, Jewelry
89126K	Pewter Casters and Finishers
89926A	Gem and Diamond Workers
93947E	Hand Painting, Coating, or Decorating Workers

50.0799 Fine Arts and Art Studies, Other

Any instructional program in fine arts and art studies not described above.

50.09   Music

A group of instructional programs (see 50.0901).

50.0901   Music, General

An instructional program that generally describes the study and appreciation of music, and the study of music performance. Includes instruction in principles of harmony, musical notation, musical styles, the historical development of music, and the fundamentals of various musical instruments.

27199C	Anthropologists
31218	Art, Drama, and Music Teachers—Postsecondary
31317	Instructors—Nonvocational Education
34002A	Columnists, Critics, and Commentators
34047A	Music Directors
34047B	Music Arrangers and Orchestrators
34047C	Singers
34047E	Composers
34047F	Prompters
34051	Musicians, Instrumental
39999B	Agents and Business Managers of Artists, Performers, and Athletes

50.0902   Music History and Literature

An instructional program that describes the study of the historical evolution of music as a social and intellectual phenomenon, the development of musical instruments and techniques, and the analysis and criticism of musical literature. Includes instruction in music history research methods, aesthetic analysis of musical compositions, history of musical writing and notation, the development of musical instruments, the development of music theory, and the study of specific periods, cultural traditions, styles, and themes.

31218	Art, Drama, and Music Teachers—Postsecondary
34002A	Columnists, Critics, and Commentators

50.0903   Music—General Performance

An instructional program that generally prepares individuals to master musical instruments and performing art as solo and/or ensemble performers. Includes instruction on one or more specific instruments.

31218	Art, Drama, and Music Teachers—Postsecondary
31317	Instructors—Nonvocational Education
34047A	Music Directors
34047C	Singers
34051	Musicians, Instrumental

50.0904   Music Theory and Composition

An instructional program that describes the study of the principles of sound manipulation as applied to the creation of music, and the techniques of creating and arranging music. Includes instruction in aural theory, melody, counterpoint, complex harmony, modulation, chromaticism, improvisation, progressions, musical writing, instrumentation, orchestration, electronic and computer applications, studies of specific musical styles, and development of original creative ability.

31218	Art, Drama, and Music Teachers—Postsecondary
34047B	Music Arrangers and Orchestrators
34047E	Composers
34047F	Prompters

50.0905   Musicology and Ethnomusicology

An instructional program that describes the systematic study of the forms and methods of music art, and the functions of music, in Western and non-Western societies and cultures. Includes instruction in music theory, musicological research methods, and studies of specific cultural styles such as jazz, folk music, rock, ethnic musical traditions, and the music of non-Western cultures.

27199C	Anthropologists
31218	Art, Drama, and Music Teachers—Postsecondary
34047A	Music Directors

50.0906   Music Conducting

An instructional program that prepares individuals to master the art of leading bands, choirs, orchestras and other ensembles in performance, and related music leadership. Includes instruction in score analysis and arranging, rehearsal and performance leadership, music coaching, arrangement and performance planning, ensemble operations management, and applications to specific school or professional ensembles.

31218	Art, Drama, and Music Teachers—Postsecondary
34047A	Music Directors

50.0907   Music—Piano and Organ Performance

An instructional program that prepares individuals to master the piano, organ, or related keyboard instruments and performing art as solo, ensemble, and/or accompanist performers. Includes instruction in piano and keyboard pedagogy, ensemble playing, accompanying, service playing, repertoire, keyboard and pedal skills, recital, and personal style development.

31218	Art, Drama, and Music Teachers—Postsecondary
34051	Musicians, Instrumental

50.0908 Music—Voice and Choral/Opera Performance

An instructional program that prepares individuals to master the human voice and performing art as solo and/or ensemble performers in concert, choir, opera, or other forms of singing. Includes instruction in voice pedagogy, diction, vocal physiology and exercise, expressive movement, repertoire, recital, and personal style development.

31218	Art, Drama, and Music Teachers—Postsecondary
34047A	Music Directors
34047C	Singers

50.0909 Music Business Management and Merchandising

An instructional program that prepares individuals to organize and manage music organizations, operations, facilities, and personnel. Includes instruction in business and financial management; marketing and fundraising; personnel management and labor relations; event promotion and management; music products merchandising; artist agency and promotion; music law; and applications to specific activities such as managing theaters, recording studios and companies, bands and other ensembles, individual artists, and music organizations.

31218	Art, Drama, and Music Teachers—Postsecondary
39999B	Agents and Business Managers of Artists, Performers, and Athletes

50.0999 Music, Other

Any instructional program in music not described above.

50.99 Visual and Performing Arts, Other

A group of instructional programs (see 50.9999).

50.9999 Visual and Performing Arts, Other

Any instructional program in visual and performing arts not described above.

51. HEALTH PROFESSIONS AND RELATED SCIENCES

A summary of groups of instructional programs that prepare individuals to provide healthcare, or related research and support services, to individuals or groups.

51.01 Chiropractic (D.C., D.C.M.)

A group of instructional programs (see 51.0101).

51.0101   Chiropractic (D.C., D.C.M.)

An instructional program that prepares individuals to be independent professional practitioners of chiropractic, either straight or progressive. Includes instruction in chiropractic theory, spinal mechanics, spinal manipulation therapy, and radiologic diagnosis; and may also include principles of neurologic health, nutrition, hydrotherapy, diet and exercise therapy, clinic and practice management, applicable regulations, and patient counseling.

31212	Health Specialties Teachers—Postsecondary
32113	Chiropractors

51.02   Communication Disorders Sciences and Services

A group of instructional programs that prepare individuals to perform research and/or healthcare services related to speech, hearing, and language problems.

51.0201   Communication Disorders, General

An instructional program that generally describes the principles and practice of identifying and treating disorders of human speech and hearing, and related problems of social communication and health. Includes instruction in developmental and acquired disorders, basic research and clinical methods, and prevention and treatment modalities.

31212	Health Specialties Teachers—Postsecondary
32314	Speech-Language Pathologists and Audiologists
39999A	Interpreters and Translators

51.0202   Audiology/Hearing Sciences

An instructional program that describes the scientific study of the anatomy and physiology of the hearing and/or speech organs, their function and malfunction, and related environmental and behavioral topics. Includes instruction in bioacoustics; neuroanatomy of speech, hearing, and language; hearing measurement; communications embryology and congenital defects; hearing aids and related technology; hearing conservation and noise reduction research; and the experimental analysis of hearing, speech, and language disorders.

31212	Health Specialties Teachers—Postsecondary
32314	Speech-Language Pathologists and Audiologists

51.0203   Speech-Language Pathology

An instructional program that prepares individuals to provide therapeutic care to persons with physical or behavioral disorders that affect speaking or comprehension.

Includes instruction in identifying and assessing speech and language disorders; specific treatment regimes; structure and development of aphasia; specific production, articulation, fluency, motor speech, and voice disorders; psychosocial and educational effects of speech/language disorders; and the planning and management of patient therapy.

| 31212 | Health Specialties Teachers—Postsecondary |
| 32314 | Speech-Language Pathologists and Audiologists |

51.0204   Speech Pathology and Audiology

An instructional program that prepares individuals to provide therapeutic care to persons with hearing and related communications disorders. Includes instruction in the principles of audiology; the structure and development of hearing and communications disorders; speech disorder and hearing loss identification and assessment; aural rehabilitation; psychosocial and educational effects of speech and hearing disorders; and the planning and management of patient therapy.

| 31212 | Health Specialties Teachers—Postsecondary |
| 32314 | Speech-Language Pathologists and Audiologists |

51.0205   Sign Language Interpreter

An instructional program that prepares individuals to interpret oral speech for the hearing impaired. Includes instruction in American Sign Language or other deaf language, fingerspelling, orientation to deaf culture, and interpreting from signing to voice as well as from voice to signing.

| 31212 | Health Specialties Teachers—Postsecondary |
| 39999A | Interpreters and Translators |

51.0299   Communication Disorders Sciences and Services, Other

Any instructional program in communication disorders sciences and services not described above.

| 15008A | Nursing Directors |
| 15008B | Medical and Health Services Managers |

51.03   Community Health Services

A group of instructional programs that prepare individuals to serve the health needs of communities and groups within communities.

51.0301   Community Health Liaison

An instructional program that prepares individuals to serve as liaisons between public health and other social services, and the recipients of health services in communities.

Includes instruction in the basics of human health and nutrition, communicable diseases, environmental health, personal hygiene, care of infants, medications, and family and community services.

19005A	Government Service Executives
21911A	Health Officers and Inspectors
31212	Health Specialties Teachers—Postsecondary
31517A	Public Health Educators

51.04 Dentistry (D.D.S., D.M.D.)

A group of instructional programs (see 51.0401).

51.0401 Dentistry (D.D.S., D.M.D.)

An instructional program that prepares individuals for the independent professional practice of dentistry. Includes instruction in the prevention, diagnosis, and treatment of diseases and abnormalities of the teeth and gums and related parts of the oral cavity; related anatomical and physiological principles; professional ethics and standards; and supervised clinical practice.

51.05 Dental Clinical Sciences/Graduate Dentistry (M.S., Ph.D.)

A group of instructional programs (see 51.0501).

51.0501 Dental Clinical Sciences/Graduate Dentistry (M.S., Ph.D.)

An instructional program that generally describes advanced study or research, by dentists or other medical doctors, in dental practice specialties and related sciences such as oral biology, endodontics, oral/maxillofacial surgery, orthodontics, pediatric dentistry, periodontics, dental materials, dental diagnostics, prosthodontics, dental nutrition, dental immunology, and dental pathology.

31212	Health Specialties Teachers—Postsecondary
32105B	Dentists

51.06 Dental Services

A group of instructional programs that prepare individuals to provide dental healthcare services.

51.0601 Dental Assistant

An instructional program that prepares individuals to assist a dentist or dental hygienist in performing the functions of a dental practice. Includes instruction in chairside assistance, patient preparation, dental office functions, selected dental office laboratory procedures, and dental radiography.

66002	Dental Assistants

51.0602   Dental Hygienist

An instructional program that prepares individuals to practice the cleaning of teeth and related oral health therapies, either independently or in collaboration with dentists. Includes instruction in basic preventive oral health care, oral health education, dental hygiene therapy, initial periodontal therapy, patient examination and counseling, dental radiography, local anesthesia, prosthetic casts, equipment operation and maintenance, and recordkeeping.

31212	Health Specialties Teachers—Postsecondary
32908	Dental Hygienists

51.0603   Dental Laboratory Technician

An instructional program that prepares individuals to make and repair dental prostheses and restorative appliances as prescribed by a dentist. Includes instruction in complete and partial denture construction, crown and fixed bridge fabrication, cast metal partial, customized porcelain and acrylic restorations, and building orthodontic appliances.

31212	Health Specialties Teachers—Postsecondary
89921	Precision Dental Laboratory Technicians
93944A	Mold Makers, Hand
93944D	Molders and Casters
93947E	Hand Painting, Coating, or Decorating Workers
93956	Assemblers and Fabricators—except Machine, Electrical, Electronic, and Precision
93997	Intermediate Hand Workers

51.0699   Dental Services, Other

Any instructional program in dental services not described above.

51.07   Health and Medical Administrative Services

A group of instructional programs that describe the management of the administrative aspects of the healthcare delivery system at the unit, office, building or system levels.

51.0701   Health Systems/Health Services Administration

An instructional program that prepares physicians and other professionals to develop, plan, and manage healthcare systems and service networks. Includes instruction in planning and coordination, business and financial management, fundraising and marketing, public relations, human resources management, technical operations of healthcare systems, resource allocation, health law, and applications to specific health-service situations.

13014B	Administrative Services Managers
15008B	Medical and Health Services Managers
19999B	Social and Community Service Managers
31212	Health Specialties Teachers—Postsecondary

51.0702   Hospital/Health Facilities Administration

An instructional program that prepares health and other professionals to apply the principles of management to the running of hospitals and similar health facilities. Includes instruction in building and facility management, planning and coordination, scheduling, business and financial management, fundraising and marketing, public relations, human resources management and labor relations, technical hospital operations, resource allocation, and health law.

15008B	Medical and Health Services Managers
19999B	Social and Community Service Managers
21911A	Health Officers and Inspectors
31212	Health Specialties Teachers—Postsecondary

51.0703   Health Unit Coordinator/Ward Clerk

An instructional program that prepares individuals to perform routine clerical and reception duties in a patient care unit within a hospital or other healthcare facility. Includes instruction in receiving and directing visitors, transcribing medical orders, preparing requisition forms, scheduling appointments and monitoring the location of patients and personnel, under the supervision of a head nurse or ward supervisor.

55347	General Office Clerks

51.0704   Health Unit Manager/Ward Supervisor

An instructional program that prepares individuals to supervise and coordinate administrative management functions for one or more patient care units in a healthcare facility, under the supervision of a nursing or medical services administrator. Includes instruction in initiating clerical procedures, supervising ward clerks, and serving as a liaison to facility administration and medical staffs.

51002A	First-Line Supervisors, Customer Service

51.0705   Medical Office Management

An instructional program that prepares individuals to manage the administrative and business aspects of a medical practice or other healthcare office. Includes instruction in policy administration, conference planning, scheduling and coordination, managing business records and reports, financial recordkeeping, personnel supervision, public relations, administrative aspects of health law, and office operations.

| 55105 | Medical Secretaries |
| 66005 | Medical Assistants |

51.0706 Medical Records Administration

An instructional program that prepares individuals to supervise and manage the preparation, storage, and use of medical records; and the management of related information systems. Includes instruction in the legal and technical aspects of medical records, the design and management of secure data systems, the role of records in medical surveys, and the supervision of medical records technicians and other related staff.

| 15008B | Medical and Health Services Managers |

51.0707 Medical Records Technology/Technician

An instructional program that prepares individuals to classify medical information and prepare records, under the supervision of a medical records administrator. Includes instruction in medical records science, medical terminology, record classification, user needs, indexing, special records systems, computer operation, and applicable laws and regulations.

| 32911 | Medical Records Technicians |
| 55328B | Medical Record Clerks |

51.0708 Medical Transcription

An instructional program that prepares individuals to execute verbatim medical minutes, reports, and orders. Includes instruction in dictation, analysis of written notes or visual evidence, computer and transcription machine operation, formal medical correspondence and report formats and requirements, and applicable laws and regulations.

| 55105 | Medical Secretaries |
| 55302B | Stenographers |

51.0799 Health and Medical Administrative Services, Other

Any instructional program in health and medical administrative services not described above.

| 13011D | Fundraising Directors |

51.08 Health and Medical Assistants

A group of instructional programs that prepare individuals to provide general or specialized assistance to physicians or other health professionals.

51.0801 Medical Assistant

An instructional program that prepares individuals to support physicians by providing assistance during patient examinations, treatment administration, and monitoring; by keeping patient and related health record information; and by performing a wide range of practice-related duties.

32999A	Orthotists and Prosthetists
66005	Medical Assistants
66099A	Morgue Attendants

51.0802 Medical Laboratory Assistant

An instructional program that prepares individuals to support laboratory directors and technicians by performing routine clinical laboratory procedures and clerical tasks.

24505A	Chemical Technicians and Technologists

51.0803 Occupational Therapy Assistant

An instructional program that prepares individuals to support occupational therapists by providing assistance during patient examinations, treatment administration, and monitoring; by keeping patient and related health record information; and by performing a wide range of practice-related duties.

66021	Occupational Therapy Assistants and Aides

51.0804 Ophthalmic Medical Assistant

An instructional program that prepares individuals to support ophthalmologists by providing assistance during patient examinations, treatment administration, and monitoring; by keeping patient and related health record information; and by performing a wide range of practice-related duties.

32999C	Optometric and Ophthalmic Technicians

51.0805 Pharmacy Technician/Assistant

An instructional program that prepares individuals to support pharmacists by providing assistance during patient consultation, counter dispensing operations, and prescription preparation; keeping patient and related health record information; and by performing a wide range of practice-related duties.

49005B	Sales Representatives, Chemical and Pharmaceutical

51.0806   Physical Therapy Assistant

An instructional program that prepares individuals to support physical therapists by providing assistance during patient examinations, treatment administration, and monitoring; by keeping patient and related health record information; and by performing a wide range of practice-related duties.

32399B	Orientation and Mobility Therapists
66017	Physical and Corrective Therapy Assistants and Aides

51.0807   Physician's Assistant

An instructional program that prepares individuals to manage the treatment of patients with routine or chronic health problems, in consultation with a physician or under indirect supervision. Includes instruction in patient interviewing and history-taking, counseling, laboratory testing and analysis, administration of medication, minor surgery, prescribing routine drugs, and preparing medical reports and referrals to physicians and other specialists.

31212	Health Specialties Teachers—Postsecondary
32511	Physician's Assistants

51.0808   Veterinarian Assistant/Animal Health Technician

An instructional program that prepares individuals to support veterinarians by providing assistance during animal examinations, treatment administration, and monitoring; by keeping animal and related health record information; and by performing a wide range of practice-related duties.

49005A	Sales Representatives, Agricultural
79806	Veterinary Assistants

51.0899   Health and Medical Assistants, Other

Any instructional program for health and medical assistants not described above.

32999C	Optometric and Ophthalmic Technicians
66005	Medical Assistants

51.09   Health and Medical Diagnostic and Treatment Services

A group of instructional programs that prepare individuals to use medical equipment and materials for diagnostic, immediate care, and treatment purposes.

51.0901 Cardiovascular Technology/Technician

An instructional program that prepares individuals to perform invasive and noninvasive tests to monitor human heart and circulatory system health, and to administer prescribed treatment therapies, under the supervision of a physician. Includes instruction in the administration of tests such as EKG, phonocardiogram, and stress tests; therapeutic procedures such as cardiac catheterization and Holter monitoring; patient preparation; equipment preparation and maintenance; and recordkeeping.

31212	Health Specialties Teachers—Postsecondary
32925	Cardiology Technologists

51.0902 Electrocardiograph Technology/Technician

An instructional program that prepares individuals to perform examinations of electro-motive variations in human heart activity using an electrocardiograph machine, under the supervision of a physician. Includes instruction in patient preparation, equipment operation and maintenance, making minor repairs, and recordkeeping.

31212	Health Specialties Teachers—Postsecondary
32926	Electrocardiograph Technicians

51.0903 Electroencephalograph Technology/Technician

An instructional program that prepares individuals to perform examinations of electro-motive variations in human brain activity using an electroencephalograph machine, and to make related data analyses, under the supervision of a physician. Includes instruction in patient preparation, equipment operation and maintenance, EEG test procedures, data analysis, determination of brain death, tumor identification, and brain injury and disorder identification.

31212	Health Specialties Teachers—Postsecondary
32923	Electroneurodiagnostic Technologists

51.0904 Emergency Medical Technology/Technician

An instructional program that prepares individuals to perform initial medical diagnosis, treatment, and comprehensive care in medical crises, under the general supervision of a coordinating physician. Includes instruction in all aspects of basic healthcare; disease, disorder, and injury symptomology and diagnosis; emergency medical treatment procedures for various injuries and disease outbreaks; basic pharmacology; anesthetics; intravenous and other drug administration procedures; obstetrics procedures; basic surgical techniques; emergency medical equipment operation and maintenance; special care of patients exposed to heat, cold, radiation, or contagious disease; and administrative aspects of emergency medicine. Programs may include emergency vehicle operation and patient transportation procedures, depending on level of training.

| 31212 | Health Specialties Teachers—Postsecondary |
| 32508 | Emergency Medical Technicians |

51.0905   Nuclear Medical Technology/Technician

An instructional program that prepares individuals to prepare and administer radio-active isotopes via injections, and to measure glandular and other bodily activity by means of in vitro and in vivo detection and specimen testing. Includes instruction in equipment operation and maintenance, materials storage and safety, patient prepara-tion, and recordkeeping.

31212	Health Specialties Teachers—Postsecondary
32913	Radiation Therapists
32914	Nuclear Medicine Technologists

51.0906   Perfusion Technology/Technician

An instructional program that prepares individuals to operate heart-lung machines and monitor patient condition under the direct supervision of a surgeon. Includes instruc-tion in patient examination and preparation, equipment operation and maintenance, anesthesia, and operating room procedures.

| 31212 | Health Specialties Teachers—Postsecondary |

51.0907   Medical Radiologic Technology/Technician

An instructional program that prepares individuals to perform diagnostic examinations, and administer therapeutic procedures, using X-rays and related radiations, under the supervision of a radiologist. Includes instruction in conducting CAT scans (computer tomography), xeradiography, thermography, and X-ray procedures; equipment opera-tion and maintenance; patient preparation; and recordkeeping.

21911T	Radiation-Protection Specialists
31212	Health Specialties Teachers—Postsecondary
32914	Nuclear Medicine Technologists
32919	Radiologic Technologists
32921	Radiologic Technicians

51.0908   Respiratory Therapy Technician

An instructional program that prepares individuals to perform therapeutic and life-support procedures using respiratory equipment, under the supervision of a physician. Includes instruction in administering inhalants via mist, mask, tent or other procedures; monitor heart-lung machines and other intensive-care therapies; anesthesia; emergency procedures; equipment operation and maintenance; storage and safety methods; and recordkeeping.

31212	Health Specialties Teachers—Postsecondary
32302	Respiratory Therapists
66097	Health Equipment Service Workers

51.0909   Surgical/Operating Room Technician

An instructional program that prepares individuals to perform general technical support tasks in the operating room before, during, and after surgery. Includes instruction in pre-operation patient and surgical team preparation, handling surgical instruments at tableside, supply inventory maintenance before and during operations, sterilization and cleaning of equipment, maintaining clean and sealed environments, operating room safety procedures, and recordkeeping.

31212	Health Specialties Teachers—Postsecondary
32928	Surgical Technologists and Technicians
66099A	Morgue Attendants

51.0910   Diagnostic Medical Sonography Technician

An instructional program that prepares individuals to perform diagnostic and monitoring procedures using acoustic energy, under the supervision of a physician. Includes instruction in patient preparation, ultrasound testing and examination procedures, sonogram evaluation, recordkeeping, and equipment operation and maintenance.

31212	Health Specialties Teachers—Postsecondary
32919	Radiologic Technologists
32925	Cardiology Technologists

51.0999   Health and Medical Diagnostic and Treatment Services, Other

Any instructional program in health and medical diagnostic and treatment services not described above.

32911	Medical Records Technicians
32919	Radiologic Technologists
32996B	Transplant Coordinators
32999B	Pheresis Technicians
32999E	Dialysis Technicians

51.10   Health and Medical Laboratory Technologies

A group of instructional programs that prepare individuals to perform diagnostic and analytical laboratory procedures that support medical research and practice.

51.1001 Blood Bank Technology/Technician

An instructional program that prepares individuals to perform classification, analysis, and related tests on banked blood under the supervision of a pathologist, physician, or laboratory director. Includes instruction in laboratory hematology; laboratory and blood bank procedures; blood donor selection; blood collection, classification, storage, and processing procedures; topological and compatibility tests; blood bank inventory and delivery procedures; recordkeeping; and personnel and volunteer supervision.

66099D   Phlebotomists

51.1002 Cytotechnologist

An instructional program that prepares individuals to perform oncological and related pathological analyses of human tissue samples, under the supervision of a pathologist. Includes instruction in pathology laboratory procedures, equipment operation and maintenance conducting Pap and other test procedures for cancer diagnosis, analytical procedures for other cell abnormalities, slide and tissue sample preparation, and recordkeeping.

32902   Medical and Clinical Laboratory Technologists

51.1003 Hematology Technology/Technician

An instructional program that prepares individuals to perform tests and analyses of patients' blood samples under the supervision of a hospital laboratory director or physician. Includes instruction in laboratory procedures; laboratory hematology; conducting quantitative, qualitative, and coagulation tests on cellular and plasma blood components; equipment operation and maintenance, and recordkeeping.

32905   Medical and Clinical Laboratory Technicians

51.1004 Medical Laboratory Technician

An instructional program that prepares individuals to perform general medical laboratory procedures and routines, under the supervision of a physician or laboratory director. Includes instruction in medical laboratory procedures; equipment operation and maintenance; principles of different bacteriological, biological, and chemical test procedures; equipment and sample inventorying and storage; laboratory safety procedures; laboratory assistant supervision; and recordkeeping.

32902   Medical and Clinical Laboratory Technologists
32905   Medical and Clinical Laboratory Technicians

51.1005 Medical Technology

An instructional program that prepares individuals as independent laboratory scientists and laboratory supervisors in the analysis of human body fluids and tissues. Includes instruction in clinical chemistry, clinical microbiology, clinical immunology, immuno-hematology, clinical hematology, chemical and physical analytic techniques, equipment technology, data and record systems maintenance, and experiment design. Also includes the preparation and interpretation of research and medical reports.

31212	Health Specialties Teachers—Postsecondary
32902	Medical and Clinical Laboratory Technologists

51.1006 Optometric/Ophthalmic Laboratory Technician

An instructional program that prepares individuals to make prescription lenses and re-lated visual aid equipment, under the supervision of an optician or optometrist. Includes instruction in optical laboratory procedures; principles of vision optics; lens grinding and polishing; contact lens fabrication; glasses construction; equipment operation and maintenance; safety procedures; precision instrument work and testing; prescription interpretation; and recordkeeping.

83005A	Production Inspectors, Testers, Graders, Sorters, Samplers, and Weighers
89917A	Precision Lens Grinders and Polishers
93951B	Etchers, Hand
93956	Assemblers and Fabricators—except Machine, Electrical, Electronic, and Precision

51.1099 Health and Medical Laboratory Technologies/Technicians, Other

Any instructional program in health and medical laboratory technologies not described above.

32902	Medical and Clinical Laboratory Technologists

51.11 Health and Medical Preparatory Programs

A group of instructional programs that prepare individuals for admission to first-professional programs in medical or other health fields.

51.1101 Pre-Dentistry Studies

An instructional program that prepares individuals for admission to a first-professional program in dentistry.

51.1102 Pre-Medicine Studies

An instructional program that prepares individuals for admission to a first-professional program in allopathic, osteopathic, or podiatric medicine.

51.1103   Pre-Pharmacy Studies

An instructional program that prepares individuals for admission to a first-professional program in pharmacy.

51.1104   Pre-Veterinary Studies

An instructional program that prepares individuals for admission to a first-professional program in veterinary medicine.

51.1199   Health and Medical Preparatory Programs, Other

Any instructional program in health and medical first-professional preparation not described above.

51.12   Medicine (M.D.)

A group of instructional programs (see 51.1201).

51.1201   Medicine (M.D.)

An instructional program that prepares individuals for the independent professional practice of allopathic medicine. Includes instruction in the principles and procedures used in the observation, diagnosis, care, and treatment of illness, disease, injury, deformity, or other anomalies in humans; ethics and professional standards; and supervised clinical practice.

31202	Life Sciences Teachers—Postsecondary
32102A	Doctors of Medicine (M.D.)

51.13   Medical Basic Sciences

A group of instructional programs that describe advanced research in the disciplines that support the clinical practice of medicine.

51.1301   Medical Anatomy

An instructional program that describes advanced research, by medical graduates and others, on the structure, substructure, and ultrastructure of the human body, and the relationship of anatomical research to the restoration and preservation of good health.

24311	Medical Scientists
31202	Life Sciences Teachers—Postsecondary

51.1302   Medical Biochemistry

An instructional program that describes advanced research, by medical graduates and others, on the nature and chemical composition of the substances that make up the human body, the changes in these substances, and the understanding and treatment of disease processes.

24308A	Biochemists
31202	Life Sciences Teachers—Postsecondary

51.1303   Medical Biomathematics and Biometrics

An instructional program that describes advanced research, by medical graduates and others, on the application of mathematical models and principles to the measurement and understanding of the human organism.

25312	Statisticians
31202	Life Sciences Teachers—Postsecondary
31224	Mathematical Sciences Teachers—Postsecondary

51.1304   Medical Physics/Biophysics

An instructional program that describes advanced research, by medical graduates and others, on the mechanics, sensory aspects, bioelectric phenomena, muscle function, genetic and molecular fine structures, and membrane transportation mechanisms of the human body.

24308C	Biophysicists
24311	Medical Scientists
31202	Life Sciences Teachers—Postsecondary

51.1305   Medical Cell Biology

An instructional program that describes advanced research, by medical graduates and others, on the biological structure and function of human cells, including cellular mechanisms, cell-to-cell communication and the pathogenesis of disease in cells.

24308G	Physiologists and Cytologists
31202	Life Sciences Teachers—Postsecondary

51.1306   Medical Genetics

An instructional program that describes advanced research, by medical graduates and others, on the relationship between inherited traits and characteristics and human health conditions, including inherited metabolic diseases, environmental damage to genetic material, human genetic engineering, and cloning.

24308F	Geneticists
31202	Life Sciences Teachers—Postsecondary

51.1307   Medical Immunology

An instructional program that describes advanced research, by medical graduates and others, on the relation between immunological system functions and human health conditions, including immune response mechanisms, immunodeficiency, antibody definition, and antibody production.

31202	Life Sciences Teachers—Postsecondary
32102A	Doctors of Medicine (M.D.)

51.1308   Medical Microbiology

An instructional program that describes advanced research, by medical graduates and others, on the nature and properties of harmful microorganisms and of the disease processes they induce in humans.

24308E	Microbiologists
31202	Life Sciences Teachers—Postsecondary

51.1309   Medical Molecular Biology

An instructional program that describes advanced research, by medical graduates and others, on the application of molecular and macromolecular studies to the investigation of genetic, hormonal, and disease problems in human organisms.

31202	Life Sciences Teachers—Postsecondary

51.1310   Medical Neurobiology

An instructional program that describes advanced research, by medical graduates and others, on the anatomy, physiology, biochemistry, and molecular biology of the brain, nerve cells, and nerve tissue and their relation to human behavior and health.

31202	Life Sciences Teachers—Postsecondary
32102A	Doctors of Medicine (M.D.)

51.1311   Medical Nutrition

An instructional program that describes advanced research, by medical graduates and others, on the chemical nature of food substances; the processes by which the human body ingests, digests, absorbs, transports, utilizes, and excretes food and nutrients; and their relation to human behavior and health.

31202	Life Sciences Teachers—Postsecondary
32521	Dietitians and Nutritionists

51.1312   Medical Pathology

An instructional program that describes advanced research, by medical graduates and others, on the causes and effects of diseases and disease mechanisms in human beings. Includes instruction in renal, cardiovascular, neuro-, pulmonary, bone, liver and gastrointestinal, surgical, autopsy, cellular, and biochemical physiology, and immuno-pathology.

24311	Medical Scientists
31202	Life Sciences Teachers—Postsecondary
32521	Dietitians and Nutritionists

51.1313   Medical Physiology

An instructional program that describes advanced research, by medical graduates and others, on the functions of the human body and its parts, and their relationship to the restoration and preservation of good health. Includes instruction in cellular, cardiovascular, renal, neuro-, endocrine, gastrointestinal, and respiratory physiology.

24308G	Physiologists and Cytologists
31202	Life Sciences Teachers—Postsecondary

51.1314   Medical Toxicology

An instructional program that describes advanced research, by medical graduates and others, on the nature and extent of adverse effects of synthetic and naturally occurring chemical substances on human beings. Includes instruction in chemical mechanisms and the specialties of reproductive, developmental, genetic, forensic, inhalation, and neurobehavioral toxicology.

24308J	Toxicologists
31202	Life Sciences Teachers—Postsecondary

51.1399   Medical Basic Sciences, Other

Any instructional program in medical basic sciences not described above.

24308B	Biologists
24308D	Botanists
24311	Medical Scientists
31202	Life Sciences Teachers—Postsecondary

51.14   Medical Clinical Sciences (M.S., Ph.D.)

A group of instructional programs (see 51.1401).

51.1401   Medical Clinical Sciences (M.S., Ph.D.)

An instructional program that describes the scientific study, by medical residents and other medical doctors, of specialized medical practice arts and related clinical research. Includes instruction in fields such as pediatrics, anesthesiology, obstetrics, gynecology, oncology, surgery, radiology, internal medicine, neurology, clinical pathology, psychiatry, and others.

31202	Life Sciences Teachers—Postsecondary
32102A	Doctors of Medicine (M.D.)
32102F	Anesthesiologists
32102U	Pathologists

51.15   Mental Health Services

A group of instructional programs that prepare individuals to provide counseling and support services related to the care and treatment of persons with mental, emotional, or behavioral disorders.

51.1501   Alcohol/Drug Abuse Counseling

An instructional program that prepares individuals to counsel drug users, addicts, family members, and associates in a wide variety of settings, using various preventive strategies and treatment regimes. Includes instruction in outreach; patient education; therapeutic intervention methods; diagnostic procedures; addiction symptomology; recordkeeping; liaison with community health, social services, law enforcement, and legal services; and applicable regulations.

13005E	Employee Assistance Specialists
19005A	Government Service Executives
27302	Social Workers, Medical and Psychiatric

51.1502   Psychiatric/Mental Health Services Technician

An instructional program that prepares individuals to assist psychiatrists, psychologists, nurses and other mental health personnel in patient care and treatment. Includes instruction in patient interviewing, data recording, taking vital signs, the supervised administration of routine medication, and assisting in examinations and treatment procedures.

31212	Health Specialties Teachers—Postsecondary
32931	Psychiatric Technicians
66014	Psychiatric Aides

51.1503   Clinical and Medical Social Work

An instructional program that prepares individuals for the independent practice of social work in mental health clinics, hospitals, and community health service organizations. Includes instruction in psychiatric case work, clinical interviewing techniques, therapeutic intervention strategies, psychological test administration, family counseling, social rehabilitation, recordkeeping, and liaison with other community support agencies and services.

| 27302 | Social Workers, Medical and Psychiatric |
| 31212 | Health Specialties Teachers—Postsecondary |

51.1599   Mental Health Services, Other

Any instructional program in mental health/human services not described above.

| 66014 | Psychiatric Aides |

51.16   Nursing

A group of instructional programs (see 51.1601).

51.1601   Nursing (R.N. Training)

An instructional program that generally prepares individuals in the knowledge, techniques, and procedures for promoting health, providing care for sick, disabled, informed, or other individuals or groups. Includes instruction in the administration of medication and treatments, assisting a physician during treatments and examinations, referring patients to physicians and other healthcare specialists, and planning education for health maintenance.

| 31114 | Nursing Instructors—Postsecondary |
| 32502 | Registered Nurses |

51.1602   Nursing Administration (Post-R.N.)

An instructional program that prepares registered nurses (R.N.) to manage nursing personnel and services in hospitals and other healthcare delivery agencies.

15005B	Educational Program Directors
15008A	Nursing Directors
15008B	Medical and Health Services Managers

19999B	Social and Community Service Managers
19999C	Association Managers and Administrators
32502	Registered Nurses

51.1603   Nursing, Adult Health (Post-R.N.)

An instructional program that prepares registered nurses (R.N.) to provide general care for adult patients, including the administration of medication and treatments, assisting a physician during treatments and examinations, referring patients to physicians and other healthcare specialists, and planning education for health maintenance.

| 31114 | Nursing Instructors—Postsecondary |
| 32502 | Registered Nurses |

51.1604   Nursing Anesthetist (Post-R.N.)

An instructional program that prepares registered nurses (R.N.) to administer anesthetics and provide care for patients before, during, and after anesthesia.

| 31114 | Nursing Instructors—Postsecondary |
| 32502 | Registered Nurses |

51.1605   Nursing, Family Practice (Post-R.N.)

An instructional program that prepares registered nurses (R.N.) to provide general care for family groups and individual health needs in the context of family living, including the administration of medication and treatments, assisting a physician during treatments and examinations, referring patients to physicians and other healthcare specialists, and planning education for health maintenance.

| 31114 | Nursing Instructors—Postsecondary |
| 32502 | Registered Nurses |

51.1606   Nursing, Maternal/Child Health (Post-R.N.)

An instructional program that prepares registered nurses (R.N.) to provide prenatal care to pregnant women and postnatal care to mothers and their infants.

| 31114 | Nursing Instructors—Postsecondary |
| 32502 | Registered Nurses |

51.1607   Nursing Midwifery (Post-R.N.)

An instructional program that prepares registered nurses (R.N.) to independently deliver babies and treat mothers in the prenatal, delivery, and post-delivery periods.

Includes instruction in predelivery screening, physician referral, and the care of infants during the delivery and immediate post-delivery phases.

31114	Nursing Instructors—Postsecondary
32502	Registered Nurses

51.1608 Nursing Science (Post-R.N.)

An instructional program in research that describes the study of advanced clinical practices, research methodologies, and the administration of complex nursing services, and that prepares nurses to further the progress of nursing research through experimentation and clinical applications.

15005B	Educational Program Directors
31114	Nursing Instructors—Postsecondary
32502	Registered Nurses

51.1609 Nursing, Pediatric (Post-R.N.)

An instructional program that prepares registered nurses (R.N.) to provide care for children from infancy through adolescence. Includes instruction in the administration of medication and treatments, assisting physicians, patient examination and referral, and planning and delivering health maintenance and health education programs.

31114	Nursing Instructors—Postsecondary
32502	Registered Nurses

51.1610 Nursing, Psychiatric/Mental Health (Post-R.N.)

An instructional program that prepares registered nurses (R.N.) to promote mental health and provide nursing care to patients with mental, emotional, or behavioral disorders, in mental institutions or other settings.

31114	Nursing Instructors—Postsecondary
32502	Registered Nurses

51.1611 Nursing, Public Health (Post-R.N)

An instructional program that prepares registered nurses (R.N.) to promote health and provide preventive and curative nursing services for individuals, groups, or communities under the supervision of a public health agency.

31114	Nursing Instructors—Postsecondary
32502	Registered Nurses

51.1612   Nursing, Surgical (Post-R.N.)

An instructional program that prepares registered nurses (R.N.) to provide care to patients before and during surgery, and provide tableside assistance to surgeons.

31114	Nursing Instructors—Postsecondary
32502	Registered Nurses

51.1613   Practical Nurse (L.P.N. Training)

An instructional program that prepares individuals to assist in providing general nursing care under the direction of a registered nurse, physician, or dentist. Includes instruction in taking patient vital signs, applying sterile dressings, patient health education, and assistance with examinations and treatment.

32505	Licensed Practical Nurses

51.1614   Nursing Assistant/Aide

An instructional program that prepares individuals to perform routine nursing-related services to patients in hospitals or long-term care facilities, under the training and supervision of a registered nurse or licensed practical nurse.

66008	Nursing Aides, Orderlies, and Attendants
66011	Home Health Aides
66014	Psychiatric Aides

51.1615   Home Health Aide

An instructional program that prepares individuals to assist elderly, convalescent, or handicapped patients in their homes by providing for their physical, mental, emotional, and/or social healthcare needs, under the supervision of a registered nurse.

66008	Nursing Aides, Orderlies, and Attendants
66011	Home Health Aides

51.1699   Nursing, Other

Any instructional program in nursing not described above.

51.17   Optometry

A group of instructional programs (see 51.1701).

51.1701   Optometry (O.D.)

An instructional program that prepares individuals for the independent professional practice of optometry and that describes the principles and techniques for examining, diagnosing, and treating conditions of the visual system. Includes instruction in prescribing glasses and contact lenses, other optical aids, corrective therapies, patient counseling, physician referral, practice management, and ethics and professional standards.

31212	Health Specialties Teachers—Postsecondary
32108	Optometrists

51.18   Ophthalmic/Optometric Services

A group of instructional programs that prepare individuals to assist ophthalmologists and/or optometrists in providing clinical services.

51.1801   Opticianry/Dispensing Optician

An instructional program that prepares individuals to fill prescriptions ordered by ophthalmologists or optometrists and to dispense optical supplies and equipment. Includes instruction in shaping and grinding lenses, frame selection and fitting, patient counseling, supervision of assistants, and the operation of a business.

32514	Opticians, Dispensing and Measuring
89917A	Precision Lens Grinders and Polishers
89917D	Optical Instrument Assemblers

51.1802   Optical Technician/Assistant

An instructional program that prepares individuals to assist optometrists or ophthalmologists in providing diagnostic, treatment, and dispensing services. Includes instruction in vision testing, corneal measurement, color screening, patient counseling, eyewear fitting and modification, and office administration duties.

89917A	Precision Lens Grinders and Polishers
89917D	Optical Instrument Assemblers
93951B	Etchers, Hand
93951C	Printers, Hand

51.1803   Ophthalmic Medical Technologist

An instructional program that prepares individuals to perform ophthalmic clinical photography and florescence angiography of the eye and ophthalmic electrophysiological and microbiological procedures, and to administer ocular motility and binocular function tests under the supervision of an ophthalmologist.

| 32999C | Optometric and Ophthalmic Technicians |
| 34023B | Photographers, Scientific |

51.1804   Orthoptics

An instructional program that prepares individuals, under the supervision of an ophthalmologist, to correct vision defects in children and adults via therapeutic exercises. Includes instruction in strabismus, amblyopia, patient care and counseling, and diagnostic testing.

| 32999C | Optometric and Ophthalmic Technicians |

51.1899   Ophthalmic/Optometric Services, Other

Any instructional program in ophthalmic/optometric services not describe above.

51.19   Osteopathic Medicine (D.O.)

A group of instructional programs (see 51.1901).

51.1901   Osteopathic Medicine (D.O.)

An instructional program that prepares individuals for the independent professional practice of osteopathy, a system of holistic diagnosis and treatment of health problems. Includes instruction in all accepted allopathic medical diagnostic and treatment methods, plus spinal manipulation, musculoskeletal and nervous system influence on body health, promoting natural defense mechanisms, and the interrelation of the various body systems.

| 31212 | Health Specialties Teachers—Postsecondary |
| 32102B | Doctors of Osteopathy (D.O.) |

51.20   Pharmacy

A group of instructional programs (see 51.2001).

51.2001   Pharmacy (B.Pharm., Pharm.D.)

An instructional program that prepares individuals for the independent professional practice of pharmacy. Includes instruction in principles of medicinal chemistry, drug behavior, and drug metabolism; mixing, preparing, and dispensing prescription medications; pharmacy practice management; patient advising; ethical and professional standards; and applicable laws and regulations.

21911A	Health Officers and Inspectors
31212	Health Specialties Teachers—Postsecondary
32517	Pharmacists

51.2002 Pharmacy Administration and Pharmaceutics

An instructional program that prepares pharmacists to manage pharmaceutical operations and programs in industrial, hospital, and other clinical settings. Includes instruction in business management principles; pharmaceutical laboratory and production operations and organization; social and economic policy aspects of pharmaceutics; and specific applications to such areas as industrial pharmaceutics, clinical pharmaceutics, hospital pharmaceutics, pharmacy industry and distribution studies, and the regulatory aspects of pharmaceutics.

21911A	Health Officers and Inspectors
31212	Health Specialties Teachers—Postsecondary
32517	Pharmacists

51.2003 Medical Pharmacology and Pharmaceutical Sciences

An instructional program that describes the scientific study, by pharmacists and other medical researchers, of drugs, drug behavior, and the actions of chemical substances on human systems and whole organisms. Includes instruction in such areas as biopharmaceutics, pharmacokinetics and dynamics, drug metabolism, bioanalytical assay, pharmacognosy, cosmetic science, neuropharmacology, behavioral effects of drugs, radiopharmacology, and pharmaceutical socioeconomic policy.

24311	Medical Scientists
31212	Health Specialties Teachers—Postsecondary

51.2099 Pharmacy, Other

Any instructional program in pharmacy not described above.

51.21 Podiatry (D.P.M., D.P., Pod.D.)

A group of instructional programs (see 51.2101).

51.2101 Podiatry (D.P.M., D.P., Pod.D.)

An instructional program that prepares individuals for the independent professional practice of podiatric medicine. Includes instruction in the principles and procedures used in the observation, diagnosis, care, and treatment of disease, injury, deformity, or other anomalies of the human foot; ethics and professional standards; and supervised clinical practice.

31212	Health Specialties Teachers—Postsecondary
32111	Podiatrists

51.22   Public Health

A group of instructional programs that prepare individuals to provide publicly supervised health services to community, regional, national, and international health services.

51.2201   Public Health, General

An instructional program that prepares individuals to plan, implement, and evaluate publicly supervised and administered healthcare programs and systems. Includes instruction in principles of epidemiology, health law and regulations, law enforcement, biostatistical methods, budget policy and economics, report-making, and personnel supervision.

21911A	Health Officers and Inspectors
31212	Health Specialties Teachers—Postsecondary

51.2202   Environmental Health

An instructional program that prepares public health specialists to monitor and evaluate potential and confirmed environmental health hazards, and to plan and manage environmental health programs. Includes instruction in environmental toxicology, genetic toxicology, biohazard research, test and evaluation procedures, measurement instrumentation and equipment operation, environmental and health law and regulations, and applications to specific environmental health problems.

19005A	Government Service Executives
24308J	Toxicologists
24311	Medical Scientists
31212	Health Specialties Teachers—Postsecondary

51.2203   Epidemiology

An instructional program that describes the scientific study, by public health scientists and other medical researchers, of the distribution of disease in human populations, patterns in the life cycles of infectious diseases, and methods of preventing disease outbreaks and promoting population health.

24311	Medical Scientists
31202	Life Sciences Teachers—Postsecondary
31212	Health Specialties Teachers—Postsecondary

51.2204   Health and Medical Biostatistics

An instructional program that describes the advanced study of the health applications of statistical models and analytical techniques. Includes instruction in descriptive and inferential studies of human populations, the human organism, and its biological components.

25312	Statisticians
31224	Mathematical Sciences Teachers—Postsecondary

51.2205   Health Physics/Radiologic Health

An instructional program that describes the scientific measurement of radiation levels and dosages affecting human beings, and that prepares individuals to monitor radiation health. Includes instruction in radiation dosimetry methods, the health effects of natural and man-made radiation, operation and maintenance of test and monitoring equipment, and applicable standards and regulations pertaining to radiation emissions.

24102A	Physicists
24311	Medical Scientists
24508B	Nuclear Monitoring Technicians
31212	Health Specialties Teachers—Postsecondary

51.2206   Occupational Health and Industrial Hygiene

An instructional program that prepares public health specialists to monitor and evaluate health standards related to industrial and commercial workplaces and locations. Includes instruction in occupational health and safety standards and regulations; requirements of particular jobs and industrial processes; test and monitoring equipment operation and maintenance; industrial toxicology; worker health and safety education; and the analysis of job-related equipment, behavior, practices, and protective gear.

21911E	Industrial and Occupational Safety and Health Inspectors
31212	Health Specialties Teachers—Postsecondary

51.2207   Public Health Education and Promotion

An instructional program that prepares public health specialists to provide specialized educational and informational services to populations affected by disease outbreak, health hazards, or who are at risk. Includes instruction in health publicity, public relations, public health campaign management, preparation of public health teaching aids and instructional materials, and applications to specific public health problems and campaign audiences.

31212	Health Specialties Teachers—Postsecondary

51.2299   Public Health, Other

Any instructional program in public health not described above.

51.23   Rehabilitation/Therapeutic Services

A group of instructional programs that prepare individuals to provide assistance in stabilizing and/or improving diagnosed health problems.

51.2301   Art Therapy

An instructional program that prepares individuals to employ art as a tool to assist patients in overcoming physical disability, resolving emotional conflicts, and enhancing communications with others.

31212	Health Specialties Teachers—Postsecondary
32317	Recreational Therapists

51.2302   Dance Therapy

An instructional program that prepares individuals to employ dance as a tool to assist patients in overcoming physical disability, resolving emotional conflicts, and enhancing communications with others.

31212	Health Specialties Teachers—Postsecondary
32317	Recreational Therapists

51.2303   Hypnotherapy

An instructional program that prepares individuals to employ hypnosis as a tool to assist patients in reducing physical pain, resolving emotional conflicts, and enhancing communications with others. Includes instruction in trance inducement and its relation to other healing arts specialties.

31212	Health Specialties Teachers—Postsecondary

51.2304   Movement Therapy

An instructional program that prepares individuals to employ hands-on repatterning and verbal instruction as a tool to assist patients in overcoming physical disability, resolving emotional conflicts, and enhancing communications with others. Includes instruction in physiological patterning/cognitive-motor functioning, movement analysis and performance, psychological/emotional expression and health maintenance and improvement.

31212   Health Specialties Teachers—Postsecondary
32308   Physical Therapists

51.2305 Music Therapy

An instructional program that prepares individuals to employ music as a tool to assist patients in overcoming physical disability, resolving emotional conflicts, and enhancing communications with others. Includes instruction in leading and monitoring individual and group musical activities with patients who suffer from physical or mental disorders.

31212   Health Specialties Teachers—Postsecondary
32317   Recreational Therapists

51.2306 Occupational Therapy

An instructional program that prepares individuals to employ self-care, work, and play activities as therapeutic regimes for patients in order to increase independent functioning, enhance development, and assist recovery from disability. Includes instruction in adapting therapeutic tasks or environments to achieve maximum independence and enhance the quality of life for each patient.

31212   Health Specialties Teachers—Postsecondary
32305   Occupational Therapists
32311A   Manual Arts Therapists

51.2307 Orthotics/Prosthetics

An instructional program that prepares individuals, under the supervision of a physician and in consultation with therapists, to make and fit orthoses and prostheses. Includes instruction in design, crafting and production techniques, properties of materials, anatomy and physiology, and patient counseling.

31212   Health Specialties Teachers—Postsecondary
32999A   Orthotists and Prosthetists
89923   Medical Appliance Makers

51.2308 Physical Therapy

An instructional program that prepares individuals, upon referral by a physician, to evaluate patients and plan and execute treatment programs to prevent or remediate physical dysfunction, relieve pain and prevent further disability. Includes instruction in patho- and therapeutic kinesiology, equipment design and maintenance, treatment regimes, and the evaluation of skeletal, neurological, and cardiovascular disorders. Also includes instruction in patient counseling, personnel supervision, and recordkeeping.

31212	Health Specialties Teachers—Postsecondary
32308	Physical Therapists
32311B	Corrective Therapists
32399B	Orientation and Mobility Therapists

51.2309   Recreational Therapy

An instructional program that prepares individuals to plan, organize, and direct medically approved programs of leisure activity to promote patient physical and mental health and functioning in social interactions. Includes instruction in volunteer and staff supervision, patient evaluation and monitoring, behavioral therapy, and recreation program and predischarge planning.

| 31212 | Health Specialties Teachers—Postsecondary |
| 32317 | Recreational Therapists |

51.2310   Vocational Rehabilitation Counseling

An instructional program that prepares individuals, under the supervision of physicians or psychologists, to assist patients in coping with physical and/or mental disabilities that affect work. Includes instruction in vocational counseling, employment assistance and placement, patient evaluation and monitoring, administering psychological and psychomotor tests, and the planning of training programs.

| 31212 | Health Specialties Teachers—Postsecondary |
| 32399B | Orientation and Mobility Therapists |

51.2399   Rehabilitation/Therapeutic Services, Other

Any instructional program in rehabilitation/therapeutic services not described above.

| 32311B | Corrective Therapists |

51.24   Veterinary Medicine (D.V.M.)

A group of instructional programs (see 51.2401).

51.2401   Veterinary Medicine (D.V.M.)

An instructional program that prepares individuals for the independent professional practice of veterinary medicine. Includes instruction in the principles and procedures used in the observation, diagnosis, care, and treatment of illness, disease, injury, deformity, or other anomalies in animals; ethics and professional standards; and supervised clinical practice.

31212	Health Specialties Teachers—Postsecondary
32114A	Veterinary Pathologists
32114B	Veterinarians
32114C	Veterinary Inspectors

51.25 Veterinary Clinical Sciences (M.S., Ph.D.)

A group of instructional programs (see 51.2501).

51.2501 Veterinary Clinical Sciences (M.S., Ph.D.)

An instructional program that describes the scientific study, by veterinarians, of the clinical specializations and supporting applied sciences related to the practice of veterinary medicine. Includes instruction in areas such as veterinary anatomy, veterinary physiology, veterinary pharmacology, veterinary radiology, veterinary pathology, veterinary toxicology, veterinary microbiology, veterinary preventive medicine, veterinary parasitology, veterinary immunology, veterinary bacteriology, veterinary virology, large animal surgery and medicine, small animal surgery and medicine, avian medicine, theriogenology, laboratory animal science, and animal nutrition.

| 31212 | Health Specialties Teachers—Postsecondary |

51.26 Miscellaneous Health Aides

A group of instructional programs (see 51.2601).

51.2601 Health Aide

Any of a group of instructional programs that prepare individuals to perform routine care and assistance duties for patients, under the direct supervision of other healthcare professionals, and/or to perform routine maintenance and general assistance duties in healthcare laboratories.

32999D	Audiometrists
66008	Nursing Aides, Orderlies, and Attendants
66011	Home Health Aides
66014	Psychiatric Aides
66017	Physical and Corrective Therapy Assistants and Aides
66021	Occupational Therapy Assistants and Aides

51.27 Miscellaneous Health Sciences and Allied Health Services

A group of instructional programs that prepare individuals in health-related subjects and fields not included in the Health Sciences and Allied Health Services series described above.

51.2701   Acupuncture and Oriental Medicine

An instructional program that prepares individuals to administer Oriental and related traditional treatment therapies and dispense traditional herbal and other medications as independent practitioners. Includes instruction in acupuncture, moxibustion, Oriental pharmacology, Oriental medical theory and principles, diagnostic procedures, patient counseling, and related healthcare arts.

31212   Health Specialties Teachers—Postsecondary

51.2702   Medical Dietician

An instructional program that prepares individuals to plan and administer special diets in clinical situations, under the supervision of or in consultation with physicians or other health professionals. Includes instruction in the principles of medical nutrition; the use of nutrition as a treatment regime; the management of healthcare facility food services; special menu planning and food preparation; and patient education and counseling.

31212   Health Specialties Teachers—Postsecondary
32521   Dietitians and Nutritionists

51.2703   Medical Illustrating

An instructional program that prepares individuals to demonstrate medical facts by the creation of illustrations such as drawings, models, photographs, and films; either independently or under physicians' supervision. Includes instruction in illustrating live treatment situations as well as working from data, notes, and samples.

31212   Health Specialties Teachers—Postsecondary
34035A   Painters and Illustrators

51.2704   Naturopathic Medicine

An instructional program that prepares individuals to provide primary care and promote patient health through the use of natural therapies and related physiological, psychological, and mechanical methods. Includes instruction in natural law, phytotherapy, electrotherapy, physiotherapy, mechanotherapy, naturopathic manipulation, minor surgery, and herbal remedies.

31212   Health Specialties Teachers—Postsecondary

51.2705   Psychoanalysis

An instructional program that prepares individuals to provide psychotherapy to individuals and groups, based on the psychodynamic theory evolved from the work of Freud, Adler, and Jung. Includes instruction in personality theory, dream analysis, free association and transference theory and techniques, psychodynamic theory, developmental processes, applications to specific clinical conditions, practice standards and management, and client relations.

27108G	Clinical Psychologists
27108H	Counseling Psychologists
31212	Health Specialties Teachers—Postsecondary
32102E	Psychiatrists

51.28 Dental Residency Programs

A group of instructional programs that prepare dentists in advanced clinical work in special areas of dental practice. Programs may lead to examination for board certification.

51.2801 Dental/Oral Surgery Specialty

A residency training program that prepares dentists and medical surgeons in advanced clinical training and practice in the surgery of the oral cavity and jaws, including the removal of cancerous and other diseased tissue, removal of teeth, and reconstruction of the jaw and related facial structure.

31212	Health Specialties Teachers—Postsecondary
32105G	Oral and Maxillofacial Surgeons

51.2802 Dental Public Health Specialty

A residency training program that prepares dentists in the formulation and delivery of public preventive and curative dental health services.

31212	Health Specialties Teachers—Postsecondary
32105B	Dentists

51.2803 Endodontics Specialty

A residency training program that prepares dentists in the etiology, diagnosis, prevention, and treatment of conditions that affect the dental and other periodontal tissues, including pulp canal therapy and root canal therapy.

31212	Health Specialties Teachers—Postsecondary
32105B	Dentists

51.2804 Oral Pathology Specialty

A residency training program that prepares dentists in the functional and structural changes that affect the oral cavity, including diagnosis of diseases, abnormalities, and tumors.

31212	Health Specialties Teachers—Postsecondary
32105A	Oral Pathologists

51.2805   Orthodontics Specialty

A residency training program that prepares dentists in the principles and techniques involved in the prevention and correction of dental malocclusions and oral cavity anomalies.

31212	Health Specialties Teachers—Postsecondary
32105D	Orthodontists

51.2806   Pedodontics Specialty

A residency training program that prepares dentists in the principles and techniques of diagnosing and treating the dental and other oral cavity conditions of children.

31212	Health Specialties Teachers—Postsecondary
32105B	Dentists

51.2807   Periodontics Specialty

A residency training program that prepares dentists in the nature and treatment of diseases which affect the mucous membranes, gums, and other soft tissues within the oral cavity.

31212	Health Specialties Teachers—Postsecondary
32105B	Dentists

51.2808   Prosthodontics Specialty

A residency training program that prepares dentists in the principles and techniques of constructing oral prostheses, and the restoration and maintenance of oral function by the replacement of missing teeth and other oral structures with such artificial devices.

31212	Health Specialties Teachers—Postsecondary
32105F	Prosthodontists

51.2899   Dental Residency Programs, Other

Any residency program in dentistry not described above.

15005B	Educational Program Directors

51.29 Medical Residency Programs

A group of instructional programs that prepare physicians in advanced clinical work in special areas of medical practice. Programs may lead to examination for board certification.

51.2901 Aerospace Medicine Residency

A residency training program that prepares physicians in the health care of operating crews and passengers of air and space vehicles, plus support personnel. Includes instruction in special conditions of physical and psychological stress, emergency medical procedures, adaptive systems, and artificial environments.

31202   Life Sciences Teachers—Postsecondary

51.2902 Allergies and Immunology Residency

A residency training program that prepares physicians in the delivery of skilled medical care to patients suffering from allergic, asthmatic, and immunologic diseases. Requires completion of a prior program in internal medicine or pediatrics.

31202   Life Sciences Teachers—Postsecondary
32102A   Doctors of Medicine (M.D.)

51.2903 Anesthesiology Residency

A residency training program that prepares physicians in the application of anesthesia for general and specialized surgery and obstetrics, critical patient care, and the care of pain problems. Includes instruction in surgical procedures, current monitoring procedures, fluid therapy, pain management, diagnostic and therapeutic procedures outside the operating room, and operating room safety (see also 51.2910).

31202   Life Sciences Teachers—Postsecondary
32102F   Anesthesiologists

51.2904 Blood Banking Residency

A residency training program that prepares physicians in the medical, technical, research, and administrative aspects of operating blood banks. Includes instruction in transfusion and transplantation procedures, logistics, and the training and supervision of blood bank technicians.

31202   Life Sciences Teachers—Postsecondary

51.2905   Cardiology Residency

A residency training program that prepares physicians in the natural history of cardio-vascular disorders in adults and the diagnosis and treatment of diseases of the heart and blood vessels. Includes instruction in coronary care, diagnostic testing and evaluation, invasive and noninvasive therapies, and pacemaker follow-up. Requires prior completion of a program in internal medicine (see also 51.2945).

31202	Life Sciences Teachers—Postsecondary
32102A	Doctors of Medicine (M.D.)

51.2906   Chemical Pathology Residency

A residency training program that prepares physicians in the development, operation, and quality control of chemical pathology laboratories and the provision of support and consultative services to other physicians. Includes instruction in instrumentation, analysis, data processing, and administration. Requires prior completion of a program in medical pathology.

31202	Life Sciences Teachers—Postsecondary
32102U	Pathologists

51.2907   Child/Pediatric Neurology Residency

A residency training program that prepares physicians in the diagnosis and management of neurological disorders of the newborn infancy, early childhood, and adolescence. Requires training in adult neurology and prior partial completion of a program in pediatrics.

31202	Life Sciences Teachers—Postsecondary
32102A	Doctors of Medicine (M.D.)

51.2908   Child Psychiatry Residency

A residency training program that prepares physicians in the diagnosis and treatment of mental, emotional, and behavioral disorders of infancy, early childhood, and adolescence. Requires completion of the initial segment of a program in psychiatry.

31202	Life Sciences Teachers—Postsecondary
32102E	Psychiatrists

51.2909   Colon and Rectal Surgery Residency

A residency training program that prepares physicians in the surgical care of patients with anorectal and colonic diseases. Also includes instruction in diagnostic and therapeutic colonoscopy. Requires prior completion of a program in general surgery.

31202	Life Sciences Teachers—Postsecondary
32102A	Doctors of Medicine (M.D.)

51.2910   Critical Care Anesthesiology Residency

A residency training program that prepares physicians in the administration of anesthesia to patients with acute, chronic, or long-term illness and who have multiple organ system derangements. Includes instruction in high-risk and trauma procedures, respiratory therapy, and biomedical engineering. Requires prior completion of a program in anesthesiology.

31202	Life Sciences Teachers—Postsecondary
32102F	Anesthesiologists

51.2911   Critical Care Medicine Residency

A residency training program that prepares physicians in the management of care for patients with acutely life-threatening conditions, which may include multiple organ failure. Includes instruction in the management of critical-care units, emergency procedures, and post-discharge care of former critical-care patients. Requires prior completion of a program in internal medicine.

31202	Life Sciences Teachers—Postsecondary
32102A	Doctors of Medicine (M.D.)

51.2912   Critical Care Surgery Residency

A residency training program that prepares physicians in surgical procedures for patients with multiple trauma, critical illness, patients on life support, and elderly or very young patients with disease complications. Requires full or partial prior completion of a program in general surgery or another surgical specialty.

31202	Life Sciences Teachers—Postsecondary
32102J	Surgeons

51.2913   Dermatology Residency

A residency training program that prepares physicians in the delivery of specialized care to patients with diseases of the skin, hair, nails, and mucous membranes. Includes instruction in dermatologic surgical procedures, cutaneous allergies, sexually transmitted diseases, and diagnostic and therapeutic techniques.

31202	Life Sciences Teachers—Postsecondary
32102A	Doctors of Medicine (M.D.)

51.2914   Dermatopathology Residency

A residency training program that prepares physicians in the clinical and microscopic diagnosis and analysis of skin diseases and disorders. Includes instruction in laboratory administration and the supervision and training of support personnel. Requires prior completion of a program in dermatology or pathology.

31202   Life Sciences Teachers—Postsecondary

51.2915   Diagnostic Radiology Residency

A residency training program that prepares physicians in the diagnostic use of roentgen, isotopic, ultrasound, and other radiant energy imaging techniques. Includes instruction in intervention procedures, safety and imaging science, and technology (see also 51.2936, 51.2958, and 51.2959).

31202   Life Sciences Teachers—Postsecondary
32102A   Doctors of Medicine (M.D.)

51.2916   Emergency Medicine Residency

A residency training program that prepares physicians in the methods, procedures, and techniques of providing and managing immediate healthcare services. Includes instruction in the initial recognition, stabilization, evaluation, and care of the acutely ill or injured patient; patient follow-up and referral; management of prehospital care; training and supervision of emergency medical personnel; emergency department management; medicolegal and ethical issues; and disaster planning.

15008B   Medical and Health Services Managers
31202   Life Sciences Teachers—Postsecondary
32102A   Doctors of Medicine (M.D.)

51.2917   Endocrinology and Metabolism Residency

A residency training program that prepares physicians in the diagnosis and treatment of diseases and disorders of the endocrine glands and metabolic system. Includes instruction in the diagnosis and care of diabetes, hypoglycemia, hormone disorders, and sexual dysfunction. Requires prior completion of a program in internal medicine (see also 51.2946).

31202   Life Sciences Teachers—Postsecondary

51.2918   Family Medicine Residency

A residency training program that prepares physicians in the provision of regular and long-term care to individuals and family members. Includes instruction in comprehensive care and specialist referral, basic surgery, emergency medical procedures, diagnostic imaging, and practice management.

31202	Life Sciences Teachers—Postsecondary
32102A	Doctors of Medicine (M.D.)

51.2919   Forensic Pathology Residency

A residency training program that prepares physicians in the performance of medical autopsies, the analysis of human remains and crime scenes, and the legal follow-up and responsibilities of public pathologists. Requires prior completion of a program in pathology.

21911P	Coroners
31202	Life Sciences Teachers—Postsecondary
32102U	Pathologists

51.2920   Gastroenterology Residency

A residency training program that prepares physicians in the diagnosis and treatment of patients with digestive and other gastrointestinal disorders. Includes instruction in surgical procedures, cancer of the digestive system, nutrition and malnutrition, and counseling the behavioral adjustment of patients with chronic problems. Requires prior completion of a program in internal medicine.

31202	Life Sciences Teachers—Postsecondary

51.2921   General Surgery Residency

A residency training program that prepares physicians in the care and treatment of diseases and disorders via invasive procedures and the etiology, pathogenesis, diagnosis, and management of physical disorders. Includes instruction in clinical and operative skills, pre-operative and post-operative care, trauma management, and endoscopic techniques (see also 51.2912, 51.2923, 51.2933, 51.2942, 51.2950, 51.2953, 51.2962, and 51.2964).

31202	Life Sciences Teachers—Postsecondary
32102J	Surgeons

51.2922   Geriatric Medicine Residency

A residency training program that prepares physicians in the care and management of elderly patients in acute, ambulatory, community, and long-term care settings, and the treatment of diseases and conditions associated with the aging process. Includes instruction in ethical and legal issues, behavioral aspects of illness, socioeconomic factors in care, and rehabilitation therapies. Requires prior completion of a program in family medicine or internal medicine.

| 31202 | Life Sciences Teachers—Postsecondary |
| 32102A | Doctors of Medicine (M.D.) |

51.2923   Hand Surgery Residency

A residency training program that prepares physicians in the investigation, preservation, and restoration by medical, surgical, or physical methods of all structures of the upper extremity that directly affect the form and function of the limb, wrist, and hand. Requires prior completion of a program in orthopedic surgery, plastic surgery, or general surgery.

| 31202 | Life Sciences Teachers—Postsecondary |
| 32102J | Surgeons |

51.2924   Hematology Residency

A residency training program that prepares physicians in the mechanisms and therapy of diseases of the blood, including patient management, diagnostic tests, biopsies, and other procedures. Requires prior completion of a program in internal medicine.

| 31202 | Life Sciences Teachers—Postsecondary |

51.2925   Hematological Pathology Residency

A residency training program that prepares physicians in the laboratory and analytical procedures for studying all facets of hematologic and coagulation disorders. Includes instruction in the management of hematology laboratories. Requires prior completion of a program in pathology.

| 31202 | Life Sciences Teachers—Postsecondary |
| 32102U | Pathologists |

51.2926   Immunopathology Residency

A residency training program that prepares physicians in the diagnosis, treatment, and laboratory management of immunologic diseases. Includes instruction in diagnostic surgical pathology, management of organ transplantation, and immunotherapy. Requires prior completion of a program in pathology.

| 31202 | Life Sciences Teachers—Postsecondary |
| 32102A | Doctors of Medicine (M.D.) |

51.2927   Infectious Disease Residency

A residency training program that prepares physicians in the natural history, prevention, and treatment of major infectious diseases, including sexually transmitted diseases, and the long-term management of patients. Includes instruction in epidemiology, identification and specimen collection techniques, quality assurance, and cost containment. Requires prior completion of a program in internal medicine.

31202	Life Sciences Teachers—Postsecondary

51.2928   Internal Medicine Residency

A residency training program that prepares physicians in the provision of general medical services to adult patients with a wide range of nonsurgical clinical problems. Includes instruction in behavioral aspects of diseases, patient and family counseling, and practice management.

31202	Life Sciences Teachers—Postsecondary
32102A	Doctors of Medicine (M.D.)

51.2929   Laboratory Medicine Residency

A residency training program that prepares physicians in the principles and practices of applied medical research and related techniques, equipment, data systems, and research design. Includes instruction in the management of medical laboratories in research and healthcare facilities.

31202	Life Sciences Teachers—Postsecondary

51.2930   Musculoskeletal Oncology Residency

A residency training program that prepares physicians in the diagnosis and treatment of musculoskeletal neoplasia, and the application of cancer therapy regimes.

31202	Life Sciences Teachers—Postsecondary

51.2931   Neonatal-Perinatal Medicine Residency

A residency training program that prepares physicians in the physiology of the normal neonate, the patho-physiology of the sick infant, and the diagnosis and management of problems of the newborn infant. Requires prior completion of a program in pediatrics and obstetrics.

31202	Life Sciences Teachers—Postsecondary
32102A	Doctors of Medicine (M.D.)

51.2932   Nephrology Residency

A residency training program that prepares physicians in the pathogenesis, natural history, and management of congenital and acquired diseases of the kidney and urinary tract and renal diseases associated with systemic disorders. Includes instruction in organ transplantation and dialysis therapy. Requires prior completion of a program in internal medicine (see also 51.2948).

31202	Life Sciences Teachers—Postsecondary

51.2933 Neurological Surgery/Neurosurgery Residency

A residency training program that prepares physicians in the diagnosis, evaluation, and treatment of disorders of the central, peripheral, and autonomic nervous systems, including their supporting systems and vascular supply; and the evaluation and treatment of pathological processes that modify function or activity of the nervous system, including the hypophysis. Includes instruction in critical-care management and rehabilitation. Requires prior partial completion of a program in general surgery and another surgical specialty.

31202	Life Sciences Teachers—Postsecondary
32102A	Doctors of Medicine (M.D.)

51.2934 Neurology Residency

A residency training program that prepares physicians in the diagnosis and nonsurgical treatment of diseases and abnormalities affecting the nervous system and nerve tissue in adults. Requires prior partial completion of a program in internal medicine (see also 51.2907).

31202	Life Sciences Teachers—Postsecondary
32102A	Doctors of Medicine (M.D.)

51.2935 Neuropathology Residency

A residency training program that prepares physicians in the laboratory analysis of nerve tissues and the clinical diagnosis of neurological and neuromuscular diseases. Includes instruction in nerve biopsies and necropsies. Requires prior completion of a program in pathology.

31202	Life Sciences Teachers—Postsecondary
32102U	Pathologists

51.2936 Nuclear Medicine Residency

A residency training program that prepares physicians in the diagnostic, therapeutic, and investigational use of radionuclides. Includes instruction in imaging and nonimaging technologies and the design and development of instrumentation, procedures, and pharmaceuticals. Requires prior partial completion of a program in radiology, pathology, or internal medicine.

31202	Life Sciences Teachers—Postsecondary

51.2937   Nuclear Radiology Residency

A residency training program that prepares physicians in the imaging by external detection of radionuclides and/or biodistribution by external detection of radionuclides for diagnosis of disease. Requires prior partial completion of a program in diagnostic radiology.

31202   Life Sciences Teachers—Postsecondary
32102A   Doctors of Medicine (M.D.)

51.2938   Obstetrics and Gynecology Residency

A residency training program that prepares physicians in the diagnosis, prevention, and treatment of diseases of women, especially those affecting the reproductive system, and the comprehensive care and treatment of women before, during, and after childbirth.

31202   Life Sciences Teachers—Postsecondary
32102A   Doctors of Medicine (M.D.)

51.2939   Occupational Medicine Residency

A residency training program that prepares physicians in the maintenance of the health of workers, the ability to perform work, the arrangements of work, and the physical and chemical environments of the workplace. Includes instruction in data collection and management and the administration and regulation of occupational medical services.

31202   Life Sciences Teachers—Postsecondary
32102A   Doctors of Medicine (M.D.)

51.2940   Oncology Residency

A residency training program that prepares physicians in the etiology, epidemiology, diagnosis, treatment, and therapeutic management of cancers and related clinical neoplastic diseases. Includes instruction in rehabilitation, supportive care, and the administration of tumor boards. Requires prior completion of a program in internal medicine (see also 51.2930, 51.2947, and 51.2958).

31202   Life Sciences Teachers—Postsecondary

51.2941   Ophthalmology Residency

A residency training program that prepares physicians in the diagnosis, prevention, and treatment of ophthalmic diseases and disorders, and ocular pathology procedures. Includes instruction in eye surgery.

31202   Life Sciences Teachers—Postsecondary
32102A   Doctors of Medicine (M.D.)

51.2942   Orthopedics/Orthopedic Surgery Residency

A residency training program that prepares physicians in the investigation, preservation, and restoration of the form and function of the extremities, spine, and associated structures by medical, surgical, and physical methods. Requires prior partial completion of a program in general surgery, internal medicine, or pediatrics (see also 51.2949).

31202	Life Sciences Teachers—Postsecondary
32102J	Surgeons

51.2943   Otolaryngology Residency

A residency training program that prepares physicians in the recognition and medical management of diseases, congenital anomalies, disorders, and traumas of the head and neck, the air and food passages, and the organs of hearing and speech. Includes instruction in regional surgery. Requires prior partial completion of a program in general surgery.

31202	Life Sciences Teachers—Postsecondary
32102A	Doctors of Medicine (M.D.)

51.2944   Pathology Residency

A residency training program that prepares physicians in the clinical laboratory analysis and diagnosis of disease and anatomic abnormalities. Includes instruction in performing general autopsies, forensic medicine, laboratory management, and quality control (see also 51.2906, 51.2914, 51.2919, 51.2925, 51.2935, and 51.2959).

31202	Life Sciences Teachers—Postsecondary
32102U	Pathologists

51.2945   Pediatric Cardiology Residency

A residency training program that prepares physicians in the diagnosis and management of diseases and disorders of the cardiovascular and cardiopulmonary systems of infants, children, and adolescents. Includes instruction in related public health and community medicine issues. Requires prior completion of a program in pediatrics.

31202	Life Sciences Teachers—Postsecondary
32102A	Doctors of Medicine (M.D.)

51.2946   Pediatric Endocrinology Residency

A residency training program that prepares physicians in the diagnosis and management of endocrine diseases and the regulation of hormone balance in childhood and adolescence. Requires prior completion of a program in pediatrics.

| 31202 | Life Sciences Teachers—Postsecondary |
| 32102A | Doctors of Medicine (M.D.) |

51.2947 Pediatric Hemato-Oncology Residency

A residency training program that prepares physicians in the diagnosis and management of hematologic disorders and malignant diseases, including blood and bone marrow function, in infancy, childhood, and adolescence. Requires prior completion of a program in pediatrics.

| 31202 | Life Sciences Teachers—Postsecondary |
| 32102A | Doctors of Medicine (M.D.) |

51.2948 Pediatric Nephrology Residency

A residency training program that prepares physicians in the diagnosis and management of infants, children, and adolescents with renal and genito-urinary problems, hypertension, and disorders of body fluid physiology. Requires prior completion of a program in pediatrics.

| 31202 | Life Sciences Teachers—Postsecondary |
| 32102A | Doctors of Medicine (M.D.) |

51.2949 Pediatric Orthopedics Residency

A residency training program that prepares physicians in the diagnosis, surgical and nonsurgical treatment, and management of musculoskeletal diseases, abnormalities, and trauma in infants, children, and adolescents. Requires prior completion of a program in orthopedic surgery.

| 31202 | Life Sciences Teachers—Postsecondary |
| 32102J | Surgeons |

51.2950 Pediatric Surgery Residency

A residency training program that prepares physicians in the diagnosis, evaluation, and surgical treatment of diseases, disorders, and trauma in infants and children. Requires prior completion of a program in general surgery.

| 31202 | Life Sciences Teachers—Postsecondary |
| 32102J | Surgeons |

51.2951 Pediatrics Residency

A residency training program that prepares physicians in the comprehensive care and treatment of all aspects of human growth and development from conception through fetal life, infancy, childhood and adolescence, including preventive and therapeutic regimes. Includes instruction in behavioral aspects of illness, related family and community medicine issues, and emergency and critical care procedures (see also 51.2945, 51.2946, 51.2947, 51.2948, 51.2949, and 51.2950).

31202	Life Sciences Teachers—Postsecondary
32102A	Doctors of Medicine (M.D.)

51.2952   Physical and Rehabilitation Medicine Residency

A residency training program that prepares physicians in the diagnosis, etiology, treatment, prevention, and rehabilitation of neuromusculoskeletal, cardiovascular, pulmonary, and other system disorders common to patients of both sexes and all ages. Includes instruction in physiatric examinations, design and prescription of rehabilitation strategies, and the supervision of rehabilitation teams.

31202	Life Sciences Teachers—Postsecondary
32102A	Doctors of Medicine (M.D.)

51.2953   Plastic Surgery Residency

A residency training program that prepares physicians in the repair, replacement, and reconstruction of defects of form and function of the integument and its underlying musculoskeletal system, with emphasis on the craniofacial structures, the oropharynx, the hand, the breast, and the external genitalia. Includes instruction in aesthetic as well as reconstructive surgery. Requires prior completion of a program in general surgery.

31202	Life Sciences Teachers—Postsecondary
32102J	Surgeons

51.2954   Preventive Medicine Residency

A residency training program that prepares physicians in the investigation of and intervention in health and disease problems of communities and defined population groups, and the simulation of behaviors that promote good health. Includes instruction in biostatistics, epidemiology, environmental control, toxicology, and the planning and administration of health programs and services. Requires prior or concurrent completion of a program in public health.

31202	Life Sciences Teachers—Postsecondary

51.2955   Psychiatry Residency

A residency training program that prepares physicians in the diagnosis, treatment, and prevention of mental, emotional, behavioral, and neurological disorders. Includes instruction in psychotherapy, family counseling, referral, clinical diagnosis, and practice management. Requires prior partial completion of a program in neurology and internal medicine, family medicine, or pediatrics (see also 51.2908).

31202	Life Sciences Teachers—Postsecondary
32102E	Psychiatrists

51.2956   Public Health Medicine Residency

A residency training program that prepares physicians in the prevention, control, and treatment of communicable and chronic diseases in communities and defined population groups, with emphasis on the administrative management of healthcare, sanitation, and applied research services.

31202	Life Sciences Teachers—Postsecondary
32102A	Doctors of Medicine (M.D.)

51.2957   Pulmonary Disease Residency

A residency training program that prepares physicians in pulmonary physiology and the treatment of lung diseases, pulmonary malignancies, related vascular diseases, respiratory disorders, diagnostic and therapeutic procedures, and pulmonary pathology. Requires prior completion of a program in internal medicine.

31202	Life Sciences Teachers—Postsecondary
32102A	Doctors of Medicine (M.D.)

51.2958   Radiation Oncology Residency

A residency training program that prepares physicians in the use of ionizing radiation to treat patients with cancer and other diseases. Includes instruction in treatment planning, instrument design and operation, radiation physics, and radiobiology.

31202	Life Sciences Teachers—Postsecondary
32102A	Doctors of Medicine (M.D.)

51.2959   Radioisotopic Pathology Residency

A residency training program that prepares physicians in the use of radionuclides in the study of body fluids, excreta, or tissues quantified outside the body. Includes instruction in laboratory management and safety, quality control, instrumentation, isotope storage, and in-vitro analyses. Requires prior completion of a program in pathology.

31202	Life Sciences Teachers—Postsecondary
32102A	Doctors of Medicine (M.D.)
32102U	Pathologists

51.2960   Rheumatology Residency

A residency training program that prepares physicians in the diagnosis and treatment of patients with acute and chronic rheumatic diseases, diffuse connective tissue diseases, systemic and metabolic diseases, and infections and complications following surgery. Requires prior completion of a program in internal medicine.

31202	Life Sciences Teachers—Postsecondary

51.2961   Sports Medicine Residency

A residency training program that prepares physicians in the pathology and biomechanics of athletic injuries and the effects of injury on the athlete, including both physical and psychological manifestations. Includes instruction in acute and chronic patient supervision, therapy and rehabilitation, and diagnostic procedures. Requires prior completion of a program in orthopedic surgery.

31202	Life Sciences Teachers—Postsecondary

51.2962   Thoracic Surgery Residency

A residency training program that prepares physicians in the evaluation and surgical treatment of pulmonary, esophageal, mediastinal, chest wall, diaphragmatic, and cardiovascular disorders. Includes instruction in bronchoscopy and esophagoscopy. Requires prior completion of a program in general surgery.

31202	Life Sciences Teachers—Postsecondary
32102A	Doctors of Medicine (M.D.)
32102J	Surgeons

51.2963   Urology Residency

A residency training program that prepares physicians in the diagnosis and treatment of diseases of the genito-urinary tract in men and women, including renal transplantation, renal-vascular disease, oncology, infertility and endocrinology, stone disease, and aerodynamics. Requires prior partial completion of a program in general surgery.

31202	Life Sciences Teachers—Postsecondary
32102A	Doctors of Medicine (M.D.)

51.2964   Vascular Surgery Residency

A residency training program that prepares physicians in the surgical treatment of diseases and disorders of the arterial, venous, and lymphatic circulatory systems and of the heart and thoracic aorta. Requires prior completion of all or a portion of a program in general surgery.

31202	Life Sciences Teachers—Postsecondary
32102J	Surgeons

51.2999   Medical Residency Programs, Other

Any residency program in medicine not described above.

32102A	Doctors of Medicine (M.D.)

51.30   Veterinary Residency Programs

A group of instructional programs that prepare veterinarians in advanced clinical work in special areas of veterinary practice. Programs may lead to examination for board certification.

51.3001   Veterinary Anesthesiology

A residency training program that prepares veterinarians in the application of anesthesia for general and specialized surgery and obstetrics, critical animal care, and the care of pain problems. Includes instruction in surgical procedures, current monitoring procedures, fluid therapy, pain management, diagnostic and therapeutic procedures outside the operating room, and operating room safety.

31212	Health Specialties Teachers—Postsecondary
32114B	Veterinarians

51.3002   Veterinary Dentistry

A residency training program that prepares veterinarians in the application of dental care procedures to the teeth, eating surfaces, and oral cavities of animals. Includes instruction in the prevention, diagnosis, and treatment of diseases and abnormalities of animal teeth and gums and related parts of the oral cavity; and related anatomical and physiological principles.

31212	Health Specialties Teachers—Postsecondary
32114B	Veterinarians

51.3003   Veterinary Dermatology

A residency training program that prepares veterinarians in the delivery of specialized care to animals with diseases of the skin, scales, feathers, hair, nails, and mucous membranes. Includes instruction in dermatologic surgical procedures, cutaneous allergies, and diagnostic and therapeutic techniques.

31212	Health Specialties Teachers—Postsecondary
32114B	Veterinarians

51.3004   Veterinary Emergency and Critical Care Medicine

A residency training program that prepares veterinarians in the emergency treatment and management of care for animals with acutely life-threatening conditions, which may include multiple organ failure. Includes instruction in the management of critical care units, emergency procedures, and long-term care of critically diseased animals.

31212	Health Specialties Teachers—Postsecondary
32114B	Veterinarians

51.3005   Veterinary Internal Medicine

A residency training program that prepares veterinarians in the provision of general medical services to animals with a wide range of nonsurgical clinical problems. Includes instruction in behavioral aspects of diseases, animal diagnosis, animal aging, and referral procedures.

31212	Health Specialties Teachers—Postsecondary
32114B	Veterinarians

51.3006   Laboratory Animal Medicine

A residency training program that prepares veterinarians in the principles and practices of applied veterinary research and related techniques, equipment, data systems, and research design. Includes instruction in the management of veterinary and other animal research laboratories and healthcare facilities.

31212	Health Specialties Teachers—Postsecondary
32114B	Veterinarians

51.3007   Veterinary Microbiology

A residency training program that prepares veterinarians in clinical applications of research on harmful microorganisms, including viruses, and of the disease processes they induce in animals.

31212	Health Specialties Teachers—Postsecondary
32114A	Veterinary Pathologists

51.3008   Veterinary Nutrition

A residency training program that prepares veterinarians to apply research on the chemical nature of food substances; the processes by which animals ingest, digest, absorb, transport, utilize, and excrete food and nutrients; and their relation to animal behavior and health.

31212	Health Specialties Teachers—Postsecondary
32114B	Veterinarians

51.3009   Veterinary Ophthalmology

A residency training program that prepares veterinarians in the diagnosis, prevention, and treatment of ophthalmic diseases and disorders in animals, and related ocular pathology procedures. Includes instruction in animal eye surgery.

31212	Health Specialties Teachers—Postsecondary
32114B	Veterinarians

51.3010   Veterinary Pathology

A residency training program that prepares veterinarians in the clinical laboratory analysis and diagnosis of diseased animal tissues and anatomic abnormalities. Includes instruction in performing general autopsies, forensic medicine, laboratory management, and quality control.

31212	Health Specialties Teachers—Postsecondary
32114A	Veterinary Pathologists

51.3011   Veterinary Practice

A residency training program that prepares veterinarians in the provision of regular and long-term care to animals, health services to owners, and the management of independent veterinary practices. Includes instruction in comprehensive care and specialist referral, basic surgery, emergency medical procedures, and diagnostic imaging.

31212	Health Specialties Teachers—Postsecondary
32114B	Veterinarians

51.3012   Veterinary Preventive Medicine

A residency training program that prepares veterinarians in the investigation of and intervention in health and disease problems of animal and related human communities; comparative medicine; and animal public health. Includes instruction in biostatistics, epidemiology, environmental control, toxicology, and the planning and administration of animal health programs and services.

31212	Health Specialties Teachers—Postsecondary
32114A	Veterinary Pathologists

51.3013   Veterinary Radiology

A residency training program that prepares veterinarians in the use of radiologic imaging and therapies to diagnose and treat animal diseases and health problems. Includes instruction in the use and handling of equipment for radionuclide detection and application.

31212   Health Specialties Teachers—Postsecondary
32114B   Veterinarians

51.3014   Veterinary Surgery

A residency training program that prepares veterinarians in the care and treatment of animal diseases and disorders via invasive procedures and the etiology, pathogenesis, diagnosis, and management of physical disorders. Includes instruction in clinical and operative skills, pre-operative and post-operative care, trauma management, endoscopic techniques, and applications to large and small animal medicine.

31212   Health Specialties Teachers—Postsecondary
32114B   Veterinarians

51.3015   Theriogenology

A residency training program that prepares veterinarians in the diagnosis, prevention, and treatment of diseases and health problems affecting the reproductive systems of animals, and the comprehensive care and treatment of parent animals, animal fetuses, and newborn or newly hatched animals throughout the gestation period.

31212   Health Specialties Teachers—Postsecondary
32114B   Veterinarians

51.3016   Veterinary Toxicology

A residency training program that prepares veterinarians in the clinical application of research on the nature and extent of adverse effects of synthetic and naturally occurring chemical substances on animals. Includes instruction in chemical mechanisms and the specialties of reproductive, developmental, genetic, forensic, inhalation, and neuro-behavioral toxicology.

31212   Health Specialties Teachers—Postsecondary
32114B   Veterinarians

51.3017   Zoological Medicine

A residency training program that prepares veterinarians in the specialized treatment and care of zoo animals, performing animals, and animals living in the wild. Includes instruction in the principles and procedures used in the observation, diagnosis, care, and treatment of illness, disease, injury, deformity, or other anomalies in nondomesticated animals.

31212   Health Specialties Teachers—Postsecondary
32114B   Veterinarians

51.3099 Veterinary Residency Programs, Other

Any residency training program in veterinary medicine not described above.

51.99   Health Professions and Related Services, Other

A group of instructional programs (see 51.9999).

51.9999 Health Professions and Related Sciences, Other

Any instructional program in health professions and related sciences not described above.

52.   BUSINESS MANAGEMENT AND ADMINISTRATIVE SERVICES

A summary of groups of instructional programs that prepare individuals to perform managerial, research, and technical support functions related to the commercial and/or non-profit production, buying, and selling of goods and services.

52.01   Business

A group of instructional programs (see 52.0101).

52.0101 Business, General

An instructional program that generally describes the world of business, including the processes of interchanging goods and services (buying, selling, and producing), business organization, and accounting as used in profit-making and nonprofit public and private institutions and agencies. Programs may prepare individuals to apply business principles and techniques in various occupational settings.

52.02   Business Administration and Management

A group of instructional programs (see 52.0201).

52.0201 Business Administration and Management, General

An instructional program that generally prepares individuals to plan, organize, direct, and control the functions and processes of a firm or organization. Includes instruction in management theory, human resources management and behavior, accounting and other quantitative methods, purchasing and logistics, organization and production, marketing, and business decision-making.

13008	Purchasing Managers
13011D	Fundraising Directors
13014A	Property Officers and Contract Administrators
13014B	Administrative Services Managers
15002	Postmasters and Mail Superintendents
15008A	Nursing Directors
15008B	Medical and Health Services Managers
15014	Industrial Production Managers
15023A	Transportation Managers
15023B	Communications Managers
15023C	Utilities Managers
15023D	Storage and Distribution Managers
19005A	Government Service Executives
19005B	Private Sector Executives
19999A	Amusement and Recreation Establishment Managers
19999B	Social and Community Service Managers
19999C	Association Managers and Administrators
19999E	Gambling Establishment Managers
21117	Budget Analysts
21308A	Purchasing Agents and Contract Specialists
21308B	Procurement Engineers
21308C	Price Analysts
21902	Cost Estimators
21905	Management Analysts
21999C	Executive Secretaries and Administrative Assistants
22514B	Electronic Drafters
27199E	Historians
28311	Title Examiners and Abstractors
51002A	First-Line Supervisors, Customer Service
51002B	First-Line Supervisors, Administrative Support
58008	Production, Planning, and Expediting Clerks
81002	First-Line Supervisors and Manager/Supervisors—Mechanics, Installers, and Repairers
81005A	First-Line Supervisors and Manager/Supervisors—Construction Trades
81008	First-Line Supervisors and Manager/Supervisors—Production and Operating Workers
81011	First-Line Supervisors and Manager/Supervisors—Transportation and Material-Moving Machine and Vehicle Operators
81017	First-Line Supervisors and Manager/Supervisors—Helpers, Laborers, and Material Movers, Hand
83008D	Freight Inspectors
97302	Railroad Conductors and Yardmasters

52.0202   Purchasing, Procurement and Contracts Management

An instructional program that prepares individuals to manage and/or administer the processes by which a firm or organization contracts for goods and services to support its operations, as well as contracts it to sell to other firms or organizations. Includes instruction in contract law, negotiations, buying procedures, government contracting, cost and price analysis, vendor relations, contract administration, auditing and inspection, relations with other firm departments, and applications to special areas such as high-technology systems, international purchasing, and construction.

13008	Purchasing Managers
13014A	Property Officers and Contract Administrators
21308A	Purchasing Agents and Contract Specialists
21308B	Procurement Engineers
21308C	Price Analysts
21902	Cost Estimators
58008	Production, Planning, and Expediting Clerks

52.0203   Logistics and Materials Management

An instructional program that prepares individuals to manage and coordinate all logistical functions in an enterprise, ranging from acquisitions to receiving and handling, through internal allocation of resources to operations units, to the handling and delivery of output. Includes instruction in acquisitions and purchasing, inventory control, storage and handling, just-in-time manufacturing, logistics planning, shipping and delivery management, transportation, quality control, resource estimation and allocation, and budgeting.

13014A	Property Officers and Contract Administrators
15023A	Transportation Managers
15023B	Communications Managers
15023C	Utilities Managers
51002A	First-Line Supervisors, Customer Service
51002B	First-Line Supervisors, Administrative Support
58008	Production, Planning, and Expediting Clerks
81002	First-Line Supervisors and Manager/Supervisors—Mechanics, Installers, and Repairers
81008	First-Line Supervisors and Manager/Supervisors—Production and Operating Workers
81011	First-Line Supervisors and Manager/Supervisors—Transportation and Material Moving Machine and Vehicle Operators
83008D	Freight Inspectors

52.0204   Office Supervision and Management

An instructional program that prepares individuals to supervise and manage the operations and personnel of business offices and management-level divisions. Includes instruction in employee supervision, management, and labor relations; budgeting; scheduling and coordination; office systems operation and maintenance; office records management, organization, and security; office facilities design and space management; preparation and evaluation of business management data; and public relations.

13014B	Administrative Services Managers
21999C	Executive Secretaries and Administrative Assistants
28311	Title Examiners and Abstractors
51002A	First-Line Supervisors, Customer Service
51002B	First-Line Supervisors, Administrative Support

52.0205   Operations Management and Supervision

An instructional program that prepares individuals to manage and direct the physical and/or technical functions of a firm or organization, particularly those relating to development, production, and manufacturing. Includes instruction in principles of general management, manufacturing and production systems, plant management, equipment maintenance management, production control, industrial labor relations and skilled trades supervision, strategic manufacturing policy, systems analysis, productivity analysis and cost control, and materials planning.

15014	Industrial Production Managers
22514B	Electronic Drafters
51002A	First-Line Supervisors, Customer Service
51002B	First-Line Supervisors, Administrative Support
81002	First-Line Supervisors and Manager/Supervisors—Mechanics, Installers, and Repairers
81005A	First-Line Supervisors and Manager/Supervisors—Construction Trades
81008	First-Line Supervisors and Manager/Supervisors—Production and Operating Workers
81017	First-Line Supervisors and Manager/Supervisors—Helpers, Laborers, and Material Movers, Hand

52.0206   Non-Profit and Public Management

An instructional program that prepares individuals to manage the business affairs of non-profit corporations, including foundations, educational institutions, associations, and other such organizations, and public agencies and governmental operations. Includes instruction in business management, principles of public administration, principles of accounting and financial management, human resources management, taxation of non-profit organizations, and business law as applied to non-profit organizations.

21117	Budget Analysts

52.0299   Business Administration and Management, Other

Any instructional program in business and administration not described above.

52.03   Accounting

A group of instructional programs (see 52.0301).

52.0301   Accounting

An instructional program that prepares individuals to practice the profession of accounting, and to perform related business functions. Includes instruction in accounting principles and theory, financial accounting, managerial accounting, cost accounting, budget control, tax accounting, legal aspects of accounting, auditing, reporting procedures, statement analysis, planning and consulting, business information systems, accounting research methods, professional standards and ethics, and applications to specific for-profit, public, and non-profit organizations.

21114A	Accountants
21114B	Auditors
21114C	Data Processing Auditors
21117	Budget Analysts
21914	Tax Examiners, Collectors, and Revenue Agents

52.0302   Accounting Technician

An instructional program that prepares individuals to provide technical administrative support to professional accountants and other financial management personnel. Includes instruction in posting transactions to accounts, recordkeeping systems, accounting software operation, and general accounting principles and practices.

21111	Tax Preparers
53108	Transit Clerks
53126	Statement Clerks
53128	Brokerage Clerks
55338A	Bookkeepers
55338B	Accounting Clerks
55341	Payroll and Timekeeping Clerks
55344	Billing, Cost, and Rate Clerks
56002	Billing, Posting, and Calculating Machine Operators
58008	Production, Planning, and Expediting Clerks

52.0399   Accounting, Other

Any instructional program in accounting not described above.

52.04   Administrative and Secretarial Services

A group of instructional programs that prepare individuals to provide administrative and office-support services.

52.0401   Administrative Assistant/Secretarial Science, General

An instructional program that generally prepares individuals to perform the duties of administrative assistants and/or secretaries and stenographers. Includes instruction in business communications, principles of business law, word processing and data entry, office machines operation and maintenance, office procedures, public relations, secretarial accounting, filing systems and records management, and report preparation.

21999C	Executive Secretaries and Administrative Assistants
53123	Adjustment Clerks
53128	Brokerage Clerks
53314	Insurance Policy Processing Clerks
53502	Welfare Eligibility Workers and Interviewers
53505	Investigators, Clerical
53508	Bill and Account Collectors
53702	Court Clerks
53705	Municipal Clerks
53708	License Clerks
53902	Library Assistants and Bookmobile Drivers
53911	Proofreaders and Copy Markers
53914	Real Estate Clerks
55102	Legal Secretaries
55105	Medical Secretaries
55108	Secretaries, except Legal and Medical
55302A	Stenotype Operators
55302B	Stenographers
55305	Receptionists and Information Clerks
55307	Typists, Including Word Processing
55317	Correspondence Clerks
55321	File Clerks
55323	Order Clerks—Materials, Merchandise, and Service
55328A	Statistical Data Clerks
55332	Interviewing Clerks, except Personnel and Social Welfare
55335	Customer Service Representatives, Utilities
55344	Billing, Cost, and Rate Clerks
55347	General Office Clerks
56005	Duplicating Machine Operators
56008	Mail Machine Operators, Preparation and Handling
56017	Data Entry Keyers, except Composing
57102	Switchboard Operators
57108	Central Office Operators
57111	Telegraph and Teletype Operators
57302	Mail Clerks, except Mail Machine Operators and Postal Service
58002	Dispatchers—Police, Fire, and Ambulance
58005	Dispatchers—except Police, Fire, and Ambulance
58008	Production, Planning, and Expediting Clerks

58017	Weighers, Measurers, Checkers, and Samplers—Recordkeeping
58099A	Engineering Clerks
58099B	Transportation Maintenance Clerks

52.0402 Executive Assistant/Secretary

An instructional program that prepares individuals to perform the duties of special assistants and/or personal secretaries for business executives and top management. Includes instruction in business communications, principles of business law, public relations, scheduling and travel management, secretarial accounting, filing systems and records management, conference and meeting recording, report preparation, office equipment and procedures, office supervisory skills, and professional standards and legal requirements.

| 21999C | Executive Secretaries and Administrative Assistants |
| 53705 | Municipal Clerks |

52.0403 Legal Administrative Assistant/Secretary

An instructional program that prepares individuals to perform the duties of special assistants and/or personal secretaries for lawyers, judges, and legal counsels. Includes instruction in business and legal communications, principles of law, public relations, scheduling and travel management, secretarial accounting, filing systems and records management, conference and meeting recording, report preparation, office equipment and procedures, office supervisory skills, legal terminology and research methods, and professional standards and legal requirements.

| 55102 | Legal Secretaries |

52.0404 Medical Administrative Assistant/Secretary

An instructional program that prepares individuals to perform the duties of special assistants and/or personal secretaries for physicians, hospital and health services administrators, and other health professionals. Includes instruction in business and medical communications, principles of health services operations, public relations, scheduling and travel management, secretarial accounting, filing systems and records management, conference and meeting recording, report preparation, office equipment and procedures, office supervisory skills, medical terminology, medical legal and business procedures, and professional standards and legal requirements.

| 55105 | Medical Secretaries |

52.0405 Court Reporter

An instructional program that prepares individuals to record examinations, testimony, judicial opinions, judges' charges to juries, judgments or sentences of courts, or other

---

formal legal proceedings by machine shorthand or other acceptable procedures. Includes instruction in specialized terminology, procedures and equipment, and professional standards and applicable regulations.

53702	Court Clerks
55302A	Stenotype Operators
55307	Typists, Including Word Processing

52.0406   Receptionist

An instructional program that prepares individuals to perform public relations duties for a business, organization, or answering service. Includes instruction in telephone answering techniques, responding to information requests, keeping caller and/or visitor records, placing business calls, operating telephone switchboards and/or other communications equipment, relaying incoming and interoffice calls, schedule maintenance, and public relations skills.

55305	Receptionists and Information Clerks
55332	Interviewing Clerks, except Personnel and Social Welfare
55335	Customer Service Representatives, Utilities
57102	Switchboard Operators
57108	Central Office Operators
57111	Telegraph and Teletype Operators
58002	Dispatchers—Police, Fire, and Ambulance
58005	Dispatchers—except Police, Fire, and Ambulance

52.0407   Information Processing/Data-Entry Technician

An instructional program that prepares individuals to support business information operations by using computer equipment to enter, process, and retrieve data for a wide variety of administrative purposes. Includes instruction in using basic business software and hardware, business computer networking, principles of desktop publishing, preparing mass mailings, compiling and editing spreadsheets, list maintenance, preparing tables and graphs, receipt control, and preparing business performance reports.

53128	Brokerage Clerks
55305	Receptionists and Information Clerks
56017	Data Entry Keyers, except Composing
58008	Production, Planning, and Expediting Clerks

52.0408   General Office/Clerical and Typing Services

An instructional program that prepares individuals to provide basic administrative support under the supervision of office managers, administrative assistants, secretaries, and other office personnel. Includes instruction in typing, keyboarding, filing, general business correspondence, office equipment operation, and communications skills.

53123	Adjustment Clerks
53314	Insurance Policy Processing Clerks
53505	Investigators, Clerical
53508	Bill and Account Collectors
53708	License Clerks
53902	Library Assistants and Bookmobile Drivers
53911	Proofreaders and Copy Markers
53914	Real Estate Clerks
55305	Receptionists and Information Clerks
55307	Typists, Including Word Processing
55317	Correspondence Clerks
55321	File Clerks
55323	Order Clerks—Materials, Merchandise, and Service
55328A	Statistical Data Clerks
55344	Billing, Cost, and Rate Clerks
55347	General Office Clerks
56005	Duplicating Machine Operators
56008	Mail Machine Operators, Preparation and Handling
57302	Mail Clerks, except Mail Machine Operators and Postal Service
58008	Production, Planning, and Expediting Clerks
58017	Weighers, Measurers, Checkers, and Samplers—Recordkeeping
58099A	Engineering Clerks
58099B	Transportation Maintenance Clerks

52.0499   Administrative and Secretarial Services, Other

Any instructional program in administrative and secretarial services not described above.

55326	Procurement Clerks
55344	Billing, Cost, and Rate Clerks
58023	Stock Clerks—Stockroom, Warehouse, or Storage Yard
58028	Shipping, Receiving, and Traffic Clerks
58099A	Engineering Clerks

52.05   Business Communications

A group of instructional programs (see 52.0501).

52.0501   Business Communications

An instructional program that prepares individuals to function in an organization as a composer, editor, and proofreader of business or business-related communications.

34002D	Editors
34005	Technical Writers
53911	Proofreaders and Copy Markers

52.06   Business/Managerial Economics

A group of instructional programs (see 52.0601).

52.0601   Business/Managerial Economics

An instructional program that describes the application of economics principles to the analysis of the organization and operation of business enterprises. Includes instruction in monetary theory, banking and financial systems, theory of competition, pricing theory, wage and salary/incentive theory, analysis of markets, and applications of econometrics and quantitative methods to the study of particular businesses and business problems.

27102A	Economists
31210	Social Science Teachers—Postsecondary

52.07   Enterprise Management and Operation

A group of instructional programs that prepare individuals to develop, own, and operate businesses.

52.0701   Enterprise Management and Operation, General

An instructional program that generally prepares individuals to perform development, marketing, and management functions associated with owning and operating a business.

19005B	Private Sector Executives

52.0702   Franchise Operation

An instructional program that prepares individuals to manage and operate franchises. Includes instruction in legal requirements, set-up costs and capitalization requirements, financing, and applications to specific franchise opportunities.

15026A	Lodging Managers
15026B	Food-Service Managers
43017	Sales Agents, Selected Business Services

52.0799   Enterprise Management and Operation, Other

Any instructional program in enterprise management and entrepreneurship not described above.

52.08   Financial Management and Services

A group of instructional programs that prepare individuals to provide financial or banking services to individuals or institutions.

52.0801   Finance, General

An instructional program that generally prepares individuals to plan, manage, and analyze the financial and monetary aspects and performance of business enterprises, banking institutions, or other organizations. Includes instruction in principles of accounting; financial instruments; capital planning; funds acquisition; asset and debt management; budgeting; financial analysis; and investments and portfolio management.

13002A	Treasurers, Controllers, and Chief Financial Officers
13002B	Financial Managers, Branch or Department
19005B	Private Sector Executives
21102	Underwriters
21105	Credit Analysts
21108	Loan Officers and Counselors
21114B	Auditors
21117	Budget Analysts
21505	Special Agents, Insurance
21911J	Financial Examiners
21921	Claims Examiners, Property and Casualty Insurance
25313	Actuaries
25315	Financial Analysts, Statistical
31224	Mathematical Sciences Teachers—Postsecondary
43002	Sales Agents and Placers, Insurance
43014A	Sales Agents, Securities and Commodities
43014B	Sales Agents, Financial Services
49023A	Cashiers, General
49023B	Cash Accounting Clerks
53102	Tellers
53105	New Accounts Clerks
53108	Transit Clerks
53114	Credit Authorizers
53121	Loan and Credit Clerks
53302	Insurance Adjusters, Examiners, and Investigators
53311	Insurance Claims Clerks
53314	Insurance Policy Processing Clerks
53505	Investigators, Clerical
53508	Bill and Account Collectors
55338A	Bookkeepers
55344	Billing, Cost, and Rate Clerks
56002	Billing, Posting, and Calculating Machine Operators

52.0802   Actuarial Science

An instructional program that describes the mathematical and statistical analysis of risk, and their applications to insurance and other business-management problems. Includes instruction in forecasting theory, quantitative and nonquantitative risk measurement methodologies, development of risk tables, secondary data analysis, and computer-assisted research methods.

25313	Actuaries
31224	Mathematical Sciences Teachers—Postsecondary

52.0803 Banking and Financial Support Services

An instructional program that prepares individuals to perform a wide variety of customer services in banks, insurance agencies, savings and loan companies, and related enterprises. Includes instruction in communications and public relations skills, business equipment operation, and technical skills applicable to the methods and operations of specific financial or insurance services.

21105	Credit Analysts
21108	Loan Officers and Counselors
49023A	Cashiers, General
49023B	Cash Accounting Clerks
53102	Tellers
53105	New Accounts Clerks
53108	Transit Clerks
53114	Credit Authorizers
53121	Loan and Credit Clerks
53302	Insurance Adjusters, Examiners, and Investigators
53311	Insurance Claims Clerks
53314	Insurance Policy Processing Clerks
53505	Investigators, Clerical
53508	Bill and Account Collectors
55338A	Bookkeepers
55344	Billing, Cost, and Rate Clerks
56002	Billing, Posting, and Calculating Machine Operators

52.0804 Financial Planning

An instructional program that prepares individuals to plan and manage the financial interests and growth of individuals and institutions. Includes instruction in portfolio management, investment management, estate planning, insurance, tax planning, strategic investing and planning, financial consulting services, and client relations.

25315	Financial Analysts, Statistical
43014A	Sales Agents, Securities and Commodities
43014B	Sales Agents, Financial Services

52.0805 Insurance and Risk Management

An instructional program that prepares individuals to manage risk in organizational settings and provide risk-aversion services to businesses, individuals, and other organizations. Includes instruction in risk theory, casualty insurance and general liability, property insurance, employee benefits, social and health insurance, loss adjustment, underwriting, and pension planning.

21102	Underwriters
21505	Special Agents, Insurance
21921	Claims Examiners, Property and Casualty Insurance
25315	Financial Analysts, Statistical
43002	Sales Agents and Placers, Insurance
53302	Insurance Adjusters, Examiners, and Investigators

52.0806   International Finance

An instructional program that prepares individuals to manage international financial operations and related currency transactions. Includes instruction in international banking, international monetary and financial policy, money and capital markets, foreign exchange, risk analysis, and international cash-flow operations.

21108	Loan Officers and Counselors

52.0807   Investments and Securities

An instructional program that prepares individuals to manage assets placed in capital markets, and related technical operations. Includes instruction in security analysis, debt and equity analysis, investment strategies, securities markets, computer-assisted research, portfolio management, portfolio performance analysis, and applications to specific investment problems and business situations.

13002A	Treasurers, Controllers, and Chief Financial Officers
13002B	Financial Managers, Branch or Department
19005B	Private Sector Executives
25315	Financial Analysts, Statistical
43014A	Sales Agents, Securities and Commodities

52.0808   Public Finance

An instructional program that prepares individuals to manage the financial assets and budgets of public-sector organizations. Includes instruction in public trusts and investments; the laws and procedures used to plan, prepare, and administer public agency budgets; and the preparation and analysis of public budget projections and policies.

21117	Budget Analysts

52.0899   Financial Management and Services, Other

Any instructional program in financial management and services not described above.

52.09   Hospitality Services Management

A group of instructional programs (see 52.0901).

52.0901   Hospitality Administration/Management

An instructional program that prepares individuals to serve as general managers and directors of hospitality operations on a system-wide basis, including both travel arrangements and promotion and the provision of traveler facilities. Includes instruction in principles of operations in the travel and tourism, hotel and lodging facilities, food services, and recreation facilities industries; hospitality marketing strategies; hospitality planning; management and coordination of franchise and unit operations; business management; accounting and financial management; hospitality transportation and logistics; and hospitality industry policies and regulations.

15026A	Lodging Managers
15026B	Food-Service Managers
19005A	Government Service Executives
19999A	Amusement and Recreation Establishment Managers
19999E	Gambling Establishment Managers
27311	Recreation Workers

52.0902   Hotel/Motel and Restaurant Management

An instructional program that prepares individuals to manage operations and facilities that provide food and/or lodging services to the traveling public. Includes instruction in hospitality industry principles; supplies purchasing, storage, and control; hotel and restaurant facilities design and planning; hospitality industry law; personnel management and labor relations; financial management; facilities management; marketing and sale promotion strategies; convention and event management; front desk operations; and applications to specific types of hotel, motel, and/or restaurant operations.

13011A	Advertising and Promotions Managers
15026A	Lodging Managers
15026B	Food-Service Managers
21999F	Meeting and Convention Planners
41002	First-Line Supervisors and Manager/Supervisors—Sales and Related Workers
43017	Sales Agents, Selected Business Services
51002A	First-Line Supervisors, Customer Service
61099C	First-Line Supervisors/Hospitality and Personal Service Workers

52.0903   Travel-Tourism Management

An instructional program that prepares individuals to manage travel-related enterprises and related convention and/or tour services. Includes instruction in travel agency management,

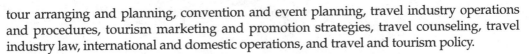

tour arranging and planning, convention and event planning, travel industry operations and procedures, tourism marketing and promotion strategies, travel counseling, travel industry law, international and domestic operations, and travel and tourism policy.

19999D	Service Establishment Managers
21999F	Meeting and Convention Planners
51002A	First-Line Supervisors, Customer Service

52.0999   Hospitality Services Management, Other

Any instructional program in hospitality services management not described above.

52.10   Human Resources Management

A group of instructional programs that prepare individuals to provide employee services and supporting research for businesses and other organizations.

52.1001   Human Resources Management

An instructional program that prepares individuals to manage the development of human capital in organizations, and to provide related services to individuals and groups. Includes instruction in personnel and organization policy, human resource dynamics and flows, labor relations, sex roles, civil rights, human resources law and regulations, motivation and compensation systems, work systems, career management, employee testing and assessment, recruitment and selection, managing employee and job training programs, and the management of human resources programs and operations.

13005A	Human Resources Managers
13005B	Training and Development Managers
13005C	Labor Relations Managers
21502	Claims Takers, Unemployment Benefits
21508	Employment Interviewers, Private or Public Employment Service
21511A	Job and Occupational Analysts
21511B	Employer Relations and Placement Specialists
21511C	Employee Relations Specialists
21511D	Employee Training Specialists
21511E	Personnel Recruiters
21511F	Labor Relations Specialists
21911F	Equal Opportunity Representatives and Officers
31314	Teachers and Instructors—Vocational Education and Training
55314	Personnel Clerks, except Payroll and Timekeeping

52.1002   Labor/Personnel Relations and Studies

An instructional program that describes the study of employee-management interactions and the management of issues and disputes regarding working conditions and worker benefit packages, and that may prepare individuals to function as labor or personnel relations specialists. Includes instruction in labor history, policies and strategies of the labor movement, union organization, labor-management negotiation, labor law and contract interpretation, labor economics, welfare and benefit packages, grievance procedures, and labor policy studies.

13005A	Human Resources Managers
13005C	Labor Relations Managers
21511C	Employee Relations Specialists
21511F	Labor Relations Specialists

52.1003   Organizational Behavior Studies

An instructional program that describes the scientific study of the behavior and motivations of individuals functioning in organized groups, and its application to business and industrial settings. Includes instruction in organization theory, industrial and organizational psychology, social psychology, sociology of organizations, reinforcement and incentive theory, employee relations strategies, organizational power and influence, organization stratification and hierarchy, leadership styles, and applications of operations research and other methodologies to organizational analysis.

21511C	Employee Relations Specialists

52.1099   Human Resources Management, Other

Any instructional program in human resources management not described above.

52.11   International Business

A group of instructional programs (see 52.1101).

52.1101   International Business

An instructional program that prepares individuals to manage international businesses and/or business operations. Includes instruction in the principles and processes of export sales, trade controls, foreign operations and related problems, monetary issues, international business policy, and applications to doing business in specific countries and markets.

15023D	Storage and Distribution Managers
21999H	Customs Brokers
41002	First-Line Supervisors and Manager/Supervisors—Sales and Related Workers

52.12 Business Information and Data Processing Services

A group of instructional programs that prepare individuals to provide computer services in business environments, and to manage such services.

52.1201 Management Information Systems and Business Data Processing, General

An instructional program that generally prepares individuals to provide and manage data systems and related facilities for processing and retrieving internal business information; select systems and train personnel; and respond to external data requests. Includes instruction in cost and accounting information systems, management control systems, personnel information systems, data storage and security, business systems networking, report preparation, computer facilities and equipment operation and maintenance, operator supervision and training, and management information systems policy and planning.

13017C	Computer and Information Systems Managers
21114C	Data Processing Auditors
21999A	Computer Security Specialists
25102	Systems Analysts, Electronic Data Processing
25103A	Database Administrators
25104	Computer Support Specialists
25105	Computer Programmers
25111	Programmers—Numerical, Tool, and Process Control
25199A	Data Communications Analysts
31226	Computer Science Teachers—Postsecondary
51002B	First-Line Supervisors, Administrative Support
56011	Computer Operators, except Peripheral Equipment
56014	Peripheral EDP Equipment Operators
58008	Production, Planning, and Expediting Clerks

52.1202 Business Computer Programming/Programmer

An instructional program that prepares individuals to apply software theory and programming methods to the solution of business data problems. Includes instruction in designing customized software applications, prototype testing, documentation, input specification, and report generation.

21114C	Data Processing Auditors
25102	Systems Analysts, Electronic Data Processing
25103A	Database Administrators
25105	Computer Programmers
25111	Programmers—Numerical, Tool, and Process Control
31226	Computer Science Teachers—Postsecondary

52.1203   Business Systems Analysis and Design

An instructional program that prepares individuals to analyze business information needs and prepare specifications and requirements for appropriate data system solutions. Includes instruction in information requirements analysis, specification development and writing, prototype evaluation, and network application interfaces.

21114C	Data Processing Auditors
21999A	Computer Security Specialists
25102	Systems Analysts, Electronic Data Processing
25103A	Database Administrators
25104	Computer Support Specialists
31226	Computer Science Teachers—Postsecondary

52.1204   Business Systems Networking and Telecommunications

An instructional program that prepares individuals to evaluate and resolve business data system hardware and software communication requirements. Includes instruction in electronic communications networks, telecommunications theory, network theory, hardware and software interfacing, computer network design and evaluation, distance communications systems, computer systems facilities and support design and evaluation, and applications to specific operational needs regarding voice, text, and data communications.

21999A	Computer Security Specialists
25104	Computer Support Specialists
25199A	Data Communications Analysts
31226	Computer Science Teachers—Postsecondary

52.1205   Business Computer Facilities Operator

An instructional program that prepares individuals to operate mainframe computers and related peripheral equipment in business settings. Includes instruction in mainframe operation and monitoring, peripheral equipment operation and monitoring, disk and tape mounting and storage, printer operations, and related computer facility operations.

21999A	Computer Security Specialists
51002B	First-Line Supervisors, Administrative Support
56011	Computer Operators, except Peripheral Equipment
56014	Peripheral EDP Equipment Operators
58008	Production, Planning, and Expediting Clerks

52.1299   Business Information and Data Processing Services, Other

Any instructional program in business information and data processing services not described above.

52.13 Business Quantitative Methods and Management Science

A group of instructional programs that describe the application of scientific and mathematical principles to the study of business problems.

52.1301 Management Science

An instructional program that describes the application of mathematical modeling, programming, forecasting, and operations research techniques to the analysis of problems of business organization and performance. Includes instruction in optimization theory and mathematical techniques, stochastic and dynamic modeling, operations analysis, and the design and testing of prototype systems and evaluation models.

25302   Operations and Systems Researchers and Analysts, except Computer

52.1302 Business Statistics

An instructional program that describes the application of mathematical statistics to the description, analysis, and forecasting of business data. Includes instruction in statistical theory and methods, computer applications, data analysis and display, long- and short-term forecasting methods, and market performance analysis.

25312   Statisticians
31224   Mathematical Sciences Teachers—Postsecondary

52.1399 Business Quantitative Methods and Management Science, Other

Any instructional program in business quantitative methods and management science not described above.

52.14 Marketing Management and Research

A group of instructional programs that prepares individuals to provide services for moving goods and services from producer to consumer, and to manage such services.

52.1401 Business Marketing and Marketing Management

An instructional program that prepares individuals to undertake and manage the process of developing consumer audiences and moving products from producers to consumers. Includes instruction in buyer behavior and dynamics, principles of marketing research, demand analysis, cost-volume and profit relationships, pricing theory, marketing campaign and strategic planning, market segments, advertising methods, sales operations and management, consumer relations, retailing, and applications to specific products and markets.

13011A	Advertising and Promotions Managers
13011B	Sales Managers
13011C	Marketing Managers
13011D	Fundraising Directors

52.1402   Marketing Research

An instructional program that prepares individuals to provide analytical descriptions of consumer behavior patterns and market environments to marketing managers and other business decision-makers. Includes instruction in survey research methods, research design, new product test marketing, exploratory marketing, consumer needs and preference analysis, geographic analysis, and applications to specific products and markets.

27102B	Market Research Analysts

52.1403   International Business Marketing

An instructional program that prepares individuals to perform marketing activities in enterprises primarily engaged in exporting or importing goods and services in world markets. Includes instruction in international trade controls, foreign trade operations, locating markets, negotiation practices, monetary issues, and international public relations.

13011B	Sales Managers
13011C	Marketing Managers
15023D	Storage and Distribution Managers
21302	Wholesale and Retail Buyers, except Farm Products
21305A	Purchasing Agents and Buyers, Farm Products
21911C	Immigration and Customs Inspectors
21999H	Customs Brokers
41002	First-Line Supervisors and Manager/Supervisors—Sales and Related Workers
53102	Tellers
55344	Billing, Cost, and Rate Clerks

52.1499   Marketing Management and Research, Other

Any instructional program in general marketing and marketing research not described above.

52.15   Real Estate

A group of instructional programs (see 52.1501).

52.1501   Real Estate

An instructional program that prepares individuals to develop, buy, sell, appraise, and manage real property. Includes instruction in land use development policy, real estate law, real estate marketing procedures, agency management, brokerage, property inspection and appraisal, real estate investing, leased and rental properties, commercial real estate, and property management.

15011A	Land Leasing and Development Managers
15011B	Property, Real Estate, and Community Association Managers
15011C	Property Records Managers
21917	Assessors
21999D	Land Leasing and Permit Agents
43008	Sales Agents, Real Estate
43011	Appraisers, Real Estate
53302	Insurance Adjusters, Examiners, and Investigators

52.16   Taxation

A group of instructional programs (see 52.1601).

52.1601   Taxation

An instructional program that prepares individuals to provide tax advice and management services to individuals and corporations. Includes instruction in tax law and regulations, tax record systems, individual and corporate income taxation, tax planning, partnerships and fiduciary relationships, estates and trusts, property depreciation, capital gains and losses, dispositions, transfers, liquidity, valuation, and applications to specific tax problems.

21111	Tax Preparers
43014A	Sales Agents, Securities and Commodities

52.99   Business Management and Administrative Services, Other

A group of instructional programs (see 52.9999).

52.9999   Business Management and Administrative Services, Other

Any instructional program in business management and administrative services not described above.

53. HIGH SCHOOL/SECONDARY DIPLOMAS AND CERTIFICATES

A summary of groups of instructional programs that describe the requirements for high school/secondary graduation.

53.01 High School/Secondary Diplomas

A group of instructional programs that describe prescribed programs of study leading to high school/secondary graduation.

53.0101 Regular High School Diploma

An instructional program that describes prescribed minimum requirements specified by a state or other jurisdiction for high school/secondary school graduation.

53.0102 College Preparatory High School Diploma

An instructional program that describes prescribed requirements, specified by a state or other jurisdiction, for high school/secondary school graduation in a program of academic subject matter designed to meet typical college entrance requirements.

53.0103 Vocational High School Diploma

An instructional program that describes prescribed requirements, specified by a state or other jurisdiction, for high school/secondary school graduation in a vocational program—together with other required subject matter, and that may prepare individuals for specific occupations.

53.0104 Honors/Regents High School Diploma

An instructional program that describes prescribed requirements, specified by a state or other jurisdiction, for high school/secondary school graduation in an academic or vocational program at a stated level of outstanding scholastic performance, or via meeting special requirements beyond the minimum.

53.0199 High School/Secondary Diplomas, Other

Any high school/secondary diploma program not described above, such as diplomas awarded to special-education students for completion of an individualized education plan (IEP).

53.02   High School/Secondary Certificates

A group of instructional programs that describe the requirements for successful completion of specified portions of high school/secondary diploma programs.

53.0201   High School Equivalence Certificate

An instructional program that describes the requirements for meeting the minimum high school/secondary graduation requirements specified by a state or other jurisdiction, either by obtaining a prescribed passing score on the national General Educational Development Test (GED), or by satisfactory completion of prescribed coursework, or both.

53.0202   High School Certificate of Competence

An instructional program that describes the requirements for meeting specified performance standards in academic or vocational program areas, as prescribed by a state or other jurisdiction, corresponding to a portion of a high school/secondary diploma program. Includes such requirements as passing a state-mandated academic achievement test, completing specified requirements for subject-matter competence, or achieving a specified high level of performance, and may be awarded independently or in conjunction with a high school/secondary diploma.

53.0203   Certificate of IEP Completion

An instructional program that describes the requirements for meeting specified goals pertaining to an individualized educational plan (IEP) established by a local school system under the authority of a state or other jurisdiction. Specific content varies by student and may or may not equal a regular high school/secondary school program.

53.0299   High School/Secondary Certificates, Other

Any certificate program at the high school/secondary instructional level not described above.

Section 2
Descriptions of All Major Occupations

This section provides descriptions for 1,122 occupations, covering all major jobs in the U.S. economy. We took the information from a database of information developed by the U.S. Department of Labor called the O*NET or Occupational Information Network.

The O*NET organizes jobs into groupings of similar occupations and we've used that structure here. Similar to the grouping structure used in Section 1, the use of groupings allows you to identify jobs that interest you, as well as jobs with similar requirements.

The occupational descriptions include information we thought would be helpful to you in understanding the education or training requirements for that job. Additional information on this section and the O*NET is provided in the Introduction to this book. Table B, following the Table of Contents, presents the O*NET groups, subgroups, and specific occupations to help you quickly locate occupations that interest you.

EXECUTIVES, MANAGERS, AND ADMINISTRATORS

General Managers

TREASURERS, CONTROLLERS, AND CHIEF FINANCIAL OFFICERS (13002A)

Plan, direct, and coordinate the financial activities of an organization at the highest level of management. Includes financial reserve officers.

Average Yearly Earnings: $54,392. **Experience:** Extensive preparation is needed. Extensive skill, knowledge, and experience are needed for this occupation. It may require more than five years of experience. **Education:** A bachelor's degree is the minimum formal education required for this group of occupations. However, many also require graduate school. For example, they may require a master's degree, and some require a Ph.D., M.D., or J.D. (law degree). **Training:** Employees in this type of occupation may need some on-the-job training, but most of these occupations assume that the person will already have the required skills, knowledge, work-related experience, and/or training. **Examples:** Other occupations like this one often involve coordinating, training, supervising, or managing the activities of others to accomplish goals. Very advanced communication and organizational skills are required. Examples include athletic trainers, lawyers, managing editors, physicists, social psychologists, and surgeons. **Standard Vocational Preparation Range:** 8.0 to 9.0—Four years to more than ten years. **Major/Instructional Program:** 52.0801 Finance, General; 52.0807 Investments and Securities. **Related Courses:** Administration and Management; Economics and Accounting; Sales and Marketing; Personnel and Human Resources; Mathematics; Psychology; English Language; History and Archeology; Philosophy and Theology; Law, Government, and Jurisprudence; Communications and Media.

FINANCIAL MANAGERS, BRANCH OR DEPARTMENT (13002B)

Direct and coordinate financial activities of workers in a branch, office, or department of an establishment, such as branch bank, brokerage firm, risk and insurance department, or credit department.

Average Yearly Earnings: $54,392. **Experience:** Considerable preparation is needed. A minimum of two to four years of work-related skill, knowledge, or experience is needed for this occupation. **Education:** This group of occupations usually requires a four-year bachelor's degree, but in some cases does not. **Training:** Employees in this type of occupation usually need several years of work-related experience, on-the-job training, and/ or vocational training. **Related Examples:** Other occupations like this one usually involve coordinating, supervising, managing, or training others. Examples include accountants, chefs and head cooks, computer programmers, historians, pharmacists, and police detectives. **Standard Vocational Preparation Range:** 7.0 to below 8.0—Two years to less than ten years. **Major/Instructional Program:** 52.0801 Finance, General; 52.0807 Investments and Securities. **Related Courses:** Administration and Management; Economics and Accounting; Sales and Marketing; Personnel and Human Resources; Mathematics; Psychology; English Language; History and Archeology; Law, Government, and Jurisprudence.

HUMAN RESOURCES MANAGERS (13005A)

Plan, direct, and coordinate human resource management activities of an organization to maximize the strategic use of human resources, and maintain functions such as employee compensation, recruitment, personnel policies, and regulatory compliance.

Average Yearly Earnings: $45,988. **Experience:** Considerable preparation is needed. A minimum of two to four years of work-related skill, knowledge, or experience is needed for this occupation. **Education:** This group of occupations usually requires a four-year bachelor's degree, but in some cases does not. **Training:** Employees in this type of occupation usually need several years of work-related experience, on-the-job training, and/ or vocational training. **Related Examples:** Other occupations like this one usually involve coordinating, supervising, managing, or training others. Examples include accountants, chefs and head cooks, computer programmers, historians, pharmacists, and police detectives. **Standard Vocational Preparation Range:** 7.0 to below 8.0—Two years to less than ten years. **Major/Instructional Program:** 52.1001 Human Resources Management, 52.1002 Labor/Personnel Relations and Studies. **Related Courses:** Administration and Management; Economics and Accounting; Personnel and Human Resources; Mathematics; Psychology; Education and Training; English Language; Law, Government, and Jurisprudence.

TRAINING AND DEVELOPMENT MANAGERS (13005B)

Plan, direct, and coordinate the training activities of an organization.

Average Yearly Earnings: $45,988. **Experience:** Considerable preparation is needed. A minimum of two to four years of work-related skill, knowledge, or experience is needed for this occupation. **Education:** This group of occupations usually requires a four-year bachelor's degree, but in some cases does not. **Training:** Employees in this type of occupation usually need several years of work-related experience, on-the-job training, and/or vocational training. **Related Examples:** Other occupations like this one usually involve coordinating, supervising, managing, or training others. Examples include accountants, chefs and head cooks, computer programmers, historians, pharmacists, and police detectives. **Standard Vocational Preparation Range:** 7.0 to below 8.0—Two years to less than ten years. **Major/Instructional Program:** 44.0401 Public Administration, 52.1001 Human Resources Management. **Related Courses:** Administration and Management; Personnel and Human Resources; Psychology; Education and Training; Law, Government, and Jurisprudence.

LABOR RELATIONS MANAGERS (13005C)

Plan, direct, and coordinate the labor relations program of an organization. Analyze and interpret collective bargaining agreements and advise management and union officials in the development, application, and interpretation of labor relations policies and practices.

Average Yearly Earnings: $45,988. **Experience:** Extensive preparation is needed. Extensive skill, knowledge, and experience are needed for this occupation. It may require more than five years of experience. **Education:** A bachelor's degree is the minimum formal education required for this group of occupations. However, many also require graduate school. For example, they may require a master's degree, and some require a Ph.D., M.D., or J.D. (law degree). **Training:** Employees in this type of occupation may need some on-the-job training, but most of these occupations assume that the person will already have the required skills, knowledge, work-related experience, and/or training. **Examples:** Other occupations like this one often involve coordinating, training, supervising, or managing the activities of others to accomplish goals. Very advanced communication and organizational skills are required. Examples include athletic trainers, lawyers, managing editors, physicists, social psychologists, and surgeons. **Standard Vocational Preparation Range:** 8.0 to 9.0—Four years to more than ten years. **Major/Instructional Program:** 52.1001 Human Resources Management, 52.1002 Labor/Personnel Relations and Studies. **Related Courses:** Administration and Management; Personnel and Human Resources; Mathematics; English Language; Law, Government, and Jurisprudence.

EMPLOYEE ASSISTANCE SPECIALISTS (13005E)

Coordinate activities of employers to set up and operate programs to help employees overcome behavioral or medical problems, such as substance abuse, that affect job performance.

Average Yearly Earnings: $36,566. **Experience:** Medium preparation is needed. Previous work-related skill, knowledge, or experience is required for this occupation. **Education:** This group of occupations usually requires training in vocational schools, related on-the-job experience, or an associate degree. A bachelor's degree may be required. **Training:** Employees in this type of occupation usually need one or two years of training involving both on-the-job experience and informal training with experienced workers. **Related**

Examples: Other occupations like this one usually involve using communication and organizational skills to coordinate, supervise, manage, or train others to accomplish goals. Examples include dental assistants, electricians, fish and game wardens, legal secretaries, personnel recruiters, and recreation workers. **Standard Vocational Preparation Range:** 6.0 to below 7.0—More than one year and less than four years. **Major/Instructional Program:** 51.1501 Alcohol/Drug Abuse Counseling. **Related Courses:** Administration and Management; Sales and Marketing; Customer and Personal Service; Personnel and Human Resources; Psychology; Sociology and Anthropology; Therapy and Counseling; Education and Training.

PURCHASING MANAGERS (13008)

Plan, direct, and coordinate the activities of buyers, purchasing officers, and related workers involved in purchasing materials, products, or services. Include wholesale or retail trade merchandising managers.

Average Yearly Earnings: $40,934. **Experience:** Considerable preparation is needed. A minimum of two to four years of work-related skill, knowledge, or experience is needed for this occupation. **Education:** This group of occupations usually requires a four-year bachelor's degree, but in some cases does not. **Training:** Employees in this type of occupation usually need several years of work-related experience, on-the-job training, and/or vocational training. **Related Examples:** Other occupations like this one usually involve coordinating, supervising, managing, or training others. Examples include accountants, chefs and head cooks, computer programmers, historians, pharmacists, and police detectives. **Standard Vocational Preparation Range:** 7.0 to below 8.0—Two years to less than ten years. **Major/Instructional Program:** 08.0705 General Retailing Operations; 52.0201 Business Administration and Management, General; 52.0202 Purchasing, Procurement and Contracts Management. **Related Courses:** Administration and Management; Economics and Accounting; Sales and Marketing; Personnel and Human Resources; Production and Processing; Mathematics; Sociology and Anthropology.

ADVERTISING AND PROMOTIONS MANAGERS (13011A)

Plan and direct advertising policies and programs or produce collateral materials, such as posters, contests, coupons, or giveaways, to create extra interest in the purchase of a product or service for a department, an entire organization, or on an account basis.

Average Yearly Earnings: $53,601. **Experience:** Considerable preparation is needed. A minimum of two to four years of work-related skill, knowledge, or experience is needed for this occupation. **Education:** This group of occupations usually requires a four-year bachelor's degree, but in some cases does not. **Training:** Employees in this type of occupation usually need several years of work-related experience, on-the-job training, and/or vocational training. **Related Examples:** Other occupations like this one usually involve coordinating, supervising, managing, or training others. Examples include accountants, chefs and head cooks, computer programmers, historians, pharmacists, and police detectives. **Standard Vocational Preparation Range:** 7.0 to below 8.0—Two years to less

than ten years. **Major/Instructional Program:** 08.0901 Hospitality and Recreation Marketing Operations, General; 08.0902 Hotel/Motel Services Marketing Operations; 09.0201 Advertising; 09.0701 Radio and Television Broadcasting; 50.0602 Film-Video Making/Cinematography and Production; 52.0902 Hotel/Motel and Restaurant Management; 52.1401 Business Marketing and Marketing Management. **Related Courses:** Administration and Management; Economics and Accounting; Sales and Marketing; Customer and Personal Service; Personnel and Human Resources; Mathematics; Psychology; Sociology and Anthropology; Geography; Education and Training; English Language; Foreign Language; Fine Arts; History and Archeology; Philosophy and Theology; Public Safety and Security; Law, Government, and Jurisprudence; Telecommunications; Communications and Media.

SALES MANAGERS (13011B)

Direct the actual distribution or movement of a product or service to customers. Coordinate sales distribution by establishing sales territories, quotas, and goals, and establish training programs for sales representatives. Analyze sales statistics gathered by staff to determine sales potential and inventory requirements, and monitor the preferences of customers.

Average Yearly Earnings: $53,601. **Experience:** Considerable preparation is needed. A minimum of two to four years of work-related skill, knowledge, or experience is needed for this occupation. **Education:** This group of occupations usually requires a four-year bachelor's degree, but in some cases does not. **Training:** Employees in this type of occupation usually need several years of work-related experience, on-the-job training, and/or vocational training. **Related Examples:** Other occupations like this one usually involve coordinating, supervising, managing, or training others. Examples include accountants, chefs and head cooks, computer programmers, historians, pharmacists, and police detectives. **Standard Vocational Preparation Range:** 7.0 to below 8.0—Two years to less than ten years. **Major/Instructional Program:** 08.0705 General Retailing Operations, 08.1208 Vehicle Marketing Operations, 09.0201 Advertising, 52.1401 Business Marketing and Marketing Management, 52.1403 International Business Marketing. **Related Courses:** Administration and Management; Clerical; Economics and Accounting; Sales and Marketing; Customer and Personal Service; Personnel and Human Resources; Mathematics; Psychology; Sociology and Anthropology; Geography; Education and Training; English Language; Foreign Language; History and Archeology; Philosophy and Theology; Public Safety and Security; Law, Government, and Jurisprudence; Communications and Media; Transportation.

MARKETING MANAGERS (13011C)

Determine the demand for products and services offered by a firm and its competitors and identify potential customers. Develop pricing strategies with the goal of maximizing the firm's profits or share of the market while ensuring the firm's customers are satisfied. Oversee product development or monitor trends that indicate the need for new products and services.

Average Yearly Earnings: $53,601. **Experience:** Considerable preparation is needed. A minimum of two to four years of work-related skill, knowledge, or experience is needed for this occupation. **Education:** This group of occupations usually requires a four-year bachelor's degree, but in some cases does not. **Training:** Employees in this type of occupation usually need several years of work-related experience, on-the-job training, and/or vocational training. **Related Examples:** Other occupations like this one usually involve coordinating, supervising, managing, or training others. Examples include accountants, chefs and head cooks, computer programmers, historians, pharmacists, and police detectives. **Standard Vocational Preparation Range:** 7.0 to below 8.0—Two years to less than ten years. **Major/Instructional Program:** 08.0101 Apparel and Accessories Marketing Operations, General; 08.0102 Fashion Merchandising; 08.0204 Business Services Marketing Operations; 20.0301 Clothing, Apparel and Textile Workers and Managers, General; 20.0306 Fashion and Fabric Consultant; 52.1401 Business Marketing and Marketing Management; 52.1403 International Business Marketing. **Related Courses:** Administration and Management; Economics and Accounting; Sales and Marketing; Customer and Personal Service; Personnel and Human Resources; Mathematics; Psychology; Sociology and Anthropology; Geography; Education and Training; English Language; Foreign Language; Fine Arts; History and Archeology; Philosophy and Theology; Law, Government, and Jurisprudence; Communications and Media; Transportation.

FUNDRAISING DIRECTORS (1301ID)

Plan and direct activities to solicit and maintain funds for special projects and nonprofit organizations, such as charities, universities, museums, and other organizations dependent upon voluntary financial contributions.

Average Yearly Earnings: $53,601. **Experience:** Considerable preparation is needed. A minimum of two to four years of work-related skill, knowledge, or experience is needed for this occupation. **Education:** This group of occupations usually requires a four-year bachelor's degree, but in some cases does not. **Training:** Employees in this type of occupation usually need several years of work-related experience, on-the-job training, and/or vocational training. **Related Examples:** Other occupations like this one usually involve coordinating, supervising, managing, or training others. Examples include accountants, chefs and head cooks, computer programmers, historians, pharmacists, and police detectives. **Standard Vocational Preparation Range:** 7.0 to below 8.0—Two years to less than ten years. **Major/Instructional Program:** 09.0501 Public Relations and Organizational Communications; 50.0701 Art, General; 50.0704 Arts Management; 51.0799 Health and Medical Administrative Services, Other; 52.0201 Business Administration and Management, General; 52.1401 Business Marketing and Marketing Management. **Related Courses:** Administration and Management; Economics and Accounting; Sales and Marketing; Psychology; Sociology and Anthropology; Geography; English Language; Foreign Language; Fine Arts; Philosophy and Theology; Law, Government, and Jurisprudence; Telecommunications; Communications and Media.

PROPERTY OFFICERS AND CONTRACT ADMINISTRATORS (13014A)

Coordinate property procurement and disposition activities of a business, agency, or other organization. Administer contracts for purchase or sale of equipment, materials, products, or services.

Average Yearly Earnings: $44,200. **Experience:** Considerable preparation is needed. A minimum of two to four years of work-related skill, knowledge, or experience is needed for this occupation. **Education:** This group of occupations usually requires a four-year bachelor's degree, but in some cases does not. **Training:** Employees in this type of occupation usually need several years of work-related experience, on-the-job training, and/or vocational training. **Related Examples:** Other occupations like this one usually involve coordinating, supervising, managing, or training others. Examples include accountants, chefs and head cooks, computer programmers, historians, pharmacists, and police detectives. **Standard Vocational Preparation Range:** 7.0 to below 8.0—Two years to less than ten years. **Major/Instructional Program:** 44.0401 Public Administration; 52.0201 Business Administration and Management, General; 52.0202 Purchasing, Procurement and Contracts Management; 52.0203 Logistics and Materials Management. **Related Courses:** Administration and Management; Economics and Accounting; Sales and Marketing; Law, Government, and Jurisprudence; Transportation.

ADMINISTRATIVE SERVICES MANAGERS (13014B)

Plan, direct, and coordinate supportive services of an organization, such as recordkeeping, mail distribution, telephone reception, and other office support services. May oversee facilities planning and maintenance and custodial operations. Includes facilities managers. Excludes procurement managers.

Average Yearly Earnings: $44,200. **Experience:** Considerable preparation is needed. A minimum of two to four years of work-related skill, knowledge, or experience is needed for this occupation. **Education:** This group of occupations usually requires a four-year bachelor's degree, but in some cases does not. **Training:** Employees in this type of occupation usually need several years of work-related experience, on-the-job training, and/or vocational training. **Related Examples:** Other occupations like this one usually involve coordinating, supervising, managing, or training others. Examples include accountants, chefs and head cooks, computer programmers, historians, pharmacists, and police detectives. **Standard Vocational Preparation Range:** 7.0 to below 8.0—Two years to less than ten years. **Major/Instructional Program:** 51.0701 Health Systems/Health Services Administration; 52.0201 Business Administration and Management, General; 52.0204 Office Supervision and Management. **Related Courses:** Administration and Management; Clerical; Economics and Accounting; Personnel and Human Resources; Mathematics; Psychology; Education and Training; English Language.

ENGINEERING MANAGERS (13017A)

Plan, direct, and coordinate activities in such fields as architecture, engineering, and related research and development. These persons spend the greatest portion of their time in managerial work, for which a background consistent with that described for engineers is required. Excludes natural science managers; mathematical managers; computer operations, information systems, computer programming, and data processing managers; as well as managers of computer-related occupations.

Average Yearly Earnings: $65,686. **Experience:** Extensive preparation is needed. Extensive skill, knowledge, and experience are needed for this occupation. It may require more than five years of experience. **Education:** A bachelor's degree is the minimum formal education required for this group of occupations. However, many also require graduate school. For example, they may require a master's degree, and some require a Ph.D., M.D., or J.D. (law degree). **Training:** Employees in this type of occupation may need some on-the-job training, but most of these occupations assume that the person will already have the required skills, knowledge, work-related experience, and/or training. **Examples:** Other occupations like this one often involve coordinating, training, supervising, or managing the activities of others to accomplish goals. Very advanced communication and organizational skills are required. Examples include athletic trainers, lawyers, managing editors, physicists, social psychologists, and surgeons. **Standard Vocational Preparation Range:** 8.0 to 9.0—Four years to more than ten years. **Major/Instructional Program:** 14.0801 Civil Engineering, General; 14.0805 Water Resources Engineering; 14.3001 Engineering/Industrial Management; 15.1102 Surveying. **Related Courses:** Administration and Management; Economics and Accounting; Sales and Marketing; Personnel and Human Resources; Engineering and Technology; Design; Building and Construction; Mechanical; Mathematics; Physics; Chemistry; Psychology; Geography; English Language; History and Archeology; Public Safety and Security; Law, Government, and Jurisprudence; Telecommunications; Communications and Media.

NATURAL SCIENCES MANAGERS (13017B)

Plan, direct, and coordinate activities in such fields as life sciences, physical sciences, mathematics, statistics, and related research and development. These persons spend the greatest portion of their time in managerial work, for which a background consistent with that described for mathematicians or natural scientists is required. Excludes engineering managers; computer operations, information systems, computer programming, and data processing managers; as well as managers of computer-related occupations.

Average Yearly Earnings: $65,686. **Experience:** Extensive preparation is needed. Extensive skill, knowledge, and experience are needed for this occupation. It may require more than five years of experience. **Education:** A bachelor's degree is the minimum formal education required for this group of occupations. However, many also require graduate

school. For example, they may require a master's degree, and some require a Ph.D., M.D., or J.D. (law degree). **Training:** Employees in this type of occupation may need some on-the-job training, but most of these occupations assume that the person will already have the required skills, knowledge, work-related experience, and/or training. **Examples:** Other occupations like this one often involve coordinating, training, supervising, or managing the activities of others to accomplish goals. Very advanced communication and organizational skills are required. Examples include athletic trainers, lawyers, managing editors, physicists, social psychologists, and surgeons. **Standard Vocational Preparation Range:** 8.0 to 9.0—Four years to more than ten years. **Major/Instructional Program:** 03.0101 Natural Resources Conservation, General; 03.0102 Environmental Science/Studies. **Related Courses:** Administration and Management; Economics and Accounting; Personnel and Human Resources; Production and Processing; Engineering and Technology; Mathematics; Physics; Chemistry; Biology; Psychology; Geography; Education and Training; English Language; Foreign Language; History and Archeology; Law, Government, and Jurisprudence.

COMPUTER AND INFORMATION SYSTEMS MANAGERS (13017C)

Plan, direct, and coordinate activities in such fields as electronic data processing, information systems, systems analysis, and computer programming. These persons spend the greatest portion of their time in managerial work, for which a background consistent with that described for computer professionals—such as computer systems analysts, computer scientists, database administrators, computer programmers, and computer support specialists—would be required.

Average Yearly Earnings: $65,686. **Experience:** Extensive preparation is needed. Extensive skill, knowledge, and experience are needed for this occupation. It may require more than five years of experience. **Education:** A bachelor's degree is the minimum formal education required for this group of occupations. However, many also require graduate school. For example, they may require a master's degree, and some require a Ph.D., M.D., or J.D. (law degree). **Training:** Employees in this type of occupation may need some on-the-job training, but most of these occupations assume that the person will already have the required skills, knowledge, work-related experience, and/or training. **Examples:** Other occupations like this one often involve coordinating, training, supervising, or managing the activities of others to accomplish goals. Very advanced communication and organizational skills are required. Examples include athletic trainers, lawyers, managing editors, physicists, social psychologists, and surgeons. **Standard Vocational Preparation Range:** 8.0 to 9.0—Four years to more than ten years. **Major/Instructional Program:** 52.1201 Management Information Systems and Business Data Processing, General. **Related Courses:** Administration and Management; Clerical; Economics and Accounting; Sales and Marketing; Customer and Personal Service; Personnel and Human Resources; Computers and Electronics; Mathematics; Psychology; Education and Training; English Language; Communications and Media.

Specialty Managers

POSTMASTERS AND MAIL SUPERINTENDENTS (15002)

Direct and coordinate operational, administrative, management, and supportive services of a U.S. post office; or coordinate activities of workers engaged in postal and related work in an assigned post office.

Average Yearly Earnings: $35,110. **Experience:** Considerable preparation is needed. A minimum of two to four years of work-related skill, knowledge, or experience is needed for this occupation. **Education:** This group of occupations usually requires a four-year bachelor's degree, but in some cases does not. **Training:** Employees in this type of occupation usually need several years of work-related experience, on-the-job training, and/or vocational training. **Related Examples:** Other occupations like this one usually involve coordinating, supervising, managing, or training others. Examples include accountants, chefs and head cooks, computer programmers, historians, pharmacists, and police detectives. **Standard Vocational Preparation Range:** 7.0 to below 8.0—Two years to less than ten years. **Major/Instructional Program:** 44.0401 Public Administration; 52.0201 Business Administration and Management, General. **Related Courses:** Administration and Management; Clerical; Economics and Accounting; Customer and Personal Service; Personnel and Human Resources; Psychology; Geography; Education and Training; Law, Government, and Jurisprudence; Transportation.

COLLEGE AND UNIVERSITY ADMINISTRATORS (15005A)

Plan, direct, and coordinate research and instructional programs at postsecondary institutions, including universities, colleges, and junior and community colleges. Excludes college presidents.

Average Yearly Earnings: $52,436. **Experience:** Extensive preparation is needed. Extensive skill, knowledge, and experience are needed for this occupation. It may require more than five years of experience. **Education:** A bachelor's degree is the minimum formal education required for this group of occupations. However, many also require graduate school. For example, they may require a master's degree, and some require a Ph.D., M.D., or J.D. (law degree). **Training:** Employees in this type of occupation may need some on-the-job training, but most of these occupations assume that the person will already have the required skills, knowledge, work-related experience, and/or training. **Examples:** Other occupations like this one often involve coordinating, training, supervising, or managing the activities of others to accomplish goals. Very advanced communication and organizational skills are required. Examples include athletic trainers, lawyers, managing editors, physicists, social psychologists, and surgeons. **Standard Vocational Preparation Range:** 8.0 to 9.0—Four years to more than ten years. **Major/Instructional Program:** 13.0101 Education, General; 13.0401 Education Administration and Supervision, General; 13.0403 Adult and Continuing Education Administration; 13.0406 Higher Education Administration; 13.0407 Community and Junior College Administration;

13.0603 Educational Statistics and Research Methods; 13.1102 College/Postsecondary Student Counseling and Personnel Services. **Related Courses:** Administration and Management; Economics and Accounting; Sales and Marketing; Customer and Personal Service; Personnel and Human Resources; Mathematics; Psychology; Sociology and Anthropology; Therapy and Counseling; Education and Training; English Language; Foreign Language; History and Archeology; Philosophy and Theology; Public Safety and Security; Law, Government, and Jurisprudence; Communications and Media.

EDUCATIONAL PROGRAM DIRECTORS (15005B)

Plan, develop, and administer programs to provide educational opportunities for students.

Average Yearly Earnings: $52,436. **Experience:** Considerable preparation is needed. A minimum of two to four years of work-related skill, knowledge, or experience is needed for this occupation. **Education:** This group of occupations usually requires a four-year bachelor's degree, but in some cases does not. **Training:** Employees in this type of occupation usually need several years of work-related experience, on-the-job training, and/or vocational training. **Related Examples:** Other occupations like this one usually involve coordinating, supervising, managing, or training others. Examples include accountants, chefs and head cooks, computer programmers, historians, pharmacists, and police detectives. **Standard Vocational Preparation Range:** 7.0 to below 8.0—Two years to less than ten years. **Major/Instructional Program:** 02.0102 Agricultural Extension; 13.0101 Education, General; 13.0301 Curriculum and Instruction; 13.0401 Education Administration and Supervision, General; 13.0402 Administration of Special Education; 13.0403 Adult and Continuing Education Administration; 13.0404 Educational Supervision; 13.0405 Elementary, Middle, and Secondary Education Administration; 13.0406 Higher Education Administration; 13.0407 Community and Junior College Administration; 13.0501 Educational/Instructional Media Design; 13.0601 Educational Evaluation and Research; 13.0604 Educational Assessment, Testing, and Measurement; 13.1001 Special Education, General; 13.1003 Education of the Deaf and Hearing Impaired; 13.1005 Education of the Emotionally Handicapped; 13.1006 Education of the Mentally Handicapped; 13.1007 Education of the Multiple Handicapped; 13.1008 Education of the Physically Handicapped; 13.1011 Education of the Specific Learning Disabled; 13.1012 Education of the Speech Impaired; 13.1101 Counselor Education/Student Counseling and Guidance Services; 13.1102 College/Postsecondary Student Counseling and Personnel Services; 13.1204 Pre-Elementary/Early Childhood/Kindergarten Teacher Education; 13.1301 Agricultural Teacher Education (Vocational); 13.1308 Home Economics Teacher Education (Vocational); 19.0901 Clothing/Apparel and Textile Studies; 20.0201 Childcare and Guidance Workers and Managers, General; 20.0203 Childcare Services Manager; 20.0501 Home Furnishings and Equipment Installers and Consultants; 51.1602 Nursing Administration (Post-R.N.); 51.1608 Nursing Science (Post-R.N.); 51.2899 Dental Residency Programs, Other. **Related Courses:** Administration and Management; Clerical; Economics and Accounting; Sales and Marketing; Customer and Personal Service; Personnel and Human Resources; Food Production; Mathematics; Psychology; Sociology and Anthropology; Therapy and

Counseling; Education and Training; English Language; History and Archeology; Philosophy and Theology; Public Safety and Security; Law, Government, and Jurisprudence; Telecommunications; Communications and Media.

NURSING DIRECTORS (15008A)

Plan, direct, and coordinate facilities or programs providing nursing care. Includes directors of schools of nursing.

Average Yearly Earnings: $48,339. **Experience:** Extensive preparation is needed. Extensive skill, knowledge, and experience are needed for this occupation. It may require more than five years of experience. **Education:** A bachelor's degree is the minimum formal education required for this group of occupations. However, many also require graduate school. For example, they may require a master's degree, and some require a Ph.D., M.D., or J.D. (law degree). **Training:** Employees in this type of occupation may need some on-the-job training, but most of these occupations assume that the person will already have the required skills, knowledge, work-related experience, and/or training. **Examples:** Other occupations like this one often involve coordinating, training, supervising, or managing the activities of others to accomplish goals. Very advanced communication and organizational skills are required. Examples include athletic trainers, lawyers, managing editors, physicists, social psychologists, and surgeons. **Standard Vocational Preparation Range:** 8.0 to 9.0—Four years to more than ten years. **Major/Instructional Program:** 51.0299 Communication Disorders Sciences and Services, Other; 51.1602 Nursing Administration (Post-R.N.); 52.0201 Business Administration and Management, General. **Related Courses:** Administration and Management; Clerical; Economics and Accounting; Sales and Marketing; Customer and Personal Service; Personnel and Human Resources; Mathematics; Biology; Psychology; Sociology and Anthropology; Medicine and Dentistry; Therapy and Counseling; Education and Training.

MEDICAL AND HEALTH SERVICES MANAGERS (15008B)

Plan, direct, and coordinate medicine and health services in hospitals, clinics, managed care organizations, public health agencies, or similar organizations. Includes hospital administrators, long-term care administrators, and other health care facility administrators.

Average Yearly Earnings: $48,339. **Experience:** Considerable preparation is needed. A minimum of two to four years of work-related skill, knowledge, or experience is needed for this occupation. **Education:** This group of occupations usually requires a four-year bachelor's degree, but in some cases does not. **Training:** Employees in this type of occupation usually need several years of work-related experience, on-the-job training, and/or vocational training. **Related Examples:** Other occupations like this one usually involve coordinating, supervising, managing, or training others. Examples include accountants, chefs and head cooks, computer programmers, historians, pharmacists, and police detectives. **Standard Vocational Preparation Range:** 7.0 to below 8.0—Two years to less

than ten years. **Major/Instructional Program:** 51.0299 Communication Disorders Sciences and Services, Other; 51.0701 Health Systems/Health Services Administration; 51.0702 Hospital/Health Facilities Administration; 51.0706 Medical Records Administration; 51.1602 Nursing Administration (Post-R.N.); 51.2916 Emergency Medicine Residency; 52.0201 Business Administration and Management, General. **Related Courses:** Administration and Management; Clerical; Economics and Accounting; Sales and Marketing; Customer and Personal Service; Personnel and Human Resources; Mathematics; Psychology; Medicine and Dentistry; Therapy and Counseling; Education and Training; Public Safety and Security; Communications and Media.

LAND LEASING AND DEVELOPMENT MANAGERS (15011A)

Plan, direct, and coordinate the acquisition or disposition of land, rights-of-way, or property rights for development, mineral, oil, or gas rights, or other special use through options, purchase, or lease agreements.

Average Yearly Earnings: $33,113. **Experience:** Extensive preparation is needed. Extensive skill, knowledge, and experience are needed for this occupation. It may require more than five years of experience. **Education:** A bachelor's degree is the minimum formal education required for this group of occupations. However, many also require graduate school. For example, they may require a master's degree, and some require a Ph.D., M.D., or J.D. (law degree). **Training:** Employees in this type of occupation may need some on-the-job training, but most of these occupations assume that the person will already have the required skills, knowledge, work-related experience, and/or training. **Examples:** Other occupations like this one often involve coordinating, training, supervising, or managing the activities of others to accomplish goals. Very advanced communication and organizational skills are required. Examples include athletic trainers, lawyers, managing editors, physicists, social psychologists, and surgeons. **Standard Vocational Preparation Range:** 8.0 to 9.0—Four years to more than ten years. **Major/Instructional Program:** 52.1501 Real Estate. **Related Courses:** Administration and Management; Economics and Accounting; Sales and Marketing; Mathematics; Geography; English Language; Law, Government, and Jurisprudence.

PROPERTY, REAL ESTATE, AND COMMUNITY ASSOCIATION MANAGERS (15011B)

Plan, direct, and coordinate selling, buying, leasing, or governance activities of commercial, industrial, or residential real estate properties. Includes managers of homeowner and condominium associations, rented or leased housing units, buildings, or land (including rights-of-way). Excludes workers whose duties are not primarily managerial. Workers who are engaged primarily in direct buying, selling, or renting of real estate are reported as sales workers.

Average Yearly Earnings: $33,113. **Experience:** Considerable preparation is needed. A minimum of two to four years of work-related skill, knowledge, or experience is needed

for this occupation. **Education:** This group of occupations usually requires a four-year bachelor's degree, but in some cases does not. **Training:** Employees in this type of occupation usually need several years of work-related experience, on-the-job training, and/or vocational training. **Related Examples:** Other occupations like this one usually involve coordinating, supervising, managing, or training others. Examples include accountants, chefs and head cooks, computer programmers, historians, pharmacists, and police detectives. **Standard Vocational Preparation Range:** 7.0 to below 8.0—Two years to less than ten years. **Major/Instructional Program:** 52.1501 Real Estate. **Related Courses:** Administration and Management; Economics and Accounting; Sales and Marketing; Personnel and Human Resources; Building and Construction; Law, Government, and Jurisprudence.

PROPERTY RECORDS MANAGERS (15011C)

Direct and coordinate activities in an organization relating to searching, examining, and recording information for property-related documents to determine the status of property titles or property rights.

Average Yearly Earnings: $33,113. **Experience:** Considerable preparation is needed. A minimum of two to four years of work-related skill, knowledge, or experience is needed for this occupation. **Education:** This group of occupations usually requires a four-year bachelor's degree, but in some cases does not. **Training:** Employees in this type of occupation usually need several years of work-related experience, on-the-job training, and/or vocational training. **Related Examples:** Other occupations like this one usually involve coordinating, supervising, managing, or training others. Examples include accountants, chefs and head cooks, computer programmers, historians, pharmacists, and police detectives. **Standard Vocational Preparation Range:** 7.0 to below 8.0—Two years to less than ten years. **Major/Instructional Program:** 22.0103 Paralegal/Legal Assistant, 52.1501 Real Estate. **Related Courses:** Administration and Management; Economics and Accounting; Personnel and Human Resources; Education and Training; English Language; Law, Government, and Jurisprudence.

INDUSTRIAL PRODUCTION MANAGERS (15014)

Plan, organize, direct, control, and coordinate the work activities and resources necessary for manufacturing products in accordance with cost, quality, and quantity specifications.

Average Yearly Earnings: $50,710. **Experience:** Considerable preparation is needed. A minimum of two to four years of work-related skill, knowledge, or experience is needed for this occupation. **Education:** This group of occupations usually requires a four-year bachelor's degree, but in some cases does not. **Training:** Employees in this type of occupation usually need several years of work-related experience, on-the-job training, and/or vocational training. **Related Examples:** Other occupations like this one usually involve coordinating, supervising, managing, or training others. Examples include

accountants, chefs and head cooks, computer programmers, historians, pharmacists, and police detectiv.es. **Standard Vocational Preparation Range:** 7.0 to below 8.0—Two years to less than ten years. **Major/Instructional Program:** 01.0401 Agricultural and Food Products Processing Operations and Management; 02.0301 Food Sciences and Technology; 13.0101 Education, General; 13.0401 Education Administration and Supervision, General; 13.0403 Adult and Continuing Education Administration; 14.2801 Textile Sciences and Engineering; 43.0102 Corrections/Correctional Administration; 52.0201 Business Administration and Management, General; 52.0205 Operations Management and Supervision. **Related Courses:** Administration and Management; Economics and Accounting; Sales and Marketing; Customer and Personal Service; Personnel and Human Resources; Production and Processing; Food Production; Chemistry; Psychology; Sociology and Anthropology; Education and Training; Law, Government, and Jurisprudence; Communications and Media; Transportation.

LANDSCAPING MANAGERS (15017A)

Plan and direct landscaping functions and sequences of work to landscape grounds of private residences, public areas, or commercial and industrial properties, according to landscape design and clients' specifications.

Average Yearly Earnings: $46,300. **Experience:** Extensive preparation is needed. Extensive skill, knowledge, and experience are needed for this occupation. It may require more than five years of experience. **Education:** A bachelor's degree is the minimum formal education required for this group of occupations. However, many also require graduate school. For example, they may require a master's degree, and some require a Ph.D., M.D., or J.D. (law degree). **Training:** Employees in this type of occupation may need some on-the-job training, but most of these occupations assume that the person will already have the required skills, knowledge, work-related experience, and/or training. **Examples:** Other occupations like this one often involve coordinating, training, supervising, or managing the activities of others to accomplish goals. Very advanced communication and organizational skills are required. Examples include athletic trainers, lawyers, managing editors, physicists, social psychologists, and surgeons. **Standard Vocational Preparation Range:** 8.0 to 9.0—Four years to more than ten years. **Major/Instructional Program:** 01.0601 Horticulture Services Operations and Management, General; 01.0605 Landscaping Operations and Management. **Related Courses:** Administration and Management; Economics and Accounting; Sales and Marketing; Customer and Personal Service; Personnel and Human Resources; Design; Chemistry; Biology.

CONSTRUCTION MANAGERS (15017B)

Plan, direct, coordinate, and budget, usually through subordinate supervisory personnel, activities concerned with the construction and maintenance of structures, facilities, and systems. Participate in the conceptual development of a construction project and oversee its organization, scheduling, and implementation. Include specialized construction fields such as carpentry or plumbing. Include general superintendents, project managers, and constructors who manage, coordinate, and supervise the construction process.

Average Yearly Earnings: $46,300. **Experience:** Considerable preparation is needed. A minimum of two to four years of work-related skill, knowledge, or experience is needed for this occupation. **Education:** This group of occupations usually requires a four-year bachelor's degree, but in some cases does not. **Training:** Employees in this type of occupation usually need several years of work-related experience, on-the-job training, and/or vocational training. **Related Examples:** Other occupations like this one usually involve coordinating, supervising, managing, or training others. Examples include accountants, chefs and head cooks, computer programmers, historians, pharmacists, and police detectives. **Standard Vocational Preparation Range:** 7.0 to below 8.0—Two years to less than ten years. **Major/Instructional Program:** No specific instructional program for this occupation. **Related Courses:** Administration and Management; Personnel and Human Resources; Design; Building and Construction; Public Safety and Security; Law, Government, and Jurisprudence.

MINING SUPERINTENDENTS AND SUPERVISORS (15021A)

Plan, direct, and coordinate mining operations to extract mineral ore or aggregate from underground or surface mines, quarries, or pits.

Average Yearly Earnings: $58,344. **Experience:** Extensive preparation is needed. Extensive skill, knowledge, and experience are needed for this occupation. It may require more than five years of experience. **Education:** A bachelor's degree is the minimum formal education required for this group of occupations. However, many also require graduate school. For example, they may require a master's degree, and some require a Ph.D., M.D., or J.D. (law degree). **Training:** Employees in this type of occupation may need some on-the-job training, but most of these occupations assume that the person will already have the required skills, knowledge, work-related experience, and/or training. **Examples:** Other occupations like this one often involve coordinating, training, supervising, or managing the activities of others to accomplish goals. Very advanced communication and organizational skills are required. Examples include athletic trainers, lawyers, managing editors, physicists, social psychologists, and surgeons. **Standard Vocational Preparation Range:** 8.0 to 9.0—Four years to more than ten years. **Major/Instructional Program:** No specific instructional program for this occupation. **Related Courses:** Administration and Management; Economics and Accounting; Personnel and Human Resources; Production and Processing; Design; Building and Construction; Geography; Public Safety and Security.

OIL AND GAS DRILLING AND PRODUCTION SUPERINTENDENTS (15021C)

Plan, direct, and coordinate activities required to erect, install, and maintain equipment for exploratory or production drilling of oil and gas. May direct technical processes and analyses to resolve drilling problems and to monitor and control operating costs and production efficiency.

Average Yearly Earnings: $58,344. **Experience:** Extensive preparation is needed. Extensive skill, knowledge, and experience are needed for this occupation. It may require more than five years of experience. **Education:** A bachelor's degree is the minimum formal education required for this group of occupations. However, many also require graduate school. For example, they may require a master's degree, and some require a Ph.D., M.D., or J.D. (law degree). **Training:** Employees in this type of occupation may need some on-the-job training, but most of these occupations assume that the person will already have the required skills, knowledge, work-related experience, and/or training. **Examples:** Other occupations like this one often involve coordinating, training, supervising, or managing the activities of others to accomplish goals. Very advanced communication and organizational skills are required. Examples include athletic trainers, lawyers, managing editors, physicists, social psychologists, and surgeons. **Standard Vocational Preparation Range:** 8.0 to 9.0—Four years to more than ten years. **Major/Instructional Program:** No specific instructional program for this occupation. **Related Courses:** Administration and Management; Production and Processing; Engineering and Technology; Building and Construction; Physics.

TRANSPORTATION MANAGERS (15023A)

Plan, direct, and coordinate the transportation operations within an organization, or the activities of organizations that provide transportation services.

Average Yearly Earnings: $48,817. **Experience:** Considerable preparation is needed. A minimum of two to four years of work-related skill, knowledge, or experience is needed for this occupation. **Education:** This group of occupations usually requires a four-year bachelor's degree, but in some cases does not. **Training:** Employees in this type of occupation usually need several years of work-related experience, on-the-job training, and/or vocational training. **Related Examples:** Other occupations like this one usually involve coordinating, supervising, managing, or training others. Examples include accountants, chefs and head cooks, computer programmers, historians, pharmacists, and police detectives. **Standard Vocational Preparation Range:** 7.0 to below 8.0—Two years to less than ten years. **Major/Instructional Program:** 01.0301 Agricultural Production Workers and Managers, General; 01.0304 Crop Production Operations and Management; 01.0501 Agricultural Supplies Retailing and Wholesaling; 08.0709 General Distribution Operations; 43.0201 Fire Protection and Safety Technology/Technician; 49.0104 Aviation Management; 52.0201 Business Administration and Management, General; 52.0203 Logistics and Materials Management. **Related Courses:** Administration and Management; Economics and Accounting; Sales and Marketing; Personnel and Human Resources; Mathematics; Geography; Public Safety and Security; Law, Government, and Jurisprudence; Transportation.

COMMUNICATIONS MANAGERS (15023B)

Plan, direct, and coordinate the communication operations within an organization, or the activities of organizations that provide communication services, such as radio and TV broadcasting or telecommunications.

Average Yearly Earnings: $48,817. **Experience:** Considerable preparation is needed. A minimum of two to four years of work-related skill, knowledge, or experience is needed for this occupation. **Education:** This group of occupations usually requires a four-year bachelor's degree, but in some cases does not. **Training:** Employees in this type of occupation usually need several years of work-related experience, on-the-job training, and/or vocational training. **Related Examples:** Other occupations like this one usually involve coordinating, supervising, managing, or training others. Examples include accountants, chefs and head cooks, computer programmers, historians, pharmacists, and police detectives. **Standard Vocational Preparation Range:** 7.0 to below 8.0—Two years to less than ten years. **Major/Instructional Program:** 52.0201 Business Administration and Management, General; 52.0203 Logistics and Materials Management. **Related Courses:** Administration and Management; Economics and Accounting; Personnel and Human Resources; Computers and Electronics; Engineering and Technology; Mathematics; Psychology; English Language; Telecommunications; Communications and Media.

UTILITIES MANAGERS (15023C)

Plan, direct, and coordinate the activities or operations of organizations that provide utility services, such as electricity, natural gas, sanitation, and water.

Average Yearly Earnings: $48,817. **Experience:** Extensive preparation is needed. Extensive skill, knowledge, and experience are needed for this occupation. It may require more than five years of experience. **Education:** A bachelor's degree is the minimum formal education required for this group of occupations. However, many also require graduate school. For example, they may require a master's degree, and some require a Ph.D., M.D., or J.D. (law degree). **Training:** Employees in this type of occupation may need some on-the-job training, but most of these occupations assume that the person will already have the required skills, knowledge, work-related experience, and/or training. **Examples:** Other occupations like this one often involve coordinating, training, supervising, or managing the activities of others to accomplish goals. Very advanced communication and organizational skills are required. Examples include athletic trainers, lawyers, managing editors, physicists, social psychologists, and surgeons. **Standard Vocational Preparation Range:** 8.0 to 9.0—Four years to more than ten years. **Major/Instructional Program:** 01.0101 Agricultural Business and Management, General; 01.0299 Agricultural Mechanization, Other; 03.0101 Natural Resources Conservation, General; 44.0401 Public Administration; 52.0201 Business Administration and Management, General; 52.0203 Logistics and Materials Management. **Related Courses:** Administration and Management; Economics and Accounting; Sales and Marketing; Personnel and Human Resources; Engineering and Technology; Design; Building and Construction; Mathematics; Physics; Psychology.

STORAGE AND DISTRIBUTION MANAGERS (15023D)

Plan, direct, and coordinate the storage and distribution operations within an organization, or the activities of organizations that are engaged in storing and distributing materials and products.

Average Yearly Earnings: $48,817. **Experience:** Considerable preparation is needed. A minimum of two to four years of work-related skill, knowledge, or experience is needed for this occupation. **Education:** This group of occupations usually requires a four-year bachelor's degree, but in some cases does not. **Training:** Employees in this type of occupation usually need several years of work-related experience, on-the-job training, and/or vocational training. **Related Examples:** Other occupations like this one usually involve coordinating, supervising, managing, or training others. Examples include accountants, chefs and head cooks, computer programmers, historians, pharmacists, and police detectives. **Standard Vocational Preparation Range:** 7.0 to below 8.0—Two years to less than ten years. **Major/Instructional Program:** 08.0709 General Distribution Operations; 52.0201 Business Administration and Management, General; 52.1101 International Business; 52.1403 International Business Marketing. **Related Courses:** Administration and Management; Economics and Accounting; Sales and Marketing; Personnel and Human Resources; Production and Processing; Design; Mathematics; Psychology; Education and Training; Public Safety and Security; Law, Government, and Jurisprudence; Communications and Media; Transportation.

LODGING MANAGERS (15026A)

Plan, direct, and coordinate activities of an organization or department that provides lodging and other accommodations. Excludes food-service managers in lodging establishments.

Average Yearly Earnings: $26,561. **Experience:** Medium preparation is needed. Previous work-related skill, knowledge, or experience is required for this occupation. **Education:** This group of occupations usually requires training in vocational schools, related on-the-job experience, or an associate degree. A bachelor's degree may be required. **Training:** Employees in this type of occupation usually need one or two years of training involving both on-the-job experience and informal training with experienced workers. **Related Examples:** Other occupations like this one usually involve using communication and organizational skills to coordinate, supervise, manage, or train others to accomplish goals. Examples include dental assistants, electricians, fish and game wardens, legal secretaries, personnel recruiters, and recreation workers. **Standard Vocational Preparation Range:** 6.0 to below 7.0—More than one year and less than four years. **Major/Instructional Program:** 12.0504 Food and Beverage/Restaurant Operations Manager; 52.0702 Franchise Operation; 52.0901 Hospitality Administration/Management; 52.0902 Hotel/Motel and Restaurant Management. **Related Courses:** Administration and Management; Clerical; Economics and Accounting; Sales and Marketing; Customer and Personal Service; Personnel and Human Resources; Food Production; Building and Construction; Psychology; Sociology and Anthropology; Geography; Medicine and Dentistry; Foreign Language; History and Archeology; Philosophy and Theology; Public Safety and Security; Law, Government, and Jurisprudence; Telecommunications.

FOOD-SERVICE MANAGERS (15026B)

Plan, direct, and coordinate the activities of an organization or department that serves food and beverages.

Average Yearly Earnings: $26,561. **Experience:** Considerable preparation is needed. A minimum of two to four years of work-related skill, knowledge, or experience is needed for this occupation. **Education:** This group of occupations usually requires a four-year bachelor's degree, but in some cases does not. **Training:** Employees in this type of occupation usually need several years of work-related experience, on-the-job training, and/or vocational training. **Related Examples:** Other occupations like this one usually involve coordinating, supervising, managing, or training others. Examples include accountants, chefs and head cooks, computer programmers, historians, pharmacists, and police detectives. **Standard Vocational Preparation Range:** 7.0 to below 8.0—Two years to less than ten years. **Major/Instructional Program:** 08.0901 Hospitality and Recreation Marketing Operations, General; 08.0906 Food Sales Operations; 12.0503 Culinary Arts/Chef Training; 12.0504 Food and Beverage/Restaurant Operations Manager; 12.0507 Waiter/Waitress and Dining Room Manager; 19.0501 Foods and Nutrition Studies, General; 19.0505 Food Systems Administration; 20.0401 Institutional Food Workers and Administrators; 20.0405 Food Catering; 20.0409 Institutional Food Services Administrator; 52.0702 Franchise Operation; 52.0901 Hospitality Administration/Management; 52.0902 Hotel/Motel and Restaurant Management. **Related Courses:** Administration and Management; Clerical; Economics and Accounting; Sales and Marketing; Customer and Personal Service; Personnel and Human Resources; Production and Processing; Food Production; Psychology; Medicine and Dentistry; Therapy and Counseling; Education and Training; Public Safety and Security; Law, Government, and Jurisprudence.

NURSERY AND GREENHOUSE MANAGERS (15031)

Plan, organize, direct, control, and coordinate the activities of workers engaged in propagating, cultivating, and harvesting horticultural specialties, such as trees, shrubs, flowers, mushrooms, and other plants. Work may involve training new employees in gardening techniques, inspecting facilities for signs of disrepair, and delegating repair duties to staff.

Average Yearly Earnings: $26,104. **Experience:** Considerable preparation is needed. A minimum of two to four years of work-related skill, knowledge, or experience is needed for this occupation. **Education:** This group of occupations usually requires a four-year bachelor's degree, but in some cases does not. **Training:** Employees in this type of occupation usually need several years of work-related experience, on-the-job training, and/or vocational training. **Related Examples:** Other occupations like this one usually involve coordinating, supervising, managing, or training others. Examples include accountants, chefs and head cooks, computer programmers, historians, pharmacists, and police detectives. **Standard Vocational Preparation Range:** 7.0 to below 8.0—Two years to less than ten years. **Major/Instructional Program:** 01.0101 Agricultural Business and Management, General; 01.0102 Agricultural Business/Agribusiness Operations; 01.0104 Farm and Ranch Management; 01.0601 Horticulture Services Operations and Management, General; 01.0604 Greenhouse Operations and Management; 01.0606 Nursery Operations and Management; 02.0401 Plant Sciences, General; 02.0403 Horticulture Science. **Related Courses:** Administration and Management; Clerical; Economics and Accounting; Sales and Marketing; Customer and Personal Service; Personnel and Human Resources; Production and Processing; Food Production; Design; Chemistry; Biology; Education and Training; Communications and Media.

LAWN SERVICE MANAGERS (15032)

Plan, organize, direct, control, and coordinate the activities of workers engaged in pruning trees and shrubs, cultivating lawns, and applying pesticides and other chemicals, according to service contract specifications. Work may involve reviewing contracts to ascertain service, machine, and workforce requirements; answering inquiries from potential customers regarding methods, material, and price ranges; and preparing service estimates according to labor, material, and machine costs.

Average Yearly Earnings: $25,916. **Experience:** Considerable preparation is needed. A minimum of two to four years of work-related skill, knowledge, or experience is needed for this occupation. **Education:** This group of occupations usually requires a four-year bachelor's degree, but in some cases does not. **Training:** Employees in this type of occupation usually need several years of work-related experience, on-the-job training, and/or vocational training. **Related Examples:** Other occupations like this one usually involve coordinating, supervising, managing, or training others. Examples include accountants, chefs and head cooks, computer programmers, historians, pharmacists, and police detectives. **Standard Vocational Preparation Range:** 7.0 to below 8.0—Two years to less than ten years. **Major/Instructional Program:** 01.0601 Horticulture Services Operations and Management, General; 01.0603 Ornamental Horticulture Operations and Management; 01.0607 Turf Management. **Related Courses:** Administration and Management; Economics and Accounting; Sales and Marketing; Customer and Personal Service; Personnel and Human Resources.

Executives

GOVERNMENT SERVICE EXECUTIVES (19005A)

Determine and formulate policies and provide overall direction of federal, state, local, or international government activities. Plan, direct, and coordinate operational activities at the highest level of management with the help of subordinate managers.

Average Yearly Earnings: NA. **Experience:** Considerable preparation is needed. A minimum of two to four years of work-related skill, knowledge, or experience is needed for this occupation. **Education:** This group of occupations usually requires a four-year bachelor's degree, but in some cases does not. **Training:** Employees in this type of occupation usually need several years of work-related experience, on-the-job training, and/or vocational training. **Related Examples:** Other occupations like this one usually involve coordinating, supervising, managing, or training others. Examples include accountants, chefs and head cooks, computer programmers, historians, pharmacists, and police detectives. **Standard Vocational Preparation Range:** 7.0 to below 8.0—Two years to less than ten years. **Major/Instructional Program:** 02.0401 Plant Sciences, General; 02.0409 Range Science and Management; 03.0101 Natural Resources Conservation, General; 03.0102 Environmental Science/Studies; 03.0203 Natural Resources Law Enforcement and Protective Services; 03.0601 Wildlife and Wildlands Management; 08.0705 General Retailing Operations; 31.0301 Parks, Recreation, and Leisure Facilities Management; 42.0601 Counseling Psychology; 43.0102 Corrections/Correctional Administration; 43.0103 Criminal Justice/Law Enforcement Administration; 43.0107 Law Enforcement/Police Science; 43.0202 Fire Services Administration; 44.0201 Community Organization, Resources and Services; 44.0401 Public Administration; 45.0601 Economics, General; 45.0604 Development Economics and International Development; 45.0605 International Economics; 45.0901 International Relations and Affairs; 50.0701 Art, General; 50.0704 Arts Management; 51.0301 Community Health Liaison; 51.1501 Alcohol/Drug Abuse Counseling; 51.2202 Environmental Health; 52.0201 Business Administration and Management, General; 52.0901 Hospitality Administration/Management. **Related Courses:** Administration and Management; Clerical; Economics and Accounting; Sales and Marketing; Customer and Personal Service; Personnel and Human Resources; Mathematics; Psychology; Sociology and Anthropology; Geography; Education and Training; English Language; Foreign Language; History and Archeology; Philosophy and Theology; Public Safety and Security; Law, Government, and Jurisprudence; Communications and Media.

PRIVATE SECTOR EXECUTIVES (19005B)

Determine and formulate policies and business strategies, and provide overall direction of private sector organizations. Plan, direct, and coordinate operational activities at the highest level of management, with the help of subordinate managers.

Average Yearly Earnings: $58,344. **Experience:** Extensive preparation is needed. Extensive skill, knowledge, and experience are needed for this occupation. It may require more than five years of experience. **Education:** A bachelor's degree is the minimum formal education required for this group of occupations. However, many also require graduate school. For example, they may require a master's degree, and some require a Ph.D., M.D., or J.D. (law degree). **Training:** Employees in this type of occupation may need some on-the-job training, but most of these occupations assume that the person will already have the required skills, knowledge, work-related experience, and/or training. **Examples:** Other occupations like this one often involve coordinating, training, supervising, or managing the activities of others to accomplish goals. Very advanced communication and organizational skills are required. Examples include athletic trainers, lawyers, managing editors, physicists, social psychologists, and surgeons. **Standard Vocational Preparation Range:** 8.0 to 9.0—Four years to more than ten years. **Major/Instructional Program:** 08.0705 General Retailing Operations; 13.0101 Education, General; 13.0401 Education Administration and Supervision, General; 13.0405 Elementary, Middle, and Secondary Education Administration; 13.0406 Higher Education Administration; 13.0407 Community and Junior College Administration; 52.0201 Business Administration and Management, General; 52.0701 Enterprise Management and Operation, General; 52.0801

Finance, General; 52.0807 Investments and Securities. **Related Courses:** Administration and Management; Economics and Accounting; Sales and Marketing; Customer and Personal Service; Personnel and Human Resources; Production and Processing; Food Production; Engineering and Technology; Building and Construction; Mathematics; Psychology; Sociology and Anthropology; Geography; Therapy and Counseling; Education and Training; English Language; Foreign Language; History and Archeology; Philosophy and Theology; Public Safety and Security; Law, Government, and Jurisprudence; Communications and Media; Transportation.

Services Managers

AMUSEMENT AND RECREATION ESTABLISHMENT MANAGERS (19999A)

Plan, direct, and coordinate the activities of organizations that provide amusement or recreational facilities or services to the public.

Average Yearly Earnings: $48,339. **Experience:** Considerable preparation is needed. A minimum of two to four years of work-related skill, knowledge, or experience is needed for this occupation. **Education:** This group of occupations usually requires a four-year bachelor's degree, but in some cases does not. **Training:** Employees in this type of occupation usually need several years of work-related experience, on-the-job training, and/or vocational training. **Related Examples:** Other occupations like this one usually involve coordinating, supervising, managing, or training others. Examples include accountants, chefs and head cooks, computer programmers, historians, pharmacists, and police detectives. **Standard Vocational Preparation Range:** 7.0 to below 8.0—Two years to less than ten years. **Major/Instructional Program:** 08.0705 General Retailing Operations; 08.0901 Hospitality and Recreation Marketing Operations, General; 08.0903 Recreation Products/Services Marketing Operations; 31.0301 Parks, Recreation, and Leisure Facilities Management; 50.0201 Crafts, Folk Art, and Artisanry; 52.0201 Business Administration and Management, General; 52.0901 Hospitality Administration/Management. **Related Courses:** Administration and Management; Economics and Accounting; Sales and Marketing; Customer and Personal Service; Personnel and Human Resources; Education and Training; Public Safety and Security; Law, Government, and Jurisprudence.

SOCIAL AND COMMUNITY SERVICE MANAGERS (19999B)

Plan, organize, and coordinate the activities of a social service program or community outreach organization. Oversee the program or organization's budget and policies regarding participant involvement, program requirements, and benefits. Work may involve directing social workers, counselors, or probation officers.

Average Yearly Earnings: $48,339. **Experience:** Considerable preparation is needed. A minimum of two to four years of work-related skill, knowledge, or experience is needed for this occupation. **Education:** This group of occupations usually requires a four-year bachelor's degree, but in some cases does not. **Training:** Employees in this type of

occupation usually need several years of work-related experience, on-the-job training, and/or vocational training. **Related Examples:** Other occupations like this one usually involve coordinating, supervising, managing, or training others. Examples include accountants, chefs and head cooks, computer programmers, historians, pharmacists, and police detectives. **Standard Vocational Preparation Range:** 7.0 to below 8.0—Two years to less than ten years. **Major/Instructional Program:** 44.0201 Community Organization, Resources, and Services; 44.0401 Public Administration; 44.0701 Social Work; 51.0701 Health Systems/Health Services Administration; 51.0702 Hospital/Health Facilities Administration; 51.1602 Nursing Administration (Post-R.N.); 52.0201 Business Administration and Management, General. **Related Courses:** Administration and Management; Economics and Accounting; Customer and Personal Service; Personnel and Human Resources; Sociology and Anthropology; Education and Training; English Language; Communications and Media.

ASSOCIATION MANAGERS AND ADMINISTRATORS (19999C)

Direct and coordinate the activities of professional, trade, or business associations to achieve the goals, objectives, and standards of the association.

Average Yearly Earnings: $48,339. **Experience:** Considerable preparation is needed. A minimum of two to four years of work-related skill, knowledge, or experience is needed for this occupation. **Education:** This group of occupations usually requires a four-year bachelor's degree, but in some cases does not. **Training:** Employees in this type of occupation usually need several years of work-related experience, on-the-job training, and/or vocational training. **Related Examples:** Other occupations like this one usually involve coordinating, supervising, managing, or training others. Examples include accountants, chefs and head cooks, computer programmers, historians, pharmacists, and police detectives. **Standard Vocational Preparation Range:** 7.0 to below 8.0—Two years to less than ten years. **Major/Instructional Program:** 51.1602 Nursing Administration (Post-R.N.); 52.0201 Business Administration and Management, General. **Related Courses:** Administration and Management; Economics and Accounting; Mathematics; Education and Training.

SERVICE ESTABLISHMENT MANAGERS (19999D)

Manage service establishment or direct and coordinate service activities within an establishment. Plan, direct, and coordinate service operations within an organization, or the activities of organizations that provide services.

Average Yearly Earnings: $48,339. **Experience:** Considerable preparation is needed. A minimum of two to four years of work-related skill, knowledge, or experience is needed for this occupation. **Education:** This group of occupations usually requires a four-year bachelor's degree, but in some cases does not. **Training:** Employees in this type of occupation usually need several years of work-related experience, on-the-job training, and/or vocational training. **Related Examples:** Other occupations like this one usually

involve coordinating, supervising, managing, or training others. Examples include accountants, chefs and head cooks, computer programmers, historians, pharmacists, and police detectives. **Standard Vocational Preparation Range:** 7.0 to below 8.0—Two years to less than ten years. **Major/Instructional Program:** 01.0201 Agricultural Mechanization, General; 08.1105 Travel Services Marketing Operations; 20.0301 Clothing, Apparel, and Textile Workers and Managers, General; 20.0309 Drycleaner and Launderer; 52.0903 Travel-Tourism Management. **Related Courses:** Administration and Management; Economics and Accounting; Sales and Marketing; Customer and Personal Service; Personnel and Human Resources; Education and Training.

GAMBLING ESTABLISHMENT MANAGERS (19999E)

Plan, direct, and coordinate the activities of organizations or establishments, such as casinos, cardrooms, and racetracks, that provide gambling or games-of-chance activities to the public.

Average Yearly Earnings: $48,339. **Experience:** Medium preparation is needed. Previous work-related skill, knowledge, or experience is required for this occupation. **Education:** This group of occupations usually requires training in vocational schools, related on-the-job experience, or an associate degree. A bachelor's degree may be required. **Training:** Employees in this type of occupation usually need one or two years of training involving both on-the-job experience and informal training with experienced workers. **Related Examples:** Other occupations like this one usually involve using communication and organizational skills to coordinate, supervise, manage, or train others to accomplish goals. Examples include dental assistants, electricians, fish and game wardens, legal secretaries, personnel recruiters, and recreation workers. **Standard Vocational Preparation Range:** 6.0 to below 7.0—More than one year and less than four years. **Major/Instructional Program:** 52.0201 Business Administration and Management, General; 52.0901 Hospitality Administration/Management. **Related Courses:** Administration and Management; Economics and Accounting; Customer and Personal Service; Personnel and Human Resources; Mathematics.

SECURITY MANAGERS (19999F)

Plan, direct, and coordinate the implementation of security procedures, systems, and personnel to protect private or public property and personnel from theft, fire, and personal injury.

Average Yearly Earnings: $48,339. **Experience:** Medium preparation is needed. Previous work-related skill, knowledge, or experience is required for this occupation. **Education:** This group of occupations usually requires training in vocational schools, related on-the-job experience, or an associate degree. A bachelor's degree may be required. **Training:** Employees in this type of occupation usually need one or two years of training involving both on-the-job experience and informal training with experienced workers. **Related Examples:** Other occupations like this one usually involve using communication and organizational skills to coordinate, supervise, manage, or train others to accomplish goals. Examples include dental assistants, electricians, fish and game wardens, legal secretaries, personnel recruiters, and recreation workers. **Standard Vocational Preparation Range:** 6.0 to below 7.0—More than one year and less than four years. **Major/Instructional Program:** 43.0109 Security and Loss Prevention Services. **Related Courses:** Administration and Management; Sales and Marketing; Customer and Personal Service; Personnel and Human Resources; Education and Training; Public Safety and Security; Law, Government, and Jurisprudence.

PROFESSIONAL AND SUPPORT SPECIALISTS—FINANCIAL SPECIALISTS, ENGINEERS, SCIENTISTS, MATHEMATICIANS, SOCIAL SCIENTISTS, SOCIAL SERVICES WORKERS, RELIGIOUS WORKERS, AND LEGAL WORKERS

Financial Specialists

UNDERWRITERS (21102)

Review individual applications for insurance to evaluate the degree of risk involved and determine acceptance of the applications.

Average Yearly Earnings: $38,792. **Experience:** Considerable preparation is needed. A minimum of two to four years of work-related skill, knowledge, or experience is needed for this occupation. **Education:** This group of occupations usually requires a four-year bachelor's degree, but in some cases does not. **Training:** Employees in this type of occupation usually need several years of work-related experience, on-the-job training, and/or vocational training. **Related Examples:** Other occupations like this one usually involve coordinating, supervising, managing, or training others. Examples include accountants, chefs and head cooks, computer programmers, historians, pharmacists, and police detectives. **Standard Vocational Preparation Range:** 7.0 to below 8.0—Two years to less than ten years. **Major/Instructional Program:** 52.0801 Finance, General; 52.0805 Insurance and Risk Management. **Related Courses:** Clerical; Economics and Accounting; Mathematics.

CREDIT ANALYSTS (21105)

Analyze current credit data and financial statements of individuals or firms to determine the degree of risk involved in extending credit or lending money. Prepare reports with this credit information for use in decision making.

Average Yearly Earnings: $36,961. **Experience:** Considerable preparation is needed. A minimum of two to four years of work-related skill, knowledge, or experience is needed for this occupation. **Education:** This group of occupations usually requires a four-year

bachelor's degree, but in some cases does not. **Training:** Employees in this type of occupation usually need several years of work-related experience, on-the-job training, and/or vocational training. **Related Examples:** Other occupations like this one usually involve coordinating, supervising, managing, or training others. Examples include accountants, chefs and head cooks, computer programmers, historians, pharmacists, and police detectives. **Standard Vocational Preparation Range:** 7.0 to below 8.0—Two years to less than ten years. **Major/Instructional Program:** 52.0801 Finance, General; 52.0803 Banking and Financial Support Services. **Related Courses:** Economics and Accounting; Personnel and Human Resources; Computers and Electronics; Mathematics; Geography; History and Archeology; Philosophy and Theology; Law, Government, and Jurisprudence.

LOAN OFFICERS AND COUNSELORS (21108)

Evaluate, authorize, or recommend approval of commercial, real estate, or credit loans. Advise borrowers on financial status and methods of payments. Include mortgage loan officers or agents, collection analysts, and loan servicing officers.

Average Yearly Earnings: $37,419. **Experience:** Considerable preparation is needed. A minimum of two to four years of work-related skill, knowledge, or experience is needed for this occupation. **Education:** This group of occupations usually requires a four-year bachelor's degree, but in some cases does not. **Training:** Employees in this type of occupation usually need several years of work-related experience, on-the-job training, and/or vocational training. **Related Examples:** Other occupations like this one usually involve coordinating, supervising, managing, or training others. Examples include accountants, chefs and head cooks, computer programmers, historians, pharmacists, and police detectives. **Standard Vocational Preparation Range:** 7.0 to below 8.0—Two years to less than ten years. **Major/Instructional Program:** 08.0401 Financial Services Marketing Operations; 52.0801 Finance, General; 52.0803 Banking and Financial Support Services; 52.0806 International Finance. **Related Courses:** Clerical; Economics and Accounting; Sales and Marketing; Customer and Personal Service; Personnel and Human Resources; Mathematics; Law, Government, and Jurisprudence; Communications and Media.

TAX PREPARERS (21111)

Prepare tax returns for individuals or small businesses, but do not have the background or responsibilities of an accredited accountant or certified public accountant. May work for established tax return firm.

Average Yearly Earnings: $22,776. **Experience:** Some preparation is needed. Some previous work-related skill, knowledge, or experience may be helpful in this occupation, but usually is not needed. **Education:** This group of occupations usually requires a high school diploma and may require some vocational training or job-related course work. In some cases, an associate or bachelor's degree is needed. **Training:** Employees in this type of occupation need anywhere from a few months to one year of working with experienced employees. **Related Examples:** Other occupations like this one often involve using your knowledge and skills to help others. Examples include drywall installers, fire inspectors, flight attendants, pharmacy technicians, retail salespersons, and tellers. **Standard Vocational Preparation Range:** 4.0 to below 6.0—Six months to less than two years. **Major/Instructional Program:** 52.0302 Accounting Technician, 52.1601 Taxation. **Related Courses:** Clerical; Economics and Accounting; Mathematics; Law, Government, and Jurisprudence.

ACCOUNTANTS (2I I I4A)

Analyze financial information and prepare financial reports to determine or maintain record of assets, liabilities, profit and loss, tax liability, or other financial activities within an organization. Excludes auditors.

Average Yearly Earnings: $38,168. **Experience:** Considerable preparation is needed. A minimum of two to four years of work-related skill, knowledge, or experience is needed for this occupation. **Education:** This group of occupations usually requires a four-year bachelor's degree, but in some cases does not. **Training:** Employees in this type of occupation usually need several years of work-related experience, on-the-job training, and/or vocational training. **Related Examples:** Other occupations like this one usually involve coordinating, supervising, managing, or training others. Examples include chefs and head cooks, computer programmers, historians, pharmacists, and police detectives. **Standard Vocational Preparation Range:** 7.0 to below 8.0—Two years to less than ten years. **Major/Instructional Program:** 52.0301 Accounting. **Related Courses:** Administration and Management; Clerical; Economics and Accounting; Personnel and Human Resources; Computers and Electronics; Mathematics; Sociology and Anthropology; Education and Training; English Language; Philosophy and Theology; Law, Government, and Jurisprudence.

AUDITORS (2I I I4B)

Examine and analyze accounting records to determine the financial status of an establishment and prepare financial reports concerning operating procedures.

Average Yearly Earnings: $38,168. **Experience:** Considerable preparation is needed. A minimum of two to four years of work-related skill, knowledge, or experience is needed for this occupation. **Education:** This group of occupations usually requires a four-year bachelor's degree, but in some cases does not. **Training:** Employees in this type of occupation usually need several years of work-related experience, on-the-job training, and/or vocational training. **Related Examples:** Other occupations like this one usually involve coordinating, supervising, managing, or training others. Examples include accountants, chefs and head cooks, computer programmers, historians, pharmacists, and police detectives. **Standard Vocational Preparation Range:** 7.0 to below 8.0—Two years to less than ten years. **Major/Instructional Program:** 52.0301 Accounting; 52.0801 Finance, General. **Related Courses:** Administration and Management; Clerical; Economics and Accounting; Computers and Electronics; Mathematics; English Language; Philosophy and Theology; Law, Government, and Jurisprudence.

DATA PROCESSING AUDITORS (21114C)

Plan and conduct audits of data processing systems and applications to safeguard assets, ensure accuracy of data, and promote operational efficiency.

Average Yearly Earnings: $38,168. **Experience:** Considerable preparation is needed. A minimum of two to four years of work-related skill, knowledge, or experience is needed for this occupation. **Education:** This group of occupations usually requires a four-year bachelor's degree, but in some cases does not. **Training:** Employees in this type of occupation usually need several years of work-related experience, on-the-job training, and/or vocational training. **Related Examples:** Other occupations like this one usually involve coordinating, supervising, managing, or training others. Examples include accountants, chefs and head cooks, computer programmers, historians, pharmacists, and police detectives. **Standard Vocational Preparation Range:** 7.0 to below 8.0—Two years to less than ten years. **Major/Instructional Program:** 11.0201 Computer Programming; 52.0301 Accounting; 52.1201 Management Information Systems and Business Data Processing, General; 52.1202 Business Computer Programming/Programmer; 52.1203 Business Systems Analysis and Design. **Related Courses:** Administration and Management; Clerical; Economics and Accounting; Computers and Electronics; Mathematics; Philosophy and Theology; Telecommunications.

BUDGET ANALYSTS (21117)

Examine budget estimates for completeness, accuracy, and conformance with procedures and regulations. Examine requests for budget revisions, recommend approval or denial, and draft correspondence. Analyze monthly department budgeting and accounting reports for the purpose of maintaining expenditure controls. Provide technical assistance to officials in the preparation of budgets.

Average Yearly Earnings: $42,057. **Experience:** Considerable preparation is needed. A minimum of two to four years of work-related skill, knowledge, or experience is needed for this occupation. **Education:** This group of occupations usually requires a four-year bachelor's degree, but in some cases does not. **Training:** Employees in this type of occupation usually need several years of work-related experience, on-the-job training, and/or vocational training. **Related Examples:** Other occupations like this one usually involve coordinating, supervising, managing, or training others. Examples include accountants, chefs and head cooks, computer programmers, historians, pharmacists, and police detectives. **Standard Vocational Preparation Range:** 7.0 to below 8.0—Two years to less than ten years. **Major/Instructional Program:** 44.0401 Public Administration; 52.0201 Business Administration and Management, General; 52.0206 Non-Profit and Public Management; 52.0301 Accounting; 52.0801 Finance, General; 52.0808 Public Finance. **Related Courses:** Administration and Management; Economics and Accounting; Personnel and Human Resources; Computers and Electronics; Mathematics; Education and Training.

FINANCIAL COUNSELORS (21199B)

Provide financial counseling to individuals regarding debt management or special financial aid for students.

Experience: Medium preparation is needed. Previous work-related skill, knowledge, or experience is required for this occupation. **Education:** This group of occupations usually requires training in vocational schools, related on-the-job experience, or an associate degree. A bachelor's degree may be required. **Training:** Employees in this type of occupation usually need one or two years of training involving both on-the-job experience and informal training with experienced workers. **Related Examples:** Other occupations like this one usually involve using communication and organizational skills to coordinate, supervise, manage, or train others to accomplish goals. Examples include dental assistants, electricians, fish and game wardens, legal secretaries, personnel recruiters, and recreation workers. **Standard Vocational Preparation Range:** 6.0 to below 7.0—More than one year and less than four years. **Major/Instructional Program:** 52.0801 Finance, General; 52.0804 Financial Planning. **Related Courses:** Economics and Accounting; Customer and Personal Service; Mathematics; Therapy and Counseling.

Purchasers and Buyers

WHOLESALE AND RETAIL BUYERS, EXCEPT FARM PRODUCTS (21302)

Buy merchandise or commodities (other than farm products) for resale to consumers at the wholesale or retail level, including both durable and nondurable goods. Analyze past buying trends, sales records, price, and quality of merchandise to determine value and yield. Select, order, and authorize payment for merchandise according to contractual agreements. May conduct meetings with sales personnel and introduce new products. Include assistant buyers.

Average Yearly Earnings: $32,531. **Experience:** Medium preparation is needed. Previous work-related skill, knowledge, or experience is required for this occupation. **Education:** This group of occupations usually requires training in vocational schools, related on-the-job experience, or an associate degree. A bachelor's degree may be required. **Training:** Employees in this type of occupation usually need one or two years of training involving both on-the-job experience and informal training with experienced workers. **Related Examples:** Other occupations like this one usually involve using communication and organizational skills to coordinate, supervise, manage, or train others to accomplish goals. Examples include dental assistants, electricians, fish and game wardens, legal secretaries, personnel recruiters, and recreation workers. **Standard Vocational Preparation Range:** 6.0 to below 7.0—More than one year and less than four years. **Major/Instructional Program:** 01.0501 Agricultural Supplies Retailing and Wholesaling; 08.0704 General Buying Operations; 08.0705 General Retailing Operations; 20.0301 Clothing, Apparel and Textile Workers and Managers, General; 20.0306 Fashion and Fabric Consultant; 20.0501 Home Furnishings and Equipment Installers and Consultants;

52.1403 International Business Marketing. **Related Courses:** Administration and Management; Economics and Accounting; Sales and Marketing; Customer and Personal Service; Personnel and Human Resources; Mathematics; Psychology; Sociology and Anthropology; Geography; Education and Training; Foreign Language; Philosophy and Theology; Communications and Media; Transportation.

PURCHASING AGENTS AND BUYERS, FARM PRODUCTS (21305A)

Arrange or contract for the purchase of farm products for further processing or resale.

Average Yearly Earnings: $38,251. **Experience:** Considerable preparation is needed. A minimum of two to four years of work-related skill, knowledge, or experience is needed for this occupation. **Education:** This group of occupations usually requires a four-year bachelor's degree, but in some cases does not. **Training:** Employees in this type of occupation usually need several years of work-related experience, on-the-job training, and/or vocational training. **Related Examples:** Other occupations like this one usually involve coordinating, supervising, managing, or training others. Examples include accountants, chefs and head cooks, computer programmers, historians, pharmacists, and police detectives. **Standard Vocational Preparation Range:** 7.0 to below 8.0—Two years to less than ten years. **Major/Instructional Program:** 01.0301 Agricultural Production Workers and Managers, General; 01.0302 Agricultural Animal Husbandry and Production Management; 01.0501 Agricultural Supplies Retailing and Wholesaling; 03.0401 Forest Harvesting and Production Technology/Technician; 08.0704 General Buying Operations; 08.0706 General Selling Skills and Sales Operations; 52.1403 International Business Marketing. **Related Courses:** Administration and Management; Clerical; Economics and Accounting; Sales and Marketing; Production and Processing; Food Production; Mathematics; Biology; English Language; Communications and Media; Transportation.

PURCHASING AGENTS AND CONTRACT SPECIALISTS (21308A)

Coordinate activities involved with procuring goods and services from suppliers. May negotiate with suppliers to draw up procurement contracts and administer, terminate, or renegotiate contracts. Exclude purchasing agents and buyers of farm products.

Average Yearly Earnings: $35,859. **Experience:** Considerable preparation is needed. A minimum of two to four years of work-related skill, knowledge, or experience is needed for this occupation. **Education:** This group of occupations usually requires a four-year bachelor's degree, but in some cases does not. **Training:** Employees in this type of occupation usually need several years of work-related experience, on-the-job training, and/or vocational training. **Related Examples:** Other occupations like this one usually involve coordinating, supervising, managing, or training others. Examples include accountants, chefs and head cooks, computer programmers, historians, pharmacists, and police detectives. **Standard Vocational Preparation Range:** 7.0 to below 8.0—Two years to less than ten years. **Major/Instructional Program:** 01.0501 Agricultural Supplies Retailing and Wholesaling; 08.0704 General Buying Operations; 20.0401 Institutional Food Workers and Administrators; 20.0409 Institutional Food Services Administrator; 52.0201 Business Administration and Management, General; 52.0202 Purchasing, Procurement and Contracts Management. **Related Courses:** Administration and Management; Clerical; Economics and Accounting; Sales and Marketing; Computers and Electronics; Law, Government, and Jurisprudence; Transportation.

PROCUREMENT ENGINEERS (21308B)

Coordinate the development and use of engineering specifications and requirements to facilitate the procurement of parts, tools, equipment, or other products or materials.

Average Yearly Earnings: $35,859. **Experience:** Considerable preparation is needed. A minimum of two to four years of work-related skill, knowledge, or experience is needed for this occupation. **Education:** This group of occupations usually requires a four-year bachelor's degree, but in some cases does not. **Training:** Employees in this type of occupation usually need several years of work-related experience, on-the-job training, and/or vocational training. **Related Examples:** Other occupations like this one usually involve coordinating, supervising, managing, or training others. Examples include accountants, chefs and head cooks, computer programmers, historians, pharmacists, and police detectives. **Standard Vocational Preparation Range:** 7.0 to below 8.0—Two years to less than ten years. **Major/Instructional Program:** 14.0201 Aerospace, Aeronautical and Astronautical Engineering; 52.0201 Business Administration and Management, General; 52.0202 Purchasing, Procurement and Contracts Management. **Related Courses:** Administration and Management; Clerical; Economics and Accounting; Sales and Marketing; Production and Processing; Engineering and Technology; Design; Mathematics; Physics.

PRICE ANALYSTS (21308C)

Compile and analyze statistical data to determine feasibility of buying products and to establish price objectives for contract transactions.

Average Yearly Earnings: $35,859. **Experience:** Considerable preparation is needed. A minimum of two to four years of work-related skill, knowledge, or experience is needed for this occupation. **Education:** This group of occupations usually requires a four-year bachelor's degree, but in some cases does not. **Training:** Employees in this type of occupation usually need several years of work-related experience, on-the-job training, and/or vocational training. **Related Examples:** Other occupations like this one usually involve coordinating, supervising, managing, or training others. Examples include accountants, chefs and head cooks, computer programmers, historians, pharmacists, and police detectives. **Standard Vocational Preparation Range:** 7.0 to below 8.0—Two years to less than ten years. **Major/Instructional Program:** 52.0201 Business Administration and Management, General; 52.0202 Purchasing, Procurement and Contracts Management. **Related Courses:** Economics and Accounting; Mathematics.

Human Resources Workers

CLAIMS TAKERS, UNEMPLOYMENT BENEFITS (21502)

Interview unemployed workers and compile data to determine eligibility for unemployment benefits.

Average Yearly Earnings: $23,795. **Experience:** Some preparation is needed. Some previous work-related skill, knowledge, or experience may be helpful in this occupation, but usually is not needed. **Education:** This group of occupations usually requires a high school diploma and may require some vocational training or job-related course work. In some cases, an associate or bachelor's degree could be needed. **Training:** Employees in this type of occupation need anywhere from a few months to one year of working with experienced employees. **Related Examples:** Other occupations like this one often involve using your knowledge and skills to help others. Examples include drywall installers, fire inspectors, flight attendants, pharmacy technicians, retail salespersons, and tellers. **Standard Vocational Preparation Range:** 4.0 to below 6.0—Six months to less than two years. **Major/Instructional Program:** 44.0401 Public Administration, 52.1001 Human Resources Management. **Related Courses:** Clerical; Customer and Personal Service; Personnel and Human Resources; Therapy and Counseling; Foreign Language.

SPECIAL AGENTS, INSURANCE (21505)

Recruit independent insurance sales agents in the field and maintain contact between them and the home office. Advise agents on matters pertaining to conduct of business, such as cancellations, overdue accounts, technical problems, claims procedures, new business contacts, and new products. May gather information for an underwriter.

Average Yearly Earnings: $38,875. **Experience:** Extensive preparation is needed. Extensive skill, knowledge, and experience are needed for this occupation. It may require more than five years of experience. **Education:** A bachelor's degree is the minimum formal education required for this group of occupations. However, many also require graduate school. For example, they may require a master's degree, and some require a Ph.D., M.D., or J.D. (law degree). **Training:** Employees in this type of occupation may need some on-the-job training, but most of these occupations assume that the person will already have the required skills, knowledge, work-related experience, and/or training. **Examples:** Other occupations like this one often involve coordinating, training, supervising, or managing the activities of others to accomplish goals. Very advanced communication and organizational skills are required. Examples include athletic trainers, lawyers, managing editors, physicists, social psychologists, and surgeons. **Standard Vocational Preparation Range:** 8.0 to 9.0—Four years to more than ten years. **Major/Instructional Program:** 08.1001 Insurance Marketing Operations; 52.0801 Finance, General; 52.0805 Insurance and Risk Management. **Related Courses:** Administration and Management; Economics and Accounting; Sales and Marketing; Personnel and Human Resources; Psychology; Geography.

EMPLOYMENT INTERVIEWERS, PRIVATE OR PUBLIC EMPLOYMENT SERVICE (21508)

Interview job applicants in the employment office and refer them to prospective employers for consideration. Search application files, notify selected applicants of job openings, and refer qualified applicants to prospective employers. Contact employers to verify referral results. Record and evaluate various pertinent data.

Average Yearly Earnings: $35,089. **Experience:** Medium preparation is needed. Previous work-related skill, knowledge, or experience is required for this occupation. **Education:** This group of occupations usually requires training in vocational schools, related on-the-job experience, or an associate degree. A bachelor's degree may be required. **Training:** Employees in this type of occupation usually need one or two years of training involving both on-the-job experience and informal training with experienced workers. **Related Examples:** Other occupations like this one usually involve using communication and organizational skills to coordinate, supervise, manage, or train others to accomplish goals. Examples include dental assistants, electricians, fish and game wardens, legal secretaries, personnel recruiters, and recreation workers. **Standard Vocational Preparation Range:** 6.0 to below 7.0—More than one year and less than four years. **Major/ Instructional Program:** 52.1001 Human Resources Management. **Related Courses:** Administration and Management; Clerical; Sales and Marketing; Customer and Personal Service; Personnel and Human Resources; Psychology; Sociology and Anthropology; Therapy and Counseling.

JOB AND OCCUPATIONAL ANALYSTS (21511A)

Collect, analyze, and classify occupational data to develop job or occupational descriptions or profiles to facilitate personnel management decision making and to develop career information.

Average Yearly Earnings: $36,566. **Experience:** Medium preparation is needed. Previous work-related skill, knowledge, or experience is required for this occupation. **Education:** This group of occupations usually requires training in vocational schools, related on-the-job experience, or an associate degree. A bachelor's degree may be required. **Training:** Employees in this type of occupation usually need one or two years of training involving both on-the-job experience and informal training with experienced workers. **Related Examples:** Other occupations like this one usually involve using communication and organizational skills to coordinate, supervise, manage, or train others to accomplish goals. Examples include dental assistants, electricians, fish and game wardens, legal secretaries, personnel recruiters, and recreation workers. **Standard Vocational Preparation Range:** 6.0 to below 7.0—More than one year and less than four years. **Major/Instructional Program:** 52.1001 Human Resources Management. **Related Courses:** Administration and Management; Clerical; Personnel and Human Resources; Food Production; Computers and Electronics; Mathematics; Psychology; Education and Training; English Language; History and Archeology; Philosophy and Theology; Communications and Media.

EMPLOYER RELATIONS AND PLACEMENT SPECIALISTS (21511B)

Develop relationships with employers to facilitate the placement of job applicants or students in employment opportunities.

Average Yearly Earnings: $36,566. **Experience:** Medium preparation is needed. Previous work-related skill, knowledge, or experience is required for this occupation. **Education:** This group of occupations usually requires training in vocational schools, related on-the-job experience, or an associate degree. A bachelor's degree may be required. **Training:** Employees in this type of occupation usually need one or two years of training involving both on-the-job experience and informal training with experienced workers. **Related Examples:** Other occupations like this one usually involve using communication and organizational skills to coordinate, supervise, manage, or train others to accomplish goals. Examples include dental assistants, electricians, fish and game wardens, legal secretaries, personnel recruiters, and recreation workers. **Standard Vocational Preparation Range:** 6.0 to below 7.0—More than one year and less than four years. **Major/Instructional Program:** 52.1001 Human Resources Management. **Related Courses:** Administration and Management; Clerical; Sales and Marketing; Customer and Personal Service; Personnel and Human Resources; Computers and Electronics; Psychology; Sociology and Anthropology; Geography; Therapy and Counseling; Education and Training.

EMPLOYEE RELATIONS SPECIALISTS (21511C)

Perform a variety of duties to promote employee welfare, such as resolving human relations problems and promoting employee health and well-being.

Average Yearly Earnings: $36,566. **Experience:** Medium preparation is needed. Previous work-related skill, knowledge, or experience is required for this occupation. **Education:** This group of occupations usually requires training in vocational schools, related on-the-job experience, or an associate degree. A bachelor's degree may be required. **Training:** Employees in this type of occupation usually need one or two years of training involving both on-the-job experience and informal training with experienced workers. **Related Examples:** Other occupations like this one usually involve using communication and organizational skills to coordinate, supervise, manage, or train others to accomplish goals. Examples include dental assistants, electricians, fish and game wardens, legal secretaries, personnel recruiters, and recreation workers. **Standard Vocational Preparation Range:** 6.0 to below 7.0—More than one year and less than four years. **Major/Instructional Program:** 52.1001 Human Resources Management, 52.1002 Labor/Personnel Relations and Studies, 52.1003 Organizational Behavior Studies. **Related Courses:** Administration and Management; Clerical; Economics and Accounting; Customer and Personal Service; Personnel and Human Resources; Computers and Electronics; Psychology; Sociology and Anthropology; Therapy and Counseling; Education and Training; Law, Government, and Jurisprudence; Communications and Media.

EMPLOYEE TRAINING SPECIALISTS (2151 ID)

Coordinate and conduct employee training programs to train new and existing employees in how to perform required work, improve work methods, or comply with policies, procedures, or regulations.

Average Yearly Earnings: $36,566. **Experience:** Considerable preparation is needed. A minimum of two to four years of work-related skill, knowledge, or experience is needed for this occupation. **Education:** This group of occupations usually requires a four-year bachelor's degree, but in some cases does not. **Training:** Employees in this type of occupation usually need several years of work-related experience, on-the-job training, and/or vocational training. **Related Examples:** Other occupations like this one usually involve coordinating, supervising, managing, or training others. Examples include accountants, chefs and head cooks, computer programmers, historians, pharmacists, and police detectives. **Standard Vocational Preparation Range:** 7.0 to below 8.0—Two years to less than ten years. **Major/Instructional Program:** 13.0401 Education Administration and Supervision, General; 13.0403 Adult and Continuing Education Administration; 44.0401 Public Administration; 52.1001 Human Resources Management. **Related Courses:** Administration and Management; Clerical; Economics and Accounting; Sales and Marketing; Customer and Personal Service; Personnel and Human Resources; Psychology; Sociology and Anthropology; Therapy and Counseling; Education and Training; Foreign Language; Communications and Media.

PERSONNEL RECRUITERS (2151 IE)

Seek out, interview, and screen applicants to fill existing and future job openings and promote career opportunities within an organization.

Average Yearly Earnings: $36,566. **Experience:** Medium preparation is needed. Previous work-related skill, knowledge, or experience is required for this occupation. **Education:** This group of occupations usually requires training in vocational schools, related on-the-job experience, or an associate degree. A bachelor's degree may be required. **Training:** Employees in this type of occupation usually need one or two years of training involving both on-the-job experience and informal training with experienced workers. **Related Examples:** Other occupations like this one usually involve using communication and organizational skills to coordinate, supervise, manage, or train others to accomplish goals. Examples include dental assistants, electricians, fish and game wardens, legal secretaries, and recreation workers. **Standard Vocational Preparation Range:** 6.0 to below 7.0—More than one year and less than four years. **Major/Instructional Program:** 13.0101 Education, General; 13.0401 Education Administration and Supervision, General; 13.0405 Elementary, Middle, and Secondary Education Administration; 13.0601 Educational Evaluation and Research; 13.0603 Educational Statistics and Research Methods; 13.0604 Educational Assessment, Testing, and Measurement; 52.1001 Human Resources Management. **Related Courses:** Administration and Management; Clerical; Sales and Marketing; Personnel and Human Resources; Computers and Electronics; Psychology; Philosophy and Theology; Law, Government, and Jurisprudence.

LABOR RELATIONS SPECIALISTS (2151 IF)

Mediate, arbitrate, and conciliate disputes over negotiations of labor agreements or labor relations disputes.

Average Yearly Earnings: $36,566. **Experience:** Extensive preparation is needed. Extensive skill, knowledge, and experience are needed for this occupation. It may require more than five years of experience. **Education:** A bachelor's degree is the minimum formal education required for this group of occupations. However, many also require graduate school. For example, they may require a master's degree, and some require a Ph.D., M.D., or J.D. (law degree). **Training:** Employees in this type of occupation may need some on-the-job training, but most of these occupations assume that the person will already have the required skills, knowledge, work-related experience, and/or training. **Examples:** Other occupations like this one often involve coordinating, training, supervising, or managing the activities of others to accomplish goals. Very advanced communication and organizational skills are required. Examples include athletic trainers, lawyers, managing editors, physicists, social psychologists, and surgeons. **Standard Vocational Preparation Range:** 8.0 to 9.0—Four years to more than ten years. **Major/Instructional Program:** 52.1001 Human Resources Management, 52.1002 Labor/Personnel Relations and Studies. **Related Courses:** Administration and Management; Customer and Personal Service; Personnel and Human Resources; Psychology; Law, Government, and Jurisprudence.

Inspectors and Compliance Officers

COST ESTIMATORS (21902)

Prepare cost estimates for product manufacturing, construction projects, or services, to aid management in bidding on or determining the price of a product or service. May specialize according to the particular service performed or the type of product manufactured.

Average Yearly Earnings: $39,894. **Experience:** Considerable preparation is needed. A minimum of two to four years of work-related skill, knowledge, or experience is needed for this occupation. **Education:** This group of occupations usually requires a four-year bachelor's degree, but in some cases does not. **Training:** Employees in this type of occupation usually need several years of work-related experience, on-the-job training, and/or vocational training. **Related Examples:** Other occupations like this one usually involve coordinating, supervising, managing, or training others. Examples include accountants, chefs and head cooks, computer programmers, historians, pharmacists, and police detectives. **Standard Vocational Preparation Range:** 7.0 to below 8.0—Two years to less than ten years. **Major/Instructional Program:** 52.0201 Business Administration and Management, General; 52.0202 Purchasing, Procurement, and Contracts Management. **Related Courses:** Administration and Management; Economics and Accounting; Production and Processing; Building and Construction; Mathematics.

MANAGEMENT ANALYSTS (21905)

Review, analyze, and suggest improvements to business and organizational systems to assist management in operating more efficiently and effectively. Conduct organizational studies and evaluations, design systems and procedures, conduct work simplification and measurement studies, and prepare operations and procedures manuals. Excludes computer systems analysts.

Average Yearly Earnings: $48,193. **Experience:** Considerable preparation is needed. A minimum of two to four years of work-related skill, knowledge, or experience is needed for this occupation. **Education:** This group of occupations usually requires a four-year bachelor's degree, but in some cases does not. **Training:** Employees in this type of occupation usually need several years of work-related experience, on-the-job training, and/ or vocational training. **Related Examples:** Other occupations like this one usually involve coordinating, supervising, managing, or training others. Examples include accountants, chefs and head cooks, computer programmers, historians, pharmacists, and police detectives. **Standard Vocational Preparation Range:** 7.0 to below 8.0—Two years to less than ten years. **Major/Instructional Program:** 52.0201 Business Administration and Management, General. **Related Courses:** Administration and Management; Clerical; Economics and Accounting; Personnel and Human Resources; Production and Processing; Mathematics; Psychology; Education and Training; English Language; Law, Government, and Jurisprudence.

CONSTRUCTION AND BUILDING INSPECTORS (21908A)

Inspect structures using engineering skills to determine structural soundness and compliance with specifications, building codes, and other regulations. Inspections may be general in nature or limited to a specific area, such as electrical systems or plumbing.

Average Yearly Earnings: $35,380. **Experience:** Medium preparation is needed. Previous work-related skill, knowledge, or experience is required for this occupation. **Education:** This group of occupations usually requires training in vocational schools, related on-the-job experience, or an associate degree. A bachelor's degree may be required. **Training:** Employees in this type of occupation usually need one or two years of training involving both on-the-job experience and informal training with experienced workers. **Related Examples:** Other occupations like this one usually involve using communication and organizational skills to coordinate, supervise, manage, or train others to accomplish goals. Examples include dental assistants, electricians, fish and game wardens, legal secretaries, personnel recruiters, and recreation workers. **Standard Vocational Preparation Range:** 6.0 to below 7.0—More than one year and less than four years. **Major/Instructional Program:** 15.0101 Architectural Engineering Technology/Technician; 15.0303 Electrical, Electronic, and Communications Engineering Technology/Technician; 15.1001 Construction/Building Technology/Technician; 43.0201 Fire Protection and Safety Technology/Technician; 46.0301 Electrical and Power Transmission Installer, General; 46.0302 Electrician; 46.0403 Construction/Building Inspector; 46.0501 Plumber and Pipefitter; 47.0201 Heating, Air Conditioning, and Refrigeration Mechanic and Repairer.

Related Courses: Economics and Accounting; Design; Building and Construction; Mathematics; Physics; Public Safety and Security; Law, Government, and Jurisprudence.

ELEVATOR INSPECTORS (21908B)

Inspect elevators and other lifting and conveying devices to verify conformance to laws and ordinances regulating design, installation, and safe operation.

Average Yearly Earnings: $35,380. **Experience:** Extensive preparation is needed. Extensive skill, knowledge, and experience are needed for this occupation. It may require more than five years of experience. **Education:** A bachelor's degree is the minimum formal education required for this group of occupations. However, many also require graduate school. For example, they may require a master's degree, and some require a Ph.D., M.D., or J.D. (law degree). **Training:** Employees in this type of occupation may need some on-the-job training, but most of these occupations assume that the person will already have the required skills, knowledge, work-related experience, and/or training. **Examples:** Other occupations like this one often involve coordinating, training, supervising, or managing the activities of others to accomplish goals. Very advanced communication and organizational skills are required. Examples include athletic trainers, lawyers, managing editors, physicists, social psychologists, and surgeons. **Standard Vocational Preparation Range:** 8.0 to 9.0—Four years to more than ten years. **Major/Instructional Program:** 46.0403 Construction/Building Inspector. **Related Courses:** Design; Building and Construction; Public Safety and Security; Law, Government, and Jurisprudence.

HEALTH OFFICERS AND INSPECTORS (21911A)

Plan, develop, and enforce health programs to maintain health and sanitation standards, regulations, and procedures designed to protect the public. May investigate cases of communicable diseases and implement programs to prevent further spread of the disease.

Average Yearly Earnings: $33,633. **Experience:** Medium preparation is needed. Previous work-related skill, knowledge, or experience is required for this occupation. **Education:** This group of occupations usually requires training in vocational schools, related on-the-job experience, or an associate degree. A bachelor's degree may be required. **Training:** Employees in this type of occupation usually need one or two years of training involving both on-the-job experience and informal training with experienced workers. **Related Examples:** Other occupations like this one usually involve using communication and organizational skills to coordinate, supervise, manage, or train others to accomplish goals. Examples include dental assistants, electricians, fish and game wardens, legal secretaries, personnel recruiters, and recreation workers. **Standard Vocational Preparation Range:** 6.0 to below 7.0—More than one year and less than four years. **Major/Instructional Program:** 02.0301 Food Sciences and Technology; 12.0301 Funeral Services and Mortuary Science; 14.1401 Environmental/Environmental Health Engineering; 15.0506 Water Quality and Wastewater Treatment Technology/Technician; 15.0507 Environmental and Pollution Control Technology/Technician; 15.0701 Occupational Safety and Health Technology/Technician; 20.0401 Institutional Food Workers and Administrators; 20.0409 Institutional Food Services Administrator; 48.0701 Woodworker, General; 48.0702 Furniture Designer and Maker; 51.0301 Community Health Liaison; 51.0702 Hospital/Health Facilities Administration; 51.2001 Pharmacy (B.Pharm., Pharm.D.); 51.2002 Pharmacy Administration and Pharmaceutics; 51.2201 Public Health, General. **Related Courses:** Food Production; Chemistry; Biology; Medicine and Dentistry; Education and Training; Public Safety and Security; Law, Government, and Jurisprudence; Communications and Media.

ENVIRONMENTAL COMPLIANCE INSPECTORS (2191 IB)

Inspect and investigate sources of pollution to protect the public and environment and ensure conformance with federal, state, and local regulations and ordinances.

Average Yearly Earnings: $33,633. **Experience:** Medium preparation is needed. Previous work-related skill, knowledge, or experience is required for this occupation. **Education:** This group of occupations usually requires training in vocational schools, related on-the-job experience, or an associate degree. A bachelor's degree may be required. **Training:** Employees in this type of occupation usually need one or two years of training involving both on-the-job experience and informal training with experienced workers. **Related Examples:** Other occupations like this one usually involve using communication and organizational skills to coordinate, supervise, manage, or train others to accomplish goals. Examples include dental assistants, electricians, fish and game wardens, legal secretaries, personnel recruiters, and recreation workers. **Standard Vocational Preparation Range:** 6.0 to below 7.0—More than one year and less than four years. **Major/Instructional Program:** 01.0401 Agricultural and Food Products Processing Operations and Management; 01.0501 Agricultural Supplies Retailing and Wholesaling; 02.0301 Food Sciences and Technology; 02.0401 Plant Sciences, General; 02.0408 Plant Protection (Pest Management); 15.0506 Water Quality and Wastewater Treatment Technology/Technician; 15.0507 Environmental and Pollution Control Technology/Technician. **Related Courses:** Production and Processing; Food Production; Mathematics; Physics; Chemistry; Biology; Public Safety and Security; Law, Government, and Jurisprudence; Communications and Media.

IMMIGRATION AND CUSTOMS INSPECTORS (2191 IC)

Investigate and inspect persons, common carriers, goods, and merchandise arriving in or departing from the United States or between states to detect violations of immigration and customs laws and regulations.

Average Yearly Earnings: $33,633. **Experience:** Medium preparation is needed. Previous work-related skill, knowledge, or experience is required for this occupation. **Education:** This group of occupations usually requires training in vocational schools, related on-the-job experience, or an associate degree. A bachelor's degree may be required. **Training:** Employees in this type of occupation usually need one or two years of training involving both on-the-job experience and informal training with experienced workers.

Related Examples: Other occupations like this one usually involve using communication and organizational skills to coordinate, supervise, manage, or train others to accomplish goals. Examples include dental assistants, electricians, fish and game wardens, legal secretaries, personnel recruiters, and recreation workers. **Standard Vocational Preparation Range:** 6.0 to below 7.0—More than one year and less than four years. **Major/Instructional Program:** 43.0107 Law Enforcement/Police Science, 43.0109 Security and Loss Prevention Services, 52.1403 International Business Marketing. **Related Courses:** Sociology and Anthropology; Geography; Foreign Language; Public Safety and Security; Law, Government, and Jurisprudence; Communications and Media; Transportation.

LICENSING EXAMINERS AND INSPECTORS (21911D)

Examine, evaluate, and investigate eligibility for, conformity with, or liability under licenses or permits.

Average Yearly Earnings: $33,633. **Experience:** Medium preparation is needed. Previous work-related skill, knowledge, or experience is required for this occupation. **Education:** This group of occupations usually requires training in vocational schools, related on-the-job experience, or an associate degree. A bachelor's degree may be required. **Training:** Employees in this type of occupation usually need one or two years of training involving both on-the-job experience and informal training with experienced workers. **Related Examples:** Other occupations like this one usually involve using communication and organizational skills to coordinate, supervise, manage, or train others to accomplish goals. Examples include dental assistants, electricians, fish and game wardens, legal secretaries, personnel recruiters, and recreation workers. **Standard Vocational Preparation Range:** 6.0 to below 7.0—More than one year and less than four years. **Major/Instructional Program:** 13.1304 Driver and Safety Teacher Education, 43.0107 Law Enforcement/Police Science, 44.0401 Public Administration, 49.0102 Aircraft Pilot and Navigator (Professional). **Related Courses:** Law, Government, and Jurisprudence; Transportation.

INDUSTRIAL AND OCCUPATIONAL SAFETY AND HEALTH INSPECTORS (21911E)

Inspect and evaluate places of employment and properties to ensure compliance with safety and health laws.

Average Yearly Earnings: $33,633. **Experience:** Medium preparation is needed. Previous work-related skill, knowledge, or experience is required for this occupation. **Education:** This group of occupations usually requires training in vocational schools, related on-the-job experience, or an associate degree. A bachelor's degree may be required. **Training:** Employees in this type of occupation usually need one or two years of training involving both on-the-job experience and informal training with experienced workers. **Related Examples:** Other occupations like this one usually involve using communication and organizational skills to coordinate, supervise, manage, or train others to accomplish goals. Examples include dental assistants, electricians, fish and game wardens, legal secretaries, personnel recruiters, and recreation workers. **Standard Vocational Preparation Range:** 6.0 to below 7.0—More than one year and less than four years. **Major/Instructional Program:** 03.0405 Logging/Timber Harvesting, 15.0701 Occupational Safety and Health Technology/Technician, 43.0201 Fire Protection and Safety Technology/Technician, 51.2206 Occupational Health and Industrial Hygiene. **Related Courses:** Administration and Management; Clerical; Production and Processing; Education and Training; English Language; Public Safety and Security; Law, Government, and Jurisprudence; Communications and Media.

EQUAL OPPORTUNITY REPRESENTATIVES AND OFFICERS (2191 IF)

Monitor and evaluate compliance with equal opportunity laws, guidelines, and policies to ensure that employment practices and contracting arrangements give equal opportunity without regard to race, religion, color, national origin, sex, age, or disability.

Average Yearly Earnings: $33,633. **Experience:** Considerable preparation is needed. A minimum of two to four years of work-related skill, knowledge, or experience is needed for this occupation. **Education:** This group of occupations usually requires a four-year bachelor's degree, but in some cases does not. **Training:** Employees in this type of occupation usually need several years of work-related experience, on-the-job training, and/or vocational training. **Related Examples:** Other occupations like this one usually involve coordinating, supervising, managing, or training others. Examples include accountants, chefs and head cooks, computer programmers, historians, pharmacists, and police detectives. **Standard Vocational Preparation Range:** 7.0 to below 8.0—Two years to less than ten years. **Major/Instructional Program:** 44.0201 Community Organization, Resources, and Services; 44.0401 Public Administration; 52.1001 Human Resources Management. **Related Courses:** Personnel and Human Resources; Sociology and Anthropology; English Language; Law, Government, and Jurisprudence.

GOVERNMENT PROPERTY INSPECTORS AND INVESTIGATORS (2191 IH)

Investigate regulated activities to ensure compliance with federal, state, or municipal laws. Investigate or inspect government property to ensure compliance with contract agreements and government regulations.

Average Yearly Earnings: $33,633. **Experience:** Medium preparation is needed. Previous work-related skill, knowledge, or experience is required for this occupation. **Education:** This group of occupations usually requires training in vocational schools, related on-the-job experience, or an associate degree. A bachelor's degree may be required. **Training:** Employees in this type of occupation usually need one or two years of training involving both on-the-job experience and informal training with experienced workers. **Related Examples:** Other occupations like this one usually involve using communication and organizational skills to coordinate, supervise, manage, or train others to accomplish goals. Examples include dental assistants, electricians, fish and game wardens, legal

secretaries, personnel recruiters, and recreation workers. **Standard Vocational Preparation Range:** 6.0 to below 7.0—More than one year and less than four years. **Major/Instructional Program:** 15.0702 Quality Control Technology/Technician, 43.0107 Law Enforcement/Police Science. **Related Courses:** Personnel and Human Resources; English Language; Public Safety and Security; Law, Government, and Jurisprudence; Communications and Media.

FINANCIAL EXAMINERS (21911J)

Enforce or ensure compliance with laws and regulations governing financial and securities institutions and financial and real estate transactions. May examine, verify the correctness of, or establish the authenticity of records.

Average Yearly Earnings: $33,633. **Experience:** Considerable preparation is needed. A minimum of two to four years of work-related skill, knowledge, or experience is needed for this occupation. **Education:** This group of occupations usually requires a four-year bachelor's degree, but in some cases does not. **Training:** Employees in this type of occupation usually need several years of work-related experience, on-the-job training, and/or vocational training. **Related Examples:** Other occupations like this one usually involve coordinating, supervising, managing, or training others. Examples include accountants, chefs and head cooks, computer programmers, historians, pharmacists, and police detectives. **Standard Vocational Preparation Range:** 7.0 to below 8.0—Two years to less than ten years. **Major/Instructional Program:** 52.0801 Finance, General. **Related Courses:** Administration and Management; Economics and Accounting; Mathematics; Education and Training; English Language; Law, Government, and Jurisprudence.

AVIATION INSPECTORS (21911K)

Inspect aircraft, maintenance procedures, air navigational aids, air traffic controls, and communications equipment to ensure conformance with federal safety regulations.

Average Yearly Earnings: $33,633. **Experience:** Considerable preparation is needed. A minimum of two to four years of work-related skill, knowledge, or experience is needed for this occupation. **Education:** This group of occupations usually requires a four-year bachelor's degree, but in some cases does not. **Training:** Employees in this type of occupation usually need several years of work-related experience, on-the-job training, and/or vocational training. **Related Examples:** Other occupations like this one usually involve coordinating, supervising, managing, or training others. Examples include accountants, chefs and head cooks, computer programmers, historians, pharmacists, and police detectives. **Standard Vocational Preparation Range:** 7.0 to below 8.0—Two years to less than ten years. **Major/Instructional Program:** 15.0801 Aeronautical and Aerospace Engineering Technology/Technician, 47.0609 Aviation Systems and Avionics Maintenance Technologist/Technician, 49.0102 Aircraft Pilot and Navigator (Professional). **Related Courses:** Personnel and Human Resources; Computers and Electronics; Engineering and Technology; Mechanical; Physics; Education and Training; English Language; Public

Safety and Security; Law, Government, and Jurisprudence; Telecommunications; Transportation.

PRESSURE VESSEL INSPECTORS (21911L)

Inspect pressure vessel equipment for conformance with safety laws and standards regulating their design, fabrication, installation, repair, and operation.

Average Yearly Earnings: $33,633. **Experience:** Considerable preparation is needed. A minimum of two to four years of work-related skill, knowledge, or experience is needed for this occupation. **Education:** This group of occupations usually requires a four-year bachelor's degree, but in some cases does not. **Training:** Employees in this type of occupation usually need several years of work-related experience, on-the-job training, and/or vocational training. **Related Examples:** Other occupations like this one usually involve coordinating, supervising, managing, or training others. Examples include accountants, chefs and head cooks, computer programmers, historians, pharmacists, and police detectives. **Standard Vocational Preparation Range:** 7.0 to below 8.0—Two years to less than ten years. **Major/Instructional Program:** 47.0303 Industrial Machinery Maintenance and Repairer, 47.0501 Stationary Energy Sources Installer and Operator. **Related Courses:** Engineering and Technology; Design; Building and Construction; Mechanical; Mathematics; Physics; Public Safety and Security; Law, Government, and Jurisprudence.

PUBLIC TRANSPORTATION INSPECTORS (21911M)

Monitor operation of public transportation systems to ensure good service and compliance with regulations. Investigate accidents, equipment failures, and complaints.

Average Yearly Earnings: $33,633. **Experience:** Considerable preparation is needed. A minimum of two to four years of work-related skill, knowledge, or experience is needed for this occupation. **Education:** This group of occupations usually requires a four-year bachelor's degree, but in some cases does not. **Training:** Employees in this type of occupation usually need several years of work-related experience, on-the-job training, and/or vocational training. **Related Examples:** Other occupations like this one usually involve coordinating, supervising, managing, or training others. Examples include accountants, chefs and head cooks, computer programmers, historians, pharmacists, and police detectives. **Standard Vocational Preparation Range:** 7.0 to below 8.0—Two years to less than ten years. **Major/Instructional Program:** 14.0801 Civil Engineering, General; 14.0804 Transportation and Highway Engineering. **Related Courses:** Administration and Management; Customer and Personal Service; Personnel and Human Resources; Geography; Public Safety and Security; Law, Government, and Jurisprudence; Transportation.

MARINE CARGO INSPECTORS (21911N)

Inspect cargoes of seagoing vessels to certify compliance with health and safety regulations in cargo handling and stowage.

Average Yearly Earnings: $33,633. **Experience:** Extensive preparation is needed. Extensive skill, knowledge, and experience are needed for this occupation. It may require more than five years of experience. **Education:** A bachelor's degree is the minimum formal education required for this group of occupations. However, many also require graduate school. For example, they may require a master's degree, and some require a Ph.D., M.D., or J.D. (law degree). **Training:** Employees in this type of occupation may need some on-the-job training, but most of these occupations assume that the person will already have the required skills, knowledge, work-related experience, and/or training. **Examples:** Other occupations like this one often involve coordinating, training, supervising, or managing the activities of others to accomplish goals. Very advanced communication and organizational skills are required. Examples include athletic trainers, lawyers, managing editors, physicists, social psychologists, and surgeons. **Standard Vocational Preparation Range:** 8.0 to 9.0—Four years to more than ten years. **Major/Instructional Program:** No specific instructional program for this occupation. **Related Courses:** Design; Mathematics; Physics; Public Safety and Security; Law, Government, and Jurisprudence; Transportation.

CORONERS (21911P)

Direct activities such as autopsies, pathological and toxicological analyses, and inquests relating to the investigation of deaths occurring within a legal jurisdiction to determine the cause of death or to fix responsibility for accidental, violent, or unexplained deaths.

Average Yearly Earnings: $33,633. **Experience:** Considerable preparation is needed. A minimum of two to four years of work-related skill, knowledge, or experience is needed for this occupation. **Education:** This group of occupations usually requires a four-year bachelor's degree, but in some cases does not. **Training:** Employees in this type of occupation usually need several years of work-related experience, on-the-job training, and/or vocational training. **Related Examples:** Other occupations like this one usually involve coordinating, supervising, managing, or training others. Examples include accountants, chefs and head cooks, computer programmers, historians, pharmacists, and police detectives. **Standard Vocational Preparation Range:** 7.0 to below 8.0—Two years to less than ten years. **Major/Instructional Program:** 51.2919 Forensic Pathology Residency. **Related Courses:** Administration and Management; Chemistry; Biology; Medicine and Dentistry; English Language; Foreign Language; Public Safety and Security; Law, Government, and Jurisprudence.

AGRICULTURAL INSPECTORS (21911R)

Inspect agricultural commodities, processing equipment, and facilities to enforce compliance with government regulations.

Average Yearly Earnings: $33,633. **Experience:** Considerable preparation is needed. A minimum of two to four years of work-related skill, knowledge, or experience is needed for this occupation. **Education:** This group of occupations usually requires a four-year bachelor's degree, but in some cases does not. **Training:** Employees in this type of

occupation usually need several years of work-related experience, on-the-job training, and/or vocational training. **Related Examples:** Other occupations like this one usually involve coordinating, supervising, managing, or training others. Examples include accountants, chefs and head cooks, computer programmers, historians, pharmacists, and police detectives. **Standard Vocational Preparation Range:** 7.0 to below 8.0—Two years to less than ten years. **Major/Instructional Program:** 01.0401 Agricultural and Food Products Processing Operations and Management; 02.0401 Plant Sciences, General; 02.0408 Plant Protection (Pest Management). **Related Courses:** Production and Processing; Food Production; Biology; Law, Government, and Jurisprudence.

RADIATION-PROTECTION SPECIALISTS (21911T)

Inspect and test X-ray or other radiation-producing equipment and utilization areas, and evaluate operating procedures to detect and control radiation hazards in hospitals, laboratories, medical offices, and other establishments that use equipment which produces radiation harmful to humans.

Average Yearly Earnings: $33,633. **Experience:** Extensive preparation is needed. Extensive skill, knowledge, and experience are needed for this occupation. It may require more than five years of experience. **Education:** A bachelor's degree is the minimum formal education required for this group of occupations. However, many also require graduate school. For example, they may require a master's degree, and some require a Ph.D., M.D., or J.D. (law degree). **Training:** Employees in this type of occupation may need some on-the-job training, but most of these occupations assume that the person will already have the required skills, knowledge, work-related experience, and/or training. **Examples:** Other occupations like this one often involve coordinating, training, supervising, or managing the activities of others to accomplish goals. Very advanced communication and organizational skills are required. Examples include athletic trainers, lawyers, managing editors, physicists, social psychologists, and surgeons. **Standard Vocational Preparation Range:** 8.0 to 9.0—Four years to more than ten years. **Major/Instructional Program:** 51.0907 Medical Radiologic Technology/Technician. **Related Courses:** Mathematics; Physics; Medicine and Dentistry; Education and Training; Public Safety and Security; Law, Government, and Jurisprudence.

TAX EXAMINERS, COLLECTORS, AND REVENUE AGENTS (21914)

Determine tax liability or collect taxes from individuals or business firms, according to prescribed laws and regulations.

Average Yearly Earnings: $32,905. **Experience:** Considerable preparation is needed. A minimum of two to four years of work-related skill, knowledge, or experience is needed for this occupation. **Education:** This group of occupations usually requires a four-year bachelor's degree, but in some cases does not. **Training:** Employees in this type of occupation usually need several years of work-related experience, on-the-job training, and/

or vocational training. **Related Examples:** Other occupations like this one usually involve coordinating, supervising, managing, or training others. Examples include accountants, chefs and head cooks, computer programmers, historians, pharmacists, and police detectives. **Standard Vocational Preparation Range:** 7.0 to below 8.0—Two years to less than ten years. **Major/Instructional Program:** 52.0301 Accounting. **Related Courses:** Economics and Accounting; Mathematics; Law, Government, and Jurisprudence.

ASSESSORS (21917)

Appraise real and personal property to determine its fair value. May assess taxes in accordance with prescribed schedules.

Average Yearly Earnings: $38,334. **Experience:** Considerable preparation is needed. A minimum of two to four years of work-related skill, knowledge, or experience is needed for this occupation. **Education:** This group of occupations usually requires a four-year bachelor's degree, but in some cases does not. **Training:** Employees in this type of occupation usually need several years of work-related experience, on-the-job training, and/or vocational training. **Related Examples:** Other occupations like this one usually involve coordinating, supervising, managing, or training others. Examples include accountants, chefs and head cooks, computer programmers, historians, pharmacists, and police detectives. **Standard Vocational Preparation Range:** 7.0 to below 8.0—Two years to less than ten years. **Major/Instructional Program:** 52.1501 Real Estate. **Related Courses:** Economics and Accounting; Mathematics; Geography; Law, Government, and Jurisprudence.

CLAIMS EXAMINERS, PROPERTY AND CASUALTY INSURANCE (21921)

Review settled insurance claims to determine that payments and settlements have been made in accordance with company practices and procedures, ensuring that adjusters have followed proper methods. Report overpayments, underpayments, and other irregularities. Confer with legal counsel on claims requiring litigation.

Average Yearly Earnings: $41,142. **Experience:** Considerable preparation is needed. A minimum of two to four years of work-related skill, knowledge, or experience is needed for this occupation. **Education:** This group of occupations usually requires a four-year bachelor's degree, but in some cases does not. **Training:** Employees in this type of occupation usually need several years of work-related experience, on-the-job training, and/or vocational training. **Related Examples:** Other occupations like this one usually involve coordinating, supervising, managing, or training others. Examples include accountants, chefs and head cooks, computer programmers, historians, pharmacists, and police detectives. **Standard Vocational Preparation Range:** 7.0 to below 8.0—Two years to less than ten years. **Major/Instructional Program:** 52.0801 Finance, General; 52.0805 Insurance and Risk Management. **Related Courses:** Law, Government, and Jurisprudence.

Management Support Workers

COMPUTER SECURITY SPECIALISTS (21999A)

Plan, coordinate, and implement security measures for information systems to regulate access to computer data files and prevent unauthorized modification, destruction, or disclosure of information.

Average Yearly Earnings: $48,360. **Experience:** Considerable preparation is needed. A minimum of two to four years of work-related skill, knowledge, or experience is needed for this occupation. **Education:** This group of occupations usually requires a four-year bachelor's degree, but in some cases does not. **Training:** Employees in this type of occupation usually need several years of work-related experience, on-the-job training, and/or vocational training. **Related Examples:** Other occupations like this one usually involve coordinating, supervising, managing, or training others. Examples include accountants, chefs and head cooks, computer programmers, historians, pharmacists, and police detectives. **Standard Vocational Preparation Range:** 7.0 to below 8.0—Two years to less than ten years. **Major/Instructional Program:** 11.0101 Computer and Information Sciences, General; 11.0501 Computer Systems Analysis; 52.1201 Management Information Systems and Business Data Processing, General; 52.1203 Business Systems Analysis and Design; 52.1204 Business Systems Networking and Telecommunications; 52.1205 Business Computer Facilities Operator. **Related Courses:** Administration and Management; Computers and Electronics; Philosophy and Theology; Public Safety and Security.

LEGISLATIVE ASSISTANTS (21999B)

Perform research into governmental laws and procedures to resolve problems or complaints of constituents or to assist a legislator in preparation of proposed legislation.

Average Yearly Earnings: $38,251. **Experience:** Medium preparation is needed. Previous work-related skill, knowledge, or experience is required for this occupation. **Education:** This group of occupations usually requires training in vocational schools, related on-the-job experience, or an associate degree. A bachelor's degree may be required. **Training:** Employees in this type of occupation usually need one or two years of training involving both on-the-job experience and informal training with experienced workers. **Related Examples:** Other occupations like this one usually involve using communication and organizational skills to coordinate, supervise, manage, or train others to accomplish goals. Examples include dental assistants, electricians, fish and game wardens, legal secretaries, personnel recruiters, and recreation workers. **Standard Vocational Preparation Range:** 6.0 to below 7.0—More than one year and less than four years. **Major/Instructional Program:** 22.0103 Paralegal/Legal Assistant, 44.0501 Public Policy Analysis. **Related Courses:** English Language; Law, Government, and Jurisprudence.

EXECUTIVE SECRETARIES AND ADMINISTRATIVE ASSISTANTS (21999C)

Aid an executive by coordinating office services, such as personnel, budget preparation and control, housekeeping, records control, and special management studies.

Average Yearly Earnings: $38,251. **Experience:** Considerable preparation is needed. A minimum of two to four years of work-related skill, knowledge, or experience is needed for this occupation. **Education:** This group of occupations usually requires a four-year bachelor's degree, but in some cases does not. **Training:** Employees in this type of occupation usually need several years of work-related experience, on-the-job training, and/or vocational training. **Related Examples:** Other occupations like this one usually involve coordinating, supervising, managing, or training others. Examples include accountants, chefs and head cooks, computer programmers, historians, pharmacists, and police detectives. **Standard Vocational Preparation Range:** 7.0 to below 8.0—Two years to less than ten years. **Major/Instructional Program:** 52.0201 Business Administration and Management, General; 52.0204 Office Supervision and Management; 52.0401 Administrative Assistant/Secretarial Science, General; 52.0402 Executive Assistant/ Secretary. **Related Courses:** Administration and Management; Clerical; Economics and Accounting.

LAND LEASING AND PERMIT AGENTS (21999D)

Arrange for property leases or permits for special use, such as mineral prospecting or movie production.

Average Yearly Earnings: $38,251. **Experience:** Medium preparation is needed. Previous work-related skill, knowledge, or experience is required for this occupation. **Education:** This group of occupations usually requires training in vocational schools, related on-the-job experience, or an associate degree. A bachelor's degree may be required. **Training:** Employees in this type of occupation usually need one or two years of training involving both on-the-job experience and informal training with experienced workers. **Related Examples:** Other occupations like this one usually involve using communication and organizational skills to coordinate, supervise, manage, or train others to accomplish goals. Examples include dental assistants, electricians, fish and game wardens, legal secretaries, personnel recruiters, and recreation workers. **Standard Vocational Preparation Range:** 6.0 to below 7.0—More than one year and less than four years. **Major/ Instructional Program:** 52.1501 Real Estate. **Related Courses:** Economics and Accounting; Geography; Law, Government, and Jurisprudence.

MEETING AND CONVENTION PLANNERS (21999F)

Coordinate activities of staff and convention personnel to make arrangements for group meetings and conventions.

Average Yearly Earnings: $38,251. **Experience:** Considerable preparation is needed. A minimum of two to four years of work-related skill, knowledge, or experience is needed for this occupation. **Education:** This group of occupations usually requires a four-year bachelor's degree, but in some cases does not. **Training:** Employees in this type of occupation usually need several years of work-related experience, on-the-job training, and/or vocational training. **Related Examples:** Other occupations like this one usually involve coordinating, supervising, managing, or training others. Examples include accountants, chefs and head cooks, computer programmers, historians, pharmacists, and police detectives. **Standard Vocational Preparation Range:** 7.0 to below 8.0—Two years to less than ten years. **Major/Instructional Program:** 19.0501 Foods and Nutrition Studies, General; 19.0505 Food Systems Administration; 20.0401 Institutional Food Workers and Administrators; 20.0405 Food Catering; 52.0902 Hotel/Motel and Restaurant Management; 52.0903 Travel-Tourism Management. **Related Courses:** Administration and Management; Economics and Accounting; Sales and Marketing; Customer and Personal Service; Sociology and Anthropology; Foreign Language; Public Safety and Security; Law, Government, and Jurisprudence; Telecommunications; Communications and Media.

GRANT COORDINATORS (21999G)

Research, develop, and coordinate development of proposals for funding and funding sources to establish or maintain grant-funded programs in public or private organizations.

Average Yearly Earnings: $53,601. **Experience:** Extensive preparation is needed. Extensive skill, knowledge, and experience are needed for this occupation. It may require more than five years of experience. **Education:** A bachelor's degree is the minimum formal education required for this group of occupations. However, many also require graduate school. For example, they may require a master's degree, and some require a Ph.D., M.D., or J.D. (law degree). **Training:** Employees in this type of occupation may need some on-the-job training, but most of these occupations assume that the person will already have the required skills, knowledge, work-related experience, and/or training. **Examples:** Other occupations like this one often involve coordinating, training, supervising, or managing the activities of others to accomplish goals. Very advanced communication and organizational skills are required. Examples include athletic trainers, lawyers, managing editors, physicists, social psychologists, and surgeons. **Standard Vocational Preparation Range:** 8.0 to 9.0—Four years to more than ten years. **Major/Instructional Program:** 44.0401 Public Administration. **Related Courses:** Administration and Management; Economics and Accounting; English Language; Law, Government, and Jurisprudence.

CUSTOMS BROKERS (21999H)

Prepare and compile documents required by federal government for discharge of foreign cargo at domestic port to serve as intermediary between importers, merchant shipping companies, airlines, railroads, trucking companies, pipeline operators, and the United States Customs Service.

Average Yearly Earnings: $38,251. **Experience:** Considerable preparation is needed. A minimum of two to four years of work-related skill, knowledge, or experience is needed for this occupation. **Education:** This group of occupations usually requires a four-year bachelor's degree, but in some cases does not. **Training:** Employees in this type of occupation usually need several years of work-related experience, on-the-job training, and/or vocational training. **Related Examples:** Other occupations like this one usually involve coordinating, supervising, managing, or training others. Examples include accountants, chefs and head cooks, computer programmers, historians, pharmacists, and police detectives. **Standard Vocational Preparation Range:** 7.0 to below 8.0—Two years to less than ten years. **Major/Instructional Program:** 52.1101 International Business, 52.1403 International Business Marketing. **Related Courses:** Economics and Accounting; Geography; Foreign Language; Law, Government, and Jurisprudence; Transportation.

Engineers

AEROSPACE ENGINEERS (22102)

Perform a variety of engineering work in designing, constructing, and testing aircraft, missiles, and spacecraft. May conduct basic and applied research to evaluate the adaptability of materials and equipment to aircraft design and manufacture. May recommend improvements in testing equipment and techniques. Includes aeronautical and astronautical engineers.

Average Yearly Earnings: $59,633. **Experience:** Extensive preparation is needed. Extensive skill, knowledge, and experience are needed for this occupation. It may require more than five years of experience. **Education:** A bachelor's degree is the minimum formal education required for this group of occupations. However, many also require graduate school. For example, they may require a master's degree, and some require a Ph.D., M.D., or J.D. (law degree). **Training:** Employees in this type of occupation may need some on-the-job training, but most of these occupations assume that the person will already have the required skills, knowledge, work-related experience, and/or training. **Examples:** Other occupations like this one often involve coordinating, training, supervising, or managing the activities of others to accomplish goals. Very advanced communication and organizational skills are required. Examples include athletic trainers, lawyers, managing editors, physicists, social psychologists, and surgeons. **Standard Vocational Preparation Range:** 8.0 to 9.0—Four years to more than ten years. **Major/Instructional Program:** 14.0201 Aerospace, Aeronautical, and Astronautical Engineering. **Related Courses:** Administration and Management; Economics and Accounting; Customer and Personal Service; Personnel and Human Resources; Production and Processing; Computers and Electronics; Engineering and Technology; Design; Building and Construction; Mechanical; Mathematics; Physics; English Language; Telecommunications; Communications and Media.

CERAMIC ENGINEERS (22105A)

Conduct research, design machinery, and develop processing techniques related to the manufacturing of ceramic products.

Average Yearly Earnings: $49,566. **Experience:** Extensive preparation is needed. Extensive skill, knowledge, and experience are needed for this occupation. It may require more than five years of experience. **Education:** A bachelor's degree is the minimum formal education required for this group of occupations. However, many also require graduate school. For example, they may require a master's degree, and some require a Ph.D., M.D., or J.D. (law degree). **Training:** Employees in this type of occupation may need some on-the-job training, but most of these occupations assume that the person will already have the required skills, knowledge, work-related experience, and/or training. **Examples:** Other occupations like this one often involve coordinating, training, supervising, or managing the activities of others to accomplish goals. Very advanced communication and organizational skills are required. Examples include athletic trainers, lawyers, managing editors, physicists, social psychologists, and surgeons. **Standard Vocational Preparation Range:** 8.0 to 9.0—Four years to more than ten years. **Major/Instructional Program:** 14.0601 Ceramic Sciences and Engineering. **Related Courses:** Administration and Management; Production and Processing; Computers and Electronics; Engineering and Technology; Design; Mathematics; Physics; Chemistry; English Language.

METALLURGISTS (22105B)

Investigate properties of metals and develop methods to produce new alloys, applications, and processes of extracting metals from their ores, and to commercially fabricate products from metals.

Average Yearly Earnings: $49,566. **Experience:** Extensive preparation is needed. Extensive skill, knowledge, and experience are needed for this occupation. It may require more than five years of experience. **Education:** A bachelor's degree is the minimum formal education required for this group of occupations. However, many also require graduate school. For example, they may require a master's degree, and some require a Ph.D., M.D., or J.D. (law degree). **Training:** Employees in this type of occupation may need some on-the-job training, but most of these occupations assume that the person will already have the required skills, knowledge, work-related experience, and/or training. **Examples:** Other occupations like this one often involve coordinating, training, supervising, or managing the activities of others to accomplish goals. Very advanced communication and organizational skills are required. Examples include athletic trainers, lawyers, managing editors, physicists, social psychologists, and surgeons. **Standard Vocational Preparation Range:** 8.0 to 9.0—Four years to more than ten years. **Major/Instructional Program:** 14.2001 Metallurgical Engineering, 40.0701 Metallurgy. **Related Courses:** Administration and Management; Production and Processing; Engineering and Technology; Design; Physics; Chemistry; Geography; English Language.

WELDING ENGINEERS (22105C)

Develop welding techniques, procedures, and applications of welding equipment to problems involving fabrication of metals.

Average Yearly Earnings: $49,566. **Experience:** Extensive preparation is needed. Extensive skill, knowledge, and experience are needed for this occupation. It may require more than five years of experience. **Education:** A bachelor's degree is the minimum formal education required for this group of occupations. However, many also require graduate school. For example, they may require a master's degree, and some require a Ph.D., M.D., or J.D. (law degree). **Training:** Employees in this type of occupation may need some on-the-job training, but most of these occupations assume that the person will already have the required skills, knowledge, work-related experience, and/or training. **Examples:** Other occupations like this one often involve coordinating, training, supervising, or managing the activities of others to accomplish goals. Very advanced communication and organizational skills are required. Examples include athletic trainers, lawyers, managing editors, physicists, social psychologists, and surgeons. **Standard Vocational Preparation Range:** 8.0 to 9.0—Four years to more than ten years. **Major/Instructional Program:** 14.2001 Metallurgical Engineering. **Related Courses:** Engineering and Technology; Design; Building and Construction; Mathematics; Physics.

MATERIALS ENGINEERS (22105D)

Evaluate materials and develop machinery and processes to manufacture materials for use in products that must meet specialized design and performance specifications. Develop new uses for known materials. Includes those working with composite materials or specializing in one type of material, such as graphite, metal and metal alloys, ceramics and glass, plastics and polymers, and naturally occurring materials. Includes metallurgists and metallurgical engineers, ceramic engineers, and welding engineers.

Average Yearly Earnings: $49,566. **Experience:** Extensive preparation is needed. Extensive skill, knowledge, and experience are needed for this occupation. It may require more than five years of experience. **Education:** A bachelor's degree is the minimum formal education required for this group of occupations. However, many also require graduate school. For example, they may require a master's degree, and some require a Ph.D., M.D., or J.D. (law degree). **Training:** Employees in this type of occupation may need some on-the-job training, but most of these occupations assume that the person will already have the required skills, knowledge, work-related experience, and/or training. **Examples:** Other occupations like this one often involve coordinating, training, supervising, or managing the activities of others to accomplish goals. Very advanced communication and organizational skills are required. Examples include athletic trainers, lawyers, managing editors, physicists, social psychologists, and surgeons. **Standard Vocational Preparation Range:** 8.0 to 9.0—Four years to more than ten years. **Major/Instructional Program:** 14.3101 Materials Science. **Related Courses:** Economics and Accounting; Production and Processing; Engineering and Technology; Design; Mathematics; Physics; Chemistry; English Language.

MINING ENGINEERS, INCLUDING MINE SAFETY (22108)

Determine the location and plan the extraction of coal, metallic ores, nonmetallic minerals, and building materials, such as stone and gravel. Work involves conducting preliminary surveys of deposits or undeveloped mines and planning their development; examining deposits or mines to determine whether they can be worked at a profit; making geological and topographical surveys; evolving methods of mining best suited to character, type, and size of deposits; and supervising mining operations.

Average Yearly Earnings: $49,836. **Experience:** Considerable preparation is needed. A minimum of two to four years of work-related skill, knowledge, or experience is needed for this occupation. **Education:** This group of occupations usually requires a four-year bachelor's degree, but in some cases does not. **Training:** Employees in this type of occupation usually need several years of work-related experience, on-the-job training, and/or vocational training. **Related Examples:** Other occupations like this one usually involve coordinating, supervising, managing, or training others. Examples include accountants, chefs and head cooks, computer programmers, historians, pharmacists, and police detectives. **Standard Vocational Preparation Range:** 7.0 to below 8.0—Two years to less than ten years. **Major/Instructional Program:** 14.2101 Mining and Mineral Engineering, 14.2501 Petroleum Engineering. **Related Courses:** Administration and Management; Economics and Accounting; Personnel and Human Resources; Production and Processing; Engineering and Technology; Design; Building and Construction; Mechanical; Mathematics; Physics; Chemistry; Geography; Education and Training; English Language; Public Safety and Security; Law, Government, and Jurisprudence; Transportation.

PETROLEUM ENGINEERS (22111)

Devise methods to improve oil and gas well production and determine the need for new or modified tool designs. Oversee drilling and offer technical advice to achieve economical and satisfactory progress.

Average Yearly Earnings: $68,224. **Experience:** Extensive preparation is needed. Extensive skill, knowledge, and experience are needed for this occupation. It may require more than five years of experience. **Education:** A bachelor's degree is the minimum formal education required for this group of occupations. However, many also require graduate school. For example, they may require a master's degree, and some require a Ph.D., M.D., or J.D. (law degree). **Training:** Employees in this type of occupation may need some on-the-job training, but most of these occupations assume that the person will already have the required skills, knowledge, work-related experience, and/or training. **Examples:** Other occupations like this one often involve coordinating, training, supervising, or managing the activities of others to accomplish goals. Very advanced communication and organizational skills are required. Examples include athletic trainers, lawyers, managing editors, physicists, social psychologists, and surgeons. **Standard Vocational Preparation Range:** 8.0 to 9.0—Four years to more than ten years. **Major/Instructional Program:** 14.2101 Mining and Mineral Engineering, 14.2501 Petroleum Engineering. **Related Courses:** Administration and Management; Personnel and Human Resources;

Production and Processing; Engineering and Technology; Design; Mechanical; Mathematics; Physics; English Language.

CHEMICAL ENGINEERS (22114)

Design chemical plant equipment and devise processes for manufacturing chemicals and products such as gasoline, synthetic rubber, plastics, detergents, cement, paper, and pulp by applying principles and technology of chemistry, physics, and engineering.

Average Yearly Earnings: $55,764. **Experience:** Extensive preparation is needed. Extensive skill, knowledge, and experience are needed for this occupation. It may require more than five years of experience. **Education:** A bachelor's degree is the minimum formal education required for this group of occupations. However, many also require graduate school. For example, they may require a master's degree, and some require a Ph.D., M.D., or J.D. (law degree). **Training:** Employees in this type of occupation may need some on-the-job training, but most of these occupations assume that the person will already have the required skills, knowledge, work-related experience, and/or training. **Examples:** Other occupations like this one often involve coordinating, training, supervising, or managing the activities of others to accomplish goals. Very advanced communication and organizational skills are required. Examples include athletic trainers, lawyers, managing editors, physicists, social psychologists, and surgeons. **Standard Vocational Preparation Range:** 8.0 to 9.0—Four years to more than ten years. **Major/Instructional Program:** 14.0701 Chemical Engineering, 14.2801 Textile Sciences and Engineering, 14.3201 Polymer/Plastics Engineering. **Related Courses:** Administration and Management; Economics and Accounting; Production and Processing; Computers and Electronics; Engineering and Technology; Design; Mechanical; Mathematics; Physics; Chemistry; Biology; English Language; Public Safety and Security; Law, Government, and Jurisprudence.

NUCLEAR ENGINEERS (22117)

Conduct research on nuclear engineering problems or apply the principles and theory of nuclear science to problems concerned with the release, control, and utilization of nuclear energy.

Average Yearly Earnings: $57,740. **Experience:** Extensive preparation is needed. Extensive skill, knowledge, and experience are needed for this occupation. It may require more than five years of experience. **Education:** A bachelor's degree is the minimum formal education required for this group of occupations. However, many also require graduate school. For example, they may require a master's degree, and some require a Ph.D., M.D., or J.D. (law degree). **Training:** Employees in this type of occupation may need some on-the-job training, but most of these occupations assume that the person will already have the required skills, knowledge, work-related experience, and/or training. **Examples:** Other occupations like this one often involve coordinating, training, supervising, or managing the activities of others to accomplish goals. Very advanced communication and organizational skills are required. Examples include athletic trainers, lawyers, managing editors, physicists, social psychologists, and surgeons. **Standard Vocational Preparation Range:** 8.0 to 9.0—Four years to more than ten years. **Major/Instructional Program:** 14.0801 Civil Engineering, General; 14.0802 Geotechnical Engineering; 14.2301 Nuclear Engineering. **Related Courses:** Administration and Management; Economics and Accounting; Computers and Electronics; Engineering and Technology; Design; Building and Construction; Mathematics; Physics; Chemistry; Education and Training; English Language; Public Safety and Security.

CIVIL ENGINEERS, INCLUDING TRAFFIC (22121)

Perform engineering duties in planning, designing, and overseeing construction and maintenance of structures and facilities such as roads, railroads, airports, bridges, harbors, channels, dams, irrigation projects, pipelines, power plants, water and sewage systems, and waste disposal units. Includes traffic engineers who specialize in studying vehicular and pedestrian traffic conditions.

Average Yearly Earnings: $49,920. **Experience:** Considerable preparation is needed. A minimum of two to four years of work-related skill, knowledge, or experience is needed for this occupation. **Education:** This group of occupations usually requires a four-year bachelor's degree, but in some cases does not. **Training:** Employees in this type of occupation usually need several years of work-related experience, on-the-job training, and/or vocational training. **Related Examples:** Other occupations like this one usually involve coordinating, supervising, managing, or training others. Examples include accountants, chefs and head cooks, computer programmers, historians, pharmacists, and police detectives. **Standard Vocational Preparation Range:** 7.0 to below 8.0—Two years to less than ten years. **Major/Instructional Program:** 01.0201 Agricultural Mechanization, General; 14.0401 Architectural Engineering; 14.0801 Civil Engineering, General; 14.0802 Geotechnical Engineering; 14.0803 Structural Engineering; 14.0804 Transportation and Highway Engineering; 14.0805 Water Resources Engineering. **Related Courses:** Administration and Management; Economics and Accounting; Computers and Electronics; Engineering and Technology; Design; Building and Construction; Mathematics; Physics; Geography; English Language; Public Safety and Security; Law, Government, and Jurisprudence; Transportation.

AGRICULTURAL ENGINEERS (22123)

Apply knowledge of engineering technology and biological science to agricultural problems concerned with power and machinery, electrification, structures, soil and water conservation, and processing of agricultural products.

Average Yearly Earnings: $54,329. **Experience:** Extensive preparation is needed. Extensive skill, knowledge, and experience are needed for this occupation. It may require more than five years of experience. **Education:** A bachelor's degree is the minimum formal education required for this group of occupations. However, many also require graduate school. For example, they may require a master's degree, and some require a Ph.D.,

M.D., or J.D. (law degree). **Training:** Employees in this type of occupation may need some on-the-job training, but most of these occupations assume that the person will already have the required skills, knowledge, work-related experience, and/or training. **Examples:** Other occupations like this one often involve coordinating, training, supervising, or managing the activities of others to accomplish goals. Very advanced communication and organizational skills are required. Examples include athletic trainers, lawyers, managing editors, physicists, social psychologists, and surgeons. **Standard Vocational Preparation Range:** 8.0 to 9.0—Four years to more than ten years. **Major/Instructional Program:** 14.0101 Engineering, General; 14.0301 Agricultural Engineering. **Related Courses:** Administration and Management; Economics and Accounting; Production and Processing; Food Production; Computers and Electronics; Engineering and Technology; Design; Building and Construction; Mechanical; Mathematics; Physics; Chemistry; Biology; Sociology and Anthropology; Geography; Education and Training; English Language; Philosophy and Theology; Law, Government, and Jurisprudence; Communications and Media; Transportation.

ELECTRICAL ENGINEERS (22126A)

Design, develop, test, or supervise the manufacturing and installation of electrical equipment, components, or systems for commercial, industrial, military, or scientific use. Excludes computer engineers.

Average Yearly Earnings: $53,227. **Experience:** Extensive preparation is needed. Extensive skill, knowledge, and experience are needed for this occupation. It may require more than five years of experience. **Education:** A bachelor's degree is the minimum formal education required for this group of occupations. However, many also require graduate school. For example, they may require a master's degree, and some require a Ph.D., M.D., or J.D. (law degree). **Training:** Employees in this type of occupation may need some on-the-job training, but most of these occupations assume that the person will already have the required skills, knowledge, work-related experience, and/or training. **Examples:** Other occupations like this one often involve coordinating, training, supervising, or managing the activities of others to accomplish goals. Very advanced communication and organizational skills are required. Examples include athletic trainers, lawyers, managing editors, physicists, social psychologists, and surgeons. **Standard Vocational Preparation Range:** 8.0 to 9.0—Four years to more than ten years. **Major/Instructional Program:** 14.1001 Electrical, Electronics, and Communications Engineering; 14.2801 Textile Sciences and Engineering. **Related Courses:** Administration and Management; Economics and Accounting; Production and Processing; Computers and Electronics; Engineering and Technology; Design; Building and Construction; Mechanical; Mathematics; Physics; Public Safety and Security; Telecommunications.

ELECTRONICS ENGINEERS, EXCEPT COMPUTER (22126B)

Research, design, develop, and test electronic components and systems for commercial, industrial, military, or scientific use, utilizing knowledge of electronic theory and materials properties. Design electronic circuits and components for use in fields such as telecommunications, aerospace guidance and propulsion control, acoustics, or instruments and controls. Excludes computer hardware engineers.

Average Yearly Earnings: $53,227. **Experience:** Extensive preparation is needed. Extensive skill, knowledge, and experience are needed for this occupation. It may require more than five years of experience. **Education:** A bachelor's degree is the minimum formal education required for this group of occupations. However, many also require graduate school. For example, they may require a master's degree, and some require a Ph.D., M.D., or J.D. (law degree). **Training:** Employees in this type of occupation may need some on-the-job training, but most of these occupations assume that the person will already have the required skills, knowledge, work-related experience, and/or training. **Examples:** Other occupations like this one often involve coordinating, training, supervising, or managing the activities of others to accomplish goals. Very advanced communication and organizational skills are required. Examples include athletic trainers, lawyers, managing editors, physicists, social psychologists, and surgeons. **Standard Vocational Preparation Range:** 8.0 to 9.0—Four years to more than ten years. **Major/Instructional Program:** 14.0901 Computer Engineering; 14.1001 Electrical, Electronics, and Communications Engineering. **Related Courses:** Administration and Management; Economics and Accounting; Customer and Personal Service; Production and Processing; Computers and Electronics; Engineering and Technology; Design; Building and Construction; Mechanical; Mathematics; Physics; English Language; Telecommunications; Communications and Media.

COMPUTER ENGINEERS (22127)

Analyze data processing requirements to plan EDP system to provide system capabilities required for projected workloads. Plan layout and installation of new system or modification of existing system. May set up and control analog or hybrid computer systems to solve scientific and engineering problems.

Average Yearly Earnings: $54,912. **Experience:** Considerable preparation is needed. A minimum of two to four years of work-related skill, knowledge, or experience is needed for this occupation. **Education:** This group of occupations usually requires a four-year bachelor's degree, but in some cases does not. **Training:** Employees in this type of occupation usually need several years of work-related experience, on-the-job training, and/or vocational training. **Related Examples:** Other occupations like this one usually involve coordinating, supervising, managing, or training others. Examples include accountants, chefs and head cooks, computer programmers, historians, pharmacists, and police detectives. **Standard Vocational Preparation Range:** 7.0 to below 8.0—Two years to less than ten years. **Major/Instructional Program:** 11.0401 Information Sciences and Systems, 14.0901 Computer Engineering. **Related Courses:** Administration and Management; Clerical; Economics and Accounting; Customer and Personal Service; Computers and Electronics; Engineering and Technology; Design; Mathematics; Education and Training; English Language; Telecommunications; Communications and Media.

INDUSTRIAL ENGINEERS, EXCEPT SAFETY (22128)

Perform engineering duties in planning and overseeing the utilization of production facilities and personnel in department or other subdivision of industrial establishment. Plan equipment layout, workflow, and accident-prevention measures to maintain efficient and safe utilization of plant facilities. Plan and oversee work, study, and training programs to promote efficient worker utilization. Develop and oversee quality control, inventory control, and production record systems. Excludes industrial product safety engineers.

Average Yearly Earnings: $51,064. **Experience:** Considerable preparation is needed. A minimum of two to four years of work-related skill, knowledge, or experience is needed for this occupation. **Education:** This group of occupations usually requires a four-year bachelor's degree, but in some cases does not. **Training:** Employees in this type of occupation usually need several years of work-related experience, on-the-job training, and/ or vocational training. **Related Examples:** Other occupations like this one usually involve coordinating, supervising, managing, or training others. Examples include accountants, chefs and head cooks, computer programmers, historians, pharmacists, and police detectives. **Standard Vocational Preparation Range:** 7.0 to below 8.0—Two years to less than ten years. **Major/Instructional Program:** 14.1701 Industrial/Manufacturing Engineering, 14.2801 Textile Sciences and Engineering, 14.3001 Engineering/Industrial Management, 15.0603 Industrial/Manufacturing Technology/Technician. **Related Courses:** Administration and Management; Clerical; Economics and Accounting; Personnel and Human Resources; Production and Processing; Engineering and Technology; Design; Mathematics; Physics; Psychology; Education and Training; Public Safety and Security.

INDUSTRIAL SAFETY AND HEALTH ENGINEERS (22132A)

Plan, implement, and coordinate safety programs to prevent or correct unsafe environmental working conditions.

Average Yearly Earnings: $54,329. **Experience:** Considerable preparation is needed. A minimum of two to four years of work-related skill, knowledge, or experience is needed for this occupation. **Education:** This group of occupations usually requires a four-year bachelor's degree, but in some cases does not. **Training:** Employees in this type of occupation usually need several years of work-related experience, on-the-job training, and/or vocational training. **Related Examples:** Other occupations like this one usually involve coordinating, supervising, managing, or training others. Examples include accountants, chefs and head cooks, computer programmers, historians, pharmacists, and police detectives. **Standard Vocational Preparation Range:** 7.0 to below 8.0—Two years to less than ten years. **Major/Instructional Program:** 14.0101 Engineering, General; 14.1401 Environmental/Environmental Health Engineering. **Related Courses:** Administration and Management; Engineering and Technology; Design; Building and Construction; Mathematics; Physics; Chemistry; Biology; Education and Training; Public Safety and Security; Law, Government, and Jurisprudence.

FIRE-PREVENTION AND PROTECTION ENGINEERS (22132B)

Research causes of fires; determine fire protection methods; and design or recommend materials or equipment, such as structural components or fire-detection equipment, to assist organizations in safeguarding life and property against fire, explosion, and related hazards.

Average Yearly Earnings: $54,329. **Experience:** Considerable preparation is needed. A minimum of two to four years of work-related skill, knowledge, or experience is needed for this occupation. **Education:** This group of occupations usually requires a four-year bachelor's degree, but in some cases does not. **Training:** Employees in this type of occupation usually need several years of work-related experience, on-the-job training, and/or vocational training. **Related Examples:** Other occupations like this one usually involve coordinating, supervising, managing, or training others. Examples include accountants, chefs and head cooks, computer programmers, historians, pharmacists, and police detectives. **Standard Vocational Preparation Range:** 7.0 to below 8.0—Two years to less than ten years. **Major/Instructional Program:** 14.0101 Engineering, General. **Related Courses:** Sales and Marketing; Engineering and Technology; Design; Building and Construction; Physics; Chemistry; Geography; Education and Training; Public Safety and Security; Law, Government, and Jurisprudence; Telecommunications; Communications and Media.

PRODUCT SAFETY ENGINEERS (22132C)

Develop and conduct tests to evaluate product safety levels, and recommend measures to reduce or eliminate hazards.

Average Yearly Earnings: $54,329. **Experience:** Extensive preparation is needed. Extensive skill, knowledge, and experience are needed for this occupation. It may require more than five years of experience. **Education:** A bachelor's degree is the minimum formal education required for this group of occupations. However, many also require graduate school. For example, they may require a master's degree, and some require a Ph.D., M.D., or J.D. (law degree). **Training:** Employees in this type of occupation may need some on-the-job training, but most of these occupations assume that the person will already have the required skills, knowledge, work-related experience, and/or training. **Examples:** Other occupations like this one often involve coordinating, training, supervising, or managing the activities of others to accomplish goals. Very advanced communication and organizational skills are required. Examples include athletic trainers, lawyers, managing editors, physicists, social psychologists, and surgeons. **Standard Vocational Preparation Range:** 8.0 to 9.0—Four years to more than ten years. **Major/Instructional Program:** 14.0101 Engineering, General. **Related Courses:** Production and Processing; Engineering and Technology; Physics; Chemistry; Biology; English Language; Public Safety and Security.

MECHANICAL ENGINEERS (22135)

Perform engineering duties in planning and designing tools, engines, machines, and other mechanically functioning equipment. Oversee installation, operation, maintenance, and repair of such equipment as centralized heat, gas, water, and steam systems.

Average Yearly Earnings: $48,900. **Experience:** Considerable preparation is needed. A minimum of two to four years of work-related skill, knowledge, or experience is needed for this occupation. **Education:** This group of occupations usually requires a four-year bachelor's degree, but in some cases does not. **Training:** Employees in this type of occupation usually need several years of work-related experience, on-the-job training, and/or vocational training. **Related Examples:** Other occupations like this one usually involve coordinating, supervising, managing, or training others. Examples include accountants, chefs and head cooks, computer programmers, historians, pharmacists, and police detectives. **Standard Vocational Preparation Range:** 7.0 to below 8.0—Two years to less than ten years. **Major/Instructional Program:** 14.1901 Mechanical Engineering, 14.2801 Textile Sciences and Engineering, 15.0505 Solar Technology/Technician, 15.0805 Mechanical Engineering/Mechanical Technology/Technician. **Related Courses:** Production and Processing; Computers and Electronics; Engineering and Technology; Design; Building and Construction; Mechanical; Mathematics; Physics.

MARINE ENGINEERS (22138)

Design, develop, and take responsibility for the installation of ship machinery and related equipment, including propulsion machines and power supply systems. Excludes marine architects.

Average Yearly Earnings: $54,329. **Experience:** Extensive preparation is needed. Extensive skill, knowledge, and experience are needed for this occupation. It may require more than five years of experience. **Education:** A bachelor's degree is the minimum formal education required for this group of occupations. However, many also require graduate school. For example, they may require a master's degree, and some require a Ph.D., M.D., or J.D. (law degree). **Training:** Employees in this type of occupation may need some on-the-job training, but most of these occupations assume that the person will already have the required skills, knowledge, work-related experience, and/or training. **Examples:** Other occupations like this one often involve coordinating, training, supervising, or managing the activities of others to accomplish goals. Very advanced communication and organizational skills are required. Examples include athletic trainers, lawyers, managing editors, physicists, social psychologists, and surgeons. **Standard Vocational Preparation Range:** 8.0 to 9.0—Four years to more than ten years. **Major/Instructional Program:** 14.0101 Engineering, General; 14.2201 Naval Architecture and Marine Engineering. **Related Courses:** Administration and Management; Economics and Accounting; Engineering and Technology; Design; Building and Construction; Mechanical; Mathematics; Physics; Chemistry; Geography; English Language; Public Safety and Security; Law, Government, and Jurisprudence; Transportation.

PRODUCTION ENGINEERS (22197)

Develop, advance, and improve products, processes, or materials, and build or supervise the building of prototypes. May operate machinery, equipment, or hand tools to produce their prototypes.

Average Yearly Earnings: $54,329. **Experience:** Considerable preparation is needed. A minimum of two to four years of work-related skill, knowledge, or experience is needed for this occupation. **Education:** This group of occupations usually requires a four-year bachelor's degree, but in some cases does not. **Training:** Employees in this type of occupation usually need several years of work-related experience, on-the-job training, and/or vocational training. **Related Examples:** Other occupations like this one usually involve coordinating, supervising, managing, or training others. Examples include accountants, chefs and head cooks, computer programmers, historians, pharmacists, and police detectives. **Standard Vocational Preparation Range:** 7.0 to below 8.0—Two years to less than ten years. **Major/Instructional Program:** 14.0101 Engineering, General; 14.0501 Bioengineering and Biomedical Engineering; 14.1101 Engineering Mechanics; 14.1201 Engineering Physics; 14.1301 Engineering Science. **Related Courses:** Administration and Management; Production and Processing; Computers and Electronics; Engineering and Technology; Design; Mechanical; Mathematics; Physics; English Language.

Architects and Surveyors

ARCHITECTS, EXCEPT LANDSCAPE AND MARINE (22302)

Plan and design structures, such as private residences, office buildings, theaters, factories, and other structural property.

Average Yearly Earnings: $46,883. **Experience:** Considerable preparation is needed. A minimum of two to four years of work-related skill, knowledge, or experience is needed for this occupation. **Education:** This group of occupations usually requires a four-year bachelor's degree, but in some cases does not. **Training:** Employees in this type of occupation usually need several years of work-related experience, on-the-job training, and/or vocational training. **Related Examples:** Other occupations like this one usually involve coordinating, supervising, managing, or training others. Examples include accountants, chefs and head cooks, computer programmers, historians, pharmacists, and police detectives. **Standard Vocational Preparation Range:** 7.0 to below 8.0—Two years to less than ten years. **Major/Instructional Program:** 04.0201 Architecture, 04.0401 Architectural Environmental Design. **Related Courses:** Administration and Management; Economics and Accounting; Sales and Marketing; Customer and Personal Service; Personnel and Human Resources; Engineering and Technology; Design; Building and Construction; Mathematics; Physics; Geography; English Language; Fine Arts; History and Archeology; Public Safety and Security; Law, Government, and Jurisprudence; Communications and Media.

MARINE ARCHITECTS (22305)

Design and oversee construction and repair of marine craft and floating structures such as ships, barges, tugs, dredges, submarines, torpedoes, floats, and buoys. May confer with marine engineers.

Average Yearly Earnings: $38,875. **Experience:** Extensive preparation is needed. Extensive skill, knowledge, and experience are needed for this occupation. It may require more than five years of experience. **Education:** A bachelor's degree is the minimum formal education required for this group of occupations. However, many also require graduate school. For example, they may require a master's degree, and some require a Ph.D., M.D., or J.D. (law degree). **Training:** Employees in this type of occupation may need some on-the-job training, but most of these occupations assume that the person will already have the required skills, knowledge, work-related experience, and/or training. **Examples:** Other occupations like this one often involve coordinating, training, supervising, or managing the activities of others to accomplish goals. Very advanced communication and organizational skills are required. Examples include athletic trainers, lawyers, managing editors, physicists, social psychologists, and surgeons. **Standard Vocational Preparation Range:** 8.0 to 9.0— Four years to more than ten years. **Major/Instructional Program:** 14.0101 Engineering, General; 14.2201 Naval Architecture and Marine Engineering. **Related Courses:** Administration and Management; Computers and Electronics; Engineering and Technology; Design; Building and Construction; Mechanical; Mathematics; Physics; Geography; English Language; Public Safety and Security; Law, Government, and Jurisprudence; Transportation.

LANDSCAPE ARCHITECTS **(22308)**

Plan and design land areas for such projects as parks and other recreational facilities, airports, highways, hospitals, schools, land subdivisions, and commercial, industrial, and residential sites.

Average Yearly Earnings: $38,875. **Experience:** Extensive preparation is needed. Extensive skill, knowledge, and experience are needed for this occupation. It may require more than five years of experience. **Education:** A bachelor's degree is the minimum formal education required for this group of occupations. However, many also require graduate school. For example, they may require a master's degree, and some require a Ph.D., M.D., or J.D. (law degree). **Training:** Employees in this type of occupation may need some on-the-job training, but most of these occupations assume that the person will already have the required skills, knowledge, work-related experience, and/or training. **Examples:** Other occupations like this one often involve coordinating, training, supervising, or managing the activities of others to accomplish goals. Very advanced communication and organizational skills are required. Examples include athletic trainers, lawyers, managing editors, physicists, social psychologists, and surgeons. **Standard Vocational Preparation Range:** 8.0 to 9.0—Four years to more than ten years. **Major/Instructional Program:** 04.0401 Architectural Environmental Design, 04.0601 Landscape Architecture. **Related Courses:** Administration and Management; Economics and Accounting; Customer and Personal Service; Engineering and Technology; Design; Building and Construction; Mathematics; Physics; Biology; Geography; English Language; Fine Arts; History and Archeology; Public Safety and Security; Law, Government, and Jurisprudence.

CARTOGRAPHERS AND PHOTOGRAMMETRISTS (2231 IA)

Collect, analyze, and interpret geographic information provided by geodetic surveys, aerial photographs, and satellite data. Research, study, and prepare maps and other spatial data in digital or graphic form for legal, social, political, educational, and design purposes.

Average Yearly Earnings: $37,793. **Experience:** Considerable preparation is needed. A minimum of two to four years of work-related skill, knowledge, or experience is needed for this occupation. **Education:** This group of occupations usually requires a four-year bachelor's degree, but in some cases does not. **Training:** Employees in this type of occupation usually need several years of work-related experience, on-the-job training, and/or vocational training. **Related Examples:** Other occupations like this one usually involve coordinating, supervising, managing, or training others. Examples include accountants, chefs and head cooks, computer programmers, historians, pharmacists, and police detectives. **Standard Vocational Preparation Range:** 7.0 to below 8.0—Two years to less than ten years. **Major/Instructional Program:** 15.1102 Surveying; 45.0702 Cartography; 48.0101 Drafting, General; 48.0103 Civil/Structural Drafting. **Related Courses:** Design; Geography; Foreign Language; History and Archeology.

SURVEYORS (2231 IB)

Make exact measurements and determine property boundaries. Provide data relevant to the shape, contour, gravitation, location, elevation, or dimension of land or land features on or near the earth's surface for engineering, mapmaking, mining, land evaluation, construction, and other purposes.

Average Yearly Earnings: $37,793. **Experience:** Considerable preparation is needed. A minimum of two to four years of work-related skill, knowledge, or experience is needed for this occupation. **Education:** This group of occupations usually requires a four-year bachelor's degree, but in some cases does not. **Training:** Employees in this type of occupation usually need several years of work-related experience, on-the-job training, and/or vocational training. **Related Examples:** Other occupations like this one usually involve coordinating, supervising, managing, or training others. Examples include accountants, chefs and head cooks, computer programmers, historians, pharmacists, and police detectives. **Standard Vocational Preparation Range:** 7.0 to below 8.0—Two years to less than ten years. **Major/Instructional Program:** 15.0805 Mechanical Engineering/Mechanical Technology/Technician, 15.1102 Surveying, 45.0701 Geography, 45.0702 Cartography. **Related Courses:** Administration and Management; Economics and Accounting; Computers and Electronics; Engineering and Technology; Design; Mathematics; Physics; Biology; Sociology and Anthropology; Geography; Education and Training; English Language; Foreign Language; History and Archeology; Philosophy and Theology; Public Safety and Security; Telecommunications; Transportation.

Engineering Technologists and Technicians

CIVIL ENGINEERING TECHNICIANS (22502)

Apply theory and principles of civil engineering in planning, designing, and overseeing construction and maintenance of structures and facilities, under the direction of engineering staff or physical scientists.

Average Yearly Earnings: $34,236. **Experience:** Considerable preparation is needed. A minimum of two to four years of work-related skill, knowledge, or experience is needed for this occupation. **Education:** This group of occupations usually requires a four-year bachelor's degree, but in some cases does not. **Training:** Employees in this type of occupation usually need several years of work-related experience, on-the-job training, and/or vocational training. **Related Examples:** Other occupations like this one usually involve coordinating, supervising, managing, or training others. Examples include accountants, chefs and head cooks, computer programmers, historians, pharmacists, and police detectives. **Standard Vocational Preparation Range:** 7.0 to below 8.0—Two years to less than ten years. **Major/Instructional Program:** 04.0501 Interior Architecture, 15.0101 Architectural Engineering Technology/Technician, 15.0201 Civil Engineering/Civil Technology/Technician, 15.1001 Construction/Building Technology/Technician. **Related Courses:** Computers and Electronics; Engineering and Technology; Design; Building and Construction; Mathematics; Law, Government, and Jurisprudence.

ELECTRONICS ENGINEERING TECHNICIANS (22505A)

Lay out, build, test, troubleshoot, repair, and modify developmental and production electronic components, parts, equipment, and systems, such as computer equipment, missile control instrumentation, electron tubes, test equipment, and machine tool numerical controls; applying principles and theories of electronics, electrical circuitry, engineering mathematics, electronic and electrical testing, and physics.

Average Yearly Earnings: $33,800. **Experience:** Considerable preparation is needed. A minimum of two to four years of work-related skill, knowledge, or experience is needed for this occupation. **Education:** This group of occupations usually requires a four-year bachelor's degree, but in some cases does not. **Training:** Employees in this type of occupation usually need several years of work-related experience, on-the-job training, and/or vocational training. **Related Examples:** Other occupations like this one usually involve coordinating, supervising, managing, or training others. Examples include accountants, chefs and head cooks, computer programmers, historians, pharmacists, and police detectives. **Standard Vocational Preparation Range:** 7.0 to below 8.0—Two years to less than ten years. **Major/Instructional Program:** 15.0301 Computer Engineering Technology/Technician; 15.0303 Electrical, Electronic, and Communications Engineering Technology/

Technician; 15.0402 Computer Maintenance Technology/Technician; 15.0403 Electro-mechanical Technology/Technician; 15.0405 Robotics Technology/Technician; 47.0101 Electrical and Electronics Equipment Installer and Repairer, General; 47.0105 Industrial Electronics Installers and Repairer. **Related Courses:** Production and Processing; Computers and Electronics; Engineering and Technology; Design; Building and Construction; Mathematics; Physics.

CALIBRATION AND INSTRUMENTATION TECHNICIANS (22505B)

Develop, test, calibrate, operate, and repair electrical, mechanical, electromechanical, electrohydraulic, or electronic measuring and recording instruments, apparatus, and equipment.

Average Yearly Earnings: $33,800. **Experience:** Considerable preparation is needed. A minimum of two to four years of work-related skill, knowledge, or experience is needed for this occupation. **Education:** This group of occupations usually requires a four-year bachelor's degree, but in some cases does not. **Training:** Employees in this type of occupation usually need several years of work-related experience, on-the-job training, and/or vocational training. **Related Examples:** Other occupations like this one usually involve coordinating, supervising, managing, or training others. Examples include accountants, chefs and head cooks, computer programmers, historians, pharmacists, and police detectives. **Standard Vocational Preparation Range:** 7.0 to below 8.0—Two years to less than ten years. **Major/Instructional Program:** 15.0303 Electrical, Electronic, and Communications Engineering Technology/Technician; 15.0403 Electromechanical Technology/Technician; 15.0404 Instrumentation Technology/Technician; 15.0801 Aeronautical and Aerospace Engineering Technology/Technician; 47.0401 Instrument Calibration and Repairer. **Related Courses:** Computers and Electronics; Engineering and Technology; Design; Mechanical; Mathematics.

ELECTRICAL ENGINEERING TECHNICIANS (22505C)

Apply electrical theory and related knowledge to test and modify developmental or operational electrical machinery and electrical control equipment and circuitry in industrial or commercial plants and laboratories.

Average Yearly Earnings: $33,800. **Experience:** Considerable preparation is needed. A minimum of two to four years of work-related skill, knowledge, or experience is needed for this occupation. **Education:** This group of occupations usually requires a four-year bachelor's degree, but in some cases does not. **Training:** Employees in this type of occupation usually need several years of work-related experience, on-the-job training, and/or vocational training. **Related Examples:** Other occupations like this one usually involve coordinating, supervising, managing, or training others. Examples include accountants, chefs and head cooks, computer programmers, historians, pharmacists, and police detectives. **Standard Vocational Preparation Range:** 7.0 to below 8.0—Two years to less than ten years. **Major/Instructional Program:** 15.0303 Electrical, Electronic, and

Communications Engineering Technology/Technician. **Related Courses:** Computers and Electronics; Engineering and Technology; Design; Mathematics; Physics.

INDUSTRIAL ENGINEERING TECHNICIANS AND TECHNOLOGISTS (22508)

Study and record time, motion, method, and speed involved in performance of production, maintenance, clerical, and other worker operations for such purposes as establishing standard production rates or improving efficiency. Usually work under the direction of engineering staff.

Average Yearly Earnings: $34,236. **Experience:** Medium preparation is needed. Previous work-related skill, knowledge, or experience is required for this occupation. **Education:** This group of occupations usually requires training in vocational schools, related on-the-job experience, or an associate degree. A bachelor's degree may be required. **Training:** Employees in this type of occupation usually need one or two years of training involving both on-the-job experience and informal training with experienced workers. **Related Examples:** Other occupations like this one usually involve using communication and organizational skills to coordinate, supervise, manage, or train others to accomplish goals. Examples include dental assistants, electricians, fish and game wardens, legal secretaries, personnel recruiters, and recreation workers. **Standard Vocational Preparation Range:** 6.0 to below 7.0—More than one year and less than four years. **Major/Instructional Program:** 15.0603 Industrial/Manufacturing Technology/Technician, 15.0702 Quality Control Technology/Technician. **Related Courses:** Administration and Management; Clerical; Economics and Accounting; Personnel and Human Resources; Production and Processing; Computers and Electronics; Engineering and Technology; Design; Mechanical; Mathematics; Physics; Psychology; Sociology and Anthropology; English Language; Philosophy and Theology; Public Safety and Security; Communications and Media.

MECHANICAL ENGINEERING TECHNICIANS AND TECHNOLOGISTS (22511)

Apply theory and principles of mechanical engineering to develop and test machinery and equipment, under the direction of engineering staff or physical scientists.

Average Yearly Earnings: $34,236. **Experience:** Considerable preparation is needed. A minimum of two to four years of work-related skill, knowledge, or experience is needed for this occupation. **Education:** This group of occupations usually requires a four-year bachelor's degree, but in some cases does not. **Training:** Employees in this type of occupation usually need several years of work-related experience, on-the-job training, and/or vocational training. **Related Examples:** Other occupations like this one usually involve coordinating, supervising, managing, or training others. Examples include accountants, chefs and head cooks, computer programmers, historians, pharmacists, and police detectives. **Standard Vocational Preparation Range:** 7.0 to below 8.0—Two years to less than ten years. **Major/Instructional Program:** 15.0501 Heating, Air Conditioning, and Refrigeration Technologies/Technicians; 15.0503 Energy Management and Systems Technology/Technician; 15.0803 Automotive Engineering Technology/Technician;

15.0805 Mechanical Engineering/Mechanical Technology/Technician; 48.0101 Drafting, General; 48.0105 Mechanical Drafting. **Related Courses:** Administration and Management; Engineering and Technology; Design; Mechanical; Mathematics; Physics.

ARCHITECTURAL DRAFTERS (22514A)

Prepare detailed drawings of architectural designs and plans for buildings and structures according to specifications provided by the architect.

Average Yearly Earnings: $32,968. **Experience:** Considerable preparation is needed. A minimum of two to four years of work-related skill, knowledge, or experience is needed for this occupation. **Education:** This group of occupations usually requires a four-year bachelor's degree, but in some cases does not. **Training:** Employees in this type of occupation usually need several years of work-related experience, on-the-job training, and/or vocational training. **Related Examples:** Other occupations like this one usually involve coordinating, supervising, managing, or training others. Examples include accountants, chefs and head cooks, computer programmers, historians, pharmacists, and police detectives. **Standard Vocational Preparation Range:** 7.0 to below 8.0—Two years to less than ten years. **Major/Instructional Program:** 15.0501 Heating, Air Conditioning, and Refrigeration Technologies/Technicians; 48.0101 Drafting, General; 48.0102 Architectural Drafting; 48.0103 Civil/Structural Drafting. **Related Courses:** Computers and Electronics; Engineering and Technology; Design; Mathematics; Physics; Fine Arts.

ELECTRONIC DRAFTERS (22514B)

Draw wiring diagrams, circuit-board assembly diagrams, schematics, and layout drawings used for manufacture, installation, and repair of electronic equipment.

Average Yearly Earnings: $32,968. **Experience:** Medium preparation is needed. Previous work-related skill, knowledge, or experience is required for this occupation. **Education:** This group of occupations usually requires training in vocational schools, related on-the-job experience, or an associate degree. A bachelor's degree may be required. **Training:** Employees in this type of occupation usually need one or two years of training involving both on-the-job experience and informal training with experienced workers. **Related Examples:** Other occupations like this one usually involve using communication and organizational skills to coordinate, supervise, manage, or train others to accomplish goals. Examples include dental assistants, electricians, fish and game wardens, legal secretaries, personnel recruiters, and recreation workers. **Standard Vocational Preparation Range:** 6.0 to below 7.0—More than one year and less than four years. **Major/Instructional Program:** 15.0301 Computer Engineering Technology/Technician; 15.0303 Electrical, Electronic, and Communications Engineering Technology/Technician; 48.0101 Drafting, General; 48.0104 Electrical/Electronics Drafting; 52.0201 Business Administration and Management, General; 52.0205 Operations Management and Supervision. **Related Courses:** Administration and Management; Computers and Electronics; Engineering and Technology; Design; Mathematics; Telecommunications.

CIVIL DRAFTERS (22514C)

Prepare drawings and topographical and relief maps used in civil engineering projects, such as highways, bridges, pipelines, flood control projects, and water and sewerage control systems.

Average Yearly Earnings: $32,968. **Experience:** Medium preparation is needed. Previous work-related skill, knowledge, or experience is required for this occupation. **Education:** This group of occupations usually requires training in vocational schools, related on-the-job experience, or an associate degree. A bachelor's degree may be required. **Training:** Employees in this type of occupation usually need one or two years of training involving both on-the-job experience and informal training with experienced workers. **Related Examples:** Other occupations like this one usually involve using communication and organizational skills to coordinate, supervise, manage, or train others to accomplish goals. Examples include dental assistants, electricians, fish and game wardens, legal secretaries, personnel recruiters, and recreation workers. **Standard Vocational Preparation Range:** 6.0 to below 7.0—More than one year and less than four years. **Major/Instructional Program:** 48.0101 Drafting, General; 48.0103 Civil/Structural Drafting. **Related Courses:** Computers and Electronics; Engineering and Technology; Design; Mathematics; Physics; Geography.

MECHANICAL DRAFTERS (22514D)

Prepare detailed working diagrams of machinery and mechanical devices, including dimensions, fastening methods, and other engineering information.

Average Yearly Earnings: $32,968. **Experience:** Considerable preparation is needed. A minimum of two to four years of work-related skill, knowledge, or experience is needed for this occupation. **Education:** This group of occupations usually requires a four-year bachelor's degree, but in some cases does not. **Training:** Employees in this type of occupation usually need several years of work-related experience, on-the-job training, and/or vocational training. **Related Examples:** Other occupations like this one usually involve coordinating, supervising, managing, or training others. Examples include accountants, chefs and head cooks, computer programmers, historians, pharmacists, and police detectives. **Standard Vocational Preparation Range:** 7.0 to below 8.0—Two years to less than ten years. **Major/Instructional Program:** 15.0403 Electromechanical Technology/Technician; 15.0404 Instrumentation Technology/Technician; 15.0805 Mechanical Engineering/Mechanical Technology/Technician; 48.0101 Drafting, General; 48.0104 Electrical/Electronics Drafting; 48.0105 Mechanical Drafting. **Related Courses:** Computers and Electronics; Engineering and Technology; Design; Mathematics; Physics; Fine Arts.

ESTIMATORS AND DRAFTERS, UTILITIES (22517)

Develop specifications and instructions for the installation of voltage transformers, overhead or underground cables, and related electrical equipment used to conduct electrical energy from transmission lines or high-voltage distribution lines to consumers.

Average Yearly Earnings: $32,968. **Experience:** Considerable preparation is needed. A minimum of two to four years of work-related skill, knowledge, or experience is needed for this occupation. **Education:** This group of occupations usually requires a four-year bachelor's degree, but in some cases does not. **Training:** Employees in this type of occupation usually need several years of work-related experience, on-the-job training, and/or vocational training. **Related Examples:** Other occupations like this one usually involve coordinating, supervising, managing, or training others. Examples include accountants, chefs and head cooks, computer programmers, historians, pharmacists, and police detectives. **Standard Vocational Preparation Range:** 7.0 to below 8.0—Two years to less than ten years. **Major/Instructional Program:** 48.0101 Drafting, General; 48.0103 Civil/Structural Drafting; 48.0104 Electrical/Electronics Drafting. **Related Courses:** Administration and Management; Economics and Accounting; Personnel and Human Resources; Engineering and Technology; Design; Building and Construction; Mathematics; Physics; Psychology; Sociology and Anthropology; Geography; English Language; Public Safety and Security.

SURVEYING TECHNICIANS (22521A)

Adjust and operate surveying instruments, such as the theodolite and electronic distance-measuring equipment, and compile notes, make sketches, and enter data into computers.

Average Yearly Earnings: $37,793. **Experience:** Considerable preparation is needed. A minimum of two to four years of work-related skill, knowledge, or experience is needed for this occupation. **Education:** This group of occupations usually requires a four-year bachelor's degree, but in some cases does not. **Training:** Employees in this type of occupation usually need several years of work-related experience, on-the-job training, and/or vocational training. **Related Examples:** Other occupations like this one usually involve coordinating, supervising, managing, or training others. Examples include accountants, chefs and head cooks, computer programmers, historians, pharmacists, and police detectives. **Standard Vocational Preparation Range:** 7.0 to below 8.0—Two years to less than ten years. **Major/Instructional Program:** 15.1102 Surveying. **Related Courses:** Engineering and Technology; Design; Mathematics; Geography.

MAPPING TECHNICIANS (22521B)

Calculate mapmaking information from field notes, and draw and verify accuracy of topographical maps.

Average Yearly Earnings: $37,793. **Experience:** Medium preparation is needed. Previous work-related skill, knowledge, or experience is required for this occupation. **Education:** This group of occupations usually requires training in vocational schools, related on-the-job experience, or an associate degree. A bachelor's degree may be required. **Training:** Employees in this type of occupation usually need one or two years of training involving both on-the-job experience and informal training with experienced workers.

Related Examples: Other occupations like this one usually involve using communication and organizational skills to coordinate, supervise, manage, or train others to accomplish goals. Examples include dental assistants, electricians, fish and game wardens, legal secretaries, personnel recruiters, and recreation workers. **Standard Vocational Preparation Range:** 6.0 to below 7.0—More than one year and less than four years. **Major/Instructional Program:** 15.1102 Surveying; 45.0702 Cartography; 48.0101 Drafting, General; 48.0103 Civil/Structural Drafting. **Related Courses:** Administration and Management; Computers and Electronics; Design; Mathematics; Geography.

SOUND ENGINEERING TECHNICIANS (22599A)

Operate machines and equipment to record, synchronize, mix, or reproduce music, voices, and previously recorded sound effects.

Average Yearly Earnings: $33,800. **Experience:** Medium preparation is needed. Previous work-related skill, knowledge, or experience is required for this occupation. **Education:** This group of occupations usually requires training in vocational schools, related on-the-job experience, or an associate degree. A bachelor's degree may be required. **Training:** Employees in this type of occupation usually need one or two years of training involving both on-the-job experience and informal training with experienced workers. **Related Examples:** Other occupations like this one usually involve using communication and organizational skills to coordinate, supervise, manage, or train others to accomplish goals. Examples include dental assistants, electricians, fish and game wardens, legal secretaries, personnel recruiters, and recreation workers. **Standard Vocational Preparation Range:** 6.0 to below 7.0—More than one year and less than four years. **Major/Instructional Program:** 10.0104 Radio and Television Broadcasting Technology/Technician. **Related Courses:** Computers and Electronics; Engineering and Technology; Telecommunications; Communications and Media.

METALLURGICAL TECHNICIANS (22599B)

Examine and test minerals and metal samples to determine their physical and chemical properties.

Average Yearly Earnings: $34,236. **Experience:** Medium preparation is needed. Previous work-related skill, knowledge, or experience is required for this occupation. **Education:** This group of occupations usually requires training in vocational schools, related on-the-job experience, or an associate degree. A bachelor's degree may be required. **Training:** Employees in this type of occupation usually need one or two years of training involving both on-the-job experience and informal training with experienced workers. **Related Examples:** Other occupations like this one usually involve using communication and organizational skills to coordinate, supervise, manage, or train others to accomplish goals. Examples include dental assistants, electricians, fish and game wardens, legal secretaries, personnel recruiters, and recreation workers. **Standard Vocational Preparation Range:** 6.0 to below 7.0—More than one year and less than four years. **Major/**

Instructional Program: 15.0611 Metallurgical Technology/Technician, 15.0702 Quality Control Technology/Technician. **Related Courses:** Engineering and Technology; Physics; Chemistry.

AEROSPACE ENGINEERING TECHNICIANS (22599C)

Operate, install, calibrate, and maintain integrated computer/communications systems consoles, simulators, and other data acquisition, test, and measurement instrument equipment, to launch, track, position, and evaluate air and space vehicles. May record and interpret test data. May fabricate, assemble, and test aircraft parts and mechanisms in a laboratory.

Average Yearly Earnings: $34,236. **Experience:** Considerable preparation is needed. A minimum of two to four years of work-related skill, knowledge, or experience is needed for this occupation. **Education:** This group of occupations usually requires a four-year bachelor's degree, but in some cases does not. **Training:** Employees in this type of occupation usually need several years of work-related experience, on-the-job training, and/or vocational training. **Related Examples:** Other occupations like this one usually involve coordinating, supervising, managing, or training others. Examples include accountants, chefs and head cooks, computer programmers, historians, pharmacists, and police detectives. **Standard Vocational Preparation Range:** 7.0 to below 8.0—Two years to less than ten years. **Major/Instructional Program:** 15.0801 Aeronautical and Aerospace Engineering Technology/Technician, 15.0805 Mechanical Engineering/Mechanical Technology/Technician. **Related Courses:** Computers and Electronics; Engineering and Technology; Mechanical; Mathematics; Physics.

AGRICULTURAL TECHNICIANS (22599D)

Lay out and complete detailed drawings of agricultural machinery and equipment, and test agricultural equipment and techniques.

Average Yearly Earnings: $34,236. **Experience:** Medium preparation is needed. Previous work-related skill, knowledge, or experience is required for this occupation. **Education:** This group of occupations usually requires training in vocational schools, related on-the-job experience, or an associate degree. A bachelor's degree may be required. **Training:** Employees in this type of occupation usually need one or two years of training involving both on-the-job experience and informal training with experienced workers. **Related Examples:** Other occupations like this one usually involve using communication and organizational skills to coordinate, supervise, manage, or train others to accomplish goals. Examples include dental assistants, electricians, fish and game wardens, legal secretaries, personnel recruiters, and recreation workers. **Standard Vocational Preparation Range:** 6.0 to below 7.0—More than one year and less than four years. **Major/**

Instructional Program: 01.0201 Agricultural Mechanization, General. **Related Courses:** Engineering and Technology; Design; Mechanical.

CHEMICAL ENGINEERING TECHNICIANS (22599E)

Conduct tests, prepare diagrams and flowcharts, and compile and record data to assist chemical engineers in developing, improving, and testing chemical plant processes, products, and equipment.

Average Yearly Earnings: $34,236. **Experience:** Extensive preparation is needed. Extensive skill, knowledge, and experience are needed for this occupation. It may require more than five years of experience. **Education:** A bachelor's degree is the minimum formal education required for this group of occupations. However, many also require graduate school. For example, they may require a master's degree, and some require a Ph.D., M.D., or J.D. (law degree). **Training:** Employees in this type of occupation may need some on-the-job training, but most of these occupations assume that the person will already have the required skills, knowledge, work-related experience, and/or training. **Examples:** Other occupations like this one often involve coordinating, training, supervising, or managing the activities of others to accomplish goals. Very advanced communication and organizational skills are required. Examples include athletic trainers, lawyers, managing editors, physicists, social psychologists, and surgeons. **Standard Vocational Preparation Range:** 8.0 to 9.0—Four years to more than ten years. **Major/Instructional Program:** 15.0506 Water Quality and Wastewater Treatment Technology/Technician, 15.0607 Plastics Technology/Technician, 15.0903 Petroleum Technology/Technician. **Related Courses:** Production and Processing; Engineering and Technology; Mechanical; Chemistry.

LASER TECHNICIANS (22599F)

Construct, install, and test gas or solid-state laser devices, according to engineering specifications and project instructions.

Average Yearly Earnings: $33,800. **Experience:** Considerable preparation is needed. A minimum of two to four years of work-related skill, knowledge, or experience is needed for this occupation. **Education:** This group of occupations usually requires a four-year bachelor's degree, but in some cases does not. **Training:** Employees in this type of occupation usually need several years of work-related experience, on-the-job training, and/or vocational training. **Related Examples:** Other occupations like this one usually involve coordinating, supervising, managing, or training others. Examples include accountants, chefs and head cooks, computer programmers, historians, pharmacists, and police detectives. **Standard Vocational Preparation Range:** 7.0 to below 8.0—Two years to less than ten years. **Major/Instructional Program:** 15.0304 Laser and Optical Technology/Technician. **Related Courses:** Computers and Electronics; Engineering and Technology; Design; Physics.

Physical Scientists

PHYSICISTS (24102A)

Conduct research into the phases of physical phenomena, develop theories and laws on the basis of observation and experiments, and devise methods to apply laws and theories to industry and other fields.

Average Yearly Earnings: $62,774. **Experience:** Extensive preparation is needed. Extensive skill, knowledge, and experience are needed for this occupation. It may require more than five years of experience. **Education:** A bachelor's degree is the minimum formal education required for this group of occupations. However, many also require graduate school. For example, they may require a master's degree, and some require a Ph.D., M.D., or J.D. (law degree). **Training:** Employees in this type of occupation may need some on-the-job training, but most of these occupations assume that the person will already have the required skills, knowledge, work-related experience, and/or training. **Examples:** Other occupations like this one often involve coordinating, training, supervising, or managing the activities of others to accomplish goals. Very advanced communication and organizational skills are required. Examples include athletic trainers, lawyers, managing editors, social psychologists, and surgeons. **Standard Vocational Preparation Range:** 8.0 to 9.0—Four years to more than ten years. **Major/Instructional Program:** 40.0201 Astronomy; 40.0301 Astrophysics; 40.0501 Chemistry, General; 40.0506 Physical and Theoretical Chemistry; 40.0703 Earth and Planetary Sciences; 40.0801 Physics, General; 40.0802 Chemical and Atomic/Molecular Physics; 40.0804 Elementary Particle Physics; 40.0805 Plasma and High-Temperature Physics; 40.0806 Nuclear Physics; 40.0807 Optics; 40.0808 Solid-State and Low-Temperature Physics; 40.0809 Acoustics; 40.0810 Theoretical and Mathematical Physics; 51.2205 Health Physics/Radiologic Health. **Related Courses:** Personnel and Human Resources; Production and Processing; Computers and Electronics; Engineering and Technology; Design; Mathematics; Physics; Chemistry; Education and Training; English Language; Foreign Language; History and Archeology; Communications and Media.

ASTRONOMERS (24102B)

Observe, research, and interpret celestial and astronomical phenomena to increase basic knowledge; and apply such information to practical problems.

Average Yearly Earnings: $62,774. **Experience:** Extensive preparation is needed. Extensive skill, knowledge, and experience are needed for this occupation. It may require more than five years of experience. **Education:** A bachelor's degree is the minimum formal education required for this group of occupations. However, many also require graduate school. For example, they may require a master's degree, and some require a Ph.D., M.D., or J.D. (law degree). **Training:** Employees in this type of occupation may need some on-the-job training, but most of these occupations assume that the person will already have the required skills, knowledge, work-related experience, and/or training.

Examples: Other occupations like this one often involve coordinating, training, supervising, or managing the activities of others to accomplish goals. Very advanced communication and organizational skills are required. Examples include athletic trainers, lawyers, managing editors, physicists, social psychologists, and surgeons. **Standard Vocational Preparation Range:** 8.0 to 9.0—Four years to more than ten years. **Major/Instructional Program:** 40.0201 Astronomy, 40.0301 Astrophysics, 40.0703 Earth and Planetary Sciences. **Related Courses:** Computers and Electronics; Engineering and Technology; Design; Mathematics; Physics; Geography; English Language; History and Archeology.

CHEMISTS, EXCEPT BIOCHEMISTS (24105)

Conduct qualitative and quantitative chemical analyses or chemical experiments in laboratories for quality or process control or to develop new products or knowledge.

Average Yearly Earnings: $43,305. **Experience:** Considerable preparation is needed. A minimum of two to four years of work-related skill, knowledge, or experience is needed for this occupation. **Education:** This group of occupations usually requires a four-year bachelor's degree, but in some cases does not. **Training:** Employees in this type of occupation usually need several years of work-related experience, on-the-job training, and/or vocational training. **Related Examples:** Other occupations like this one usually involve coordinating, supervising, managing, or training others. Examples include accountants, chefs and head cooks, computer programmers, historians, pharmacists, and police detectives. **Standard Vocational Preparation Range:** 7.0 to below 8.0—Two years to less than ten years. **Major/Instructional Program:** 40.0501 Chemistry, General; 40.0502 Analytical Chemistry; 40.0503 Inorganic Chemistry; 40.0504 Organic Chemistry; 40.0505 Medicinal/Pharmaceutical Chemistry; 40.0506 Physical and Theoretical Chemistry; 40.0801 Physics, General; 40.0802 Chemical and Atomic/Molecular Physics. **Related Courses:** Administration and Management; Production and Processing; Computers and Electronics; Engineering and Technology; Mathematics; Physics; Chemistry; Biology; English Language.

ATMOSPHERIC AND SPACE SCIENTISTS (24108)

Investigate atmospheric phenomena and interpret meteorological data gathered by surface and air stations, satellites, and radar, to prepare reports and forecasts for public and other uses. Include weather analysts and forecasters who work for radio and TV stations and whose functions require the detailed knowledge of a meteorologist.

Average Yearly Earnings: $47,673. **Experience:** Considerable preparation is needed. A minimum of two to four years of work-related skill, knowledge, or experience is needed for this occupation. **Education:** This group of occupations usually requires a four-year bachelor's degree, but in some cases does not. **Training:** Employees in this type of occupation usually need several years of work-related experience, on-the-job training, and/or vocational training. **Related Examples:** Other occupations like this one usually involve coordinating, supervising, managing, or training others. Examples include

accountants, chefs and head cooks, computer programmers, historians, pharmacists, and police detectives. **Standard Vocational Preparation Range:** 7.0 to below 8.0—Two years to less than ten years. **Major/Instructional Program:** 40.0401 Atmospheric Sciences and Meteorology. **Related Courses:** Administration and Management; Clerical; Personnel and Human Resources; Computers and Electronics; Mathematics; Physics; Sociology and Anthropology; Geography; Education and Training; English Language; Foreign Language; Telecommunications; Communications and Media.

GEOLOGISTS (24111A)

Study the composition, structure, and history of the earth's crust; examine rocks, minerals, and fossil remains to identify and determine the sequence of processes affecting the development of the earth; apply knowledge of chemistry, physics, biology, and mathematics to explain these phenomena and to help locate mineral and petroleum deposits and underground water resources; prepare geologic reports and maps; and interpret research data to recommend further action for study.

Average Yearly Earnings: $52,083. **Experience:** Extensive preparation is needed. Extensive skill, knowledge, and experience are needed for this occupation. It may require more than five years of experience. **Education:** A bachelor's degree is the minimum formal education required for this group of occupations. However, many also require graduate school. For example, they may require a master's degree, and some require a Ph.D., M.D., or J.D. (law degree). **Training:** Employees in this type of occupation may need some on-the-job training, but most of these occupations assume that the person will already have the required skills, knowledge, work-related experience, and/or training. **Examples:** Other occupations like this one often involve coordinating, training, supervising, or managing the activities of others to accomplish goals. Very advanced communication and organizational skills are required. Examples include athletic trainers, lawyers, managing editors, physicists, social psychologists, and surgeons. **Standard Vocational Preparation Range:** 8.0 to 9.0—Four years to more than ten years. **Major/Instructional Program:** 15.0901 Mining Technology/Technician, 40.0601 Geology, 40.0602 Geochemistry, 40.0603 Geophysics and Seismology, 40.0604 Paleontology, 40.0702 Oceanography, 45.0201 Anthropology, 45.0701 Geography. **Related Courses:** Administration and Management; Engineering and Technology; Design; Mechanical; Mathematics; Physics; Chemistry; Biology; Psychology; Sociology and Anthropology; Geography; English Language; History and Archeology; Communications and Media.

GEOPHYSICISTS (24111B)

Study physical aspects of the earth, including the atmosphere and hydrosphere. Investigate and measure seismic, gravitational, electrical, thermal, and magnetic forces affecting the earth, utilizing principles of physics, mathematics, and chemistry.

Average Yearly Earnings: $52,083. **Experience:** Extensive preparation is needed. Extensive skill, knowledge, and experience are needed for this occupation. It may require more

than five years of experience. **Education:** A bachelor's degree is the minimum formal education required for this group of occupations. However, many also require graduate school. For example, they may require a master's degree, and some require a Ph.D., M.D., or J.D. (law degree). **Training:** Employees in this type of occupation may need some on-the-job training, but most of these occupations assume that the person will already have the required skills, knowledge, work-related experience, and/or training. **Examples:** Other occupations like this one often involve coordinating, training, supervising, or managing the activities of others to accomplish goals. Very advanced communication and organizational skills are required. Examples include athletic trainers, lawyers, managing editors, physicists, social psychologists, and surgeons. **Standard Vocational Preparation Range:** 8.0 to 9.0—Four years to more than ten years. **Major/Instructional Program:** 40.0601 Geology, 40.0603 Geophysics and Seismology, 40.0702 Oceanography. **Related Courses:** Mathematics; Physics; Chemistry; Geography; English Language; History and Archeology; Communications and Media.

GEOGRAPHERS (24199A)

Study nature and the use of areas of the earth's surface, relating and interpreting interactions of physical and cultural phenomena. Conduct research on physical aspects of a region, including land forms, climates, soils, plants, and animals; and conduct research on the spatial implications of human activities within a given area, including social characteristics, economic activities, and political organization, as well as researching interdependence between regions at scales ranging from local to global.

Average Yearly Earnings: $36,296. **Experience:** Considerable preparation is needed. A minimum of two to four years of work-related skill, knowledge, or experience is needed for this occupation. **Education:** This group of occupations usually requires a four-year bachelor's degree, but in some cases does not. **Training:** Employees in this type of occupation usually need several years of work-related experience, on-the-job training, and/or vocational training. **Related Examples:** Other occupations like this one usually involve coordinating, supervising, managing, or training others. Examples include accountants, chefs and head cooks, computer programmers, historians, pharmacists, and police detectives. **Standard Vocational Preparation Range:** 7.0 to below 8.0—Two years to less than ten years. **Major/Instructional Program:** 45.0701 Geography. **Related Courses:** Physics; Biology; Sociology and Anthropology; Geography; Foreign Language; History and Archeology.

ENVIRONMENTAL SCIENTISTS (24199B)

Conduct research to develop methods of abating, controlling, or remediating sources of environmental pollutants, utilizing knowledge of various scientific disciplines. Identify and analyze sources of pollution to determine their effects. Collect and synthesize data derived from pollution-emission measurements, atmospheric monitoring, meteorological and mineralogical information, or soil and water samples. Exclude wildlife conservationists and natural resource scientists.

Average Yearly Earnings: $36,649. **Experience:** Extensive preparation is needed. Extensive skill, knowledge, and experience are needed for this occupation. It may require more than five years of experience. **Education:** A bachelor's degree is the minimum formal education required for this group of occupations. However, many also require graduate school. For example, they may require a master's degree, and some require a Ph.D., M.D., or J.D. (law degree). **Training:** Employees in this type of occupation may need some on-the-job training, but most of these occupations assume that the person will already have the required skills, knowledge, work-related experience, and/or training. **Examples:** Other occupations like this one often involve coordinating, training, supervising, or managing the activities of others to accomplish goals. Very advanced communication and organizational skills are required. Examples include athletic trainers, lawyers, managing editors, physicists, social psychologists, and surgeons. **Standard Vocational Preparation Range:** 8.0 to 9.0—Four years to more than ten years. **Major/Instructional Program:** 03.0101 Natural Resources Conservation, General; 03.0102 Environmental Science/Studies. **Related Courses:** Mathematics; Physics; Chemistry; Biology.

MATERIALS SCIENTISTS (24199C)

Research and study the structures and chemical properties of various natural and manmade materials, including metals, alloys, rubber, ceramics, semiconductors, polymers, and glass. Determine ways to strengthen or combine materials, or develop new materials with new or specific properties for use in a variety of products and applications. Include glass scientists, ceramic scientists, metallurgical scientists, and polymer scientists.

Average Yearly Earnings: $47,632. **Experience:** Considerable preparation is needed. A minimum of two to four years of work-related skill, knowledge, or experience is needed for this occupation. **Education:** This group of occupations usually requires a four-year bachelor's degree, but in some cases does not. **Training:** Employees in this type of occupation usually need several years of work-related experience, on-the-job training, and/or vocational training. **Related Examples:** Other occupations like this one usually involve coordinating, supervising, managing, or training others. Examples include accountants, chefs and head cooks, computer programmers, historians, pharmacists, and police detectives. **Standard Vocational Preparation Range:** 7.0 to below 8.0—Two years to less than ten years. **Major/Instructional Program:** 14.3101 Materials Science. **Related Courses:** Administration and Management; Engineering and Technology; Mathematics; Physics; Chemistry; English Language; Foreign Language; Communications and Media.

Life Scientists

FORESTERS (24302A)

Plan, develop, and control environmental factors affecting forests and their resources for economic and recreation purposes.

Average Yearly Earnings: $36,649. Experience: Considerable preparation is needed. A minimum of two to four years of work-related skill, knowledge, or experience is needed for this occupation. Education: This group of occupations usually requires a four-year bachelor's degree, but in some cases does not. Training: Employees in this type of occupation usually need several years of work-related experience, on-the-job training, and/or vocational training. Related Examples: Other occupations like this one usually involve coordinating, supervising, managing, or training others. Examples include accountants, chefs and head cooks, computer programmers, historians, pharmacists, and police detectives. Standard Vocational Preparation Range: 7.0 to below 8.0—Two years to less than ten years. Major/Instructional Program: 01.0601 Horticulture Services Operations and Management, General; 01.0606 Nursery Operations and Management; 03.0101 Natural Resources Conservation, General; 03.0401 Forest Harvesting and Production Technology/Technician; 03.0501 Forestry, General; 03.0502 Forestry Sciences; 03.0506 Forest Management. Related Courses: Administration and Management; Economics and Accounting; Sale and Marketing; Personnel and Human Resources; Production and Processing; Engineering and Technology; Design; Building and Construction; Mathematics; Physics; Chemistry; Biology; Sociology and Anthropology; Geography; Education and Training; English Language; History and Archeology; Philosophy and Theology; Public Safety and Security; Law, Government, and Jurisprudence; Telecommunications; Communications and Media; Transportation.

SOIL CONSERVATIONISTS (24302B)

Plan and develop coordinated practices for soil erosion control, soil and water conservation, and sound land use.

Average Yearly Earnings: $36,649. Experience: Considerable preparation is needed. A minimum of two to four years of work-related skill, knowledge, or experience is needed for this occupation. Education: This group of occupations usually requires a four-year bachelor's degree, but in some cases does not. Training: Employees in this type of occupation usually need several years of work-related experience, on-the-job training, and/or vocational training. Related Examples: Other occupations like this one usually involve coordinating, supervising, managing, or training others. Examples include accountants, chefs and head cooks, computer programmers, historians, pharmacists, and police detectives. Standard Vocational Preparation Range: 7.0 to below 8.0—Two years to less than ten years. Major/Instructional Program: 02.0501 Soil Sciences; 03.0101 Natural Resources Conservation, General; 03.0501 Forestry, General; 03.0502 Forestry Sciences; 03.0506 Forest Management. Related Courses: Administration and Management; Economics and Accounting; Food Production; Engineering and Technology; Design; Building and Construction; Mathematics; Physics; Chemistry; Biology; Geography; Education and Training; English Language; History and Archeology; Philosophy and Theology.

WOOD TECHNOLOGISTS (24302C)

Conduct research to determine composition, properties, behavior, utilization, development, treatments, and processing methods of wood and wood products.

Average Yearly Earnings: $36,649. **Experience:** Extensive preparation is needed. Extensive skill, knowledge, and experience are needed for this occupation. It may require more than five years of experience. **Education:** A bachelor's degree is the minimum formal education required for this group of occupations. However, many also require graduate school. For example, they may require a master's degree, and some require a Ph.D., M.D., or J.D. (law degree). **Training:** Employees in this type of occupation may need some on-the-job training, but most of these occupations assume that the person will already have the required skills, knowledge, work-related experience, and/or training. **Examples:** Other occupations like this one often involve coordinating, training, supervising, or managing the activities of others to accomplish goals. Very advanced communication and organizational skills are required. Examples include athletic trainers, lawyers, managing editors, physicists, social psychologists, and surgeons. **Standard Vocational Preparation Range:** 8.0 to 9.0—Four years to more than ten years. **Major/Instructional Program:** 03.0404 Forest Products Technology/Technician; 03.0501 Forestry, General; 03.0509 Wood Science and Pulp/Paper Technology. **Related Courses:** Production and Processing; Engineering and Technology; Building and Construction; Mathematics; Physics; Chemistry; Biology; Geography; English Language.

RANGE MANAGERS (24302D)

Research or study rangeland management practices to provide sustained production of forage, livestock, and wildlife.

Average Yearly Earnings: $36,649. **Experience:** Extensive preparation is needed. Extensive skill, knowledge, and experience are needed for this occupation. It may require more than five years of experience. **Education:** A bachelor's degree is the minimum formal education required for this group of occupations. However, many also require graduate school. For example, they may require a master's degree, and some require a Ph.D., M.D., or J.D. (law degree). **Training:** Employees in this type of occupation may need some on-the-job training, but most of these occupations assume that the person will already have the required skills, knowledge, work-related experience, and/or training. **Examples:** Other occupations like this one often involve coordinating, training, supervising, or managing the activities of others to accomplish goals. Very advanced communication and organizational skills are required. Examples include athletic trainers, lawyers, managing editors, physicists, social psychologists, and surgeons. **Standard Vocational Preparation Range:** 8.0 to 9.0—Four years to more than ten years. **Major/Instructional Program:** 02.0401 Plant Sciences, General; 02.0409 Range Science and Management; 03.0101 Natural Resources Conservation, General. **Related Courses:** Administration and Management; Economics and Accounting; Food Production; Building and Construction; Biology; Geography; Law, Government, and Jurisprudence.

PARK NATURALISTS (24302E)

Plan, develop, and conduct programs to inform the public of historical, natural, and scientific features of national, state, or local parks.

Average Yearly Earnings: $36,649. Experience: Considerable preparation is needed. A minimum of two to four years of work-related skill, knowledge, or experience is needed for this occupation. Education: This group of occupations usually requires a four-year bachelor's degree, but in some cases does not. Training: Employees in this type of occupation usually need several years of work-related experience, on-the-job training, and/or vocational training. Related Examples: Other occupations like this one usually involve coordinating, supervising, managing, or training others. Examples include accountants, chefs and head cooks, computer programmers, historians, pharmacists, and police detectives. Standard Vocational Preparation Range: 7.0 to below 8.0—Two years to less than ten years. Major/Instructional Program: 02.0401 Plant Sciences, General; 02.0409 Range Science and Management. Related Courses: Administration and Management; Biology; Geography; Education and Training; English Language; Fine Arts; History and Archeology; Communications and Media.

ANIMAL SCIENTISTS (24305A)

Research or study selection, breeding, feeding, management, and marketing of livestock, pets, or other economically important animals.

Average Yearly Earnings: $35,942. Experience: Extensive preparation is needed. Extensive skill, knowledge, and experience are needed for this occupation. It may require more than five years of experience. Education: A bachelor's degree is the minimum formal education required for this group of occupations. However, many also require graduate school. For example, they may require a master's degree, and some require a Ph.D., M.D., or J.D. (law degree). Training: Employees in this type of occupation may need some on-the-job training, but most of these occupations assume that the person will already have the required skills, knowledge, work-related experience, and/or training. Examples: Other occupations like this one often involve coordinating, training, supervising, or managing the activities of others to accomplish goals. Very advanced communication and organizational skills are required. Examples include athletic trainers, lawyers, managing editors, physicists, social psychologists, and surgeons. Standard Vocational Preparation Range: 8.0 to 9.0—Four years to more than ten years. Major/Instructional Program: 02.0101 Agriculture/Agricultural Sciences, General; 02.0201 Animal Sciences, General; 02.0202 Agricultural Animal Breeding and Genetics; 02.0203 Agricultural Animal Health; 02.0204 Agricultural Animal Nutrition; 02.0206 Dairy Science; 02.0209 Poultry Science. Related Courses: Food Production; Chemistry; Biology; Medicine and Dentistry; History and Archeology.

PLANT SCIENTISTS (24305B)

Conduct research in the breeding, production, and yield of plants or crops, and control of pests.

Average Yearly Earnings: $35,942. Experience: Extensive preparation is needed. Extensive skill, knowledge, and experience are needed for this occupation. It may require more than five years of experience. **Education:** A bachelor's degree is the minimum formal education required for this group of occupations. However, many also require graduate school. For example, they may require a master's degree, and some require a Ph.D., M.D., or J.D. (law degree). **Training:** Employees in this type of occupation may need some on-the-job training, but most of these occupations assume that the person will already have the required skills, knowledge, work-related experience, and/or training. **Examples:** Other occupations like this one often involve coordinating, training, supervising, or managing the activities of others to accomplish goals. Very advanced communication and organizational skills are required. Examples include athletic trainers, lawyers, managing editors, physicists, social psychologists, and surgeons. **Standard Vocational Preparation Range:** 8.0 to 9.0—Four years to more than ten years. **Major/Instructional Program:** 02.0101 Agriculture/Agricultural Sciences, General; 02.0201 Animal Sciences, General; 02.0202 Agricultural Animal Breeding and Genetics; 02.0401 Plant Sciences, General; 02.0402 Agronomy and Crop Science; 02.0403 Horticulture Science; 02.0405 Plant Breeding and Genetics; 02.0406 Agricultural Plant Pathology; 02.0408 Plant Protection (Pest Management); 26.0701 Zoology, General; 26.0702 Entomology. **Related Courses:** Food Production; Chemistry; Biology; Geography; Education and Training; English Language; History and Archeology; Communications and Media.

FOOD SCIENTISTS (24305C)

Apply scientific and engineering principles in the research, development, production, packaging, and processing of foods.

Average Yearly Earnings: $35,942. **Experience:** Considerable preparation is needed. A minimum of two to four years of work-related skill, knowledge, or experience is needed for this occupation. **Education:** This group of occupations usually requires a four-year bachelor's degree, but in some cases does not. **Training:** Employees in this type of occupation usually need several years of work-related experience, on-the-job training, and/or vocational training. **Related Examples:** Other occupations like this one usually involve coordinating, supervising, managing, or training others. Examples include accountants, chefs and head cooks, computer programmers, historians, pharmacists, and police detectives. **Standard Vocational Preparation Range:** 7.0 to below 8.0—Two years to less than ten years. **Major/Instructional Program:** 02.0101 Agriculture/Agricultural Sciences, General; 02.0301 Food Sciences and Technology; 19.0501 Foods and Nutrition Studies, General; 19.0502 Foods and Nutrition Science. **Related Courses:** Production and Processing; Food Production; Chemistry; Biology; Law, Government, and Jurisprudence.

SOIL SCIENTISTS (24305D)

Research or study soil characteristics, map soil types, and investigate the responses of soils to known management practices to determine use capabilities of soils and the effects of alternative practices on soil productivity.

Average Yearly Earnings: $35,942. **Experience:** Extensive preparation is needed. Extensive skill, knowledge, and experience are needed for this occupation. It may require more

than five years of experience. **Education:** A bachelor's degree is the minimum formal education required for this group of occupations. However, many also require graduate school. For example, they may require a master's degree, and some require a Ph.D., M.D., or J.D. (law degree). **Training:** Employees in this type of occupation may need some on-the-job training, but most of these occupations assume that the person will already have the required skills, knowledge, work-related experience, and/or training. **Examples:** Other occupations like this one often involve coordinating, training, supervising, or managing the activities of others to accomplish goals. Very advanced communication and organizational skills are required. Examples include athletic trainers, lawyers, managing editors, physicists, social psychologists, and surgeons. **Standard Vocational Preparation Range:** 8.0 to 9.0—Four years to more than ten years. **Major/Instructional Program:** 02.0501 Soil Sciences. **Related Courses:** Food Production; Chemistry; Biology; Geography.

BIOCHEMISTS **(24308A)**

Research or study chemical composition and processes of living organisms that affect vital processes such as growth and aging, to determine chemical actions and effects on organisms, such as the action of foods, drugs, or other substances on body functions and tissues.

Average Yearly Earnings: $41,828. **Experience:** Extensive preparation is needed. Extensive skill, knowledge, and experience are needed for this occupation. It may require more than five years of experience. **Education:** A bachelor's degree is the minimum formal education required for this group of occupations. However, many also require graduate school. For example, they may require a master's degree, and some require a Ph.D., M.D., or J.D. (law degree). **Training:** Employees in this type of occupation may need some on-the-job training, but most of these occupations assume that the person will already have the required skills, knowledge, work-related experience, and/or training. **Examples:** Other occupations like this one often involve coordinating, training, supervising, or managing the activities of others to accomplish goals. Very advanced communication and organizational skills are required. Examples include athletic trainers, lawyers, managing editors, physicists, social psychologists, and surgeons. **Standard Vocational Preparation Range:** 8.0 to 9.0—Four years to more than ten years. **Major/Instructional Program:** 26.0202 Biochemistry; 26.0203 Biophysics; 26.0616 Biotechnology Research; 26.0701 Zoology, General; 26.0705 Pharmacology, Human and Animal; 51.1302 Medical Biochemistry. **Related Courses:** Building and Construction; Mathematics; Chemistry; Biology.

BIOLOGISTS **(24308B)**

Study the relationship among organisms and between organisms and their environment.

Average Yearly Earnings: $41,828. **Experience:** Extensive preparation is needed. Extensive skill, knowledge, and experience are needed for this occupation. It may require more than five years of experience. **Education:** A bachelor's degree is the minimum formal

education required for this group of occupations. However, many also require graduate school. For example, they may require a master's degree, and some require a Ph.D., M.D., or J.D. (law degree). **Training:** Employees in this type of occupation may need some on-the-job training, but most of these occupations assume that the person will already have the required skills, knowledge, work-related experience, and/or training. **Examples:** Other occupations like this one often involve coordinating, training, supervising, or managing the activities of others to accomplish goals. Very advanced communication and organizational skills are required. Examples include athletic trainers, lawyers, managing editors, physicists, social psychologists, and surgeons. **Standard Vocational Preparation Range:** 8.0 to 9.0—Four years to more than ten years. **Major/Instructional Program:** 26.0607 Marine/Aquatic Biology; 26.0701 Zoology, General; 51.1399 Medical Basic Sciences, Other. **Related Courses:** Food Production; Mathematics; Physics; Chemistry; Biology; English Language.

BIOPHYSICISTS (24308C)

Research or study physical principles of living cells and organisms, their electrical and mechanical energy, and related phenomena.

Average Yearly Earnings: $41,828. **Experience:** Extensive preparation is needed. Extensive skill, knowledge, and experience are needed for this occupation. It may require more than five years of experience. **Education:** A bachelor's degree is the minimum formal education required for this group of occupations. However, many also require graduate school. For example, they may require a master's degree, and some require a Ph.D., M.D., or J.D. (law degree). **Training:** Employees in this type of occupation may need some on-the-job training, but most of these occupations assume that the person will already have the required skills, knowledge, work-related experience, and/or training. **Examples:** Other occupations like this one often involve coordinating, training, supervising, or managing the activities of others to accomplish goals. Very advanced communication and organizational skills are required. Examples include athletic trainers, lawyers, managing editors, physicists, social psychologists, and surgeons. **Standard Vocational Preparation Range:** 8.0 to 9.0—Four years to more than ten years. **Major/Instructional Program:** 26.0202 Biochemistry, 26.0203 Biophysics, 51.1304 Medical Physics/Biophysics. **Related Courses:** Mathematics; Physics; Chemistry; Biology.

BOTANISTS (24308D)

Research or study the development of life processes, physiology, heredity, environment, distribution, morphology, and the economic value of plants for application in such fields as agronomy, forestry, horticulture, and pharmacology.

Average Yearly Earnings: $41,828. **Experience:** Extensive preparation is needed. Extensive skill, knowledge, and experience are needed for this occupation. It may require more than five years of experience. **Education:** A bachelor's degree is the minimum formal education required for this group of occupations. However, many also require graduate

school. For example, they may require a master's degree, and some require a Ph.D., M.D., or J.D. (law degree). **Training:** Employees in this type of occupation may need some on-the-job training, but most of these occupations assume that the person will already have the required skills, knowledge, work-related experience, and/or training. **Examples:** Other occupations like this one often involve coordinating, training, supervising, or managing the activities of others to accomplish goals. Very advanced communication and organizational skills are required. Examples include athletic trainers, lawyers, managing editors, physicists, social psychologists, and surgeons. **Standard Vocational Preparation Range:** 8.0 to 9.0—Four years to more than ten years. **Major/Instructional Program:** 02.0401 Plant Sciences, General; 02.0406 Agricultural Plant Pathology; 02.0408 Plant Protection (Pest Management); 26.0202 Biochemistry; 26.0301 Botany, General; 26.0305 Plant Pathology; 26.0307 Plant Physiology; 26.0399 Botany, Other; 26.0610 Parasitology; 51.1399 Medical Basic Sciences, Other. **Related Courses:** Chemistry; Biology.

MICROBIOLOGISTS (24308E)

Research or study the growth, structure, development, and general characteristics of bacteria and other microorganisms.

Average Yearly Earnings: $41,828. **Experience:** Extensive preparation is needed. Extensive skill, knowledge, and experience are needed for this occupation. It may require more than five years of experience. **Education:** A bachelor's degree is the minimum formal education required for this group of occupations. However, many also require graduate school. For example, they may require a master's degree, and some require a Ph.D., M.D., or J.D. (law degree). **Training:** Employees in this type of occupation may need some on-the-job training, but most of these occupations assume that the person will already have the required skills, knowledge, work-related experience, and/or training. **Examples:** Other occupations like this one often involve coordinating, training, supervising, or managing the activities of others to accomplish goals. Very advanced communication and organizational skills are required. Examples include athletic trainers, lawyers, managing editors, physicists, social psychologists, and surgeons. **Standard Vocational Preparation Range:** 8.0 to 9.0—Four years to more than ten years. **Major/Instructional Program:** 26.0202 Biochemistry, 26.0401 Cell Biology, 26.0501 Microbiology/ Bacteriology, 26.0619 Virology, 51.1308 Medical Microbiology. **Related Courses:** Mathematics; Chemistry; Biology; English Language.

GENETICISTS (24308F)

Research or study the inheritance and variation of characteristics on forms of life to determine laws, mechanisms, and environmental factors in origin, transmission, and the development of inherited traits.

Average Yearly Earnings: $41,828. **Experience:** Extensive preparation is needed. Extensive skill, knowledge, and experience are needed for this occupation. It may require more than five years of experience. **Education:** A bachelor's degree is the minimum formal

education required for this group of occupations. However, many also require graduate school. For example, they may require a master's degree, and some require a Ph.D., M.D., or J.D. (law degree). **Training:** Employees in this type of occupation may need some on-the-job training, but most of these occupations assume that the person will already have the required skills, knowledge, work-related experience, and/or training. **Examples:** Other occupations like this one often involve coordinating, training, supervising, or managing the activities of others to accomplish goals. Very advanced communication and organizational skills are required. Examples include athletic trainers, lawyers, managing editors, physicists, social psychologists, and surgeons. **Standard Vocational Preparation Range:** 8.0 to 9.0—Four years to more than ten years. **Major/Instructional Program:** 26.0202 Biochemistry; 26.0401 Cell Biology; 26.0402 Molecular Biology; 26.0613 Genetics, Plant and Animal; 26.0616 Biotechnology Research; 26.0617 Evolutionary Biology; 51.1306 Medical Genetics. **Related Courses:** Administration and Management; Mathematics; Chemistry; Biology; Medicine and Dentistry; Therapy and Counseling; Foreign Language.

PHYSIOLOGISTS AND CYTOLOGISTS (24308G)

Research or study cellular structure and functions, or organ-system functions, of plants and animals.

Average Yearly Earnings: $41,828. **Experience:** Extensive preparation is needed. Extensive skill, knowledge, and experience are needed for this occupation. It may require more than five years of experience. **Education:** A bachelor's degree is the minimum formal education required for this group of occupations. However, many also require graduate school. For example, they may require a master's degree, and some require a Ph.D., M.D., or J.D. (law degree). **Training:** Employees in this type of occupation may need some on-the-job training, but most of these occupations assume that the person will already have the required skills, knowledge, work-related experience, and/or training. **Examples:** Other occupations like this one often involve coordinating, training, supervising, or managing the activities of others to accomplish goals. Very advanced communication and organizational skills are required. Examples include athletic trainers, lawyers, managing editors, physicists, social psychologists, and surgeons. **Standard Vocational Preparation Range:** 8.0 to 9.0—Four years to more than ten years. **Major/Instructional Program:** 02.0401 Plant Sciences, General; 02.0407 Agricultural Plant Physiology; 26.0202 Biochemistry; 26.0301 Botany, General; 26.0307 Plant Physiology; 26.0401 Cell Biology; 26.0601 Anatomy; 26.0608 Neuroscience; 26.0616 Biotechnology Research; 26.0701 Zoology, General; 26.0706 Physiology, Human and Animal; 51.1305 Medical Cell Biology; 51.1313 Medical Physiology. **Related Courses:** Administration and Management; Chemistry; Biology.

ZOOLOGISTS (24308H)

Research or study origins, interrelationships, classification, habits, life histories, life processes, diseases, relation to environment, growth, development, genetics, and distribution of animals.

Average Yearly Earnings: $41,828. **Experience:** Extensive preparation is needed. Extensive skill, knowledge, and experience are needed for this occupation. It may require more than five years of experience. **Education:** A bachelor's degree is the minimum formal education required for this group of occupations. However, many also require graduate school. For example, they may require a master's degree, and some require a Ph.D., M.D., or J.D. (law degree). **Training:** Employees in this type of occupation may need some on-the-job training, but most of these occupations assume that the person will already have the required skills, knowledge, work-related experience, and/or training. **Examples:** Other occupations like this one often involve coordinating, training, supervising, or managing the activities of others to accomplish goals. Very advanced communication and organizational skills are required. Examples include athletic trainers, lawyers, managing editors, physicists, social psychologists, and surgeons. **Standard Vocational Preparation Range:** 8.0 to 9.0—Four years to more than ten years. **Major/Instructional Program:** 26.0701 Zoology, General. **Related Courses:** Chemistry; Biology.

TOXICOLOGISTS (24308J)

Research or study the effects of toxic substances on the physiological functions of humans, animals, and plants.

Average Yearly Earnings: $41,828. **Experience:** Extensive preparation is needed. Extensive skill, knowledge, and experience are needed for this occupation. It may require more than five years of experience. **Education:** A bachelor's degree is the minimum formal education required for this group of occupations. However, many also require graduate school. For example, they may require a master's degree, and some require a Ph.D., M.D., or J.D. (law degree). **Training:** Employees in this type of occupation may need some on-the-job training, but most of these occupations assume that the person will already have the required skills, knowledge, work-related experience, and/or training. **Examples:** Other occupations like this one often involve coordinating, training, supervising, or managing the activities of others to accomplish goals. Very advanced communication and organizational skills are required. Examples include athletic trainers, lawyers, managing editors, physicists, social psychologists, and surgeons. **Standard Vocational Preparation Range:** 8.0 to 9.0—Four years to more than ten years. **Major/Instructional Program:** 26.0202 Biochemistry; 26.0612 Toxicology; 40.0501 Chemistry, General; 40.0505 Medicinal/Pharmaceutical Chemistry; 51.1314 Medical Toxicology; 51.2202 Environmental Health. **Related Courses:** Mathematics; Chemistry; Biology; English Language.

MEDICAL SCIENTISTS (24311)

Conduct research dealing with the understanding of human diseases and the improvement of human health. Engage in clinical investigation or other research, production, technical writing, or related activities. Includes medical scientists such as physicians, dentists, public health specialists, pharmacologists, and medical pathologists. Excludes practitioners who provide medical care or dispense drugs.

Average Yearly Earnings: $56,659. **Experience:** Considerable preparation is needed. A minimum of two to four years of work-related skill, knowledge, or experience is needed for this occupation. **Education:** This group of occupations usually requires a four-year bachelor's degree, but in some cases does not. **Training:** Employees in this type of occupation usually need several years of work-related experience, on-the-job training, and/or vocational training. **Related Examples:** Other occupations like this one usually involve coordinating, supervising, managing, or training others. Examples include accountants, chefs and head cooks, computer programmers, historians, pharmacists, and police detectives. **Standard Vocational Preparation Range:** 7.0 to below 8.0—Two years to less than ten years. **Major/Instructional Program:** 26.0202 Biochemistry; 26.0203 Biophysics; 26.0501 Microbiology/Bacteriology; 26.0601 Anatomy; 26.0610 Parasitology; 26.0612 Toxicology; 26.0616 Biotechnology Research; 26.0618 Biological Immunology; 26.0701 Zoology, General; 26.0705 Pharmacology, Human and Animal; 51.1301 Medical Anatomy; 51.1304 Medical Physics/Biophysics; 51.1312 Medical Pathology; 51.1399 Medical Basic Sciences, Other; 51.2003 Medical Pharmacology and Pharmaceutical Sciences; 51.2202 Environmental Health; 51.2203 Epidemiology; 51.2205 Health Physics/Radiologic Health. **Related Courses:** Food Production; Mathematics; Physics; Chemistry; Biology; Psychology; Medicine and Dentistry; Therapy and Counseling; Education and Training; Foreign Language; History and Archeology; Public Safety and Security; Law, Government, and Jurisprudence; Telecommunications; Communications and Media; Transportation.

Life and Physical Sciences Technologists and Technicians

BIOLOGICAL AND AGRICULTURAL TECHNOLOGISTS (24502A)

Study and apply biological and agricultural principles to experiment, test, and develop new and improved methods in the production, preservation, and processing of plant and animal life.

Average Yearly Earnings: $34,465. **Experience:** Extensive preparation is needed. Extensive skill, knowledge, and experience are needed for this occupation. It may require more than five years of experience. **Education:** A bachelor's degree is the minimum formal education required for this group of occupations. However, many also require graduate school. For example, they may require a master's degree, and some require a Ph.D., M.D., or J.D. (law degree). **Training:** Employees in this type of occupation may need some on-the-job training, but most of these occupations assume that the person will already have the required skills, knowledge, work-related experience, and/or training. **Examples:** Other occupations like this one often involve coordinating, training, supervising, or managing the activities of others to accomplish goals. Very advanced communication and organizational skills are required. Examples include athletic trainers, lawyers, managing editors, physicists, social psychologists, and surgeons. **Standard Vocational Preparation Range:** 8.0 to 9.0—Four years to more than ten years. **Major/Instructional Program:** 02.0201 Animal Sciences, General; 02.0206 Dairy Science; 41.0101 Biological Technology/Technician. **Related Courses:** Production and Processing; Food Production; Mathematics; Chemistry; Biology.

ARTIFICIAL BREEDING TECHNICIANS (24502B)

Collect, inject, measure, or test animal semen to breed livestock or to develop improved artificial insemination methods.

Average Yearly Earnings: $34,465. **Experience:** Some preparation is needed. Some previous work-related skill, knowledge, or experience may be helpful in this occupation, but usually is not needed. **Education:** This group of occupations usually requires a high school diploma and may require some vocational training or job-related course work. In some cases, an associate or bachelor's degree could be needed. **Training:** Employees in this type of occupation need anywhere from a few months to one year of working with experienced employees. **Related Examples:** Other occupations like this one often involve using your knowledge and skills to help others. Examples include drywall installers, fire inspectors, flight attendants, pharmacy technicians, retail salespersons, and tellers. **Standard Vocational Preparation Range:** 4.0 to below 6.0—Six months to less than two years. **Major/Instructional Program:** 01.0301 Agricultural Production Workers and Managers, General; 01.0302 Agricultural Animal Husbandry and Production Management; 01.0501 Agricultural Supplies Retailing and Wholesaling; 02.0201 Animal Sciences, General; 02.0202 Agricultural Animal Breeding and Genetics. **Related Courses:** Food Production; Chemistry; Biology; Medicine and Dentistry.

BIOLOGICAL AND AGRICULTURAL TECHNICIANS (24502C)

Set up and maintain the laboratory, and collect and record data to assist scientists in biology, plant pathology, and related agricultural science experiments.

Average Yearly Earnings: $34,465. **Experience:** Some preparation is needed. Some previous work-related skill, knowledge, or experience may be helpful in this occupation, but usually is not needed. **Education:** This group of occupations usually requires a high school diploma and may require some vocational training or job-related course work. In some cases, an associate or bachelor's degree could be needed. **Training:** Employees in this type of occupation need anywhere from a few months to one year of working with experienced employees. **Related Examples:** Other occupations like this one often involve using your knowledge and skills to help others. Examples include drywall installers, fire inspectors, flight attendants, pharmacy technicians, retail salespersons, and tellers. **Standard Vocational Preparation Range:** 4.0 to below 6.0—Six months to less than two years. **Major/Instructional Program:** 01.0301 Agricultural Production Workers and Managers, General; 01.0302 Agricultural Animal Husbandry and Production Management; 01.0304 Crop Production Operations and Management; 02.0201 Animal Sciences, General; 02.0204 Agricultural Animal Nutrition; 02.0401 Plant Sciences, General; 02.0402 Agronomy and Crop Science; 41.0101 Biological Technology/Technician. **Related Courses:** Food Production; Biology.

BIOLOGY SPECIMEN TECHNICIANS (24502D)

Prepare biological specimens of plant and animal life for use as instructional aids in schools, museums, and other institutions.

Average Yearly Earnings: $34,465. **Experience:** Medium preparation is needed. Previous work-related skill, knowledge, or experience is required for this occupation. **Education:** This group of occupations usually requires training in vocational schools, related on-the-job experience, or an associate degree. A bachelor's degree may be required. **Training:** Employees in this type of occupation usually need one or two years of training involving both on-the-job experience and informal training with experienced workers. **Related Examples:** Other occupations like this one usually involve using communication and organizational skills to coordinate, supervise, manage, or train others to accomplish goals. Examples include dental assistants, electricians, fish and game wardens, legal secretaries, personnel recruiters, and recreation workers. **Standard Vocational Preparation Range:** 6.0 to below 7.0—More than one year and less than four years. **Major/Instructional Program:** 41.0101 Biological Technology/Technician. **Related Courses:** Chemistry; Biology.

CHEMICAL TECHNICIANS AND TECHNOLOGISTS (24505A)

Conduct chemical and physical laboratory tests to assist scientists in making qualitative and quantitative analyses of solids, liquids, and gaseous materials.

Average Yearly Earnings: $34,465. **Experience:** Medium preparation is needed. Previous work-related skill, knowledge, or experience is required for this occupation. **Education:** This group of occupations usually requires training in vocational schools, related on-the-job experience, or an associate degree. A bachelor's degree may be required. **Training:** Employees in this type of occupation usually need one or two years of training involving both on-the-job experience and informal training with experienced workers. **Related Examples:** Other occupations like this one usually involve using communication and organizational skills to coordinate, supervise, manage, or train others to accomplish goals. Examples include dental assistants, electricians, fish and game wardens, legal secretaries, personnel recruiters, and recreation workers. **Standard Vocational Preparation Range:** 6.0 to below 7.0—More than one year and less than four years. **Major/Instructional Program:** 02.0301 Food Sciences and Technology, 15.0702 Quality Control Technology/Technician, 15.0803 Automotive Engineering Technology/Technician, 15.0903 Petroleum Technology/Technician, 41.0301 Chemical Technology/Technician, 51.0802 Medical Laboratory Assistant. **Related Courses:** Mathematics; Chemistry; Biology; English Language.

FOOD SCIENCE TECHNICIANS AND TECHNOLOGISTS (24505B)

Perform standardized qualitative and quantitative tests to determine the physical or chemical properties of food or beverage products.

Average Yearly Earnings: $34,465. **Experience:** Some preparation is needed. Some previous work-related skill, knowledge, or experience may be helpful in this occupation, but usually is not needed. **Education:** This group of occupations usually requires a high school diploma and may require some vocational training or job-related course work.

In some cases, an associate or bachelor's degree could be needed. **Training:** Employees in this type of occupation need anywhere from a few months to one year of working with experienced employees. **Related Examples:** Other occupations like this one often involve using your knowledge and skills to help others. Examples include drywall installers, fire inspectors, flight attendants, pharmacy technicians, retail salespersons, and tellers. **Standard Vocational Preparation Range:** 4.0 to below 6.0—Six months to less than two years. **Major/Instructional Program:** 02.0301 Food Sciences and Technology, 15.0701 Occupational Safety and Health Technology/Technician, 41.0301 Chemical Technology/Technician. **Related Courses:** Production and Processing; Food Production; Mathematics; Chemistry; Biology; English Language.

ASSAYERS **(24505C)**

Test ores and minerals and analyze the results to determine value and properties.

Average Yearly Earnings: $34,465. **Experience:** Considerable preparation is needed. A minimum of two to four years of work-related skill, knowledge, or experience is needed for this occupation. **Education:** This group of occupations usually requires a four-year bachelor's degree, but in some cases does not. **Training:** Employees in this type of occupation usually need several years of work-related experience, on-the-job training, and/or vocational training. **Related Examples:** Other occupations like this one usually involve coordinating, supervising, managing, or training others. Examples include accountants, chefs and head cooks, computer programmers, historians, pharmacists, and police detectives. **Standard Vocational Preparation Range:** 7.0 to below 8.0—Two years to less than ten years. **Major/Instructional Program:** 41.0301 Chemical Technology/Technician. **Related Courses:** History and Archeology.

TEXTILE SCIENCE TECHNICIANS AND TECHNOLOGISTS **(24505D)**

Conduct tests to determine characteristics of textile products, fibers, and related materials and adherence to specifications. May develop and test color formulas.

Average Yearly Earnings: $34,465. **Experience:** Some preparation is needed. Some previous work-related skill, knowledge, or experience may be helpful in this occupation, but usually is not needed. **Education:** This group of occupations usually requires a high school diploma and may require some vocational training or job-related course work. In some cases, an associate or bachelor's degree could be needed. **Training:** Employees in this type of occupation need anywhere from a few months to one year of working with experienced employees. **Related Examples:** Other occupations like this one often involve using your knowledge and skills to help others. Examples include drywall installers, fire inspectors, flight attendants, pharmacy technicians, retail salespersons, and tellers. **Standard Vocational Preparation Range:** 4.0 to below 6.0—Six months to less than two years. **Major/Instructional Program:** 41.0301 Chemical Technology/Technician. **Related Courses:** Production and Processing; Chemistry; Fine Arts.

ENVIRONMENTAL SCIENCE TECHNICIANS (24505E)

Perform laboratory and field tests to monitor environmental resources and determine sources of pollution, under the direction of an environmental scientist. Collect samples of gases, soil, water, and other materials for testing. May recommend remediation treatment to resolve pollution problems.

Average Yearly Earnings: $34,465. **Experience:** Medium preparation is needed. Previous work-related skill, knowledge, or experience is required for this occupation. **Education:** This group of occupations usually requires training in vocational schools, related on-the-job experience, or an associate degree. A bachelor's degree may be required. **Training:** Employees in this type of occupation usually need one or two years of training involving both on-the-job experience and informal training with experienced workers. **Related Examples:** Other occupations like this one usually involve using communication and organizational skills to coordinate, supervise, manage, or train others to accomplish goals. Examples include dental assistants, electricians, fish and game wardens, legal secretaries, personnel recruiters, and recreation workers. **Standard Vocational Preparation Range:** 6.0 to below 7.0—More than one year and less than four years. **Major/Instructional Program:** 15.0599 Environmental Control Technologies/Technicians, Other; 41.0301 Chemical Technology/Technician. **Related Courses:** Mathematics; Physics; Chemistry; Biology; English Language; Public Safety and Security; Communications and Media.

NUCLEAR EQUIPMENT OPERATION TECHNICIANS (24508A)

Operate equipment used for the release, control, and utilization of nuclear energy to assist scientists in laboratory and production activities.

Average Yearly Earnings: $34,465. **Experience:** Medium preparation is needed. Previous work-related skill, knowledge, or experience is required for this occupation. **Education:** This group of occupations usually requires training in vocational schools, related on-the-job experience, or an associate degree. A bachelor's degree may be required. **Training:** Employees in this type of occupation usually need one or two years of training involving both on-the-job experience and informal training with experienced workers. **Related Examples:** Other occupations like this one usually involve using communication and organizational skills to coordinate, supervise, manage, or train others to accomplish goals. Examples include dental assistants, electricians, fish and game wardens, legal secretaries, personnel recruiters, and recreation workers. **Standard Vocational Preparation Range:** 6.0 to below 7.0—More than one year and less than four years. **Major/Instructional Program:** 41.0204 Industrial Radiologic Technology/Technician; 41.0299 Nuclear and Industrial Radiologic Technologies/Technicians, Other. **Related Courses:** Production and Processing; Engineering and Technology; Design; Mathematics; Physics; Chemistry; Public Safety and Security.

NUCLEAR MONITORING TECHNICIANS (24508B)

Collect and test samples to monitor the results of nuclear experiments and the contamination of humans, facilities, and environment.

Average Yearly Earnings: $34,465. **Experience:** Medium preparation is needed. Previous work-related skill, knowledge, or experience is required for this occupation. **Education:** This group of occupations usually requires training in vocational schools, related on-the-job experience, or an associate degree. A bachelor's degree may be required. **Training:** Employees in this type of occupation usually need one or two years of training involving both on-the-job experience and informal training with experienced workers. **Related Examples:** Other occupations like this one usually involve using communication and organizational skills to coordinate, supervise, manage, or train others to accomplish goals. Examples include dental assistants, electricians, fish and game wardens, legal secretaries, personnel recruiters, and recreation workers. **Standard Vocational Preparation Range:** 6.0 to below 7.0—More than one year and less than four years. **Major/Instructional Program:** 41.0205 Nuclear/Nuclear Power Technology/Technician; 41.0299 Nuclear and Industrial Radiologic Technologies/Technicians, Other; 51.2205 Health Physics/Radiologic Health. **Related Courses:** Computers and Electronics; Engineering and Technology; Mathematics; Physics; Chemistry; Biology; Medicine and Dentistry; Education and Training; English Language; Public Safety and Security; Communications and Media.

GEOLOGICAL DATA TECHNICIANS (2451 IB)

Measure, record, and evaluate geological data, such as core samples and cuttings, used in prospecting for oil or gas.

Average Yearly Earnings: $34,465. **Experience:** Medium preparation is needed. Previous work-related skill, knowledge, or experience is required for this occupation. **Education:** This group of occupations usually requires training in vocational schools, related on-the-job experience, or an associate degree. A bachelor's degree may be required. **Training:** Employees in this type of occupation usually need one or two years of training involving both on-the-job experience and informal training with experienced workers. **Related Examples:** Other occupations like this one usually involve using communication and organizational skills to coordinate, supervise, manage, or train others to accomplish goals. Examples include dental assistants, electricians, fish and game wardens, legal secretaries, personnel recruiters, and recreation workers. **Standard Vocational Preparation Range:** 6.0 to below 7.0—More than one year and less than four years. **Major/Instructional Program:** 15.0903 Petroleum Technology/Technician. **Related Courses:** Administration and Management; Clerical; Production and Processing; Engineering and Technology; Physics.

GEOLOGICAL SAMPLE TEST TECHNICIANS (24511E)

Test and analyze geological samples, crude oil, or petroleum products to detect the presence of petroleum, gas, or mineral deposits indicating potential for exploration and production, or to determine physical and chemical properties to ensure that products meet quality standards.

Average Yearly Earnings: $34,465. **Experience:** Medium preparation is needed. Previous work-related skill, knowledge, or experience is required for this occupation. **Education:** This group of occupations usually requires training in vocational schools, related on-the-job experience, or an associate degree. A bachelor's degree may be required. **Training:** Employees in this type of occupation usually need one or two years of training involving both on-the-job experience and informal training with experienced workers. **Related Examples:** Other occupations like this one usually involve using communication and organizational skills to coordinate, supervise, manage, or train others to accomplish goals. Examples include dental assistants, electricians, fish and game wardens, legal secretaries, personnel recruiters, and recreation workers. **Standard Vocational Preparation Range:** 6.0 to below 7.0—More than one year and less than four years. **Major/ Instructional Program:** 15.0903 Petroleum Technology/Technician; 41.0301 Chemical Technology/Technician; 41.0399 Physical Science Technologies/Technicians, Other. **Related Courses:** Personnel and Human Resources; Mechanical; Physics; Chemistry.

METEOROLOGICAL TECHNICIANS (24599A)

Analyze and record oceanographic and meteorological data to forecast changes in weather or sea conditions, and to determine trends in the movement and utilization of water.

Average Yearly Earnings: $34,465. **Experience:** Medium preparation is needed. Previous work-related skill, knowledge, or experience is required for this occupation. **Education:** This group of occupations usually requires training in vocational schools, related on-the-job experience, or an associate degree. A bachelor's degree may be required. **Training:** Employees in this type of occupation usually need one or two years of training involving both on-the-job experience and informal training with experienced workers. **Related Examples:** Other occupations like this one usually involve using communication and organizational skills to coordinate, supervise, manage, or train others to accomplish goals. Examples include dental assistants, electricians, fish and game wardens, legal secretaries, personnel recruiters, and recreation workers. **Standard Vocational Preparation Range:** 6.0 to below 7.0—More than one year and less than four years. **Major/ Instructional Program:** 03.0101 Natural Resources Conservation, General; 41.0399 Physical Science Technologies/Technicians, Other; 49.0304 Diver (Professional). **Related Courses:** Computers and Electronics; Design; Mathematics; Physics; Geography; English Language; Communications and Media; Transportation.

CRIMINALISTS AND BALLISTICS EXPERTS (24599B)

Examine, identify, classify, and analyze evidence related to criminology.

Average Yearly Earnings: $34,465. **Experience:** Considerable preparation is needed. A minimum of two to four years of work-related skill, knowledge, or experience is needed for this occupation. **Education:** This group of occupations usually requires a four-year bachelor's degree, but in some cases does not. **Training:** Employees in this type of occupation usually need several years of work-related experience, on-the-job training, and/or vocational training. **Related Examples:** Other occupations like this one usually involve coordinating, supervising, managing, or training others. Examples include accountants, chefs and head cooks, computer programmers, historians, pharmacists, and police detectives. **Standard Vocational Preparation Range:** 7.0 to below 8.0—Two years to less than ten years. **Major/Instructional Program:** 43.0106 Forensic Technology/Technician, 45.0401 Criminology. **Related Courses:** Computers and Electronics; Chemistry; Biology; Medicine and Dentistry; English Language; Public Safety and Security; Law, Government, and Jurisprudence.

SCIENTIFIC HELPERS (24599C)

Assist supervising scientists to research problems and conduct experiments and tests.

Average Yearly Earnings: $34,465. **Experience:** Some preparation is needed. Some previous work-related skill, knowledge, or experience may be helpful in this occupation, but usually is not needed. **Education:** This group of occupations usually requires a high school diploma and may require some vocational training or job-related course work. In some cases, an associate or bachelor's degree could be needed. **Training:** Employees in this type of occupation need anywhere from a few months to one year of working with experienced employees. **Related Examples:** Other occupations like this one often involve using your knowledge and skills to help others. Examples include drywall installers, fire inspectors, flight attendants, pharmacy technicians, retail salespersons, and tellers. **Standard Vocational Preparation Range:** 4.0 to below 6.0—Six months to less than two years. **Major/Instructional Program:** 03.0404 Forest Products Technology/Technician; 15.0702 Quality Control Technology/Technician; 15.0903 Petroleum Technology/Technician; 41.0101 Biological Technology/Technician; 41.0204 Industrial Radiologic Technology/Technician; 41.0205 Nuclear/Nuclear Power Technology/Technician; 41.0301 Chemical Technology/Technician; 41.0399 Physical Science Technologies/Technicians, Other. **Related Courses:** Production and Processing; Physics; Geography; History and Archeology.

Computer Scientists

SYSTEMS ANALYSTS, ELECTRONIC DATA PROCESSING (25102)

Analyze business, scientific, and technical problems for application to electronic data processing systems. Excludes persons working primarily as engineers, mathematicians, or scientists.

Average Yearly Earnings: $48,360. **Experience:** Medium preparation is needed. Previous work-related skill, knowledge, or experience is required for this occupation.

Education: This group of occupations usually requires training in vocational schools, related on-the-job experience, or an associate degree. A bachelor's degree may be required. **Training:** Employees in this type of occupation usually need one or two years of training involving both on-the-job experience and informal training with experienced workers. **Related Examples:** Other occupations like this one usually involve using communication and organizational skills to coordinate, supervise, manage, or train others to accomplish goals. Examples include dental assistants, electricians, fish and game wardens, legal secretaries, personnel recruiters, and recreation workers. **Standard Vocational Preparation Range:** 6.0 to below 7.0—More than one year and less than four years. **Major/Instructional Program:** 11.0101 Computer and Information Sciences, General; 11.0201 Computer Programming; 11.0501 Computer Systems Analysis; 52.1201 Management Information Systems and Business Data Processing, General; 52.1202 Business Computer Programming/ Programmer; 52.1203 Business Systems Analysis and Design. **Related Courses:** Clerical; Customer and Personal Service; Computers and Electronics; Mathematics; Education and Training; English Language; Telecommunications; Communications and Media.

DATABASE ADMINISTRATORS (25103A)

Coordinate changes to computer databases; test and implement the database, applying knowledge of database management systems. May plan, coordinate, and implement security measures to safeguard computer databases.

Average Yearly Earnings: $48,630. **Experience:** Considerable preparation is needed. A minimum of two to four years of work-related skill, knowledge, or experience is needed for this occupation. **Education:** This group of occupations usually requires a four-year bachelor's degree, but in some cases does not. **Training:** Employees in this type of occupation usually need several years of work-related experience, on-the-job training, and/ or vocational training. **Related Examples:** Other occupations like this one usually involve coordinating, supervising, managing, or training others. Examples include accountants, chefs and head cooks, computer programmers, historians, pharmacists, and police detectives. **Standard Vocational Preparation Range:** 7.0 to below 8.0—Two years to less than ten years. **Major/Instructional Program:** 11.0101 Computer and Information Sciences, General; 11.0201 Computer Programming; 11.0401 Information Sciences and Systems; 52.1201 Management Information Systems and Business Data Processing, General; 52.1202 Business Computer Programming/Programmer; 52.1203 Business Systems Analysis and Design. **Related Courses:** Administration and Management; Computers and Electronics; Mathematics; Education and Training.

GEOGRAPHIC INFORMATION SYSTEM SPECIALISTS (25103B)

Design and coordinate the development of an integrated geographic information system database of spatial and nonspatial data; develop analyses and presentation of this data, applying knowledge of the geographic information system.

Average Yearly Earnings: $48,360. **Experience:** Extensive preparation is needed. Extensive skill, knowledge, and experience are needed for this occupation. It may require more

than five years of experience. **Education:** A bachelor's degree is the minimum formal education required for this group of occupations. However, many also require graduate school. For example, they may require a master's degree, and some require a Ph.D., M.D., or J.D. (law degree). **Training:** Employees in this type of occupation may need some on-the-job training, but most of these occupations assume that the person will already have the required skills, knowledge, work-related experience, and/or training. **Examples:** Other occupations like this one often involve coordinating, training, supervising, or managing the activities of others to accomplish goals. Very advanced communication and organizational skills are required. Examples include athletic trainers, lawyers, managing editors, physicists, social psychologists, and surgeons. **Standard Vocational Preparation Range:** 8.0 to 9.0—Four years to more than ten years. **Related Courses:** Administration and Management; Sales and Marketing; Computers and Electronics; Design; Mathematics; Physics; Sociology and Anthropology; Geography; English Language; Transportation.

COMPUTER SUPPORT SPECIALISTS (25104)

Provide technical assistance and training to system users. Investigate and resolve computer software and hardware problems of users. Answer clients' inquiries in person and via telephone concerning the use of computer hardware and software, including printing, word processing, programming languages, electronic mail, and operating systems.

Average Yearly Earnings: $48,360. **Experience:** Considerable preparation is needed. A minimum of two to four years of work-related skill, knowledge, or experience is needed for this occupation. **Education:** This group of occupations usually requires a four-year bachelor's degree, but in some cases does not. **Training:** Employees in this type of occupation usually need several years of work-related experience, on-the-job training, and/or vocational training. **Related Examples:** Other occupations like this one usually involve coordinating, supervising, managing, or training others. Examples include accountants, chefs and head cooks, computer programmers, historians, pharmacists, and police detectives. **Standard Vocational Preparation Range:** 7.0 to below 8.0—Two years to less than ten years. **Major/Instructional Program:** 11.0401 Information Sciences and Systems; 11.0701 Computer Science; 47.0101 Electrical and Electronics Equipment Installer and Repairer, General; 47.0104 Computer Installer and Repairer; 52.1201 Management Information Systems and Business Data Processing, General; 52.1203 Business Systems Analysis and Design; 52.1204 Business Systems Networking and Telecommunications. **Related Courses:** Administration and Management; Economics and Accounting; Sales and Marketing; Customer and Personal Service; Computers and Electronics; Mathematics; Education and Training; Telecommunications.

COMPUTER PROGRAMMERS (25105)

Convert project specifications and statements of problems and procedures to detailed logical flowcharts for coding into computer language. Develop and write computer programs to store, locate, and retrieve specific documents, data, and information.

Average Yearly Earnings: $48,360. **Experience:** Considerable preparation is needed. A minimum of two to four years of work-related skill, knowledge, or experience is needed for this occupation. **Education:** This group of occupations usually requires a four-year bachelor's degree, but in some cases does not. **Training:** Employees in this type of occupation usually need several years of work-related experience, on-the-job training, and/or vocational training. **Related Examples:** Other occupations like this one usually involve coordinating, supervising, managing, or training others. Examples include accountants, chefs and head cooks, historians, pharmacists, and police detectives. **Standard Vocational Preparation Range:** 7.0 to below 8.0—Two years to less than ten years. **Major/Instructional Program:** 11.0201 Computer Programming; 52.1201 Management Information Systems and Business Data Processing, General; 52.1202 Business Computer Programming/Programmer. **Related Courses:** Administration and Management; Clerical; Personnel and Human Resources; Computers and Electronics; Design; Mathematics; Education and Training; English Language; Communications and Media.

PROGRAMMERS—NUMERICAL, TOOL, AND PROCESS CONTROL (25111)

Develop numerical control tape programs to control machining or processing of parts by automatic machine tools, equipment, or systems.

Average Yearly Earnings: $39,083. **Experience:** Medium preparation is needed. Previous work-related skill, knowledge, or experience is required for this occupation. **Education:** This group of occupations usually requires training in vocational schools, related on-the-job experience, or an associate degree. A bachelor's degree may be required. **Training:** Employees in this type of occupation usually need one or two years of training involving both on-the-job experience and informal training with experienced workers. **Related Examples:** Other occupations like this one usually involve using communication and organizational skills to coordinate, supervise, manage, or train others to accomplish goals. Examples include dental assistants, electricians, fish and game wardens, legal secretaries, personnel recruiters, and recreation workers. **Standard Vocational Preparation Range:** 6.0 to below 7.0—More than one year and less than four years. **Major/Instructional Program:** 11.0201 Computer Programming; 11.0301 Data Processing Technology/Technician; 11.0501 Computer Systems Analysis; 48.0501 Machinist/Machine Technologist; 52.1201 Management Information Systems and Business Data Processing, General; 52.1202 Business Computer Programming/Programmer. **Related Courses:** Production and Processing; Computers and Electronics; Design; Mathematics; Foreign Language.

DATA COMMUNICATIONS ANALYSTS (25199A)

Research, test, evaluate, and recommend data communications hardware and software.

Average Yearly Earnings: $48,360. **Experience:** Considerable preparation is needed. A minimum of two to four years of work-related skill, knowledge, or experience is needed for this occupation. **Education:** This group of occupations usually requires a four-year bachelor's degree, but in some cases does not. **Training:** Employees in this type of

occupation usually need several years of work-related experience, on-the-job training, and/ or vocational training. **Related Examples:** Other occupations like this one usually involve coordinating, supervising, managing, or training others. Examples include accountants, chefs and head cooks, computer programmers, historians, pharmacists, and police detectives. **Standard Vocational Preparation Range:** 7.0 to below 8.0—Two years to less than ten years. **Major/Instructional Program:** 11.0301 Data Processing Technology/Technician; 52.1201 Management Information Systems and Business Data Processing, General; 52.1204 Business Systems Networking and Telecommunications. **Related Courses:** Sales and Marketing; Customer and Personal Service; Computers and Electronics; Mathematics; Psychology; Education and Training; Telecommunications; Communications and Media.

Mathematical Scientists and Technicians

OPERATIONS AND SYSTEMS RESEARCHERS AND ANALYSTS, EXCEPT COMPUTER (25302)

Conduct analyses of management and operational problems in terms of management information and concepts. Formulate mathematical or simulation models of the problem for solution by a computer or other method. May develop and supply time and cost networks, such as program evaluation and review techniques.

Average Yearly Earnings: $45,760. **Experience:** Considerable preparation is needed. A minimum of two to four years of work-related skill, knowledge, or experience is needed for this occupation. **Education:** This group of occupations usually requires a four-year bachelor's degree, but in some cases does not. **Training:** Employees in this type of occupation usually need several years of work-related experience, on-the-job training, and/ or vocational training. **Related Examples:** Other occupations like this one usually involve coordinating, supervising, managing, or training others. Examples include accountants, chefs and head cooks, computer programmers, historians, pharmacists, and police detectives. **Standard Vocational Preparation Range:** 7.0 to below 8.0—Two years to less than ten years. **Major/Instructional Program:** 27.0301 Applied Mathematics, General; 27.0302 Operations Research; 52.1301 Management Science. **Related Courses:** Administration and Management; Clerical; Economics and Accounting; Sales and Marketing; Personnel and Human Resources; Production and Processing; Computers and Electronics; Mathematics; Communications and Media.

STATISTICIANS (25312)

Plan surveys and collect, organize, interpret, summarize, and analyze numerical data, applying statistical theory and methods to provide usable information in scientific, business, economic, and other fields. Data derived from surveys may represent either complete enumeration or statistical samples. Include mathematical statisticians who are engaged in the development of mathematical theory associated with the application of statistical techniques.

Average Yearly Earnings: $47,507. **Experience:** Considerable preparation is needed. A minimum of two to four years of work-related skill, knowledge, or experience is needed for this occupation. **Education:** This group of occupations usually requires a four-year bachelor's degree, but in some cases does not. **Training:** Employees in this type of occupation usually need several years of work-related experience, on-the-job training, and/or vocational training. **Related Examples:** Other occupations like this one usually involve coordinating, supervising, managing, or training others. Examples include accountants, chefs and head cooks, computer programmers, historians, pharmacists, and police detectives. **Standard Vocational Preparation Range:** 7.0 to below 8.0—Two years to less than ten years. **Major/Instructional Program:** 26.0615 Biostatistics; 27.0101 Mathematics; 27.0301 Applied Mathematics, General; 27.0501 Mathematical Statistics; 45.0501 Demography and Population Studies; 45.0601 Economics, General; 45.0603 Econometrics and Quantitative Economics; 51.1303 Medical Biomathematics and Biometrics; 51.2204 Health and Medical Biostatistics, 52.1302 Business Statistics. **Related Courses:** Administration and Management; Economics and Accounting; Computers and Electronics; Mathematics; English Language; Philosophy and Theology.

ACTUARIES (25313)

Apply knowledge of mathematics, probability, statistics, and principles of finance and business to problems in life, health, social, and casualty insurance, annuities, and pensions.

Average Yearly Earnings: $66,352. **Experience:** Extensive preparation is needed. Extensive skill, knowledge, and experience are needed for this occupation. It may require more than five years of experience. **Education:** A bachelor's degree is the minimum formal education required for this group of occupations. However, many also require graduate school. For example, they may require a master's degree, and some require a Ph.D., M.D., or J.D. (law degree). **Training:** Employees in this type of occupation may need some on-the-job training, but most of these occupations assume that the person will already have the required skills, knowledge, work-related experience, and/or training. **Examples:** Other occupations like this one often involve coordinating, training, supervising, or managing the activities of others to accomplish goals. Very advanced communication and organizational skills are required. Examples include athletic trainers, lawyers, managing editors, physicists, social psychologists, and surgeons. **Standard Vocational Preparation Range:** 8.0 to 9.0—Four years to more than ten years. **Major/Instructional Program:** 52.0801 Finance, General; 52.0802 Actuarial Science. **Related Courses:** Clerical; Economics and Accounting; Mathematics; Sociology and Anthropology; History and Archeology; Philosophy and Theology; Law, Government, and Jurisprudence.

FINANCIAL ANALYSTS, STATISTICAL (25315)

Conduct statistical analyses of information affecting investment programs of public or private institutions and private individuals.

Average Yearly Earnings: $47,507. **Experience:** Extensive preparation is needed. Extensive skill, knowledge, and experience are needed for this occupation. It may require more

than five years of experience. **Education:** A bachelor's degree is the minimum formal education required for this group of occupations. However, many also require graduate school. For example, they may require a master's degree, and some require a Ph.D., M.D., or J.D. (law degree). **Training:** Employees in this type of occupation may need some on-the-job training, but most of these occupations assume that the person will already have the required skills, knowledge, work-related experience, and/or training. **Examples:** Other occupations like this one often involve coordinating, training, supervising, or managing the activities of others to accomplish goals. Very advanced communication and organizational skills are required. Examples include athletic trainers, lawyers, managing editors, physicists, social psychologists, and surgeons. **Standard Vocational Preparation Range:** 8.0 to 9.0—Four years to more than ten years. **Major/Instructional Program:** 52.0801 Finance, General; 52.0804 Financial Planning; 52.0805 Insurance and Risk Management; 52.0807 Investments and Securities. **Related Courses:** Economics and Accounting; Sales and Marketing; Computers and Electronics; Mathematics; Foreign Language; History and Archeology; Law, Government, and Jurisprudence.

MATHEMATICIANS (25319A)

Conduct research in fundamental mathematics or in the application of mathematical techniques to science, management, and other fields. Solve or direct solutions to problems in various fields by mathematical methods.

Average Yearly Earnings: $46,342. **Experience:** Extensive preparation is needed. Extensive skill, knowledge, and experience are needed for this occupation. It may require more than five years of experience. **Education:** A bachelor's degree is the minimum formal education required for this group of occupations. However, many also require graduate school. For example, they may require a master's degree, and some require a Ph.D., M.D., or J.D. (law degree). **Training:** Employees in this type of occupation may need some on-the-job training, but most of these occupations assume that the person will already have the required skills, knowledge, work-related experience, and/or training. **Examples:** Other occupations like this one often involve coordinating, training, supervising, or managing the activities of others to accomplish goals. Very advanced communication and organizational skills are required. Examples include athletic trainers, lawyers, managing editors, physicists, social psychologists, and surgeons. **Standard Vocational Preparation Range:** 8.0 to 9.0—Four years to more than ten years. **Major/Instructional Program:** 27.0101 Mathematics; 27.0301 Applied Mathematics, General; 40.0801 Physics, General; 40.0810 Theoretical and Mathematical Physics. **Related Courses:** Administration and Management; Economics and Accounting; Computers and Electronics; Engineering and Technology; Mathematics; Physics.

WEIGHT ANALYSTS (25319B)

Analyze and calculate weight data of structural assemblies, components, and loads for purposes of weight, balance, loading, and operational functions of ships, aircraft, space vehicles, missiles, research instrumentation, and commercial and industrial products and systems.

Average Yearly Earnings: $46,342. **Experience:** Considerable preparation is needed. A minimum of two to four years of work-related skill, knowledge, or experience is needed for this occupation. **Education:** This group of occupations usually requires a four-year bachelor's degree, but in some cases does not. **Training:** Employees in this type of occupation usually need several years of work-related experience, on-the-job training, and/ or vocational training. **Related Examples:** Other occupations like this one usually involve coordinating, supervising, managing, or training others. Examples include accountants, chefs and head cooks, computer programmers, historians, pharmacists, and police detectives. **Standard Vocational Preparation Range:** 7.0 to below 8.0—Two years to less than ten years. **Major/Instructional Program:** 27.0301 Applied Mathematics, General. **Related Courses:** Production and Processing; Computers and Electronics; Engineering and Technology; Design; Mathematics; Physics; Transportation.

MATHEMATICAL TECHNICIANS (25323)

Apply standardized mathematical formulas, principles, and methodologies to technical problems in engineering and physical science in relation to specific industrial and research objectives, processes, equipment, and products.

Average Yearly Earnings: $34,465. **Experience:** Considerable preparation is needed. A minimum of two to four years of work-related skill, knowledge, or experience is needed for this occupation. **Education:** This group of occupations usually requires a four-year bachelor's degree, but in some cases does not. **Training:** Employees in this type of occupation usually need several years of work-related experience, on-the-job training, and/or vocational training. **Related Examples:** Other occupations like this one usually involve coordinating, supervising, managing, or training others. Examples include accountants, chefs and head cooks, computer programmers, historians, pharmacists, and police detectives. **Standard Vocational Preparation Range:** 7.0 to below 8.0—Two years to less than ten years. **Major/Instructional Program:** 27.0301 Applied Mathematics, General. **Related Courses:** Computers and Electronics; Engineering and Technology; Mathematics; English Language.

Social Scientists

ECONOMISTS (27102A)

Conduct research, prepare reports, or formulate plans to aid in the solution of economic problems arising from the production and distribution of goods and services. May collect and process economic and statistical data using econometric and sampling techniques. Exclude market research analysts.

Average Yearly Earnings: $50,544. **Experience:** Extensive preparation is needed. Extensive skill, knowledge, and experience are needed for this occupation. It may require more than five years of experience. **Education:** A bachelor's degree is the minimum formal education required for this group of occupations. However, many also require graduate

school. For example, they may require a master's degree, and some require a Ph.D., M.D., or J.D. (law degree). **Training:** Employees in this type of occupation may need some on-the-job training, but most of these occupations assume that the person will already have the required skills, knowledge, work-related experience, and/or training. **Examples:** Other occupations like this one often involve coordinating, training, supervising, or managing the activities of others to accomplish goals. Very advanced communication and organizational skills are required. Examples include athletic trainers, lawyers, managing editors, physicists, social psychologists, and surgeons. **Standard Vocational Preparation Range:** 8.0 to 9.0—Four years to more than ten years. **Major/Instructional Program:** 01.0101 Agricultural Business and Management, General; 01.0103 Agricultural Economics; 45.0601 Economics, General; 45.0602 Applied and Resource Economics; 45.0603 Econometrics and Quantitative Economics; 45.0604 Development Economics and International Development; 45.0605 International Economics; 45.0699 Economics, Other; 52.0601 Business/Managerial Economics. **Related Courses:** Economics and Accounting; Personnel and Human Resources; Production and Processing; Food Production; Computers and Electronics; Mathematics; Geography; Education and Training; History and Archeology; Philosophy and Theology; Law, Government, and Jurisprudence.

MARKET RESEARCH ANALYSTS (27102B)

Research market conditions in local, regional, or national areas to determine potential sales of a product or service. May gather information on competitors, prices, sales, and methods of marketing and distribution. May use survey results to create a marketing campaign based on regional preferences and buying habits.

Average Yearly Earnings: $50,544. **Experience:** Considerable preparation is needed. A minimum of two to four years of work-related skill, knowledge, or experience is needed for this occupation. **Education:** This group of occupations usually requires a four-year bachelor's degree, but in some cases does not. **Training:** Employees in this type of occupation usually need several years of work-related experience, on-the-job training, and/or vocational training. **Related Examples:** Other occupations like this one usually involve coordinating, supervising, managing, or training others. Examples include accountants, chefs and head cooks, computer programmers, historians, pharmacists, and police detectives. **Standard Vocational Preparation Range:** 7.0 to below 8.0—Two years to less than ten years. **Major/Instructional Program:** 45.0601 Economics, General; 45.0602 Applied and Resource Economics; 45.0603 Econometrics and Quantitative Economics; 52.1402 Marketing Research. **Related Courses:** Economics and Accounting; Sales and Marketing; Customer and Personal Service; Food Production; Computers and Electronics; Mathematics; Psychology; Geography; Philosophy and Theology.

URBAN AND REGIONAL PLANNERS (27105)

Develop comprehensive plans and programs for the use of land and physical facilities of cities, counties, and metropolitan areas.

Average Yearly Earnings: $40,934. **Experience:** Considerable preparation is needed. A minimum of two to four years of work-related skill, knowledge, or experience is needed for this occupation. **Education:** This group of occupations usually requires a four-year bachelor's degree, but in some cases does not. **Training:** Employees in this type of occupation usually need several years of work-related experience, on-the-job training, and/ or vocational training. **Related Examples:** Other occupations like this one usually involve coordinating, supervising, managing, or training others. Examples include accountants, chefs and head cooks, computer programmers, historians, pharmacists, and police detectives. **Standard Vocational Preparation Range:** 7.0 to below 8.0—Two years to less than ten years. **Major/Instructional Program:** 04.0301 City/Urban, Community and Regional Planning, 04.0701 Architectural Urban Design and Planning, 44.0501 Public Policy Analysis. **Related Courses:** Administration and Management; Clerical; Economics and Accounting; Sales and Marketing; Computers and Electronics; Engineering and Technology; Design; Building and Construction; Mathematics; Biology; Sociology and Anthropology; Geography; Education and Training; English Language; History and Archeology; Philosophy and Theology; Public Safety and Security; Law, Government, and Jurisprudence; Communications and Media; Transportation.

DEVELOPMENTAL PSYCHOLOGISTS (27108A)

Study and research the emotional, mental, physical, and social growth and development of individuals, from birth to death, to increase the understanding of human behavior and the processes of human growth and decline.

Average Yearly Earnings: $48,089. **Experience:** Considerable preparation is needed. A minimum of two to four years of work-related skill, knowledge, or experience is needed for this occupation. **Education:** This group of occupations usually requires a four-year bachelor's degree, but in some cases does not. **Training:** Employees in this type of occupation usually need several years of work-related experience, on-the-job training, and/ or vocational training. **Related Examples:** Other occupations like this one usually involve coordinating, supervising, managing, or training others. Examples include accountants, chefs and head cooks, computer programmers, historians, pharmacists, and police detectives. **Standard Vocational Preparation Range:** 7.0 to below 8.0—Two years to less than ten years. **Major/Instructional Program:** 42.0101 Psychology, General; 42.0301 Cognitive Psychology and Psycholinguistics; 42.0701 Developmental and Child Psychology. **Related Courses:** Mathematics; Biology; Psychology; Sociology and Anthropology; Therapy and Counseling; Education and Training; English Language; Philosophy and Theology.

EXPERIMENTAL PSYCHOLOGISTS (27108C)

Plan, design, and conduct, laboratory experiments to investigate animal or human physiology, perception, memory, learning, personality, and cognitive processes. Conduct interdisciplinary studies with scientists in such fields as physiology, biology, and sociology.

Average Yearly Earnings: $48,089. **Experience:** Extensive preparation is needed. Extensive skill, knowledge, and experience are needed for this occupation. It may require more than five years of experience. **Education:** A bachelor's degree is the minimum formal education required for this group of occupations. However, many also require graduate school. For example, they may require a master's degree, and some require a Ph.D., M.D., or J.D. (law degree). **Training:** Employees in this type of occupation may need some on-the-job training, but most of these occupations assume that the person will already have the required skills, knowledge, work-related experience, and/or training. **Examples:** Other occupations like this one often involve coordinating, training, supervising, or managing the activities of others to accomplish goals. Very advanced communication and organizational skills are required. Examples include athletic trainers, lawyers, managing editors, physicists, social psychologists, and surgeons. **Standard Vocational Preparation Range:** 8.0 to 9.0—Four years to more than ten years. **Major/Instructional Program:** 42.0101 Psychology, General; 42.0301 Cognitive Psychology and Psycholinguistics; 42.0801 Experimental Psychology; 42.1101 Physiological Psychology/ Psychobiology. **Related Courses:** Mathematics; Biology; Psychology; Sociology and Anthropology; English Language.

EDUCATIONAL PSYCHOLOGISTS (27108D)

Investigate processes of learning and teaching, and develop psychological principles and techniques applicable to educational problems.

Average Yearly Earnings: $48,089. **Experience:** Considerable preparation is needed. A minimum of two to four years of work-related skill, knowledge, or experience is needed for this occupation. **Education:** This group of occupations usually requires a four-year bachelor's degree, but in some cases does not. **Training:** Employees in this type of occupation usually need several years of work-related experience, on-the-job training, and/ or vocational training. **Related Examples:** Other occupations like this one usually involve coordinating, supervising, managing, or training others. Examples include accountants, chefs and head cooks, computer programmers, historians, pharmacists, and police detectives. **Standard Vocational Preparation Range:** 7.0 to below 8.0—Two years to less than ten years. **Major/Instructional Program:** 13.0604 Educational Assessment, Testing, and Measurement; 13.0802 Educational Psychology; 42.0101 Psychology, General; 42.0201 Clinical Psychology; 42.0301 Cognitive Psychology and Psycholinguistics; 42.0601 Counseling Psychology; 42.0901 Industrial and Organizational Psychology; 42.1601 Social Psychology; 42.1701 School Psychology. **Related Courses:** Administration and Management; Mathematics; Psychology; Sociology and Anthropology; Therapy and Counseling; Education and Training; English Language.

SOCIAL PSYCHOLOGISTS (27108E)

Investigate psychological aspects of human interrelationships to gain an understanding of individual and group thought, feeling, and behavior. Conduct research to analyze attitude, motivation, opinion, and group behavior, using behavioral observation, experimentation, or survey techniques.

Average Yearly Earnings: $48,089. **Experience:** Extensive preparation is needed. Extensive skill, knowledge, and experience are needed for this occupation. It may require more than five years of experience. **Education:** A bachelor's degree is the minimum formal education required for this group of occupations. However, many also require graduate school. For example, they may require a master's degree, and some require a Ph.D., M.D., or J.D. (law degree). **Training:** Employees in this type of occupation may need some on-the-job training, but most of these occupations assume that the person will already have the required skills, knowledge, work-related experience, and/or training. **Examples:** Other occupations like this one often involve coordinating, training, supervising, or managing the activities of others to accomplish goals. Very advanced communication and organizational skills are required. Examples include athletic trainers, lawyers, managing editors, physicists, and surgeons. **Standard Vocational Preparation Range:** 8.0 to 9.0—Four years to more than ten years. **Major/Instructional Program:** 42.0101 Psychology, General; 42.0401 Community Psychology; 42.0901 Industrial and Organizational Psychology; 42.1601 Social Psychology. **Related Courses:** Administration and Management; Mathematics; Psychology; Sociology and Anthropology; English Language; Philosophy and Theology.

CLINICAL PSYCHOLOGISTS (27108G)

Diagnose or evaluate mental and emotional disorders of individuals through observation, interview, and psychological tests; formulate and administer programs of treatment.

Average Yearly Earnings: $48,089. **Experience:** Considerable preparation is needed. A minimum of two to four years of work-related skill, knowledge, or experience is needed for this occupation. **Education:** This group of occupations usually requires a four-year bachelor's degree, but in some cases does not. **Training:** Employees in this type of occupation usually need several years of work-related experience, on-the-job training, and/or vocational training. **Related Examples:** Other occupations like this one usually involve coordinating, supervising, managing, or training others. Examples include accountants, chefs and head cooks, computer programmers, historians, pharmacists, and police detectives. **Standard Vocational Preparation Range:** 7.0 to below 8.0—Two years to less than ten years. **Major/Instructional Program:** 42.0101 Psychology, General; 42.0201 Clinical Psychology; 42.0601 Counseling Psychology; 51.2705 Psychoanalysis. **Related Courses:** Administration and Management; Customer and Personal Service; Personnel and Human Resources; Biology; Psychology; Sociology and Anthropology; Medicine and Dentistry; Therapy and Counseling; Education and Training; English Language.

COUNSELING PSYCHOLOGISTS (27108H)

Assess and evaluate individuals' problems through the use of case histories, interviews, and observation, and provide individual or group counseling services to assist individuals in achieving more effective personal, social, educational, and vocational development and adjustment.

Average Yearly Earnings: $48,089. **Experience:** Extensive preparation is needed. Extensive skill, knowledge, and experience are needed for this occupation. It may require more than five years of experience. **Education:** A bachelor's degree is the minimum formal education required for this group of occupations. However, many also require graduate school. For example, they may require a master's degree, and some require a Ph.D., M.D., or J.D. (law degree). **Training:** Employees in this type of occupation may need some on-the-job training, but most of these occupations assume that the person will already have the required skills, knowledge, work-related experience, and/or training. **Examples:** Other occupations like this one often involve coordinating, training, supervising, or managing the activities of others to accomplish goals. Very advanced communication and organizational skills are required. Examples include athletic trainers, lawyers, managing editors, physicists, social psychologists, and surgeons. **Standard Vocational Preparation Range:** 8.0 to 9.0—Four years to more than ten years. **Major/Instructional Program:** 13.1101 Counselor Education/Student Counseling and Guidance Services; 13.1102 College/Postsecondary Student Counseling and Personnel Services; 42.0101 Psychology, General; 42.0201 Clinical Psychology; 42.0601 Counseling Psychology; 51.2705 Psychoanalysis. **Related Courses:** Psychology; Sociology and Anthropology; Therapy and Counseling; Education and Training; Philosophy and Theology.

INDUSTRIAL-ORGANIZATIONAL PSYCHOLOGISTS (27108J)

Apply principles of psychology and human behavior to personnel, administration, management, sales, and marketing problems. Develop personnel policies, instruments, and programs for the selection, placement, training and development, and evaluation of employees. Conduct organizational analysis and programs for organizational development. Conduct research studies of leadership, supervision, morale, motivation, and worker productivity.

Average Yearly Earnings: $48,089. **Experience:** Extensive preparation is needed. Extensive skill, knowledge, and experience are needed for this occupation. It may require more than five years of experience. **Education:** A bachelor's degree is the minimum formal education required for this group of occupations. However, many also require graduate school. For example, they may require a master's degree, and some require a Ph.D., M.D., or J.D. (law degree). **Training:** Employees in this type of occupation may need some on-the-job training, but most of these occupations assume that the person will already have the required skills, knowledge, work-related experience, and/or training. **Examples:** Other occupations like this one often involve coordinating, training, supervising, or managing the activities of others to accomplish goals. Very advanced communication and organizational skills are required. Examples include athletic trainers, lawyers, managing editors, physicists, social psychologists, and surgeons. **Standard Vocational Preparation Range:** 8.0 to 9.0—Four years to more than ten years. **Major/Instructional Program:** 42.0101 Psychology, General; 42.0901 Industrial and Organizational Psychology; 42.1601 Social Psychology. **Related Courses:** Administration and Management; Sales and Marketing; Personnel and Human Resources; Mathematics; Psychology; Sociology and Anthropology; Therapy and Counseling; Education and Training; Philosophy and Theology.

POLITICAL SCIENTISTS (27199A)

Study the origin, development, and operation of political systems. Research a wide range of subjects, such as relations between the United States and foreign countries, the beliefs and institutions of foreign nations, or the politics of small towns or a major metropolis. May study topics such as public opinion, political decision making, and ideology. May analyze the structure and operation of governments as well as various political entities. May conduct public opinion surveys, analyze election results, or analyze public documents.

Average Yearly Earnings: $36,296. **Experience:** Extensive preparation is needed. Extensive skill, knowledge, and experience are needed for this occupation. It may require more than five years of experience. **Education:** A bachelor's degree is the minimum formal education required for this group of occupations. However, many also require graduate school. For example, they may require a master's degree, and some require a Ph.D., M.D., or J.D. (law degree). **Training:** Employees in this type of occupation may need some on-the-job training, but most of these occupations assume that the person will already have the required skills, knowledge, work-related experience, and/or training. **Examples:** Other occupations like this one often involve coordinating, training, supervising, or managing the activities of others to accomplish goals. Very advanced communication and organizational skills are required. Examples include athletic trainers, lawyers, managing editors, physicists, social psychologists, and surgeons. **Standard Vocational Preparation Range:** 8.0 to 9.0—Four years to more than ten years. **Major/Instructional Program:** 45.0901 International Relations and Affairs; 45.1001 Political Science and Government, General; 45.1002 American Government and Politics (United States). **Related Courses:** Psychology; Sociology and Anthropology; Geography; English Language; Foreign Language; History and Archeology; Philosophy and Theology; Law, Government, and Jurisprudence; Communications and Media.

SOCIOLOGISTS (27199B)

Conduct research into the development, structure, and behavior of groups of human beings and patterns of culture and social organization.

Average Yearly Earnings: $36,296. **Experience:** Medium preparation is needed. Previous work-related skill, knowledge, or experience is required for this occupation. **Education:** This group of occupations usually requires training in vocational schools, related on-the-job experience, or an associate degree. A bachelor's degree may be required. **Training:** Employees in this type of occupation usually need one or two years of training involving both on-the-job experience and informal training with experienced workers. **Related Examples:** Other occupations like this one usually involve using communication and organizational skills to coordinate, supervise, manage, or train others to accomplish goals. Examples include dental assistants, electricians, fish and game wardens, legal secretaries, personnel recruiters, and recreation workers. **Standard Vocational Preparation Range:** 6.0 to below 7.0—More than one year and less than four years. **Major/Instructional Program:** 43.0104 Criminal Justice Studies; 45.0201 Anthropology; 45.0401 Criminology; 45.0501 Demography and Population Studies; 45.1001 Political Science and Government, General; 45.1101 Sociology; 45.1201 Urban Studies/Affairs. **Related Courses:** Administration and Management; Psychology; Sociology and Anthropology; Geography; Education and Training; English Language; Foreign Language; History and Archeology; Philosophy and Theology; Law, Government, and Jurisprudence; Communications and Media.

ANTHROPOLOGISTS (27199C)

Research or study the origins and physical, social, and cultural development and behavior of humans, and the cultures and organizations they have created.

Average Yearly Earnings: $36,296. **Experience:** Considerable preparation is needed. A minimum of two to four years of work-related skill, knowledge, or experience is needed for this occupation. **Education:** This group of occupations usually requires a four-year bachelor's degree, but in some cases does not. **Training:** Employees in this type of occupation usually need several years of work-related experience, on-the-job training, and/or vocational training. **Related Examples:** Other occupations like this one usually involve coordinating, supervising, managing, or training others. Examples include accountants, chefs and head cooks, computer programmers, historians, pharmacists, and police detectives. **Standard Vocational Preparation Range:** 7.0 to below 8.0—Two years to less than ten years. **Major/Instructional Program:** 45.0201 Anthropology; 45.0301 Archeology; 45.0501 Demography and Population Studies; 45.0901 International Relations and Affairs; 45.1101 Sociology; 50.0901 Music, General; 50.0905 Musicology and Ethnomusicology. **Related Courses:** Administration and Management; Biology; Psychology; Sociology and Anthropology; Geography; Education and Training; English Language; Foreign Language; Fine Arts; History and Archeology; Philosophy and Theology; Communications and Media.

LINGUISTIC SCIENTISTS (27199D)

Study the structure and development of a specific language or language group.

Average Yearly Earnings: $36,296. **Experience:** Extensive preparation is needed. Extensive skill, knowledge, and experience are needed for this occupation. It may require more than five years of experience. **Education:** A bachelor's degree is the minimum formal education required for this group of occupations. However, many also require graduate school. For example, they may require a master's degree, and some require a Ph.D., M.D., or J.D. (law degree). **Training:** Employees in this type of occupation may need some on-the-job training, but most of these occupations assume that the person will

already have the required skills, knowledge, work-related experience, and/or training. **Examples:** Other occupations like this one often involve coordinating, training, supervising, or managing the activities of others to accomplish goals. Very advanced communication and organizational skills are required. Examples include athletic trainers, lawyers, managing editors, physicists, social psychologists, and surgeons. **Standard Vocational Preparation Range:** 8.0 to 9.0—Four years to more than ten years. **Major/Instructional Program:** 16.0101 Foreign Languages and Literatures, General; 16.0102 Linguistics; 45.0201 Anthropology; 45.0301 Archeology; 45.0901 International Relations and Affairs. **Related Courses:** Sociology and Anthropology; Geography; Education and Training; English Language; Foreign Language; History and Archeology; Philosophy and Theology.

HISTORIANS (27199E)

Research, analyze, record, and interpret the past as recorded in sources such as government and institutional records, newspapers and other periodicals, photographs, interviews, films, and unpublished manuscripts, such as personal diaries and letters.

Average Yearly Earnings: $36,296. **Experience:** Considerable preparation is needed. A minimum of two to four years of work-related skill, knowledge, or experience is needed for this occupation. **Education:** This group of occupations usually requires a four-year bachelor's degree, but in some cases does not. **Training:** Employees in this type of occupation usually need several years of work-related experience, on-the-job training, and/or vocational training. **Related Examples:** Other occupations like this one usually involve coordinating, supervising, managing, or training others. Examples include accountants, chefs and head cooks, computer programmers, pharmacists, and police detectives. **Standard Vocational Preparation Range:** 7.0 to below 8.0—Two years to less than ten years. **Major/Instructional Program:** 45.0801 History, General; 45.0802 American (United States) History; 45.0803 European History; 45.0804 History and Philosophy of Science; 45.0805 Public/Applied History and Archival Administration; 45.0901 International Relations and Affairs; 45.1001 Political Science and Government, General; 50.0501 Drama/Theater Arts, General; 50.0505 Drama/Theater Literature, History, and Criticism; 50.0701 Art, General; 50.0704 Arts Management; 52.0201 Business Administration and Management, General. **Related Courses:** Administration and Management; Economics and Accounting; Sales and Marketing; Personnel and Human Resources; Sociology and Anthropology; Geography; Education and Training; English Language; Foreign Language; Fine Arts; History and Archeology; Philosophy and Theology; Communications and Media.

INTELLIGENCE SPECIALISTS (27199F)

Collect, record, analyze, and disseminate tactical, political, strategic, or technical intelligence information to facilitate the development of military or political strategies.

Average Yearly Earnings: $36,296. **Experience:** Considerable preparation is needed. A minimum of two to four years of work-related skill, knowledge, or experience is needed for this occupation. **Education:** This group of occupations usually requires a four-year

bachelor's degree, but in some cases does not. **Training:** Employees in this type of occupation usually need several years of work-related experience, on-the-job training, and/or vocational training. **Related Examples:** Other occupations like this one usually involve coordinating, supervising, managing, or training others. Examples include accountants, chefs and head cooks, computer programmers, historians, pharmacists, and police detectives. **Standard Vocational Preparation Range:** 7.0 to below 8.0—Two years to less than ten years. **Major/Instructional Program:** 45.0901 International Relations and Affairs; 45.1001 Political Science and Government, General; 45.1101 Sociology. **Related Courses:** Administration and Management; Clerical; Economics and Accounting; Psychology; Sociology and Anthropology; Geography; Education and Training; Foreign Language; History and Archeology; Philosophy and Theology; Public Safety and Security; Law, Government, and Jurisprudence; Telecommunications; Communications and Media; Transportation.

GENEALOGISTS (27199G)

Research genealogical background of an individual or family to establish descent from a specific ancestor or to identify the forebears of an individual or family.

Average Yearly Earnings: $36,296. **Experience:** Considerable preparation is needed. A minimum of two to four years of work-related skill, knowledge, or experience is needed for this occupation. **Education:** This group of occupations usually requires a four-year bachelor's degree, but in some cases does not. **Training:** Employees in this type of occupation usually need several years of work-related experience, on-the-job training, and/or vocational training. **Related Examples:** Other occupations like this one usually involve coordinating, supervising, managing, or training others. Examples include accountants, chefs and head cooks, computer programmers, historians, pharmacists, and police detectives. **Standard Vocational Preparation Range:** 7.0 to below 8.0—Two years to less than ten years. **Major/Instructional Program:** 45.0801 History, General; 45.0805 Public/Applied History and Archival Administration. **Related Courses:** Sociology and Anthropology; Geography; English Language; Foreign Language; History and Archeology.

ARCHEOLOGISTS (27199H)

Conduct research to reconstruct the record of past human life and culture from human remains, artifacts, architectural features, and structures recovered through excavation, underwater recovery, or other means of discovery.

Average Yearly Earnings: $36,296. **Experience:** Considerable preparation is needed. A minimum of two to four years of work-related skill, knowledge, or experience is needed for this occupation. **Education:** This group of occupations usually requires a four-year bachelor's degree, but in some cases does not. **Training:** Employees in this type of occupation usually need several years of work-related experience, on-the-job training, and/or vocational training. **Related Examples:** Other occupations like this one usually involve coordinating, supervising, managing, or training others. Examples include

accountants, chefs and head cooks, computer programmers, historians, pharmacists, and police detectives. **Standard Vocational Preparation Range:** 7.0 to below 8.0—Two years to less than ten years. **Major/Instructional Program:** 45.0201 Anthropology, 45.0301 Archeology. **Related Courses:** Sociology and Anthropology; Geography; Foreign Language; History and Archeology; Philosophy and Theology.

Social Services Workers

SOCIAL WORKERS, MEDICAL AND PSYCHIATRIC (27302)

Counsel and aid individuals and families with problems that may arise during or following the recovery from physical or mental illness, by providing supportive services designed to help the persons understand, accept, and follow medical recommendations. Includes chemical dependency counselors.

Average Yearly Earnings: $31,865. **Experience:** Considerable preparation is needed. A minimum of two to four years of work-related skill, knowledge, or experience is needed for this occupation. **Education:** This group of occupations usually requires a four-year bachelor's degree, but in some cases does not. **Training:** Employees in this type of occupation usually need several years of work-related experience, on-the-job training, and/or vocational training. **Related Examples:** Other occupations like this one usually involve coordinating, supervising, managing, or training others. Examples include accountants, chefs and head cooks, computer programmers, historians, pharmacists, and police detectives. **Standard Vocational Preparation Range:** 7.0 to below 8.0—Two years to less than ten years. **Major/Instructional Program:** 42.0201 Clinical Psychology, 42.0601 Counseling Psychology, 44.0701 Social Work, 51.1501 Alcohol/Drug Abuse Counseling, 51.1503 Clinical and Medical Social Work. **Related Courses:** Customer and Personal Service; Personnel and Human Resources; Psychology; Sociology and Anthropology; Medicine and Dentistry; Therapy and Counseling; Education and Training; Philosophy and Theology; Communications and Media.

COMMUNITY ORGANIZATION SOCIAL WORKERS (27305A)

Plan, organize, and work with community groups to help solve social problems and deliver specialized social services.

Average Yearly Earnings: $31,220. **Experience:** Considerable preparation is needed. A minimum of two to four years of work-related skill, knowledge, or experience is needed for this occupation. **Education:** This group of occupations usually requires a four-year bachelor's degree, but in some cases does not. **Training:** Employees in this type of occupation usually need several years of work-related experience, on-the-job training, and/or vocational training. **Related Examples:** Other occupations like this one usually involve coordinating, supervising, managing, or training others. Examples include accountants, chefs and head cooks, computer programmers, historians, pharmacists, and police detectives. **Standard Vocational Preparation Range:** 7.0 to below 8.0—Two years to less than ten years. **Major/Instructional Program:** 13.0101 Education, General; 13.1001 Special Education, General; 13.1005 Education of the Emotionally Handicapped; 13.1006 Education of the Mentally Handicapped; 13.1007 Education of the Multiple Handicapped; 13.1008 Education of the Physically Handicapped; 13.1011 Education of the Specific Learning Disabled; 13.1012 Education of the Speech Impaired; 44.0201 Community Organization, Resources, and Services; 44.0701 Social Work. **Related Courses:** Administration and Management; Sales and Marketing; Customer and Personal Service; Personnel and Human Resources; Psychology; Sociology and Anthropology; Therapy and Counseling; Education and Training; English Language; Communications and Media.

SOCIAL WORKERS (27305B)

Counsel and aid individuals and families with problems relating to personal and family adjustments, finances, employment, food, clothing, housing, or other human needs and conditions.

Average Yearly Earnings: $31,220. **Experience:** Considerable preparation is needed. A minimum of two to four years of work-related skill, knowledge, or experience is needed for this occupation. **Education:** This group of occupations usually requires a four-year bachelor's degree, but in some cases does not. **Training:** Employees in this type of occupation usually need several years of work-related experience, on-the-job training, and/or vocational training. **Related Examples:** Other occupations like this one usually involve coordinating, supervising, managing, or training others. Examples include accountants, chefs and head cooks, computer programmers, historians, pharmacists, and police detectives. **Standard Vocational Preparation Range:** 7.0 to below 8.0—Two years to less than ten years. **Major/Instructional Program:** 42.0201 Clinical Psychology, 44.0701 Social Work. **Related Courses:** Administration and Management; Clerical; Customer and Personal Service; Psychology; Sociology and Anthropology; Therapy and Counseling; Foreign Language; Philosophy and Theology; Law, Government, and Jurisprudence.

PROBATION AND CORRECTIONAL TREATMENT SPECIALISTS (27305C)

Provide social services to assist in the rehabilitation of law offenders in custody or on probation. Includes probation and parole officers.

Average Yearly Earnings: $31,220. **Experience:** Medium preparation is needed. Previous work-related skill, knowledge, or experience is required for this occupation. **Education:** This group of occupations usually requires training in vocational schools, related on-the-job experience, or an associate degree. A bachelor's degree may be required. **Training:** Employees in this type of occupation usually need one or two years of training involving both on-the-job experience and informal training with experienced workers. **Related Examples:** Other occupations like this one usually involve using communication and organizational skills to coordinate, supervise, manage, or train others to accomplish goals. Examples include dental assistants, electricians, fish and game wardens, legal

secretaries, personnel recruiters, and recreation workers. **Standard Vocational Preparation Range:** 6.0 to below 7.0—More than one year and less than four years. **Major/Instructional Program:** 44.0701 Social Work. **Related Courses:** Psychology; Sociology and Anthropology; Therapy and Counseling; Public Safety and Security; Law, Government, and Jurisprudence.

RESIDENTIAL COUNSELORS (27307)

Coordinate activities for residents of care and treatment institutions, boarding schools, college fraternities or sororities, children's homes, or similar establishments. Work includes developing or assisting in the development of program plans for individuals, maintaining household records, and assigning rooms. Counsel residents in identifying and resolving social or other problems. Order supplies and determine need for maintenance, repairs, and furnishings.

Average Yearly Earnings: $19,260. **Experience:** Medium preparation is needed. Previous work-related skill, knowledge, or experience is required for this occupation. **Education:** This group of occupations usually requires training in vocational schools, related on-the-job experience, or an associate degree. A bachelor's degree may be required. **Training:** Employees in this type of occupation usually need one or two years of training involving both on-the-job experience and informal training with experienced workers. **Related Examples:** Other occupations like this one usually involve using communication and organizational skills to coordinate, supervise, manage, or train others to accomplish goals. Examples include dental assistants, electricians, fish and game wardens, legal secretaries, personnel recruiters, and recreation workers. **Standard Vocational Preparation Range:** 6.0 to below 7.0—More than one year and less than four years. **Major/Instructional Program:** 20.0201 Childcare and Guidance Workers and Managers, General; 20.0202 Childcare Provider/Assistant; 20.0203 Childcare Services Manager. **Related Courses:** Administration and Management; Customer and Personal Service; Personnel and Human Resources; Psychology; Sociology and Anthropology; Medicine and Dentistry; Therapy and Counseling; Philosophy and Theology; Transportation.

HUMAN SERVICES WORKERS (27308)

Assist social group workers and caseworkers with developing, organizing, and conducting programs to prevent and resolve problems relevant to substance abuse and human relationships. Aid families and clients in obtaining information on the use of social and community services. May recommend additional services. Excludes residential counselors and psychiatric technicians.

Average Yearly Earnings: $21,112. **Experience:** Some preparation is needed. Some previous work-related skill, knowledge, or experience may be helpful in this occupation, but usually is not needed. **Education:** This group of occupations usually requires a high school diploma and may require some vocational training or job-related course work. In some cases, an associate or bachelor's degree could be needed. **Training:** Employees in this type of occupation need anywhere from a few months to one year of working with experienced employees. **Related Examples:** Other occupations like this one often involve using your knowledge and skills to help others. Examples include drywall installers, fire inspectors, flight attendants, pharmacy technicians, retail salespersons, and tellers. **Standard Vocational Preparation Range:** 4.0 to below 6.0—Six months to less than two years. **Major/Instructional Program:** 20.0601 Custodial, Housekeeping, and Home Services Workers and Managers, General; 20.0602 Elder Care Provider/Companion; 20.0606 Homemaker's Aide. **Related Courses:** Administration and Management; Clerical; Customer and Personal Service; Food Production; Psychology; Sociology and Anthropology; Therapy and Counseling; Education and Training; Philosophy and Theology; Transportation.

RECREATION WORKERS (27311)

Conduct recreation activities with groups in public, private, or volunteer agencies or recreation facilities. Organize and promote activities such as arts and crafts, sports, games, music, dramatics, social recreation, camping, and hobbies, taking into account the needs and interests of individual members.

Average Yearly Earnings: $17,139. **Experience:** Medium preparation is needed. Previous work-related skill, knowledge, or experience is required for this occupation. **Education:** This group of occupations usually requires training in vocational schools, related on-the-job experience, or an associate degree. A bachelor's degree may be required. **Training:** Employees in this type of occupation usually need one or two years of training involving both on-the-job experience and informal training with experienced workers. **Related Examples:** Other occupations like this one usually involve using communication and organizational skills to coordinate, supervise, manage, or train others to accomplish goals. Examples include dental assistants, electricians, fish and game wardens, legal secretaries, and personnel recruiters. **Standard Vocational Preparation Range:** 6.0 to below 7.0—More than one year and less than four years. **Major/Instructional Program:** 20.0201 Child Care and Guidance Workers and Managers, General; 20.0202 Childcare Provider/Assistant; 31.0101 Parks, Recreation, and Leisure Studies; 31.0301 Parks, Recreation, and Leisure Facilities Management; 52.0901 Hospitality Administration/Management. **Related Courses:** Administration and Management; Customer and Personal Service; Personnel and Human Resources; Psychology; Sociology and Anthropology; Medicine and Dentistry; Therapy and Counseling; Education and Training; Foreign Language; Fine Arts; Public Safety and Security; Law, Government, and Jurisprudence; Communications and Media.

Religious Workers

CLERGY (27502)

Conduct religious worship and perform other spiritual functions associated with the beliefs and practices of a religious faith or denomination, as delegated by ordinance, license, or other authorization. Provide spiritual and moral guidance and assistance to members.

Average Yearly Earnings: $28,870. **Experience:** Extensive preparation is needed. Extensive skill, knowledge, and experience are needed for this occupation. It may require more than five years of experience. **Education:** A bachelor's degree is the minimum formal education required for this group of occupations. However, many also require graduate school. For example, they may require a master's degree, and some require a Ph.D., M.D., or J.D. (law degree). **Training:** Employees in this type of occupation may need some on-the-job training, but most of these occupations assume that the person will already have the required skills, knowledge, work-related experience, and/or training. **Examples:** Other occupations like this one often involve coordinating, training, supervising, or managing the activities of others to accomplish goals. Very advanced communication and organizational skills are required. Examples include athletic trainers, lawyers, managing editors, physicists, social psychologists, and surgeons. **Standard Vocational Preparation Range:** 8.0 to 9.0—Four years to more than ten years. **Major/Instructional Program:** 39.0201 Bible/Biblical Studies, 39.0301 Missions/Missionary Studies and Misology, 39.0602 Divinity/Ministry (B.D., M.Div.), 39.0701 Pastoral Counseling and Specialized Ministries. **Related Courses:** Psychology; Sociology and Anthropology; Therapy and Counseling; Education and Training; English Language; History and Archeology; Philosophy and Theology; Communications and Media.

DIRECTORS, RELIGIOUS ACTIVITIES AND EDUCATION (27505)

Direct and coordinate the activities of a denominational group to meet the religious needs of students. Plan, organize, and direct church school programs designed to promote religious education among church membership. Provide counseling and guidance relative to marital, health, financial, and religious problems.

Average Yearly Earnings: $24,169. **Experience:** Extensive preparation is needed. Extensive skill, knowledge, and experience are needed for this occupation. It may require more than five years of experience. **Education:** A bachelor's degree is the minimum formal education required for this group of occupations. However, many also require graduate school. For example, they may require a master's degree, and some require a Ph.D., M.D., or J.D. (law degree). **Training:** Employees in this type of occupation may need some on-the-job training, but most of these occupations assume that the person will already have the required skills, knowledge, work-related experience, and/or training. **Examples:** Other occupations like this one often involve coordinating, training, supervising, or managing the activities of others to accomplish goals. Very advanced communication and organizational skills are required. Examples include athletic trainers, lawyers, managing editors, physicists, social psychologists, and surgeons. **Standard Vocational Preparation Range:** 8.0 to 9.0—Four years to more than ten years. **Major/Instructional Program:** 39.0201 Bible/Biblical Studies, 39.0301 Missions/Missionary Studies and Misology, 39.0401 Religious Education, 39.0701 Pastoral Counseling and Specialized Ministries. **Related Courses:** Administration and Management; Economics and Accounting;

Psychology; Sociology and Anthropology; Therapy and Counseling; Education and Training; English Language; Philosophy and Theology; Communications and Media.

Lawyers and Judges

JUDGES AND MAGISTRATES (28102)

Judges arbitrate, advise, and administer justice in a court of law. Sentence defendant in criminal cases according to statutes of state or federal government. May determine liability of defendant in civil cases. Magistrates adjudicate criminal cases not involving penitentiary sentences and civil cases concerning damages below a sum specified by state law. May issue marriage licenses and perform wedding ceremonies.

Average Yearly Earnings: $51,667. **Experience:** Extensive preparation is needed. Extensive skill, knowledge, and experience are needed for this occupation. It may require more than five years of experience. **Education:** A bachelor's degree is the minimum formal education required for this group of occupations. However, many also require graduate school. For example, they may require a master's degree, and some require a Ph.D., M.D., or J.D. (law degree). **Training:** Employees in this type of occupation may need some on-the-job training, but most of these occupations assume that the person will already have the required skills, knowledge, work-related experience, and/or training. **Examples:** Other occupations like this one often involve coordinating, training, supervising, or managing the activities of others to accomplish goals. Very advanced communication and organizational skills are required. Examples include athletic trainers, lawyers, managing editors, physicists, social psychologists, and surgeons. **Standard Vocational Preparation Range:** 8.0 to 9.0—Four years to more than ten years. **Major/Instructional Program:** 22.0101 Law (L.L.B., J.D.). **Related Courses:** Economics and Accounting; Personnel and Human Resources; Psychology; Sociology and Anthropology; Geography; English Language; History and Archeology; Philosophy and Theology; Public Safety and Security; Law, Government, and Jurisprudence; Communications and Media.

ADJUDICATORS, HEARINGS OFFICERS, AND JUDICIAL REVIEWERS (28105)

Conduct hearings to review and decide claims filed by the government against individuals or organizations, or individual eligibility issues concerning social programs, disability, or unemployment benefits. Determine the existence and the amount of liability; recommend the acceptance or rejection of claims; or compromise settlements according to laws, regulations, policies, and precedent decisions. Confer with persons or organizations involved, and prepare written decisions.

Average Yearly Earnings: $51,667. **Experience:** Extensive preparation is needed. Extensive skill, knowledge, and experience are needed for this occupation. It may require more than five years of experience. **Education:** A bachelor's degree is the minimum formal education required for this group of occupations. However, many also require graduate

school. For example, they may require a master's degree, and some require a Ph.D., M.D., or J.D. (law degree). **Training:** Employees in this type of occupation may need some on-the-job training, but most of these occupations assume that the person will already have the required skills, knowledge, work-related experience, and/or training. **Examples:** Other occupations like this one often involve coordinating, training, supervising, or managing the activities of others to accomplish goals. Very advanced communication and organizational skills are required. Examples include athletic trainers, lawyers, managing editors, physicists, social psychologists, and surgeons. **Standard Vocational Preparation Range:** 8.0 to 9.0—Four years to more than ten years. **Major/Instructional Program:** 22.0101 Law (L.L.B., J.D.), 44.0701 Social Work. **Related Courses:** Administration and Management; Psychology; Sociology and Anthropology; Therapy and Counseling; English Language; History and Archeology; Philosophy and Theology; Law, Government, and Jurisprudence.

LAWYERS **(28108)**

Conduct criminal and civil lawsuits, draw up legal documents, advise clients as to legal rights, and practice other phases of law. May represent the client in court or before quasi-judicial or administrative agencies of government. May specialize in a single area of law, such as patent law, corporate law, or criminal law.

Average Yearly Earnings: $70,116. **Experience:** Extensive preparation is needed. Extensive skill, knowledge, and experience are needed for this occupation. It may require more than five years of experience. **Education:** A bachelor's degree is the minimum formal education required for this group of occupations. However, many also require graduate school. For example, they may require a master's degree, and some require a Ph.D., M.D., or J.D. (law degree). **Training:** Employees in this type of occupation may need some on-the-job training, but most of these occupations assume that the person will already have the required skills, knowledge, work-related experience, and/or training. **Examples:** Other occupations like this one often involve coordinating, training, supervising, or managing the activities of others to accomplish goals. Very advanced communication and organizational skills are required. Examples include athletic trainers, managing editors, physicists, social psychologists, and surgeons. **Standard Vocational Preparation Range:** 8.0 to 9.0—Four years to more than ten years. **Major/Instructional Program:** 22.0101 Law (L.L.B., J.D.), 22.0104 Juridical Science/Legal Specialization (L.L.M., M.C.L., J.S.D., S.J.D.). **Related Courses:** Administration and Management; Clerical; Computers and Electronics; Psychology; Sociology and Anthropology; Therapy and Counseling; Education and Training; English Language; Public Safety and Security; Law, Government, and Jurisprudence.

Legal Assistants

LAW CLERKS **(28302)**

Research legal data for a brief or argument based on statutory law or decisions. Search for and study legal records and documents to obtain data applicable to the case under consideration. Prepare rough drafts of briefs or arguments. File pleadings for the firm with the court clerk. Serve copies of pleading on the opposing counsel. Prepare affidavits of documents and keep the document file and correspondence of cases.

Average Yearly Earnings: $26,748. **Experience:** Considerable preparation is needed. A minimum of two to four years of work-related skill, knowledge, or experience is needed for this occupation. **Education:** This group of occupations usually requires a four-year bachelor's degree, but in some cases does not. **Training:** Employees in this type of occupation usually need several years of work-related experience, on-the-job training, and/or vocational training. **Related Examples:** Other occupations like this one usually involve coordinating, supervising, managing, or training others. Examples include accountants, chefs and head cooks, computer programmers, historians, pharmacists, and police detectives. **Standard Vocational Preparation Range:** 7.0 to below 8.0—Two years to less than ten years. **Major/Instructional Program:** 22.0103 Paralegal/Legal Assistant. **Related Courses:** Administration and Management; Clerical; Economics and Accounting; Personnel and Human Resources; English Language; Law, Government, and Jurisprudence; Communications and Media.

PARALEGALS AND LEGAL ASSISTANTS (28305)

Assist lawyers by researching legal precedent, investigating facts, or preparing legal documents. Conduct research to support a legal proceeding, to formulate a defense, or to initiate legal action.

Average Yearly Earnings: $32,032. **Experience:** Considerable preparation is needed. A minimum of two to four years of work-related skill, knowledge, or experience is needed for this occupation. **Education:** This group of occupations usually requires a four-year bachelor's degree, but in some cases does not. **Training:** Employees in this type of occupation usually need several years of work-related experience, on-the-job training, and/or vocational training. **Related Examples:** Other occupations like this one usually involve coordinating, supervising, managing, or training others. Examples include accountants, chefs and head cooks, computer programmers, historians, pharmacists, and police detectives. **Standard Vocational Preparation Range:** 7.0 to below 8.0—Two years to less than ten years. **Major/Instructional Program:** 22.0103 Paralegal/Legal Assistant. **Related Courses:** Administration and Management; Clerical; Economics and Accounting; Personnel and Human Resources; Computers and Electronics; Sociology and Anthropology; English Language; Law, Government, and Jurisprudence.

TITLE SEARCHERS (28308)

Compile a list of mortgages, deeds, contracts, judgments, and other instruments pertaining to title, by searching public and private records of a real estate or title insurance company.

Average Yearly Earnings: $26,000. **Experience:** Some preparation is needed. Some previous work-related skill, knowledge, or experience may be helpful in this occupation, but usually is not needed. **Education:** This group of occupations usually requires a high school diploma and may require some vocational training or job-related course work. In some cases, an associate or bachelor's degree could be needed. **Training:** Employees in this type of occupation need anywhere from a few months to one year of working with experienced employees. **Related Examples:** Other occupations like this one often involve using your knowledge and skills to help others. Examples include drywall installers, fire inspectors, flight attendants, pharmacy technicians, retail salespersons, and tellers. **Standard Vocational Preparation Range:** 4.0 to below 6.0—Six months to less than two years. **Major/Instructional Program:** 22.0103 Paralegal/Legal Assistant. **Related Courses:** Clerical; Economics and Accounting; Computers and Electronics; Sociology and Anthropology; Geography; English Language; History and Archeology; Law, Government, and Jurisprudence.

TITLE EXAMINERS AND ABSTRACTORS (28311)

Title examiners search public records and examine titles to determine the legal condition of a property title. Copy or summarize (abstract) recorded documents that affect the condition of title to property (e.g., mortgages, trust deeds, and contracts). May prepare and issue a policy that guarantees the legality of title. Abstractors summarize pertinent legal or insurance details or sections of statutes or case law from reference books for the purpose of examination, proof, or ready reference. Search out titles to determine whether title deed is correct.

Average Yearly Earnings: $26,000. **Experience:** Medium preparation is needed. Previous work-related skill, knowledge, or experience is required for this occupation. **Education:** This group of occupations usually requires training in vocational schools, related on-the-job experience, or an associate degree. A bachelor's degree may be required. **Training:** Employees in this type of occupation usually need one or two years of training involving both on-the-job experience and informal training with experienced workers. **Related Examples:** Other occupations like this one usually involve using communication and organizational skills to coordinate, supervise, manage, or train others to accomplish goals. Examples include dental assistants, electricians, fish and game wardens, legal secretaries, personnel recruiters, and recreation workers. **Standard Vocational Preparation Range:** 6.0 to below 7.0—More than one year and less than four years. **Major/Instructional Program:** 22.0103 Paralegal/Legal Assistant; 52.0201 Business Administration and Management, General; 52.0204 Office Supervision and Management. **Related Courses:** Administration and Management; Clerical; Economics and Accounting; Geography; English Language; Law, Government, and Jurisprudence.

PROFESSIONAL AND SUPPORT SPECIALTIES—EDUCATORS, LIBRARIANS, COUNSELORS, HEALTHCARE WORKERS, ARTISTS, WRITERS, PERFORMERS, AND OTHER PROFESSIONAL WORKERS

College and University Faculty

NURSING INSTRUCTORS—POSTSECONDARY (31114)

Demonstrate and teach patient care in classroom and clinical units to nursing students. Instruct students in principles and application of physical, biological, and psychological subjects related to nursing. Conduct and supervise laboratory experiments. Issue assignments, direct seminars, etc. Participate in planning curriculum with medical and nursing personnel and in evaluating and improving teaching and nursing practices. May specialize in specific subjects, such as anatomy or chemistry, or in a type of nursing activity, such as nursing of surgical patients.

Average Yearly Earnings: $44,800. **Experience:** Extensive preparation is needed. Extensive skill, knowledge, and experience are needed for this occupation. It may require more than five years of experience. **Education:** A bachelor's degree is the minimum formal education required for this group of occupations. However, many also require graduate school. For example, they may require a master's degree, and some require a Ph.D., M.D., or J.D. (law degree). **Training:** Employees in this type of occupation may need some on-the-job training, but most of these occupations assume that the person will already have the required skills, knowledge, work-related experience, and/or training. **Examples:** Other occupations like this one often involve coordinating, training, supervising, or managing the activities of others to accomplish goals. Very advanced communication and organizational skills are required. Examples include athletic trainers, lawyers, managing editors, physicists, social psychologists, and surgeons. **Standard Vocational Preparation Range:** 8.0 to 9.0—Four years to more than ten years. **Major/Instructional Program:** 51.1601 Nursing (R.N.); 51.1603 Nursing, Adult Health (Post-R.N.); 51.1604 Nursing Anesthetist (Post-R.N.); 51.1605 Nursing, Family Practice (Post-R.N.); 51.1606 Nursing, Maternal/Child Health (Post-R.N.); 51.1607 Nursing Midwifery (Post-R.N.); 51.1608 Nursing Science (Post-R.N.); 51.1609 Nursing, Pediatric (Post-R.N.); 51.1610 Nursing, Psychiatric/Mental Health (Post-R.N.); 51.1611 Nursing, Public Health (Post-R.N.); 51.1612 Nursing, Surgical (Post-R.N.). **Related Courses:** Administration and Management; Customer and Personal Service; Personnel and Human Resources; Chemistry; Biology; Psychology; Sociology and Anthropology; Medicine and Dentistry; Therapy and Counseling; Education and Training; English Language; Philosophy and Theology; Public Safety and Security; Law, Government, and Jurisprudence.

GRADUATE ASSISTANTS, TEACHING (31117)

Assist department chairperson, faculty members, or other professional staff members in a college or university by performing teaching or teaching-related duties, such as teaching lower-level courses, developing teaching materials, preparing and giving examinations, and grading examinations or papers. Graduate assistants who primarily perform nonteaching duties, such as laboratory research, are included in the occupational category related to the work performed.

Experience: Extensive preparation is needed. Extensive skill, knowledge, and experience are needed for this occupation. It may require more than five years of experience. **Education:** A bachelor's degree is the minimum formal education required for this group of occupations. However, many also require graduate school. For example, they may require a master's degree, and some require a Ph.D., M.D., or J.D. (law degree). **Training:** Employees in this type of occupation may need some on-the-job training, but most of these occupations assume that the person will already have the required skills, knowledge, work-related experience, and/or training. **Examples:** Other occupations like this one often involve coordinating, training, supervising, or managing the activities of others to accomplish goals. Very advanced communication and organizational skills are required. Examples include athletic trainers, lawyers, managing editors, physicists, social psychologists, and surgeons. **Standard Vocational Preparation Range:** 8.0 to 9.0— Four years to more than ten years. **Major/Instructional Program:** 13.0101 Education, General. **Related Courses:** Clerical; Education and Training; English Language.

LIFE SCIENCES TEACHERS—POSTSECONDARY (31202)

Teach courses pertaining to living organisms, such as biological sciences, agricultural sciences, and medical sciences. Includes teachers of subjects such as botany, zoology, agronomy, biochemistry, biophysics, soil conservation, forestry, psychiatry, surgery, and obstetrics.

Average Yearly Earnings: $44,800. **Experience:** Extensive preparation is needed. Extensive skill, knowledge, and experience are needed for this occupation. It may require more than five years of experience. **Education:** A bachelor's degree is the minimum formal education required for this group of occupations. However, many also require graduate school. For example, they may require a master's degree, and some require a Ph.D., M.D., or J.D. (law degree). **Training:** Employees in this type of occupation may need some on-the-job training, but most of these occupations assume that the person will already have the required skills, knowledge, work-related experience, and/or training. **Examples:** Other occupations like this one often involve coordinating, training, supervising, or managing the activities of others to accomplish goals. Very advanced communication and organizational skills are required. Examples include athletic trainers, lawyers, managing editors, physicists, social psychologists, and surgeons. **Standard Vocational Preparation Range:** 8.0 to 9.0—Four years to more than ten years. **Major/Instructional Program:** 02.0101 Agriculture/Agricultural Sciences, General; 02.0201 Animal Sciences, General; 02.0202 Agricultural Animal Breeding and Genetics; 02.0203 Agricultural Animal Health; 02.0204 Agricultural Animal Nutrition; 02.0205 Agricultural Animal Physiology; 02.0206 Dairy Science; 02.0209 Poultry Science; 02.0301 Food Sciences and Technology; 02.0401 Plant Sciences, General; 02.0402 Agronomy and Crop Science; 02.0403 Horticulture Science; 02.0405 Plant Breeding and Genetics; 02.0406 Agricultural Plant Pathology; 02.0407 Agricultural Plant Physiology; 02.0408 Plant Protection (Pest Management); 02.0409 Range Science and Management; 02.0501 Soil Sciences; 03.0101 Natural Resources Conservation, General; 03.0102 Environmental Science/Studies; 03.0201 Natural Resources Management and Policy; 03.0301 Fishing and Fisheries Sciences and Management; 03.0501 Forestry, General; 03.0502 Forestry Sciences; 03.0506 Forest Management; 03.0601 Wildlife and Wildlands Management; 26.0101 Biology, General; 26.0202 Biochemistry; 26.0203 Biophysics; 26.0301 Botany, General; 26.0305 Plant Pathology; 26.0307 Plant Physiology; 26.0401 Cell Biology; 26.0402 Molecular Biology; 26.0501 Microbiology/Bacteriology; 26.0601 Anatomy; 26.0603 Ecology; 26.0607 Marine/Aquatic Biology; 26.0608 Neuroscience; 26.0609 Nutritional Sciences; 26.0610 Parasitology; 26.0611 Radiation Biology/Radiobiology; 26.0612 Toxicology; 26.0613 Genetics, Plant and

Animal; 26.0614 Biometrics; 26.0616 Biotechnology Research; 26.0617 Evolutionary Biology; 26.0618 Biological Immunology; 26.0619 Virology; 26.0701 Zoology, General; 26.0702 Entomology; 26.0704 Pathology, Human and Animal; 26.0705 Pharmacology, Human and Animal; 26.0706 Physiology, Human and Animal; 30.0101 Biological and Physical Sciences; 30.1001 Biopsychology; 30.1101 Gerontology; 51.1201 Medicine (M.D.); 51.1301 Medical Anatomy; 51.1302 Medical Biochemistry; 51.1303 Medical Biomathematics and Biometrics; 51.1304 Medical Physics/Biophysics; 51.1305 Medical Cell Biology; 51.1306 Medical Genetics; 51.1307 Medical Immunology; 51.1308 Medical Microbiology; 51.1309 Medical Molecular Biology; 51.1310 Medical Neurobiology; 51.1311 Medical Nutrition; 51.1312 Medical Pathology; 51.1313 Medical Physiology; 51.1314 Medical Toxicology; 51.1399 Medical Basic Sciences, Other; 51.1401 Medical Clinical Sciences (M.S., Ph.D.); 51.2203 Epidemiology; 51.2901 Aerospace Medicine Residency; 51.2902 Allergies and Immunology Residency; 51.2903 Anesthesiology Residency; 51.2904 Blood Banking Residency; 51.2905 Cardiology Residency; 51.2906 Chemical Pathology Residency; 51.2907 Child/Pediatric Neurology Residency; 51.2908 Child Psychiatry Residency; 51.2909 Colon and Rectal Surgery Residency; 51.2910 Critical Care Anesthesiology Residency; 51.2911 Critical Care Medicine Residency; 51.2912 Critical Care Surgery Residency; 51.2913 Dermatology Residency; 51.2914 Dermatopathology Residency; 51.2915 Diagnostic Radiology Residency; 51.2916 Emergency Medicine Residency; 51.2917 Endocrinology and Metabolism Residency; 51.2918 Family Medicine Residency; 51.2919 Forensic Pathology Residency; 51.2920 Gastroenterology Residency; 51.2921 General Surgery Residency; 51.2922 Geriatric Medicine Residency; 51.2923 Hand Surgery Residency; 51.2924 Hematology Residency; 51.2925 Hematological Pathology Residency; 51.2926 Immunopathology Residency; 51.2927 Infectious Disease Residency; 51.2928 Internal Medicine Residency; 51.2929 Laboratory Medicine Residency; 51.2930 Musculoskeletal Oncology Residency; 51.2931 Neonatal-Perinatal Medicine Residency; 51.2932 Nephrology Residency; 51.2933 Neurological Surgery/Neurosurgery Residency; 51.2934 Neurology Residency; 51.2935 Neuropathology Residency; 51.2936 Nuclear Medicine Residency; 51.2937 Nuclear Radiology Residency; 51.2938 Obstetrics and Gynecology Residency; 51.2939 Occupational Medicine Residency; 51.2940 Oncology Residency; 51.2941 Ophthalmology Residency; 51.2942 Orthopedics/Orthopedic Surgery Residency; 51.2943 Otolaryngology Residency; 51.2944 Pathology Residency; 51.2945 Pediatric Cardiology Residency; 51.2946 Pediatric Endocrinology Residency; 51.2947 Pediatric Hemato-Oncology Residency; 51.2948 Pediatric Nephrology Residency; 51.2949 Pediatric Orthopedics Residency; 51.2950 Pediatric Surgery Residency; 51.2951 Pediatrics Residency; 51.2952 Physical and Rehabilitation Medicine Residency; 51.2953 Plastic Surgery Residency; 51.2954 Preventive Medicine Residency; 51.2955 Psychiatry Residency; 51.2956 Public Health Medicine Residency; 51.2957 Pulmonary Disease Residency; 51.2958 Radiation Oncology Residency; 51.2959 Radioisotopic Pathology Residency; 51.2960 Rheumatology Residency; 51.2961 Sports Medicine Residency; 51.2962 Thoracic Surgery Residency; 51.2963 Urology Residency; 51.2964 Vascular Surgery Residency. **Related Courses:** Administration and Management; Clerical; Food Production; Computers and Electronics; Mathematics; Physics; Chemistry; Biology; Psychology; Medicine and Dentistry; Therapy and Counseling; Education and Training; English Language; Communications and Media.

CHEMISTRY TEACHERS—POSTSECONDARY (31204)

Teach courses pertaining to the chemical and physical properties and compositional changes of substances. Work may include instruction in the methods of qualitative and quantitative chemical analysis.

Average Yearly Earnings: $44,800. **Experience:** Extensive preparation is needed. Extensive skill, knowledge, and experience are needed for this occupation. It may require more than five years of experience. **Education:** A bachelor's degree is the minimum formal education required for this group of occupations. However, many also require graduate school. For example, they may require a master's degree, and some require a Ph.D., M.D., or J.D. (law degree). **Training:** Employees in this type of occupation may need some on-the-job training, but most of these occupations assume that the person will already have the required skills, knowledge, work-related experience, and/or training. **Examples:** Other occupations like this one often involve coordinating, training, supervising, or managing the activities of others to accomplish goals. Very advanced communication and organizational skills are required. Examples include athletic trainers, lawyers, managing editors, physicists, social psychologists, and surgeons. **Standard Vocational Preparation Range:** 8.0 to 9.0—Four years to more than ten years. **Major/Instructional Program:** 40.0101 Physical Sciences, General; 40.0501 Chemistry, General; 40.0502 Analytical Chemistry; 40.0503 Inorganic Chemistry; 40.0504 Organic Chemistry; 40.0505 Medicinal/Pharmaceutical Chemistry; 40.0506 Physical and Theoretical Chemistry; 40.0507 Polymer Chemistry. **Related Courses:** Administration and Management; Computers and Electronics; Engineering and Technology; Mathematics; Physics; Chemistry; Biology; Psychology; Sociology and Anthropology; Education and Training; English Language; Foreign Language.

PHYSICS TEACHERS—POSTSECONDARY (31206)

Teach courses pertaining to the laws of matter and energy.

Average Yearly Earnings: $44,800. **Experience:** Extensive preparation is needed. Extensive skill, knowledge, and experience are needed for this occupation. It may require more than five years of experience. **Education:** A bachelor's degree is the minimum formal education required for this group of occupations. However, many also require graduate school. For example, they may require a master's degree, and some require a Ph.D., M.D., or J.D. (law degree). **Training:** Employees in this type of occupation may need some on-the-job training, but most of these occupations assume that the person will already have the required skills, knowledge, work-related experience, and/or training. **Examples:** Other occupations like this one often involve coordinating, training, supervising, or managing the activities of others to accomplish goals. Very advanced communication and organizational skills are required. Examples include athletic trainers, lawyers, managing editors, physicists, social psychologists, and surgeons. **Standard Vocational Preparation Range:** 8.0 to 9.0—Four years to more than ten years. **Major/Instructional Program:** 30.0101 Biological and Physical Sciences; 40.0101 Physical Sciences, General; 40.0801 Physics, General; 40.0802 Chemical and Atomic/Molecular Physics;

40.0804 Elementary Particle Physics; 40.0805 Plasma and High-Temperature Physics; 40.0806 Nuclear Physics; 40.0807 Optics; 40.0808 Solid-State and Low-Temperature Physics; 40.0809 Acoustics; 40.0810 Theoretical and Mathematical Physics. **Related Courses:** Administration and Management; Engineering and Technology; Mathematics; Physics; Chemistry; Psychology; Sociology and Anthropology; Therapy and Counseling; Education and Training; English Language; Foreign Language; History and Archeology; Philosophy and Theology.

SOCIAL SCIENCE TEACHERS—POSTSECONDARY (31210)

Teach courses pertaining to human society and its characteristic elements, with economic and social relations and with scientific data relating to human behavior and mental processes. Includes teachers of subjects such as psychology, economics, history, political science, and sociology.

Average Yearly Earnings: $44,800. **Experience:** Extensive preparation is needed. Extensive skill, knowledge, and experience are needed for this occupation. It may require more than five years of experience. **Education:** A bachelor's degree is the minimum formal education required for this group of occupations. However, many also require graduate school. For example, they may require a master's degree, and some require a Ph.D., M.D., or J.D. (law degree). **Training:** Employees in this type of occupation may need some on-the-job training, but most of these occupations assume that the person will already have the required skills, knowledge, work-related experience, and/or training. **Examples:** Other occupations like this one often involve coordinating, training, supervising, or managing the activities of others to accomplish goals. Very advanced communication and organizational skills are required. Examples include athletic trainers, lawyers, managing editors, physicists, social psychologists, and surgeons. **Standard Vocational Preparation Range:** 8.0 to 9.0—Four years to more than ten years. **Major/Instructional Program:** 01.0101 Agricultural Business and Management, General; 01.0103 Agricultural Economics; 05.0101 African Studies; 05.0102 American Studies/Civilization; 05.0103 Asian Studies; 05.0104 East Asian Studies; 05.0105 Eastern European Area Studies; 05.0106 European Studies; 05.0107 Latin American Studies; 05.0108 Middle Eastern Studies; 05.0109 Pacific Area Studies; 05.0110 Russian and Slavic Area Studies; 05.0111 Scandinavian Area Studies; 05.0112 South Asian Studies; 05.0113 Southeast Asian Studies; 05.0114 Western European Studies; 05.0115 Canadian Studies; 05.0201 Afro-American (Black) Studies; 05.0202 American Indian/Native American Studies; 05.0203 Hispanic-American Studies; 05.0204 Islamic Studies; 05.0205 Jewish/Judaic Studies; 05.0206 Asian-American Studies; 05.0207 Women's Studies; 30.0501 Peace and Conflict Studies; 30.1101 Gerontology; 30.1301 Medieval and Renaissance Studies; 30.1501 Science, Technology and Society; 31.0501 Health and Physical Education, General; 31.0506 Socio-Psychological Sports Studies; 42.0101 Psychology, General; 42.0201 Clinical Psychology; 42.0301 Cognitive Psychology and Psycholinguistics; 42.0401 Community Psychology; 42.0601 Counseling Psychology; 42.0701 Developmental and Child Psychology; 42.0801 Experimental Psychology; 42.0901 Industrial and Organizational Psychology; 42.1101 Physiological Psychology/Psychobiology; 42.1601 Social Psychology; 42.1701 School Psychology;

43.0102 Corrections/Correctional Administration; 43.0103 Criminal Justice/Law Enforcement Administration; 43.0104 Criminal Justice Studies; 45.0101 Social Sciences, General; 45.0201 Anthropology; 45.0301 Archeology; 45.0401 Criminology; 45.0501 Demography and Population Studies; 45.0601 Economics, General; 45.0602 Applied and Resource Economics; 45.0603 Econometrics and Quantitative Economics; 45.0604 Development Economics and International Development; 45.0605 International Economics; 45.0801 History, General; 45.0802 American (United States) History; 45.0803 European History; 45.0804 History and Philosophy of Science; 45.0805 Public/Applied History and Archival Administration; 45.0901 International Relations and Affairs; 45.1001 Political Science and Government, General; 45.1002 American Government and Politics (United States); 45.1101 Sociology; 45.1201 Urban Studies/Affairs; 52.0601 Business/Managerial Economics. **Related Courses:** Administration and Management; Clerical; Economics and Accounting; Personnel and Human Resources; Computers and Electronics; Mathematics; Psychology; Sociology and Anthropology; Geography; Therapy and Counseling; Education and Training; English Language; History and Archeology; Philosophy and Theology; Law, Government, and Jurisprudence; Communications and Media.

HEALTH SPECIALTIES TEACHERS—POSTSECONDARY (31212)

Teach courses in health specialties such as veterinary medicine, dentistry, pharmacy, therapy, laboratory technology, and public health. Exclude nursing instructors and medical sciences teachers.

Average Yearly Earnings: $44,800. **Experience:** Extensive preparation is needed. Extensive skill, knowledge, and experience are needed for this occupation. It may require more than five years of experience. **Education:** A bachelor's degree is the minimum formal education required for this group of occupations. However, many also require graduate school. For example, they may require a master's degree, and some require a Ph.D., M.D., or J.D. (law degree). **Training:** Employees in this type of occupation may need some on-the-job training, but most of these occupations assume that the person will already have the required skills, knowledge, work-related experience, and/or training. **Examples:** Other occupations like this one often involve coordinating, training, supervising, or managing the activities of others to accomplish goals. Very advanced communication and organizational skills are required. Examples include athletic trainers, lawyers, managing editors, physicists, social psychologists, and surgeons. **Standard Vocational Preparation Range:** 8.0 to 9.0—Four years to more than ten years. **Major/Instructional Program:** 30.1101 Gerontology; 31.0501 Health and Physical Education, General; 31.0502 Adapted Physical Education/Therapeutic Recreation; 31.0503 Athletic Training and Sports Medicine; 31.0505 Exercise Sciences/Physiology and Movement Studies; 51.0101 Chiropractic (D.C., D.C.M.); 51.0201 Communication Disorders, General; 51.0202 Audiology/Hearing Sciences; 51.0203 Speech-Language Pathology; 51.0204 Speech Pathology and Audiology; 51.0205 Sign Language Interpreter; 51.0301 Community Health Liaison; 51.0501 Dentistry (D.D.S., D.M.D.); 51.0602 Dental Hygienist; 51.0603 Dental Laboratory Technician; 51.0701 Health Systems/Health Services Administration; 51.0702 Hospital/Health Facilities Administration; 51.0807 Physician Assistant; 51.0901 Cardiovascular

Technology/Technician; 51.0902 Electrocardiograph Technology/Technician; 51.0903 Electroencephalograph Technology/Technician; 51.0904 Emergency Medical Technology/Technician; 51.0905 Nuclear Medical Technology/Technician; 51.0906 Perfusion Technology/Technician; 51.0907 Medical Radiologic Technology/Technician; 51.0908 Respiratory Therapy Technician; 51.0909 Surgical/Operating Room Technician; 51.0910 Diagnostic Medical Sonography Technician; 51.1005 Medical Technology; 51.1502 Psychiatric/Mental Health Services Technician; 51.1503 Clinical and Medical Social Work; 51.1701 Optometry (O.D.).; 51.1901 Osteopathic Medicine (D.O.).; 51.2001 Pharmacy (B.Pharm., Pharm.D.).; 51.2002 Pharmacy Administration and Pharmaceutics; 51.2003 Medical Pharmacology and Pharmaceutical Sciences; 51.2101 Podiatry (D.P.M., D.P., Pod.D.); 51.2201 Public Health, General; 51.2202 Environmental Health; 51.2203 Epidemiology; 51.2205 Health Physics/Radiologic Health; 51.2206 Occupational Health and Industrial Hygiene; 51.2207 Public Health Education and Promotion; 51.2301 Art Therapy; 51.2302 Dance Therapy; 51.2303 Hypnotherapy; 51.2304 Movement Therapy; 51.2305 Music Therapy; 51.2306 Occupational Therapy; 51.2307 Orthotics/Prosthetics; 51.2308 Physical Therapy; 51.2309 Recreational Therapy; 51.2310 Vocational Rehabilitation Counseling; 51.2399 Rehabilitation/Therapeutic Services, Other; 51.2401 Veterinary Medicine (D.V.M.).; 51.2501 Veterinary Clinical Sciences (M.S., Ph.D.); 51.2701 Acupuncture and Oriental Medicine; 51.2702 Medical Dietician; 51.2703 Medical Illustrating; 51.2704 Naturopathic Medicine; 51.2705 Psychoanalysis; 51.2801 Dental/Oral Surgery Specialty; 51.2802 Dental Public Health Specialty; 51.2803 Endodontics Specialty; 51.2804 Oral Pathology Specialty; 51.2805 Orthodontics Specialty; 51.2806 Pedodontics Specialty; 51.2807 Periodontics Specialty; 51.2808 Prosthodontics Specialty; 51.3001 Veterinary Anesthesiology; 51.3002 Veterinary Dentistry; 51.3003 Veterinary Dermatology; 51.3004 Veterinary Emergency and Critical Care Medicine; 51.3005 Veterinary Internal Medicine; 51.3006 Laboratory Animal Medicine; 51.3007 Veterinary Microbiology; 51.3008 Veterinary Nutrition; 51.3009 Veterinary Ophthalmology; 51.3010 Veterinary Pathology; 51.3011 Veterinary Practice; 51.3012 Veterinary Preventive Medicine; 51.3013 Veterinary Radiology; 51.3014 Veterinary Surgery; 51.3015 Theriogenology; 51.3016 Veterinary Toxicology; 51.3017 Zoological Medicine. **Related Courses:** Administration and Management; Clerical; Computers and Electronics; Mathematics; Chemistry; Biology; Psychology; Sociology and Anthropology; Medicine and Dentistry; Therapy and Counseling; Education and Training; English Language; Philosophy and Theology; Law, Government, and Jurisprudence; Communications and Media.

ENGLISH AND FOREIGN LANGUAGE TEACHERS—POSTSECONDARY (31216)

Teach courses in English language and literature or in foreign languages and literature. Includes teachers of subjects such as journalism, classics, and linguistics.

Average Yearly Earnings: $44,800. **Experience:** Extensive preparation is needed. Extensive skill, knowledge, and experience are needed for this occupation. It may require more than five years of experience. **Education:** A bachelor's degree is the minimum formal education required for this group of occupations. However, many also require graduate

school. For example, they may require a master's degree, and some require a Ph.D., M.D., or J.D. (law degree). **Training:** Employees in this type of occupation may need some on-the-job training, but most of these occupations assume that the person will already have the required skills, knowledge, work-related experience, and/or training. **Examples:** Other occupations like this one often involve coordinating, training, supervising, or managing the activities of others to accomplish goals. Very advanced communication and organizational skills are required. Examples include athletic trainers, lawyers, managing editors, physicists, social psychologists, and surgeons. **Standard Vocational Preparation Range:** 8.0 to 9.0—Four years to more than ten years. **Major/Instructional Program:** 09.0401 Journalism; 16.0101 Foreign Languages and Literatures, General; 16.0102 Linguistics; 16.0103 Foreign Language Interpretation and Translation; 16.0301 Chinese Language and Literature; 16.0302 Japanese Language and Literature; 16.0399 East and Southeast Asian Languages and Literatures, Other; 16.0402 Russian Language and Literature; 16.0403 Slavic Languages and Literatures (Other than Russian); 16.0499 East European Languages and Literatures, Other; 16.0501 German Language and Literature; 16.0502 Scandinavian Languages and Literatures; 16.0599 Germanic Languages and Literatures, Other; 16.0601 Greek Language and Literature (Modern); 16.0703 South Asian Languages and Literatures; 16.0901 French Language and Literature; 16.0902 Italian Language and Literature; 16.0904 Portuguese Language and Literature; 16.0905 Spanish Language and Literature; 16.0999 Romance Languages and Literatures, Other; 16.1101 Arabic Language and Literature; 16.1102 Hebrew Language and Literature; 16.1199 Middle Eastern Languages and Literatures, Other; 16.1201 Classics and Classical Languages and Literatures; 16.1202 Greek Language and Literature (Ancient and Medieval); 16.1203 Latin Language and Literature (Ancient and Medieval); 16.1299 Classical and Ancient Near Eastern Languages and Literatures, Other; 23.0101 English Language and Literature, General; 23.0301 Comparative Literature; 23.0401 English Composition; 23.0501 English Creative Writing; 23.0701 American Literature (United States); 23.0801 English Literature (British and Commonwealth); 23.1001 Speech and Rhetorical Studies; 23.1101 English Technical and Business Writing. **Related Courses:** Clerical; Computers and Electronics; Sociology and Anthropology; Therapy and Counseling; Education and Training; English Language; Foreign Language; History and Archeology; Philosophy and Theology; Communications and Media.

ART, DRAMA, AND MUSIC TEACHERS—POSTSECONDARY (31218)

Teach courses in art, drama, and music, including painting and sculpture.

Average Yearly Earnings: $44,800. **Experience:** Extensive preparation is needed. Extensive skill, knowledge, and experience are needed for this occupation. It may require more than five years of experience. **Education:** A bachelor's degree is the minimum formal education required for this group of occupations. However, many also require graduate school. For example, they may require a master's degree, and some require a Ph.D., M.D., or J.D. (law degree). **Training:** Employees in this type of occupation may need some on-the-job training, but most of these occupations assume that the person will already have the required skills, knowledge, work-related experience, and/or training.

Examples: Other occupations like this one often involve coordinating, training, supervising, or managing the activities of others to accomplish goals. Very advanced communication and organizational skills are required. Examples include athletic trainers, lawyers, managing editors, physicists, social psychologists, and surgeons. **Standard Vocational Preparation Range:** 8.0 to 9.0—Four years to more than ten years. **Major/Instructional Program:** 50.0201 Crafts, Folk Art, and Artisanry; 50.0301 Dance; 50.0501 Drama/Theater Arts, General; 50.0502 Technical Theater/Theater Design and Stagecraft; 50.0503 Acting and Directing; 50.0504 Playwriting and Screenwriting; 50.0505 Drama/Theater Literature, History, and Criticism; 50.0601 Film/Cinema Studies; 50.0602 Film-Video Making/Cinematography and Production; 50.0605 Photography; 50.0701 Art, General; 50.0702 Fine/Studio Arts; 50.0703 Art History, Criticism, and Conservation; 50.0704 Arts Management; 50.0705 Drawing; 50.0706 Intermedia; 50.0708 Painting; 50.0709 Sculpture; 50.0710 Printmaking; 50.0711 Ceramic Arts and Ceramics; 50.0712 Fiber, Textile, and Weaving Arts; 50.0713 Metal and Jewelry Arts; 50.0901 Music, General; 50.0902 Music History and Literature; 50.0903 Music—General Performance; 50.0904 Music Theory and Composition; 50.0905 Musicology and Ethnomusicology; 50.0906 Music Conducting; 50.0907 Music—Piano and Organ Performance; 50.0908 Music—Voice and Choral/Opera Performance; 50.0909 Music Business Management and Merchandising. **Related Courses:** Administration and Management; Clerical; Sociology and Anthropology; Therapy and Counseling; Education and Training; English Language; Fine Arts; History and Archeology; Philosophy and Theology; Communications and Media.

ENGINEERING TEACHERS—POSTSECONDARY (31222)

Teach courses pertaining to the application of physical laws and principles of engineering for the development of machines, materials, instruments, processes, and services. Includes teachers of subjects such as chemical, civil, electrical, industrial, mechanical, mineral, and petroleum engineering.

Average Yearly Earnings: $44,800. **Experience:** Extensive preparation is needed. Extensive skill, knowledge, and experience are needed for this occupation. It may require more than five years of experience. **Education:** A bachelor's degree is the minimum formal education required for this group of occupations. However, many also require graduate school. For example, they may require a master's degree, and some require a Ph.D., M.D., or J.D. (law degree). **Training:** Employees in this type of occupation may need some on-the-job training, but most of these occupations assume that the person will already have the required skills, knowledge, work-related experience, and/or training. **Examples:** Other occupations like this one often involve coordinating, training, supervising, or managing the activities of others to accomplish goals. Very advanced communication and organizational skills are required. Examples include athletic trainers, lawyers, managing editors, physicists, social psychologists, and surgeons. **Standard Vocational Preparation Range:** 8.0 to 9.0—Four years to more than ten years. **Major/Instructional Program:** 14.0101 Engineering, General; 14.0201 Aerospace, Aeronautical, and Astronautical Engineering; 14.0301 Agricultural Engineering; 14.0401 Architectural Engineering; 14.0501 Bioengineering and Biomedical Engineering; 14.0601 Ceramic Sciences and

Engineering; 14.0701 Chemical Engineering; 14.0801 Civil Engineering, General; 14.0802 Geotechnical Engineering; 14.0803 Structural Engineering; 14.0804 Transportation and Highway Engineering; 14.0805 Water Resources Engineering; 14.0901 Computer Engineering; 14.1001 Electrical, Electronics, and Communications Engineering; 14.1101 Engineering Mechanics; 14.1201 Engineering Physics; 14.1301 Engineering Science; 14.1401 Environmental/Environmental Health Engineering; 14.1501 Geological Engineering; 14.1601 Geophysical Engineering; 14.1701 Industrial/Manufacturing Engineering; 14.1801 Materials Engineering; 14.1901 Mechanical Engineering; 14.2001 Metallurgical Engineering; 14.2101 Mining and Mineral Engineering; 14.2201 Naval Architecture and Marine Engineering; 14.2301 Nuclear Engineering; 14.2401 Ocean Engineering; 14.2501 Petroleum Engineering; 14.2701 Systems Engineering; 14.2801 Textile Sciences and Engineering; 14.2901 Engineering Design; 14.3001 Engineering/Industrial Management; 14.3101 Materials Science; 14.3201 Polymer/Plastics Engineering; 15.1101 Engineering Technology/Technician, General. **Related Courses:** Administration and Management; Clerical; Computers and Electronics; Engineering and Technology; Design; Building and Construction; Mathematics; Physics; Chemistry; Therapy and Counseling; Education and Training; English Language; Telecommunications; Communications and Media.

MATHEMATICAL SCIENCES TEACHERS—POSTSECONDARY (31224)

Teach courses pertaining to mathematical concepts, statistics, and actuarial science and to the application of original and standardized mathematical techniques in solving specific problems and situations.

Average Yearly Earnings: $44,800. **Experience:** Extensive preparation is needed. Extensive skill, knowledge, and experience are needed for this occupation. It may require more than five years of experience. **Education:** A bachelor's degree is the minimum formal education required for this group of occupations. However, many also require graduate school. For example, they may require a master's degree, and some require a Ph.D., M.D., or J.D. (law degree). **Training:** Employees in this type of occupation may need some on-the-job training, but most of these occupations assume that the person will already have the required skills, knowledge, work-related experience, and/or training. **Examples:** Other occupations like this one often involve coordinating, training, supervising, or managing the activities of others to accomplish goals. Very advanced communication and organizational skills are required. Examples include athletic trainers, lawyers, managing editors, physicists, social psychologists, and surgeons. **Standard Vocational Preparation Range:** 8.0 to 9.0—Four years to more than ten years. **Major/Instructional Program:** 26.0615 Biostatistics; 27.0101 Mathematics; 27.0301 Applied Mathematics, General; 27.0302 Operations Research; 27.0501 Mathematical Statistics; 30.0801 Mathematics and Computer Science; 51.1303 Medical Biomathematics and Biometrics; 51.2204 Health and Medical Biostatistics; 52.0801 Finance, General; 52.0802 Actuarial Science; 52.1302 Business Statistics. **Related Courses:** Administration and Management; Clerical; Computers and Electronics; Mathematics; Education and Training; English Language; Philosophy and Theology; Communications and Media.

COMPUTER SCIENCE TEACHERS—POSTSECONDARY (31226)

Teach courses in computer science. May specialize in a field of computer science, such as the design and function of computers or operations and research analysis.

Average Yearly Earnings: $44,800. **Experience:** Extensive preparation is needed. Extensive skill, knowledge, and experience are needed for this occupation. It may require more than five years of experience. **Education:** A bachelor's degree is the minimum formal education required for this group of occupations. However, many also require graduate school. For example, they may require a master's degree, and some require a Ph.D., M.D., or J.D. (law degree). **Training:** Employees in this type of occupation may need some on-the-job training, but most of these occupations assume that the person will already have the required skills, knowledge, work-related experience, and/or training. **Examples:** Other occupations like this one often involve coordinating, training, supervising, or managing the activities of others to accomplish goals. Very advanced communication and organizational skills are required. Examples include athletic trainers, lawyers, managing editors, physicists, social psychologists, and surgeons. **Standard Vocational Preparation Range:** 8.0 to 9.0—Four years to more than ten years. **Major/Instructional Program:** 11.0101 Computer and Information Sciences, General; 11.0201 Computer Programming; 11.0401 Information Sciences and Systems; 11.0501 Computer Systems Analysis; 11.0701 Computer Science; 30.0801 Mathematics and Computer Science; 52.1201 Management Information Systems and Business Data Processing, General; 52.1202 Business Computer Programming/Programmer; 52.1203 Business Systems Analysis and Design; 52.1204 Business Systems Networking and Telecommunications. **Related Courses:** Administration and Management; Clerical; Computers and Electronics; Engineering and Technology; Design; Mathematics; Physics; Psychology; Sociology and Anthropology; Therapy and Counseling; Education and Training; English Language; Philosophy and Theology; Telecommunications; Communications and Media.

Preschool, Kindergarten, Elementary, Secondary, and Special Education Teachers and Instructors

TEACHERS—PRESCHOOL (31303)

Instruct children (normally up to five years of age) in activities designed to promote social, physical, and intellectual growth needed for primary school in preschool, day-care center, or other child development facility. May be required to hold state certification.

Average Yearly Earnings: $30,180. **Experience:** Considerable preparation is needed. A minimum of two to four years of work-related skill, knowledge, or experience is needed for this occupation. **Education:** This group of occupations usually requires a four-year bachelor's degree, but in some cases does not. **Training:** Employees in this type of occupation usually need several years of work-related experience, on-the-job training,

and/or vocational training. **Related Examples:** Other occupations like this one usually involve coordinating, supervising, managing, or training others. Examples include accountants, chefs and head cooks, computer programmers, historians, pharmacists, and police detectives. **Standard Vocational Preparation Range:** 7.0 to below 8.0—Two years to less than ten years. **Major/Instructional Program:** 13.0101 Education, General; 13.0201 Bilingual/Bicultural Education; 13.0401 Education Administration and Supervision, General; 13.0404 Educational Supervision; 13.1204 Pre-Elementary/Early Childhood/Kindergarten Teacher Education; 13.1206 Teacher Education, Multiple Levels; 13.1302 Art Teacher Education; 13.1305 English Teacher Education; 13.1306 Foreign Languages Teacher Education; 13.1311 Mathematics Teacher Education; 13.1312 Music Teacher Education; 13.1314 Physical Education Teaching and Coaching; 13.1315 Reading Teacher Education; 13.1316 Science Teacher Education, General; 13.1318 Social Studies Teacher Education; 13.1324 Drama and Dance Teacher Education; 13.1325 French Language Teacher Education; 13.1326 German Language Teacher Education; 13.1330 Spanish Language Teacher Education; 13.1331 Speech Teacher Education; 13.1399 Teacher Education, Specific Academic and Vocational Programs, Other; 20.0201 Childcare and Guidance Workers and Managers, General; 20.0203 Childcare Services Manager. **Related Courses:** Customer and Personal Service; Psychology; Sociology and Anthropology; Therapy and Counseling; Education and Training; Foreign Language; Fine Arts; History and Archeology; Philosophy and Theology.

TEACHERS—KINDERGARTEN (31304)

Teach elemental natural and social science, personal hygiene, music, art, and literature to children from four to six years old. Promote physical, mental, and social development. May be required to hold state certification.

Average Yearly Earnings: $30,180. **Experience:** Considerable preparation is needed. A minimum of two to four years of work-related skill, knowledge, or experience is needed for this occupation. **Education:** This group of occupations usually requires a four-year bachelor's degree, but in some cases does not. **Training:** Employees in this type of occupation usually need several years of work-related experience, on-the-job training, and/or vocational training. **Related Examples:** Other occupations like this one usually involve coordinating, supervising, managing, or training others. Examples include accountants, chefs and head cooks, computer programmers, historians, pharmacists, and police detectives. **Standard Vocational Preparation Range:** 7.0 to below 8.0—Two years to less than ten years. **Major/Instructional Program:** 13.0101 Education, General; 13.0201 Bilingual/Bicultural Education; 13.0401 Education Administration and Supervision, General; 13.0404 Educational Supervision; 13.1202 Elementary Teacher Education; 13.1204 Pre-Elementary/Early Childhood/Kindergarten Teacher Education; 13.1206 Teacher Education, Multiple Levels; 13.1302 Art Teacher Education; 13.1305 English Teacher Education; 13.1306 Foreign Languages Teacher Education; 13.1311 Mathematics Teacher Education; 13.1312 Music Teacher Education; 13.1314 Physical Education Teaching and Coaching; 13.1315 Reading Teacher Education; 13.1316 Science Teacher Education, General; 13.1318 Social Studies Teacher Education; 13.1324 Drama and Dance Teacher

Education; 13.1325 French Language Teacher Education; 13.1326 German Language Teacher Education; 13.1330 Spanish Language Teacher Education; 13.1331 Speech Teacher Education; 13.1399 Teacher Education, Specific Academic and Vocational Programs, Other. **Related Courses:** Customer and Personal Service; Psychology; Sociology and Anthropology; Geography; Medicine and Dentistry; Therapy and Counseling; Education and Training; English Language; Foreign Language; Fine Arts; History and Archeology; Philosophy and Theology; Law, Government, and Jurisprudence; Communications and Media.

TEACHERS—ELEMENTARY SCHOOL (31305)

Teach elementary pupils in public or private schools basic academic, social, and other formulative skills. Excludes special education teachers of the handicapped.

Average Yearly Earnings: $35,280. **Experience:** Considerable preparation is needed. A minimum of two to four years of work-related skill, knowledge, or experience is needed for this occupation. **Education:** This group of occupations usually requires a four-year bachelor's degree, but in some cases does not. **Training:** Employees in this type of occupation usually need several years of work-related experience, on-the-job training, and/or vocational training. **Related Examples:** Other occupations like this one usually involve coordinating, supervising, managing, or training others. Examples include accountants, chefs and head cooks, computer programmers, historians, pharmacists, and police detectives. **Standard Vocational Preparation Range:** 7.0 to below 8.0—Two years to less than ten years. **Major/Instructional Program:** 13.0101 Education, General; 13.0201 Bilingual/Bicultural Education; 13.0401 Education Administration and Supervision, General; 13.0404 Educational Supervision; 13.1202 Elementary Teacher Education; 13.1203 Junior High/Intermediate/Middle School Teacher Education; 13.1204 Pre-Elementary/ Early Childhood/Kindergarten Teacher Education; 13.1206 Teacher Education, Multiple Levels; 13.1301 Agricultural Teacher Education (Vocational); 13.1302 Art Teacher Education; 13.1303 Business Teacher Education (Vocational); 13.1305 English Teacher Education; 13.1306 Foreign Languages Teacher Education; 13.1307 Health Teacher Education; 13.1308 Home Economics Teacher Education (Vocational); 13.1309 Technology Teacher Education/Industrial Arts Teacher Education; 13.1311 Mathematics Teacher Education; 13.1312 Music Teacher Education; 13.1314 Physical Education Teaching and Coaching; 13.1315 Reading Teacher Education; 13.1316 Science Teacher Education, General; 13.1317 Social Science Teacher Education; 13.1318 Social Studies Teacher Education; 13.1321 Computer Teacher Education; 13.1324 Drama and Dance Teacher Education; 13.1325 French Language Teacher Education; 13.1326 German Language Teacher Education; 13.1328 History Teacher Education; 13.1330 Spanish Language Teacher Education; 13.1331 Speech Teacher Education; 13.1399 Teacher Education, Specific Academic and Vocational Programs, Other. **Related Courses:** Administration and Management; Clerical; Customer and Personal Service; Mathematics; Chemistry; Biology; Psychology; Sociology and Anthropology; Geography; Medicine and Dentistry; Therapy and Counseling; Education and Training; English Language; Foreign Language; Fine Arts; History and Archeology; Philosophy and Theology; Law, Government, and Jurisprudence; Transportation.

TEACHERS—SECONDARY SCHOOL (31308)

Instruct students in public or private schools in one or more subjects, such as English, mathematics, or social studies. May be designated according to subject matter specialty, such as typing instructors, commercial teachers, or English teachers. Includes vocational high school teachers.

Average Yearly Earnings: $36,784. **Experience:** Considerable preparation is needed. A minimum of two to four years of work-related skill, knowledge, or experience is needed for this occupation. **Education:** This group of occupations usually requires a four-year bachelor's degree, but in some cases does not. **Training:** Employees in this type of occupation usually need several years of work-related experience, on-the-job training, and/or vocational training. **Related Examples:** Other occupations like this one usually involve coordinating, supervising, managing, or training others. Examples include accountants, chefs and head cooks, computer programmers, historians, pharmacists, and police detectives. **Standard Vocational Preparation Range:** 7.0 to below 8.0—Two years to less than ten years. **Major/Instructional Program:** 13.0101 Education, General; 13.0201 Bilingual/Bicultural Education; 13.0401 Education Administration and Supervision, General; 13.0404 Educational Supervision; 13.1203 Junior High/Intermediate/Middle School Teacher Education; 13.1205 Secondary Teacher Education; 13.1206 Teacher Education, Multiple Levels; 13.1301 Agricultural Teacher Education (Vocational); 13.1302 Art Teacher Education; 13.1303 Business Teacher Education (Vocational); 13.1304 Driver and Safety Teacher Education; 13.1305 English Teacher Education; 13.1306 Foreign Languages Teacher Education; 13.1307 Health Teacher Education; 13.1308 Home Economics Teacher Education (Vocational); 13.1309 Technology Teacher Education/Industrial Arts Teacher Education; 13.1310 Marketing Operations Teacher Education/Marketing and Distributive Teacher Education (Vocational); 13.1311 Mathematics Teacher Education; 13.1312 Music Teacher Education; 13.1314 Physical Education Teaching and Coaching; 13.1315 Reading Teacher Education; 13.1316 Science Teacher Education, General; 13.1317 Social Science Teacher Education; 13.1318 Social Studies Teacher Education; 13.1319 Technical Teacher Education (Vocational); 13.1320 Trade and Industrial Teacher Education (Vocational); 13.1321 Computer Teacher Education; 13.1322 Biology Teacher Education; 13.1323 Chemistry Teacher Education; 13.1324 Drama and Dance Teacher Education; 13.1325 French Language Teacher Education; 13.1326 German Language Teacher Education; 13.1327 Health Occupations Teacher Education (Vocational); 13.1328 History Teacher Education; 13.1329 Physics Teacher Education; 13.1330 Spanish Language Teacher Education; 13.1331 Speech Teacher Education; 13.1399 Teacher Education, Specific Academic and Vocational Programs, Other. **Related Courses:** Administration and Management; Clerical; Psychology; Sociology and Anthropology; Geography; Therapy and Counseling; Education and Training; English Language; Foreign Language; History and Archeology; Philosophy and Theology.

SPECIAL EDUCATION VOCATIONAL TRAINING TEACHERS (31311A)

Plan and conduct special education work and study programs or teach vocational skills to handicapped students.

Average Yearly Earnings: $37,104. **Experience:** Considerable preparation is needed. A minimum of two to four years of work-related skill, knowledge, or experience is needed for this occupation. **Education:** This group of occupations usually requires a four-year bachelor's degree, but in some cases does not. **Training:** Employees in this type of occupation usually need several years of work-related experience, on-the-job training, and/or vocational training. **Related Examples:** Other occupations like this one usually involve coordinating, supervising, managing, or training others. Examples include accountants, chefs and head cooks, computer programmers, historians, pharmacists, and police detectives. **Standard Vocational Preparation Range:** 7.0 to below 8.0—Two years to less than ten years. **Major/Instructional Program:** 13.0101 Education, General; 13.0401 Education Administration and Supervision, General; 13.0402 Administration of Special Education; 13.1001 Special Education, General; 13.1003 Education of the Deaf and Hearing Impaired; 13.1005 Education of the Emotionally Handicapped; 13.1006 Education of the Mentally Handicapped; 13.1007 Education of the Multiple Handicapped; 13.1008 Education of the Physically Handicapped; 13.1009 Education of the Blind and Visually Handicapped; 13.1011 Education of the Specific Learning Disabled; 13.1012 Education of the Speech Impaired. **Related Courses:** Administration and Management; Sales and Marketing; Customer and Personal Service; Personnel and Human Resources; Psychology; Sociology and Anthropology; Therapy and Counseling; Education and Training; Philosophy and Theology.

TEACHERS—EMOTIONALLY IMPAIRED, MENTALLY IMPAIRED, AND LEARNING DISABLED (31311B)

Teach basic academic and living skills to students with emotional or mental impairments or learning disabilities.

Average Yearly Earnings: $37,104. **Experience:** Considerable preparation is needed. A minimum of two to four years of work-related skill, knowledge, or experience is needed for this occupation. **Education:** This group of occupations usually requires a four-year bachelor's degree, but in some cases does not. **Training:** Employees in this type of occupation usually need several years of work-related experience, on-the-job training, and/or vocational training. **Related Examples:** Other occupations like this one usually involve coordinating, supervising, managing, or training others. Examples include accountants, chefs and head cooks, computer programmers, historians, pharmacists, and police detectives. **Standard Vocational Preparation Range:** 7.0 to below 8.0—Two years to less than ten years. **Major/Instructional Program:** 13.0101 Education, General; 13.0201 Bilingual/Bicultural Education; 13.0401 Education Administration and Supervision, General; 13.0402 Administration of Special Education; 13.0404 Educational Supervision; 13.1001 Special Education, General; 13.1003 Education of the Deaf and Hearing Impaired; 13.1005 Education of the Emotionally Handicapped; 13.1006 Education of the Mentally Handicapped; 13.1007 Education of the Multiple Handicapped; 13.1008 Education of the Physically Handicapped; 13.1009 Education of the Blind and Visually Handicapped; 13.1011 Education of the Specific Learning Disabled; 13.1012 Education of the Speech Impaired; 13.1013 Education of the Autistic. **Related Courses:** Customer and Personal Service; Psychology; Sociology and Anthropology; Medicine and Dentistry; Therapy and Counseling; Education and Training; English Language; Foreign Language.

TEACHERS—PHYSICALLY, VISUALLY, AND HEARING IMPAIRED (31311C)

Teach elementary and secondary school subjects to physically, visually, and hearing impaired students.

Average Yearly Earnings: $37,104. **Experience:** Considerable preparation is needed. A minimum of two to four years of work-related skill, knowledge, or experience is needed for this occupation. **Education:** This group of occupations usually requires a four-year bachelor's degree, but in some cases does not. **Training:** Employees in this type of occupation usually need several years of work-related experience, on-the-job training, and/or vocational training. **Related Examples:** Other occupations like this one usually involve coordinating, supervising, managing, or training others. Examples include accountants, chefs and head cooks, computer programmers, historians, pharmacists, and police detectives. **Standard Vocational Preparation Range:** 7.0 to below 8.0—Two years to less than ten years. **Major/Instructional Program:** 13.0101 Education, General; 13.0401 Education Administration and Supervision, General; 13.0402 Administration of Special Education; 13.1001 Special Education, General; 13.1003 Education of the Deaf and Hearing Impaired; 13.1008 Education of the Physically Handicapped; 13.1009 Education of the Blind and Visually Handicapped. **Related Courses:** Administration and Management; Clerical; Customer and Personal Service; Biology; Psychology; Sociology and Anthropology; Therapy and Counseling; Education and Training; English Language; Foreign Language; History and Archeology; Philosophy and Theology.

SPECIAL EDUCATION EVALUATORS (31311D)

Assess type and degree of disability of handicapped children to aid in determining special programs and services required to meet educational needs.

Average Yearly Earnings: $37,104. **Experience:** Considerable preparation is needed. A minimum of two to four years of work-related skill, knowledge, or experience is needed for this occupation. **Education:** This group of occupations usually requires a four-year bachelor's degree, but in some cases does not. **Training:** Employees in this type of occupation usually need several years of work-related experience, on-the-job training, and/or vocational training. **Related Examples:** Other occupations like this one usually involve coordinating, supervising, managing, or training others. Examples include accountants, chefs and head cooks, computer programmers, historians, pharmacists, and police detectives. **Standard Vocational Preparation Range:** 7.0 to below 8.0—Two years to less than ten years. **Major/Instructional Program:** 13.0101 Education, General; 13.0401 Education Administration and Supervision, General; 13.0402 Administration of Special Education; 13.0604 Educational Assessment, Testing, and Measurement; 13.1001 Special Education, General; 13.1003 Education of the Deaf and Hearing Impaired; 13.1005 Education of the Emotionally Handicapped; 13.1006 Education of the Mentally Handicapped; 13.1007 Education of the Multiple Handicapped; 13.1008 Education of the Physically Handicapped; 13.1009 Education of the Blind and Visually Handicapped; 13.1011 Education of the Specific Learning Disabled; 13.1012 Education of the Speech Impaired.

Related Courses: Customer and Personal Service; Psychology; Sociology and Anthropology; Therapy and Counseling; Education and Training.

PARENT INSTRUCTORS—CHILD DEVELOPMENT AND REHABILITATION (31311E)

Instruct parents of mentally and physically handicapped children in therapy techniques and behavior modification.

Average Yearly Earnings: $37,104. **Experience:** Considerable preparation is needed. A minimum of two to four years of work-related skill, knowledge, or experience is needed for this occupation. **Education:** This group of occupations usually requires a four-year bachelor's degree, but in some cases does not. **Training:** Employees in this type of occupation usually need several years of work-related experience, on-the-job training, and/or vocational training. **Related Examples:** Other occupations like this one usually involve coordinating, supervising, managing, or training others. Examples include accountants, chefs and head cooks, computer programmers, historians, pharmacists, and police detectives. **Standard Vocational Preparation Range:** 7.0 to below 8.0—Two years to less than ten years. **Major/Instructional Program:** 13.0101 Education, General; 13.1001 Special Education, General; 13.1003 Education of the Deaf and Hearing Impaired; 13.1005 Education of the Emotionally Handicapped; 13.1006 Education of the Mentally Handicapped; 13.1007 Education of the Multiple Handicapped; 13.1008 Education of the Physically Handicapped; 13.1009 Education of the Blind and Visually Handicapped; 13.1011 Education of the Specific Learning Disabled; 13.1012 Education of the Speech Impaired; 19.0701 Individual and Family Development Studies, General; 19.0706 Child Growth, Care, and Development Studies. **Related Courses:** Customer and Personal Service; Psychology; Sociology and Anthropology; Medicine and Dentistry; Therapy and Counseling; Education and Training.

TEACHERS AND INSTRUCTORS—VOCATIONAL EDUCATION AND TRAINING (31314)

Teach or instruct vocational and/or occupational subjects at the postsecondary level (but at less than the baccalaureate) to students who have graduated or left high school. Subjects include business, secretarial science, data processing, trades, and practical nursing. Includes correspondence school instructors; industrial, commercial, and government training instructors; and adult education teachers and instructors who prepare persons to operate industrial machinery and equipment and transportation and communications equipment. Teaching may take place in public or private schools whose primary business is education or in a school associated with an organization whose primary business is other than education.

Average Yearly Earnings: $33,800. **Experience:** Considerable preparation is needed. A minimum of two to four years of work-related skill, knowledge, or experience is needed

for this occupation. **Education:** This group of occupations usually requires a four-year bachelor's degree, but in some cases does not. **Training:** Employees in this type of occupation usually need several years of work-related experience, on-the-job training, and/ or vocational training. **Related Examples:** Other occupations like this one usually involve coordinating, supervising, managing, or training others. Examples include accountants, chefs and head cooks, computer programmers, historians, pharmacists, and police detectives. **Standard Vocational Preparation Range:** 7.0 to below 8.0—Two years to less than ten years. **Major/Instructional Program:** 01.0401 Agricultural and Food Products Processing Operations and Management; 13.0101 Education, General; 13.0401 Education Administration and Supervision, General; 13.0404 Educational Supervision; 13.1201 Adult and Continuing Teacher Education; 13.1205 Secondary Teacher Education; 13.1206 Teacher Education, Multiple Levels; 13.1301 Agricultural Teacher Education (Vocational); 13.1303 Business Teacher Education (Vocational); 13.1308 Home Economics Teacher Education (Vocational); 13.1310 Marketing Operations Teacher Education/Marketing and Distributive Teacher Education (Vocational); 13.1319 Technical Teacher Education (Vocational); 13.1320 Trade and Industrial Teacher Education (Vocational); 13.1327 Health Occupations Teacher Education (Vocational); 43.0107 Law Enforcement/Police Science; 47.0408 Watch, Clock, and Jewelry Repairer; 47.0608 Aircraft Mechanic/Technician Powerplant; 49.0205 Truck, Bus, and Other Commercial Vehicle Operator; 52.1001 Human Resources Management. **Related Courses:** Sociology and Anthropology; Education and Training; English Language; History and Archeology; Philosophy and Theology.

INSTRUCTORS—NONVOCATIONAL EDUCATION (31317)

Teach or instruct out-of-school youths and adults in courses other than those that normally lead to an occupational objective and are less than the baccalaureate level. Subjects may include self-improvement and nonvocational courses such as Americanization, basic education, art, drama, music, bridge, homemaking, stock market analysis, languages, modeling, flying, dancing, and automobile driving. Teaching may take place in public or private schools or in an organization whose primary business is other than education.

Average Yearly Earnings: $27,372. **Experience:** Considerable preparation is needed. A minimum of two to four years of work-related skill, knowledge, or experience is needed for this occupation. **Education:** This group of occupations usually requires a four-year bachelor's degree, but in some cases does not. **Training:** Employees in this type of occupation usually need several years of work-related experience, on-the-job training, and/ or vocational training. **Related Examples:** Other occupations like this one usually involve coordinating, supervising, managing, or training others. Examples include accountants, chefs and head cooks, computer programmers, historians, pharmacists, and police detectives. **Standard Vocational Preparation Range:** 7.0 to below 8.0—Two years to less than ten years. **Major/Instructional Program:** 13.0101 Education, General; 13.0201 Bilingual/Bicultural Education; 13.1201 Adult and Continuing Teacher Education; 13.1206 Teacher Education, Multiple Levels; 13.1302 Art Teacher Education; 13.1304 Driver and Safety Teacher Education; 13.1310 Marketing Operations Teacher Education/Marketing and Distributive Teacher Education (Vocational); 13.1312 Music Teacher Education;

13.1324 Drama and Dance Teacher Education; 13.1399 Teacher Education, Specific Academic and Vocational Programs, Other; 13.1401 Teaching English as a Second Language/ Foreign Language; 43.0203 Fire Science/Firefighting; 50.0501 Drama/Theater Arts, General; 50.0503 Acting and Directing; 50.0901 Music, General; 50.0903 Music—General Performance. **Related Courses:** Economics and Accounting; Sociology and Anthropology; Education and Training; English Language; Foreign Language; Fine Arts; History and Archeology; Philosophy and Theology.

INSTRUCTORS AND COACHES, SPORTS AND PHYSICAL TRAINING (31321)

Instruct or coach groups or individuals in the fundamentals of sports. Demonstrate techniques and methods of participation. Observe and inform participants of corrective measures necessary to improve their skills. Those required to hold teaching degrees are included in the appropriate teaching category.

Average Yearly Earnings: $22,900. **Experience:** Medium preparation is needed. Previous work-related skill, knowledge, or experience is required for this occupation. **Education:** This group of occupations usually requires training in vocational schools, related on-the-job experience, or an associate degree. A bachelor's degree may be required. **Training:** Employees in this type of occupation usually need one or two years of training involving both on-the-job experience and informal training with experienced workers. **Related Examples:** Other occupations like this one usually involve using communication and organizational skills to coordinate, supervise, manage, or train others to accomplish goals. Examples include dental assistants, electricians, fish and game wardens, legal secretaries, personnel recruiters, and recreation workers. **Standard Vocational Preparation Range:** 6.0 to below 7.0—More than one year and less than four years. **Major/ Instructional Program:** 13.0101 Education, General; 13.0401 Education Administration and Supervision, General; 13.0404 Educational Supervision; 13.1201 Adult and Continuing Teacher Education; 13.1314 Physical Education Teaching and Coaching; 31.0501 Health and Physical Education, General. **Related Courses:** Customer and Personal Service; Psychology; Sociology and Anthropology; Medicine and Dentistry; Therapy and Counseling; Education and Training; History and Archeology.

FARM AND HOME MANAGEMENT ADVISORS (31323)

Advise, instruct, and assist individuals and families engaged in agriculture, agricultural-related processes, or home economics activities. Demonstrate procedures and apply research findings to solve problems; instruct and train in product development, sales, and the utilization of machinery and equipment to promote general welfare. Includes county agricultural agents, feed and farm management advisers, home economists, and extension service advisers.

Average Yearly Earnings: $48,505. **Experience:** Considerable preparation is needed. A minimum of two to four years of work-related skill, knowledge, or experience is needed for this occupation. **Education:** This group of occupations usually requires a four-year

bachelor's degree, but in some cases does not. **Training:** Employees in this type of occupation usually need several years of work-related experience, on-the-job training, and/or vocational training. **Related Examples:** Other occupations like this one usually involve coordinating, supervising, managing, or training others. Examples include accountants, chefs and head cooks, computer programmers, historians, pharmacists, and police detectives. **Standard Vocational Preparation Range:** 7.0 to below 8.0—Two years to less than ten years. **Major/Instructional Program:** 01.0101 Agricultural Business and Management, General; 01.0104 Farm and Ranch Management; 01.0301 Agricultural Production Workers and Managers, General; 01.0302 Agricultural Animal Husbandry and Production Management; 01.0304 Crop Production Operations and Management; 01.0501 Agricultural Supplies Retailing and Wholesaling; 02.0102 Agricultural Extension; 02.0201 Animal Sciences, General; 02.0204 Agricultural Animal Nutrition; 13.0101 Education, General; 13.1301 Agricultural Teacher Education (Vocational); 13.1308 Home Economics Teacher Education (Vocational); 19.0501 Foods and Nutrition Studies, General; 19.0503 Dietetics/Human Nutritional Services; 19.0901 Clothing/Apparel and Textile Studies. **Related Courses:** Administration and Management; Economics and Accounting; Sales and Marketing; Personnel and Human Resources; Food Production; Computers and Electronics; Mathematics; Chemistry; Biology; Education and Training; Communications and Media; Transportation.

Librarians, Curators, and Counselors

LIBRARIANS (31502A)

Administer library services; provide library patrons access to or instruction in accessing library resources; and select, acquire, process, and organize library materials and collections for patron use.

Average Yearly Earnings: $36,628. **Experience:** Considerable preparation is needed. A minimum of two to four years of work-related skill, knowledge, or experience is needed for this occupation. **Education:** This group of occupations usually requires a four-year bachelor's degree, but in some cases does not. **Training:** Employees in this type of occupation usually need several years of work-related experience, on-the-job training, and/or vocational training. **Related Examples:** Other occupations like this one usually involve coordinating, supervising, managing, or training others. Examples include accountants, chefs and head cooks, computer programmers, historians, pharmacists, and police detectives. **Standard Vocational Preparation Range:** 7.0 to below 8.0—Two years to less than ten years. **Major/Instructional Program:** 13.0501 Educational/Instructional Media Design, 25.0101 Library Science/Librarianship. **Related Courses:** Administration and Management; Clerical; Sales and Marketing; Customer and Personal Service; Personnel and Human Resources; Computers and Electronics; Psychology; Sociology and Anthropology; Geography; Education and Training; English Language; Foreign Language; Fine Arts; History and Archeology; Philosophy and Theology; Communications and Media.

LIBRARY RESEARCH WORKERS (31502B)

Research specific subjects and make information available to library patrons on an individual basis.

Average Yearly Earnings: $36,628. **Experience:** Medium preparation is needed. Previous work-related skill, knowledge, or experience is required for this occupation. **Education:** This group of occupations usually requires training in vocational schools, related on-the-job experience, or an associate degree. A bachelor's degree may be required. **Training:** Employees in this type of occupation usually need one or two years of training involving both on-the-job experience and informal training with experienced workers. **Related Examples:** Other occupations like this one usually involve using communication and organizational skills to coordinate, supervise, manage, or train others to accomplish goals. Examples include dental assistants, electricians, fish and game wardens, legal secretaries, personnel recruiters, and recreation workers. **Standard Vocational Preparation Range:** 6.0 to below 7.0—More than one year and less than four years. **Major/Instructional Program:** 25.0301 Library Assistant. **Related Courses:** Customer and Personal Service; English Language; Foreign Language; Philosophy and Theology; Communications and Media.

TECHNICAL ASSISTANTS, LIBRARY (31505)

Assist librarians by furnishing information on library sciences, facilities, and rules; by assisting readers in the use of card catalogs and indexes to locate books and other materials; and by answering questions that require only brief consultation of standard reference. May catalog books or train and supervise clerical staff.

Average Yearly Earnings: $20,945. **Experience:** Some preparation is needed. Some previous work-related skill, knowledge, or experience may be helpful in this occupation, but usually is not needed. **Education:** This group of occupations usually requires a high school diploma and may require some vocational training or job-related course work. In some cases, an associate or bachelor's degree could be needed. **Training:** Employees in this type of occupation need anywhere from a few months to one year of working with experienced employees. **Related Examples:** Other occupations like this one often involve using your knowledge and skills to help others. Examples include drywall installers, fire inspectors, flight attendants, pharmacy technicians, retail salespersons, and tellers. **Standard Vocational Preparation Range:** 4.0 to below 6.0—Six months to less than two years. **Major/Instructional Program:** 25.0301 Library Assistant. **Related Courses:** Clerical; Customer and Personal Service; English Language; Communications and Media.

AUDIO-VISUAL SPECIALISTS (31508)

Plan and prepare audio-visual teaching aids and methods for use in a school system.

Average Yearly Earnings: $20,945. **Experience:** Considerable preparation is needed. A minimum of two to four years of work-related skill, knowledge, or experience is needed for this occupation. **Education:** This group of occupations usually requires a four-year bachelor's degree, but in some cases does not. **Training:** Employees in this type of occupation usually need several years of work-related experience, on-the-job training, and/or vocational training. **Related Examples:** Other occupations like this one usually involve coordinating, supervising, managing, or training others. Examples include accountants, chefs and head cooks, computer programmers, historians, pharmacists, and police detectives. **Standard Vocational Preparation Range:** 7.0 to below 8.0—Two years to less than ten years. **Major/Instructional Program:** 10.0101 Educational/Instructional Media Technology/Technician, 13.0501 Educational/Instructional Media Design. **Related Courses:** Administration and Management; Economics and Accounting; Personnel and Human Resources; Computers and Electronics; Building and Construction; Psychology; Education and Training; English Language; Fine Arts; History and Archeology; Telecommunications; Communications and Media.

CURATORS (31511A)

Plan, direct, and coordinate the activities of an exhibiting institution, such as a museum, art gallery, botanical garden, zoo, or historic site. Direct the instructional, acquisition, exhibitory, safekeeping, research, and public-service activities of the institution.

Average Yearly Earnings: $30,035. **Experience:** Considerable preparation is needed. A minimum of two to four years of work-related skill, knowledge, or experience is needed for this occupation. **Education:** This group of occupations usually requires a four-year bachelor's degree, but in some cases does not. **Training:** Employees in this type of occupation usually need several years of work-related experience, on-the-job training, and/or vocational training. **Related Examples:** Other occupations like this one usually involve coordinating, supervising, managing, or training others. Examples include accountants, chefs and head cooks, computer programmers, historians, pharmacists, and police detectives. **Standard Vocational Preparation Range:** 7.0 to below 8.0—Two years to less than ten years. **Major/Instructional Program:** 13.0101 Education, General; 13.0301 Curriculum and Instruction; 13.0501 Educational/Instructional Media Design; 30.1401 Museology/Museum Studies; 45.0801 History, General; 45.0805 Public/Applied History and Archival Administration; 50.0701 Art, General; 50.0703 Art History, Criticism, and Conservation. **Related Courses:** Administration and Management; Clerical; Economics and Accounting; Sales and Marketing; Sociology and Anthropology; Geography; English Language; Foreign Language; Fine Arts; History and Archeology; Philosophy and Theology; Communications and Media.

ARCHIVISTS (31511B)

Appraise, edit, and direct the safekeeping of permanent records and historically valuable documents. Participate in research activities based on archival materials.

Average Yearly Earnings: $30,035. **Experience:** Extensive preparation is needed. Extensive skill, knowledge, and experience are needed for this occupation. It may require more than five years of experience. **Education:** A bachelor's degree is the minimum formal education required for this group of occupations. However, many also require graduate school. For example, they may require a master's degree, and some require a Ph.D., M.D., or J.D. (law degree). **Training:** Employees in this type of occupation may need some on-the-job training, but most of these occupations assume that the person will already have the required skills, knowledge, work-related experience, and/or training. **Examples:** Other occupations like this one often involve coordinating, training, supervising, or managing the activities of others to accomplish goals. Very advanced communication and organizational skills are required. Examples include athletic trainers, lawyers, managing editors, physicists, social psychologists, and surgeons. **Standard Vocational Preparation Range:** 8.0 to 9.0—Four years to more than ten years. **Major/Instructional Program:** 30.1401 Museology/Museum Studies; 45.0801 History, General; 45.0805 Public/Applied History and Archival Administration; 50.0701 Art, General; 50.0703 Art History, Criticism, and Conservation. **Related Courses:** Administration and Management; Clerical; Sociology and Anthropology; English Language; History and Archeology; Philosophy and Theology; Communications and Media.

MUSEUM RESEARCH WORKERS (3151 IC)

Plan, organize, and conduct research in scientific, historical, cultural, or artistic fields to document or support exhibits in museums and museum publications.

Average Yearly Earnings: $30,035. **Experience:** Considerable preparation is needed. A minimum of two to four years of work-related skill, knowledge, or experience is needed for this occupation. **Education:** This group of occupations usually requires a four-year bachelor's degree, but in some cases does not. **Training:** Employees in this type of occupation usually need several years of work-related experience, on-the-job training, and/or vocational training. **Related Examples:** Other occupations like this one usually involve coordinating, supervising, managing, or training others. Examples include accountants, chefs and head cooks, computer programmers, historians, pharmacists, and police detectives. **Standard Vocational Preparation Range:** 7.0 to below 8.0—Two years to less than ten years. **Major/Instructional Program:** 30.1401 Museology/Museum Studies; 45.0801 History, General; 45.0805 Public/Applied History and Archival Administration; 50.0701 Art, General; 50.0703 Art History, Criticism, and Conservation. **Related Courses:** Administration and Management; Computers and Electronics; Mathematics; Psychology; Sociology and Anthropology; Geography; English Language; Foreign Language; Fine Arts; History and Archeology; Philosophy and Theology; Telecommunications; Communications and Media.

MUSEUM TECHNICIANS AND CONSERVATORS (3151 ID)

Prepare specimens, such as fossils, skeletal parts, and textiles, for museum collection and exhibits. May restore documents or install, arrange, and exhibit materials.

Average Yearly Earnings: $30,035. **Experience:** Medium preparation is needed. Previous work-related skill, knowledge, or experience is required for this occupation. **Education:** This group of occupations usually requires training in vocational schools, related on-the-job experience, or an associate degree. A bachelor's degree may be required. **Training:** Employees in this type of occupation usually need one or two years of training involving both on-the-job experience and informal training with experienced workers. **Related Examples:** Other occupations like this one usually involve using communication and organizational skills to coordinate, supervise, manage, or train others to accomplish goals. Examples include dental assistants, electricians, fish and game wardens, legal secretaries, personnel recruiters, and recreation workers. **Standard Vocational Preparation Range:** 6.0 to below 7.0—More than one year and less than four years. **Major/Instructional Program:** 30.1401 Museology/Museum Studies; 45.0801 History, General; 45.0805 Public/Applied History and Archival Administration; 50.0201 Crafts, Folk Art, and Artisanry; 50.0701 Art, General; 50.0703 Art History, Criticism, and Conservation; 50.0711 Ceramic Arts and Ceramics. **Related Courses:** Building and Construction; Chemistry; Sociology and Anthropology; Fine Arts; History and Archeology; Philosophy and Theology.

CRAFT DEMONSTRATORS (31511E)

Demonstrate and explain the techniques and purposes of historic crafts.

Average Yearly Earnings: $30,035. **Experience:** Some preparation is needed. Some previous work-related skill, knowledge, or experience may be helpful in this occupation, but usually is not needed. **Education:** This group of occupations usually requires a high school diploma and may require some vocational training or job-related course work. In some cases, an associate or bachelor's degree could be needed. **Training:** Employees in this type of occupation need anywhere from a few months to one year of working with experienced employees. **Related Examples:** Other occupations like this one often involve using your knowledge and skills to help others. Examples include drywall installers, fire inspectors, flight attendants, pharmacy technicians, retail salespersons, and tellers. **Standard Vocational Preparation Range:** 4.0 to below 6.0—Six months to less than two years. **Major/Instructional Program:** 50.0201 Crafts, Folk Art, and Artisanry. **Related Courses:** Sociology and Anthropology; Geography; Fine Arts; History and Archeology; Philosophy and Theology.

VOCATIONAL AND EDUCATIONAL COUNSELORS (31514)

Counsel individuals and provide group educational and vocational guidance services.

Average Yearly Earnings: $36,566. **Experience:** Considerable preparation is needed. A minimum of two to four years of work-related skill, knowledge, or experience is needed for this occupation. **Education:** This group of occupations usually requires a four-year bachelor's degree, but in some cases does not. **Training:** Employees in this type of occupation usually need several years of work-related experience, on-the-job training,

and/or vocational training. **Related Examples:** Other occupations like this one usually involve coordinating, supervising, managing, or training others. Examples include accountants, chefs and head cooks, computer programmers, historians, pharmacists, and police detectives. **Standard Vocational Preparation Range:** 7.0 to below 8.0—Two years to less than ten years. **Major/Instructional Program:** 13.0201 Bilingual/Bicultural Education; 13.0401 Education Administration and Supervision, General; 13.0406 Higher Education Administration; 13.0407 Community and Junior College Administration; 13.1101 Counselor Education/Student Counseling and Guidance Services; 13.1102 College/Postsecondary Student Counseling and Personnel Services; 42.1701 School Psychology. **Related Courses:** Personnel and Human Resources; Psychology; Sociology and Anthropology; Therapy and Counseling; Education and Training; English Language.

PUBLIC HEALTH EDUCATORS (31517A)

Plan, organize, and direct health education programs for group and community needs.

Average Yearly Earnings: $26,000. **Experience:** Extensive preparation is needed. Extensive skill, knowledge, and experience are needed for this occupation. It may require more than five years of experience. **Education:** A bachelor's degree is the minimum formal education required for this group of occupations. However, many also require graduate school. For example, they may require a master's degree, and some require a Ph.D., M.D., or J.D. (law degree). **Training:** Employees in this type of occupation may need some on-the-job training, but most of these occupations assume that the person will already have the required skills, knowledge, work-related experience, and/or training. **Examples:** Other occupations like this one often involve coordinating, training, supervising, or managing the activities of others to accomplish goals. Very advanced communication and organizational skills are required. Examples include athletic trainers, lawyers, managing editors, physicists, social psychologists, and surgeons. **Standard Vocational Preparation Range:** 8.0 to 9.0—Four years to more than ten years. **Major/Instructional Program:** 13.0301 Curriculum and Instruction, 51.0301 Community Health Liaison. **Related Courses:** Administration and Management; Sales and Marketing; Customer and Personal Service; Biology; Psychology; Sociology and Anthropology; Medicine and Dentistry; Therapy and Counseling; Education and Training; English Language; Philosophy and Theology; Communications and Media.

VOCATIONAL REHABILITATION COORDINATORS (31517B)

Develop and coordinate the implementation of vocational rehabilitation programs.

Average Yearly Earnings: $36,566. **Experience:** Extensive preparation is needed. Extensive skill, knowledge, and experience are needed for this occupation. It may require more than five years of experience. **Education:** A bachelor's degree is the minimum formal education required for this group of occupations. However, many also require graduate school. For example, they may require a master's degree, and some require a Ph.D., M.D., or J.D. (law degree). **Training:** Employees in this type of occupation may need some on-the-job training, but most of these occupations assume that the person will already have the required skills, knowledge, work-related experience, and/or training. **Examples:** Other occupations like this one often involve coordinating, training, supervising, or managing the activities of others to accomplish goals. Very advanced communication and organizational skills are required. Examples include athletic trainers, lawyers, managing editors, physicists, social psychologists, and surgeons. **Standard Vocational Preparation Range:** 8.0 to 9.0—Four years to more than ten years. **Major/Instructional Program:** 13.0401 Education Administration and Supervision, General; 13.0402 Administration of Special Education; 13.1001 Special Education, General. **Related Courses:** Administration and Management; Personnel and Human Resources; Psychology; Sociology and Anthropology; Therapy and Counseling; Education and Training; English Language; Philosophy and Theology; Law, Government, and Jurisprudence.

LABORATORY MANAGERS (31517C)

Coordinate the activities of a university science laboratory to assist faculty in teaching and research programs.

Average Yearly Earnings: $65,686. **Experience:** Considerable preparation is needed. A minimum of two to four years of work-related skill, knowledge, or experience is needed for this occupation. **Education:** This group of occupations usually requires a four-year bachelor's degree, but in some cases does not. **Training:** Employees in this type of occupation usually need several years of work-related experience, on-the-job training, and/ or vocational training. **Related Examples:** Other occupations like this one usually involve coordinating, supervising, managing, or training others. Examples include accountants, chefs and head cooks, computer programmers, historians, pharmacists, and police detectives. **Standard Vocational Preparation Range:** 7.0 to below 8.0—Two years to less than ten years. **Major/Instructional Program:** No specific instructional program for this occupation. **Related Courses:** Administration and Management; Economics and Accounting; Computers and Electronics; Engineering and Technology; Mathematics; Physics; Chemistry; Biology; Education and Training; English Language.

INSTRUCTIONAL COORDINATORS (31517D)

Develop instructional material, educational content, and instructional methods to provide guidelines to educators and instructors for developing curricula, conducting courses, and incorporating current technology.

Average Yearly Earnings: $52,436. **Experience:** Extensive preparation is needed. Extensive skill, knowledge, and experience are needed for this occupation. It may require more than five years of experience. **Education:** A bachelor's degree is the minimum formal education required for this group of occupations. However, many also require graduate school. For example, they may require a master's degree, and some require a Ph.D., M.D., or J.D. (law degree). **Training:** Employees in this type of occupation may need some on-the-job training, but most of these occupations assume that the person will

already have the required skills, knowledge, work-related experience, and/or training. **Examples:** Other occupations like this one often involve coordinating, training, supervising, or managing the activities of others to accomplish goals. Very advanced communication and organizational skills are required. Examples include athletic trainers, lawyers, managing editors, physicists, social psychologists, and surgeons. **Standard Vocational Preparation Range:** 8.0 to 9.0—Four years to more than ten years. **Major/Instructional Program:** 13.0101 Education, General; 13.0201 Bilingual/Bicultural Education; 13.0301 Curriculum and Instruction; 13.0401 Education Administration and Supervision, General; 13.0402 Administration of Special Education; 13.0404 Educational Supervision; 13.0405 Elementary, Middle, and Secondary Education Administration; 13.0501 Educational/Instructional Media Design; 13.0601 Educational Evaluation and Research; 13.0603 Educational Statistics and Research Methods; 13.0604 Educational Assessment, Testing, and Measurement; 13.0701 International and Comparative Education; 13.1001 Special Education, General; 13.1003 Education of the Deaf and Hearing Impaired; 13.1004 Education of the Gifted and Talented; 13.1005 Education of the Emotionally Handicapped; 13.1006 Education of the Mentally Handicapped; 13.1007 Education of the Multiple Handicapped; 13.1008 Education of the Physically Handicapped; 13.1009 Education of the Blind and Visually Handicapped; 13.1011 Education of the Specific Learning Disabled; 13.1012 Education of the Speech Impaired. **Related Courses:** Administration and Management; Economics and Accounting; Sales and Marketing; Personnel and Human Resources; Psychology; Sociology and Anthropology; Therapy and Counseling; Education and Training; English Language; Foreign Language; Fine Arts; History and Archeology; Philosophy and Theology; Law, Government, and Jurisprudence; Communications and Media.

TEACHER AIDES, PARAPROFESSIONAL (31521)

Perform duties that are instructional in nature, or deliver direct services to students and/ or parents. Serve in a position for which a teacher or another professional has ultimate responsibility for the design and implementation of educational programs and services.

Average Yearly Earnings: $15,974. **Experience:** Medium preparation is needed. Previous work-related skill, knowledge, or experience is required for this occupation. **Education:** This group of occupations usually requires training in vocational schools, related on-the-job experience, or an associate degree. A bachelor's degree may be required. **Training:** Employees in this type of occupation usually need one or two years of training involving both on-the-job experience and informal training with experienced workers. **Related Examples:** Other occupations like this one usually involve using communication and organizational skills to coordinate, supervise, manage, or train others to accomplish goals. Examples include dental assistants, electricians, fish and game wardens, legal secretaries, personnel recruiters, and recreation workers. **Standard Vocational Preparation Range:** 6.0 to below 7.0—More than one year and less than four years. **Major/Instructional Program:** 13.0101 Education, General; 13.0201 Bilingual/Bicultural Education; 13.1501 Teacher Assistant/Aide. **Related Courses:** Psychology; Sociology and Anthropology; Education and Training; English Language; History and Archeology; Philosophy and Theology.

Diagnosing and Treating Practitioners

DOCTORS OF MEDICINE (M.D.) **(32102A)**

Diagnose illness and prescribe and administer treatment for injury and disease. Exclude doctors of osteopathy, psychiatrists, anesthesiologists, surgeons, and pathologists.

Average Yearly Earnings: $96,636. **Experience:** Extensive preparation is needed. Extensive skill, knowledge, and experience are needed for this occupation. It may require more than five years of experience. **Education:** A bachelor's degree is the minimum formal education required for this group of occupations. However, many also require graduate school. For example, they may require a master's degree, and some require a Ph.D., M.D., or J.D. (law degree). **Training:** Employees in this type of occupation may need some on-the-job training, but most of these occupations assume that the person will already have the required skills, knowledge, work-related experience, and/or training. **Examples:** Other occupations like this one often involve coordinating, training, supervising, or managing the activities of others to accomplish goals. Very advanced communication and organizational skills are required. Examples include athletic trainers, lawyers, managing editors, physicists, social psychologists, and surgeons. **Standard Vocational Preparation Range:** 8.0 to 9.0—Four years to more than ten years. **Major/Instructional Program:** 51.1201 Medicine (M.D.); 51.1307 Medical Immunology; 51.1310 Medical Neurobiology; 51.1401 Medical Clinical Sciences (M.S., Ph.D.); 51.2902 Allergies and Immunology Residency; 51.2905 Cardiology Residency; 51.2907 Child/Pediatric Neurology Residency; 51.2909 Colon and Rectal Surgery Residency; 51.2911 Critical Care Medicine Residency; 51.2913 Dermatology Residency; 51.2915 Diagnostic Radiology Residency; 51.2916 Emergency Medicine Residency; 51.2918 Family Medicine Residency; 51.2922 Geriatric Medicine Residency; 51.2926 Immunopathology Residency; 51.2928 Internal Medicine Residency; 51.2931 Neonatal-Perinatal Medicine Residency; 51.2933 Neurological Surgery/Neurosurgery Residency; 51.2934 Neurology Residency; 51.2937 Nuclear Radiology Residency; 51.2938 Obstetrics and Gynecology Residency; 51.2939 Occupational Medicine Residency; 51.2941 Ophthalmology Residency; 51.2943 Otolaryngology Residency; 51.2945 Pediatric Cardiology Residency; 51.2946 Pediatric Endocrinology Residency; 51.2947 Pediatric Hemato-Oncology Residency; 51.2948 Pediatric Nephrology Residency; 51.2951 Pediatrics Residency; 51.2952 Physical and Rehabilitation Medicine Residency; 51.2956 Public Health Medicine Residency; 51.2957 Pulmonary Disease Residency; 51.2958 Radiation Oncology Residency; 51.2959 Radioisotopic Pathology Residency; 51.2962 Thoracic Surgery Residency; 51.2963 Urology Residency; 51.2999 Medical Residency Programs, Other. **Related Courses:** Administration and Management; Personnel and Human Resources; Mathematics; Physics; Chemistry; Biology; Psychology; Sociology and Anthropology; Medicine and Dentistry; Therapy and Counseling; Education and Training; English Language; Foreign Language; Law, Government, and Jurisprudence.

DOCTORS OF OSTEOPATHY (D.O.) **(32102B)**

Diagnose illness and prescribe and administer treatment for injury and disease with emphasis on body's musculoskeletal system.

Average Yearly Earnings: $96,636. **Experience:** Extensive preparation is needed. Extensive skill, knowledge, and experience are needed for this occupation. It may require more than five years of experience. **Education:** A bachelor's degree is the minimum formal education required for this group of occupations. However, many also require graduate school. For example, they may require a master's degree, and some require a Ph.D., M.D., or J.D. (law degree). **Training:** Employees in this type of occupation may need some on-the-job training, but most of these occupations assume that the person will already have the required skills, knowledge, work-related experience, and/or training. **Examples:** Other occupations like this one often involve coordinating, training, supervising, or managing the activities of others to accomplish goals. Very advanced communication and organizational skills are required. Examples include athletic trainers, lawyers, managing editors, physicists, social psychologists, and surgeons. **Standard Vocational Preparation Range:** 8.0 to 9.0—Four years to more than ten years. **Major/Instructional Program:** 51.1901 Osteopathic Medicine (D.O.). **Related Courses:** Customer and Personal Service; Mathematics; Chemistry; Biology; Psychology; Sociology and Anthropology; Medicine and Dentistry; Therapy and Counseling; English Language.

PSYCHIATRISTS (32102E)

Diagnose mental, emotional, and behavioral disorders and prescribe medication or administer psychotherapeutic treatments to treat disorders.

Average Yearly Earnings: $96,636. **Experience:** Extensive preparation is needed. Extensive skill, knowledge, and experience are needed for this occupation. It may require more than five years of experience. **Education:** A bachelor's degree is the minimum formal education required for this group of occupations. However, many also require graduate school. For example, they may require a master's degree, and some require a Ph.D., M.D., or J.D. (law degree). **Training:** Employees in this type of occupation may need some on-the-job training, but most of these occupations assume that the person will already have the required skills, knowledge, work-related experience, and/or training. **Examples:** Other occupations like this one often involve coordinating, training, supervising, or managing the activities of others to accomplish goals. Very advanced communication and organizational skills are required. Examples include athletic trainers, lawyers, managing editors, physicists, social psychologists, and surgeons. **Standard Vocational Preparation Range:** 8.0 to 9.0—Four years to more than ten years. **Major/Instructional Program:** 51.2705 Psychoanalysis, 51.2908 Child Psychiatry Residency, 51.2955 Psychiatry Residency. **Related Courses:** Customer and Personal Service; Chemistry; Biology; Psychology; Sociology and Anthropology; Medicine and Dentistry; Therapy and Counseling; Education and Training; English Language; Philosophy and Theology; Law, Government, and Jurisprudence; Communications and Media.

ANESTHESIOLOGISTS (32102F)

Administer anesthetic during surgery or other medical procedures.

Average Yearly Earnings: $96,636. **Experience:** Extensive preparation is needed. Extensive skill, knowledge, and experience are needed for this occupation. It may require more

than five years of experience. **Education:** A bachelor's degree is the minimum formal education required for this group of occupations. However, many also require graduate school. For example, they may require a master's degree, and some require a Ph.D., M.D., or J.D. (law degree). **Training:** Employees in this type of occupation may need some on-the-job training, but most of these occupations assume that the person will already have the required skills, knowledge, work-related experience, and/or training. **Examples:** Other occupations like this one often involve coordinating, training, supervising, or managing the activities of others to accomplish goals. Very advanced communication and organizational skills are required. Examples include athletic trainers, lawyers, managing editors, physicists, social psychologists, and surgeons. **Standard Vocational Preparation Range:** 8.0 to 9.0—Four years to more than ten years. **Major/Instructional Program:** 51.1401 Medical Clinical Sciences (M.S., Ph.D.), 51.2903 Anesthesiology Residency, 51.2910 Critical Care Anesthesiology Residency. **Related Courses:** Chemistry; Biology; Medicine and Dentistry; English Language.

SURGEONS (32102J)

Perform surgery to repair injuries; remove or repair diseased organs, bones, or tissue; correct deformities, or improve function in patients.

Average Yearly Earnings: $96,636. **Experience:** Extensive preparation is needed. Extensive skill, knowledge, and experience are needed for this occupation. It may require more than five years of experience. **Education:** A bachelor's degree is the minimum formal education required for this group of occupations. However, many also require graduate school. For example, they may require a master's degree, and some require a Ph.D., M.D., or J.D. (law degree). **Training:** Employees in this type of occupation may need some on-the-job training, but most of these occupations assume that the person will already have the required skills, knowledge, work-related experience, and/or training. **Examples:** Other occupations like this one often involve coordinating, training, supervising, or managing the activities of others to accomplish goals. Very advanced communication and organizational skills are required. Examples include athletic trainers, lawyers, managing editors, physicists, and social psychologists. **Standard Vocational Preparation Range:** 8.0 to 9.0—Four years to more than ten years. **Major/Instructional Program:** 51.2912 Critical Care Surgery Residency, 51.2921 General Surgery Residency, 51.2923 Hand Surgery Residency, 51.2942 Orthopedics/Orthopedic Surgery Residency, 51.2949 Pediatric Orthopedics Residency, 51.2950 Pediatric Surgery Residency, 51.2953 Plastic Surgery Residency, 51.2962 Thoracic Surgery Residency, 51.2964 Vascular Surgery Residency. **Related Courses:** Administration and Management; Physics; Chemistry; Biology; Psychology; Medicine and Dentistry; Therapy and Counseling; English Language.

PATHOLOGISTS (32102U)

Research or study the nature, cause, effects, and development of diseases; and determine the presence and extent of disease in body tissue, fluids, secretions, and other specimens.

Average Yearly Earnings: $96,636. **Experience:** Extensive preparation is needed. Extensive skill, knowledge, and experience are needed for this occupation. It may require more than five years of experience. **Education:** A bachelor's degree is the minimum formal education required for this group of occupations. However, many also require graduate school. For example, they may require a master's degree, and some require a Ph.D., M.D., or J.D. (law degree). **Training:** Employees in this type of occupation may need some on-the-job training, but most of these occupations assume that the person will already have the required skills, knowledge, work-related experience, and/or training. **Examples:** Other occupations like this one often involve coordinating, training, supervising, or managing the activities of others to accomplish goals. Very advanced communication and organizational skills are required. Examples include athletic trainers, lawyers, managing editors, physicists, social psychologists, and surgeons. **Standard Vocational Preparation Range:** 8.0 to 9.0—Four years to more than ten years. **Major/Instructional Program:** 26.0701 Zoology, General; 26.0704 Pathology, Human, and Animal; 51.1401 Medical Clinical Sciences (M.S., Ph.D.); 51.2906 Chemical Pathology Residency; 51.2919 Forensic Pathology Residency; 51.2925 Hematological Pathology Residency; 51.2935 Neuropathology Residency; 51.2944 Pathology Residency; 51.2959 Radioisotopic Pathology Residency. **Related Courses:** Administration and Management; Mathematics; Chemistry; Biology; Medicine and Dentistry; Therapy and Counseling; Education and Training; English Language.

ORAL PATHOLOGISTS (32105A)

Research or study the nature, cause, effects, and development of diseases associated with the mouth. Examine oral tissue specimens of patients to determine pathological conditions such as tumors and lesions.

Average Yearly Earnings: $85,508. **Experience:** Extensive preparation is needed. Extensive skill, knowledge, and experience are needed for this occupation. It may require more than five years of experience. **Education:** A bachelor's degree is the minimum formal education required for this group of occupations. However, many also require graduate school. For example, they may require a master's degree, and some require a Ph.D., M.D., or J.D. (law degree). **Training:** Employees in this type of occupation may need some on-the-job training, but most of these occupations assume that the person will already have the required skills, knowledge, work-related experience, and/or training. **Examples:** Other occupations like this one often involve coordinating, training, supervising, or managing the activities of others to accomplish goals. Very advanced communication and organizational skills are required. Examples include athletic trainers, lawyers, managing editors, physicists, social psychologists, and surgeons. **Standard Vocational Preparation Range:** 8.0 to 9.0—Four years to more than ten years. **Major/Instructional Program:** 51.2804 Oral Pathology Specialty. **Related Courses:** Chemistry; Biology; Psychology; Medicine and Dentistry; Therapy and Counseling; English Language.

DENTISTS (32105B)

Diagnose, prevent, and treat problems of the teeth and tissue of the mouth. Excludes orthodontists, prosthodontists, oral and maxillofacial surgeons, and oral pathologists.

Average Yearly Earnings: $85,508. **Experience:** Extensive preparation is needed. Extensive skill, knowledge, and experience are needed for this occupation. It may require more than five years of experience. **Education:** A bachelor's degree is the minimum formal education required for this group of occupations. However, many also require graduate school. For example, they may require a master's degree, and some require a Ph.D., M.D., or J.D. (law degree). **Training:** Employees in this type of occupation may need some on-the-job training, but most of these occupations assume that the person will already have the required skills, knowledge, work-related experience, and/or training. **Examples:** Other occupations like this one often involve coordinating, training, supervising, or managing the activities of others to accomplish goals. Very advanced communication and organizational skills are required. Examples include athletic trainers, lawyers, managing editors, physicists, social psychologists, and surgeons. **Standard Vocational Preparation Range:** 8.0 to 9.0—Four years to more than ten years. **Major/Instructional Program:** 51.0401 Dentistry (D.D.S., D.M.D.); 51.0501 Dental Clinical Sciences/Graduate Dentistry (M.S., Ph.D.); 51.2802 Dental Public Health Specialty, 51.2803 Endodontics Specialty, 51.2806 Pedodontics Specialty, 51.2807 Periodontics Specialty. **Related Courses:** Chemistry; Biology; Medicine and Dentistry; English Language.

ORTHODONTISTS (32105D)

Examine, diagnose, and treat dental malocclusions and oral cavity anomalies. Design and fabricate appliances to realign teeth and jaws to produce and maintain normal function and to improve appearance.

Average Yearly Earnings: $85,508. **Experience:** Extensive preparation is needed. Extensive skill, knowledge, and experience are needed for this occupation. It may require more than five years of experience. **Education:** A bachelor's degree is the minimum formal education required for this group of occupations. However, many also require graduate school. For example, they may require a master's degree, and some require a Ph.D., M.D., or J.D. (law degree). **Training:** Employees in this type of occupation may need some on-the-job training, but most of these occupations assume that the person will already have the required skills, knowledge, work-related experience, and/or training. **Examples:** Other occupations like this one often involve coordinating, training, supervising, or managing the activities of others to accomplish goals. Very advanced communication and organizational skills are required. Examples include athletic trainers, lawyers, managing editors, physicists, social psychologists, and surgeons. **Standard Vocational Preparation Range:** 8.0 to 9.0—Four years to more than ten years. **Major/Instructional Program:** 51.2805 Orthodontics Specialty. **Related Courses:** Customer and Personal Service; Chemistry; Biology; Medicine and Dentistry; Therapy and Counseling.

PROSTHODONTISTS (32105F)

Construct oral prostheses to replace missing teeth and other oral structures; to correct natural and acquired deformation of mouth and jaws; to restore and maintain oral function, such as chewing and speaking; and to improve appearance.

Average Yearly Earnings: $85,508. **Experience:** Extensive preparation is needed. Extensive skill, knowledge, and experience are needed for this occupation. It may require more than five years of experience. **Education:** A bachelor's degree is the minimum formal education required for this group of occupations. However, many also require graduate school. For example, they may require a master's degree, and some require a Ph.D., M.D., or J.D. (law degree). **Training:** Employees in this type of occupation may need some on-the-job training, but most of these occupations assume that the person will already have the required skills, knowledge, work-related experience, and/or training. **Examples:** Other occupations like this one often involve coordinating, training, supervising, or managing the activities of others to accomplish goals. Very advanced communication and organizational skills are required. Examples include athletic trainers, lawyers, managing editors, physicists, social psychologists, and surgeons. **Standard Vocational Preparation Range:** 8.0 to 9.0—Four years to more than ten years. **Major/Instructional Program:** 51.2808 Prosthodontics Specialty. **Related Courses:** Chemistry; Biology; Medicine and Dentistry.

ORAL AND MAXILLOFACIAL SURGEONS (32105G)

Perform surgery on mouth, jaws, and related head and neck structure to execute difficult and multiple extractions of teeth, to remove tumors and other abnormal growths; to correct abnormal jaw relations by mandibular or maxillary revision; to prepare the mouth for the insertion of dental prosthesis; or to treat fractured jaws.

Average Yearly Earnings: $85,508. **Experience:** Extensive preparation is needed. Extensive skill, knowledge, and experience are needed for this occupation. It may require more than five years of experience. **Education:** A bachelor's degree is the minimum formal education required for this group of occupations. However, many also require graduate school. For example, they may require a master's degree, and some require a Ph.D., M.D., or J.D. (law degree). **Training:** Employees in this type of occupation may need some on-the-job training, but most of these occupations assume that the person will already have the required skills, knowledge, work-related experience, and/or training. **Examples:** Other occupations like this one often involve coordinating, training, supervising, or managing the activities of others to accomplish goals. Very advanced communication and organizational skills are required. Examples include athletic trainers, lawyers, managing editors, physicists, social psychologists, and surgeons. **Standard Vocational Preparation Range:** 8.0 to 9.0—Four years to more than ten years. **Major/Instructional Program:** 51.2801 Dental/Oral Surgery Specialty. **Related Courses:** Chemistry; Biology; Psychology; Medicine and Dentistry; Therapy and Counseling; English Language.

OPTOMETRISTS (32108)

Diagnose, manage, and treat conditions and diseases of the human eye and visual system. Examine eyes to determine visual efficiency and performance by the use of instruments and observation. Prescribe corrective procedures.

Average Yearly Earnings: $64,209. **Experience:** Considerable preparation is needed. A minimum of two to four years of work-related skill, knowledge, or experience is needed for this occupation. **Education:** This group of occupations usually requires a four-year bachelor's degree, but in some cases does not. **Training:** Employees in this type of occupation usually need several years of work-related experience, on-the-job training, and/or vocational training. **Related Examples:** Other occupations like this one usually involve coordinating, supervising, managing, or training others. Examples include accountants, chefs and head cooks, computer programmers, historians, pharmacists, and police detectives. **Standard Vocational Preparation Range:** 7.0 to below 8.0—Two years to less than ten years. **Major/Instructional Program:** 51.1701 Optometry (O.D.). **Related Courses:** Chemistry; Biology; Medicine and Dentistry; Therapy and Counseling; Education and Training; Foreign Language.

PODIATRISTS (32111)

Diagnose and treat diseases and deformities of the human foot.

Average Yearly Earnings: $85,134. **Experience:** Considerable preparation is needed. A minimum of two to four years of work-related skill, knowledge, or experience is needed for this occupation. **Education:** This group of occupations usually requires a four-year bachelor's degree, but in some cases does not. **Training:** Employees in this type of occupation usually need several years of work-related experience, on-the-job training, and/or vocational training. **Related Examples:** Other occupations like this one usually involve coordinating, supervising, managing, or training others. Examples include accountants, chefs and head cooks, computer programmers, historians, pharmacists, and police detectives. **Standard Vocational Preparation Range:** 7.0 to below 8.0—Two years to less than ten years. **Major/Instructional Program:** 51.2101 Podiatry (D.P.M., D.P., Pod.D.). **Related Courses:** Customer and Personal Service; Physics; Chemistry; Biology; Psychology; Sociology and Anthropology; Medicine and Dentistry; Therapy and Counseling; English Language; Philosophy and Theology.

CHIROPRACTORS (32113)

Adjust the spinal column and other articulations of the body to prevent disease and correct abnormalities of the human body believed to be caused by interference with the nervous system. Examine patient to determine the nature and extent of the disorder. Manipulate the spine or other involved area. May utilize supplementary measures such as exercise, rest, water, light, heat, and nutritional therapy.

Average Yearly Earnings: $63,211. **Experience:** Extensive preparation is needed. Extensive skill, knowledge, and experience are needed for this occupation. It may require more than five years of experience. **Education:** A bachelor's degree is the minimum formal education required for this group of occupations. However, many also require graduate school. For example, they may require a master's degree, and some require a Ph.D., M.D., or J.D. (law degree). **Training:** Employees in this type of occupation may need some on-the-job training, but most of these occupations assume that the person will already have the required skills, knowledge, work-related experience, and/or training. **Examples:** Other occupations like this one often involve coordinating, training, supervising, or managing the activities of others to accomplish goals. Very advanced communication and organizational skills are required. Examples include athletic trainers, lawyers, managing editors, physicists, social psychologists, and surgeons. **Standard Vocational Preparation Range:** 8.0 to 9.0—Four years to more than ten years. **Major/Instructional Program:** 51.0101 Chiropractic (D.C., D.C.M.). **Related Courses:** Customer and Personal Service; Physics; Chemistry; Biology; Psychology; Sociology and Anthropology; Medicine and Dentistry; Therapy and Counseling; English Language; Philosophy and Theology.

VETERINARY PATHOLOGISTS (32114A)

Study the nature, cause, and development of animal diseases; the form and structure of animals; or drugs related to veterinary medicine.

Average Yearly Earnings: $52,936. **Experience:** Extensive preparation is needed. Extensive skill, knowledge, and experience are needed for this occupation. It may require more than five years of experience. **Education:** A bachelor's degree is the minimum formal education required for this group of occupations. However, many also require graduate school. For example, they may require a master's degree, and some require a Ph.D., M.D., or J.D. (law degree). **Training:** Employees in this type of occupation may need some on-the-job training, but most of these occupations assume that the person will already have the required skills, knowledge, work-related experience, and/or training. **Examples:** Other occupations like this one often involve coordinating, training, supervising, or managing the activities of others to accomplish goals. Very advanced communication and organizational skills are required. Examples include athletic trainers, lawyers, managing editors, physicists, social psychologists, and surgeons. **Standard Vocational Preparation Range:** 8.0 to 9.0—Four years to more than ten years. **Major/Instructional Program:** 51.2401 Veterinary Medicine (D.V.M.), 51.3007 Veterinary Microbiology, 51.3010 Veterinary Pathology, 51.3012 Veterinary Preventive Medicine. **Related Courses:** Administration and Management; Food Production; Mathematics; Chemistry; Biology; Medicine and Dentistry; Therapy and Counseling; Education and Training; English Language; Philosophy and Theology; Public Safety and Security.

VETERINARIANS (32114B)

Diagnose and treat medical problems in animals. Excludes veterinary inspectors and veterinary pathologists.

Average Yearly Earnings: $52,936. **Experience:** Extensive preparation is needed. Extensive skill, knowledge, and experience are needed for this occupation. It may require more than five years of experience. **Education:** A bachelor's degree is the minimum formal education required for this group of occupations. However, many also require graduate school. For example, they may require a master's degree, and some require a Ph.D., M.D., or J.D. (law degree). **Training:** Employees in this type of occupation may need some on-the-job training, but most of these occupations assume that the person will

already have the required skills, knowledge, work-related experience, and/or training. **Examples:** Other occupations like this one often involve coordinating, training, supervising, or managing the activities of others to accomplish goals. Very advanced communication and organizational skills are required. Examples include athletic trainers, lawyers, managing editors, physicists, social psychologists, and surgeons. **Standard Vocational Preparation Range:** 8.0 to 9.0—Four years to more than ten years. **Major/Instructional Program:** 51.2401 Veterinary Medicine (D.V.M.), 51.3001 Veterinary Anesthesiology, 51.3002 Veterinary Dentistry, 51.3003 Veterinary Dermatology, 51.3004 Veterinary Emergency and Critical Care Medicine, 51.3005 Veterinary Internal Medicine, 51.3006 Laboratory Animal Medicine, 51.3008 Veterinary Nutrition, 51.3009 Veterinary Ophthalmology, 51.3011 Veterinary Practice, 51.3013 Veterinary Radiology, 51.3014 Veterinary Surgery, 51.3015 Theriogenology, 51.3016 Veterinary Toxicology, 51.3017 Zoological Medicine. **Related Courses:** Mathematics; Chemistry; Biology; Psychology; Medicine and Dentistry; Therapy and Counseling; Education and Training; English Language; Philosophy and Theology; Public Safety and Security.

VETERINARY INSPECTORS (32114C)

Inspect animals for the presence of disease in facilities such as laboratories, livestock sites, and livestock slaughter or meat-processing facilities.

Average Yearly Earnings: $52,936. **Experience:** Considerable preparation is needed. A minimum of two to four years of work-related skill, knowledge, or experience is needed for this occupation. **Education:** This group of occupations usually requires a four-year bachelor's degree, but in some cases does not. **Training:** Employees in this type of occupation usually need several years of work-related experience, on-the-job training, and/or vocational training. **Related Examples:** Other occupations like this one usually involve coordinating, supervising, managing, or training others. Examples include accountants, chefs and head cooks, computer programmers, historians, pharmacists, and police detectives. **Standard Vocational Preparation Range:** 7.0 to below 8.0—Two years to less than ten years. **Major/Instructional Program:** 51.2401 Veterinary Medicine (D.V.M.). **Related Courses:** Economics and Accounting; Production and Processing; Food Production; Chemistry; Biology; Geography; Medicine and Dentistry; English Language; Philosophy and Theology; Public Safety and Security; Law, Government, and Jurisprudence.

Medical Therapists

RESPIRATORY THERAPISTS (32302)

Set up and operate various types of equipment, such as ventilators, oxygen tents, resuscitators, and incubators, to administer oxygen and other gases to patients.

Average Yearly Earnings: $32,780. **Experience:** Medium preparation is needed. Previous work-related skill, knowledge, or experience is required for this occupation.

Education: This group of occupations usually requires training in vocational schools, related on-the-job experience, or an associate degree. A bachelor's degree may be required. **Training:** Employees in this type of occupation usually need one or two years of training involving both on-the-job experience and informal training with experienced workers. **Related Examples:** Other occupations like this one usually involve using communication and organizational skills to coordinate, supervise, manage, or train others to accomplish goals. Examples include dental assistants, electricians, fish and game wardens, legal secretaries, personnel recruiters, and recreation workers. **Standard Vocational Preparation Range:** 6.0 to below 7.0—More than one year and less than four years. **Major/Instructional Program:** 51.0908 Respiratory Therapy Technician. **Related Courses:** Chemistry; Biology; Psychology; Medicine and Dentistry; Therapy and Counseling; Education and Training.

OCCUPATIONAL THERAPISTS (32305)

Plan, organize, and participate in medically oriented occupational programs in a hospital or similar institution to rehabilitate patients who are physically or mentally ill.

Average Yearly Earnings: $46,779. **Experience:** Considerable preparation is needed. A minimum of two to four years of work-related skill, knowledge, or experience is needed for this occupation. **Education:** This group of occupations usually requires a four-year bachelor's degree, but in some cases does not. **Training:** Employees in this type of occupation usually need several years of work-related experience, on-the-job training, and/or vocational training. **Related Examples:** Other occupations like this one usually involve coordinating, supervising, managing, or training others. Examples include accountants, chefs and head cooks, computer programmers, historians, pharmacists, and police detectives. **Standard Vocational Preparation Range:** 7.0 to below 8.0—Two years to less than ten years. **Major/Instructional Program:** 51.2306 Occupational Therapy. **Related Courses:** Administration and Management; Clerical; Economics and Accounting; Customer and Personal Service; Personnel and Human Resources; Biology; Psychology; Sociology and Anthropology; Medicine and Dentistry; Therapy and Counseling; Education and Training; Foreign Language.

PHYSICAL THERAPISTS (32308)

Apply techniques and treatments that help relieve pain, increase the patient's strength, and decrease or prevent deformity and crippling.

Average Yearly Earnings: $52,811. **Experience:** Considerable preparation is needed. A minimum of two to four years of work-related skill, knowledge, or experience is needed for this occupation. **Education:** This group of occupations usually requires a four-year bachelor's degree, but in some cases does not. **Training:** Employees in this type of occupation usually need several years of work-related experience, on-the-job training, and/or vocational training. **Related Examples:** Other occupations like this one usually involve coordinating, supervising, managing, or training others. Examples include

accountants, chefs and head cooks, computer programmers, historians, pharmacists, and police detectives. **Standard Vocational Preparation Range:** 7.0 to below 8.0—Two years to less than ten years. **Major/Instructional Program:** 31.0501 Health and Physical Education, General; 31.0505 Exercise Sciences/Physiology and Movement Studies; 51.2304 Movement Therapy; 51.2308 Physical Therapy. **Related Courses:** Administration and Management; Customer and Personal Service; Biology; Psychology; Medicine and Dentistry; Therapy and Counseling; Education and Training; English Language.

MANUAL ARTS THERAPISTS (3231 IA)

Instruct patients in prescribed manual arts activities, such as woodworking, photography, or graphic arts, to prevent anatomical and physiological deconditioning and to assist in maintaining, improving, or developing work skills.

Average Yearly Earnings: $46,779. **Experience:** Considerable preparation is needed. A minimum of two to four years of work-related skill, knowledge, or experience is needed for this occupation. **Education:** This group of occupations usually requires a four-year bachelor's degree, but in some cases does not. **Training:** Employees in this type of occupation usually need several years of work-related experience, on-the-job training, and/or vocational training. **Related Examples:** Other occupations like this one usually involve coordinating, supervising, managing, or training others. Examples include accountants, chefs and head cooks, computer programmers, historians, pharmacists, and police detectives. **Standard Vocational Preparation Range:** 7.0 to below 8.0—Two years to less than ten years. **Major/Instructional Program:** 51.2306 Occupational Therapy. **Related Courses:** Customer and Personal Service; Psychology; Therapy and Counseling; Education and Training; Fine Arts.

CORRECTIVE THERAPISTS (3231 IB)

Apply techniques and treatments designed to prevent muscular deconditioning resulting from long convalescence or inactivity due to chronic illness.

Average Yearly Earnings: $52,811. **Experience:** Medium preparation is needed. Previous work-related skill, knowledge, or experience is required for this occupation. **Education:** This group of occupations usually requires training in vocational schools, related on-the-job experience, or an associate degree. A bachelor's degree may be required. **Training:** Employees in this type of occupation usually need one or two years of training involving both on-the-job experience and informal training with experienced workers. **Related Examples:** Other occupations like this one usually involve using communication and organizational skills to coordinate, supervise, manage, or train others to accomplish goals. Examples include dental assistants, electricians, fish and game wardens, legal secretaries, personnel recruiters, and recreation workers. **Standard Vocational Preparation Range:** 6.0 to below 7.0—More than one year and less than four years. **Major/Instructional Program:** 31.0501 Health and Physical Education, General; 31.0502 Adapted Physical Education/Therapeutic Recreation; 31.0505 Exercise Sciences/Physiology and

Movement Studies; 51.2308 Physical Therapy; 51.2399 Rehabilitation/Therapeutic Services, Other. **Related Courses:** Customer and Personal Service; Biology; Psychology; Medicine and Dentistry; Therapy and Counseling; Education and Training; Communications and Media.

SPEECH-LANGUAGE PATHOLOGISTS AND AUDIOLOGISTS (32314)

Examine and provide remedial services for persons with speech and hearing disorders. Perform research related to speech and language problems.

Average Yearly Earnings: $42,702. **Experience:** Considerable preparation is needed. A minimum of two to four years of work-related skill, knowledge, or experience is needed for this occupation. **Education:** This group of occupations usually requires a four-year bachelor's degree, but in some cases does not. **Training:** Employees in this type of occupation usually need several years of work-related experience, on-the-job training, and/or vocational training. **Related Examples:** Other occupations like this one usually involve coordinating, supervising, managing, or training others. Examples include accountants, chefs and head cooks, computer programmers, historians, pharmacists, and police detectives. **Standard Vocational Preparation Range:** 7.0 to below 8.0—Two years to less than ten years. **Major/Instructional Program:** 51.0201 Communication Disorders, General; 51.0202 Audiology/Hearing Sciences; 51.0203 Speech-Language Pathology; 51.0204 Speech Pathology and Audiology. **Related Courses:** Administration and Management; Economics and Accounting; Customer and Personal Service; Personnel and Human Resources; Biology; Psychology; Medicine and Dentistry; Therapy and Counseling; Education and Training; English Language; Foreign Language; Telecommunications.

RECREATIONAL THERAPISTS (32317)

Plan, organize, and direct medically approved recreation programs for patients in hospitals, nursing homes, or other institutions. Activities include sports, trips, dramatics, social activities, and arts and crafts.

Average Yearly Earnings: $26,769. **Experience:** Considerable preparation is needed. A minimum of two to four years of work-related skill, knowledge, or experience is needed for this occupation. **Education:** This group of occupations usually requires a four-year bachelor's degree, but in some cases does not. **Training:** Employees in this type of occupation usually need several years of work-related experience, on-the-job training, and/or vocational training. **Related Examples:** Other occupations like this one usually involve coordinating, supervising, managing, or training others. Examples include accountants, chefs and head cooks, computer programmers, historians, pharmacists, and police detectives. **Standard Vocational Preparation Range:** 7.0 to below 8.0—Two years to less than ten years. **Major/Instructional Program:** 31.0501 Health and Physical Education, General; 31.0502 Adapted Physical Education/Therapeutic Recreation; 51.2301 Art Therapy; 51.2302 Dance Therapy; 51.2305 Music Therapy; 51.2309 Recreational Therapy. **Related Courses:** Administration and Management; Customer and Personal Service;

Biology; Psychology; Sociology and Anthropology; Medicine and Dentistry; Therapy and Counseling; Education and Training; English Language; Philosophy and Theology.

EXERCISE PHYSIOLOGISTS (32399A)

Develop, implement, and coordinate exercise programs and administer medical tests, under a physician's supervision, to program participants to promote physical fitness.

Average Yearly Earnings: $31,865. **Experience:** Considerable preparation is needed. A minimum of two to four years of work-related skill, knowledge, or experience is needed for this occupation. **Education:** This group of occupations usually requires a four-year bachelor's degree, but in some cases does not. **Training:** Employees in this type of occupation usually need several years of work-related experience, on-the-job training, and/ or vocational training. **Related Examples:** Other occupations like this one usually involve coordinating, supervising, managing, or training others. Examples include accountants, chefs and head cooks, computer programmers, historians, pharmacists, and police detectives. **Standard Vocational Preparation Range:** 7.0 to below 8.0—Two years to less than ten years. **Major/Instructional Program:** 31.0501 Health and Physical Education, General; 31.0502 Adapted Physical Education/Therapeutic Recreation; 31.0503 Athletic Training and Sports Medicine; 31.0505 Exercise Sciences/Physiology and Movement Studies. **Related Courses:** Customer and Personal Service; Chemistry; Biology; Psychology; Medicine and Dentistry; Therapy and Counseling; Education and Training; Foreign Language.

ORIENTATION AND MOBILITY THERAPISTS (32399B)

Train blind and visually impaired clients in the techniques of daily living to maximize independence and personal adjustment.

Average Yearly Earnings: $31,865. **Experience:** Medium preparation is needed. Previous work-related skill, knowledge, or experience is required for this occupation. **Education:** This group of occupations usually requires training in vocational schools, related on-the-job experience, or an associate degree. A bachelor's degree may be required. **Training:** Employees in this type of occupation usually need one or two years of training involving both on-the-job experience and informal training with experienced workers. **Related Examples:** Other occupations like this one usually involve using communication and organizational skills to coordinate, supervise, manage, or train others to accomplish goals. Examples include dental assistants, electricians, fish and game wardens, legal secretaries, personnel recruiters, and recreation workers. **Standard Vocational Preparation Range:** 6.0 to below 7.0—More than one year and less than four years. **Major/ Instructional Program:** 13.1001 Special Education, General; 13.1009 Education of the Blind and Visually Handicapped; 44.0701 Social Work; 51.0806 Physical Therapy Assistant; 51.2308 Physical Therapy; 51.2310 Vocational Rehabilitation Counseling. **Related Courses:** Customer and Personal Service; Psychology; Medicine and Dentistry; Therapy and Counseling; Education and Training; Foreign Language; Fine Arts; Telecommunications.

Healthcare Providers

REGISTERED NURSES (32502)

Administer nursing care to ill or injured persons. Licensing or registration required. Include administrative, public health, industrial, private duty, and surgical nurses.

Average Yearly Earnings: $40,310. **Experience:** Considerable preparation is needed. A minimum of two to four years of work-related skill, knowledge, or experience is needed for this occupation. **Education:** This group of occupations usually requires a four-year bachelor's degree, but in some cases does not. **Training:** Employees in this type of occupation usually need several years of work-related experience, on-the-job training, and/or vocational training. **Related Examples:** Other occupations like this one usually involve coordinating, supervising, managing, or training others. Examples include accountants, chefs and head cooks, computer programmers, historians, pharmacists, and police detectives. **Standard Vocational Preparation Range:** 7.0 to below 8.0—Two years to less than ten years. **Major/Instructional Program:** 51.1601 Nursing (R.N.); 51.1602 Nursing Administration (Post-R.N.); 51.1603 Nursing, Adult Health (Post-R.N.); 51.1604 Nursing Anesthetist (Post-R.N.); 51.1605 Nursing, Family Practice (Post-R.N.); 51.1606 Nursing, Maternal/Child Health (Post-R.N.); 51.1607 Nursing Midwifery (Post-R.N.); 51.1608 Nursing Science (Post-R.N.); 51.1609 Nursing, Pediatric (Post-R.N.); 51.1610 Nursing, Psychiatric/Mental Health (Post-R.N.); 51.1611 Nursing, Public Health (Post-R.N.); 51.1612 Nursing, Surgical (Post-R.N.); 51.1699 Nursing, Other. **Related Courses:** Administration and Management; Clerical; Customer and Personal Service; Personnel and Human Resources; Chemistry; Biology; Psychology; Sociology and Anthropology; Medicine and Dentistry; Therapy and Counseling; Education and Training; English Language; Foreign Language; Philosophy and Theology; Public Safety and Security; Law, Government, and Jurisprudence; Communications and Media.

LICENSED PRACTICAL NURSES (32505)

Care for ill, injured, convalescent, and handicapped persons in hospitals, clinics, private homes, sanitariums, and similar institutions.

Average Yearly Earnings: $26,020. **Experience:** Medium preparation is needed. Previous work-related skill, knowledge, or experience is required for this occupation. **Education:** This group of occupations usually requires training in vocational schools, related on-the-job experience, or an associate degree. A bachelor's degree may be required. **Training:** Employees in this type of occupation usually need one or two years of training involving both on-the-job experience and informal training with experienced workers. **Related Examples:** Other occupations like this one usually involve using communication and organizational skills to coordinate, supervise, manage, or train others to accomplish goals. Examples include dental assistants, electricians, fish and game wardens, legal secretaries, personnel recruiters, and recreation workers. **Standard Vocational Preparation Range:** 6.0 to below 7.0—More than one year and less than four years.

Major/Instructional Program: 51.1613 Practical Nurse (L.P.N.). **Related Courses:** Customer and Personal Service; Chemistry; Biology; Psychology; Sociology and Anthropology; Medicine and Dentistry; Therapy and Counseling.

EMERGENCY MEDICAL TECHNICIANS (32508)

Administer first-aid treatment and transport sick or injured persons to a medical facility, working as members of an emergency medical team.

Average Yearly Earnings: $21,361. **Experience:** Some preparation is needed. Some previous work-related skill, knowledge, or experience may be helpful in this occupation, but usually is not needed. **Education:** This group of occupations usually requires a high school diploma and may require some vocational training or job-related course work. In some cases, an associate or bachelor's degree could be needed. **Training:** Employees in this type of occupation need anywhere from a few months to one year of working with experienced employees. **Related Examples:** Other occupations like this one often involve using your knowledge and skills to help others. Examples include drywall installers, fire inspectors, flight attendants, pharmacy technicians, retail salespersons, and tellers. **Standard Vocational Preparation Range:** 4.0 to below 6.0—Six months to less than two years. **Major/Instructional Program:** 51.0904 Emergency Medical Technology/Technician. **Related Courses:** Chemistry; Biology; Psychology; Geography; Medicine and Dentistry; Therapy and Counseling; Foreign Language; Telecommunications; Transportation.

PHYSICIAN'S ASSISTANTS (32511)

Provide patient services under the direct supervision and responsibility of a doctor of medicine or osteopathy. Elicit detailed patient histories and make complete physical examinations. Reach tentative diagnoses and order appropriate laboratory tests. May require certification. Excludes nurses and ambulance attendants, whose training is limited to the application of first aid.

Average Yearly Earnings: $40,310. **Experience:** Considerable preparation is needed. A minimum of two to four years of work-related skill, knowledge, or experience is needed for this occupation. **Education:** This group of occupations usually requires a four-year bachelor's degree, but in some cases does not. **Training:** Employees in this type of occupation usually need several years of work-related experience, on-the-job training, and/or vocational training. **Related Examples:** Other occupations like this one usually involve coordinating, supervising, managing, or training others. Examples include accountants, chefs and head cooks, computer programmers, historians, pharmacists, and police detectives. **Standard Vocational Preparation Range:** 7.0 to below 8.0—Two years to less than ten years. **Major/Instructional Program:** 51.0807 Physician Assistant. **Related Courses:** Chemistry; Biology; Psychology; Medicine and Dentistry; Therapy and Counseling.

OPTICIANS, DISPENSING AND MEASURING (32514)

Design, measure, fit, and adapt lenses and frames for the client, according to a written optical prescription or specification. Assist the client with selecting frames. Measure the customer for size of eyeglasses and coordinate frames with facial and eye measurements and optical prescription. Prepare work order for optical laboratory containing instructions for grinding and mounting lenses in frames. Verify exactness of finished lens spectacles. Adjust frame and lens position to fit the client. May shape or reshape frames. Includes contact lens opticians.

Average Yearly Earnings: $22,547. **Experience:** Considerable preparation is needed. A minimum of two to four years of work-related skill, knowledge, or experience is needed for this occupation. **Education:** This group of occupations usually requires a four-year bachelor's degree, but in some cases does not. **Training:** Employees in this type of occupation usually need several years of work-related experience, on-the-job training, and/or vocational training. **Related Examples:** Other occupations like this one usually involve coordinating, supervising, managing, or training others. Examples include accountants, chefs and head cooks, computer programmers, historians, pharmacists, and police detectives. **Standard Vocational Preparation Range:** 7.0 to below 8.0—Two years to less than ten years. **Major/Instructional Program:** 51.1801 Opticianry/Dispensing Optician. **Related Courses:** Administration and Management; Economics and Accounting; Sales and Marketing; Customer and Personal Service; Personnel and Human Resources.

PHARMACISTS (32517)

Compound and dispense medications following prescriptions issued by physicians, dentists, or other authorized medical practitioners.

Average Yearly Earnings: $55,328. **Experience:** Considerable preparation is needed. A minimum of two to four years of work-related skill, knowledge, or experience is needed for this occupation. **Education:** This group of occupations usually requires a four-year bachelor's degree, but in some cases does not. **Training:** Employees in this type of occupation usually need several years of work-related experience, on-the-job training, and/or vocational training. **Related Examples:** Other occupations like this one usually involve coordinating, supervising, managing, or training others. Examples include accountants, chefs and head cooks, computer programmers, historians, pharmacists, and police detectives. **Standard Vocational Preparation Range:** 7.0 to below 8.0—Two years to less than ten years. **Major/Instructional Program:** 51.2001 Pharmacy (B.Pharm., Pharm.D.), 51.2002 Pharmacy Administration and Pharmaceutics. **Related Courses:** Administration and Management; Clerical; Economics and Accounting; Personnel and Human Resources; Computers and Electronics; Chemistry; Biology; Medicine and Dentistry; Therapy and Counseling; Education and Training; English Language; Foreign Language; Law, Government, and Jurisprudence.

PHARMACY TECHNICIANS (32518)

Fill orders for unit doses and prepackaged pharmaceuticals and perform other related duties under the supervision and direction of a pharmacy supervisor or staff pharmacist. Duties include keeping records of drugs delivered to the pharmacy, storing incoming merchandise in proper locations, and informing the supervisor of stock needs and shortages. May clean equipment used in the performance of duties and assist in the care and maintenance of equipment and supplies.

Average Yearly Earnings: $31,054. **Experience:** Some preparation is needed. Some previous work-related skill, knowledge, or experience may be helpful in this occupation, but usually is not needed. **Education:** This group of occupations usually requires a high school diploma and may require some vocational training or job-related course work. In some cases, an associate or bachelor's degree could be needed. **Training:** Employees in this type of occupation need anywhere from a few months to one year of working with experienced employees. **Related Examples:** Other occupations like this one often involve using your knowledge and skills to help others. Examples include drywall installers, fire inspectors, flight attendants, retail salespersons, and tellers. **Standard Vocational Preparation Range:** 4.0 to below 6.0—Six months to less than two years. **Major/ Instructional Program:** No specific instructional program for this occupation. **Related Courses:** Clerical; Chemistry; Medicine and Dentistry.

DIETITIANS AND NUTRITIONISTS (32521)

Organize, plan, and conduct food service or nutritional programs to assist in the promotion of health and control of disease. May administer activities of the department in providing quantity food service. May plan, organize, and conduct programs in nutritional research.

Average Yearly Earnings: $32,406. **Experience:** Considerable preparation is needed. A minimum of two to four years of work-related skill, knowledge, or experience is needed for this occupation. **Education:** This group of occupations usually requires a four-year bachelor's degree, but in some cases does not. **Training:** Employees in this type of occupation usually need several years of work-related experience, on-the-job training, and/ or vocational training. **Related Examples:** Other occupations like this one usually involve coordinating, supervising, managing, or training others. Examples include accountants, chefs and head cooks, computer programmers, historians, pharmacists, and police detectives. **Standard Vocational Preparation Range:** 7.0 to below 8.0—Two years to less than ten years. **Major/Instructional Program:** 19.0501 Foods and Nutrition Studies, General; 19.0502 Foods and Nutrition Science; 19.0503 Dietetics/Human Nutritional Services; 19.0505 Food Systems Administration; 20.0401 Institutional Food Workers and Administrators; 20.0409 Institutional Food Services Administrator; 51.1311 Medical Nutrition; 51.1312 Medical Pathology; 51.2702 Medical Dietician. **Related Courses:** Food Production; Computers and Electronics; Chemistry; Biology; Psychology; Medicine and Dentistry; Education and Training; English Language; History and Archeology.

DIETETIC TECHNICIANS (32523)

Provide service in assigned areas of food service management. Teach principles of food and nutrition and provide dietary counseling under the direction of dietitians.

Average Yearly Earnings: $31,054. **Experience:** Considerable preparation is needed. A minimum of two to four years of work-related skill, knowledge, or experience is needed for this occupation. **Education:** This group of occupations usually requires a four-year bachelor's degree, but in some cases does not. **Training:** Employees in this type of occupation usually need several years of work-related experience, on-the-job training, and/or vocational training. **Related Examples:** Other occupations like this one usually involve coordinating, supervising, managing, or training others. Examples include accountants, chefs and head cooks, computer programmers, historians, pharmacists, and police detectives. **Standard Vocational Preparation Range:** 7.0 to below 8.0—Two years to less than ten years. **Major/Instructional Program:** 19.0501 Foods and Nutrition Studies, General; 19.0502 Foods and Nutrition Science; 19.0503 Dietetics/Human Nutritional Services; 20.0401 Institutional Food Workers and Administrators; 20.0404 Dietician Assistant. **Related Courses:** Administration and Management; Economics and Accounting; Customer and Personal Service; Personnel and Human Resources; Food Production; Chemistry; Biology; Psychology; Sociology and Anthropology; Medicine and Dentistry; Education and Training.

Medical Technologists and Technicians

MEDICAL AND CLINICAL LABORATORY TECHNOLOGISTS (32902)

Perform a wide range of complex procedures in the general area of the clinical laboratory, or perform specialized procedures in such areas as cytology, histology, and microbiology. Duties may include supervising and coordinating the activities of workers engaged in laboratory testing. Include workers who teach medical technology when teaching is not their primary activity.

Average Yearly Earnings: $30,804. **Experience:** Considerable preparation is needed. A minimum of two to four years of work-related skill, knowledge, or experience is needed for this occupation. **Education:** This group of occupations usually requires a four-year bachelor's degree, but in some cases does not. **Training:** Employees in this type of occupation usually need several years of work-related experience, on-the-job training, and/or vocational training. **Related Examples:** Other occupations like this one usually involve coordinating, supervising, managing, or training others. Examples include accountants, chefs and head cooks, computer programmers, historians, pharmacists, and police detectives. **Standard Vocational Preparation Range:** 7.0 to below 8.0—Two years to less than ten years. **Major/Instructional Program:** 51.1002 Cytotechnologist, 51.1004 Medical Laboratory Technician, 51.1005 Medical Technology, 51.1099 Health and Medical Laboratory Technologies/Technicians, Other. **Related Courses:** Clerical; Personnel and Human

Resources; Chemistry; Biology; Psychology; Medicine and Dentistry; Therapy and Counseling; Education and Training; English Language; Philosophy and Theology; Communications and Media.

MEDICAL AND CLINICAL LABORATORY TECHNICIANS (32905)

Perform routine tests in a medical laboratory for use in the treatment and diagnosis of disease. Prepare vaccines, biologicals, and serums for the prevention of disease. Prepare tissue samples for pathologists, take blood samples, and execute such laboratory tests as urinalysis and blood counts. May work under the general supervision of a medical laboratory technologist.

Average Yearly Earnings: $30,804. **Experience:** Some preparation is needed. Some previous work-related skill, knowledge, or experience may be helpful in this occupation, but usually is not needed. **Education:** This group of occupations usually requires a high school diploma and may require some vocational training or job-related course work. In some cases, an associate or bachelor's degree could be needed. **Training:** Employees in this type of occupation need anywhere from a few months to one year of working with experienced employees. **Related Examples:** Other occupations like this one often involve using your knowledge and skills to help others. Examples include drywall installers, fire inspectors, flight attendants, pharmacy technicians, retail salespersons, and tellers. **Standard Vocational Preparation Range:** 4.0 to below 6.0—Six months to less than two years. **Major/Instructional Program:** 51.1003 Hematology Technology/Technician, 51.1004 Medical Laboratory Technician. **Related Courses:** Mathematics; Chemistry; Biology; Medicine and Dentistry; Philosophy and Theology.

DENTAL HYGIENISTS (32908)

Perform dental prophylactic treatments and instruct groups and individuals in the care of the teeth and mouth.

Average Yearly Earnings: $42,432. **Experience:** Medium preparation is needed. Previous work-related skill, knowledge, or experience is required for this occupation. **Education:** This group of occupations usually requires training in vocational schools, related on-the-job experience, or an associate degree. A bachelor's degree may be required. **Training:** Employees in this type of occupation usually need one or two years of training involving both on-the-job experience and informal training with experienced workers. **Related Examples:** Other occupations like this one usually involve using communication and organizational skills to coordinate, supervise, manage, or train others to accomplish goals. Examples include electricians, fish and game wardens, legal secretaries, personnel recruiters, and recreation workers. **Standard Vocational Preparation Range:** 6.0 to below 7.0—More than one year and less than four years. **Major/Instructional Program:** 51.0602 Dental Hygienist. **Related Courses:** Biology; Medicine and Dentistry.

MEDICAL RECORDS TECHNICIANS (32911)

Compile and maintain medical records of hospital and clinic patients.

Average Yearly Earnings: $20,488. **Experience:** Medium preparation is needed. Previous work-related skill, knowledge, or experience is required for this occupation. **Education:** This group of occupations usually requires training in vocational schools, related on-the-job experience, or an associate degree. A bachelor's degree may be required. **Training:** Employees in this type of occupation usually need one or two years of training involving both on-the-job experience and informal training with experienced workers. **Related Examples:** Other occupations like this one usually involve using communication and organizational skills to coordinate, supervise, manage, or train others to accomplish goals. Examples include dental assistants, electricians, fish and game wardens, legal secretaries, personnel recruiters, and recreation workers. **Standard Vocational Preparation Range:** 6.0 to below 7.0—More than one year and less than four years. **Major/Instructional Program:** 51.0707 Medical Records Technology/Technician, 51.0999 Health and Medical Diagnostic and Treatment Services, Other. **Related Courses:** Clerical; Computers and Electronics; Mathematics; Medicine and Dentistry.

RADIATION THERAPISTS (32913)

Provide radiation therapy to patients as prescribed by a radiologist, according to established practices and standards. Duties may include reviewing prescription and diagnosis; acting as liaison with physician and supportive care personnel; preparing equipment, such as immobilization, treatment, and protection devices; and maintaining records, reports, and files. May assist in dosimetry procedures and tumor localization.

Average Yearly Earnings: $31,969. **Experience:** Considerable preparation is needed. A minimum of two to four years of work-related skill, knowledge, or experience is needed for this occupation. **Education:** This group of occupations usually requires a four-year bachelor's degree, but in some cases does not. **Training:** Employees in this type of occupation usually need several years of work-related experience, on-the-job training, and/or vocational training. **Related Examples:** Other occupations like this one usually involve coordinating, supervising, managing, or training others. Examples include accountants, chefs and head cooks, computer programmers, historians, pharmacists, and police detectives. **Standard Vocational Preparation Range:** 7.0 to below 8.0—Two years to less than ten years. **Major/Instructional Program:** 51.0905 Nuclear Medical Technology/Technician. **Related Courses:** Clerical; Customer and Personal Service; Computers and Electronics; Biology; Medicine and Dentistry; Therapy and Counseling.

NUCLEAR MEDICINE TECHNOLOGISTS (32914)

Prepare, administer, and measure radioactive isotopes in therapeutic, diagnostic, and tracer studies utilizing a variety of radioisotope equipment. Prepare stock solutions of radioactive materials and calculate doses to be administered by radiologist. Subject patients to radiation. Execute blood volume, red cell survival, and fat absorption studies following standard laboratory techniques.

Average Yearly Earnings: $38,604. **Experience:** Considerable preparation is needed. A minimum of two to four years of work-related skill, knowledge, or experience is needed for this occupation. **Education:** This group of occupations usually requires a four-year bachelor's degree, but in some cases does not. **Training:** Employees in this type of occupation usually need several years of work-related experience, on-the-job training, and/or vocational training. **Related Examples:** Other occupations like this one usually involve coordinating, supervising, managing, or training others. Examples include accountants, chefs and head cooks, computer programmers, historians, pharmacists, and police detectives. **Standard Vocational Preparation Range:** 7.0 to below 8.0—Two years to less than ten years. **Major/Instructional Program:** 51.0905 Nuclear Medical Technology/Technician, 51.0907 Medical Radiologic Technology/Technician. **Related Courses:** Clerical; Computers and Electronics; Physics; Chemistry; Biology; Medicine and Dentistry; Therapy and Counseling.

RADIOLOGIC TECHNOLOGISTS (32919)

Take X-rays and CAT scans or administer nonradioactive materials into patient's blood stream for diagnostic purposes. Includes technologists who specialize in other modalities, such as computed tomography, ultrasound, and magnetic resonance. Include workers whose primary duties are to demonstrate portions of the human body on X-ray film or fluoroscopic screen.

Average Yearly Earnings: $31,969. **Experience:** Considerable preparation is needed. A minimum of two to four years of work-related skill, knowledge, or experience is needed for this occupation. **Education:** This group of occupations usually requires a four-year bachelor's degree, but in some cases does not. **Training:** Employees in this type of occupation usually need several years of work-related experience, on-the-job training, and/or vocational training. **Related Examples:** Other occupations like this one usually involve coordinating, supervising, managing, or training others. Examples include accountants, chefs and head cooks, computer programmers, historians, pharmacists, and police detectives. **Standard Vocational Preparation Range:** 7.0 to below 8.0—Two years to less than ten years. **Major/Instructional Program:** 51.0907 Medical Radiologic Technology/Technician, 51.0910 Diagnostic Medical Sonography Technician, 51.0999 Health and Medical Diagnostic and Treatment Services, Other. **Related Courses:** Computers and Electronics; Chemistry; Biology; Psychology; Medicine and Dentistry.

RADIOLOGIC TECHNICIANS (32921)

Maintain and use the equipment and supplies necessary to demonstrate portions of the human body on X-ray film or fluoroscopic screen for diagnostic purposes.

Average Yearly Earnings: $31,969. **Experience:** Considerable preparation is needed. A minimum of two to four years of work-related skill, knowledge, or experience is needed for this occupation. **Education:** This group of occupations usually requires a four-year bachelor's degree, but in some cases does not. **Training:** Employees in this type of occupation usually need several years of work-related experience, on-the-job training, and/ or vocational training. **Related Examples:** Other occupations like this one usually involve coordinating, supervising, managing, or training others. Examples include accountants, chefs and head cooks, computer programmers, historians, pharmacists, and police detectives. **Standard Vocational Preparation Range:** 7.0 to below 8.0—Two years to less than ten years. **Major/Instructional Program:** 51.0907 Medical Radiologic Technology/ Technician. **Related Courses:** Customer and Personal Service; Biology; Medicine and Dentistry.

ELECTRONEURODIAGNOSTIC TECHNOLOGISTS (32923)

Record electrical activity of the brain and other nervous system functions using a variety of techniques and equipment. May prepare patients for the test, obtain medical history, calculate results, and maintain equipment.

Average Yearly Earnings: $30,992. **Experience:** Some preparation is needed. Some previous work-related skill, knowledge, or experience may be helpful in this occupation, but usually is not needed. **Education:** This group of occupations usually requires a high school diploma and may require some vocational training or job-related course work. In some cases, an associate or bachelor's degree could be needed. **Training:** Employees in this type of occupation need anywhere from a few months to one year of working with experienced employees. **Related Examples:** Other occupations like this one often involve using your knowledge and skills to help others. Examples include drywall installers, fire inspectors, flight attendants, pharmacy technicians, retail salespersons, and tellers. **Standard Vocational Preparation Range:** 4.0 to below 6.0—Six months to less than two years. **Major/Instructional Program:** 51.0903 Electroencephalograph Technology/Technician. **Related Courses:** Computers and Electronics; Biology; Medicine and Dentistry; English Language.

CARDIOLOGY TECHNOLOGISTS (32925)

Conduct tests on the pulmonary and/or cardiovascular systems of patients for diagnostic purposes. May conduct or assist in electrocardiograms, cardiac catheterizations, and pulmonary function, lung capacity and similar tests.

Average Yearly Earnings: $33,696. **Experience:** Medium preparation is needed. Previous work-related skill, knowledge, or experience is required for this occupation. **Education:** This group of occupations usually requires training in vocational schools, related on-the-job experience, or an associate degree. A bachelor's degree may be required. **Training:** Employees in this type of occupation usually need one or two years of training involving both on-the-job experience and informal training with experienced workers. **Related Examples:** Other occupations like this one usually involve using communication and organizational skills to coordinate, supervise, manage, or train others to accomplish goals. Examples include dental assistants, electricians, fish and game wardens, legal secretaries, personnel recruiters, and recreation workers. **Standard Vocational Preparation Range:** 6.0 to below 7.0—More than one year and less than four years. **Major/Instructional Program:** 51.0901 Cardiovascular Technology/Technician, 51.0910 Diagnostic Medical Sonography Technician. **Related Courses:** Clerical; Computers and Electronics; Physics; Chemistry; Biology; Psychology; Medicine and Dentistry; Therapy and Counseling; English Language; Foreign Language.

ELECTROCARDIOGRAPH TECHNICIANS (32926)

Record electromotive variations in heart muscle using an electrocardiograph, to provide data for the diagnosis of heart ailments.

Average Yearly Earnings: $33,696. **Experience:** Some preparation is needed. Some previous work-related skill, knowledge, or experience may be helpful in this occupation, but usually is not needed. **Education:** This group of occupations usually requires a high school diploma and may require some vocational training or job-related course work. In some cases, an associate or bachelor's degree could be needed. **Training:** Employees in this type of occupation need anywhere from a few months to one year of working with experienced employees. **Related Examples:** Other occupations like this one often involve using your knowledge and skills to help others. Examples include drywall installers, fire inspectors, flight attendants, pharmacy technicians, retail salespersons, and tellers. **Standard Vocational Preparation Range:** 4.0 to below 6.0—Six months to less than two years. **Major/Instructional Program:** 51.0902 Electrocardiograph Technology/Technician. **Related Courses:** Clerical; Customer and Personal Service; Computers and Electronics; Biology; Psychology; Medicine and Dentistry; Therapy and Counseling; Philosophy and Theology.

SURGICAL TECHNOLOGISTS AND TECHNICIANS (32928)

Perform any combination of the following tasks, either before, during, or after an operation: prepare patient by washing, shaving, etc.; place equipment and supplies in operating room according to surgeon's instructions; arrange instruments under the direction of a nurse; maintain specified supply of fluids for use during operation; adjust lights and equipment as directed; hand instruments and supplies to surgeon, hold retractors, and cut sutures as directed; count the sponges, needles, and instruments used during operation; and clean the operating room.

Average Yearly Earnings: $25,001. **Experience:** Medium preparation is needed. Previous work-related skill, knowledge, or experience is required for this occupation. **Education:** This group of occupations usually requires training in vocational schools, related on-the-job experience, or an associate degree. A bachelor's degree may be required.

Training: Employees in this type of occupation usually need one or two years of training involving both on-the-job experience and informal training with experienced workers. **Related Examples:** Other occupations like this one usually involve using communication and organizational skills to coordinate, supervise, manage, or train others to accomplish goals. Examples include dental assistants, electricians, fish and game wardens, legal secretaries, personnel recruiters, and recreation workers. **Standard Vocational Preparation Range:** 6.0 to below 7.0—More than one year and less than four years. **Major/Instructional Program:** 51.0909 Surgical/Operating Room Technician. **Related Courses:** Biology; Medicine and Dentistry.

PSYCHIATRIC TECHNICIANS (32931)

Provide nursing care to mentally ill, emotionally disturbed, or mentally retarded patients. Participate in rehabilitation and treatment programs. Help with personal hygiene. Administer oral medications and hypodermic injections, following physician's prescriptions and hospital procedures. Monitor patient's physical and emotional well-being and report to medical staff.

Average Yearly Earnings: $20,217. **Experience:** Medium preparation is needed. Previous work-related skill, knowledge, or experience is required for this occupation. **Education:** This group of occupations usually requires training in vocational schools, related on-the-job experience, or an associate degree. A bachelor's degree may be required. **Training:** Employees in this type of occupation usually need one or two years of training involving both on-the-job experience and informal training with experienced workers. **Related Examples:** Other occupations like this one usually involve using communication and organizational skills to coordinate, supervise, manage, or train others to accomplish goals. Examples include dental assistants, electricians, fish and game wardens, legal secretaries, personnel recruiters, and recreation workers. **Standard Vocational Preparation Range:** 6.0 to below 7.0—More than one year and less than four years. **Major/Instructional Program:** 51.1502 Psychiatric/Mental Health Services Technician. **Related Courses:** Clerical; Customer and Personal Service; Biology; Psychology; Medicine and Dentistry; Therapy and Counseling.

HEALTH SERVICE COORDINATORS (32996A)

Conduct or coordinate health programs or services in hospitals, private homes, businesses, or other institutions.

Average Yearly Earnings: $31,054. **Experience:** Medium preparation is needed. Previous work-related skill, knowledge, or experience is required for this occupation. **Education:** This group of occupations usually requires training in vocational schools, related on-the-job experience, or an associate degree. A bachelor's degree may be required. **Training:** Employees in this type of occupation usually need one or two years of training involving both on-the-job experience and informal training with experienced workers. **Related Examples:** Other occupations like this one usually involve using communication and organizational skills to coordinate, supervise, manage, or train others to accomplish goals. Examples include dental assistants, electricians, fish and game wardens, legal secretaries, personnel recruiters, and recreation workers. **Standard Vocational Preparation Range:** 6.0 to below 7.0—More than one year and less than four years. **Related Courses:** Administration and Management; Clerical; Customer and Personal Service; Personnel and Human Resources; Medicine and Dentistry; Therapy and Counseling; Education and Training.

TRANSPLANT COORDINATORS (32996B)

Plan and coordinate organ and tissue services and solicit medical and community groups for organ and tissue donors.

Average Yearly Earnings: $31,054. **Experience:** Extensive preparation is needed. Extensive skill, knowledge, and experience are needed for this occupation. It may require more than five years of experience. **Education:** A bachelor's degree is the minimum formal education required for this group of occupations. However, many also require graduate school. For example, they may require a master's degree, and some require a Ph.D., M.D., or J.D. (law degree). **Training:** Employees in this type of occupation may need some on-the-job training, but most of these occupations assume that the person will already have the required skills, knowledge, work-related experience, and/or training. **Examples:** Other occupations like this one often involve coordinating, training, supervising, or managing the activities of others to accomplish goals. Very advanced communication and organizational skills are required. Examples include athletic trainers, lawyers, managing editors, physicists, social psychologists, and surgeons. **Standard Vocational Preparation Range:** 8.0 to 9.0—Four years to more than ten years. **Major/Instructional Program:** 51.0999 Health and Medical Diagnostic and Treatment Services, Other. **Related Courses:** Administration and Management; Clerical; Customer and Personal Service; Mathematics; Biology; Psychology; Medicine and Dentistry; Therapy and Counseling.

OCCUPATIONAL HEALTH AND SAFETY SPECIALISTS (32996C)

Review, evaluate, and analyze work environments and design programs and procedures to control, eliminate, and prevent disease or injury caused by chemical, physical, and biological agents or ergonomic factors.

Average Yearly Earnings: $31,054. **Experience:** Extensive preparation is needed. Extensive skill, knowledge, and experience are needed for this occupation. It may require more than five years of experience. **Education:** A bachelor's degree is the minimum formal education required for this group of occupations. However, many also require graduate school. For example, they may require a master's degree, and some require a Ph.D., M.D., or J.D. (law degree). **Training:** Employees in this type of occupation may need some on-the-job training, but most of these occupations assume that the person will already have the required skills, knowledge, work-related experience, and/or training. **Examples:** Other occupations like this one often involve coordinating, training, supervising, or managing the activities of others to accomplish goals. Very advanced communication and organizational skills are required. Examples include athletic trainers, lawyers, managing editors, physicists, social psychologists, and surgeons. **Standard Vocational Preparation Range:** 8.0 to 9.0—Four years to more than ten years. **Major/ Instructional Program:** 15.0701 Occupational Safety and Health Technology/Technician. **Related Courses:** Economics and Accounting; Physics; Chemistry; Biology; Medicine and Dentistry; Education and Training; Public Safety and Security; Law, Government, and Jurisprudence.

ORTHOTISTS AND PROSTHETISTS (32999A)

Fabricate and fit orthopedic braces or prostheses to assist patients with disabling conditions of the limbs and spine, or with partial or total absence of a limb.

Average Yearly Earnings: $31,054. **Experience:** Medium preparation is needed. Previous work-related skill, knowledge, or experience is required for this occupation. **Education:** This group of occupations usually requires training in vocational schools, related on-the-job experience, or an associate degree. A bachelor's degree may be required. **Training:** Employees in this type of occupation usually need one or two years of training involving both on-the-job experience and informal training with experienced workers. **Related Examples:** Other occupations like this one usually involve using communication and organizational skills to coordinate, supervise, manage, or train others to accomplish goals. Examples include dental assistants, electricians, fish and game wardens, legal secretaries, personnel recruiters, and recreation workers. **Standard Vocational Preparation Range:** 6.0 to below 7.0—More than one year and less than four years. **Major/ Instructional Program:** 51.0801 Medical Assistant, 51.2307 Orthotics/Prosthetics. **Related Courses:** Customer and Personal Service; Engineering and Technology; Design; Building and Construction; Psychology; Medicine and Dentistry; Therapy and Counseling; Education and Training.

PHERESIS TECHNICIANS (32999B)

Collect blood components and provide therapeutic treatment, such as the replacement of plasma or removal of white blood cells or platelets, using blood cell separator equipment.

Average Yearly Earnings: $31,054. **Experience:** Considerable preparation is needed. A minimum of two to four years of work-related skill, knowledge, or experience is needed for this occupation. **Education:** This group of occupations usually requires a four-year bachelor's degree, but in some cases does not. **Training:** Employees in this type of occupation usually need several years of work-related experience, on-the-job training, and/ or vocational training. **Related Examples:** Other occupations like this one usually involve coordinating, supervising, managing, or training others. Examples include accountants, chefs and head cooks, computer programmers, historians, pharmacists, and police detectives. **Standard Vocational Preparation Range:** 7.0 to below 8.0—Two years to less than ten years. **Major/Instructional Program:** 51.0999 Health and Medical Diagnostic and Treatment Services, Other. **Related Courses:** Biology; Psychology; Medicine and Dentistry; Therapy and Counseling.

OPTOMETRIC AND OPHTHALMIC TECHNICIANS (32999C)

Test and measure eye function to assist with the diagnosis and treatment of disease.

Average Yearly Earnings: $31,054. **Experience:** Medium preparation is needed. Previous work-related skill, knowledge, or experience is required for this occupation. **Education:** This group of occupations usually requires training in vocational schools, related on-the-job experience, or an associate degree. A bachelor's degree may be required. **Training:** Employees in this type of occupation usually need one or two years of training involving both on-the-job experience and informal training with experienced workers. **Related Examples:** Other occupations like this one usually involve using communication and organizational skills to coordinate, supervise, manage, or train others to accomplish goals. Examples include dental assistants, electricians, fish and game wardens, legal secretaries, personnel recruiters, and recreation workers. **Standard Vocational Preparation Range:** 6.0 to below 7.0—More than one year and less than four years. **Major/Instructional Program:** 51.0804 Ophthalmic Medical Assistant; 51.0899 Health and Medical Assistants, Other; 51.1803 Ophthalmic Medical Technologist; 51.1804 Orthoptics. **Related Courses:** Customer and Personal Service; Biology; Medicine and Dentistry; Therapy and Counseling.

AUDIOMETRISTS (32999D)

Administer audiometric screening and threshold tests under the supervision of an audiologist or otolaryngologist and refer an individual to an audiologist or other health professional for test interpretation or further examination.

Average Yearly Earnings: $31,054. **Experience:** Medium preparation is needed. Previous work-related skill, knowledge, or experience is required for this occupation. **Education:** This group of occupations usually requires training in vocational schools, related on-the-job experience, or an associate degree. A bachelor's degree may be required. **Training:** Employees in this type of occupation usually need one or two years of training involving both on-the-job experience and informal training with experienced workers. **Related Examples:** Other occupations like this one usually involve using communication and organizational skills to coordinate, supervise, manage, or train others to accomplish goals. Examples include dental assistants, electricians, fish and game wardens, legal secretaries, personnel recruiters, and recreation workers. **Standard Vocational Preparation Range:** 6.0 to below 7.0—More than one year and less than four years. **Major/Instructional Program:** 51.2601 Health Aide. **Related Courses:** No related courses listed in the database for this occupation.

DIALYSIS TECHNICIANS (32999E)

Set up and operate a hemodialysis machine to provide dialysis treatment for patients with kidney failure.

Average Yearly Earnings: $31,054. **Experience:** Medium preparation is needed. Previous work-related skill, knowledge, or experience is required for this occupation. **Education:** This group of occupations usually requires training in vocational schools, related on-the-job experience, or an associate degree. A bachelor's degree may be required. **Training:** Employees in this type of occupation usually need one or two years of training involving both on-the-job experience and informal training with experienced workers. **Related Examples:** Other occupations like this one usually involve using communication and organizational skills to coordinate, supervise, manage, or train others to accomplish goals. Examples include dental assistants, electricians, fish and game wardens, legal secretaries, personnel recruiters, and recreation workers. **Standard Vocational Preparation Range:** 6.0 to below 7.0—More than one year and less than four years. **Major/Instructional Program:** 51.0999 Health and Medical Diagnostic and Treatment Services, Other. **Related Courses:** Customer and Personal Service; Chemistry; Biology; Medicine and Dentistry; Therapy and Counseling.

Artistic, Creative, and Entertainment Providers

COLUMNISTS, CRITICS, AND COMMENTATORS (34002A)

Write commentaries or critical reviews based on the analysis of news items or literary, musical, or artistic works and performances.

Average Yearly Earnings: $38,355. **Experience:** Considerable preparation is needed. A minimum of two to four years of work-related skill, knowledge, or experience is needed for this occupation. **Education:** This group of occupations usually requires a four-year bachelor's degree, but in some cases does not. **Training:** Employees in this type of occupation usually need several years of work-related experience, on-the-job training, and/or vocational training. **Related Examples:** Other occupations like this one usually involve coordinating, supervising, managing, or training others. Examples include accountants, chefs and head cooks, computer programmers, historians, pharmacists, and police detectives. **Standard Vocational Preparation Range:** 7.0 to below 8.0—Two years to less than ten years. **Major/Instructional Program:** 09.0401 Journalism; 09.0402 Broadcast Journalism; 23.0501 English Creative Writing; 50.0501 Drama/Theater Arts, General; 50.0505 Drama/Theater Literature, History, and Criticism; 50.0601 Film/Cinema Studies; 50.0901 Music, General; 50.0902 Music History and Literature. **Related Courses:** Computers and Electronics; English Language; Fine Arts; Communications and Media.

POETS AND LYRICISTS (34002B)

Write poetry or song lyrics for publication or performance.

Average Yearly Earnings: $38,355. **Experience:** Considerable preparation is needed. A minimum of two to four years of work-related skill, knowledge, or experience is needed for this occupation. **Education:** This group of occupations usually requires a four-year bachelor's degree, but in some cases does not. **Training:** Employees in this type of occupation usually need several years of work-related experience, on-the-job training, and/or vocational training. **Related Examples:** Other occupations like this one usually involve coordinating, supervising, managing, or training others. Examples include accountants, chefs and head cooks, computer programmers, historians, pharmacists, and police detectives. **Standard Vocational Preparation Range:** 7.0 to below 8.0—Two years to less than ten years. **Major/Instructional Program:** 23.0501 English Creative Writing. **Related Courses:** English Language; Fine Arts; Communications and Media.

CREATIVE WRITERS (34002C)

Create original written works, such as plays or prose, for publication or performance.

Average Yearly Earnings: $38,355. **Experience:** Considerable preparation is needed. A minimum of two to four years of work-related skill, knowledge, or experience is needed for this occupation. **Education:** This group of occupations usually requires a four-year bachelor's degree, but in some cases does not. **Training:** Employees in this type of occupation usually need several years of work-related experience, on-the-job training, and/or vocational training. **Related Examples:** Other occupations like this one usually involve coordinating, supervising, managing, or training others. Examples include accountants, chefs and head cooks, computer programmers, historians, pharmacists, and police detectives. **Standard Vocational Preparation Range:** 7.0 to below 8.0—Two years to less than ten years. **Major/Instructional Program:** 09.0401 Journalism; 09.0402 Broadcast Journalism; 09.0701 Radio and Television Broadcasting; 23.0501 English Creative Writing; 23.1101 English Technical and Business Writing; 50.0501 Drama/Theater Arts, General; 50.0504 Playwriting and Screenwriting. **Related Courses:** Sociology and Anthropology; English Language; Fine Arts; Communications and Media.

EDITORS (34002D)

Perform a variety of editorial duties, such as laying out, indexing, and revising the content of written materials in preparation for final publication. Excludes managing editors, programming and script editors, book editors, and film editors.

Average Yearly Earnings: $38,355. **Experience:** Considerable preparation is needed. A minimum of two to four years of work-related skill, knowledge, or experience is needed for this occupation. **Education:** This group of occupations usually requires a four-year bachelor's degree, but in some cases does not. **Training:** Employees in this type of occupation usually need several years of work-related experience, on-the-job training,

and/or vocational training. **Related Examples:** Other occupations like this one usually involve coordinating, supervising, managing, or training others. Examples include accountants, chefs and head cooks, computer programmers, historians, pharmacists, and police detectives. **Standard Vocational Preparation Range:** 7.0 to below 8.0—Two years to less than ten years. **Major/Instructional Program:** 09.0401 Journalism, 09.0402 Broadcast Journalism, 09.0701 Radio and Television Broadcasting, 23.0501 English Creative Writing, 23.1101 English Technical and Business Writing, 52.0501 Business Communications. **Related Courses:** English Language; Communications and Media.

MANAGING EDITORS (34002E)

Direct and coordinate the editorial operations of a newspaper, newspaper department, or magazine. Includes workers who formulate editorial policy.

Average Yearly Earnings: $38,355. **Experience:** Extensive preparation is needed. Extensive skill, knowledge, and experience are needed for this occupation. It may require more than five years of experience. **Education:** A bachelor's degree is the minimum formal education required for this group of occupations. However, many also require graduate school. For example, they may require a master's degree, and some require a Ph.D., M.D., or J.D. (law degree). **Training:** Employees in this type of occupation may need some on-the-job training, but most of these occupations assume that the person will already have the required skills, knowledge, work-related experience, and/or training. **Examples:** Other occupations like this one often involve coordinating, training, supervising, or managing the activities of others to accomplish goals. Very advanced communication and organizational skills are required. Examples include athletic trainers, lawyers, physicists, social psychologists, and surgeons. **Standard Vocational Preparation Range:** 8.0 to 9.0—Four years to more than ten years. **Major/Instructional Program:** 09.0401 Journalism, 09.0402 Broadcast Journalism, 23.0501 English Creative Writing, 23.1101 English Technical and Business Writing. **Related Courses:** Administration and Management; Personnel and Human Resources; Computers and Electronics; English Language; Communications and Media.

PROGRAMMING AND SCRIPT EDITORS AND COORDINATORS (34002F)

Direct and coordinate activities of workers who prepare scripts for radio, television, or motion picture productions. Includes workers who develop, write, and edit proposals for new radio or television programs.

Average Yearly Earnings: $38,355. **Experience:** Considerable preparation is needed. A minimum of two to four years of work-related skill, knowledge, or experience is needed for this occupation. **Education:** This group of occupations usually requires a four-year bachelor's degree, but in some cases does not. **Training:** Employees in this type of occupation usually need several years of work-related experience, on-the-job training, and/or vocational training. **Related Examples:** Other occupations like this one usually involve coordinating, supervising, managing, or training others. Examples include accountants, chefs and head cooks, computer programmers, historians, pharmacists, and police detectives. **Standard Vocational Preparation Range:** 7.0 to below 8.0—Two years to less than ten years. **Major/Instructional Program:** 09.0402 Broadcast Journalism; 09.0701 Radio and Television Broadcasting; 23.0501 English Creative Writing; 50.0501 Drama/Theater Arts, General; 50.0504 Playwriting and Screenwriting. **Related Courses:** Administration and Management; Economics and Accounting; Personnel and Human Resources; English Language; Fine Arts; Communications and Media.

BOOK EDITORS (34002G)

Secure, select, and coordinate the publication of manuscripts in book form.

Average Yearly Earnings: $38,355. **Experience:** Extensive preparation is needed. Extensive skill, knowledge, and experience are needed for this occupation. It may require more than five years of experience. **Education:** A bachelor's degree is the minimum formal education required for this group of occupations. However, many also require graduate school. For example, they may require a master's degree, and some require a Ph.D., M.D., or J.D. (law degree). **Training:** Employees in this type of occupation may need some on-the-job training, but most of these occupations assume that the person will already have the required skills, knowledge, work-related experience, and/or training. **Examples:** Other occupations like this one often involve coordinating, training, supervising, or managing the activities of others to accomplish goals. Very advanced communication and organizational skills are required. Examples include athletic trainers, lawyers, managing editors, physicists, social psychologists, and surgeons. **Standard Vocational Preparation Range:** 8.0 to 9.0—Four years to more than ten years. **Major/Instructional Program:** 23.0501 English Creative Writing, 23.1101 English Technical and Business Writing. **Related Courses:** Administration and Management; Sales and Marketing; English Language; Communications and Media.

READERS (34002H)

Read books, plays, or scripts to prepare synopses for review by editorial staff or to recommend content revisions.

Average Yearly Earnings: $38,355. **Experience:** Medium preparation is needed. Previous work-related skill, knowledge, or experience is required for this occupation. **Education:** This group of occupations usually requires training in vocational schools, related on-the-job experience, or an associate degree. A bachelor's degree may be required. **Training:** Employees in this type of occupation usually need one or two years of training involving both on-the-job experience and informal training with experienced workers. **Related Examples:** Other occupations like this one usually involve using communication and organizational skills to coordinate, supervise, manage, or train others to accomplish goals. Examples include dental assistants, electricians, fish and game wardens, legal secretaries, personnel recruiters, and recreation workers. **Standard Vocational Preparation Range:** 6.0 to below 7.0—More than one year and less than four years. **Major/Instructional Program:** 09.0402 Broadcast Journalism, 09.0701 Radio and Television Broadcasting. **Related Courses:** English Language; Communications and Media.

CAPTION WRITERS (34002J)

Write caption phrases of dialogue for hearing-impaired and foreign language-speaking viewers of movie or television productions.

Average Yearly Earnings: $38,355. **Experience:** Medium preparation is needed. Previous work-related skill, knowledge, or experience is required for this occupation. **Education:** This group of occupations usually requires training in vocational schools, related on-the-job experience, or an associate degree. A bachelor's degree may be required. **Training:** Employees in this type of occupation usually need one or two years of training involving both on-the-job experience and informal training with experienced workers. **Related Examples:** Other occupations like this one usually involve using communication and organizational skills to coordinate, supervise, manage, or train others to accomplish goals. Examples include dental assistants, electricians, fish and game wardens, legal secretaries, personnel recruiters, and recreation workers. **Standard Vocational Preparation Range:** 6.0 to below 7.0—More than one year and less than four years. **Major/Instructional Program:** 16.0101 Foreign Languages and Literatures, General; 16.0103 Foreign Language Interpretation and Translation. **Related Courses:** Computers and Electronics; English Language; Foreign Language; Communications and Media.

COPY WRITERS (34002L)

Write advertising copy for use by a publication or broadcast media to promote the sale of goods and services.

Average Yearly Earnings: $38,355. **Experience:** Considerable preparation is needed. A minimum of two to four years of work-related skill, knowledge, or experience is needed for this occupation. **Education:** This group of occupations usually requires a four-year bachelor's degree, but in some cases does not. **Training:** Employees in this type of occupation usually need several years of work-related experience, on-the-job training, and/or vocational training. **Related Examples:** Other occupations like this one usually involve coordinating, supervising, managing, or training others. Examples include accountants, chefs and head cooks, computer programmers, historians, pharmacists, and police detectives. **Standard Vocational Preparation Range:** 7.0 to below 8.0—Two years to less than ten years. **Major/Instructional Program:** 09.0201 Advertising. **Related Courses:** Sales and Marketing; Computers and Electronics; English Language; Communications and Media.

DICTIONARY EDITORS (34002M)

Research information about words, and write and review definitions for publication in a dictionary.

Average Yearly Earnings: $38,355. **Experience:** Extensive preparation is needed. Extensive skill, knowledge, and experience are needed for this occupation. It may require more than five years of experience. **Education:** A bachelor's degree is the minimum formal

education required for this group of occupations. However, many also require graduate school. For example, they may require a master's degree, and some require a Ph.D., M.D., or J.D. (law degree). **Training:** Employees in this type of occupation may need some on-the-job training, but most of these occupations assume that the person will already have the required skills, knowledge, work-related experience, and/or training. **Examples:** Other occupations like this one often involve coordinating, training, supervising, or managing the activities of others to accomplish goals. Very advanced communication and organizational skills are required. Examples include athletic trainers, lawyers, managing editors, physicists, social psychologists, and surgeons. **Standard Vocational Preparation Range:** 8.0 to 9.0—Four years to more than ten years. **Major/Instructional Program:** 23.0501 English Creative Writing, 23.1101 English Technical and Business Writing. **Related Courses:** English Language.

TECHNICAL WRITERS (34005)

Write or edit technical materials, such as equipment manuals, appendices, and operating and maintenance instructions. May oversee the preparation of illustrations, photographs, diagrams, and charts; and assist in layout work.

Average Yearly Earnings: $38,355. **Experience:** Extensive preparation is needed. Extensive skill, knowledge, and experience are needed for this occupation. It may require more than five years of experience. **Education:** A bachelor's degree is the minimum formal education required for this group of occupations. However, many also require graduate school. For example, they may require a master's degree, and some require a Ph.D., M.D., or J.D. (law degree). **Training:** Employees in this type of occupation may need some on-the-job training, but most of these occupations assume that the person will already have the required skills, knowledge, work-related experience, and/or training. **Examples:** Other occupations like this one often involve coordinating, training, supervising, or managing the activities of others to accomplish goals. Very advanced communication and organizational skills are required. Examples include athletic trainers, lawyers, managing editors, physicists, social psychologists, and surgeons. **Standard Vocational Preparation Range:** 8.0 to 9.0—Four years to more than ten years. **Major/Instructional Program:** 23.0501 English Creative Writing, 23.1101 English Technical and Business Writing, 52.0501 Business Communications. **Related Courses:** Administration and Management; Clerical; Computers and Electronics; Engineering and Technology; Design; Sociology and Anthropology; Education and Training; English Language; Telecommunications; Communications and Media.

PUBLIC RELATIONS SPECIALISTS AND PUBLICITY WRITERS (34008)

Engage in promoting or creating goodwill for individuals, groups, or organizations by writing or selecting favorable publicity material and releasing it through various communications media. Prepare and arrange displays, make speeches, and perform related publicity efforts.

Average Yearly Earnings: $33,862. **Experience:** Considerable preparation is needed. A minimum of two to four years of work-related skill, knowledge, or experience is needed for this occupation. **Education:** This group of occupations usually requires a four-year bachelor's degree, but in some cases does not. **Training:** Employees in this type of occupation usually need several years of work-related experience, on-the-job training, and/or vocational training. **Related Examples:** Other occupations like this one usually involve coordinating, supervising, managing, or training others. Examples include accountants, chefs and head cooks, computer programmers, historians, pharmacists, and police detectives. **Standard Vocational Preparation Range:** 7.0 to below 8.0—Two years to less than ten years. **Major/Instructional Program:** 08.0204 Business Services Marketing Operations, 09.0501 Public Relations and Organizational Communications. **Related Courses:** Clerical; Sales and Marketing; Personnel and Human Resources; Computers and Electronics; Psychology; Sociology and Anthropology; Therapy and Counseling; Education and Training; Communications and Media.

REPORTERS AND CORRESPONDENTS (34011)

Collect and analyze facts about newsworthy events by interview, investigation, or observation. Report and write stories for newspaper, news magazine, radio, or television. Excludes correspondents who broadcast news for radio and television.

Average Yearly Earnings: $28,329. **Experience:** Considerable preparation is needed. A minimum of two to four years of work-related skill, knowledge, or experience is needed for this occupation. **Education:** This group of occupations usually requires a four-year bachelor's degree, but in some cases does not. **Training:** Employees in this type of occupation usually need several years of work-related experience, on-the-job training, and/or vocational training. **Related Examples:** Other occupations like this one usually involve coordinating, supervising, managing, or training others. Examples include accountants, chefs and head cooks, computer programmers, historians, pharmacists, and police detectives. **Standard Vocational Preparation Range:** 7.0 to below 8.0—Two years to less than ten years. **Major/Instructional Program:** 09.0401 Journalism, 09.0402 Broadcast Journalism. **Related Courses:** Computers and Electronics; Sociology and Anthropology; Geography; English Language; Telecommunications; Communications and Media.

BROADCAST NEWS ANALYSTS (34014)

Analyze, interpret, and broadcast news received from various sources.

Average Yearly Earnings: $24,148. **Experience:** Considerable preparation is needed. A minimum of two to four years of work-related skill, knowledge, or experience is needed for this occupation. **Education:** This group of occupations usually requires a four-year bachelor's degree, but in some cases does not. **Training:** Employees in this type of occupation usually need several years of work-related experience, on-the-job training, and/or vocational training. **Related Examples:** Other occupations like this one usually

involve coordinating, supervising, managing, or training others. Examples include accountants, chefs and head cooks, computer programmers, historians, pharmacists, and police detectives. **Standard Vocational Preparation Range:** 7.0 to below 8.0—Two years to less than ten years. **Major/Instructional Program:** 09.0401 Journalism, 09.0402 Broadcast Journalism, 23.0501 English Creative Writing. **Related Courses:** Computers and Electronics; Sociology and Anthropology; Geography; English Language; Foreign Language; Fine Arts; History and Archeology; Philosophy and Theology; Telecommunications; Communications and Media.

ANNOUNCERS, RADIO AND TELEVISION (34017)

Introduce various types of radio or television programs, interview or question guests, or act as master of ceremonies. Read news flashes and identify the station by giving call letters.

Average Yearly Earnings: $24,148. **Experience:** Some preparation is needed. Some previous work-related skill, knowledge, or experience may be helpful in this occupation, but usually is not needed. **Education:** This group of occupations usually requires a high school diploma and may require some vocational training or job-related course work. In some cases, an associate or bachelor's degree could be needed. **Training:** Employees in this type of occupation need anywhere from a few months to one year of working with experienced employees. **Related Examples:** Other occupations like this one often involve using your knowledge and skills to help others. Examples include drywall installers, fire inspectors, flight attendants, pharmacy technicians, retail salespersons, and tellers. **Standard Vocational Preparation Range:** 4.0 to below 6.0—Six months to less than two years. **Major/Instructional Program:** 09.0402 Broadcast Journalism, 09.0701 Radio and Television Broadcasting. **Related Courses:** Sales and Marketing; Computers and Electronics; English Language; Telecommunications; Communications and Media.

ANNOUNCERS, EXCEPT RADIO AND TELEVISION (34021)

Announce information to patrons of sporting and other entertainment events using a public address system.

Average Yearly Earnings: $35,339. **Experience:** Medium preparation is needed. Previous work-related skill, knowledge, or experience is required for this occupation. **Education:** This group of occupations usually requires training in vocational schools, related on-the-job experience, or an associate degree. A bachelor's degree may be required. **Training:** Employees in this type of occupation usually need one or two years of training involving both on-the-job experience and informal training with experienced workers. **Related Examples:** Other occupations like this one usually involve using communication and organizational skills to coordinate, supervise, manage, or train others to accomplish goals. Examples include dental assistants, electricians, fish and game wardens, legal secretaries, personnel recruiters, and recreation workers. **Standard Vocational Preparation Range:** 6.0 to below 7.0—More than one year and less than four years. **Major/Instructional Program:** 09.0101 Communications, General. **Related Courses:** Communications and Media.

PROFESSIONAL PHOTOGRAPHERS (34023A)

Photograph subjects or newsworthy events, using still cameras, color or black-and-white film, and a variety of photographic accessories. Excludes scientific photographers.

Average Yearly Earnings: $23,379. **Experience:** Medium preparation is needed. Previous work-related skill, knowledge, or experience is required for this occupation. **Education:** This group of occupations usually requires training in vocational schools, related on-the-job experience, or an associate degree. A bachelor's degree may be required. **Training:** Employees in this type of occupation usually need one or two years of training involving both on-the-job experience and informal training with experienced workers. **Related Examples:** Other occupations like this one usually involve using communication and organizational skills to coordinate, supervise, manage, or train others to accomplish goals. Examples include dental assistants, electricians, fish and game wardens, legal secretaries, personnel recruiters, and recreation workers. **Standard Vocational Preparation Range:** 6.0 to below 7.0—More than one year and less than four years. **Major/Instructional Program:** 50.0406 Commercial Photography, 50.0605 Photography. **Related Courses:** Chemistry; Geography; Fine Arts; History and Archeology; Communications and Media.

PHOTOGRAPHERS, SCIENTIFIC (34023B)

Photograph a variety of subject materials to illustrate or record scientific/medical data or phenomena, utilizing knowledge of scientific procedures and photographic technology and techniques.

Average Yearly Earnings: $23,379. **Experience:** Medium preparation is needed. Previous work-related skill, knowledge, or experience is required for this occupation. **Education:** This group of occupations usually requires training in vocational schools, related on-the-job experience, or an associate degree. A bachelor's degree may be required. **Training:** Employees in this type of occupation usually need one or two years of training involving both on-the-job experience and informal training with experienced workers. **Related Examples:** Other occupations like this one usually involve using communication and organizational skills to coordinate, supervise, manage, or train others to accomplish goals. Examples include dental assistants, electricians, fish and game wardens, legal secretaries, personnel recruiters, and recreation workers. **Standard Vocational Preparation Range:** 6.0 to below 7.0—More than one year and less than four years. **Major/Instructional Program:** 50.0406 Commercial Photography, 50.0605 Photography, 51.1803 Ophthalmic Medical Technologist. **Related Courses:** Engineering and Technology; Physics; Chemistry; Medicine and Dentistry; Fine Arts; Communications and Media.

CAMERA OPERATORS, TELEVISION AND MOTION PICTURE (34026)

Operate a television or motion picture camera to photograph scenes for TV broadcasts, advertising, or motion pictures.

Average Yearly Earnings: $25,792. **Experience:** Considerable preparation is needed. A minimum of two to four years of work-related skill, knowledge, or experience is needed

for this occupation. **Education:** This group of occupations usually requires a four-year bachelor's degree, but in some cases does not. **Training:** Employees in this type of occupation usually need several years of work-related experience, on-the-job training, and/or vocational training. **Related Examples:** Other occupations like this one usually involve coordinating, supervising, managing, or training others. Examples include accountants, chefs and head cooks, computer programmers, historians, pharmacists, and police detectives. **Standard Vocational Preparation Range:** 7.0 to below 8.0—Two years to less than ten years. **Major/Instructional Program:** 10.0103 Photographic Technology/Technician, 50.0406 Commercial Photography, 50.0602 Film-Video Making/Cinematography and Production, 50.0605 Photography. **Related Courses:** Physics; Fine Arts; Telecommunications; Communications and Media.

BROADCAST TECHNICIANS (34028B)

Set up, operate, and maintain electrical and electronic equipment used in radio and television broadcasts.

Average Yearly Earnings: $31,033. **Experience:** Considerable preparation is needed. A minimum of two to four years of work-related skill, knowledge, or experience is needed for this occupation. **Education:** This group of occupations usually requires a four-year bachelor's degree, but in some cases does not. **Training:** Employees in this type of occupation usually need several years of work-related experience, on-the-job training, and/or vocational training. **Related Examples:** Other occupations like this one usually involve coordinating, supervising, managing, or training others. Examples include accountants, chefs and head cooks, computer programmers, historians, pharmacists, and police detectives. **Standard Vocational Preparation Range:** 7.0 to below 8.0—Two years to less than ten years. **Major/Instructional Program:** 10.0103 Photographic Technology/Technician, 10.0104 Radio and Television Broadcasting Technology/Technician. **Related Courses:** Computers and Electronics; Geography; Education and Training; Telecommunications; Communications and Media; Transportation.

TRANSMITTER ENGINEERS (34028C)

Operate and maintain a radio transmitter to broadcast radio and television programs.

Average Yearly Earnings: $31,033. **Experience:** Considerable preparation is needed. A minimum of two to four years of work-related skill, knowledge, or experience is needed for this occupation. **Education:** This group of occupations usually requires a four-year bachelor's degree, but in some cases does not. **Training:** Employees in this type of occupation usually need several years of work-related experience, on-the-job training, and/or vocational training. **Related Examples:** Other occupations like this one usually involve coordinating, supervising, managing, or training others. Examples include accountants, chefs and head cooks, computer programmers, historians, pharmacists, and police detectives. **Standard Vocational Preparation Range:** 7.0 to below 8.0—Two years to less than ten years. **Major/Instructional Program:** 10.0104 Radio and Television Broadcasting Technology/Technician. **Related Courses:** Computers and Electronics; Telecommunications; Communications and Media.

FILM EDITORS (34032)

Edit motion picture film and soundtracks.

Average Yearly Earnings: $35,339. **Experience:** Considerable preparation is needed. A minimum of two to four years of work-related skill, knowledge, or experience is needed for this occupation. **Education:** This group of occupations usually requires a four-year bachelor's degree, but in some cases does not. **Training:** Employees in this type of occupation usually need several years of work-related experience, on-the-job training, and/or vocational training. **Related Examples:** Other occupations like this one usually involve coordinating, supervising, managing, or training others. Examples include accountants, chefs and head cooks, computer programmers, historians, pharmacists, and police detectives. **Standard Vocational Preparation Range:** 7.0 to below 8.0—Two years to less than ten years. **Major/Instructional Program:** 10.0104 Radio and Television Broadcasting Technology/Technician, 50.0602 Film-Video Making/Cinematography and Production. **Related Courses:** Computers and Electronics; English Language; Fine Arts; Telecommunications; Communications and Media.

PAINTERS AND ILLUSTRATORS (34035A)

Paint or draw subject material to produce original artwork or provide illustrations to explain or adorn the written or spoken word, using watercolors, oils, acrylics, tempera, or other paint mediums.

Average Yearly Earnings: $33,113. **Experience:** Considerable preparation is needed. A minimum of two to four years of work-related skill, knowledge, or experience is needed for this occupation. **Education:** This group of occupations usually requires a four-year bachelor's degree, but in some cases does not. **Training:** Employees in this type of occupation usually need several years of work-related experience, on-the-job training, and/or vocational training. **Related Examples:** Other occupations like this one usually involve coordinating, supervising, managing, or training others. Examples include accountants, chefs and head cooks, computer programmers, historians, pharmacists, and police detectives. **Standard Vocational Preparation Range:** 7.0 to below 8.0—Two years to less than ten years. **Major/Instructional Program:** 50.0402 Graphic Design, Commercial Art and Illustration; 50.0501 Drama/Theater Arts, General; 50.0502 Technical Theater/Theater Design and Stagecraft; 50.0701 Art, General; 50.0702 Fine/Studio Arts; 50.0705 Drawing; 50.0708 Painting; 50.0710 Printmaking; 51.2703 Medical Illustrating. **Related Courses:** Design; Chemistry; Fine Arts; History and Archeology.

SKETCH ARTISTS (34035B)

Sketch likenesses of subjects according to observation or descriptions, either to assist law-enforcement agencies in identifying suspects or for the entertainment purposes of patrons, using mediums such as pencil, charcoal, and pastels.

Average Yearly Earnings: $33,113. **Experience:** Medium preparation is needed. Previous work-related skill, knowledge, or experience is required for this occupation. **Education:**

This group of occupations usually requires training in vocational schools, related on-the-job experience, or an associate degree. A bachelor's degree may be required. **Training:** Employees in this type of occupation usually need one or two years of training involving both on-the-job experience and informal training with experienced workers. **Related Examples:** Other occupations like this one usually involve using communication and organizational skills to coordinate, supervise, manage, or train others to accomplish goals. Examples include dental assistants, electricians, fish and game wardens, legal secretaries, personnel recruiters, and recreation workers. **Standard Vocational Preparation Range:** 6.0 to below 7.0—More than one year and less than four years. **Major/Instructional Program:** 43.0106 Forensic Technology/Technician; 50.0402 Graphic Design, Commercial Art and Illustration; 50.0701 Art, General; 50.0705 Drawing; 50.0708 Painting. **Related Courses:** Design; Fine Arts.

GRAPHIC DESIGNERS (34035C)

Design art and copy layouts for material to be presented by visual communications media, such as books, magazines, newspapers, television, and packaging.

Average Yearly Earnings: $33,113. **Experience:** Considerable preparation is needed. A minimum of two to four years of work-related skill, knowledge, or experience is needed for this occupation. **Education:** This group of occupations usually requires a four-year bachelor's degree, but in some cases does not. **Training:** Employees in this type of occupation usually need several years of work-related experience, on-the-job training, and/or vocational training. **Related Examples:** Other occupations like this one usually involve coordinating, supervising, managing, or training others. Examples include accountants, chefs and head cooks, computer programmers, historians, pharmacists, and police detectives. **Standard Vocational Preparation Range:** 7.0 to below 8.0—Two years to less than ten years. **Major/Instructional Program:** 50.0402 Graphic Design, Commercial Art and Illustration; 50.0701 Art, General; 50.0710 Printmaking. **Related Courses:** Computers and Electronics; Design; Fine Arts; Telecommunications; Communications and Media.

CARTOONISTS AND ANIMATORS (34035D)

Draw cartoons or other animated images by hand for publication, motion pictures, or television. May specialize in creating storyboards, laying out scenes, painting, inbetweening, developing characters, or cleanup.

Average Yearly Earnings: $33,113. **Experience:** Considerable preparation is needed. A minimum of two to four years of work-related skill, knowledge, or experience is needed for this occupation. **Education:** This group of occupations usually requires a four-year bachelor's degree, but in some cases does not. **Training:** Employees in this type of occupation usually need several years of work-related experience, on-the-job training, and/or vocational training. **Related Examples:** Other occupations like this one usually involve coordinating, supervising, managing, or training others. Examples include

accountants, chefs and head cooks, computer programmers, historians, pharmacists, and police detectives. **Standard Vocational Preparation Range:** 7.0 to below 8.0—Two years to less than ten years. **Major/Instructional Program:** 50.0201 Crafts, Folk Art, and Artisanry; 50.0402 Graphic Design, Commercial Art, and Illustration. **Related Courses:** Sales and Marketing; Fine Arts; Communications and Media.

SCULPTORS (34035E)

Design and construct three-dimensional artworks, using materials such as stone, wood, plaster, and metal and employing various manual and tool techniques.

Average Yearly Earnings: $33,113. **Experience:** Extensive preparation is needed. Extensive skill, knowledge, and experience are needed for this occupation. It may require more than five years of experience. **Education:** A bachelor's degree is the minimum formal education required for this group of occupations. However, many also require graduate school. For example, they may require a master's degree, and some require a Ph.D., M.D., or J.D. (law degree). **Training:** Employees in this type of occupation may need some on-the-job training, but most of these occupations assume that the person will already have the required skills, knowledge, work-related experience, and/or training. **Examples:** Other occupations like this one often involve coordinating, training, supervising, or managing the activities of others to accomplish goals. Very advanced communication and organizational skills are required. Examples include athletic trainers, lawyers, managing editors, physicists, social psychologists, and surgeons. **Standard Vocational Preparation Range:** 8.0 to 9.0—Four years to more than ten years. **Major/Instructional Program:** 50.0701 Art, General; 50.0702 Fine/Studio Arts; 50.0709 Sculpture. **Related Courses:** Design; Fine Arts.

FASHION DESIGNERS (34038A)

Design clothing and accessories. Create original garments or design garments that follow well-established fashion trends. May develop the line of color and kinds of materials.

Average Yearly Earnings: $30,867. **Experience:** Medium preparation is needed. Previous work-related skill, knowledge, or experience is required for this occupation. **Education:** This group of occupations usually requires training in vocational schools, related on-the-job experience, or an associate degree. A bachelor's degree may be required. **Training:** Employees in this type of occupation usually need one or two years of training involving both on-the-job experience and informal training with experienced workers. **Related Examples:** Other occupations like this one usually involve using communication and organizational skills to coordinate, supervise, manage, or train others to accomplish goals. Examples include dental assistants, electricians, fish and game wardens, legal secretaries, personnel recruiters, and recreation workers. **Standard Vocational Preparation Range:** 6.0 to below 7.0—More than one year and less than four years. **Major/Instructional Program:** 20.0301 Clothing, Apparel, and Textile Workers and Managers, General; 20.0305 Custom Tailor; 50.0402 Graphic Design, Commercial Art, and

Illustration; 50.0407 Fashion Design and Illustration. **Related Courses:** Sales and Marketing; Customer and Personal Service; Production and Processing; Design; Education and Training; Fine Arts.

COMMERCIAL AND INDUSTRIAL DESIGNERS (34038B)

Develop and design manufactured products, such as cars, home appliances, and children's toys. Combine artistic talent with research on product use, marketing, and materials, to create the most functional and appealing product design.

Average Yearly Earnings: $30,867. **Experience:** Considerable preparation is needed. A minimum of two to four years of work-related skill, knowledge, or experience is needed for this occupation. **Education:** This group of occupations usually requires a four-year bachelor's degree, but in some cases does not. **Training:** Employees in this type of occupation usually need several years of work-related experience, on-the-job training, and/or vocational training. **Related Examples:** Other occupations like this one usually involve coordinating, supervising, managing, or training others. Examples include accountants, chefs and head cooks, computer programmers, historians, pharmacists, and police detectives. **Standard Vocational Preparation Range:** 7.0 to below 8.0—Two years to less than ten years. **Major/Instructional Program:** 20.0501 Home Furnishings and Equipment Installers and Consultants; 50.0402 Graphic Design, Commercial Art, and Illustration; 50.0404 Industrial Design; 50.0407 Fashion Design and Illustration. **Related Courses:** Sales and Marketing; Production and Processing; Design; Education and Training; Fine Arts; History and Archeology.

SET DESIGNERS (34038C)

Design sets for theatrical, motion picture, and television productions.

Average Yearly Earnings: $30,867. **Experience:** Extensive preparation is needed. Extensive skill, knowledge, and experience are needed for this occupation. It may require more than five years of experience. **Education:** A bachelor's degree is the minimum formal education required for this group of occupations. However, many also require graduate school. For example, they may require a master's degree, and some require a Ph.D., M.D., or J.D. (law degree). **Training:** Employees in this type of occupation may need some on-the-job training, but most of these occupations assume that the person will already have the required skills, knowledge, work-related experience, and/or training. **Examples:** Other occupations like this one often involve coordinating, training, supervising, or managing the activities of others to accomplish goals. Very advanced communication and organizational skills are required. Examples include athletic trainers, lawyers, managing editors, physicists, social psychologists, and surgeons. **Standard Vocational Preparation Range:** 8.0 to 9.0—Four years to more than ten years. **Major/Instructional Program:** 50.0408 Interior Design; 50.0501 Drama/Theater Arts, General; 50.0502 Technical Theater/Theater Design and Stagecraft; 50.0599 Dramatic/Theater Arts and Stagecraft, Other. **Related Courses:** Design; Building and Construction; Geography; Fine Arts; History and Archeology; Communications and Media.

EXHIBIT DESIGNERS (34038D)

Plan, design, and oversee the construction and installation of permanent and temporary exhibits and displays.

Average Yearly Earnings: $30,867. **Experience:** Considerable preparation is needed. A minimum of two to four years of work-related skill, knowledge, or experience is needed for this occupation. **Education:** This group of occupations usually requires a four-year bachelor's degree, but in some cases does not. **Training:** Employees in this type of occupation usually need several years of work-related experience, on-the-job training, and/or vocational training. **Related Examples:** Other occupations like this one usually involve coordinating, supervising, managing, or training others. Examples include accountants, chefs and head cooks, computer programmers, historians, pharmacists, and police detectives. **Standard Vocational Preparation Range:** 7.0 to below 8.0—Two years to less than ten years. **Major/Instructional Program:** 20.0501 Home Furnishings and Equipment Installers and Consultants; 50.0402 Graphic Design; Commercial Art and Illustration; 50.0408 Interior Design; 50.0501 Drama/Theater Arts, General; 50.0502 Technical Theater/Theater Design and Stagecraft. **Related Courses:** Sales and Marketing; Customer and Personal Service; Computers and Electronics; Design; Building and Construction; Fine Arts.

ART DIRECTORS (34038E)

Formulate design concepts and presentation approaches, and direct workers engaged in artwork, layout design, and copy writing for visual communications media, such as magazines, books, newspapers, and packaging.

Average Yearly Earnings: $30,867. **Experience:** Considerable preparation is needed. A minimum of two to four years of work-related skill, knowledge, or experience is needed for this occupation. **Education:** This group of occupations usually requires a four-year bachelor's degree, but in some cases does not. **Training:** Employees in this type of occupation usually need several years of work-related experience, on-the-job training, and/or vocational training. **Related Examples:** Other occupations like this one usually involve coordinating, supervising, managing, or training others. Examples include accountants, chefs and head cooks, computer programmers, historians, pharmacists, and police detectives. **Standard Vocational Preparation Range:** 7.0 to below 8.0—Two years to less than ten years. **Major/Instructional Program:** 09.0201 Advertising; 50.0402 Graphic Design, Commercial Art, and Illustration. **Related Courses:** Administration and Management; Sales and Marketing; Production and Processing; Design; Psychology; Fine Arts; Communications and Media.

FLORAL DESIGNERS (34038F)

Design and fashion live, cut, dried, and artificial floral and foliar arrangements for events, such as holidays, anniversaries, weddings, balls, and funerals.

Average Yearly Earnings: $30,867. **Experience:** Some preparation is needed. Some previous work-related skill, knowledge, or experience may be helpful in this occupation, but usually is not needed. **Education:** This group of occupations usually requires a high school diploma and may require some vocational training or job-related course work. In some cases, an associate or bachelor's degree could be needed. **Training:** Employees in this type of occupation need anywhere from a few months to one year of working with experienced employees. **Related Examples:** Other occupations like this one often involve using your knowledge and skills to help others. Examples include drywall installers, fire inspectors, flight attendants, pharmacy technicians, retail salespersons, and tellers. **Standard Vocational Preparation Range:** 4.0 to below 6.0—Six months to less than two years. **Major/Instructional Program:** 08.0503 Floristry Marketing Operations, 20.0501 Home Furnishings and Equipment Installers and Consultants. **Related Courses:** Customer and Personal Service; Fine Arts.

INTERIOR DESIGNERS (34041)

Plan, design, and furnish interiors of residential, commercial, or industrial buildings. Formulate a design that is practical, aesthetic, and conducive to intended purposes, such as raising productivity, selling merchandise, or improving lifestyle. May specialize in a particular field, style, or phase of interior design. Excludes merchandise display designers.

Average Yearly Earnings: $32,094. **Experience:** Considerable preparation is needed. A minimum of two to four years of work-related skill, knowledge, or experience is needed for this occupation. **Education:** This group of occupations usually requires a four-year bachelor's degree, but in some cases does not. **Training:** Employees in this type of occupation usually need several years of work-related experience, on-the-job training, and/or vocational training. **Related Examples:** Other occupations like this one usually involve coordinating, supervising, managing, or training others. Examples include accountants, chefs and head cooks, computer programmers, historians, pharmacists, and police detectives. **Standard Vocational Preparation Range:** 7.0 to below 8.0—Two years to less than ten years. **Major/Instructional Program:** 04.0501 Interior Architecture; 19.0601 Housing Studies, General; 19.0603 Interior Environments; 20.0501 Home Furnishings and Equipment Installers and Consultants; 50.0408 Interior Design. **Related Courses:** Administration and Management; Sales and Marketing; Customer and Personal Service; Design; Fine Arts.

MERCHANDISE DISPLAYERS AND WINDOW TRIMMERS (34044)

Plan and erect commercial displays, such as those in windows and interiors of retail stores and at trade exhibitions.

Average Yearly Earnings: $30,867. **Experience:** Medium preparation is needed. Previous work-related skill, knowledge, or experience is required for this occupation. **Education:** This group of occupations usually requires training in vocational schools, related

on-the-job experience, or an associate degree. A bachelor's degree may be required. **Training:** Employees in this type of occupation usually need one or two years of training involving both on-the-job experience and informal training with experienced workers. **Related Examples:** Other occupations like this one usually involve using communication and organizational skills to coordinate, supervise, manage, or train others to accomplish goals. Examples include dental assistants, electricians, fish and game wardens, legal secretaries, personnel recruiters, and recreation workers. **Standard Vocational Preparation Range:** 6.0 to below 7.0—More than one year and less than four years. **Major/Instructional Program:** 20.0501 Home Furnishings and Equipment Installers and Consultants, 50.0401 Design and Visual Communications. **Related Courses:** Sales and Marketing; Design; Sociology and Anthropology; Fine Arts; Communications and Media.

MUSIC DIRECTORS (34047A)

Direct and conduct instrumental or vocal performances by musical groups, such as orchestras or choirs.

Average Yearly Earnings: $30,888. **Experience:** Extensive preparation is needed. Extensive skill, knowledge, and experience are needed for this occupation. It may require more than five years of experience. **Education:** A bachelor's degree is the minimum formal education required for this group of occupations. However, many also require graduate school. For example, they may require a master's degree, and some require a Ph.D., M.D., or J.D. (law degree). **Training:** Employees in this type of occupation may need some on-the-job training, but most of these occupations assume that the person will already have the required skills, knowledge, work-related experience, and/or training. **Examples:** Other occupations like this one often involve coordinating, training, supervising, or managing the activities of others to accomplish goals. Very advanced communication and organizational skills are required. Examples include athletic trainers, lawyers, managing editors, physicists, social psychologists, and surgeons. **Standard Vocational Preparation Range:** 8.0 to 9.0—Four years to more than ten years. **Major/Instructional Program:** 39.0501 Religious/Sacred Music; 50.0901 Music, General; 50.0903 Music—General Performance; 50.0905 Musicology and Ethnomusicology; 50.0906 Music Conducting; 50.0908 Music—Voice and Choral/Opera Performance. **Related Courses:** Administration and Management; Personnel and Human Resources; Foreign Language; Fine Arts.

MUSIC ARRANGERS AND ORCHESTRATORS (34047B)

Write and transcribe musical scores.

Average Yearly Earnings: $30,888. **Experience:** Considerable preparation is needed. A minimum of two to four years of work-related skill, knowledge, or experience is needed for this occupation. **Education:** This group of occupations usually requires a four-year bachelor's degree, but in some cases does not. **Training:** Employees in this type of

occupation usually need several years of work-related experience, on-the-job training, and/or vocational training. **Related Examples:** Other occupations like this one usually involve coordinating, supervising, managing, or training others. Examples include accountants, chefs and head cooks, computer programmers, historians, pharmacists, and police detectives. **Standard Vocational Preparation Range:** 7.0 to below 8.0—Two years to less than ten years. **Major/Instructional Program:** 50.0901 Music, General; 50.0904 Music Theory and Composition. **Related Courses:** Foreign Language; Fine Arts.

SINGERS (34047C)

Sing songs on stage, radio, television, or motion pictures.

Average Yearly Earnings: $30,888. **Experience:** Some preparation is needed. Some previous work-related skill, knowledge, or experience may be helpful in this occupation, but usually is not needed. **Education:** This group of occupations usually requires a high school diploma and may require some vocational training or job-related course work. In some cases, an associate or bachelor's degree could be needed. **Training:** Employees in this type of occupation need anywhere from a few months to one year of working with experienced employees. **Related Examples:** Other occupations like this one often involve using your knowledge and skills to help others. Examples include drywall installers, fire inspectors, flight attendants, pharmacy technicians, retail salespersons, and tellers. **Standard Vocational Preparation Range:** 4.0 to below 6.0—Six months to less than two years. **Major/Instructional Program:** 50.0901 Music, General; 50.0903 Music—General Performance; 50.0908 Music—Voice and Choral/Opera Performance. **Related Courses:** Foreign Language; Fine Arts.

COMPOSERS (34047E)

Compose music for orchestras, choral groups, or bands.

Average Yearly Earnings: $30,888. **Experience:** Extensive preparation is needed. Extensive skill, knowledge, and experience are needed for this occupation. It may require more than five years of experience. **Education:** A bachelor's degree is the minimum formal education required for this group of occupations. However, many also require graduate school. For example, they may require a master's degree, and some require a Ph.D., M.D., or J.D. (law degree). **Training:** Employees in this type of occupation may need some on-the-job training, but most of these occupations assume that the person will already have the required skills, knowledge, work-related experience, and/or training. **Examples:** Other occupations like this one often involve coordinating, training, supervising, or managing the activities of others to accomplish goals. Very advanced communication and organizational skills are required. Examples include athletic trainers, lawyers, managing editors, physicists, social psychologists, and surgeons. **Standard Vocational Preparation Range:** 8.0 to 9.0—Four years to more than ten years. **Major/Instructional Program:** 50.0901 Music, General; 50.0904 Music Theory and Composition. **Related Courses:** Fine Arts; History and Archeology.

PROMPTERS (34047F)

Prompt performers in stage productions.

Average Yearly Earnings: $30,888. **Experience:** Considerable preparation is needed. A minimum of two to four years of work-related skill, knowledge, or experience is needed for this occupation. **Education:** This group of occupations usually requires a four-year bachelor's degree, but in some cases does not. **Training:** Employees in this type of occupation usually need several years of work-related experience, on-the-job training, and/or vocational training. **Related Examples:** Other occupations like this one usually involve coordinating, supervising, managing, or training others. Examples include accountants, chefs and head cooks, computer programmers, historians, pharmacists, and police detectives. **Standard Vocational Preparation Range:** 7.0 to below 8.0—Two years to less than ten years. **Major/Instructional Program:** 50.0901 Music, General; 50.0904 Music Theory and Composition. **Related Courses:** Foreign Language; Fine Arts.

MUSICIANS, INSTRUMENTAL (34051)

Play one or more musical instruments in recital, in accompaniment, or as members of an orchestra, band, or other musical group.

Average Yearly Earnings: $30,888. **Experience:** Extensive preparation is needed. Extensive skill, knowledge, and experience are needed for this occupation. It may require more than five years of experience. **Education:** A bachelor's degree is the minimum formal education required for this group of occupations. However, many also require graduate school. For example, they may require a master's degree, and some require a Ph.D., M.D., or J.D. (law degree). **Training:** Employees in this type of occupation may need some on-the-job training, but most of these occupations assume that the person will already have the required skills, knowledge, work-related experience, and/or training. **Examples:** Other occupations like this one often involve coordinating, training, supervising, or managing the activities of others to accomplish goals. Very advanced communication and organizational skills are required. Examples include athletic trainers, lawyers, managing editors, physicists, social psychologists, and surgeons. **Standard Vocational Preparation Range:** 8.0 to 9.0—Four years to more than ten years. **Major/Instructional Program:** 39.0501 Religious/Sacred Music; 50.0901 Music, General; 50.0903 Music—General Performance; 50.0907 Music—Piano and Organ Performance. **Related Courses:** Psychology; Education and Training; Fine Arts; History and Archeology.

DANCERS (34053A)

Dance alone, with partners, or in a group to entertain audiences.

Average Yearly Earnings: $28,017. **Experience:** Considerable preparation is needed. A minimum of two to four years of work-related skill, knowledge, or experience is needed for this occupation. **Education:** This group of occupations usually requires a four-year

bachelor's degree, but in some cases does not. **Training:** Employees in this type of occupation usually need several years of work-related experience, on-the-job training, and/or vocational training. **Related Examples:** Other occupations like this one usually involve coordinating, supervising, managing, or training others. Examples include accountants, chefs and head cooks, computer programmers, historians, pharmacists, and police detectives. **Standard Vocational Preparation Range:** 7.0 to below 8.0—Two years to less than ten years. **Major/Instructional Program:** 50.0301 Dance. **Related Courses:** Fine Arts.

CHOREOGRAPHERS (34053B)

Create and teach original dances for a ballet, musical, or revue to be performed for a stage, television, motion picture, or nightclub production.

Average Yearly Earnings: $28,017. **Experience:** Extensive preparation is needed. Extensive skill, knowledge, and experience are needed for this occupation. It may require more than five years of experience. **Education:** A bachelor's degree is the minimum formal education required for this group of occupations. However, many also require graduate school. For example, they may require a master's degree, and some require a Ph.D., M.D., or J.D. (law degree). **Training:** Employees in this type of occupation may need some on-the-job training, but most of these occupations assume that the person will already have the required skills, knowledge, work-related experience, and/or training. **Examples:** Other occupations like this one often involve coordinating, training, supervising, or managing the activities of others to accomplish goals. Very advanced communication and organizational skills are required. Examples include athletic trainers, lawyers, managing editors, physicists, social psychologists, and surgeons. **Standard Vocational Preparation Range:** 8.0 to 9.0—Four years to more than ten years. **Major/Instructional Program:** 50.0301 Dance. **Related Courses:** Personnel and Human Resources; Education and Training; Fine Arts; Communications and Media.

ACTORS AND PERFORMERS (34056A)

Perform dramatic roles, comedic routines, or tricks of illusion to entertain audiences.

Average Yearly Earnings: $35,339. **Experience:** Medium preparation is needed. Previous work-related skill, knowledge, or experience is required for this occupation. **Education:** This group of occupations usually requires training in vocational schools, related on-the-job experience, or an associate degree. A bachelor's degree may be required. **Training:** Employees in this type of occupation usually need one or two years of training involving both on-the-job experience and informal training with experienced workers. **Related Examples:** Other occupations like this one usually involve using communication and organizational skills to coordinate, supervise, manage, or train others to accomplish goals. Examples include dental assistants, electricians, fish and game wardens, legal secretaries, personnel recruiters, and recreation workers. **Standard Vocational Preparation Range:** 6.0 to below 7.0—More than one year and less than four years. **Major/Instructional Program:** 50.0501 Drama/Theater Arts, General; 50.0503 Acting and Directing. **Related Courses:** Fine Arts; Communications and Media.

EXTRAS/STAND-INS (34056B)

Perform as a nonspeaking member of scenes in stage, motion picture, or television productions.

Average Yearly Earnings: $35,339. **Experience:** Little or no preparation is needed. No previous work-related skill, knowledge, or experience is needed for this occupation. **Education:** This group of occupations may require a high school diploma or GED certificate. A formal training course to obtain a license may be required. **Training:** Employees in this type of occupation need anywhere from a few days to a few months of training. Usually, an experienced worker could show you how to do the job. **Related Examples:** Other occupations like this one involve following instructions and helping others. Examples include bus drivers, forest and conservation workers, general office clerks, home health aides, and waiters/waitresses. **Standard Vocational Preparation Range:** Below 4.0—Less than six months. **Major/Instructional Program:** 50.0501 Drama/Theater Arts, General; 50.0503 Acting and Directing. **Related Courses:** Fine Arts.

AMUSEMENT ENTERTAINERS (34056D)

Entertain audiences by exhibiting special skills, such as juggling, diving, swimming, or acrobatics, or by performing daredevil feats.

Average Yearly Earnings: $35,339. **Experience:** Some preparation is needed. Some previous work-related skill, knowledge, or experience may be helpful in this occupation, but usually is not needed. **Education:** This group of occupations usually requires a high school diploma and may require some vocational training or job-related course work. In some cases, an associate or bachelor's degree could be needed. **Training:** Employees in this type of occupation need anywhere from a few months to one year of working with experienced employees. **Related Examples:** Other occupations like this one often involve using your knowledge and skills to help others. Examples include drywall installers, fire inspectors, flight attendants, pharmacy technicians, retail salespersons, and tellers. **Standard Vocational Preparation Range:** 4.0 to below 6.0—Six months to less than two years. **Major/Instructional Program:** 49.0304 Diver (Professional). **Related Courses:** No specific related courses in database.

EQUESTRIAN PERFORMERS (34056E)

Ride horses at a circus, carnival, exhibition, or rodeo, performing feats of equestrian skills and daring to entertain audiences.

Average Yearly Earnings: $35,339. **Experience:** Some preparation is needed. Some previous work-related skill, knowledge, or experience may be helpful in this occupation, but usually is not needed. **Education:** This group of occupations usually requires a high school diploma and may require some vocational training or job-related course work. In some cases, an associate or bachelor's degree could be needed. **Training:** Employees in this type of occupation need anywhere from a few months to one year of working with experienced employees. **Related Examples:** Other occupations like this one often involve using your knowledge and skills to help others. Examples include drywall installers, fire inspectors, flight attendants, pharmacy technicians, retail salespersons, and tellers. **Standard Vocational Preparation Range:** 4.0 to below 6.0—Six months to less than two years. **Major/Instructional Program:** 01.0507 Equestrian/Equine Studies, Horse Management and Training. **Related Courses:** No related courses listed in the database for this occupation.

PRODUCERS (34056F)

Plan and coordinate various aspects of radio, television, stage, or motion picture production, such as selecting scripts, coordinating writing, directing, and editing; and arranging financing.

Average Yearly Earnings: $35,339. **Experience:** Considerable preparation is needed. A minimum of two to four years of work-related skill, knowledge, or experience is needed for this occupation. **Education:** This group of occupations usually requires a four-year bachelor's degree, but in some cases does not. **Training:** Employees in this type of occupation usually need several years of work-related experience, on-the-job training, and/or vocational training. **Related Examples:** Other occupations like this one usually involve coordinating, supervising, managing, or training others. Examples include accountants, chefs and head cooks, computer programmers, historians, pharmacists, and police detectives. **Standard Vocational Preparation Range:** 7.0 to below 8.0—Two years to less than ten years. **Major/Instructional Program:** 09.0701 Radio and Television Broadcasting; 50.0501 Drama/Theater Arts, General; 50.0502 Technical Theater/Theater Design and Stagecraft; 50.0503 Acting and Directing; 50.0602 Film-Video Making/Cinematography and Production. **Related Courses:** Administration and Management; Economics and Accounting; Personnel and Human Resources; English Language; Fine Arts; Communications and Media.

DIRECTORS—STAGE, MOTION PICTURE, TELEVISION, AND RADIO (34056G)

Interpret script, conduct rehearsals, and direct the activities of the cast and technical crew for stage, motion picture, television, or radio programs.

Average Yearly Earnings: $35,339. **Experience:** Considerable preparation is needed. A minimum of two to four years of work-related skill, knowledge, or experience is needed for this occupation. **Education:** This group of occupations usually requires a four-year bachelor's degree, but in some cases does not. **Training:** Employees in this type of occupation usually need several years of work-related experience, on-the-job training, and/or vocational training. **Related Examples:** Other occupations like this one usually involve coordinating, supervising, managing, or training others. Examples include accountants, chefs and head cooks, computer programmers, historians, pharmacists, and police detectives. **Standard Vocational Preparation Range:** 7.0 to below 8.0—Two years to less

than ten years. **Major/Instructional Program:** 09.0701 Radio and Television Broadcasting; 31.0301 Parks, Recreation, and Leisure Facilities Management; 50.0501 Drama/Theater Arts, General; 50.0502 Technical Theater/Theater Design and Stagecraft; 50.0503 Acting and Directing; 50.0602 Film-Video Making/Cinematography and Production. **Related Courses:** Administration and Management; Fine Arts; Communications and Media.

PROGRAM DIRECTORS (34056H)

Direct and coordinate the activities of personnel engaged in the preparation of radio or television station program schedules and programs, such as sports or news.

Average Yearly Earnings: $35,339. **Experience:** Extensive preparation is needed. Extensive skill, knowledge, and experience are needed for this occupation. It may require more than five years of experience. **Education:** A bachelor's degree is the minimum formal education required for this group of occupations. However, many also require graduate school. For example, they may require a master's degree, and some require a Ph.D., M.D., or J.D. (law degree). **Training:** Employees in this type of occupation may need some on-the-job training, but most of these occupations assume that the person will already have the required skills, knowledge, work-related experience, and/or training. **Examples:** Other occupations like this one often involve coordinating, training, supervising, or managing the activities of others to accomplish goals. Very advanced communication and organizational skills are required. Examples include athletic trainers, lawyers, managing editors, physicists, social psychologists, and surgeons. **Standard Vocational Preparation Range:** 8.0 to 9.0—Four years to more than ten years. **Major/Instructional Program:** 50.0501 Drama/Theater Arts, General; 50.0503 Acting and Directing; 50.0602 Film-Video Making/Cinematography and Production. **Related Courses:** Administration and Management; Economics and Accounting; Personnel and Human Resources; Communications and Media.

TALENT DIRECTORS (34056J)

Audition and interview performers to select the most appropriate talent for parts in stage, television, radio, or motion picture productions.

Average Yearly Earnings: $35,339. **Experience:** Medium preparation is needed. Previous work-related skill, knowledge, or experience is required for this occupation. **Education:** This group of occupations usually requires training in vocational schools, related on-the-job experience, or an associate degree. A bachelor's degree may be required. **Training:** Employees in this type of occupation usually need one or two years of training involving both on-the-job experience and informal training with experienced workers. **Related Examples:** Other occupations like this one usually involve using communication and organizational skills to coordinate, supervise, manage, or train others to accomplish goals. Examples include dental assistants, electricians, fish and game wardens, legal secretaries, personnel recruiters, and recreation workers. **Standard Vocational**

Preparation Range: 6.0 to below 7.0—More than one year and less than four years. **Major/Instructional Program:** 50.0501 Drama/Theater Arts, General; 50.0503 Acting and Directing. **Related Courses:** Administration and Management; Sales and Marketing; Personnel and Human Resources; Fine Arts; Communications and Media.

TECHNICAL DIRECTORS/MANAGERS (34056K)

Coordinate the activities of technical departments, such as taping, editing, engineering, and maintenance, to produce radio or television programs.

Average Yearly Earnings: $35,339. **Experience:** Considerable preparation is needed. A minimum of two to four years of work-related skill, knowledge, or experience is needed for this occupation. **Education:** This group of occupations usually requires a four-year bachelor's degree, but in some cases does not. **Training:** Employees in this type of occupation usually need several years of work-related experience, on-the-job training, and/or vocational training. **Related Examples:** Other occupations like this one usually involve coordinating, supervising, managing, or training others. Examples include accountants, chefs and head cooks, computer programmers, historians, pharmacists, and police detectives. **Standard Vocational Preparation Range:** 7.0 to below 8.0—Two years to less than ten years. **Major/Instructional Program:** 09.0701 Radio and Television Broadcasting, 50.0602 Film-Video Making/Cinematography and Production. **Related Courses:** Administration and Management; Personnel and Human Resources; Education and Training; Fine Arts; Telecommunications; Communications and Media.

COACHES AND SCOUTS (34058A)

Analyze performance or instruct athletes of professional sporting events. May evaluate athletes' strengths and weaknesses as possible recruits or to improve the athletes' technique to prepare them for competition.

Average Yearly Earnings: $28,995. **Experience:** Extensive preparation is needed. Extensive skill, knowledge, and experience are needed for this occupation. It may require more than five years of experience. **Education:** A bachelor's degree is the minimum formal education required for this group of occupations. However, many also require graduate school. For example, they may require a master's degree, and some require a Ph.D., M.D., or J.D. (law degree). **Training:** Employees in this type of occupation may need some on-the-job training, but most of these occupations assume that the person will already have the required skills, knowledge, work-related experience, and/or training. **Examples:** Other occupations like this one often involve coordinating, training, supervising, or managing the activities of others to accomplish goals. Very advanced communication and organizational skills are required. Examples include athletic trainers, lawyers, managing editors, physicists, social psychologists, and surgeons. **Standard Vocational Preparation Range:** 8.0 to 9.0—Four years to more than ten years. **Major/Instructional Program:** 13.1314 Physical Education Teaching and Coaching. **Related Courses:** Administration and Management; Sales and Marketing; Personnel and Human Resources; Psychology; Therapy and Counseling; Education and Training.

ATHLETIC TRAINERS **(34058B)**

Evaluate, advise, and treat athletes to maintain physical fitness.

Average Yearly Earnings: $28,995. **Experience:** Extensive preparation is needed. Extensive skill, knowledge, and experience are needed for this occupation. It may require more than five years of experience. **Education:** A bachelor's degree is the minimum formal education required for this group of occupations. However, many also require graduate school. For example, they may require a master's degree, and some require a Ph.D., M.D., or J.D. (law degree). **Training:** Employees in this type of occupation may need some on-the-job training, but most of these occupations assume that the person will already have the required skills, knowledge, work-related experience, and/or training. **Examples:** Other occupations like this one often involve coordinating, training, supervising, or managing the activities of others to accomplish goals. Very advanced communication and organizational skills are required. Examples include lawyers, managing editors, physicists, social psychologists, and surgeons. **Standard Vocational Preparation Range:** 8.0 to 9.0—Four years to more than ten years. **Major/Instructional Program:** 31.0501 Health and Physical Education, General; 31.0503 Athletic Training and Sports Medicine. **Related Courses:** Customer and Personal Service; Biology; Psychology; Medicine and Dentistry; Therapy and Counseling.

PROFESSIONAL ATHLETES **(34058C)**

Participate in physical, competitive athletic events.

Average Yearly Earnings: $28,995. **Experience:** Medium preparation is needed. Previous work-related skill, knowledge, or experience is required for this occupation. **Education:** This group of occupations usually requires training in vocational schools, related on-the-job experience, or an associate degree. A bachelor's degree may be required. **Training:** Employees in this type of occupation usually need one or two years of training involving both on-the-job experience and informal training with experienced workers. **Related Examples:** Other occupations like this one usually involve using communication and organizational skills to coordinate, supervise, manage, or train others to accomplish goals. Examples include dental assistants, electricians, fish and game wardens, legal secretaries, personnel recruiters, and recreation workers. **Standard Vocational Preparation Range:** 6.0 to below 7.0—More than one year and less than four years. **Major/Instructional Program:** No specific instructional program for this occupation. **Related Courses:** No related courses listed in the database for this occupation.

MOTOR RACERS **(34058E)**

Drive automobiles or ride motorcycles in competitive races.

Average Yearly Earnings: $28,995. **Experience:** Some preparation is needed. Some previous work-related skill, knowledge, or experience may be helpful in this occupation, but usually is not needed. **Education:** This group of occupations usually requires a high school diploma and may require some vocational training or job-related course work. In some cases, an associate or bachelor's degree could be needed. **Training:** Employees in this type of occupation need anywhere from a few months to one year of working with experienced employees. **Related Examples:** Other occupations like this one often involve using your knowledge and skills to help others. Examples include drywall installers, fire inspectors, flight attendants, pharmacy technicians, retail salespersons, and tellers. **Standard Vocational Preparation Range:** 4.0 to below 6.0—Six months to less than two years. **Major/Instructional Program:** No specific instructional program for this occupation. **Related Courses:** Mechanical; Transportation.

JOCKEYS AND SULKY DRIVERS (34058F)

Ride racehorses or drive sulkies in horse or harness races.

Average Yearly Earnings: $28,995. **Experience:** Medium preparation is needed. Previous work-related skill, knowledge, or experience is required for this occupation. **Education:** This group of occupations usually requires training in vocational schools, related on-the-job experience, or an associate degree. A bachelor's degree may be required. **Training:** Employees in this type of occupation usually need one or two years of training involving both on-the-job experience and informal training with experienced workers. **Related Examples:** Other occupations like this one usually involve using communication and organizational skills to coordinate, supervise, manage, or train others to accomplish goals. Examples include dental assistants, electricians, fish and game wardens, legal secretaries, personnel recruiters, and recreation workers. **Standard Vocational Preparation Range:** 6.0 to below 7.0—More than one year and less than four years. **Major/Instructional Program:** No specific instructional program for this occupation. **Related Courses:** No related courses listed in the database for this occupation.

HORSE RIDERS/EXERCISERS (34058G)

Ride horses to exercise, condition, or lead other horses.

Average Yearly Earnings: $28,995. **Experience:** Little or no preparation is needed. No previous work-related skill, knowledge, or experience is needed for this occupation. **Education:** This group of occupations may require a high school diploma or GED certificate. A formal training course to obtain a license may be required. **Training:** Employees in this type of occupation need anywhere from a few days to a few months of training. Usually, an experienced worker could show you how to do the job. **Related Examples:** Other occupations like this one involve following instructions and helping others. Examples include bus drivers, forest and conservation workers, general office clerks, home health aides, and waiters/waitresses. **Standard Vocational Preparation Range:** Below 4.0—Less than six months. **Major/Instructional Program:** 01.0507 Equestrian/Equine Studies, Horse Management and Training. **Related Courses:** Medicine and Dentistry.

UMPIRES, REFEREES, AND OTHER SPORTS OFFICIALS (34058L)

Officiate at competitive athletic or sporting events. Detect infractions of rules and decide penalties according to established regulations. Includes all sporting officials, referees, and competition judges.

Average Yearly Earnings: $28,995. **Experience:** Medium preparation is needed. Previous work-related skill, knowledge, or experience is required for this occupation. **Education:** This group of occupations usually requires training in vocational schools, related on-the-job experience, or an associate degree. A bachelor's degree may be required. **Training:** Employees in this type of occupation usually need one or two years of training involving both on-the-job experience and informal training with experienced workers. **Related Examples:** Other occupations like this one usually involve using communication and organizational skills to coordinate, supervise, manage, or train others to accomplish goals. Examples include dental assistants, electricians, fish and game wardens, legal secretaries, personnel recruiters, and recreation workers. **Standard Vocational Preparation Range:** 6.0 to below 7.0—More than one year and less than four years. **Major/Instructional Program:** 01.0505 Animal Trainer; 01.0507 Equestrian/Equine Studies, Horse Management and Training; 12.0204 Umpires and Other Sport Officials. **Related Courses:** No related courses listed in the database for this occupation.

Other Professional, Paraprofessional, and Technical Workers

AIRPLANE DISPATCHERS AND AIR TRAFFIC CONTROLLERS (39002)

Control air traffic on and within the vicinity of an airport and the movement of air traffic between altitude sectors and control centers, according to established procedures and policies. Authorize, regulate, and control commercial airline flights, according to government or company regulations, to expedite and ensure flight safety.

Average Yearly Earnings: $45,739. **Experience:** Considerable preparation is needed. A minimum of two to four years of work-related skill, knowledge, or experience is needed for this occupation. **Education:** This group of occupations usually requires a four-year bachelor's degree, but in some cases does not. **Training:** Employees in this type of occupation usually need several years of work-related experience, on-the-job training, and/or vocational training. **Related Examples:** Other occupations like this one usually involve coordinating, supervising, managing, or training others. Examples include accountants, chefs and head cooks, computer programmers, historians, pharmacists, and police detectives. **Standard Vocational Preparation Range:** 7.0 to below 8.0—Two years to less than ten years. **Major/Instructional Program:** 49.0105 Air Traffic Controller. **Related Courses:** Computers and Electronics; Physics; Geography; Telecommunications; Transportation.

TRAFFIC TECHNICIANS (39005)

Conduct field studies to determine traffic volume and speed, effectiveness of signals, adequacy of lighting, and other factors influencing traffic conditions, under the direction of a traffic engineer.

Average Yearly Earnings: $34,236. **Experience:** Considerable preparation is needed. A minimum of two to four years of work-related skill, knowledge, or experience is needed for this occupation. **Education:** This group of occupations usually requires a four-year bachelor's degree, but in some cases does not. **Training:** Employees in this type of occupation usually need several years of work-related experience, on-the-job training, and/or vocational training. **Related Examples:** Other occupations like this one usually involve coordinating, supervising, managing, or training others. Examples include accountants, chefs and head cooks, computer programmers, historians, pharmacists, and police detectives. **Standard Vocational Preparation Range:** 7.0 to below 8.0—Two years to less than ten years. **Major/Instructional Program:** 15.0201 Civil Engineering/Civil Technology/Technician. **Related Courses:** Computers and Electronics; Engineering and Technology; Design; Mathematics; Sociology and Anthropology; Geography; Public Safety and Security; Law, Government, and Jurisprudence; Telecommunications; Transportation.

RADIO OPERATORS (39008)

Receive and transmit communications using radiotelegraph or radiotelephone equipment, in accordance with government regulations. May repair equipment.

Average Yearly Earnings: $33,800. **Experience:** Medium preparation is needed. Previous work-related skill, knowledge, or experience is required for this occupation. **Education:** This group of occupations usually requires training in vocational schools, related on-the-job experience, or an associate degree. A bachelor's degree may be required. **Training:** Employees in this type of occupation usually need one or two years of training involving both on-the-job experience and informal training with experienced workers. **Related Examples:** Other occupations like this one usually involve using communication and organizational skills to coordinate, supervise, manage, or train others to accomplish goals. Examples include dental assistants, electricians, fish and game wardens, legal secretaries, personnel recruiters, and recreation workers. **Standard Vocational Preparation Range:** 6.0 to below 7.0—More than one year and less than four years. **Major/Instructional Program:** 47.0101 Electrical and Electronics Equipment Installer and Repairer, General; 47.0103 Communications Systems Installer and Repairer. **Related Courses:** Computers and Electronics; Geography; Telecommunications; Communications and Media.

FUNERAL DIRECTORS AND MORTICIANS (39011)

Perform various tasks to arrange and direct funeral services, such as coordinating the transportation of the body to the mortuary for embalming, interviewing family or other authorized persons to arrange details, selecting pallbearers, procuring an official for religious rites, and providing transportation for mourners.

Average Yearly Earnings: $37,356. Experience: Considerable preparation is needed. A minimum of two to four years of work-related skill, knowledge, or experience is needed for this occupation. Education: This group of occupations usually requires a four-year bachelor's degree, but in some cases does not. Training: Employees in this type of occupation usually need several years of work-related experience, on-the-job training, and/or vocational training. Related Examples: Other occupations like this one usually involve coordinating, supervising, managing, or training others. Examples include accountants, chefs and head cooks, computer programmers, historians, pharmacists, and police detectives. Standard Vocational Preparation Range: 7.0 to below 8.0—Two years to less than ten years. Major/Instructional Program: 12.0301 Funeral Services and Mortuary Science. Related Courses: Administration and Management; Sales and Marketing; Customer and Personal Service; Psychology; Transportation.

EMBALMERS (39014)

Prepare bodies for interment in conformity with legal requirements.

Average Yearly Earnings: $37,356. Experience: Considerable preparation is needed. A minimum of two to four years of work-related skill, knowledge, or experience is needed for this occupation. Education: This group of occupations usually requires a four-year bachelor's degree, but in some cases does not. Training: Employees in this type of occupation usually need several years of work-related experience, on-the-job training, and/or vocational training. Related Examples: Other occupations like this one usually involve coordinating, supervising, managing, or training others. Examples include accountants, chefs and head cooks, computer programmers, historians, pharmacists, and police detectives. Standard Vocational Preparation Range: 7.0 to below 8.0—Two years to less than ten years. Major/Instructional Program: 12.0301 Funeral Services and Mortuary Science. Related Courses: Customer and Personal Service; Chemistry; Biology; Sociology and Anthropology; Medicine and Dentistry; Philosophy and Theology; Law, Government, and Jurisprudence.

INTERPRETERS AND TRANSLATORS (39999A)

Translate and interpret written or spoken communications from one language to another or from spoken to manual sign language used by hearing-impaired.

Average Yearly Earnings: $35,339. Experience: Medium preparation is needed. Previous work-related skill, knowledge, or experience is required for this occupation. Education: This group of occupations usually requires training in vocational schools, related on-the-job experience, or an associate degree. A bachelor's degree may be required. Training: Employees in this type of occupation usually need one or two years of training involving both on-the-job experience and informal training with experienced workers. Related Examples: Other occupations like this one usually involve using communication and organizational skills to coordinate, supervise, manage, or train others to accomplish goals. Examples include dental assistants, electricians, fish and game wardens, legal secretaries, personnel recruiters, and recreation workers. Standard Vocational

Preparation Range: 6.0 to below 7.0—More than one year and less than four years. **Major/Instructional Program:** 16.0101 Foreign Languages and Literatures, General; 16.0103 Foreign Language Interpretation and Translation; 51.0201 Communication Disorders, General; 51.0205 Sign Language Interpreter. **Related Courses:** Sociology and Anthropology; English Language; Foreign Language; History and Archeology; Communications and Media.

AGENTS AND BUSINESS MANAGERS OF ARTISTS, PERFORMERS, AND ATHLETES (39999B)

Represent and promote artists, performers, and athletes to prospective employers. May handle contract negotiations and other business matters for clients.

Average Yearly Earnings: $53,601. **Experience:** Medium preparation is needed. Previous work-related skill, knowledge, or experience is required for this occupation. **Education:** This group of occupations usually requires training in vocational schools, related on-the-job experience, or an associate degree. A bachelor's degree may be required. **Training:** Employees in this type of occupation usually need one or two years of training involving both on-the-job experience and informal training with experienced workers. **Related Examples:** Other occupations like this one usually involve using communication and organizational skills to coordinate, supervise, manage, or train others to accomplish goals. Examples include dental assistants, electricians, fish and game wardens, legal secretaries, personnel recruiters, and recreation workers. **Standard Vocational Preparation Range:** 6.0 to below 7.0—More than one year and less than four years. **Major/Instructional Program:** 08.0299 Business and Personal Services Marketing Operations, Other; 08.0901 Hospitality and Recreation Marketing Operations, General; 08.0903 Recreation Products/Services Marketing Operations; 09.0501 Public Relations and Organizational Communications; 50.0901 Music, General; 50.0909 Music Business Management and Merchandising. **Related Courses:** Administration and Management; Economics and Accounting; Sales and Marketing; Personnel and Human Resources; Fine Arts; Law, Government, and Jurisprudence.

CITY PLANNING AIDES (39999C)

Compile data from various sources, such as maps, reports, and field and file investigations, for use by the city planner in making planning studies.

Average Yearly Earnings: $35,339. **Experience:** Medium preparation is needed. Previous work-related skill, knowledge, or experience is required for this occupation. **Education:** This group of occupations usually requires training in vocational schools, related on-the-job experience, or an associate degree. A bachelor's degree may be required. **Training:** Employees in this type of occupation usually need one or two years of training involving both on-the-job experience and informal training with experienced workers. **Related Examples:** Other occupations like this one usually involve using communication and organizational skills to coordinate, supervise, manage, or train others to accomplish goals. Examples include dental assistants, electricians, fish and game wardens, legal secretaries, personnel recruiters, and recreation workers. **Standard Vocational Preparation Range:** 6.0 to below 7.0—More than one year and less than four years. **Major/Instructional Program:** 15.0201 Civil Engineering/Civil Technology/Technician. **Related Courses:** Clerical; Mathematics; Geography.

STUDIO, STAGE, AND SPECIAL EFFECTS TECHNICIANS (39999D)

Install, operate, and maintain special equipment used in stage, television, or motion picture production.

Average Yearly Earnings: $35,339. **Experience:** Medium preparation is needed. Previous work-related skill, knowledge, or experience is required for this occupation. **Education:** This group of occupations usually requires training in vocational schools, related on-the-job experience, or an associate degree. A bachelor's degree may be required. **Training:** Employees in this type of occupation usually need one or two years of training involving both on-the-job experience and informal training with experienced workers. **Related Examples:** Other occupations like this one usually involve using communication and organizational skills to coordinate, supervise, manage, or train others to accomplish goals. Examples include dental assistants, electricians, fish and game wardens, legal secretaries, personnel recruiters, and recreation workers. **Standard Vocational Preparation Range:** 6.0 to below 7.0—More than one year and less than four years. **Major/Instructional Program:** 10.0101 Educational/Instructional Media Technology/Technician; 10.0104 Radio and Television Broadcasting Technology/Technician; 46.0201 Carpenter; 46.0301 Electrical and Power Transmission Installer, General; 46.0302 Electrician; 50.0501 Drama/Theater Arts, General; 50.0502 Technical Theater/Theater Design and Stagecraft; 50.0602 Film-Video Making/Cinematography and Production. **Related Courses:** Computers and Electronics; Design; Building and Construction; Physics; Fine Arts.

TAXIDERMISTS (39999E)

Prepare, stuff, and mount skins of birds, fish, or mammals in lifelike form.

Average Yearly Earnings: $34,465. **Experience:** Considerable preparation is needed. A minimum of two to four years of work-related skill, knowledge, or experience is needed for this occupation. **Education:** This group of occupations usually requires a four-year bachelor's degree, but in some cases does not. **Training:** Employees in this type of occupation usually need several years of work-related experience, on-the-job training, and/or vocational training. **Related Examples:** Other occupations like this one usually involve coordinating, supervising, managing, or training others. Examples include accountants, chefs and head cooks, computer programmers, historians, pharmacists, and police detectives. **Standard Vocational Preparation Range:** 7.0 to below 8.0—Two years to less than ten years. **Major/Instructional Program:** No specific instructional program for this occupation. **Related Courses:** Biology.

POLYGRAPH EXAMINERS (39999G)

Interrogate and screen individuals to detect deception, using polygraph equipment.

Average Yearly Earnings: $41,267. **Experience:** Some preparation is needed. Some previous work-related skill, knowledge, or experience may be helpful in this occupation, but usually is not needed. **Education:** This group of occupations usually requires a high school diploma and may require some vocational training or job-related course work. In some cases, an associate or bachelor's degree could be needed. **Training:** Employees in this type of occupation need anywhere from a few months to one year of working with experienced employees. **Related Examples:** Other occupations like this one often involve using your knowledge and skills to help others. Examples include drywall installers, fire inspectors, flight attendants, pharmacy technicians, retail salespersons, and tellers. **Standard Vocational Preparation Range:** 4.0 to below 6.0—Six months to less than two years. **Major/Instructional Program:** 43.0106 Forensic Technology/Technician. **Related Courses:** Biology; Psychology; Education and Training; Law, Government, and Jurisprudence.

 SALES WORKERS

Sales Supervisors and Managers

FIRST-LINE SUPERVISORS AND MANAGER/SUPERVISORS— SALES AND RELATED WORKERS (41002)

Directly supervise and coordinate the activities of marketing, sales, and related workers. May perform management functions, such as budgeting, accounting, marketing, and personnel work, in addition to their supervisory duties.

Average Yearly Earnings: $32,718. **Experience:** Medium preparation is needed. Previous work-related skill, knowledge, or experience is required for this occupation. **Education:** This group of occupations usually requires training in vocational schools, related on-the-job experience, or an associate degree. A bachelor's degree may be required. **Training:** Employees in this type of occupation usually need one or two years of training involving both on-the-job experience and informal training with experienced workers. **Related Examples:** Other occupations like this one usually involve using communication and organizational skills to coordinate, supervise, manage, or train others to accomplish goals. Examples include dental assistants, electricians, fish and game wardens, legal secretaries, personnel recruiters, and recreation workers. **Standard Vocational Preparation Range:** 6.0 to below 7.0—More than one year and less than four years. **Major/Instructional Program:** 01.0201 Agricultural Mechanization, General; 01.0204 Agricultural Power Machinery Operator; 01.0501 Agricultural Supplies Retailing and Wholesaling; 08.0101 Apparel and Accessories Marketing Operations, General; 08.0204 Business Services Marketing Operations; 08.0299 Business and Personal Services Marketing

Operations, Other; 08.0601 Food Products Retailing and Wholesaling Operations; 08.0705 General Retailing Operations; 08.0706 General Selling Skills and Sales Operations; 08.0708 General Marketing Operations; 08.0709 General Distribution Operations; 08.0809 Home Products Marketing Operations; 08.0810 Office Products Marketing Operations; 08.0901 Hospitality and Recreation Marketing Operations, General; 08.0903 Recreation Products/ Services Marketing Operations; 08.1001 Insurance Marketing Operations; 08.1203 Vehicle Parts and Accessories Marketing Operations; 08.1209 Petroleum Products Retailing Operations; 08.1301 Health Products and Services Marketing Operations; 12.0504 Food and Beverage/Restaurant Operations Manager; 19.0901 Clothing/Apparel and Textile Studies; 20.0301 Clothing, Apparel, and Textile Workers and Managers, General; 52.0902 Hotel/Motel and Restaurant Management; 52.1101 International Business; 52.1403 International Business Marketing. **Related Courses:** Administration and Management; Economics and Accounting; Sales and Marketing; Customer and Personal Service; Personnel and Human Resources; Mathematics; Psychology; Education and Training; Communications and Media.

Sales Agents

SALES AGENTS AND PLACERS, INSURANCE (43002)

Sell or advise clients on life, endowments, fire, accident, and other types of insurance. May refer clients to independent brokers, work as independent brokers, or be employed by an insurance company.

Average Yearly Earnings: $38,875. **Experience:** Medium preparation is needed. Previous work-related skill, knowledge, or experience is required for this occupation. **Education:** This group of occupations usually requires training in vocational schools, related on-the-job experience, or an associate degree. A bachelor's degree may be required. **Training:** Employees in this type of occupation usually need one or two years of training involving both on-the-job experience and informal training with experienced workers. **Related Examples:** Other occupations like this one usually involve using communication and organizational skills to coordinate, supervise, manage, or train others to accomplish goals. Examples include dental assistants, electricians, fish and game wardens, legal secretaries, personnel recruiters, and recreation workers. **Standard Vocational Preparation Range:** 6.0 to below 7.0—More than one year and less than four years. **Major/ Instructional Program:** 08.1001 Insurance Marketing Operations; 52.0801 Finance, General; 52.0805 Insurance and Risk Management. **Related Courses:** Clerical; Economics and Accounting; Sales and Marketing.

SALES AGENTS, REAL ESTATE (43008)

Rent, buy, and sell property to clients. Perform duties such as studying property listings, interviewing prospective clients, accompanying clients to property site, discussing conditions of sale, and drawing up real estate contracts.

Average Yearly Earnings: $45,219. **Experience:** Some preparation is needed. Some previous work-related skill, knowledge, or experience may be helpful in this occupation, but usually is not needed. **Education:** This group of occupations usually requires a high school diploma and may require some vocational training or job-related course work. In some cases, an associate or bachelor's degree could be needed. **Training:** Employees in this type of occupation need anywhere from a few months to one year of working with experienced employees. **Related Examples:** Other occupations like this one often involve using your knowledge and skills to help others. Examples include drywall installers, fire inspectors, flight attendants, pharmacy technicians, retail salespersons, and tellers. **Standard Vocational Preparation Range:** 4.0 to below 6.0—Six months to less than two years. **Major/Instructional Program:** 08.0706 General Selling Skills and Sales Operations, 52.1501 Real Estate. **Related Courses:** Economics and Accounting; Sales and Marketing; Mathematics; Sociology and Anthropology; Geography; Law, Government, and Jurisprudence; Communications and Media.

APPRAISERS, REAL ESTATE (43011)

Appraise real property to determine its value for purchase, sales, investment, mortgage, or loan purposes.

Average Yearly Earnings: $38,334. **Experience:** Considerable preparation is needed. A minimum of two to four years of work-related skill, knowledge, or experience is needed for this occupation. **Education:** This group of occupations usually requires a four-year bachelor's degree, but in some cases does not. **Training:** Employees in this type of occupation usually need several years of work-related experience, on-the-job training, and/or vocational training. **Related Examples:** Other occupations like this one usually involve coordinating, supervising, managing, or training others. Examples include accountants, chefs and head cooks, computer programmers, historians, pharmacists, and police detectives. **Standard Vocational Preparation Range:** 7.0 to below 8.0—Two years to less than ten years. **Major/Instructional Program:** 52.1501 Real Estate. **Related Courses:** Administration and Management; Clerical; Economics and Accounting; Personnel and Human Resources; Building and Construction; Geography; Public Safety and Security; Law, Government, and Jurisprudence; Communications and Media.

SALES AGENTS, SECURITIES AND COMMODITIES (43014A)

Buy and sell securities in investment and trading firms and develop and implement financial plans for individuals, businesses, and organizations.

Average Yearly Earnings: $59,633. **Experience:** Considerable preparation is needed. A minimum of two to four years of work-related skill, knowledge, or experience is needed for this occupation. **Education:** This group of occupations usually requires a four-year bachelor's degree, but in some cases does not. **Training:** Employees in this type of occupation usually need several years of work-related experience, on-the-job training, and/or vocational training. **Related Examples:** Other occupations like this one usually

involve coordinating, supervising, managing, or training others. Examples include accountants, chefs and head cooks, computer programmers, historians, pharmacists, and police detectives. **Standard Vocational Preparation Range:** 7.0 to below 8.0—Two years to less than ten years. **Major/Instructional Program:** 08.0401 Financial Services Marketing Operations; 52.0801 Finance, General; 52.0804 Financial Planning; 52.0807 Investments and Securities; 52.1601 Taxation. **Related Courses:** Economics and Accounting; Sales and Marketing; Customer and Personal Service; Personnel and Human Resources; Computers and Electronics; Mathematics.

SALES AGENTS, FINANCIAL SERVICES (43014B)

Sell financial services, such as loan, tax, and securities counseling, to customers of financial institutions and business establishments.

Average Yearly Earnings: $59,633. **Experience:** Medium preparation is needed. Previous work-related skill, knowledge, or experience is required for this occupation. **Education:** This group of occupations usually requires training in vocational schools, related on-the-job experience, or an associate degree. A bachelor's degree may be required. **Training:** Employees in this type of occupation usually need one or two years of training involving both on-the-job experience and informal training with experienced workers. **Related Examples:** Other occupations like this one usually involve using communication and organizational skills to coordinate, supervise, manage, or train others to accomplish goals. Examples include dental assistants, electricians, fish and game wardens, legal secretaries, personnel recruiters, and recreation workers. **Standard Vocational Preparation Range:** 6.0 to below 7.0—More than one year and less than four years. **Major/Instructional Program:** 08.0204 Business Services Marketing Operations; 08.0401 Financial Services Marketing Operations; 52.0801 Finance, General; 52.0804 Financial Planning. **Related Courses:** Economics and Accounting; Sales and Marketing; Customer and Personal Service; Computers and Electronics; Law, Government, and Jurisprudence.

SALES AGENTS, SELECTED BUSINESS SERVICES (43017)

Sell selected services, such as building maintenance, credit reporting, bookkeeping, security, printing, and storage space, to businesses. Exclude advertising, insurance, financial, and real estate sales agents.

Average Yearly Earnings: $24,502. **Experience:** Medium preparation is needed. Previous work-related skill, knowledge, or experience is required for this occupation. **Education:** This group of occupations usually requires training in vocational schools, related on-the-job experience, or an associate degree. A bachelor's degree may be required. **Training:** Employees in this type of occupation usually need one or two years of training involving both on-the-job experience and informal training with experienced workers. **Related Examples:** Other occupations like this one usually involve using communication and organizational skills to coordinate, supervise, manage, or train others to accomplish goals. Examples include dental assistants, electricians, fish and game wardens, legal

secretaries, personnel recruiters, and recreation workers. **Standard Vocational Preparation Range:** 6.0 to below 7.0—More than one year and less than four years. **Major/ Instructional Program:** 01.0501 Agricultural Supplies Retailing and Wholesaling; 02.0401 Plant Sciences, General; 02.0408 Plant Protection (Pest Management); 08.0204 Business Services Marketing Operations; 08.0706 General Selling Skills and Sales Operations; 08.0901 Hospitality and Recreation Marketing Operations, General; 08.0902 Hotel/ Motel Services Marketing Operations; 52.0702 Franchise Operation; 52.0902 Hotel/ Motel and Restaurant Management. **Related Courses:** Administration and Management; Clerical; Economics and Accounting; Sales and Marketing; Customer and Personal Service; English Language; Communications and Media.

TRAVEL AGENTS (43021)

Plan trips for travel agency customers. Duties include determining destination, modes of transportation, travel dates, costs, and accommodations required; and planning, describing, or selling itinerary package tours. May specialize in foreign or domestic service, individual or group travel, a specific geographical area, airplane charters, or package tours.

Average Yearly Earnings: $21,964. **Experience:** Some preparation is needed. Some previous work-related skill, knowledge, or experience may be helpful in this occupation, but usually is not needed. **Education:** This group of occupations usually requires a high school diploma and may require some vocational training or job-related course work. In some cases, an associate or bachelor's degree could be needed. **Training:** Employees in this type of occupation need anywhere from a few months to one year of working with experienced employees. **Related Examples:** Other occupations like this one often involve using your knowledge and skills to help others. Examples include drywall installers, fire inspectors, flight attendants, pharmacy technicians, retail salespersons, and tellers. **Standard Vocational Preparation Range:** 4.0 to below 6.0—Six months to less than two years. **Major/Instructional Program:** 08.1105 Travel Services Marketing Operations. **Related Courses:** Clerical; Sales and Marketing; Customer and Personal Service; Sociology and Anthropology; Geography; Foreign Language; Transportation.

SITE LEASING AND PROMOTION AGENTS (43023A)

Promote products by obtaining leases for outdoor advertising sites or permission to display product promotional items in establishments.

Average Yearly Earnings: $24,502. **Experience:** Little or no preparation is needed. No previous work-related skill, knowledge, or experience is needed for this occupation. **Education:** This group of occupations may require a high school diploma or GED certificate. A formal training course to obtain a license may be required. **Training:** Employees in this type of occupation need anywhere from a few days to a few months of training. Usually, an experienced worker could show you how to do the job. **Related Examples:** Other occupations like this one involve following instructions and helping others. Examples include bus drivers, forest and conservation workers, general office clerks, home health aides, and waiters/waitresses. **Standard Vocational Preparation Range:** Below 4.0—Less than six months. **Major/Instructional Program:** 08.0706 General Selling Skills and Sales Operations, 09.0201 Advertising. **Related Courses:** Sales and Marketing; Psychology; Geography; Law, Government, and Jurisprudence; Communications and Media.

SALES AGENTS, ADVERTISING (43023B)

Sell or solicit advertising, such as graphic art, advertising space in publications, custom-made signs, and air time on TV and radio.

Average Yearly Earnings: $24,502. **Experience:** Medium preparation is needed. Previous work-related skill, knowledge, or experience is required for this occupation. **Education:** This group of occupations usually requires training in vocational schools, related on-the-job experience, or an associate degree. A bachelor's degree may be required. **Training:** Employees in this type of occupation usually need one or two years of training involving both on-the-job experience and informal training with experienced workers. **Related Examples:** Other occupations like this one usually involve using communication and organizational skills to coordinate, supervise, manage, or train others to accomplish goals. Examples include dental assistants, electricians, fish and game wardens, legal secretaries, personnel recruiters, and recreation workers. **Standard Vocational Preparation Range:** 6.0 to below 7.0—More than one year and less than four years. **Major/Instructional Program:** 08.0204 Business Services Marketing Operations, 08.0706 General Selling Skills and Sales Operations, 09.0201 Advertising. **Related Courses:** Sales and Marketing; Psychology; English Language; Fine Arts; Communications and Media.

SALES REPRESENTATIVES, SERVICE (43099A)

Contact prospective customers to sell services, such as educational courses, dance instructions, cable television, furniture repair, auto leasing, and burial needs.

Average Yearly Earnings: $24,502. **Experience:** Some preparation is needed. Some previous work-related skill, knowledge, or experience may be helpful in this occupation, but usually is not needed. **Education:** This group of occupations usually requires a high school diploma and may require some vocational training or job-related course work. In some cases, an associate or bachelor's degree could be needed. **Training:** Employees in this type of occupation need anywhere from a few months to one year of working with experienced employees. **Related Examples:** Other occupations like this one often involve using your knowledge and skills to help others. Examples include drywall installers, fire inspectors, flight attendants, pharmacy technicians, retail salespersons, and tellers. **Standard Vocational Preparation Range:** 4.0 to below 6.0—Six months to less than two years. **Major/Instructional Program:** 08.0204 Business Services Marketing Operations; 08.0205 Personal Services Marketing Operations; 08.0299 Business and Personal Services Marketing Operations, Other; 08.0705 General Retailing Operations; 08.0706 General Selling Skills and Sales Operations; 08.0901 Hospitality and Recreation Marketing

Operations, General; 08.0903 Recreation Products/Services Marketing Operations; 08.1104 Tourism Promotion Operations; 08.1208 Vehicle Marketing Operations; 12.0301 Funeral Services and Mortuary Science; 20.0501 Home Furnishings and Equipment Installers and Consultants. **Related Courses:** Administration and Management; Economics and Accounting; Sales and Marketing; Customer and Personal Service.

FUNDRAISERS AND SOLICITORS (43099B)

Solicit contributions to support a nonprofit organization, such as a charity or university. May encourage individuals to join or participate in activities of the organization.

Average Yearly Earnings: $24,502. **Experience:** Little or no preparation is needed. No previous work-related skill, knowledge, or experience is needed for this occupation. **Education:** This group of occupations may require a high school diploma or GED certificate. A formal training course to obtain a license may be required. **Training:** Employees in this type of occupation need anywhere from a few days to a few months of training. Usually, an experienced worker could show you how to do the job. **Related Examples:** Other occupations like this one involve following instructions and helping others. Examples include bus drivers, forest and conservation workers, general office clerks, home health aides, and waiters/waitresses. **Standard Vocational Preparation Range:** Below 4.0—Less than 6 months. **Major/Instructional Program:** 08.0299 Business and Personal Services Marketing Operations, Other; 08.0706 General Selling Skills and Sales Operations; 08.0901 Hospitality and Recreation Marketing Operations, General; 08.0903 Recreation Products/Services Marketing Operations; 50.0701 Art, General; 50.0704 Arts Management. **Related Courses:** Administration and Management; Clerical; Economics and Accounting; Sales and Marketing; Psychology; Sociology and Anthropology; Education and Training; Communications and Media.

Technical, Wholesale, and Retail Sales Workers

SALES ENGINEERS (49002)

Sell business goods or services that require a technical background equivalent to a baccalaureate degree in engineering. Excludes engineers whose primary function is not marketing or sales.

Average Yearly Earnings: $24,502. **Experience:** Extensive preparation is needed. Extensive skill, knowledge, and experience are needed for this occupation. It may require more than five years of experience. **Education:** A bachelor's degree is the minimum formal education required for this group of occupations. However, many also require graduate school. For example, they may require a master's degree, and some require a Ph.D., M.D., or J.D. (law degree). **Training:** Employees in this type of occupation may need some on-the-job training, but most of these occupations assume that the person will already have the required skills, knowledge, work-related experience, and/or training.

Examples: Other occupations like this one often involve coordinating, training, supervising, or managing the activities of others to accomplish goals. Very advanced communication and organizational skills are required. Examples include athletic trainers, lawyers, managing editors, physicists, social psychologists, and surgeons. **Standard Vocational Preparation Range:** 8.0 to 9.0—Four years to more than ten years. **Major/Instructional Program:** 14.0201 Aerospace, Aeronautical, and Astronautical Engineering; 14.0301 Agricultural Engineering; 14.0601 Ceramic Sciences and Engineering; 14.0701 Chemical Engineering; 14.1001 Electrical, Electronics, and Communications Engineering; 14.1901 Mechanical Engineering; 14.2101 Mining and Mineral Engineering; 14.2201 Naval Architecture and Marine Engineering; 14.2301 Nuclear Engineering; 14.2701 Systems Engineering. **Related Courses:** Economics and Accounting; Sales and Marketing; Customer and Personal Service; Production and Processing; Computers and Electronics; Engineering and Technology; Design; Mechanical; Mathematics; Physics; Psychology; Education and Training; English Language; History and Archeology; Telecommunications.

SALES REPRESENTATIVES, AGRICULTURAL (49005A)

Sell agricultural products and services, such as animal feeds, farm and garden equipment, and dairy, poultry, and veterinarian supplies.

Average Yearly Earnings: $24,502. **Experience:** Some preparation is needed. Some previous work-related skill, knowledge, or experience may be helpful in this occupation, but usually is not needed. **Education:** This group of occupations usually requires a high school diploma and may require some vocational training or job-related course work. In some cases, an associate or bachelor's degree could be needed. **Training:** Employees in this type of occupation need anywhere from a few months to one year of working with experienced employees. **Related Examples:** Other occupations like this one often involve using your knowledge and skills to help others. Examples include drywall installers, fire inspectors, flight attendants, pharmacy technicians, retail salespersons, and tellers. **Standard Vocational Preparation Range:** 4.0 to below 6.0—Six months to less than two years. **Major/Instructional Program:** 01.0501 Agricultural Supplies Retailing and Wholesaling; 02.0201 Animal Sciences, General; 02.0204 Agricultural Animal Nutrition; 02.0209 Poultry Science; 08.0706 General Selling Skills and Sales Operations; 51.0808 Veterinarian Assistant/Animal Health Technician. **Related Courses:** Economics and Accounting; Sales and Marketing; Customer and Personal Service; Food Production.

SALES REPRESENTATIVES, CHEMICAL AND PHARMACEUTICAL (49005B)

Sell chemical or pharmaceutical products or services, such as acids, industrial chemicals, agricultural chemicals, medicines, drugs, and water treatment supplies.

Average Yearly Earnings: $24,502. **Experience:** Medium preparation is needed. Previous work-related skill, knowledge, or experience is required for this occupation. **Education:** This group of occupations usually requires training in vocational schools, related on-the-job experience, or an associate degree. A bachelor's degree may be required.

Training: Employees in this type of occupation usually need one or two years of training involving both on-the-job experience and informal training with experienced workers. **Related Examples:** Other occupations like this one usually involve using communication and organizational skills to coordinate, supervise, manage, or train others to accomplish goals. Examples include dental assistants, electricians, fish and game wardens, legal secretaries, personnel recruiters, and recreation workers. **Standard Vocational Preparation Range:** 6.0 to below 7.0—More than one year and less than four years. **Major/Instructional Program:** 01.0501 Agricultural Supplies Retailing and Wholesaling, 08.0706 General Selling Skills and Sales Operations, 15.0506 Water Quality and Wastewater Treatment Technology/Technician, 41.0301 Chemical Technology/Technician, 51.0805 Pharmacy Technician/Assistant. **Related Courses:** Sales and Marketing; Chemistry.

SALES REPRESENTATIVES, ELECTRICAL/ELECTRONIC (49005C)

Sell electrical, electronic, or related products or services, such as communication equipment, radiographic-inspection equipment and services, ultrasonic equipment, electronics parts, computers, and EDP systems.

Average Yearly Earnings: $24,502. **Experience:** Some preparation is needed. Some previous work-related skill, knowledge, or experience may be helpful in this occupation, but usually is not needed. **Education:** This group of occupations usually requires a high school diploma and may require some vocational training or job-related course work. In some cases, an associate or bachelor's degree could be needed. **Training:** Employees in this type of occupation need anywhere from a few months to one year of working with experienced employees. **Related Examples:** Other occupations like this one often involve using your knowledge and skills to help others. Examples include drywall installers, fire inspectors, flight attendants, pharmacy technicians, retail salespersons, and tellers. **Standard Vocational Preparation Range:** 4.0 to below 6.0—Six months to less than two years. **Major/Instructional Program:** 08.0706 General Selling Skills and Sales Operations; 08.0810 Office Products Marketing Operations; 15.0301 Computer Engineering Technology/Technician; 15.0303 Electrical, Electronic, and Communications Engineering Technology/Technician; 15.0402 Computer Maintenance Technology/Technician; 15.0404 Instrumentation Technology/Technician; 15.0611 Metallurgical Technology/Technician. **Related Courses:** Economics and Accounting; Sales and Marketing; Computers and Electronics; Psychology; Education and Training; Telecommunications.

SALES REPRESENTATIVES, MECHANICAL EQUIPMENT AND SUPPLIES (49005D)

Sell mechanical equipment, machinery, materials, and supplies, such as aircraft and railroad equipment and parts, construction machinery, material-handling equipment, industrial machinery, and welding equipment.

Average Yearly Earnings: $24,502. **Experience:** Some preparation is needed. Some previous work-related skill, knowledge, or experience may be helpful in this occupation, but usually is not needed. **Education:** This group of occupations usually requires a high school diploma and may require some vocational training or job-related course work. In some cases, an associate or bachelor's degree could be needed. **Training:** Employees in this type of occupation need anywhere from a few months to one year of working with experienced employees. **Related Examples:** Other occupations like this one often involve using your knowledge and skills to help others. Examples include drywall installers, fire inspectors, flight attendants, pharmacy technicians, retail salespersons, and tellers. **Standard Vocational Preparation Range:** 4.0 to below 6.0—Six months to less than two years. **Major/Instructional Program:** 01.0501 Agricultural Supplies Retailing and Wholesaling, 08.0706 General Selling Skills and Sales Operations, 15.0603 Industrial/Manufacturing Technology/Technician, 15.0607 Plastics Technology/Technician, 15.0611 Metallurgical Technology/Technician, 15.0801 Aeronautical and Aerospace Engineering Technology/Technician, 15.0903 Petroleum Technology/Technician, 15.1001 Construction/Building Technology/Technician, 47.0303 Industrial Machinery Maintenance and Repairer, 48.0501 Machinist/Machine Technologist, 48.0508 Welder/Welding Technologist, 49.0202 Construction Equipment Operator. **Related Courses:** Economics and Accounting; Sales and Marketing; Customer and Personal Service; Mathematics.

SALES REPRESENTATIVES, MEDICAL (49005F)

Sell medical equipment, products, and services. Does not include pharmaceutical sales representatives.

Average Yearly Earnings: $24,502. **Experience:** Medium preparation is needed. Previous work-related skill, knowledge, or experience is required for this occupation. **Education:** This group of occupations usually requires training in vocational schools, related on-the-job experience, or an associate degree. A bachelor's degree may be required. **Training:** Employees in this type of occupation usually need one or two years of training involving both on-the-job experience and informal training with experienced workers. **Related Examples:** Other occupations like this one usually involve using communication and organizational skills to coordinate, supervise, manage, or train others to accomplish goals. Examples include dental assistants, electricians, fish and game wardens, legal secretaries, personnel recruiters, and recreation workers. **Standard Vocational Preparation Range:** 6.0 to below 7.0—More than one year and less than four years. **Major/Instructional Program:** 08.0706 General Selling Skills and Sales Operations, 08.1301 Health Products and Services Marketing Operations, 15.0401 Biomedical Engineering-Related Technology/Technician. **Related Courses:** Economics and Accounting; Sales and Marketing; Design; Mathematics; Medicine and Dentistry.

SALES REPRESENTATIVES, INSTRUMENTS (49005G)

Sell precision instruments, such as dynamometers and spring scales, and laboratory, navigation, and surveying instruments.

Average Yearly Earnings: $24,502. **Experience:** Medium preparation is needed. Previous work-related skill, knowledge, or experience is required for this occupation. **Education:** This group of occupations usually requires training in vocational schools, related

on-the-job experience, or an associate degree. A bachelor's degree may be required. **Training:** Employees in this type of occupation usually need one or two years of training involving both on-the-job experience and informal training with experienced workers. **Related Examples:** Other occupations like this one usually involve using communication and organizational skills to coordinate, supervise, manage, or train others to accomplish goals. Examples include dental assistants, electricians, fish and game wardens, legal secretaries, personnel recruiters, and recreation workers. **Standard Vocational Preparation Range:** 6.0 to below 7.0—More than one year and less than four years. **Major/Instructional Program:** 08.0706 General Selling Skills and Sales Operations, 15.0404 Instrumentation Technology/Technician. **Related Courses:** Sales and Marketing.

SALES REPRESENTATIVES, EXCEPT RETAIL AND SCIENTIFIC AND RELATED PRODUCTS AND SERVICES (49008)

Sell goods or services for wholesalers or manufacturers to businesses or groups of individuals. Solicit orders from established clients or secure new customers. Work requires substantial knowledge of the items sold.

Average Yearly Earnings: $24,502. **Experience:** Some preparation is needed. Some previous work-related skill, knowledge, or experience may be helpful in this occupation, but usually is not needed. **Education:** This group of occupations usually requires a high school diploma and may require some vocational training or job-related course work. In some cases, an associate or bachelor's degree could be needed. **Training:** Employees in this type of occupation need anywhere from a few months to one year of working with experienced employees. **Related Examples:** Other occupations like this one often involve using your knowledge and skills to help others. Examples include drywall installers, fire inspectors, flight attendants, pharmacy technicians, retail salespersons, and tellers. **Standard Vocational Preparation Range:** 4.0 to below 6.0—Six months to less than two years. **Major/Instructional Program:** 01.0501 Agricultural Supplies Retailing and Wholesaling; 08.0101 Apparel and Accessories Marketing Operations, General; 08.0102 Fashion Merchandising; 08.0199 Apparel and Accessories Marketing Operations, Other; 08.0299 Business and Personal Services Marketing Operations, Other; 08.0503 Floristry Marketing Operations; 08.0601 Food Products Retailing and Wholesaling Operations; 08.0705 General Retailing Operations; 08.0706 General Selling Skills and Sales Operations; 08.0810 Office Products Marketing Operations; 08.0901 Hospitality and Recreation Marketing Operations, General; 08.0903 Recreation Products/Services Marketing Operations; 08.9999 Marketing Operations/Marketing and Distribution, Other; 15.0101 Architectural Engineering Technology/Technician; 20.0301 Clothing, Apparel, and Textile Workers and Managers, General; 20.0306 Fashion and Fabric Consultant. **Related Courses:** Economics and Accounting; Sales and Marketing; Customer and Personal Service; Mathematics; Psychology; Sociology and Anthropology; Education and Training; Foreign Language; Philosophy and Theology; Communications and Media; Transportation.

SALESPERSONS, RETAIL (49011)

Sell to the public any of a wide variety of merchandise, such as furniture, motor vehicles, appliances, or apparel. Includes workers who sell less expensive merchandise, where a knowledge of the item sold is not a primary requirement. Excludes cashiers.

Average Yearly Earnings: $17,180. **Experience:** Some preparation is needed. Some previous work-related skill, knowledge, or experience may be helpful in this occupation, but usually is not needed. **Education:** This group of occupations usually requires a high school diploma and may require some vocational training or job-related course work. In some cases, an associate or bachelor's degree could be needed. **Training:** Employees in this type of occupation need anywhere from a few months to one year of working with experienced employees. **Related Examples:** Other occupations like this one often involve using your knowledge and skills to help others. Examples include drywall installers, fire inspectors, flight attendants, pharmacy technicians, and tellers. **Standard Vocational Preparation Range:** 4.0 to below 6.0—Six months to less than two years. **Major/Instructional Program:** 01.0501 Agricultural Supplies Retailing and Wholesaling; 01.0601 Horticulture Services Operations and Management, General; 01.0603 Ornamental Horticulture Operations and Management; 01.0604 Greenhouse Operations and Management; 01.0606 Nursery Operations and Management; 08.0101 Apparel and Accessories Marketing Operations, General; 08.0102 Fashion Merchandising; 08.0199 Apparel and Accessories Marketing Operations, Other; 08.0503 Floristry Marketing Operations; 08.0705 General Retailing Operations; 08.0706 General Selling Skills and Sales Operations; 08.0809 Home Products Marketing Operations; 08.0901 Hospitality and Recreation Marketing Operations, General; 08.0903 Recreation Products/Services Marketing Operations; 08.1203 Vehicle Parts and Accessories Marketing Operations; 08.1208 Vehicle Marketing Operations; 08.1301 Health Products and Services Marketing Operations; 08.9999 Marketing Operations/Marketing and Distribution, Other; 20.0301 Clothing, Apparel and Textile Workers and Managers, General; 20.0306 Fashion and Fabric Consultant; 20.0501 Home Furnishings and Equipment Installers and Consultants. **Related Courses:** Economics and Accounting; Sales and Marketing; Customer and Personal Service.

SALESPERSONS, PARTS (49014)

Sell spare and replaceable parts and equipment from behind a counter in an agency, repair shop, or parts store. Determine the make, year, and type of part needed by observing the damaged part or listening to a description of the malfunction. Read a catalog to find the stock number, price, etc., and fill the customer's order from stock. Excludes workers whose primary responsibilities are to receive, store, and issue materials, equipment, and other items from the stockroom.

Average Yearly Earnings: $17,180. **Experience:** Some preparation is needed. Some previous work-related skill, knowledge, or experience may be helpful in this occupation, but usually is not needed. **Education:** This group of occupations usually requires a high school diploma and may require some vocational training or job-related course work. In some cases, an associate or bachelor's degree could be needed. **Training:** Employees in this type of occupation need anywhere from a few months to one year of working with experienced employees. **Related Examples:** Other occupations like this one often involve using your knowledge and skills to help others. Examples include drywall installers, fire inspectors, flight attendants, pharmacy technicians, retail salespersons, and tellers. **Standard Vocational Preparation Range:** 4.0 to below 6.0—Six months to less than two years. **Major/Instructional Program:** 01.0501 Agricultural Supplies Retailing and Wholesaling, 08.0705 General Retailing Operations, 08.0706 General Selling Skills and Sales Operations, 08.1203 Vehicle Parts and Accessories Marketing Operations. **Related Courses:** Sales and Marketing; Customer and Personal Service; Mechanical; Telecommunications.

COUNTER AND RENTAL CLERKS (49017)

Receive orders for services, such as rentals, repairs, dry-cleaning, and storage. May compute the cost and accept payment.

Average Yearly Earnings: $14,580. **Experience:** Little or no preparation is needed. No previous work-related skill, knowledge, or experience is needed for this occupation. **Education:** This group of occupations may require a high school diploma or GED certificate. A formal training course to obtain a license may be required. **Training:** Employees in this type of occupation need anywhere from a few days to a few months of training. Usually, an experienced worker could show you how to do the job. **Related Examples:** Other occupations like this one involve following instructions and helping others. Examples include bus drivers, forest and conservation workers, general office clerks, home health aides, and waiters/waitresses. **Standard Vocational Preparation Range:** Below 4.0—Less than six months. **Major/Instructional Program:** 08.0705 General Retailing Operations; 08.0706 General Selling Skills and Sales Operations; 08.1105 Travel Services Marketing Operations; 08.1299 Vehicle and Petroleum Products Marketing Operations, Other; 20.0301 Clothing, Apparel, and Textile Workers and Managers, General; 20.0309 Drycleaner and Launderer; 47.0408 Watch, Clock, and Jewelry Repairer. **Related Courses:** Clerical; Sales and Marketing; Customer and Personal Service; Telecommunications.

STOCK CLERKS, SALES FLOOR (49021)

Receive, store, and issue sales floor merchandise. Stock shelves, racks, cases, bins, and tables with merchandise, and arrange merchandise displays to attract customers. May periodically take physical count of stock or check and mark merchandise.

Average Yearly Earnings: $19,344. **Experience:** Little or no preparation is needed. No previous work-related skill, knowledge, or experience is needed for this occupation. **Education:** This group of occupations may require a high school diploma or GED certificate. A formal training course to obtain a license may be required. **Training:** Employees in this type of occupation need anywhere from a few days to a few months of training.

Usually, an experienced worker could show you how to do the job. **Related Examples:** Other occupations like this one involve following instructions and helping others. Examples include bus drivers, forest and conservation workers, general office clerks, home health aides, and waiters/waitresses. **Standard Vocational Preparation Range:** Below 4.0—Less than six months. **Major/Instructional Program:** 08.0601 Food Products Retailing and Wholesaling Operations; 08.0705 General Retailing Operations; 08.9999 Marketing Operations/Marketing and Distribution, Other. **Related Courses:** Clerical; Sales and Marketing.

CASHIERS, GENERAL (49023A)

Receive payments, issue receipts, handle credit transactions, account for the amounts received, and perform related clerical duties in a wide variety of business establishments.

Average Yearly Earnings: $13,686. **Experience:** Little or no preparation is needed. No previous work-related skill, knowledge, or experience is needed for this occupation. **Education:** This group of occupations may require a high school diploma or GED certificate. A formal training course to obtain a license may be required. **Training:** Employees in this type of occupation need anywhere from a few days to a few months of training. Usually, an experienced worker could show you how to do the job. **Related Examples:** Other occupations like this one involve following instructions and helping others. Examples include bus drivers, forest and conservation workers, general office clerks, home health aides, and waiters/waitresses. **Standard Vocational Preparation Range:** Below 4.0—Less than six months. **Major/Instructional Program:** 08.0601 Food Products Retailing and Wholesaling Operations; 08.0705 General Retailing Operations; 52.0801 Finance, General; 52.0803 Banking and Financial Support Services. **Related Courses:** Clerical; Sales and Marketing; Customer and Personal Service.

CASH ACCOUNTING CLERKS (49023B)

Receive payments, issue receipts, handle credit transactions, account for the amounts received, and perform related clerical duties in a wide variety of business establishments. Operate office machines, such as a typewriter, computer terminal, and adding, calculating, bookkeeping, and check-writing machines.

Average Yearly Earnings: $13,686. **Experience:** Some preparation is needed. Some previous work-related skill, knowledge, or experience may be helpful in this occupation, but usually is not needed. **Education:** This group of occupations usually requires a high school diploma and may require some vocational training or job-related course work. In some cases, an associate or bachelor's degree could be needed. **Training:** Employees in this type of occupation need anywhere from a few months to one year of working with experienced employees. **Related Examples:** Other occupations like this one often involve using your knowledge and skills to help others. Examples include drywall installers, fire inspectors, flight attendants, pharmacy technicians, retail salespersons, and tellers. **Standard Vocational Preparation Range:** 4.0 to below 6.0—Six months to less than two years. **Major/Instructional Program:** 08.0705 General Retailing Operations; 52.0801 Finance, General; 52.0803 Banking and Financial Support Services. **Related Courses:** Clerical; Economics and Accounting; Computers and Electronics.

TELEMARKETERS, DOOR-TO-DOOR SALES WORKERS, NEWS AND STREET VENDORS, AND OTHER RELATED WORKERS (49026)

Solicit orders for goods or services over the telephone; sell goods or services door-to-door or on the street.

Average Yearly Earnings: $17,180. **Experience:** Little or no preparation is needed. No previous work-related skill, knowledge, or experience is needed for this occupation. **Education:** This group of occupations may require a high school diploma or GED certificate. A formal training course to obtain a license may be required. **Training:** Employees in this type of occupation need anywhere from a few days to a few months of training. Usually, an experienced worker could show you how to do the job. **Related Examples:** Other occupations like this one involve following instructions and helping others. Examples include bus drivers, forest and conservation workers, general office clerks, home health aides, and waiters/waitresses. **Standard Vocational Preparation Range:** Below 4.0—Less than six months. **Major/Instructional Program:** 08.0705 General Retailing Operations, 08.0708 General Marketing Operations, 08.0809 Home Products Marketing Operations. **Related Courses:** Sales and Marketing; Customer and Personal Service.

DEMONSTRATORS AND PROMOTERS (49032A)

Demonstrate merchandise and answer questions for the purpose of creating public interest in buying the products.

Average Yearly Earnings: $17,180. **Experience:** Little or no preparation is needed. No previous work-related skill, knowledge, or experience is needed for this occupation. **Education:** This group of occupations may require a high school diploma or GED certificate. A formal training course to obtain a license may be required. **Training:** Employees in this type of occupation need anywhere from a few days to a few months of training. Usually, an experienced worker could show you how to do the job. **Related Examples:** Other occupations like this one involve following instructions and helping others. Examples include bus drivers, forest and conservation workers, general office clerks, home health aides, and waiters/waitresses. **Standard Vocational Preparation Range:** Below 4.0—Less than six months. **Major/Instructional Program:** 08.0299 Business and Personal Services Marketing Operations, Other; 08.0705 General Retailing Operations; 08.0706 General Selling Skills and Sales Operations; 08.0809 Home Products Marketing Operations; 20.0301 Clothing, Apparel, and Textile Workers and Managers, General; 20.0306 Fashion and Fabric Consultant; 20.0501 Home Furnishings and Equipment Installers and Consultants; 50.0701 Art, General; 50.0708 Painting; 50.0712 Fiber, Textile, and Weaving Arts. **Related Courses:** Clerical; Sales and Marketing; Customer and Personal Service;

Sociology and Anthropology; Education and Training; English Language; Communications and Media.

MODELS **(49032B)**

Model for photographers or artists, or display merchandise or depict characters.

Average Yearly Earnings: $35,339. **Experience:** Little or no preparation is needed. No previous work-related skill, knowledge, or experience is needed for this occupation. **Education:** This group of occupations may require a high school diploma or GED certificate. A formal training course to obtain a license may be required. **Training:** Employees in this type of occupation need anywhere from a few days to a few months of training. Usually, an experienced worker could show you how to do the job. **Related Examples:** Other occupations like this one involve following instructions and helping others. Examples include bus drivers, forest and conservation workers, general office clerks, home health aides, and waiters/waitresses. **Standard Vocational Preparation Range:** Below 4.0—Less than six months. **Major/Instructional Program:** 08.0101 Apparel and Accessories Marketing Operations, General; 08.0102 Fashion Merchandising; 08.0103 Fashion Modeling. **Related Courses:** Sales and Marketing; Sociology and Anthropology; Fine Arts; Communications and Media.

Sales Consultants and Estimators

MERCHANDISE APPRAISERS AND AUCTIONEERS **(49999A)**

Appraise and estimate the value of items, such as paintings, antiques, jewelry, cameras, musical instruments, machinery, and fixtures for loan, insurance, or sale purposes. May sell merchandise at auction.

Average Yearly Earnings: $24,502. **Experience:** Medium preparation is needed. Previous work-related skill, knowledge, or experience is required for this occupation. **Education:** This group of occupations usually requires training in vocational schools, related on-the-job experience, or an associate degree. A bachelor's degree may be required. **Training:** Employees in this type of occupation usually need one or two years of training involving both on-the-job experience and informal training with experienced workers. **Related Examples:** Other occupations like this one usually involve using communication and organizational skills to coordinate, supervise, manage, or train others to accomplish goals. Examples include dental assistants, electricians, fish and game wardens, legal secretaries, personnel recruiters, and recreation workers. **Standard Vocational Preparation Range:** 6.0 to below 7.0—More than one year and less than four years. **Major/Instructional Program:** 01.0501 Agricultural Supplies Retailing and Wholesaling; 08.0701 Auctioneering; 08.0705 General Retailing Operations; 08.0706 General Selling Skills and Sales Operations; 08.0708 General Marketing Operations; 50.0701 Art, General; 50.0704 Arts Management. **Related Courses:** Economics and Accounting; Sales and Marketing; Fine Arts; History and Archeology; Law, Government, and Jurisprudence.

HOME FURNISHINGS ESTIMATORS (49999B)

Measure dimensions and estimate the price of making and installing household accessories.

Average Yearly Earnings: $24,502. **Experience:** Some preparation is needed. Some previous work-related skill, knowledge, or experience may be helpful in this occupation, but usually is not needed. **Education:** This group of occupations usually requires a high school diploma and may require some vocational training or job-related course work. In some cases, an associate or bachelor's degree could be needed. **Training:** Employees in this type of occupation need anywhere from a few months to one year of working with experienced employees. **Related Examples:** Other occupations like this one often involve using your knowledge and skills to help others. Examples include drywall installers, fire inspectors, flight attendants, pharmacy technicians, retail salespersons, and tellers. **Standard Vocational Preparation Range:** 4.0 to below 6.0—Six months to less than two years. **Major/Instructional Program:** 20.0501 Home Furnishings and Equipment Installers and Consultants, 20.0502 Window Treatment Maker and Installer, 48.0303 Upholsterers. **Related Courses:** Sales and Marketing; Customer and Personal Service; Design; Building and Construction.

SALES CONSULTANTS (49999C)

Select, recommend, or purchase merchandise or services for customers shopping either in person or by telephone at department or specialty stores. Include personal shoppers and wedding consultants.

Average Yearly Earnings: $24,502. **Experience:** Some preparation is needed. Some previous work-related skill, knowledge, or experience may be helpful in this occupation, but usually is not needed. **Education:** This group of occupations usually requires a high school diploma and may require some vocational training or job-related course work. In some cases, an associate or bachelor's degree could be needed. **Training:** Employees in this type of occupation need anywhere from a few months to one year of working with experienced employees. **Related Examples:** Other occupations like this one often involve using your knowledge and skills to help others. Examples include drywall installers, fire inspectors, flight attendants, pharmacy technicians, retail salespersons, and tellers. **Standard Vocational Preparation Range:** 4.0 to below 6.0—Six months to less than two years. **Major/Instructional Program:** 08.0101 Apparel and Accessories Marketing Operations, General; 08.0102 Fashion Merchandising; 08.0205 Personal Services Marketing Operations; 08.0705 General Retailing Operations; 08.0706 General Selling Skills and Sales Operations; 20.0301 Clothing, Apparel, and Textile Workers and Managers, General; 20.0306 Fashion and Fabric Consultant; 20.0601 Custodial, Housekeeping, and Home Services Workers and Managers, General; 20.0606 Homemaker's Aide. **Related Courses:** Sales and Marketing; Customer and Personal Service.

ADMINISTRATIVE SUPPORT WORKERS

Administrative Supervisors

FIRST-LINE SUPERVISORS, CUSTOMER SERVICE (51002A)

Supervise and coordinate the activities of workers involved in providing customer service.

Average Yearly Earnings: $31,012. **Experience:** Medium preparation is needed. Previous work-related skill, knowledge, or experience is required for this occupation. **Education:** This group of occupations usually requires training in vocational schools, related on-the-job experience, or an associate degree. A bachelor's degree may be required. **Training:** Employees in this type of occupation usually need one or two years of training involving both on-the-job experience and informal training with experienced workers. **Related Examples:** Other occupations like this one usually involve using communication and organizational skills to coordinate, supervise, manage, or train others to accomplish goals. Examples include dental assistants, electricians, fish and game wardens, legal secretaries, personnel recruiters, and recreation workers. **Standard Vocational Preparation Range:** 6.0 to below 7.0—More than one year and less than four years. **Major/Instructional Program:** 08.0709 General Distribution Operations; 08.1104 Tourism Promotion Operations; 08.1105 Travel Services Marketing Operations; 12.0504 Food and Beverage/Restaurant Operations Manager; 43.0103 Criminal Justice/Law Enforcement Administration; 51.0704 Health Unit Manager/Ward Supervisor; 52.0201 Business Administration and Management, General; 52.0203 Logistics and Materials Management; 52.0204 Office Supervision and Management; 52.0205 Operations Management and Supervision; 52.0902 Hotel/Motel and Restaurant Management; 52.0903 Travel-Tourism Management. **Related Courses:** Administration and Management; Clerical; Economics and Accounting; Customer and Personal Service; Personnel and Human Resources; Psychology; Sociology and Anthropology; Therapy and Counseling; Education and Training; Law, Government, and Jurisprudence; Communications and Media.

FIRST-LINE SUPERVISORS, ADMINISTRATIVE SUPPORT (51002B)

Supervise and coordinate the activities of workers involved in providing administrative support.

Average Yearly Earnings: $31,012. **Experience:** Medium preparation is needed. Previous work-related skill, knowledge, or experience is required for this occupation. **Education:** This group of occupations usually requires training in vocational schools, related on-the-job experience, or an associate degree. A bachelor's degree may be required.

Training: Employees in this type of occupation usually need one or two years of training involving both on-the-job experience and informal training with experienced workers. **Related Examples:** Other occupations like this one usually involve using communication and organizational skills to coordinate, supervise, manage, or train others to accomplish goals. Examples include dental assistants, electricians, fish and game wardens, legal secretaries, personnel recruiters, and recreation workers. **Standard Vocational Preparation Range:** 6.0 to below 7.0—More than one year and less than four years. **Major/Instructional Program:** 08.0709 General Distribution Operations; 11.0301 Data Processing Technology/Technician; 20.0301 Clothing, Apparel, and Textile Workers and Managers, General; 20.0303 Commercial Garment and Apparel Worker; 43.0103 Criminal Justice/Law Enforcement Administration; 52.0201 Business Administration and Management, General; 52.0203 Logistics and Materials Management; 52.0204 Office Supervision and Management; 52.0205 Operations Management and Supervision; 52.1201 Management Information Systems and Business Data Processing, General; 52.1205 Business Computer Facilities Operator. **Related Courses:** Administration and Management; Clerical; Economics and Accounting; Customer and Personal Service; Personnel and Human Resources; Mathematics; Psychology; Education and Training; Philosophy and Theology; Public Safety and Security; Law, Government, and Jurisprudence; Transportation.

Financial Transaction Workers

TELLERS (53102)

Receive and pay out money. Keep records of money and negotiable instruments involved in a financial institution's various transactions.

Average Yearly Earnings: $16,536. **Experience:** Some preparation is needed. Some previous work-related skill, knowledge, or experience may be helpful in this occupation, but usually is not needed. **Education:** This group of occupations usually requires a high school diploma and may require some vocational training or job-related course work. In some cases, an associate or bachelor's degree could be needed. **Training:** Employees in this type of occupation need anywhere from a few months to one year of working with experienced employees. **Related Examples:** Other occupations like this one often involve using your knowledge and skills to help others. Examples include drywall installers, fire inspectors, flight attendants, pharmacy technicians, and retail salespersons. **Standard Vocational Preparation Range:** 4.0 to below 6.0—Six months to less than two years. **Major/Instructional Program:** 08.0401 Financial Services Marketing Operations; 52.0801 Finance, General; 52.0803 Banking and Financial Support Services; 52.1403 International Business Marketing. **Related Courses:** Clerical; Economics and Accounting; Sales and Marketing; Customer and Personal Service; Foreign Language; Law, Government, and Jurisprudence.

NEW ACCOUNTS CLERKS (53105)

Interview persons desiring to open bank accounts. Explain the banking services available to prospective customers and assist them in preparing the application form.

Average Yearly Earnings: $20,550. **Experience:** Some preparation is needed. Some previous work-related skill, knowledge, or experience may be helpful in this occupation, but usually is not needed. **Education:** This group of occupations usually requires a high school diploma and may require some vocational training or job-related course work. In some cases, an associate or bachelor's degree could be needed. **Training:** Employees in this type of occupation need anywhere from a few months to one year of working with experienced employees. **Related Examples:** Other occupations like this one often involve using your knowledge and skills to help others. Examples include drywall installers, fire inspectors, flight attendants, pharmacy technicians, retail salespersons, and tellers. **Standard Vocational Preparation Range:** 4.0 to below 6.0—Six months to less than two years. **Major/Instructional Program:** 52.0801 Finance, General; 52.0803 Banking and Financial Support Services. **Related Courses:** Clerical; Economics and Accounting; Sales and Marketing; Customer and Personal Service; Computers and Electronics.

TRANSIT CLERKS (53108)

Sort, record, prove, and prepare transit items for mailing to or from out-of-city banks to ensure correct routing and prompt collection.

Average Yearly Earnings: $21,756. **Experience:** Some preparation is needed. Some previous work-related skill, knowledge, or experience may be helpful in this occupation, but usually is not needed. **Education:** This group of occupations usually requires a high school diploma and may require some vocational training or job-related course work. In some cases, an associate or bachelor's degree could be needed. **Training:** Employees in this type of occupation need anywhere from a few months to one year of working with experienced employees. **Related Examples:** Other occupations like this one often involve using your knowledge and skills to help others. Examples include drywall installers, fire inspectors, flight attendants, pharmacy technicians, retail salespersons, and tellers. **Standard Vocational Preparation Range:** 4.0 to below 6.0—Six months to less than two years. **Major/Instructional Program:** 52.0302 Accounting Technician; 52.0801 Finance, General; 52.0803 Banking and Financial Support Services. **Related Courses:** Clerical; Computers and Electronics.

CREDIT AUTHORIZERS (53114)

Authorize credit charges against customers' accounts.

Average Yearly Earnings: $22,817. **Experience:** Little or no preparation is needed. No previous work-related skill, knowledge, or experience is needed for this occupation. **Education:** This group of occupations may require a high school diploma or GED certificate. A formal training course to obtain a license may be required. **Training:** Employees in this type of occupation need anywhere from a few days to a few months of training. Usually, an experienced worker could show you how to do the job. **Related Examples:** Other occupations like this one involve following instructions and helping others. Examples include bus drivers, forest and conservation workers, general office clerks, home health aides, and waiters/waitresses. **Standard Vocational Preparation Range:** Below

4.0—Less than six months. **Major/Instructional Program:** 52.0801 Finance, General; 52.0803 Banking and Financial Support Services. **Related Courses:** Clerical.

CREDIT CHECKERS (53117)

Investigate the history and credit standing of individuals or business establishments applying for credit. Telephone or write to credit departments of business and service establishments to obtain information about an applicant's credit standing.

Average Yearly Earnings: $22,568. **Experience:** Little or no preparation is needed. No previous work-related skill, knowledge, or experience is needed for this occupation. **Education:** This group of occupations may require a high school diploma or GED certificate. A formal training course to obtain a license may be required. **Training:** Employees in this type of occupation need anywhere from a few days to a few months of training. Usually, an experienced worker could show you how to do the job. **Related Examples:** Other occupations like this one involve following instructions and helping others. Examples include bus drivers, forest and conservation workers, general office clerks, home health aides, and waiters/waitresses. **Standard Vocational Preparation Range:** Below 4.0—Less than six months. **Major/Instructional Program:** No specific instructional program for this occupation. **Related Courses:** No related courses listed in the database for this occupation.

LOAN AND CREDIT CLERKS (53121)

Assemble documents, prepare papers, process applications, and complete transactions of individuals applying for loans and credit. Loan clerks review loan papers to ensure completeness; operate typewriters to prepare correspondence, reports, and loan documents from drafts; and complete transactions between the loan establishment, borrowers, and sellers upon approval of the loan. Credit clerks interview applicants to obtain personal and financial data, determine credit worthiness, process applications, and notify the customer of acceptance or rejection of credit. Excludes loan interviewers.

Average Yearly Earnings: $22,089. **Experience:** Some preparation is needed. Some previous work-related skill, knowledge, or experience may be helpful in this occupation, but usually is not needed. **Education:** This group of occupations usually requires a high school diploma and may require some vocational training or job-related course work. In some cases, an associate or bachelor's degree could be needed. **Training:** Employees in this type of occupation need anywhere from a few months to one year of working with experienced employees. **Related Examples:** Other occupations like this one often involve using your knowledge and skills to help others. Examples include drywall installers, fire inspectors, flight attendants, pharmacy technicians, retail salespersons, and tellers. **Standard Vocational Preparation Range:** 4.0 to below 6.0—Six months to less than two years. **Major/Instructional Program:** 52.0801 Finance, General; 52.0803 Banking and Financial Support Services. **Related Courses:** Clerical; Economics and Accounting; Customer and Personal Service; Law, Government, and Jurisprudence.

ADJUSTMENT CLERKS (53123)

Investigate and resolve customers' inquiries concerning merchandise, service, billing, or credit rating. Examine pertinent information to determine the accuracy of customers' complaints and responsibility for errors. Notify customers and appropriate personnel of findings, adjustments, and recommendations, such as exchange of merchandise, refund of money, credit to customers' accounts, or adjustment to customers' bills.

Average Yearly Earnings: $22,422. **Experience:** Some preparation is needed. Some previous work-related skill, knowledge, or experience may be helpful in this occupation, but usually is not needed. **Education:** This group of occupations usually requires a high school diploma and may require some vocational training or job-related course work. In some cases, an associate or bachelor's degree could be needed. **Training:** Employees in this type of occupation need anywhere from a few months to one year of working with experienced employees. **Related Examples:** Other occupations like this one often involve using your knowledge and skills to help others. Examples include drywall installers, fire inspectors, flight attendants, pharmacy technicians, retail salespersons, and tellers. **Standard Vocational Preparation Range:** 4.0 to below 6.0—Six months to less than two years. **Major/Instructional Program:** 08.1203 Vehicle Parts and Accessories Marketing Operations; 52.0401 Administrative Assistant/Secretarial Science, General; 52.0408 General Office/Clerical and Typing Services. **Related Courses:** Economics and Accounting.

STATEMENT CLERKS (53126)

Prepare and distribute bank statements to customers, answer inquiries, and reconcile discrepancies in records and accounts.

Average Yearly Earnings: $18,928. **Experience:** Some preparation is needed. Some previous work-related skill, knowledge, or experience may be helpful in this occupation, but usually is not needed. **Education:** This group of occupations usually requires a high school diploma and may require some vocational training or job-related course work. In some cases, an associate or bachelor's degree could be needed. **Training:** Employees in this type of occupation need anywhere from a few months to one year of working with experienced employees. **Related Examples:** Other occupations like this one often involve using your knowledge and skills to help others. Examples include drywall installers, fire inspectors, flight attendants, pharmacy technicians, retail salespersons, and tellers. **Standard Vocational Preparation Range:** 4.0 to below 6.0—Six months to less than two years. **Major/Instructional Program:** 52.0302 Accounting Technician. **Related Courses:** Clerical; Economics and Accounting; Computers and Electronics.

BROKERAGE CLERKS (53128)

Perform clerical duties involving the purchase or sale of securities. Duties include writing orders for stock purchases and sales, computing transfer taxes, verifying stock transactions, accepting and delivering securities, informing customers of stock price fluctuations, computing equity, distributing dividends, and keeping records of daily transactions and holdings.

Average Yearly Earnings: $28,766. **Experience:** Some preparation is needed. Some previous work-related skill, knowledge, or experience may be helpful in this occupation, but usually is not needed. **Education:** This group of occupations usually requires a high school diploma and may require some vocational training or job-related course work. In some cases, an associate or bachelor's degree could be needed. **Training:** Employees in this type of occupation need anywhere from a few months to one year of working with experienced employees. **Related Examples:** Other occupations like this one often involve using your knowledge and skills to help others. Examples include drywall installers, fire inspectors, flight attendants, pharmacy technicians, retail salespersons, and tellers. **Standard Vocational Preparation Range:** 4.0 to below 6.0—Six months to less than two years. **Major/Instructional Program:** 52.0302 Accounting Technician; 52.0401 Administrative Assistant/Secretarial Science, General; 52.0407 Information Processing/Data Entry Technician. **Related Courses:** Clerical; Economics and Accounting; Sales and Marketing; Computers and Electronics; Mathematics; Communications and Media.

Insurance Specialists

INSURANCE ADJUSTERS, EXAMINERS, AND INVESTIGATORS (53302)

Investigate, analyze, and determine the extent of an insurance company's liability concerning personal, casualty, or property loss or damages, and attempt to effect settlement with claimants. Correspond with or interview medical specialists, agents, witnesses, or claimants to compile information. Calculate benefit payments and approve the payment of claims within a certain monetary limit. Excludes insurance sales agents, insurance policy processing clerks, and claims clerks.

Average Yearly Earnings: $38,230. **Experience:** Medium preparation is needed. Previous work-related skill, knowledge, or experience is required for this occupation. **Education:** This group of occupations usually requires training in vocational schools, related on-the-job experience, or an associate degree. A bachelor's degree may be required. **Training:** Employees in this type of occupation usually need one or two years of training involving both on-the-job experience and informal training with experienced workers. **Related Examples:** Other occupations like this one usually involve using communication and organizational skills to coordinate, supervise, manage, or train others to accomplish goals. Examples include dental assistants, electricians, fish and game wardens, legal secretaries, personnel recruiters, and recreation workers. **Standard Vocational Preparation Range:** 6.0 to below 7.0—More than one year and less than four years. **Major/Instructional Program:** 08.1001 Insurance Marketing Operations; 52.0801 Finance, General; 52.0803 Banking and Financial Support Services; 52.0805 Insurance and Risk Management; 52.1501 Real Estate. **Related Courses:** Economics and Accounting; Personnel and Human Resources; Public Safety and Security; Law, Government, and Jurisprudence.

INSURANCE APPRAISERS, AUTO DAMAGE (53305)

Appraise automobile or other vehicle damage to determine the cost of repair for insurance claim settlement and seek agreement with the automotive repair shop on the cost of the repair. Prepare insurance forms to indicate the repair cost or cost estimates and recommendations.

Average Yearly Earnings: $38,230. **Experience:** Considerable preparation is needed. A minimum of two to four years of work-related skill, knowledge, or experience is needed for this occupation. **Education:** This group of occupations usually requires a four-year bachelor's degree, but in some cases does not. **Training:** Employees in this type of occupation usually need several years of work-related experience, on-the-job training, and/ or vocational training. **Related Examples:** Other occupations like this one usually involve coordinating, supervising, managing, or training others. Examples include accountants, chefs and head cooks, computer programmers, historians, pharmacists, and police detectives. **Standard Vocational Preparation Range:** 7.0 to below 8.0—Two years to less than ten years. **Major/Instructional Program:** 08.1001 Insurance Marketing Operations. **Related Courses:** Economics and Accounting.

INSURANCE CLAIMS CLERKS (53311)

Obtain information from insured or designated persons for the purpose of settling the claim with the insurance carrier.

Average Yearly Earnings: $22,089. **Experience:** Some preparation is needed. Some previous work-related skill, knowledge, or experience may be helpful in this occupation, but usually is not needed. **Education:** This group of occupations usually requires a high school diploma and may require some vocational training or job-related course work. In some cases, an associate or bachelor's degree could be needed. **Training:** Employees in this type of occupation need anywhere from a few months to one year of working with experienced employees. **Related Examples:** Other occupations like this one often involve using your knowledge and skills to help others. Examples include drywall installers, fire inspectors, flight attendants, pharmacy technicians, retail salespersons, and tellers. **Standard Vocational Preparation Range:** 4.0 to below 6.0—Six months to less than two years. **Major/Instructional Program:** 52.0801 Finance, General; 52.0803 Banking and Financial Support Services. **Related Courses:** Clerical; Economics and Accounting; Law, Government, and Jurisprudence.

INSURANCE POLICY PROCESSING CLERKS (53314)

Process applications for, changes to, reinstatement of, and cancellation of insurance policies. Duties include reviewing insurance applications to ensure that all questions have been answered, compiling data on insurance policy changes, changing policy records to conform to insured party's specifications, compiling data on lapsed insurance policies to determine automatic reinstatement according to company policies, canceling insurance policies as requested by agents, and verifying the accuracy of insurance company records. Excludes insurance claims clerks and banking insurance clerks.

Average Yearly Earnings: $22,089. **Experience:** Some preparation is needed. Some previous work-related skill, knowledge, or experience may be helpful in this occupation, but usually is not needed. **Education:** This group of occupations usually requires a high school diploma and may require some vocational training or job-related course work. In some cases, an associate or bachelor's degree could be needed. **Training:** Employees in this type of occupation need anywhere from a few months to one year of working with experienced employees. **Related Examples:** Other occupations like this one often involve using your knowledge and skills to help others. Examples include drywall installers, fire inspectors, flight attendants, pharmacy technicians, retail salespersons, and tellers. **Standard Vocational Preparation Range:** 4.0 to below 6.0—Six months to less than two years. **Major/Instructional Program:** 52.0401 Administrative Assistant/Secretarial Science, General; 52.0408 General Office/Clerical and Typing Services; 52.0801 Finance, General; 52.0803 Banking and Financial Support Services. **Related Courses:** Clerical.

Investigators and Collectors

WELFARE ELIGIBILITY WORKERS AND INTERVIEWERS (53502)

Interview and investigate applicants and recipients to determine eligibility for the use of social programs and agency resources. Duties include recording and evaluating personal and financial data obtained from individuals; initiating procedures to grant, modify, deny, or terminate eligibility for various aid programs; authorizing grant amounts; and preparing reports. These workers generally receive specialized training and assist social service caseworkers.

Average Yearly Earnings: $28,080. **Experience:** Some preparation is needed. Some previous work-related skill, knowledge, or experience may be helpful in this occupation, but usually is not needed. **Education:** This group of occupations usually requires a high school diploma and may require some vocational training or job-related course work. In some cases, an associate or bachelor's degree could be needed. **Training:** Employees in this type of occupation need anywhere from a few months to one year of working with experienced employees. **Related Examples:** Other occupations like this one often involve using your knowledge and skills to help others. Examples include drywall installers, fire inspectors, flight attendants, pharmacy technicians, retail salespersons, and tellers. **Standard Vocational Preparation Range:** 4.0 to below 6.0—Six months to less than two years. **Major/Instructional Program:** 44.0201 Community Organization, Resources, and Services; 44.0701 Social Work; 52.0401 Administrative Assistant/Secretarial Science, General. **Related Courses:** Clerical; Psychology; Sociology and Anthropology; Therapy and Counseling; Law, Government, and Jurisprudence.

INVESTIGATORS, CLERICAL (53505)

Contact persons or businesses by telephone to verify employment records, health history, and moral and social behavior. Examine city directories and public records. Write reports on findings and recommendations. Excludes insurance, credit, and welfare investigators.

Average Yearly Earnings: $21,819. **Experience:** Little or no preparation is needed. No previous work-related skill, knowledge, or experience is needed for this occupation. **Education:** This group of occupations may require a high school diploma or GED certificate. A formal training course to obtain a license may be required. **Training:** Employees in this type of occupation need anywhere from a few days to a few months of training. Usually, an experienced worker could show you how to do the job. **Related Examples:** Other occupations like this one involve following instructions and helping others. Examples include bus drivers, forest and conservation workers, general office clerks, home health aides, and waiters/waitresses. **Standard Vocational Preparation Range:** Below 4.0—Less than six months. **Major/Instructional Program:** 01.0501 Agricultural Supplies Retailing and Wholesaling; 08.1001 Insurance Marketing Operations; 52.0401 Administrative Assistant/Secretarial Science, General; 52.0408 General Office/Clerical and Typing Services; 52.0801 Finance, General; 52.0803 Banking and Financial Support Services. **Related Courses:** Clerical; Computers and Electronics.

BILL AND ACCOUNT COLLECTORS (53508)

Locate and notify customers of delinquent accounts by mail, telephone, or personal visit to solicit payment. Duties include receiving payment and posting the amount to the customers' account; preparing statements to the credit department if the customer fails to respond; initiating repossession proceedings or service disconnection; and keeping records of collection and status of accounts. Excludes workers who collect money from coin boxes.

Average Yearly Earnings: $22,401. **Experience:** Some preparation is needed. Some previous work-related skill, knowledge, or experience may be helpful in this occupation, but usually is not needed. **Education:** This group of occupations usually requires a high school diploma and may require some vocational training or job-related course work. In some cases, an associate or bachelor's degree could be needed. **Training:** Employees in this type of occupation need anywhere from a few months to one year of working with experienced employees. **Related Examples:** Other occupations like this one often involve using your knowledge and skills to help others. Examples include drywall installers, fire inspectors, flight attendants, pharmacy technicians, retail salespersons, and tellers. **Standard Vocational Preparation Range:** 4.0 to below 6.0—Six months to less than two years. **Major/Instructional Program:** 52.0401 Administrative Assistant/Secretarial Science, General; 52.0408 General Office/Clerical and Typing Services; 52.0801 Finance, General; 52.0803 Banking and Financial Support Services. **Related Courses:** Clerical; Economics and Accounting; Law, Government, and Jurisprudence.

Government Clerks

COURT CLERKS (53702)

Perform clerical duties in court of law; prepare the docket of cases to be called; secure information for judges; and contact witnesses, attorneys, and litigants to obtain information for the court.

Average Yearly Earnings: $24,585. **Experience:** Medium preparation is needed. Previous work-related skill, knowledge, or experience is required for this occupation. **Education:** This group of occupations usually requires training in vocational schools, related on-the-job experience, or an associate degree. A bachelor's degree may be required. **Training:** Employees in this type of occupation usually need one or two years of training involving both on-the-job experience and informal training with experienced workers. **Related Examples:** Other occupations like this one usually involve using communication and organizational skills to coordinate, supervise, manage, or train others to accomplish goals. Examples include dental assistants, electricians, fish and game wardens, legal secretaries, personnel recruiters, and recreation workers. **Standard Vocational Preparation Range:** 6.0 to below 7.0—More than one year and less than four years. **Major/Instructional Program:** 52.0401 Administrative Assistant/Secretarial Science, General; 52.0405 Court Reporter. **Related Courses:** Clerical; Law, Government, and Jurisprudence.

MUNICIPAL CLERKS (53705)

Draft agendas and bylaws for a town or city council, record minutes of council meetings, answer official correspondence, keep fiscal records and accounts, and prepare reports on civic needs.

Average Yearly Earnings: $23,753. **Experience:** Some preparation is needed. Some previous work-related skill, knowledge, or experience may be helpful in this occupation, but usually is not needed. **Education:** This group of occupations usually requires a high school diploma and may require some vocational training or job-related course work. In some cases, an associate or bachelor's degree could be needed. **Training:** Employees in this type of occupation need anywhere from a few months to one year of working with experienced employees. **Related Examples:** Other occupations like this one often involve using your knowledge and skills to help others. Examples include drywall installers, fire inspectors, flight attendants, pharmacy technicians, retail salespersons, and tellers. **Standard Vocational Preparation Range:** 4.0 to below 6.0—Six months to less than two years. **Major/Instructional Program:** 52.0401 Administrative Assistant/Secretarial Science, General; 52.0402 Executive Assistant/Secretary. **Related Courses:** Administration and Management; Clerical; Economics and Accounting; Mathematics; Sociology and Anthropology; Geography; English Language; History and Archeology; Philosophy and Theology; Law, Government, and Jurisprudence; Communications and Media.

LICENSE CLERKS (53708)

Issue licenses or permits to qualified applicants. Obtain necessary information, record data, advise applicants on requirements, collect fees, and issue licenses. May conduct oral, written, visual, or performance testing.

Average Yearly Earnings: $23,753. **Experience:** Some preparation is needed. Some previous work-related skill, knowledge, or experience may be helpful in this occupation, but usually is not needed. **Education:** This group of occupations usually requires a high school diploma and may require some vocational training or job-related course work. In some cases, an associate or bachelor's degree could be needed. **Training:** Employees in this type of occupation need anywhere from a few months to one year of working with experienced employees. **Related Examples:** Other occupations like this one often involve using your knowledge and skills to help others. Examples include drywall installers, fire inspectors, flight attendants, pharmacy technicians, retail salespersons, and tellers. **Standard Vocational Preparation Range:** 4.0 to below 6.0—Six months to less than two years. **Major/Instructional Program:** 52.0401 Administrative Assistant/Secretarial Science, General; 52.0408 General Office/Clerical and Typing Services. **Related Courses:** Clerical; Law, Government, and Jurisprudence.

Travel and Hotel Clerks

TRAVEL CLERKS (53802)

Provide tourists with travel information, such as points of interest, restaurants, rates, and emergency service. Duties include answering inquiries; offering suggestions; and providing literature pertaining to trips, excursions, sporting events, concerts, and plays. May make reservations, deliver tickets, arrange for visas, or contact individuals and groups to inform them of package tours. Excludes travel agents.

Average Yearly Earnings: $24,502. **Experience:** Some preparation is needed. Some previous work-related skill, knowledge, or experience may be helpful in this occupation, but usually is not needed. **Education:** This group of occupations usually requires a high school diploma and may require some vocational training or job-related course work. In some cases, an associate or bachelor's degree could be needed. **Training:** Employees in this type of occupation need anywhere from a few months to one year of working with experienced employees. **Related Examples:** Other occupations like this one often involve using your knowledge and skills to help others. Examples include drywall installers, fire inspectors, flight attendants, pharmacy technicians, retail salespersons, and tellers. **Standard Vocational Preparation Range:** 4.0 to below 6.0—Six months to less than two years. **Major/Instructional Program:** 08.1104 Tourism Promotion Operations, 08.1105 Travel Services Marketing Operations. **Related Courses:** Customer and Personal Service; Geography; Transportation.

RESERVATION AND TRANSPORTATION TICKET AGENTS **(53805)**

Make and confirm reservations for passengers and sell tickets for transportation agencies such as airlines, bus companies, railroads, and steamship lines. May check baggage and direct passengers to the designated concourse, pier, or track. Excludes workers selling tickets for subways, city buses, ferry boats, and street railways.

Average Yearly Earnings: $24,502. **Experience:** Some preparation is needed. Some previous work-related skill, knowledge, or experience may be helpful in this occupation, but usually is not needed. **Education:** This group of occupations usually requires a high school diploma and may require some vocational training or job-related course work. In some cases, an associate or bachelor's degree could be needed. **Training:** Employees in this type of occupation need anywhere from a few months to one year of working with experienced employees. **Related Examples:** Other occupations like this one often involve using your knowledge and skills to help others. Examples include drywall installers, fire inspectors, flight attendants, pharmacy technicians, retail salespersons, and tellers. **Standard Vocational Preparation Range:** 4.0 to below 6.0—Six months to less than two years. **Major/Instructional Program:** 08.1105 Travel Services Marketing Operations, 49.0106 Flight Attendant. **Related Courses:** Clerical; Sales and Marketing; Customer and Personal Service; Computers and Electronics; Geography; Foreign Language; Philosophy and Theology; Transportation.

HOTEL DESK CLERKS **(53808)**

Accommodate hotel patrons by registering and assigning rooms to guests, issuing room keys, transmitting and receiving messages, keeping records of occupied rooms and guests' accounts, making and confirming reservations, and presenting statements to and collecting payments from departing guests.

Average Yearly Earnings: $14,643. **Experience:** Some preparation is needed. Some previous work-related skill, knowledge, or experience may be helpful in this occupation, but usually is not needed. **Education:** This group of occupations usually requires a high school diploma and may require some vocational training or job-related course work. In some cases, an associate or bachelor's degree could be needed. **Training:** Employees in this type of occupation need anywhere from a few months to one year of working with experienced employees. **Related Examples:** Other occupations like this one often involve using your knowledge and skills to help others. Examples include drywall installers, fire inspectors, flight attendants, pharmacy technicians, retail salespersons, and tellers. **Standard Vocational Preparation Range:** 4.0 to below 6.0—Six months to less than two years. **Major/Instructional Program:** 08.0901 Hospitality and Recreation Marketing Operations, General; 08.0902 Hotel/Motel Services Marketing Operations. **Related Courses:** Clerical; Customer and Personal Service; Transportation.

Other Clerical Workers

LIBRARY ASSISTANTS AND BOOKMOBILE DRIVERS (53902)

Library assistants compile records; sort and shelve books; issue and receive library materials, such as pictures, cards, slides, phonograph records, and microfilm; and handle tape decks. Locate library materials for loan, and replace materials in shelving area (stacks) or files according to identification number and title. Register patrons to permit them to borrow books, periodicals, and other library materials. Bookmobile drivers operate a bookmobile or light truck that pulls a book trailer to specific locations on a predetermined schedule and assist with providing services in the mobile library.

Average Yearly Earnings: $17,472. **Experience:** Little or no preparation is needed. No previous work-related skill, knowledge, or experience is needed for this occupation. **Education:** This group of occupations may require a high school diploma or GED certificate. A formal training course to obtain a license may be required. **Training:** Employees in this type of occupation need anywhere from a few days to a few months of training. Usually, an experienced worker could show you how to do the job. **Related Examples:** Other occupations like this one involve following instructions and helping others. Examples include bus drivers, forest and conservation workers, general office clerks, home health aides, and waiters/waitresses. **Standard Vocational Preparation Range:** Below 4.0—Less than six months. **Major/Instructional Program:** 25.0301 Library Assistant; 52.0401 Administrative Assistant/Secretarial Science, General; 52.0408 General Office/Clerical and Typing Services. **Related Courses:** Clerical; Customer and Personal Service; History and Archeology.

TEACHER AIDES AND EDUCATIONAL ASSISTANTS, CLERICAL (53905)

Arrange work materials, supervise students at play, and operate audio-visual equipment under the guidance of a teacher.

Average Yearly Earnings: $15,974. **Experience:** Little or no preparation is needed. No previous work-related skill, knowledge, or experience is needed for this occupation. **Education:** This group of occupations may require a high school diploma or GED certificate. A formal training course to obtain a license may be required. **Training:** Employees in this type of occupation need anywhere from a few days to a few months of training. Usually, an experienced worker could show you how to do the job. **Related Examples:** Other occupations like this one involve following instructions and helping others. Examples include bus drivers, forest and conservation workers, general office clerks, home health aides, and waiters/waitresses. **Standard Vocational Preparation Range:** Below 4.0—Less than six months. **Major/Instructional Program:** 13.0101 Education, General; 13.0201 Bilingual/Bicultural Education; 13.1501 Teacher Assistant/Aide. **Related Courses:**

Clerical; Customer and Personal Service; Psychology; Sociology and Anthropology; Therapy and Counseling; Education and Training; English Language; Foreign Language; History and Archeology; Telecommunications; Communications and Media.

ADVERTISING CLERKS (53908)

Receive orders for classified advertising in a newspaper or magazine from customers in person or by telephone. Examine and mark classified advertisements according to copy sheet specifications to guide the composing room in assembling type. Verify conformance of published advertisements to specifications for billing purposes.

Average Yearly Earnings: $20,737. **Experience:** Some preparation is needed. Some previous work-related skill, knowledge, or experience may be helpful in this occupation, but usually is not needed. **Education:** This group of occupations usually requires a high school diploma and may require some vocational training or job-related course work. In some cases, an associate or bachelor's degree could be needed. **Training:** Employees in this type of occupation need anywhere from a few months to one year of working with experienced employees. **Related Examples:** Other occupations like this one often involve using your knowledge and skills to help others. Examples include drywall installers, fire inspectors, flight attendants, pharmacy technicians, retail salespersons, and tellers. **Standard Vocational Preparation Range:** 4.0 to below 6.0—Six months to less than two years. **Major/Instructional Program:** 09.0201 Advertising. **Related Courses:** Clerical; Economics and Accounting; Sales and Marketing; Production and Processing.

PROOFREADERS AND COPY MARKERS (53911)

Read transcript or proof type set-up to detect and mark for correction any grammatical, typographical, or compositional errors. Excludes workers whose primary duty is editing copy. Includes proofreaders of Braille.

Average Yearly Earnings: $20,633. **Experience:** Some preparation is needed. Some previous work-related skill, knowledge, or experience may be helpful in this occupation, but usually is not needed. **Education:** This group of occupations usually requires a high school diploma and may require some vocational training or job-related course work. In some cases, an associate or bachelor's degree could be needed. **Training:** Employees in this type of occupation need anywhere from a few months to one year of working with experienced employees. **Related Examples:** Other occupations like this one often involve using your knowledge and skills to help others. Examples include drywall installers, fire inspectors, flight attendants, pharmacy technicians, retail salespersons, and tellers. **Standard Vocational Preparation Range:** 4.0 to below 6.0—Six months to less than two years. **Major/Instructional Program:** 52.0401 Administrative Assistant/Secretarial Science, General; 52.0408 General Office/Clerical and Typing Services; 52.0501 Business Communications. **Related Courses:** English Language.

REAL ESTATE CLERKS (53914)

Perform duties concerned with the rental, sale, and management of real estate, such as typing copies of listings, computing interest or penalty owed, holding collateral in escrow, and checking due notices on taxes and renewal dates of insurance and mortgage loans.

Average Yearly Earnings: $19,385. **Experience:** Some preparation is needed. Some previous work-related skill, knowledge, or experience may be helpful in this occupation, but usually is not needed. **Education:** This group of occupations usually requires a high school diploma and may require some vocational training or job-related course work. In some cases, an associate or bachelor's degree could be needed. **Training:** Employees in this type of occupation need anywhere from a few months to one year of working with experienced employees. **Related Examples:** Other occupations like this one often involve using your knowledge and skills to help others. Examples include drywall installers, fire inspectors, flight attendants, pharmacy technicians, retail salespersons, and tellers. **Standard Vocational Preparation Range:** 4.0 to below 6.0—Six months to less than two years. **Major/Instructional Program:** 52.0401 Administrative Assistant/Secretarial Science, General; 52.0408 General Office/Clerical and Typing Services. **Related Courses:** Clerical; Economics and Accounting; Sales and Marketing; Computers and Electronics; Mathematics; Geography; English Language; Law, Government, and Jurisprudence; Communications and Media.

Secretaries

LEGAL SECRETARIES (55102)

Prepare legal papers and correspondence, such as summonses, complaints, motions, and subpoenas. May review law journals and other legal publications to identify court decisions pertinent to pending cases and submit articles to company officials. Must be familiar with legal terminology, procedures, and documents, as well as legal research.

Average Yearly Earnings: $29,348. **Experience:** Medium preparation is needed. Previous work-related skill, knowledge, or experience is required for this occupation. **Education:** This group of occupations usually requires training in vocational schools, related on-the-job experience, or an associate degree. A bachelor's degree may be required. **Training:** Employees in this type of occupation usually need one or two years of training involving both on-the-job experience and informal training with experienced workers. **Related Examples:** Other occupations like this one usually involve using communication and organizational skills to coordinate, supervise, manage, or train others to accomplish goals. Examples include dental assistants, electricians, fish and game wardens, personnel recruiters, and recreation workers. **Standard Vocational Preparation Range:** 6.0 to below 7.0—More than one year and less than four years. **Major/Instructional Program:** 52.0401 Administrative Assistant/Secretarial Science, General; 52.0403 Legal Administrative Assistant/Secretary. **Related Courses:** Clerical; Economics and Accounting; Computers and Electronics; Law, Government, and Jurisprudence.

MEDICAL SECRETARIES (55105)

Perform secretarial duties utilizing specific knowledge of medical terminology and hospital, clinic, or laboratory procedures. Duties include taking dictation and compiling and recording medical charts, reports, and correspondence, using a typewriter or computer. Duties also may include preparing and sending bills to patients or recording appointments.

Average Yearly Earnings: $21,756. **Experience:** Medium preparation is needed. Previous work-related skill, knowledge, or experience is required for this occupation. **Education:** This group of occupations usually requires training in vocational schools, related on-the-job experience, or an associate degree. A bachelor's degree may be required. **Training:** Employees in this type of occupation usually need one or two years of training involving both on-the-job experience and informal training with experienced workers. **Related Examples:** Other occupations like this one usually involve using communication and organizational skills to coordinate, supervise, manage, or train others to accomplish goals. Examples include dental assistants, electricians, fish and game wardens, legal secretaries, personnel recruiters, and recreation workers. **Standard Vocational Preparation Range:** 6.0 to below 7.0—More than one year and less than four years. **Major/Instructional Program:** 51.0705 Medical Office Management; 51.0708 Medical Transcription; 52.0401 Administrative Assistant/Secretarial Science, General; 52.0404 Medical Administrative Assistant/Secretary. **Related Courses:** Clerical; Computers and Electronics.

SECRETARIES, EXCEPT LEGAL AND MEDICAL (55108)

Relieve officials of clerical work and minor administrative and business details by scheduling appointments, giving information to callers, taking dictation, composing and typing routine correspondence (using a typewriter or computer), reading and routing incoming mail, filing correspondence and other records, and performing other assigned clerical duties. Excludes executive secretaries.

Average Yearly Earnings: $23,129. **Experience:** Some preparation is needed. Some previous work-related skill, knowledge, or experience may be helpful in this occupation, but usually is not needed. **Education:** This group of occupations usually requires a high school diploma and may require some vocational training or job-related course work. In some cases, an associate or bachelor's degree could be needed. **Training:** Employees in this type of occupation need anywhere from a few months to one year of working with experienced employees. **Related Examples:** Other occupations like this one often involve using your knowledge and skills to help others. Examples include drywall installers, fire inspectors, flight attendants, pharmacy technicians, retail salespersons, and tellers. **Standard Vocational Preparation Range:** 4.0 to below 6.0—Six months to less than two years. **Major/Instructional Program:** 52.0401 Administrative Assistant/Secretarial Science, General. **Related Courses:** Clerical; Economics and Accounting; Customer and Personal Service; Computers and Electronics; Geography; English Language; Communications and Media; Transportation.

General Office Support Workers

STENOTYPE OPERATORS (55302A)

Operate a stenotype machine to take dictation, record proceedings, or provide captions.

Average Yearly Earnings: $26,540. **Experience:** Medium preparation is needed. Previous work-related skill, knowledge, or experience is required for this occupation. **Education:** This group of occupations usually requires training in vocational schools, related on-the-job experience, or an associate degree. A bachelor's degree may be required. **Training:** Employees in this type of occupation usually need one or two years of training involving both on-the-job experience and informal training with experienced workers. **Related Examples:** Other occupations like this one usually involve using communication and organizational skills to coordinate, supervise, manage, or train others to accomplish goals. Examples include dental assistants, electricians, fish and game wardens, legal secretaries, personnel recruiters, and recreation workers. **Standard Vocational Preparation Range:** 6.0 to below 7.0—More than one year and less than four years. **Major/Instructional Program:** 09.0701 Radio and Television Broadcasting; 52.0401 Administrative Assistant/Secretarial Science, General; 52.0405 Court Reporter. **Related Courses:** Clerical; Computers and Electronics.

STENOGRAPHERS (55302B)

Take dictation in shorthand and transcribe dictated material.

Average Yearly Earnings: $26,540. **Experience:** Some preparation is needed. Some previous work-related skill, knowledge, or experience may be helpful in this occupation, but usually is not needed. **Education:** This group of occupations usually requires a high school diploma and may require some vocational training or job-related course work. In some cases, an associate or bachelor's degree could be needed. **Training:** Employees in this type of occupation need anywhere from a few months to one year of working with experienced employees. **Related Examples:** Other occupations like this one often involve using your knowledge and skills to help others. Examples include drywall installers, fire inspectors, flight attendants, pharmacy technicians, retail salespersons, and tellers. **Standard Vocational Preparation Range:** 4.0 to below 6.0—Six months to less than two years. **Major/Instructional Program:** 51.0708 Medical Transcription; 52.0401 Administrative Assistant/Secretarial Science, General. **Related Courses:** Clerical.

RECEPTIONISTS AND INFORMATION CLERKS (55305)

Answer inquiries and obtain information for the general public (customers, visitors, and other interested parties). Provide information regarding the activities conducted at the establishment; the location of departments, offices, and employees within the organization; or the services in a hotel. May perform other clerical duties as assigned. Excludes receptionists who operate switchboards.

Average Yearly Earnings: $18,075. **Experience:** Little or no preparation is needed. No previous work-related skill, knowledge, or experience is needed for this occupation. **Education:** This group of occupations may require a high school diploma or GED certificate. A formal training course to obtain a license may be required. **Training:** Employees in this type of occupation need anywhere from a few days to a few months of training. Usually, an experienced worker could show you how to do the job. **Related Examples:** Other occupations like this one involve following instructions and helping others. Examples include bus drivers, forest and conservation workers, general office clerks, home health aides, and waiters/waitresses. **Standard Vocational Preparation Range:** Below 4.0—Less than six months. **Major/Instructional Program:** 08.1104 Tourism Promotion Operations; 52.0401 Administrative Assistant/Secretarial Science, General; 52.0406 Receptionist; 52.0407 Information Processing/Data Entry Technician; 52.0408 General Office/Clerical and Typing Services. **Related Courses:** Clerical; Customer and Personal Service; Geography; Foreign Language; History and Archeology; Telecommunications.

TYPISTS, INCLUDING WORD PROCESSING (55307)

Use a typewriter or computer to type letters, reports, forms, or other straight copy material from a rough draft, corrected copy, or a voice recording. May perform other clerical duties as assigned. Excludes keypunchers, secretaries, and stenographers.

Average Yearly Earnings: $21,403. **Experience:** Some preparation is needed. Some previous work-related skill, knowledge, or experience may be helpful in this occupation, but usually is not needed. **Education:** This group of occupations usually requires a high school diploma and may require some vocational training or job-related course work. In some cases, an associate or bachelor's degree could be needed. **Training:** Employees in this type of occupation need anywhere from a few months to one year of working with experienced employees. **Related Examples:** Other occupations like this one often involve using your knowledge and skills to help others. Examples include drywall installers, fire inspectors, flight attendants, pharmacy technicians, retail salespersons, and tellers. **Standard Vocational Preparation Range:** 4.0 to below 6.0—Six months to less than two years. **Major/Instructional Program:** 52.0401 Administrative Assistant/Secretarial Science, General; 52.0405 Court Reporter; 52.0408 General Office/Clerical and Typing Services. **Related Courses:** Clerical; Computers and Electronics; English Language.

PERSONNEL CLERKS, EXCEPT PAYROLL AND TIMEKEEPING (55314)

Compile and keep personnel records. Record data for each employee, such as address, weekly earnings, absences, amount of sales or production, supervisory reports on ability, and date of and reason for termination. Compile and type reports from employment records. File employment records. Search employee files and furnish information to authorized persons.

Average Yearly Earnings: $24,003. Experience: Some preparation is needed. Some previous work-related skill, knowledge, or experience may be helpful in this occupation, but usually is not needed. Education: This group of occupations usually requires a high school diploma and may require some vocational training or job-related course work. In some cases, an associate or bachelor's degree could be needed. Training: Employees in this type of occupation need anywhere from a few months to one year of working with experienced employees. Related Examples: Other occupations like this one often involve using your knowledge and skills to help others. Examples include drywall installers, fire inspectors, flight attendants, pharmacy technicians, retail salespersons, and tellers. Standard Vocational Preparation Range: 4.0 to below 6.0—Six months to less than two years. Major/Instructional Program: 52.1001 Human Resources Management. Related Courses: Clerical; Personnel and Human Resources.

CORRESPONDENCE CLERKS (55317)

Compose letters in reply to requests for merchandise, damage claims, credit and other information, delinquent accounts, incorrect billings, or unsatisfactory services. Duties may include gathering data to formulate reply and typing correspondence.

Average Yearly Earnings: $22,110. Experience: Some preparation is needed. Some previous work-related skill, knowledge, or experience may be helpful in this occupation, but usually is not needed. Education: This group of occupations usually requires a high school diploma and may require some vocational training or job-related course work. In some cases, an associate or bachelor's degree could be needed. Training: Employees in this type of occupation need anywhere from a few months to one year of working with experienced employees. Related Examples: Other occupations like this one often involve using your knowledge and skills to help others. Examples include drywall installers, fire inspectors, flight attendants, pharmacy technicians, retail salespersons, and tellers. Standard Vocational Preparation Range: 4.0 to below 6.0—Six months to less than two years. Major/Instructional Program: 52.0401 Administrative Assistant/Secretarial Science, General; 52.0408 General Office/Clerical and Typing Services. Related Courses: Clerical.

FILE CLERKS (55321)

File correspondence, cards, invoices, receipts, and other records in alphabetical or numerical order or according to the filing system used. Locate and remove material from the file when requested. May be required to classify and file new material.

Average Yearly Earnings: $16,348. Experience: Little or no preparation is needed. No previous work-related skill, knowledge, or experience is needed for this occupation. Education: This group of occupations may require a high school diploma or GED certificate. A formal training course to obtain a license may be required. Training: Employees in this type of occupation need anywhere from a few days to a few months of training. Usually, an experienced worker could show you how to do the job. Related Examples:

Other occupations like this one involve following instructions and helping others. Examples include bus drivers, forest and conservation workers, general office clerks, home health aides, and waiters/waitresses. **Standard Vocational Preparation Range:** Below 4.0—Less than six months. **Major/Instructional Program:** 52.0401 Administrative Assistant/Secretarial Science, General; 52.0408 General Office/Clerical and Typing Services. **Related Courses:** Clerical.

ORDER CLERKS—MATERIALS, MERCHANDISE, AND SERVICE (55323)

Receive and process incoming orders for materials, merchandise, or services such as repairs, installations, or rental of facilities. Duties include informing customers of order receipt, prices, shipping dates, and delays; preparing contracts; and handling complaints. Excludes workers who dispatch as well as take orders for services.

Average Yearly Earnings: $21,652. **Experience:** Some preparation is needed. Some previous work-related skill, knowledge, or experience may be helpful in this occupation, but usually is not needed. **Education:** This group of occupations usually requires a high school diploma and may require some vocational training or job-related course work. In some cases, an associate or bachelor's degree could be needed. **Training:** Employees in this type of occupation need anywhere from a few months to one year of working with experienced employees. **Related Examples:** Other occupations like this one often involve using your knowledge and skills to help others. Examples include drywall installers, fire inspectors, flight attendants, pharmacy technicians, retail salespersons, and tellers. **Standard Vocational Preparation Range:** 4.0 to below 6.0—Six months to less than two years. **Major/Instructional Program:** 52.0401 Administrative Assistant/Secretarial Science, General; 52.0408 General Office/Clerical and Typing Services. **Related Courses:** Clerical; Economics and Accounting; Sales and Marketing; Transportation.

PROCUREMENT CLERKS (55326)

Compile information and records to draw up purchase orders for the procurement of materials.

Average Yearly Earnings: $21,569. **Experience:** Little or no preparation is needed. No previous work-related skill, knowledge, or experience is needed for this occupation. **Education:** This group of occupations may require a high school diploma or GED certificate. A formal training course to obtain a license may be required. **Training:** Employees in this type of occupation need anywhere from a few days to a few months of training. Usually, an experienced worker could show you how to do the job. **Related Examples:** Other occupations like this one involve following instructions and helping others. Examples include bus drivers, forest and conservation workers, general office clerks, home health aides, and waiters/waitresses. **Standard Vocational Preparation Range:** Below 4.0—Less than six months. **Major/Instructional Program:** 52.0499 Administrative and Secretarial Services, Other. **Related Courses:** Clerical; Economics and Accounting; Transportation.

STATISTICAL DATA CLERKS **(55328A)**

Compile and compute data for use in statistical studies.

Average Yearly Earnings: $23,316. **Experience:** Some preparation is needed. Some previous work-related skill, knowledge, or experience may be helpful in this occupation, but usually is not needed. **Education:** This group of occupations usually requires a high school diploma and may require some vocational training or job-related course work. In some cases, an associate or bachelor's degree could be needed. **Training:** Employees in this type of occupation need anywhere from a few months to one year of working with experienced employees. **Related Examples:** Other occupations like this one often involve using your knowledge and skills to help others. Examples include drywall installers, fire inspectors, flight attendants, pharmacy technicians, retail salespersons, and tellers. **Standard Vocational Preparation Range:** 4.0 to below 6.0—Six months to less than two years. **Major/Instructional Program:** 52.0401 Administrative Assistant/Secretarial Science, General; 52.0408 General Office/Clerical and Typing Services. **Related Courses:** Clerical; Computers and Electronics; Mathematics.

MEDICAL RECORD CLERKS **(55328B)**

Compile medical statistical data, such as diagnoses, treatments, deaths, and births.

Average Yearly Earnings: $16,348. **Experience:** Some preparation is needed. Some previous work-related skill, knowledge, or experience may be helpful in this occupation, but usually is not needed. **Education:** This group of occupations usually requires a high school diploma and may require some vocational training or job-related course work. In some cases, an associate or bachelor's degree could be needed. **Training:** Employees in this type of occupation need anywhere from a few months to one year of working with experienced employees. **Related Examples:** Other occupations like this one often involve using your knowledge and skills to help others. Examples include drywall installers, fire inspectors, flight attendants, pharmacy technicians, retail salespersons, and tellers. **Standard Vocational Preparation Range:** 4.0 to below 6.0—Six months to less than two years. **Major/Instructional Program:** 51.0707 Medical Records Technology/Technician. **Related Courses:** Clerical.

INTERVIEWING CLERKS, EXCEPT PERSONNEL AND SOCIAL WELFARE **(55332)**

Interview the public to obtain information. Contact persons by telephone, mail, or in person for the purpose of completing forms, applications, or questionnaires. Ask specific questions, record answers, and assist persons with completing forms. May sort, classify, and file forms. Excludes workers whose primary duty is processing applications.

Average Yearly Earnings: $18,075. **Experience:** Little or no preparation is needed. No previous work-related skill, knowledge, or experience is needed for this occupation.

Education: This group of occupations may require a high school diploma or GED certificate. A formal training course to obtain a license may be required. **Training:** Employees in this type of occupation need anywhere from a few days to a few months of training. Usually, an experienced worker could show you how to do the job. **Related Examples:** Other occupations like this one involve following instructions and helping others. Examples include bus drivers, forest and conservation workers, general office clerks, home health aides, and waiters/waitresses. **Standard Vocational Preparation Range:** Below 4.0—Less than six months. **Major/Instructional Program:** 52.0401 Administrative Assistant/Secretarial Science, General; 52.0406 Receptionist. **Related Courses:** Clerical; Personnel and Human Resources.

CUSTOMER SERVICE REPRESENTATIVES, UTILITIES (55335)

Interview applicants for water, gas, electric, or telephone service. Talk with the customer by phone or in person, and receive orders for installation, turn-on, discontinuance, or change in services.

Average Yearly Earnings: $27,060. **Experience:** Some preparation is needed. Some previous work-related skill, knowledge, or experience may be helpful in this occupation, but usually is not needed. **Education:** This group of occupations usually requires a high school diploma and may require some vocational training or job-related course work. In some cases, an associate or bachelor's degree could be needed. **Training:** Employees in this type of occupation need anywhere from a few months to one year of working with experienced employees. **Related Examples:** Other occupations like this one often involve using your knowledge and skills to help others. Examples include drywall installers, fire inspectors, flight attendants, pharmacy technicians, retail salespersons, and tellers. **Standard Vocational Preparation Range:** 4.0 to below 6.0—Six months to less than two years. **Major/Instructional Program:** 52.0401 Administrative Assistant/Secretarial Science, General; 52.0406 Receptionist. **Related Courses:** Sales and Marketing; Customer and Personal Service.

BOOKKEEPERS (55338A)

Classify, record, and summarize numerical data to compile and maintain financial records.

Average Yearly Earnings: $22,776. **Experience:** Some preparation is needed. Some previous work-related skill, knowledge, or experience may be helpful in this occupation, but usually is not needed. **Education:** This group of occupations usually requires a high school diploma and may require some vocational training or job-related course work. In some cases, an associate or bachelor's degree could be needed. **Training:** Employees in this type of occupation need anywhere from a few months to one year of working with experienced employees. **Related Examples:** Other occupations like this one often involve using your knowledge and skills to help others. Examples include drywall installers, fire inspectors, flight attendants, pharmacy technicians, retail salespersons, and tellers.

Standard Vocational Preparation Range: 4.0 to below 6.0—Six months to less than two years. **Major/Instructional Program:** 12.0504 Food and Beverage/Restaurant Operations Manager; 52.0302 Accounting Technician; 52.0801 Finance, General; 52.0803 Banking and Financial Support Services. **Related Courses:** Clerical; Economics and Accounting; Computers and Electronics; Mathematics; Law, Government, and Jurisprudence.

ACCOUNTING CLERKS (55338B)

Compute, calculate, and post financial, statistical, and numerical data to maintain accounting records.

Average Yearly Earnings: $22,776. **Experience:** Little or no preparation is needed. No previous work-related skill, knowledge, or experience is needed for this occupation. **Education:** This group of occupations may require a high school diploma or GED certificate. A formal training course to obtain a license may be required. **Training:** Employees in this type of occupation need anywhere from a few days to a few months of training. Usually, an experienced worker could show you how to do the job. **Related Examples:** Other occupations like this one involve following instructions and helping others. Examples include bus drivers, forest and conservation workers, general office clerks, home health aides, and waiters/waitresses. **Standard Vocational Preparation Range:** Below 4.0—Less than six months. **Major/Instructional Program:** 52.0302 Accounting Technician. **Related Courses:** Clerical; Economics and Accounting; Computers and Electronics; Mathematics; English Language.

PAYROLL AND TIMEKEEPING CLERKS (55341)

Compute wages and post wage data to payroll records. Keep daily records showing employees' time of arrival and departure from work. Compute earnings from timesheets and work tickets using a calculator. Operate a posting machine to compute and subtract payroll deductions. Enter net wages on earnings record card, check stub, and payroll sheet.

Average Yearly Earnings: $23,691. **Experience:** Some preparation is needed. Some previous work-related skill, knowledge, or experience may be helpful in this occupation, but usually is not needed. **Education:** This group of occupations usually requires a high school diploma and may require some vocational training or job-related course work. In some cases, an associate or bachelor's degree could be needed. **Training:** Employees in this type of occupation need anywhere from a few months to one year of working with experienced employees. **Related Examples:** Other occupations like this one often involve using your knowledge and skills to help others. Examples include drywall installers, fire inspectors, flight attendants, pharmacy technicians, retail salespersons, and tellers. **Standard Vocational Preparation Range:** 4.0 to below 6.0—Six months to less than two years. **Major/Instructional Program:** 52.0302 Accounting Technician. **Related Courses:** Clerical; Economics and Accounting; Personnel and Human Resources.

BILLING, COST, AND RATE CLERKS (55344)

Compile data, compute fees and charges, and prepare invoices for billing purposes. Duties include computing costs and calculating rates for goods, services, and shipment of goods; posting data; and keeping other relevant records. May involve the use of a computer or typewriter, a calculator, and adding and bookkeeping machines. Excludes workers whose primary duty is operation of special office machines or workers who calculate charges for passenger transportation.

Average Yearly Earnings: $22,027. **Experience:** Some preparation is needed. Some previous work-related skill, knowledge, or experience may be helpful in this occupation, but usually is not needed. **Education:** This group of occupations usually requires a high school diploma and may require some vocational training or job-related course work. In some cases, an associate or bachelor's degree could be needed. **Training:** Employees in this type of occupation need anywhere from a few months to one year of working with experienced employees. **Related Examples:** Other occupations like this one often involve using your knowledge and skills to help others. Examples include drywall installers, fire inspectors, flight attendants, pharmacy technicians, retail salespersons, and tellers. **Standard Vocational Preparation Range:** 4.0 to below 6.0—Six months to less than two years. **Major/Instructional Program:** 08.0709 General Distribution Operations; 52.0302 Accounting Technician; 52.0401 Administrative Assistant/Secretarial Science, General; 52.0408 General Office/Clerical and Typing Services; 52.0499 Administrative and Secretarial Services, Other; 52.0801 Finance, General; 52.0803 Banking and Financial Support Services; 52.1403 International Business Marketing. **Related Courses:** Clerical; Economics and Accounting; Mathematics; Law, Government, and Jurisprudence; Transportation.

GENERAL OFFICE CLERKS (55347)

Perform duties too varied and diverse to be classified in any specific office clerical occupation. Clerical duties may be assigned in accordance with the office procedures of individual establishments and may include a combination of bookkeeping, typing, stenography, office machine operation, and filing.

Average Yearly Earnings: $19,281. **Experience:** Little or no preparation is needed. No previous work-related skill, knowledge, or experience is needed for this occupation. **Education:** This group of occupations may require a high school diploma or GED certificate. A formal training course to obtain a license may be required. **Training:** Employees in this type of occupation need anywhere from a few days to a few months of training. Usually, an experienced worker could show you how to do the job. **Related Examples:** Other occupations like this one involve following instructions and helping others. Examples include bus drivers, forest and conservation workers, home health aides, and waiters/waitresses. **Standard Vocational Preparation Range:** Below 4.0—Less than six months. **Major/Instructional Program:** 51.0703 Health Unit Coordinator/Ward Clerk; 52.0401 Administrative Assistant/Secretarial Science, General; 52.0408 General Office/Clerical and Typing Services. **Related Courses:** Clerical; Economics and Accounting; Customer and Personal Service; Telecommunications.

Office Machine Operators

BILLING, POSTING, AND CALCULATING MACHINE OPERATORS (56002)

Operate machines that automatically perform mathematical processes, such as addition, subtraction, multiplication, and division, to calculate and record billing, accounting, statistical, and other numerical data. Duties include operating special billing machines to prepare statements, bills, and invoices; and operating bookkeeping machines to copy and post data, make computations, and compile records of transactions.

Average Yearly Earnings: $19,760. **Experience:** Little or no preparation is needed. No previous work-related skill, knowledge, or experience is needed for this occupation. **Education:** This group of occupations may require a high school diploma or GED certificate. A formal training course to obtain a license may be required. **Training:** Employees in this type of occupation need anywhere from a few days to a few months of training. Usually, an experienced worker could show you how to do the job. **Related Examples:** Other occupations like this one involve following instructions and helping others. Examples include bus drivers, forest and conservation workers, general office clerks, home health aides, and waiters/waitresses. **Standard Vocational Preparation Range:** Below 4.0—Less than six months. **Major/Instructional Program:** 52.0302 Accounting Technician; 52.0801 Finance, General; 52.0803 Banking and Financial Support Services. **Related Courses:** Clerical; Economics and Accounting.

DUPLICATING MACHINE OPERATORS (56005)

Operate one of a variety of office machines, such as photocopying, photographic, mimeograph, and duplicating machines, to make copies. Excludes blueprinting machine operators and operators of offset printing machines and presses.

Average Yearly Earnings: $18,990. **Experience:** Little or no preparation is needed. No previous work-related skill, knowledge, or experience is needed for this occupation. **Education:** This group of occupations may require a high school diploma or GED certificate. A formal training course to obtain a license may be required. **Training:** Employees in this type of occupation need anywhere from a few days to a few months of training. Usually, an experienced worker could show you how to do the job. **Related Examples:** Other occupations like this one involve following instructions and helping others. Examples include bus drivers, forest and conservation workers, general office clerks, home health aides, and waiters/waitresses. **Standard Vocational Preparation Range:** Below 4.0—Less than six months. **Major/Instructional Program:** 52.0401 Administrative Assistant/Secretarial Science, General; 52.0408 General Office/Clerical and Typing Services. **Related Courses:** No related courses listed in the database for this occupation.

MAIL MACHINE OPERATORS, PREPARATION AND HANDLING (56008)

Operate machines that emboss names, addresses, and other matter onto metal plates for use in addressing machines; print names, addresses, and similar information onto items such as envelopes, accounting forms, and advertising literature; address, fold, stuff, seal, and stamp mail; and open envelopes. Excludes workers who prepare incoming and outgoing mail for distribution by hand.

Average Yearly Earnings: $18,990. **Experience:** Little or no preparation is needed. No previous work-related skill, knowledge, or experience is needed for this occupation. **Education:** This group of occupations may require a high school diploma or GED certificate. A formal training course to obtain a license may be required. **Training:** Employees in this type of occupation need anywhere from a few days to a few months of training. Usually, an experienced worker could show you how to do the job. **Related Examples:** Other occupations like this one involve following instructions and helping others. Examples include bus drivers, forest and conservation workers, general office clerks, home health aides, and waiters/waitresses. **Standard Vocational Preparation Range:** Below 4.0—Less than six months. **Major/Instructional Program:** 52.0401 Administrative Assistant/Secretarial Science, General; 52.0408 General Office/Clerical and Typing Services. **Related Courses:** No related courses listed in the database for this occupation.

COMPUTER OPERATORS, EXCEPT PERIPHERAL EQUIPMENT (56011)

Monitor and control computer to process business, scientific, engineering, and other data according to operating instructions. Excludes operators who control peripheral equipment only.

Average Yearly Earnings: $24,897. **Experience:** Medium preparation is needed. Previous work-related skill, knowledge, or experience is required for this occupation. **Education:** This group of occupations usually requires training in vocational schools, related on-the-job experience, or an associate degree. A bachelor's degree may be required. **Training:** Employees in this type of occupation usually need one or two years of training involving both on-the-job experience and informal training with experienced workers. **Related Examples:** Other occupations like this one usually involve using communication and organizational skills to coordinate, supervise, manage, or train others to accomplish goals. Examples include dental assistants, electricians, fish and game wardens, legal secretaries, personnel recruiters, and recreation workers. **Standard Vocational Preparation Range:** 6.0 to below 7.0—More than one year and less than four years. **Major/Instructional Program:** 11.0301 Data Processing Technology/Technician; 52.1201 Management Information Systems and Business Data Processing, General; 52.1205 Business Computer Facilities Operator. **Related Courses:** Clerical; Customer and Personal Service; Computers and Electronics; Telecommunications.

PERIPHERAL EDP EQUIPMENT OPERATORS (56014)

Operate computer peripheral equipment, such as tape or disk drives, printers, card-to-tape or tabulating machines, sorters, or interpreters. Exclude computer operators and data-entry keyers.

Average Yearly Earnings: $22,027. **Experience:** Some preparation is needed. Some previous work-related skill, knowledge, or experience may be helpful in this occupation, but usually is not needed. **Education:** This group of occupations usually requires a high school diploma and may require some vocational training or job-related course work. In some cases, an associate or bachelor's degree could be needed. **Training:** Employees in this type of occupation need anywhere from a few months to one year of working with experienced employees. **Related Examples:** Other occupations like this one often involve using your knowledge and skills to help others. Examples include drywall installers, fire inspectors, flight attendants, pharmacy technicians, retail salespersons, and tellers. **Standard Vocational Preparation Range:** 4.0 to below 6.0—Six months to less than two years. **Major/Instructional Program:** 11.0301 Data Processing Technology/Technician; 52.1201 Management Information Systems and Business Data Processing, General; 52.1205 Business Computer Facilities Operator; 52.1299 Business Information and Data Processing Services, Other. **Related Courses:** Computers and Electronics; Telecommunications.

DATA-ENTRY KEYERS, EXCEPT COMPOSING (56017)

Operate keyboard or other data-entry devices to prepare data processing input on cards, disk, or tape. Duties include coding and verifying alphabetic or numeric data.

Average Yearly Earnings: $18,470. **Experience:** Some preparation is needed. Some previous work-related skill, knowledge, or experience may be helpful in this occupation, but usually is not needed. **Education:** This group of occupations usually requires a high school diploma and may require some vocational training or job-related course work. In some cases, an associate or bachelor's degree could be needed. **Training:** Employees in this type of occupation need anywhere from a few months to one year of working with experienced employees. **Related Examples:** Other occupations like this one often involve using your knowledge and skills to help others. Examples include drywall installers, fire inspectors, flight attendants, pharmacy technicians, retail salespersons, and tellers. **Standard Vocational Preparation Range:** 4.0 to below 6.0—Six months to less than two years. **Major/Instructional Program:** 52.0401 Administrative Assistant/Secretarial Science, General; 52.0407 Information Processing/Data Entry Technician. **Related Courses:** Clerical; Computers and Electronics.

DATA KEYERS, COMPOSING (56021)

Operate photocomposing perforator or comparable data-entry composing machines (similar in operation to an electric typewriter) to prepare materials for printing or publication.

Average Yearly Earnings: $21,236. **Experience:** Some preparation is needed. Some previous work-related skill, knowledge, or experience may be helpful in this occupation, but usually is not needed. **Education:** This group of occupations usually requires a high school diploma and may require some vocational training or job-related course work. In some cases, an associate or bachelor's degree could be needed. **Training:** Employees in this type of occupation need anywhere from a few months to one year of working with experienced employees. **Related Examples:** Other occupations like this one often involve using your knowledge and skills to help others. Examples include drywall installers, fire inspectors, flight attendants, pharmacy technicians, retail salespersons, and tellers. **Standard Vocational Preparation Range:** 4.0 to below 6.0—Six months to less than two years. **Major/Instructional Program:** 48.0201 Graphic and Printing Equipment Operator, General; 48.0205 Mechanical Typesetter and Composer; 48.0211 Computer Typography and Composition Equipment Operator. **Related Courses:** Clerical; Computers and Electronics.

Communications Equipment Operators

SWITCHBOARD OPERATORS (57102)

Operate cord or cordless switchboard to relay incoming, outgoing, and interoffice calls. May supply information to callers and record messages. May also act as receptionist, perform routine clerical work, and type.

Average Yearly Earnings: $17,555. **Experience:** Little or no preparation is needed. No previous work-related skill, knowledge, or experience is needed for this occupation. **Education:** This group of occupations may require a high school diploma or GED certificate. A formal training course to obtain a license may be required. **Training:** Employees in this type of occupation need anywhere from a few days to a few months of training. Usually, an experienced worker could show you how to do the job. **Related Examples:** Other occupations like this one involve following instructions and helping others. Examples include bus drivers, forest and conservation workers, general office clerks, home health aides, and waiters/waitresses. **Standard Vocational Preparation Range:** Below 4.0—Less than six months. **Major/Instructional Program:** 52.0401 Administrative Assistant/Secretarial Science, General; 52.0406 Receptionist. **Related Courses:** Clerical; Foreign Language; Telecommunications.

DIRECTORY ASSISTANCE OPERATORS (57105)

Provide telephone information from a central office switchboard. Refer to alphabetical or geographical reels or directories to answer questions or suggest answer sources.

Average Yearly Earnings: $27,934. **Experience:** Little or no preparation is needed. No previous work-related skill, knowledge, or experience is needed for this occupation. **Education:** This group of occupations may require a high school diploma or GED certificate. A formal training course to obtain a license may be required. **Training:** Employees in this type of occupation need anywhere from a few days to a few months of training. Usually, an experienced worker could show you how to do the job. **Related Examples:** Other occupations like this one involve following instructions and helping others.

Examples include bus drivers, forest and conservation workers, general office clerks, home health aides, and waiters/waitresses. **Standard Vocational Preparation Range:** Below 4.0—Less than six months. **Major/Instructional Program:** No specific instructional program for this occupation. **Related Courses:** Clerical; Customer and Personal Service; Computers and Electronics; Geography; Foreign Language; Telecommunications.

CENTRAL OFFICE OPERATORS (57108)

Operate telephone switchboard to establish or assist customers in establishing local or long-distance telephone connections.

Average Yearly Earnings: $17,555. **Experience:** Little or no preparation is needed. No previous work-related skill, knowledge, or experience is needed for this occupation. **Education:** This group of occupations may require a high school diploma or GED certificate. A formal training course to obtain a license may be required. **Training:** Employees in this type of occupation need anywhere from a few days to a few months of training. Usually, an experienced worker could show you how to do the job. **Related Examples:** Other occupations like this one involve following instructions and helping others. Examples include bus drivers, forest and conservation workers, general office clerks, home health aides, and waiters/waitresses. **Standard Vocational Preparation Range:** Below 4.0—Less than six months. **Major/Instructional Program:** 52.0401 Administrative Assistant/Secretarial Science, General; 52.0406 Receptionist. **Related Courses:** Telecommunications.

TELEGRAPH AND TELETYPE OPERATORS (57111)

Operate telegraphic typewriter, telegraph key, teletype machine facsimile, and related equipment to transmit and receive signals or messages. Prepare messages according to prescribed formats. Verify and correct errors in messages. May adjust equipment for proper operation.

Average Yearly Earnings: $24,232. **Experience:** Some preparation is needed. Some previous work-related skill, knowledge, or experience may be helpful in this occupation, but usually is not needed. **Education:** This group of occupations usually requires a high school diploma and may require some vocational training or job-related course work. In some cases, an associate or bachelor's degree could be needed. **Training:** Employees in this type of occupation need anywhere from a few months to one year of working with experienced employees. **Related Examples:** Other occupations like this one often involve using your knowledge and skills to help others. Examples include drywall installers, fire inspectors, flight attendants, pharmacy technicians, retail salespersons, and tellers. **Standard Vocational Preparation Range:** 4.0 to below 6.0—Six months to less than two years. **Major/Instructional Program:** 52.0401 Administrative Assistant/Secretarial Science, General; 52.0406 Receptionist. **Related Courses:** Clerical; Computers and Electronics; Telecommunications.

Mail Clerks, Carriers, and Messengers

MAIL CLERKS, EXCEPT MAIL MACHINE OPERATORS AND POSTAL SERVICE (57302)

Prepare incoming and outgoing mail for distribution. Duties include time-stamping, opening, reading, sorting, and routing incoming mail; sealing, stamping, and affixing postage to outgoing mail or packages; and keeping necessary records and completed forms. Exclude workers whose primary duty is mail distribution or the operation of mail-preparing and mail-handling machines.

Average Yearly Earnings: $17,888. **Experience:** Little or no preparation is needed. No previous work-related skill, knowledge, or experience is needed for this occupation. **Education:** This group of occupations may require a high school diploma or GED certificate. A formal training course to obtain a license may be required. **Training:** Employees in this type of occupation need anywhere from a few days to a few months of training. Usually, an experienced worker could show you how to do the job. **Related Examples:** Other occupations like this one involve following instructions and helping others. Examples include bus drivers, forest and conservation workers, general office clerks, home health aides, and waiters/waitresses. **Standard Vocational Preparation Range:** Below 4.0—Less than six months. **Major/Instructional Program:** 52.0401 Administrative Assistant/Secretarial Science, General; 52.0408 General Office/Clerical and Typing Services. **Related Courses:** Clerical; Geography.

POSTAL MAIL CARRIERS (57305)

Sort mail for delivery. Deliver mail on an established route by vehicle or on foot.

Average Yearly Earnings: $28,371. **Experience:** Little or no preparation is needed. No previous work-related skill, knowledge, or experience is needed for this occupation. **Education:** This group of occupations may require a high school diploma or GED certificate. A formal training course to obtain a license may be required. **Training:** Employees in this type of occupation need anywhere from a few days to a few months of training. Usually, an experienced worker could show you how to do the job. **Related Examples:** Other occupations like this one involve following instructions and helping others. Examples include bus drivers, forest and conservation workers, general office clerks, home health aides, and waiters/waitresses. **Standard Vocational Preparation Range:** Below 4.0—Less than six months. **Major/Instructional Program:** No specific instructional program for this occupation. **Related Courses:** Geography; Transportation.

POSTAL SERVICE CLERKS (57308)

Perform any combination of tasks in a post office, such as receive letters and parcels; sell postage and revenue stamps, postal cards, and stamped envelopes; fill out and sell money orders; place mail in pigeonholes of a mail rack or in bags according to state, address, or other scheme; and examine mail for correct postage.

Average Yearly Earnings: $28,371. **Experience:** Some preparation is needed. Some previous work-related skill, knowledge, or experience may be helpful in this occupation, but usually is not needed. **Education:** This group of occupations usually requires a high school diploma and may require some vocational training or job-related course work. In some cases, an associate or bachelor's degree could be needed. **Training:** Employees in this type of occupation need anywhere from a few months to one year of working with experienced employees. **Related Examples:** Other occupations like this one often involve using your knowledge and skills to help others. Examples include drywall installers, fire inspectors, flight attendants, pharmacy technicians, retail salespersons, and tellers. **Standard Vocational Preparation Range:** 4.0 to below 6.0—Six months to less than two years. **Major/Instructional Program:** No specific instructional program for this occupation. **Related Courses:** Clerical; Customer and Personal Service; Geography.

COURIERS AND MESSENGERS (57311A)

Pick up and carry messages, documents, packages, and other items between offices or departments within an establishment or to other business concerns, traveling by foot, bicycle, motorcycle, automobile, or public conveyance.

Average Yearly Earnings: $17,118. **Experience:** Little or no preparation is needed. No previous work-related skill, knowledge, or experience is needed for this occupation. **Education:** This group of occupations may require a high school diploma or GED certificate. A formal training course to obtain a license may be required. **Training:** Employees in this type of occupation need anywhere from a few days to a few months of training. Usually, an experienced worker could show you how to do the job. **Related Examples:** Other occupations like this one involve following instructions and helping others. Examples include bus drivers, forest and conservation workers, general office clerks, home health aides, and waiters/waitresses. **Standard Vocational Preparation Range:** Below 4.0—Less than six months. **Major/Instructional Program:** No specific instructional program for this occupation. **Related Courses:** No related courses listed in the database for this occupation.

Material Recording, Scheduling, and Distributing Workers

DISPATCHERS—POLICE, FIRE, AND AMBULANCE (58002)

Receive complaints from the public concerning crimes and police emergencies. Broadcast orders to police radio patrol units in the vicinity of the complaint to investigate. Operate radio and telephone equipment to receive reports of fires and medical emergencies, and relay information or orders to the proper officials.

Average Yearly Earnings: $22,942. **Experience:** Some preparation is needed. Some previous work-related skill, knowledge, or experience may be helpful in this occupation,

but usually is not needed. **Education:** This group of occupations usually requires a high school diploma and may require some vocational training or job-related course work. In some cases, an associate or bachelor's degree could be needed. **Training:** Employees in this type of occupation need anywhere from a few months to one year of working with experienced employees. **Related Examples:** Other occupations like this one often involve using your knowledge and skills to help others. Examples include drywall installers, fire inspectors, flight attendants, pharmacy technicians, retail salespersons, and tellers. **Standard Vocational Preparation Range:** 4.0 to below 6.0—Six months to less than two years. **Major/Instructional Program:** 52.0401 Administrative Assistant/Secretarial Science, General; 52.0406 Receptionist. **Related Courses:** Computers and Electronics; Geography; Therapy and Counseling; Public Safety and Security; Telecommunications.

DISPATCHERS—EXCEPT POLICE, FIRE, AND AMBULANCE (58005)

Schedule and dispatch workers, work crews, equipment, or service vehicles for conveyance of materials, freight, or passengers or for normal installation, service, or emergency repairs rendered outside the place of business. Duties may include the use of a radio or telephone to transmit assignments and compiling statistics and reports on work progress.

Average Yearly Earnings: $26,561. **Experience:** Some preparation is needed. Some previous work-related skill, knowledge, or experience may be helpful in this occupation, but usually is not needed. **Education:** This group of occupations usually requires a high school diploma and may require some vocational training or job-related course work. In some cases, an associate or bachelor's degree could be needed. **Training:** Employees in this type of occupation need anywhere from a few months to one year of working with experienced employees. **Related Examples:** Other occupations like this one often involve using your knowledge and skills to help others. Examples include drywall installers, fire inspectors, flight attendants, pharmacy technicians, retail salespersons, and tellers. **Standard Vocational Preparation Range:** 4.0 to below 6.0—Six months to less than two years. **Major/Instructional Program:** 08.0709 General Distribution Operations; 41.0205 Nuclear/Nuclear Power Technology/Technician; 47.0501 Stationary Energy Sources Installer and Operator; 49.0399 Water Transportation Workers, Other; 52.0401 Administrative Assistant/Secretarial Science, General; 52.0406 Receptionist. **Related Courses:** Customer and Personal Service; Geography; Telecommunications; Transportation.

PRODUCTION, PLANNING, AND EXPEDITING CLERKS (58008)

Coordinate and expedite the flow of work and materials within or between departments of an establishment, according to the production schedule. Duties, which are primarily clerical in nature, include reviewing and distributing production schedules and work orders; conferring with department supervisors to determine the progress of the work and completion dates; and compiling reports on the progress of the work and production problems. Work may also include scheduling workers and estimating costs; routing and delivering parts to ensure production quotas are met; scheduling shipment of parts;

keeping an inventory of material in departments; ensuring that vendors ship merchandise on the promised date; and writing special orders for services and merchandise.

Average Yearly Earnings: $27,060. **Experience:** Some preparation is needed. Some previous work-related skill, knowledge, or experience may be helpful in this occupation, but usually is not needed. **Education:** This group of occupations usually requires a high school diploma and may require some vocational training or job-related course work. In some cases, an associate or bachelor's degree could be needed. **Training:** Employees in this type of occupation need anywhere from a few months to one year of working with experienced employees. **Related Examples:** Other occupations like this one often involve using your knowledge and skills to help others. Examples include drywall installers, fire inspectors, flight attendants, pharmacy technicians, retail salespersons, and tellers. **Standard Vocational Preparation Range:** 4.0 to below 6.0—Six months to less than two years. **Major/Instructional Program:** 20.0301 Clothing, Apparel, and Textile Workers and Managers, General; 20.0303 Commercial Garment and Apparel Worker; 47.0408 Watch, Clock, and Jewelry Repairer; 48.0201 Graphic and Printing Equipment Operator, General; 48.0205 Mechanical Typesetter and Composer; 52.0201 Business Administration and Management, General; 52.0202 Purchasing, Procurement, and Contracts Management; 52.0203 Logistics and Materials Management; 52.0302 Accounting Technician; 52.0401 Administrative Assistant/Secretarial Science, General; 52.0407 Information Processing/ Data Entry Technician; 52.0408 General Office/Clerical and Typing Services; 52.1201 Management Information Systems and Business Data Processing, General; 52.1205 Business Computer Facilities Operator. **Related Courses:** Clerical; Economics and Accounting; Production and Processing; Computers and Electronics; Mathematics.

TRANSPORTATION AGENTS (58011)

Expedite the movement of freight, mail, baggage, and passengers through airline terminals. Route inbound and outbound air freight shipments. May prepare an airway bill of lading on freight and record baggage, mail, freight, weights, and the number of passengers on an airplane.

Average Yearly Earnings: $22,568. **Experience:** Some preparation is needed. Some previous work-related skill, knowledge, or experience may be helpful in this occupation, but usually is not needed. **Education:** This group of occupations usually requires a high school diploma and may require some vocational training or job-related course work. In some cases, an associate or bachelor's degree could be needed. **Training:** Employees in this type of occupation need anywhere from a few months to one year of working with experienced employees. **Related Examples:** Other occupations like this one often involve using your knowledge and skills to help others. Examples include drywall installers, fire inspectors, flight attendants, pharmacy technicians, retail salespersons, and tellers. **Standard Vocational Preparation Range:** 4.0 to below 6.0—Six months to less than two years. **Major/Instructional Program:** 08.0709 General Distribution Operations. **Related Courses:** Clerical; Customer and Personal Service; Geography; Telecommunications; Transportation.

METER READERS, UTILITIES (58014)

Read electric, gas, water, or steam consumption meters and record the volume used by residential and commercial customers.

Average Yearly Earnings: $24,627. **Experience:** Little or no preparation is needed. No previous work-related skill, knowledge, or experience is needed for this occupation. **Education:** This group of occupations may require a high school diploma or GED certificate. A formal training course to obtain a license may be required. **Training:** Employees in this type of occupation need anywhere from a few days to a few months of training. Usually, an experienced worker could show you how to do the job. **Related Examples:** Other occupations like this one involve following instructions and helping others. Examples include bus drivers, forest and conservation workers, general office clerks, home health aides, and waiters/waitresses. **Standard Vocational Preparation Range:** Below 4.0—Less than six months. **Major/Instructional Program:** No specific instructional program for this occupation. **Related Courses:** No related courses listed in the database for this occupation.

WEIGHERS, MEASURERS, CHECKERS, AND SAMPLERS—RECORDKEEPING (58017)

Weigh, measure, and check materials, supplies, and equipment for the purpose of keeping relevant records. Duties are primarily clerical in nature. Includes workers who collect and keep records of samples of products or materials. Excludes production samplers and weighers.

Average Yearly Earnings: $23,795. **Experience:** Little or no preparation is needed. No previous work-related skill, knowledge, or experience is needed for this occupation. **Education:** This group of occupations may require a high school diploma or GED certificate. A formal training course to obtain a license may be required. **Training:** Employees in this type of occupation need anywhere from a few days to a few months of training. Usually, an experienced worker could show you how to do the job. **Related Examples:** Other occupations like this one involve following instructions and helping others. Examples include bus drivers, forest and conservation workers, general office clerks, home health aides, and waiters/waitresses. **Standard Vocational Preparation Range:** Below 4.0—Less than six months. **Major/Instructional Program:** 08.0705 General Retailing Operations; 52.0401 Administrative Assistant/Secretarial Science, General; 52.0408 General Office/Clerical and Typing Services. **Related Courses:** Clerical; Design; Transportation.

MARKING CLERKS (58021)

Print and attach price tickets to articles of merchandise using one of several methods, such as marking price on tickets by hand or using a ticket-printing machine.

Average Yearly Earnings: $22,568. **Experience:** Little or no preparation is needed. No previous work-related skill, knowledge, or experience is needed for this occupation.

Education: This group of occupations may require a high school diploma or GED certificate. A formal training course to obtain a license may be required. **Training:** Employees in this type of occupation need anywhere from a few days to a few months of training. Usually, an experienced worker could show you how to do the job. **Related Examples:** Other occupations like this one involve following instructions and helping others. Examples include bus drivers, forest and conservation workers, general office clerks, home health aides, and waiters/waitresses. **Standard Vocational Preparation Range:** Below 4.0—Less than six months. **Major/Instructional Program:** No specific instructional program for this occupation. **Related Courses:** Clerical.

STOCK CLERKS—STOCKROOM, WAREHOUSE, OR STORAGE YARD (58023)

Receive, store, and issue materials, equipment, and other items from a stockroom, warehouse, or storage yard. Keep records and compile stock reports. Excludes stockroom laborers and workers whose primary duties involve shipping, weighing, and checking.

Average Yearly Earnings: $19,344. **Experience:** Some preparation is needed. Some previous work-related skill, knowledge, or experience may be helpful in this occupation, but usually is not needed. **Education:** This group of occupations usually requires a high school diploma and may require some vocational training or job-related course work. In some cases, an associate or bachelor's degree could be needed. **Training:** Employees in this type of occupation need anywhere from a few months to one year of working with experienced employees. **Related Examples:** Other occupations like this one often involve using your knowledge and skills to help others. Examples include drywall installers, fire inspectors, flight attendants, pharmacy technicians, retail salespersons, and tellers. **Standard Vocational Preparation Range:** 4.0 to below 6.0—Six months to less than two years. **Major/Instructional Program:** 08.0709 General Distribution Operations; 08.1203 Vehicle Parts and Accessories Marketing Operations; 52.0499 Administrative and Secretarial Services, Other. **Related Courses:** Clerical; Computers and Electronics.

ORDER FILLERS, WHOLESALE AND RETAIL SALES (58026)

Fill customers' mail and telephone orders from stored merchandise in accordance with specifications on sales slips or order forms. Duties include computing prices of items, completing order receipts, keeping records of outgoing orders, and requisitioning additional materials, supplies, and equipment. Excludes laborers, stock clerks, and workers whose primary duties involve weighing and checking.

Average Yearly Earnings: $19,344. **Experience:** Some preparation is needed. Some previous work-related skill, knowledge, or experience may be helpful in this occupation, but usually is not needed. **Education:** This group of occupations usually requires a high school diploma and may require some vocational training or job-related course work. In some cases, an associate or bachelor's degree could be needed. **Training:** Employees in this type of occupation need anywhere from a few months to one year of working with experienced employees. **Related Examples:** Other occupations like this one often involve using your knowledge and skills to help others. Examples include drywall installers, fire inspectors, flight attendants, pharmacy technicians, retail salespersons, and tellers. **Standard Vocational Preparation Range:** 4.0 to below 6.0—Six months to less than two years. **Major/Instructional Program:** No specific instructional program for this occupation. **Related Courses:** No related courses listed in the database for this occupation.

SHIPPING, RECEIVING, AND TRAFFIC CLERKS (58028)

Verify and keep records on incoming and outgoing shipments. Prepare items for shipment. Duties include assembling, addressing, stamping, and shipping merchandise or material; receiving, unpacking, verifying, and recording incoming merchandise or material; and arranging for the transportation of products. Excludes laborers, stock clerks, and workers whose primary duties involve weighing and checking.

Average Yearly Earnings: $21,881. **Experience:** Little or no preparation is needed. No previous work-related skill, knowledge, or experience is needed for this occupation. **Education:** This group of occupations may require a high school diploma or GED certificate. A formal training course to obtain a license may be required. **Training:** Employees in this type of occupation need anywhere from a few days to a few months of training. Usually, an experienced worker could show you how to do the job. **Related Examples:** Other occupations like this one involve following instructions and helping others. Examples include bus drivers, forest and conservation workers, general office clerks, home health aides, and waiters/waitresses. **Standard Vocational Preparation Range:** Below 4.0—Less than six months. **Major/Instructional Program:** 52.0499 Administrative and Secretarial Services, Other. **Related Courses:** Clerical; Economics and Accounting; Philosophy and Theology; Transportation.

ENGINEERING CLERKS (58099A)

Compile, maintain, check, release, and distribute engineering control records, such as blueprints, drawings, engineering documents, parts listings, and catalogs.

Average Yearly Earnings: $22,568. **Experience:** Medium preparation is needed. Previous work-related skill, knowledge, or experience is required for this occupation. **Education:** This group of occupations usually requires training in vocational schools, related on-the-job experience, or an associate degree. A bachelor's degree may be required. **Training:** Employees in this type of occupation usually need one or two years of training involving both on-the-job experience and informal training with experienced workers. **Related Examples:** Other occupations like this one usually involve using communication and organizational skills to coordinate, supervise, manage, or train others to accomplish goals. Examples include dental assistants, electricians, fish and game wardens, legal secretaries, personnel recruiters, and recreation workers. **Standard Vocational Preparation Range:** 6.0 to below 7.0—More than one year and less than four years. **Major/Instructional Program:** 52.0401 Administrative Assistant/Secretarial Science, General; 52.0408 General Office/Clerical and Typing Services; 52.0499 Administrative and Secretarial Services, Other. **Related Courses:** Clerical.

TRANSPORTATION MAINTENANCE CLERKS (58099B)

Compile and record information, such as amount of equipment usage, time between inspections, repairs made, materials used, and hours of work expended, to document the maintenance of transportation equipment.

Average Yearly Earnings: $22,568. **Experience:** Some preparation is needed. Some previous work-related skill, knowledge, or experience may be helpful in this occupation, but usually is not needed. **Education:** This group of occupations usually requires a high school diploma and may require some vocational training or job-related course work. In some cases, an associate or bachelor's degree could be needed. **Training:** Employees in this type of occupation need anywhere from a few months to one year of working with experienced employees. **Related Examples:** Other occupations like this one often involve using your knowledge and skills to help others. Examples include drywall installers, fire inspectors, flight attendants, pharmacy technicians, retail salespersons, and tellers. **Standard Vocational Preparation Range:** 4.0 to below 6.0—Six months to less than two years. **Major/Instructional Program:** 52.0401 Administrative Assistant/Secretarial Science, General; 52.0408 General Office/Clerical and Typing Services. **Related Courses:** Clerical; Transportation.

SERVICE WORKERS

Service Supervisors and Managers

MUNICIPAL FIREFIGHTING AND PREVENTION SUPERVISORS (61002A)

Supervise firefighters who control and extinguish municipal fires, protect life and property, and conduct rescue efforts.

Average Yearly Earnings: $40,981. **Experience:** Considerable preparation is needed. A minimum of two to four years of work-related skill, knowledge, or experience is needed for this occupation. **Education:** This group of occupations usually requires a four-year bachelor's degree, but in some cases does not. **Training:** Employees in this type of occupation usually need several years of work-related experience, on-the-job training, and/or vocational training. **Related Examples:** Other occupations like this one usually involve coordinating, supervising, managing, or training others. Examples include accountants, chefs and head cooks, computer programmers, historians, pharmacists, and police detectives. **Standard Vocational Preparation Range:** 7.0 to below 8.0—Two years to less than ten years. **Major/Instructional Program:** 43.0201 Fire Protection and Safety Technology/Technician, 43.0202 Fire Services Administration. **Related Courses:** Administration and Management; Personnel and Human Resources; Building and Construction; Geography; Medicine and Dentistry; Education and Training; Public Safety and Security; Telecommunications.

FOREST FIREFIGHTING AND PREVENTION SUPERVISORS (61002B)

Supervise firefighters who control and suppress fires in forests or on vacant public land.

Average Yearly Earnings: $40,981. **Experience:** Extensive preparation is needed. Extensive skill, knowledge, and experience are needed for this occupation. It may require more than five years of experience. **Education:** A bachelor's degree is the minimum formal education required for this group of occupations. However, many also require graduate school. For example, they may require a master's degree, and some require a Ph.D., M.D., or J.D. (law degree). **Training:** Employees in this type of occupation may need some on-the-job training, but most of these occupations assume that the person will already have the required skills, knowledge, work-related experience, and/or training. **Examples:** Other occupations like this one often involve coordinating, training, supervising, or managing the activities of others to accomplish goals. Very advanced communication and organizational skills are required. Examples include athletic trainers, lawyers, managing editors, physicists, social psychologists, and surgeons. **Standard Vocational Preparation Range:** 8.0 to 9.0—Four years to more than ten years. **Major/Instructional Program:** 03.0203 Natural Resources Law Enforcement and Protective Services, 43.0202 Fire Services Administration, 43.0203 Fire Science/Firefighting. **Related Courses:** Administration and Management; Chemistry; Geography; Education and Training; Public Safety and Security; Transportation.

POLICE AND DETECTIVE SUPERVISORS (61005)

Supervise and coordinate the activities of members of the police force.

Average Yearly Earnings: $44,928. **Experience:** Considerable preparation is needed. A minimum of two to four years of work-related skill, knowledge, or experience is needed for this occupation. **Education:** This group of occupations usually requires a four-year bachelor's degree, but in some cases does not. **Training:** Employees in this type of occupation usually need several years of work-related experience, on-the-job training, and/or vocational training. **Related Examples:** Other occupations like this one usually involve coordinating, supervising, managing, or training others. Examples include accountants, chefs and head cooks, computer programmers, historians, pharmacists, and police detectives. **Standard Vocational Preparation Range:** 7.0 to below 8.0—Two years to less than ten years. **Major/Instructional Program:** 43.0102 Corrections/Correctional Administration, 43.0103 Criminal Justice/Law Enforcement Administration. **Related Courses:** Administration and Management; Clerical; Economics and Accounting; Sales and Marketing; Customer and Personal Service; Personnel and Human Resources; Psychology; Sociology and Anthropology; Geography; Medicine and Dentistry; Therapy and Counseling; Education and Training; English Language; Foreign Language; Philosophy and Theology; Public Safety and Security; Law, Government, and Jurisprudence; Telecommunications; Communications and Media; Transportation.

HOUSEKEEPING SUPERVISORS **(61008)**

Supervise the work activities of cleaning personnel to ensure clean, orderly, and attractive rooms in hotels, hospitals, educational institutions, and similar establishments. Assign duties, inspect work, investigate complaints regarding housekeeping service and equipment, and take corrective action. May purchase housekeeping supplies and equipment, take periodic inventories, screen applicants, train new employees, and recommend dismissals.

Average Yearly Earnings: $28,121. **Experience:** Considerable preparation is needed. A minimum of two to four years of work-related skill, knowledge, or experience is needed for this occupation. **Education:** This group of occupations usually requires a four-year bachelor's degree, but in some cases does not. **Training:** Employees in this type of occupation usually need several years of work-related experience, on-the-job training, and/or vocational training. **Related Examples:** Other occupations like this one usually involve coordinating, supervising, managing, or training others. Examples include accountants, chefs and head cooks, computer programmers, historians, pharmacists, and police detectives. **Standard Vocational Preparation Range:** 7.0 to below 8.0—Two years to less than ten years. **Major/Instructional Program:** 20.0601 Custodial, Housekeeping, and Home Services Workers and Managers, General; 20.0605 Executive Housekeeper. **Related Courses:** Administration and Management; Clerical; Customer and Personal Service; Personnel and Human Resources; Education and Training; Foreign Language.

CHEFS AND HEAD COOKS **(61099A)**

Direct the preparation, seasoning, and cooking of salads, soups, fish, meats, vegetables, desserts, or other foods. May plan and price menu items, order supplies, and keep records and accounts. May participate in cooking.

Average Yearly Earnings: $26,561. **Experience:** Considerable preparation is needed. A minimum of two to four years of work-related skill, knowledge, or experience is needed for this occupation. **Education:** This group of occupations usually requires a four-year bachelor's degree, but in some cases does not. **Training:** Employees in this type of occupation usually need several years of work-related experience, on-the-job training, and/or vocational training. **Related Examples:** Other occupations like this one usually involve coordinating, supervising, managing, or training others. Examples include accountants, computer programmers, historians, pharmacists, and police detectives. **Standard Vocational Preparation Range:** 7.0 to below 8.0—Two years to less than ten years. **Major/Instructional Program:** 12.0501 Baker/Pastry Chef, 12.0503 Culinary Arts/Chef Training, 20.0401 Institutional Food Workers and Administrators. **Related Courses:** Administration and Management; Economics and Accounting; Personnel and Human Resources; Food Production; Education and Training.

FIRST-LINE SUPERVISORS/MANAGERS OF FOOD PREPARATION AND SERVING WORKERS (61099B)

Supervise workers engaged in serving and preparing food.

Average Yearly Earnings: $26,561. **Experience:** Medium preparation is needed. Previous work-related skill, knowledge, or experience is required for this occupation. **Education:** This group of occupations usually requires training in vocational schools, related on-the-job experience, or an associate degree. A bachelor's degree may be required. **Training:** Employees in this type of occupation usually need one or two years of training involving both on-the-job experience and informal training with experienced workers. **Related Examples:** Other occupations like this one usually involve using communication and organizational skills to coordinate, supervise, manage, or train others to accomplish goals. Examples include dental assistants, electricians, fish and game wardens, legal secretaries, personnel recruiters, and recreation workers. **Standard Vocational Preparation Range:** 6.0 to below 7.0—More than one year and less than four years. **Major/Instructional Program:** 12.0507 Waiter/Waitress and Dining Room Manager; 19.0501 Foods and Nutrition Studies, General; 19.0505 Food Systems Administration; 20.0401 Institutional Food Workers and Administrators; 20.0404 Dietician Assistant; 20.0405 Food Catering; 20.0409 Institutional Food Services Administrator. **Related Courses:** Administration and Management; Customer and Personal Service; Personnel and Human Resources; Production and Processing; Food Production.

FIRST-LINE SUPERVISORS/HOSPITALITY AND PERSONAL SERVICE WORKERS (61099C)

Supervise workers engaged in providing hospitality and personal services.

Average Yearly Earnings: $26,561. **Experience:** Medium preparation is needed. Previous work-related skill, knowledge, or experience is required for this occupation. **Education:** This group of occupations usually requires training in vocational schools, related on-the-job experience, or an associate degree. A bachelor's degree may be required. **Training:** Employees in this type of occupation usually need one or two years of training involving both on-the-job experience and informal training with experienced workers. **Related Examples:** Other occupations like this one usually involve using communication and organizational skills to coordinate, supervise, manage, or train others to accomplish goals. Examples include dental assistants, electricians, fish and game wardens, legal secretaries, personnel recruiters, and recreation workers. **Standard Vocational Preparation Range:** 6.0 to below 7.0—More than one year and less than four years. **Major/Instructional Program:** 08.1104 Tourism Promotion Operations; 20.0601 Custodial, Housekeeping, and Home Services Workers and Managers, General; 20.0604 Custodian/Caretaker; 20.0605 Executive Housekeeper; 49.0106 Flight Attendant; 52.0902 Hotel/Motel and Restaurant Management. **Related Courses:** Administration and Management; Customer and Personal Service; Personnel and Human Resources; Psychology; Education and Training.

FIRST-LINE SUPERVISORS/MANAGERS OF HOUSEKEEPING AND JANITORIAL WORKERS **(61099D)**

Supervise work activities of cleaning personnel in hotels, hospitals, offices, and other establishments.

Average Yearly Earnings: $28,121. **Experience:** Medium preparation is needed. Previous work-related skill, knowledge, or experience is required for this occupation. **Education:** This group of occupations usually requires training in vocational schools, related on-the-job experience, or an associate degree. A bachelor's degree may be required. **Training:** Employees in this type of occupation usually need one or two years of training involving both on-the-job experience and informal training with experienced workers. **Related Examples:** Other occupations like this one usually involve using communication and organizational skills to coordinate, supervise, manage, or train others to accomplish goals. Examples include dental assistants, electricians, fish and game wardens, legal secretaries, personnel recruiters, and recreation workers. **Standard Vocational Preparation Range:** 6.0 to below 7.0—More than one year and less than four years. **Major/Instructional Program:** 20.0601 Custodial, Housekeeping, and Home Services Workers and Managers, General; 20.0604 Custodian/Caretaker. **Related Courses:** Administration and Management; Customer and Personal Service; Personnel and Human Resources.

Private Household Workers

HOUSEKEEPERS, PRIVATE HOUSEHOLD **(62031)**

Manage, maintain, and clean a private home and render personal services to family members.

Average Yearly Earnings: $14,227. **Experience:** Little or no preparation is needed. No previous work-related skill, knowledge, or experience is needed for this occupation. **Education:** This group of occupations may require a high school diploma or GED certificate. A formal training course to obtain a license may be required. **Training:** Employees in this type of occupation need anywhere from a few days to a few months of training. Usually, an experienced worker could show you how to do the job. **Related Examples:** Other occupations like this one involve following instructions and helping others. Examples include bus drivers, forest and conservation workers, general office clerks, home health aides, and waiters/waitresses. **Standard Vocational Preparation Range:** Below 4.0—Less than six months. **Major/Instructional Program:** 20.0601 Custodial, Housekeeping, and Home Services Workers and Managers, General; 20.0604 Custodian/Caretaker; 20.0605 Executive Housekeeper; 20.0606 Homemaker's Aide. **Related Courses:** Customer and Personal Service; Food Production.

CHILD MONITORS, PRIVATE HOUSEHOLD **(62041)**

Attend to and care for children in a private home.

Average Yearly Earnings: $13,998. **Experience:** Little or no preparation is needed. No previous work-related skill, knowledge, or experience is needed for this occupation. **Education:** This group of occupations may require a high school diploma or GED certificate. A formal training course to obtain a license may be required. **Training:** Employees in this type of occupation need anywhere from a few days to a few months of training. Usually, an experienced worker could show you how to do the job. **Related Examples:** Other occupations like this one involve following instructions and helping others. Examples include bus drivers, forest and conservation workers, general office clerks, home health aides, and waiters/waitresses. **Standard Vocational Preparation Range:** Below 4.0—Less than six months. **Major/Instructional Program:** 13.0101 Education, General; 20.0201 Childcare and Guidance Workers and Managers, General; 20.0202 Childcare Provider/Assistant; 20.0601 Custodial, Housekeeping and Home Services Workers and Managers, General; 20.0604 Custodian/Caretaker; 20.0606 Homemaker's Aide. **Related Courses:** Customer and Personal Service; Psychology.

PERSONAL ATTENDANTS, PRIVATE HOUSEHOLD (62061)

Provide personal services and companionship to persons in a private household.

Average Yearly Earnings: $14,227. **Experience:** Some preparation is needed. Some previous work-related skill, knowledge, or experience may be helpful in this occupation, but usually is not needed. **Education:** This group of occupations usually requires a high school diploma and may require some vocational training or job-related course work. In some cases, an associate or bachelor's degree could be needed. **Training:** Employees in this type of occupation need anywhere from a few months to one year of working with experienced employees. **Related Examples:** Other occupations like this one often involve using your knowledge and skills to help others. Examples include drywall installers, fire inspectors, flight attendants, pharmacy technicians, retail salespersons, and tellers. **Standard Vocational Preparation Range:** 4.0 to below 6.0—Six months to less than two years. **Major/Instructional Program:** 20.0301 Clothing, Apparel, and Textile Workers and Managers, General; 20.0601 Custodial, Housekeeping, and Home Services Workers and Managers, General; 20.0602 Elder Care Provider/Companion; 20.0604 Custodian/Caretaker; 20.0606 Homemaker's Aide. **Related Courses:** Customer and Personal Service; Food Production.

Protective Service Workers

FIRE INSPECTORS (63002A)

Inspect buildings and equipment to detect fire hazards and enforce state and local regulations.

Average Yearly Earnings: $39,416. **Experience:** Some preparation is needed. Some previous work-related skill, knowledge, or experience may be helpful in this occupation,

but usually is not needed. **Education:** This group of occupations usually requires a high school diploma and may require some vocational training or job-related course work. In some cases, an associate or bachelor's degree could be needed. **Training:** Employees in this type of occupation need anywhere from a few months to one year of working with experienced employees. **Related Examples:** Other occupations like this one often involve using your knowledge and skills to help others. Examples include drywall installers, flight attendants, pharmacy technicians, retail salespersons, and tellers. **Standard Vocational Preparation Range:** 4.0 to below 6.0—Six months to less than two years. **Major/Instructional Program:** 43.0201 Fire Protection and Safety Technology/Technician. **Related Courses:** Medicine and Dentistry; Therapy and Counseling; Education and Training; Public Safety and Security; Law, Government, and Jurisprudence.

FIRE INVESTIGATORS (63002B)

Conduct investigations to determine the causes of fires and explosions.

Average Yearly Earnings: $39,416. **Experience:** Considerable preparation is needed. A minimum of two to four years of work-related skill, knowledge, or experience is needed for this occupation. **Education:** This group of occupations usually requires a four-year bachelor's degree, but in some cases does not. **Training:** Employees in this type of occupation usually need several years of work-related experience, on-the-job training, and/or vocational training. **Related Examples:** Other occupations like this one usually involve coordinating, supervising, managing, or training others. Examples include accountants, chefs and head cooks, computer programmers, historians, pharmacists, and police detectives. **Standard Vocational Preparation Range:** 7.0 to below 8.0—Two years to less than ten years. **Major/Instructional Program:** 43.0109 Security and Loss Prevention Services, 43.0201 Fire Protection and Safety Technology/Technician, 43.0202 Fire Services Administration, 43.0203 Fire Science/Firefighting. **Related Courses:** Building and Construction; Chemistry; Psychology; Education and Training; Public Safety and Security; Law, Government, and Jurisprudence; Telecommunications.

FOREST FIRE INSPECTORS AND PREVENTION SPECIALISTS (63005)

Administer fire regulations. Locate and report forest fires and weather conditions, usually from remote locations within a forest or logging area. Inspect the area for fire hazards and equipment for serviceability. May work from a station or patrol area.

Average Yearly Earnings: $39,416. **Experience:** Some preparation is needed. Some previous work-related skill, knowledge, or experience may be helpful in this occupation, but usually is not needed. **Education:** This group of occupations usually requires a high school diploma and may require some vocational training or job-related course work. In some cases, an associate or bachelor's degree could be needed. **Training:** Employees in this type of occupation need anywhere from a few months to one year of working with experienced employees. **Related Examples:** Other occupations like this one often involve using your knowledge and skills to help others. Examples include drywall installers, fire inspectors, flight attendants, pharmacy technicians, retail salespersons, and tellers. **Standard Vocational Preparation Range:** 4.0 to below 6.0—Six months to less than two years. **Major/Instructional Program:** 03.0203 Natural Resources Law Enforcement and Protective Services, 43.0202 Fire Services Administration, 43.0203 Fire Science/Firefighting. **Related Courses:** Customer and Personal Service; Physics; Chemistry; Biology; Sociology and Anthropology; Geography; Medicine and Dentistry; Education and Training; Public Safety and Security; Law, Government, and Jurisprudence; Telecommunications.

MUNICIPAL FIREFIGHTERS (63008A)

Control and extinguish municipal fires, protect life and property, and conduct rescue efforts.

Average Yearly Earnings: $29,681. **Experience:** Some preparation is needed. Some previous work-related skill, knowledge, or experience may be helpful in this occupation, but usually is not needed. **Education:** This group of occupations usually requires a high school diploma and may require some vocational training or job-related course work. In some cases, an associate or bachelor's degree could be needed. **Training:** Employees in this type of occupation need anywhere from a few months to one year of working with experienced employees. **Related Examples:** Other occupations like this one often involve using your knowledge and skills to help others. Examples include drywall installers, fire inspectors, flight attendants, pharmacy technicians, retail salespersons, and tellers. **Standard Vocational Preparation Range:** 4.0 to below 6.0—Six months to less than two years. **Major/Instructional Program:** 43.0203 Fire Science/Firefighting. **Related Courses:** Geography; Medicine and Dentistry; Therapy and Counseling; Public Safety and Security; Telecommunications; Transportation.

FOREST FIREFIGHTERS (63008B)

Control and suppress fires in forests or on vacant public land.

Average Yearly Earnings: $29,681. **Experience:** Some preparation is needed. Some previous work-related skill, knowledge, or experience may be helpful in this occupation, but usually is not needed. **Education:** This group of occupations usually requires a high school diploma and may require some vocational training or job-related course work. In some cases, an associate or bachelor's degree could be needed. **Training:** Employees in this type of occupation need anywhere from a few months to one year of working with experienced employees. **Related Examples:** Other occupations like this one often involve using your knowledge and skills to help others. Examples include drywall installers, fire inspectors, flight attendants, pharmacy technicians, retail salespersons, and tellers. **Standard Vocational Preparation Range:** 4.0 to below 6.0—Six months to less than two years. **Major/Instructional Program:** 03.0203 Natural Resources Law Enforcement and Protective Services, 43.0203 Fire Science/Firefighting. **Related Courses:** Geography; Therapy and Counseling; Public Safety and Security; Telecommunications; Transportation.

POLICE DETECTIVES (6301 IA)

Conduct investigations to prevent crimes or to solve criminal cases.

Average Yearly Earnings: $41,267. **Experience:** Considerable preparation is needed. A minimum of two to four years of work-related skill, knowledge, or experience is needed for this occupation. **Education:** This group of occupations usually requires a four-year bachelor's degree, but in some cases does not. **Training:** Employees in this type of occupation usually need several years of work-related experience, on-the-job training, and/or vocational training. **Related Examples:** Other occupations like this one usually involve coordinating, supervising, managing, or training others. Examples include accountants, chefs and head cooks, computer programmers, historians, and pharmacists. **Standard Vocational Preparation Range:** 7.0 to below 8.0—Two years to less than ten years. **Major/Instructional Program:** 43.0107 Law Enforcement/Police Science. **Related Courses:** Clerical; Psychology; Sociology and Anthropology; Geography; Foreign Language; Public Safety and Security; Law, Government, and Jurisprudence; Telecommunications.

POLICE IDENTIFICATION AND RECORDS OFFICERS (6301 IB)

Collect evidence at a crime scene, classify and identify fingerprints, and photograph evidence for use in criminal and civil cases.

Average Yearly Earnings: $41,267. **Experience:** Medium preparation is needed. Previous work-related skill, knowledge, or experience is required for this occupation. **Education:** This group of occupations usually requires training in vocational schools, related on-the-job experience, or an associate degree. A bachelor's degree may be required. **Training:** Employees in this type of occupation usually need one or two years of training involving both on-the-job experience and informal training with experienced workers. **Related Examples:** Other occupations like this one usually involve using communication and organizational skills to coordinate, supervise, manage, or train others to accomplish goals. Examples include dental assistants, electricians, fish and game wardens, legal secretaries, personnel recruiters, and recreation workers. **Standard Vocational Preparation Range:** 6.0 to below 7.0—More than one year and less than four years. **Major/Instructional Program:** 43.0107 Law Enforcement/Police Science. **Related Courses:** Clerical; Chemistry; Public Safety and Security; Law, Government, and Jurisprudence.

POLICE INVESTIGATORS—PATROLLERS (63014A)

Patrol an assigned area to enforce laws and ordinances, regulate traffic, control crowds, prevent crime, and arrest violators.

Average Yearly Earnings: $35,484. **Experience:** Medium preparation is needed. Previous work-related skill, knowledge, or experience is required for this occupation. **Education:** This group of occupations usually requires training in vocational schools, related

on-the-job experience, or an associate degree. A bachelor's degree may be required. **Training:** Employees in this type of occupation usually need one or two years of training involving both on-the-job experience and informal training with experienced workers. **Related Examples:** Other occupations like this one usually involve using communication and organizational skills to coordinate, supervise, manage, or train others to accomplish goals. Examples include dental assistants, electricians, fish and game wardens, legal secretaries, personnel recruiters, and recreation workers. **Standard Vocational Preparation Range:** 6.0 to below 7.0—More than one year and less than four years. **Major/Instructional Program:** 43.0107 Law Enforcement/Police Science. **Related Courses:** Clerical; Customer and Personal Service; Psychology; Sociology and Anthropology; Geography; Medicine and Dentistry; Therapy and Counseling; Foreign Language; Philosophy and Theology; Public Safety and Security; Law, Government, and Jurisprudence; Telecommunications; Transportation.

HIGHWAY PATROL PILOTS (63014B)

Pilot aircraft to patrol highways and enforce traffic laws.

Average Yearly Earnings: $35,484. **Experience:** Medium preparation is needed. Previous work-related skill, knowledge, or experience is required for this occupation. **Education:** This group of occupations usually requires training in vocational schools, related on-the-job experience, or an associate degree. A bachelor's degree may be required. **Training:** Employees in this type of occupation usually need one or two years of training involving both on-the-job experience and informal training with experienced workers. **Related Examples:** Other occupations like this one usually involve using communication and organizational skills to coordinate, supervise, manage, or train others to accomplish goals. Examples include dental assistants, electricians, fish and game wardens, legal secretaries, personnel recruiters, and recreation workers. **Standard Vocational Preparation Range:** 6.0 to below 7.0—More than one year and less than four years. **Major/Instructional Program:** 49.0102 Aircraft Pilot and Navigator (Professional). **Related Courses:** Customer and Personal Service; Psychology; Sociology and Anthropology; Geography; Medicine and Dentistry; Therapy and Counseling; Foreign Language; Philosophy and Theology; Public Safety and Security; Law, Government, and Jurisprudence; Telecommunications; Transportation.

CORRECTION OFFICERS AND JAILERS (63017)

Guard inmates in penal or rehabilitative institutions, in accordance with established regulations and procedures. May guard prisoners in transit between the jail, courtroom, prison, or other point, traveling by automobile or public transportation. Includes deputy sheriffs who spend the majority of their time guarding prisoners in county correctional institutions.

Average Yearly Earnings: $28,787. **Experience:** Some preparation is needed. Some previous work-related skill, knowledge, or experience may be helpful in this occupation,

but usually is not needed. **Education:** This group of occupations usually requires a high school diploma and may require some vocational training or job-related course work. In some cases, an associate or bachelor's degree could be needed. **Training:** Employees in this type of occupation need anywhere from a few months to one year of working with experienced employees. **Related Examples:** Other occupations like this one often involve using your knowledge and skills to help others. Examples include drywall installers, fire inspectors, flight attendants, pharmacy technicians, retail salespersons, and tellers. **Standard Vocational Preparation Range:** 4.0 to below 6.0—Six months to less than two years. **Major/Instructional Program:** 43.0102 Corrections/Correctional Administration; 43.0107 Law Enforcement/Police Science; 43.0199 Corrections and Criminal Justice, Other. **Related Courses:** Psychology; Sociology and Anthropology; Medicine and Dentistry; Public Safety and Security; Law, Government, and Jurisprudence.

PARKING ENFORCEMENT OFFICERS (63021)

Patrol an assigned area such as a public parking lot or section of the city, to issue tickets to overtime parking violators and illegally parked vehicles.

Average Yearly Earnings: $18,678. **Experience:** Little or no preparation is needed. No previous work-related skill, knowledge, or experience is needed for this occupation. **Education:** This group of occupations may require a high school diploma or GED certificate. A formal training course to obtain a license may be required. **Training:** Employees in this type of occupation need anywhere from a few days to a few months of training. Usually, an experienced worker could show you how to do the job. **Related Examples:** Other occupations like this one involve following instructions and helping others. Examples include bus drivers, forest and conservation workers, general office clerks, home health aides, and waiters/waitresses. **Standard Vocational Preparation Range:** Below 4.0—Less than six months. **Major/Instructional Program:** No related courses listed in the database for this occupation. **Related Courses:** No related courses listed in the database for this occupation.

BAILIFFS (63023)

Open court by announcing the entrance of the judge. Seat witnesses and jurors in specified areas of the courtroom. Eject or arrest individuals disturbing the proceedings.

Average Yearly Earnings: $18,678. **Experience:** Little or no preparation is needed. No previous work-related skill, knowledge, or experience is needed for this occupation. **Education:** This group of occupations may require a high school diploma or GED certificate. A formal training course to obtain a license may be required. **Training:** Employees in this type of occupation need anywhere from a few days to a few months of training. Usually, an experienced worker could show you how to do the job. **Related Examples:** Other occupations like this one involve following instructions and helping others. Examples include bus drivers, forest and conservation workers, general office clerks, home health aides, and waiters/waitresses. **Standard Vocational Preparation Range:** Below

4.0—Less than six months. **Major/Instructional Program:** 43.0107 Law Enforcement/Police Science. **Related Courses:** Psychology; Sociology and Anthropology; Public Safety and Security; Law, Government, and Jurisprudence.

UNITED STATES MARSHALS **(63026)**

Perform such law-enforcement activities as serve civil writs and criminal warrants issued by federal courts; trace and arrest persons wanted under court warrants; seize and dispose of property under court orders; safeguard and transport prisoners and jurors; and maintain order in the courtroom.

Average Yearly Earnings: $28,017. **Experience:** Some preparation is needed. Some previous work-related skill, knowledge, or experience may be helpful in this occupation, but usually is not needed. **Education:** This group of occupations usually requires a high school diploma and may require some vocational training or job-related course work. In some cases, an associate or bachelor's degree could be needed. **Training:** Employees in this type of occupation need anywhere from a few months to one year of working with experienced employees. **Related Examples:** Other occupations like this one often involve using your knowledge and skills to help others. Examples include drywall installers, fire inspectors, flight attendants, pharmacy technicians, retail salespersons, and tellers. **Standard Vocational Preparation Range:** 4.0 to below 6.0—Six months to less than two years. **Major/Instructional Program:** 43.0107 Law Enforcement/Police Science. **Related Courses:** Psychology; Sociology and Anthropology; Geography; Philosophy and Theology; Public Safety and Security; Law, Government, and Jurisprudence; Transportation.

CRIMINAL INVESTIGATORS AND SPECIAL AGENTS **(63028A)**

Investigate alleged or suspected criminal violations of federal, state, or local laws to determine if evidence is sufficient to recommend prosecution.

Average Yearly Earnings: $41,267. **Experience:** Considerable preparation is needed. A minimum of two to four years of work-related skill, knowledge, or experience is needed for this occupation. **Education:** This group of occupations usually requires a four-year bachelor's degree, but in some cases does not. **Training:** Employees in this type of occupation usually need several years of work-related experience, on-the-job training, and/or vocational training. **Related Examples:** Other occupations like this one usually involve coordinating, supervising, managing, or training others. Examples include accountants, chefs and head cooks, computer programmers, historians, pharmacists, and police detectives. **Standard Vocational Preparation Range:** 7.0 to below 8.0—Two years to less than ten years. **Major/Instructional Program:** 43.0107 Law Enforcement/Police Science. **Related Courses:** Psychology; Sociology and Anthropology; Geography; Philosophy and Theology; Public Safety and Security; Law, Government, and Jurisprudence; Telecommunications.

CHILD SUPPORT, MISSING PERSONS, AND UNEMPLOYMENT INSURANCE FRAUD INVESTIGATORS (63028B)

Conduct investigations to locate, arrest, and return fugitives and persons wanted for nonpayment of child support and unemployment insurance fraud, and to locate missing persons.

Average Yearly Earnings: $18,678. **Experience:** Considerable preparation is needed. A minimum of two to four years of work-related skill, knowledge, or experience is needed for this occupation. **Education:** This group of occupations usually requires a four-year bachelor's degree, but in some cases does not. **Training:** Employees in this type of occupation usually need several years of work-related experience, on-the-job training, and/or vocational training. **Related Examples:** Other occupations like this one usually involve coordinating, supervising, managing, or training others. Examples include accountants, chefs and head cooks, computer programmers, historians, pharmacists, and police detectives. **Standard Vocational Preparation Range:** 7.0 to below 8.0—Two years to less than ten years. **Major/Instructional Program:** 43.0107 Law Enforcement/Police Science, 44.0701 Social Work. **Related Courses:** Sociology and Anthropology; Geography; Therapy and Counseling; Public Safety and Security; Law, Government, and Jurisprudence.

SHERIFFS AND DEPUTY SHERIFFS (63032)

Enforce law and order in rural or unincorporated districts or serve legal processes of courts. May patrol the courthouse, guard the court or grand jury, or escort defendants. Excludes deputy sheriffs who spend the majority of their time guarding prisoners in county correctional institutions.

Average Yearly Earnings: $28,017. **Experience:** Some preparation is needed. Some previous work-related skill, knowledge, or experience may be helpful in this occupation, but usually is not needed. **Education:** This group of occupations usually requires a high school diploma and may require some vocational training or job-related course work. In some cases, an associate or bachelor's degree could be needed. **Training:** Employees in this type of occupation need anywhere from a few months to one year of working with experienced employees. **Related Examples:** Other occupations like this one often involve using your knowledge and skills to help others. Examples include drywall installers, fire inspectors, flight attendants, pharmacy technicians, retail salespersons, and tellers. **Standard Vocational Preparation Range:** 4.0 to below 6.0—Six months to less than two years. **Major/Instructional Program:** 43.0107 Law Enforcement/Police Science. **Related Courses:** Administration and Management; Clerical; Psychology; Sociology and Anthropology; Geography; Therapy and Counseling; Foreign Language; Philosophy and Theology; Public Safety and Security; Law, Government, and Jurisprudence; Telecommunications; Transportation.

DETECTIVES AND INVESTIGATORS, EXCEPT PUBLIC (63035)

Protect property, merchandise, and money of a store or similar establishment by detecting theft, shoplifting, or other unlawful practices by public or employees. Perform necessary action to preserve order and enforce the standards of decorum established by management. Includes investigators who conduct private investigations, such as obtaining confidential information, seeking missing persons, or investigating crimes and thefts.

Average Yearly Earnings: $24,648. **Experience:** Some preparation is needed. Some previous work-related skill, knowledge, or experience may be helpful in this occupation, but usually is not needed. **Education:** This group of occupations usually requires a high school diploma and may require some vocational training or job-related course work. In some cases, an associate or bachelor's degree could be needed. **Training:** Employees in this type of occupation need anywhere from a few months to one year of working with experienced employees. **Related Examples:** Other occupations like this one often involve using your knowledge and skills to help others. Examples include drywall installers, fire inspectors, flight attendants, pharmacy technicians, retail salespersons, and tellers. **Standard Vocational Preparation Range:** 4.0 to below 6.0—Six months to less than two years. **Major/Instructional Program:** 12.0203 Card Dealer, 43.0109 Security and Loss Prevention Services. **Related Courses:** Psychology; Therapy and Counseling; Public Safety and Security; Law, Government, and Jurisprudence; Telecommunications.

RAILROAD AND TRANSIT POLICE AND SPECIAL AGENTS (63038)

Protect and police railroad and transit property, employees, or passengers. Includes workers who coordinate security staff.

Average Yearly Earnings: $18,678. **Experience:** Some preparation is needed. Some previous work-related skill, knowledge, or experience may be helpful in this occupation, but usually is not needed. **Education:** This group of occupations usually requires a high school diploma and may require some vocational training or job-related course work. In some cases, an associate or bachelor's degree could be needed. **Training:** Employees in this type of occupation need anywhere from a few months to one year of working with experienced employees. **Related Examples:** Other occupations like this one often involve using your knowledge and skills to help others. Examples include drywall installers, fire inspectors, flight attendants, pharmacy technicians, retail salespersons, and tellers. **Standard Vocational Preparation Range:** 4.0 to below 6.0—Six months to less than two years. **Major/Instructional Program:** 43.0109 Security and Loss Prevention Services. **Related Courses:** Public Safety and Security; Law, Government, and Jurisprudence; Transportation.

FISH AND GAME WARDENS (63041)

Patrol assigned area to prevent game law violations. Investigate reports of damage to crops or property by wildlife. Compile biological data.

Average Yearly Earnings: $18,678. **Experience:** Medium preparation is needed. Previous work-related skill, knowledge, or experience is required for this occupation. **Education:** This group of occupations usually requires training in vocational schools, related on-the-job experience, or an associate degree. A bachelor's degree may be required. **Training:** Employees in this type of occupation usually need one or two years of training involving both on-the-job experience and informal training with experienced workers. **Related Examples:** Other occupations like this one usually involve using communication and organizational skills to coordinate, supervise, manage, or train others to accomplish goals. Examples include dental assistants, electricians, legal secretaries, personnel recruiters, and recreation workers. **Standard Vocational Preparation Range:** 6.0 to below 7.0—More than one year and less than four years. **Major/Instructional Program:** 03.0203 Natural Resources Law Enforcement and Protective Services, 03.0301 Fishing and Fisheries Sciences and Management, 03.0601 Wildlife and Wildlands Management. **Related Courses:** Administration and Management; Economics and Accounting; Food Production; Chemistry; Biology; Sociology and Anthropology; Geography; Medicine and Dentistry; Education and Training; History and Archeology; Philosophy and Theology; Public Safety and Security; Law, Government, and Jurisprudence; Communications and Media; Transportation.

CROSSING GUARDS (63044)

Guide or control vehicular or pedestrian traffic at such places as street and railroad crossings and construction sites.

Average Yearly Earnings: $14,955. **Experience:** Little or no preparation is needed. No previous work-related skill, knowledge, or experience is needed for this occupation. **Education:** This group of occupations may require a high school diploma or GED certificate. A formal training course to obtain a license may be required. **Training:** Employees in this type of occupation need anywhere from a few days to a few months of training. Usually, an experienced worker could show you how to do the job. **Related Examples:** Other occupations like this one involve following instructions and helping others. Examples include bus drivers, forest and conservation workers, general office clerks, home health aides, and waiters/waitresses. **Standard Vocational Preparation Range:** Below 4.0—Less than six months. **Major/Instructional Program:** 43.0109 Security and Loss Prevention Services. **Related Courses:** No related courses listed in the database for this occupation.

GUARDS AND WATCH GUARDS (63047)

Stand guard at an entrance gate or walk about the premises of a business or industrial establishment to prevent theft, violence, or infractions of rules. Guard property against fire, theft, vandalism, and illegal entry. Direct patrons or employees and answer questions relative to the services of the establishment. Control traffic to and from buildings and grounds. Includes workers who perform these functions using a car patrol.

Average Yearly Earnings: $16,640. **Experience:** Little or no preparation is needed. No previous work-related skill, knowledge, or experience is needed for this occupation. **Education:** This group of occupations may require a high school diploma or GED certificate. A formal training course to obtain a license may be required. **Training:** Employees in this type of occupation need anywhere from a few days to a few months of training. Usually, an experienced worker could show you how to do the job. **Related Examples:** Other occupations like this one involve following instructions and helping others. Examples include bus drivers, forest and conservation workers, general office clerks, home health aides, and waiters/waitresses. **Standard Vocational Preparation Range:** Below 4.0—Less than six months. **Major/Instructional Program:** 43.0109 Security and Loss Prevention Services. **Related Courses:** Customer and Personal Service; Psychology; Geography; Public Safety and Security; Law, Government, and Jurisprudence; Telecommunications; Transportation.

PROTECTIVE SERVICE WORKERS, RECREATIONAL (63099B)

Monitor recreational areas, such as pools, beaches, or ski slopes, to provide assistance and protection to participants.

Average Yearly Earnings: $18,678. **Experience:** Some preparation is needed. Some previous work-related skill, knowledge, or experience may be helpful in this occupation, but usually is not needed. **Education:** This group of occupations usually requires a high school diploma and may require some vocational training or job-related course work. In some cases, an associate or bachelor's degree could be needed. **Training:** Employees in this type of occupation need anywhere from a few months to one year of working with experienced employees. **Related Examples:** Other occupations like this one often involve using your knowledge and skills to help others. Examples include drywall installers, fire inspectors, flight attendants, pharmacy technicians, retail salespersons, and tellers. **Standard Vocational Preparation Range:** 4.0 to below 6.0—Six months to less than two years. **Major/Instructional Program:** 43.0199 Corrections and Criminal Justice, Other. **Related Courses:** Medicine and Dentistry; Public Safety and Security.

ANIMAL CONTROL WORKERS (63099C)

Handle animals for the purpose of investigations of mistreatment, or control of abandoned or unattended animals.

Average Yearly Earnings: $18,678. **Experience:** Some preparation is needed. Some previous work-related skill, knowledge, or experience may be helpful in this occupation, but usually is not needed. **Education:** This group of occupations usually requires a high school diploma and may require some vocational training or job-related course work. In some cases, an associate or bachelor's degree could be needed. **Training:** Employees in this type of occupation need anywhere from a few months to one year of working with experienced employees. **Related Examples:** Other occupations like this one often involve using your knowledge and skills to help others. Examples include drywall installers, fire inspectors, flight attendants, pharmacy technicians, retail salespersons, and tellers. **Standard Vocational Preparation Range:** 4.0 to below 6.0—Six months to less than two years. **Major/Instructional Program:** 01.0505 Animal Trainer; 43.0107 Law Enforcement/Police Science; 43.0199 Corrections and Criminal Justice, Other; 43.9999 Protective Services, Other. **Related Courses:** Biology; Education and Training.

AUTOMATIC TELLER MACHINE SERVICERS (63099D)

Collect deposits and replenish automatic teller machines with cash and supplies.

Average Yearly Earnings: $18,678. **Experience:** Medium preparation is needed. Previous work-related skill, knowledge, or experience is required for this occupation. **Education:** This group of occupations usually requires training in vocational schools, related on-the-job experience, or an associate degree. A bachelor's degree may be required. **Training:** Employees in this type of occupation usually need one or two years of training involving both on-the-job experience and informal training with experienced workers. **Related Examples:** Other occupations like this one usually involve using communication and organizational skills to coordinate, supervise, manage, or train others to accomplish goals. Examples include dental assistants, electricians, fish and game wardens, legal secretaries, personnel recruiters, and recreation workers. **Standard Vocational Preparation Range:** 6.0 to below 7.0—More than one year and less than four years. **Related Courses:** Philosophy and Theology.

Alphabetic Index of Instructional Programs

This index provides an alphabetic listing of the instructional programs and groupings that are included in Section 1 of this book. Names of major instructional groupings are presented in all capital letters. The index includes the page number where you can find the related descriptions. Table A, following the Table of Contents, lists the same instructional programs within related groupings—an approach that may be more useful than this Index if you are exploring educational options.

Index

Dictionary of Instructional Programs and Careers

Alphabetic Index of Occupations

This index lists, in alphabetic order, all job titles and groupings that are described in Section 2 of this book along with the page number where you can find the description. Names of major occupational groupings are presented in capital letters. Table B, following the Table of Contents, lists the same occupations within groupings of related jobs—a more useful arrangement if you are exploring career options.

Index

Index

The Quick Resume & Cover Letter Book,

Second Edition

Write and Use an Effective Resume in Only One Day

J. Michael Farr

This unique book will help you write a solid resume in just a few hours and improve it later, in stages, as you have time. This edition features over 90 sample resumes from professional resume writers, plus notes on the resumes highlighting easy-to-imitate techniques. Special sections cover career planning, other correspondence, and the most effective job search techniques.

ISBN 1-56370-634-2 / Order Code LP-J6342
$14.95

America's Top Resumes for America's Top Jobs®

J. Michael Farr

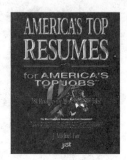

The only book with sample resumes for all major occupations covering 85 percent of the workforce. Here you'll find nearly 400 of the best resumes submitted by professional resume writers, grouped by occupation, and annotated by the author to highlight their best features. Also includes career planning and job search advice.

ISBN 1-56370-288-6 / Order Code LP-J2886
$19.95

Gallery of Best Resumes

A Collection of Quality Resumes by Professional Resume Writers

David F. Noble, Ph.D.

Sample more than 200 great resumes with an expansive range of styles, formats, occupations, and situations–all arranged in easy-to-find groups and written by professional resume writers. You also get the author's 101 best resume tips on design, layout, writing style, and mistakes to avoid.

ISBN 1-56370-144-8 / Order Code LP-GBR
$17.95

Gallery of Best Cover Letters

A Collection of Quality Cover Letters by Professional Resume Writers

David F. Noble, Ph.D.

This new Gallery showcases 292 superior cover letters for a wide range of job seekers–from entry-level workers to senior staff members–in 38 occupational fields. Instructive comments point out distinctive situations, features, and strategies to help you focus your thinking about your own cover letters.

ISBN 1-56370-551-6 / Order Code LP-J5516
$18.95

The Enhanced Occupational Outlook Handbook

*Based on data from the U.S. Department of Labor
Compiled by J. Michael Farr and LaVerne L. Ludden, Ed.D.,
with database work by Paul Mangin*

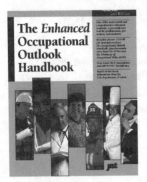

This award-winning book combines the best features of America's three most authoritative occupational references—the *Occupational Outlook Handbook*, the *Dictionary of Occupational Titles*, and now for the first time, the O*NET (the Department of Labor's Occupational Information Network). This is a huge 888-page reference with over 3,600 job descriptions. It helps readers identify major jobs of interest and then obtain information on these jobs and the many more specialized jobs related to them.

ISBN 1-56370-523-0 / Order Code LP-J5230 / **$37.95**

The Guide for Occupational Exploration, 2000 Edition

*J. Michael Farr, LaVerne L. Ludden Ed.D., and
Laurence Shatkin, Ph.D.*

The first major revision since the *GOE* was released in 1977 by the U.S. Department of Labor! It still uses the same approach of exploration based on major interest areas but is updated to reflect the many changes in our labor market. The new *GOE* also uses the recently released O*NET database of occupational information developed by the U.S. Department of Labor. An essential career reference!

ISBN 1-56370-636-9 / Order Code LP-J6369 / **$39.95**

Career Guide to Industries, 2000-2001 Edition

A Companion Reference to the Occupational Outlook Handbook
U.S. Department of Labor

This information-packed review of 40 top industries discusses careers from an industry perspective and covers employment trends, earnings, types of jobs available, working conditions, training required, and more.

ISBN 1-56370-804-3 / Order Code LP-J8043 / **$16.95**